the CONCISE
Gastronomy
of Italy

the CONCISE
Gastronomy
of Italy

ANNA DEL CONTE

PAVILION

FOR OLIVER

THIS CONCISE PAPERBACK EDITION FIRST PUBLISHED IN
GREAT BRITAIN IN 2004 BY
PAVILION BOOKS
ORIGINAL EDITION FIRST PUBLISHED IN HARDBACK IN GREAT BRITAIN IN 2001

An imprint of **Chrysalis** Books Group

THE CHRYSALIS BUILDING, BRAMLEY ROAD
LONDON W10 6SP

TEXT © 2001 ANNA DEL CONTE
TEXT PP371-395 © 2001 DR BRUNO RONCARATI
MAP (P26) © 2001 EMMA GARNER
DESIGN AND LAYOUT © PAVILION BOOKS

THE MORAL RIGHT OF THE AUTHOR AND ILLUSTRATOR
HAS BEEN ASSERTED

ORIGINAL EDITION DESIGNED BY DAVID FORDHAM
ORIGINAL EDITION EDITED BY JANE BAMFORTH, BEVERLY LEBLANC, KATE OLDFIELD
CONCISE EDITION COPY EDITED BY LINDA DOESER
WINE EDITOR SUE MORONY

A CIP CATALOGUE RECORD FOR THIS BOOK IS AVAILABLE
FROM THE BRITISH LIBRARY.

ISBN 1 86205 658 7

SET IN CENTAUR
PRINTED IN SINGAPORE BY KYODO

2 4 6 8 10 9 7 5 3 1

THIS BOOK CAN BE ORDERED DIRECT FROM THE PUBLISHER. PLEASE CONTACT
THE MARKETING DEPARTMENT. BUT TRY YOUR BOOKSHOP FIRST.

Contents

Acknowledgements

M Y WARMEST THANKS must go to Colin Webb, who was managing director of Pavilion Books when the idea for this book first came about, and to Vivien James, who at the time was the publishing director at Pavilion, for pointing me in the right direction. Others to whom I owe special thanks are Jeni Wright who has looked through every entry and each recipe with extreme care, to check, for instance, that the parsley in the list of ingredients did eventually go into the dish, to Kate Oldfield, the book's editor, to David Fordham who designed it, and the whole team at Pavilion and beyond who helped to make this such a beautiful book. I also want to thank my agent Vivien Green who was always ready at the other end of the telephone to support me with her enthusiasm and humour and her faith in me and my cooking. Special thanks for this new edition go to Lizzy Gray and Katherine Morton at Pavilion and to Linda Doeser, the copy editor, who was kind enough to spend the whole of a Sunday afternoon in the Spring on the telephone with me discussing the final revisions.

And finally I have to thank my husband, Oliver Waley, without whom this book would never have seen its dawn.

Anna Del Conte

Foreword

BY THE LATE
COUNT CAPNIST,
PRESIDENT OF
THE ACCADEMIA ITALIANA DELLA CUCINA
1996–2001

As President of the Accademia Italiana Della Cucina I am happy to have this opportunity to recognize the important contribution Anna Del Conte has made to the interest in, and knowledge of Italian food and cooking.

This book covers every aspect of this intricate, often convoluted, and always delightful subject. It is at once an authoritative work of reference for those wishing to know more about Italian food, and a fascinating read for many thousands who already count Italian food among their loves.

The recipes, written in a way that is clear and helpful, never fail to produce the most excellent results.

This is an easy-to-use, practical, and beautiful volume. Anna has been fortunate in having secured the cooperation of Dr Bruno Roncarati, an acknowledged expert, to write the comprehensive and informative section on Italian wines, now more popular than ever around the world.

"*Insomma*" as we say in Italian, it gives me great pleasure to associate the Accademia Italiana della Cucina with this valuable and important book.

Introduction

ABOUT THE BOOK

T HE GASTRONOMY OF ITALY is the culmination of my long love affair with the food of Italy and the culture that lies behind it.

It has been said that Italians love to eat. I certainly do, and it is my fondest hope that this passion will glow through the words – words that will tell you everything you might want to know about the wonderful food of my country.

The book is divided into seven chapters (see page 5), the first of which traces Italian cuisine's history through the centuries. While the entries on ingredients, dishes and terms and techniques are comprehensive, the choice of recipes is personal. Readers have asked me before, and will no doubt do so again, why the recipe for this or that is not included, to which my answer can only be that I had to choose just 200 recipes out of a possible total of several thousand. I have also chosen a considerable number of classic recipes that are representative of the region from which they come. Others are more modern and a few are my particular favourites, often variations on a theme.

The A-Z of Ingredients was originally conceived 20 years ago as an index to the ingredients of Italian cuisine with recipes interspersed, because I felt that then – in the 1980s – authentic Italian food was new in Britain, where I lived. People were interested, and keen to know more. My task was very ambitious as there were only a few books on Italian gastronomic history and even fewer on the food itself. I researched, read, talked, asked, listened... and eventually wrote.

This index of ingredients was fully expanded in 2001 to become the *Gastronomy of Italy*, which includes a detailed introductory chapter exploring the origins and history of Italian cuisine; a section on the 20 regions of Italy and their specialities; a 200-recipe section; a full A-Z reference guide to Italian food; an explanation of terms and techniques and a comprehensive wine directory. This concise edition has been further updated and revised and also includes a section on modern-day Italian shopping and eating habits.

I was very lucky to meet the man who gave me more valuable advice than I can ever remember, who led me in the right direction and told me which books to consult. The man in question is the late Massimo Alberini, the great Italian food historian who was an inspiration to the younger generation. He advised me to avoid writing on current, but ephemeral, topics and not to refer to statistics or trends, all things that make a book obsolete in a matter of months.

So many other people have helped me in this project that it would be impossible to name them all. My thanks go to every one of them. In particular I must thank many members of the Accademia Italiana della Cucina in Italy and many colleagues in Italy and England.

A NOTE ON SYMBOLS USED:

₵	refers to a mention of the Author in the Development of Italian Gastronomy
✲✲	refers to entry in the Recipe section
✲	refers to an entry in the A – Z of Ingredients
†	refers to entry in Terms and Techniques
•	refers to entry in the Wine Index

the Development of Italian Gastronomy

THE ORIGINS OF ITALIAN COOKING

L OOKING FAR BACK INTO THE PAST, it is possible to uphold the claim that the roots of European cooking are to be found in Italy. The first known food writer was Archestratus, a Sicilian Greek who lived in Syracuse in the fourth century BC. He wrote a poem about food, and although the original was lost, part of it has been passed down to us through Atheneus who quoted it in his *Deipnosophists*. Archestratus was concerned that the ingredients should be fresh, of top quality and seasonal, and that their flavour should be distinct and not masked by the addition of spices, herbs and seasonings. This is particularly stressed in the preparation of fish.

A few centuries later these precepts seem to have been totally forgotten when one reads *De Re Coquinaria*, a collection of about 470 recipes collected by Apicius. We know nothing of the author, but he was certainly not the originator of the recipes. We can only presume that he was Gavius Apicius, a great gourmet who lived in the first century AD. The recipes, which probably came from many different sources, list a huge number of different spices and herbs, that would totally hide the intrinsic flavour of the main ingredients. The bulk of the recipes consist of sauces and garnishes, most of them containing a selection of at least six or seven herbs plus honey and spices, the final results of which seem rather questionable. They do give us, however, a fairly good idea of what was eaten in a patrician household at this time.

Some people have suggested that this copious use of strong seasonings was intended to hide unwanted flavours in food that was not as fresh as it should be, but I do not agree. The Romans knew about good food and had access to the best produce. They had oysters from the Gulf of Taranto, fish from the port of Ostia, game from the hills near Rome, and the freshest fruit and vegetables brought into the city every day by the produce growers themselves, as they still are today 2000 years later. Their pecorini* were produced in Sicily because the Sicilians were known to be the best cheese-makers, and they employed Greeks to bake their bread – the Greeks having the reputation of being excellent bakers. But the most important legacy that was passed down from the Romans to the Italians was their love for the land and their knowledge of how, for example, to grow an artichoke or a leek, and how to raise and butcher a pig.

THE SICILIAN INFLUENCE

IN THE FOLLOWING CENTURIES northern Italy was invaded by barbarians from northern Europe who brought with them destruction and desolation, while Sicily, on the other hand, was invaded by the Saracens, who brought with them their culture and their highly civilized way of life. It is on this island that the origins of Italian, and thus to a large extent European cooking, can be traced. The Sicilians had already fused together the cooking of Athens and Rome, and in the ninth century AD they began to absorb the traditional foods and the cooking methods of the Arabs and made them their own.

The Saracens came with an array of new produce, from spinach to almonds and rice. They may well also have been the people who introduced the Italian food *par excellence* to Italy: spaghetti. While lasagne was known to the Romans, the first mention of spaghetti appears in a document written by a geographer who, in the twelfth century AD, was commissioned by the Norman king to make a survey of the island. The geographer reported that in north-east Sicily he saw people drawing a flour and water mixture into long strings, which they called *atriya*, the local word for unleavened bread cut into strips. The word became *tria*, and even today *trii* is another term for spaghetti in southern Italy.

More new influences in the melting pot of Sicilian cooking came with the Normans who brought with them both a new method of cooking (casseroling) and also two new ingredients – salt cod (baccalà) and stockfish. They quickly became the most popular fish all over the peninsula. To the fish-loving Italians stockfish and baccalà had the unique advantage of being always available regardless of distance from the sea, climate or the time of year.

INFLUENCES DURING THE RENAISSANCE

MEANWHILE, ON THE CONTINENT LIFE WAS SETTLING DOWN, and cooking took its rightful place again, as it does in all civilized societies. Two manuscripts have survived from this period, written in the fourteenth century by a Tuscan and a Venetian cook, but they are eclipsed by a manuscript written by Maestro Martino, a fifteenth-century cook from Como who became chef to the Patriarch of Aquileia at the Vatican. Martino's manuscript, *Libro de Arte Coquinaria*, manifests a kind of cuisine that is no longer burdened by roughness, taking on a light and elegant character; it is indeed the earliest medieval Renaissance cuisine. In it there is a recipe for *Maccaroni Siciliani* made by wrapping dough around a thin iron rod. The maccaroni are then "dried in the sun and will last two or three years, especially when made during the August moon". The recipe for maccaroni is a blueprint for a modern recipe, except that Martino cooks the maccaroni in capon stock "made yellow by a little saffron" (a popular spice). Particularly fascinating is the chapter on fish, with 69 recipes, and the one on savoury pies and tarts. He replaces the heavy Eastern spices of previous centuries with fresh herbs, a touch that still continues to characterize Italian cooking today.

This manuscript was incorporated in its entirety into an important treaty on food and health, *De Honesta Voluntate et Valetudine* written by Platina. This, the first food book ever printed, was published in Venice in 1475, and soon after appeared in translation in France and Germany. The book is in two parts, the first dedicated to diet and health while the second is a literary rendition of Martino's manuscript. Platina's work is not plagiarism; he refers to Martino as "prince of all chefs of our time from whom I learned how to cook every kind of food". It is a rewriting of the manuscript, enriching it and giving it the status of a classical text written by a humanist, as Platina was.

THE GREATEST CENTURY

THE IMPORTANCE OF A GOOD AND LAVISH TABLE grew in the sixteenth century with the power of the many princes, and from Florence, Rome, Venice or Ferrara the importance of good food reached first France and then Germany and the rest of Europe. But as in the arts, Italian cooking was influenced by the foreigners who invaded their country, or just came to learn about the arts and the art of good living.

In Ferrara the court of the Estes was one of the focal points of this culture. A book widely considered to be of great importance in the history of Italian gastronomy was indeed written by a nobleman of Ferrara, Christoforo Messisbugo, steward to Ippolito d'Este. The first part of his work, *Banchetti Composizioni di Vivande*, published in 1549, contains descriptions of the banquets, while the second part is given over to those recipes which Messisbugo judges worthy of a great chef. In the extensive section on pies and tarts, for instance, there are no less than 124 recipes in which the filling varies from cream cheese and ricotta to meat, fish, vegetables and fruit, and every tart or pie is brimming with melted butter. It is in this book that there are the first recipes of French, German and even English origin, which arose from the cosmopolitan ambience of the Este court. Although Messisbugo tends sometimes to look to the past with his lavish use of Eastern spices and sugar, his contribution cannot be ignored.

Another great work followed in 1570: *Opera* by Bartolomeo Scappi, the personal chef to Pope Pius V. *Opera* is the most exhaustive and comprehensive cookery manual ever written in Italian and is one volume divided into five books. It contains more than 1000 recipes, plus arrangements and menus for banquets, as well as illustrations of kitchen and table utensils, which add much to our knowledge of that period. As an example I would like to mention the second book of this huge work, which includes 151 recipes devoted to meat. Scappi avoids the previous trend of attaching great importance to game, the meat of the court tables. Instead he brings domestic animals and courtyard birds into the limelight, taking his cue from the cooking of a much more modest household. He describes ways of cooking even the poorest cuts of meat – tongues, head and shoulders, and he explains how to clean and prepare the meat, which cut to use, from which animal and at what age.

The same exhaustive approach is applied to fish in the third book, dealing with food for Lent. Scappi cooks fish in very simple ways, mostly poached, grilled (broiled) or fried and often marinated first, just as it is today. He indicates the optimum size of the fish, in which season it should be caught and in which sea or river, referring to the oysters of Ancona and Chioggia, the freshwater shrimp of Brescia and Verona and the trout of the Tiber. The second section of this book is dedicated to soups and vegetables, thus covering the whole range of dishes for Lent.

There is a recipe for cooking soft-boiled eggs, giving detailed instructions on how to check if the egg is ready. Thus, the cooking time should be as long as it takes to recite a Credo, after which you can check if it is done by tapping it hard with the blunt edge of a knife; it should not break.

The fifth book contains 237 recipes for pies, tarts and fritters etc. There is a recipe for a pie which Scappi calls a Neapolitan pizza, although, unlike today's pizza, it is a sweet preparation. But after all, the tomato had not yet invaded Italy, and was still largely unknown. He does, however, include some recipes that use ingredients from the New World, such as maize (corn) and turkey.

Scappi taught cooking techniques which, although now commonplace, were then new. He explains the preparation of dishes in great detail and imparts his unique knowledge of ingredients in a way that had not been done before, and has seldom been done since. His recipes are inventive and written in a clear, precise way, even including suggestions of alternatives and substitutions. All in all, Scappi's contribution, not only to the Italian, but also to the whole European gastronomic scenario is immense.

THE TWILIGHT YEARS

IT IS SAD THAT, against that brilliant background of art and culture, Italy was torn apart, becoming the battleground of wars among her more powerful neighbours, the French, Spanish and Germans. As a result there began the decline of Italy from her leading role in every art, and in the seventeenth century the leadership of European gastronomy moved across the Alps to France. While up to the sixteenth century French chefs took their lead from Italy, from the seventeenth century onwards the Italians were influenced by their neighbours. That said, however, Italian cooking has always been rooted in the use of a wide variety of local ingredients and has always had local characteristics. This is apparent even in the books written by the chefs to grand households, where local produce was much in evidence, just as it is today.

THE INFLUENCE OF CASTELVETRO

A BOOK OF PARTICULAR INTEREST has the somewhat lengthy title of *Brieve Racconto di Tutte le Radici di Tutte l'Herbe et di Tutti i Frutti* (*A Brief Account of all Vegetables, Herbs and Fruit*) by Giangiacomo Castelvetro, and translated into English by Gillian Riley. The book was written in the first decade of the seventeenth century by a man from Modena who moved to England because of his Protestant leaning. More than a recipe book, it is an extensive account of the fruit and vegetables of Italy, of his love for them (including an exhortation to the English to eat more of them!) and the various ways in which they should be eaten.

Castelvetro's treatment of vegetables was very modern. Sometimes the vegetables are the centrepiece of a course, although his favourite way of serving them — still popular today in Italy — is to boil the vegetables in salted water and serve them warm or cold, with olive oil, salt and freshly ground black pepper and a little lemon juice, verjuice or bitter orange juice. Another method, for cooking root vegetables or cabbage, is to blanch them and then finish them off in a rich stock thickened with egg and/or breadcrumbs and seasoned with cheese and various spices. Then he gives instructions for roasting vegetables, wrapped in damp paper, over charcoal or in embers and then drizzled with a little olive oil – roasting vegetables is popular today and figures prominently in modern cookery books.

Castelvetro's book is divided according to the four seasons, starting in spring with hop shoots served as a cooked vegetable and finishing in the winter with truffles, plus an account of a truffle hunt, at that time done with pigs. He gives detailed instructions on how to make a good salad – *Insalata ben salata/poco aceto e ben oliata* or, in Gillian Riley's translation: "Salt the salad quite a lot/then generous oil put in the pot/and vinegar but just a jot". He adds, "And whosoever transgresses this benign commandment is condemned never to enjoy a decent salad in his life, a fate which I fear lies in store for most of the inhabitants of this kingdom".

In the section on spinach he suggests cooking it "in salted water and serve with oil, pepper, a little verjuice and raisins" or "cook first in plain water, drain and chop it very fine with a large knife and finish cooking it on a low heat with oil or butter, seasoned with salt and pepper and raisins". He concludes, "This makes a delicious dish". Both still remain classic methods of preparing spinach.

There is no mention in the book of maize (corn), potatoes, tomatoes or (bell) peppers – all essential ingredients in Italian cookery today. These only began to become popular later in the seventeenth century, with the exception of maize which was the first ingredient from the New World to be widely grown and consumed.

BANQUETS AND GOOD MANNERS

A NEW APPROACH TO COOKERY WRITING is revealed in a book written in Mantova in 1662. It is *L'Arte di Ben Cucinare*, written by Bartolomeo Stefani, chef to the Gonzagas. He was the last cookery writer to adhere strictly to Italian traditions and, at the same time, the first to include a section dedicated to *vitto ordinario* (ordinary food), as opposed to the food of the grand tables. He even gives the cost of a menu: six lire for 5 kg/11 lb of meat, pasta, cheese, lard, eggs, salad, ricotta, oil, pepper, vinegar and raisins!

Stefani also devotes a section of his book to the preparation and serving of banquets, as indeed every previous cookery book had done. In this section the banquet given by the Gonzagas for Queen Christina of Sweden, who was on her way to the Vatican, is described in detail. It shows that up to that time Italy led the way in the organization of banquets, as well as in the preparation of the food. It was, after all, first in Italy that each diner was given a knife, fork and spoon, their own glass, a plate instead of a bowl and a napkin. The Italians were also renowned for their knowledge of good wine and their elegant manner of drinking it.

While at this time France began to take the lead on matters of cuisine, thanks mainly to La Varenne, Italian writers became obsessed with the work of the *scalco* (steward). The eating and serving at tables took on a ceremonial aspect which became increasingly refined. The first important book on table manners is *Galatheo* by Giovanni della Casa, in which are listed many do's and don'ts. For instance: the waiters must not scratch their heads or other parts of the body, they must not spit, cough or sneeze while serving; the diners must not put their fingers in their mouths, not use their fingers for eating and not wipe their sweat with their napkins. It is strange to read these maxims given to people who were at grand banquets, where the tables were covered by precious tablecloths, with gold or silver cutlery (silverware) and plates, chiselled glasses and array after array of dishes sufficient to keep a modern diner happy for weeks. It was also at this time that the banquets became theatrical events, involving architects, sculptors, choreographers, musicians and playwrights.

While this was going on in the grand houses, we know little of what happened in ordinary households. All the cookery books were written by chefs for chefs and in Italy we have to wait another century or two before any writer produced a book written for the ordinary person.

THE SIGNIFICANCE OF THE NEW WORLD

IT WAS NOT UNTIL THE BEGINNING OF THE EIGHTEENTH CENTURY that produce from the New World began to feature in Italian cuisine. The first recipes for tomatoes were written by Antonio Latini in his book *Lo Scalco alla Moderna*, which was published in Naples in 1692. Latini became Principal Steward to the First Minister of the King of Naples – a suitable place to be writing about tomatoes. In one of his recipes, *Altro Piatto di Cassuola di Pomodoro*, the tomatoes, previously roasted on charcoal, are "added with the above ingredients" (mainly chicken and pigeon) "being careful that they should not be cooked for long because they need quick cooking". They were added as the main ingredient in a tomato sauce, much as we would use them today. In another of Latini's recipes tomatoes are combined with (bell) peppers for the first time, in a sauce. Latini was also the first Italian writer to mention chocolate as a drink.

Of the other imports from America, the turkey had been one of the first to appear on the Italian table. It featured in the sixteenth-century recipes by Messisbugo and Scappi. Scappi, a great innovator, was also the first chef to mention maize (corn), which he used not as flour, but in grains; he cooks it in a rich stock. But peppers, potatoes and tomatoes, although already known, were cultivated mainly as ornamental plants and took longer to become popular as culinary ingredients. They were in fact regarded with suspicion, all being members of the *Solanaceae* family, which includes deadly nightshade.

It was during the seventeenth century that two new drinks became the fashion: coffee and chocolate. Coffee, which came from the Yemen, was immediately adopted by the Venetians; indeed Venice claims to have been the first city in Europe to open a caffè in Piazza San Marco in 1645. A few years later, chocolate, the drink of the Aztecs, arrived in Italy, being already popular in the rest of Europe. First consumed as a drink, by the end of the century it was also used as a flavouring in both sweet and savoury dishes – see the recipe for Lepre in Salmì on page 113.

THE NEW ITALIAN STYLE

THE END OF THE EIGHTEENTH CENTURY saw a rebirth of Italian culinary art. Although most of Italy was governed by France, Spain and Austria, and the cultural atmosphere was influenced by that of the European capitals, the cookery books hint at the beginning of the regionality of Italian food, which is indeed its intrinsic strength. The books are no longer written by chefs for chefs of grand households, they are addressed to the bourgeois housewife, and through her to her cook. This approach is still evident up to the time of the Second World War, so that one can still read, "Have the dish brought to the table…".

The first chef of note trying to shake off French influences was Antonio Nebbia from Marche. In his 1779 book *Il Cuoco Maceratese*, he gives importance to local vegetables as well as pasta and gnocchi, signalling the leading role that the last two are going to have in the future. Soups are no longer puréed in the French style, but based on Mediterranean vegetables with pasta or rice. Meat stock, which only the wealthy could afford, gives way to vegetable and chicken stock.

The same attitude can be seen in another important book, *Il Cucoco Galante* by Vincenzo Corrado, published in Naples in 1773. Although Corrado uses several French words, he remains faithful to Italian, or rather Neapolitan, tradition. His recipes, grouped according to ingredients, are succinctly yet clearly described even though – like so many recipes of the past – they do not specify quantities. Corrado shows the characteristic Italian emphasis on the essential flavour.

In one of his recipes for pigeon he suggests stuffing the boned birds with sweetbread bound with egg, stewing them in stock with lemon rind and cinnamon and serving them with a light cream sauce. In the chapter on red mullet there are five recipes which are now classics in the Italian repertoire for cooking such fine fish. I particularly like "in bianco", in which the fish, wrapped in paper, are poached with flavourings and then dressed with butter or oil. They are served unwrapped with a sauce of pine nuts pounded in oil.

But Corrado's most remarkable contribution is the importance he attached to *Vitto Pitagorico* (vegetarian food). He opens with these words, music to the ear of a vegetarian: "Pitagoric food consists of fresh herbs, roots, flowers, fruits, seeds and all that is produced in the earth for our nourishment. It is so called because Pythagoras, as is well known, only used such produce. There is no doubt that this kind of food appears to be more natural to man, and the use of meat is noxious".

INTRODUCING THE TOMATO AND THE POTATO

FOR THE FIRST TIME IN ANY CULINARY BOOK the tomato takes a leading position in *Il Cuoco Galante*, with 13 recipes. The *Zuppa alli Pomidoro* is the Neapolitan precursor of the Tuscan Pappa al Pomodoro**. There is also a sauce combining tomatoes with peppers, garlic, spices and vinegar, to be served with lamb, which is similar to the Piedmontese salsa rossa for boiled meats. In the 1798 edition of *Il Cuoco Galante* there is a "Treatise on the Potato", the root having also achieved popularity in Italy after Parmentier's success in getting the royal approval in France. In Corrado's treatise the potatoes are cooked in the oven or in hot embers and served with different sauces, one combining almonds, chilli, coriander (cilantro) and chicken livers, which could be an inspiration to any contemporary chef. I could go on quoting Corrado's recipes, they are so readable, but that would not do justice to other writers of the period such as Francesco Leonardi.

Leonardi wrote a scholarly but uninspiring and rather repetitive, encyclopedic tome called *L'Apicio Moderno*, published in six volumes in Rome in 1790. Leonardi had ended his successful career as chef to Catherine the Great. The volume devoted to timbales and pies is the most interesting because it describes many dishes of undoubted Italian origin. The recipe for *Polenta alla Milanese* is particularly appetizing:

the polenta, cooked in buttered milk, is layered with butter, grated Parmesan, cinnamon and truffles. Another recipe I like is that for *Gamberetto all'Italiana* in which the prawns (shrimp) are cooked in oil, white wine and lemon juice with a mixture of chopped parsley, chives, shallot, garlic, tarragon and basil. The cooking juices are reduced after the prawns are cooked. Both recipes are still part of the Italian culinary repertoire today.

REGIONALITY AND DOMESTICITY

LEONARDI WAS WITHOUT A DOUBT A GREAT MASTER, and his teachings influenced the future generation of chefs. At the same time, in France, a great chef, but an even greater self-publicist, Antonin Carême was hailed as the unparalleled genius of haute cuisine and no chef could ignore him. Yet some Italians seem to have been able to produce recipes which had very little in common with the grandiose creations of Carême. And it is in these works that we can see the development of the Italian cuisine and written testimony of its regionality. In every cookery book from this time onwards, for the first time, food and dishes are placed in the context of a domestic household.

Gone for ever were the days of the banquets when live birds were wrapped in napkins so that they could liven the last course of the banquet cooked by Scappi for his master, Cardinal Campeggi who was entertaining the Holy Roman Emperor Charles V. Gone too were the days such as those, in 1581, when, for the wedding of the Duke of Mantova, the tables were adorned with animals made of citrons, castles made of turnips and walls made of lemons, all decorated with caviar, prosciutto, bottarga* and other gourmandises. Now, in the nineteenth century, even the chef to the first king of Italy, Giovanni Vialardi, included recipes "suitable for a modest household" in his book of *A Treatise of Modern Cookery and Patisserie*, published in Turin in 1854. Perhaps not modest in the modern sense of the word, but certainly not royal. Many of his recipes show Italian characteristics, thus side-tracking the French influence that, in Turin, was even stronger than in the rest of the country. Vialardi's recipe for *Cappone detto in Galera* is a blueprint for the Genoese *Cappon Magro**, one of the great, traditional local dishes. And his recipe for *Tomatiche alla Provenzale* is just like today's recipe for Pomodori Ammollicati. The book also contains twelve recipes for potatoes, including one for *Patate all'Inglese* (boiled potatoes), "beautiful and good" served in a linen cloth, with butter "eaten fresh" on the side, as they still are, even though the linen cloth might not be there.

In every region at this time we see how the chefs are searching for traditional, regional recipes. In Milan, in 1829, *Il Nuovo Cuoco Milanese Economico*, written by Giovanni Felice Luraschi, has many recipes that are the precursors of the modern equivalent. The recipes for Kidney with Anchovies and Lemon featured on page 140 and that for Gnocchi alla Romana on page 87 are identical to those clearly set down by Luraschi.

La Cucina Genovese by Gian Battista and Giovanni Ratto, published in 1871, is the first and still reputedly the best book on Ligurian cooking. Liguria, bounded by the sea on one side, is totally surrounded by mountains on the inland side. Its food had not travelled over the mountains, and this book is the first to show how strong the regionality of the local cooking was. It contains the first recipe for pesto, made with a little butter, as quite a few Italians (myself among them) still do. In a book of 526 recipes from a region with a long coastline it seems odd that there are only 38 recipes for fish. But the Ligurians do not need recipes for fish. They have always cooked it in the simplest ways, sautéed, deep-fried or boiled, and as long as the fish is fresh that's all that is needed. Most of the fish recipes are for baccalà and stockfish which, because of their unusual flavour and dry texture, need more complicated methods of cooking in combination with other ingredients.

Of all the output of the nineteenth century, one of the most fascinating and readable books is, to my mind, *La Cucina Teorico-Pratica* by Ippolito Cavalcanti, Duke of Buonvicino, published in Naples in 1837. Cavalcanti is the first writer to jot down his recipes in a more personal, chatty way which makes them appealing. He is also the first writer to give a recipe for pasta dressed with tomatoes. This baked dish consists of a layer of tomatoes cut in half, a layer of raw vermicelli covered by another layer of tomatoes. The recipe works well as long as at least twice the quantity of tomatoes to pasta is used. Another timpano (pie) is made exactly like the Sicilian *Pasta 'Ncasciata***. The maccaroni is served with a tomato sauce studded with tiny meatballs (or fishballs in Lent) and topped with a layer of fried aubergine (eggplant) slices.

THE INFLUENCE OF ARTUSI

SOME 50 YEARS LATER THIS DIRECT STYLE OF WRITING was taken up by Pellegrino Artusi in his splendid book *La Scienza in Cucina e l'Arte di Mangiar Bene*. Artusi is the first writer to gather recipes from all over Italy, although the bulk of them are from the Po Valley – he was born in Romagna – and from Tuscany where he lived, in Florence. The book was first published, in 1891, at Artusi's own expense but it soon became a bestseller, with over one million copies sold. When the book first came out its success was in part due to the inclusion, for the first time, of recipes from the north and the south. This happened at an opportune time, just after Italy had at last become a united nation. The success of the book in subsequent decades – published in over 100 editions by the end of the millennium – was due to the creativity, practicality and validity of the recipes, as well as to the easy, confidential and often jocular style of writing. The recipes, clearly described, are enriched by anecdotes, jokes and stories. They are all chosen with great care to represent the wealth of the Italian culinary tradition.

Let me just quote you the opening paragraph of the recipe for Pigeon, English-Style: "I want to warn you once and for all that in my kind of cooking names have no importance, nor do I care about pompous titles. If an Englishman should tell me that this dish is not cooked according to the custom of his nation, I wouldn't care two hoots. The only thing I care is that he would like it." The recipe is for a pigeon pie which receives the benefit of Artusi's master-touch – a little wine and lemon juice is added to the pastry and "to give the dish a more national character, I would previously sauté the pigeon in butter and season it with salt and pepper and spices. And you could also add a few chicken livers, sweetbreads and truffles."

The chapter on first courses is particularly interesting, listing for the first time soups and foods of peasant and foreign origin (couscous is one of them), together with many sophisticated and delicate broths characteristic of the bourgeois cuisine of northern Italy. The section on *Minestre Asciutte* (pasta, risotti and gnocchi etc) includes most of the classic dishes, from *Tagliatelle Verdi* to three recipes for *Risotto alla Milanese***, *Risotto Nero* (with cuttlefish) and *Cappelletti* and *Ravioli* with a selection of different stuffings.

The chapter on cakes, biscuits (cookies) and desserts is comprehensive, which shows just how wide Artusi's knowledge of cooking was, since most cooks can manage to produce a decent sauce or a good *Pollo alla Cacciatora***, but a cake needs accurately measured quantities, a well-balanced mixture and perfect timing. It also shows that Artusi seemed to know the downfall of many Italian cooks – the preparation of sweet recipes. The chapter includes a variety of foreign dishes such as plum pudding, plum cake, apple pie, Spanish custard and *kugelhupf*. The recipe for strudel opens with this jocular but charming warning, "Do not panic if this cake seems a messy mixture in its preparation and once baked it appears to you downright ugly, like a huge leech or a shapeless snake. You will love its flavour." This is the relaxed and down-to-earth style of writing that makes *La Scienza in Cucina* the most loved cookery book in Italy!

Artusi can be enthusiastic about some recipes and just as dismissive about others, as in the introduction for *Braciole alla Contadina*. "These are not for me and I prefer to leave them to the peasants. But since some people might like them I'd better describe them, and for the moment, I am an unremitting peasant." In the introduction to the recipe for *Quenelles* the dish is described as "probably invented by a cook whose master has no teeth".

Fun to read it may be, but the book stands as the foundation stone of modern Italian cooking. Artusi's recipes show a controlled combination of the flavours used to enhance – and not distract from – the intrinsic flavour of the main ingredient. This is the second commandment in good Italian cooking, the first being the use of top quality ingredients, which Artusi took for granted.

The only drawback to Artusi's recipes, for our health-conscious diet in the twenty-first century, is the generous use of butter, a fat which he considers to be indispensable to the success of a dish.

THE TWENTIETH CENTURY AND BEYOND…

THE FIRST HALF OF THE TWENTIETH CENTURY saw the publication of another classic, *Il Talismano della Felicità* by Ada Boni. An abridged edition in English was published in 1978. Boni was a dedicated teacher, and the strength of this book lies in the methodical instructions for each and every dish from the most basic to the very elaborate, including all the French preparations that are popular throughout Italy. The recipes are written in clear, although rather didactic, prose.

It is in the second half of the twentieth century that Italian cooking developed in a way that was to influence the rest of the world. Regional cooking in all its versions and versatility comes to the fore thanks to the publication in 1967 of a monumental work by Anna Gosetti della Salda. The book, *Le Ricette Regionali Italiane*, contains more than 2000 recipes divided by region. The recipes are all regional, traditional and totally and faultlessly workable. It also contains footnotes on the origins of recipes, and anecdotes related to the food in question. This book best represents, in a single volume, regional Italian cooking.

At the same time a series of works on the regional cuisines were published by Franco Muzzio of Padova. This series includes literary and gastronomic gems such as *La Cucina del Piemonte* by Giovanni Goria, *La Cucina Veronese* by Giovanni Capnist, *La Cucina Milanese* by Marco Guarnaschelli Gotti and *Dolci di Siena e della Toscana* by Giovanni Righi Parenti. All these books and the many others in the series contain recipes, as well as historical and social notes, and comments on the sometimes legendary or apocryphal origins of the recipes and ingredients.

Part of the credit for keeping Italian cooking within the bounds of tradition must go to the *Accademia Italiana della Cucina*. This gastronomic academy was founded in 1953 by the journalist Orio Vergani together with a group of journalists and writers concerned both with safeguarding Italian culinary traditions and with trying to improve Italian cooking through cultural and historical research. The Academy is strongly represented abroad and its members publish a critical guide to Italian restaurants in Italy and abroad.

I have recounted the history of Italian gastronomy as seen through the writings of the last six centuries. But although much is learnt about its development over that time, the fact remains that Italian cooking has always been to a large extent based on home cooking. This is the *cucina casalinga*† passed down from one generation to the next, by word of mouth and by the family recipe book. The family, after all, is the one social unit that counts for everything in Italy. And, when it comes to food, the Italians are very sure about what they like: they like the food they are used to, they like the food they see growing and being produced around them, which means home cooking and, of course, regional cooking.

Several factors account for the great popularity of Italian cooking abroad. Its simple, straightforward appeal is much in keeping with the spirit of our time. But above all else, perhaps, this popularity is due to the contemporary concern with the health-giving properties of what we eat. The Mediterranean diet has been scientifically proclaimed as *the* healthy diet, and of all the Mediterranean countries it is the food of Italy that offers more variety, more delight in its flavours and, as a result, greater pleasures.

the Italian Culture of Food

ITALIAN SHOPPING HABITS HAVE CHANGED SINCE the nineties, because more and more women go out to work. More and more people now shop in suburban supermarkets, but only once a week and only for certain things: all the household goods, plus sugar, salt, dried pasta and cereals. Most people tend to buy fresh products: fruit, vegetables, cheese, meat and fish in local shops, markets or small supermarkets dotted around the town.

This type of "spesa" – food shopping – is done at least three or four times a week. Indeed, any self-respecting Italian buys his or her bread everyday, so that fresh bread is on the table at every meal. Very few people make their own bread; they buy it in the Panetteria, usually white and occasionally brown, but seldom the dressed type which is eaten more as a snack and not as the essential accompaniment to a meal. Other daily, or at least very frequent, purchases are the cheeses and all the salumi, often bought at the local *salumeria* – deli.

The discerning customer will order their best olive oil directly from a *frantoio* – oil mill, and their wine from a *cantina* – winery. But for the run-of-the-mill oil or wine they will go to the supermarket and the *enoteca* – large wine shop.

There are of course exceptions to all this, and a minority of shoppers buy everything in the large supermarkets, but here the point must be made that even in the largest hypermarket all the food is of an excellent quality. From time to time I have bought seafood and other fish in supermarkets (something I seldom do in England) and found everything as fresh as I could wish.

Shopping for food is one of the joys of living in Italy. Time becomes immaterial. The man or woman behind the counter is at the disposal of the very discerning customer. This is at its most notable in a *macelleria* – butcher's, where the butcher – standing behind the counter on a higher level – selects and cuts whatever the customer wants. And the customer does know exactly what he or she wants, and demands it. You stand there and listen to these exchanges and, I promise, you learn a lot. And then you ask somebody how they cook this particular piece of meat and the whole shop will be the scene of a lengthy discussion of recipes and ideas.

Seasonality is paramount, especially with fruit and vegetables. Only in big cities can you buy out of season produce from abroad, which is never as good as the locally grown. Italians always prefer to cook and eat the produce they see growing around them. For this reason, if they have a piece of land, however small, they would rather grow their salad leaves and herbs than beautiful roses. They particularly like to grow herbs, either in the soil or in pots on the window sill.

MARKETS

WHEN IN ITALY, TRY TO SHOP IN THE MARKETS. Every town, large or small, has a weekly market selling everything from fake Fendi and Gucci to real (bell) peppers and swordfish and it is here that you will learn the rich culinary culture of the region. Not only the best places to buy anything and everything, they are also the places to enjoy a preprandial snack, be it piadina with squacquerone in Emilia Romagna, farinata in Liguria, porchetta in central Italy or fried calamari in Le Marche.

Markets are also the place where you can learn how to cook the Italian way. People are always willing – quite proud, indeed – to share their culinary secrets and to give you their recipes. Here are a few markets and specialist shops I can recommend.

VENICE – **THE RIALTO MARKET**

The most attractive display of fruit, vegetables and fish in the most stunning location.

PADUA – **IL MERCATO**

Near the Piazza della Frutta. Stalls and little shops selling excellent products.

FLORENCE – **THE SAN LORENZO MARKET**

Not only T-shirts and jeans but also fruit and vegetables and other good products.

ROME – **TESTACCIO MARKET**

The best place to learn how the Romans live and eat. A fascinating experience.

PALERMO – **THE VUCCIRIA MARKET**

A perfect combination of an Italian market and a North African souk.

SHOPS

TURIN PEYRANO – **CORSO MONCALIERI 47**

Where you can buy the best Piedmontese chocolate, which is saying a lot.

MILAN – **PECK**

This food purveyor has food shops for fish, cheeses, salumi, meats and wine in a few streets near the Piazza del Duomo. The famous Gastronomia is at Via Spadari 9, where the most exquisitely prepared food is sold.

BOLOGNA

Impossible to name any one shop. Go to the district around Via Drapperie and Via Caprarie and do not miss Tamburini in Via Caprarie, where the best of the region's salumi and cheeses can be bought.

FERRARA – **PANIFICIO ORSATTI, VIA CORTE VECCHIA 13**

The best bakery in a city famous for its bread.

ROME – **GASTRONOMIA VOLPETTI, VIA DELLA SCROFA 11**

Go there to buy a memorable picnic.

NAPLES – **PASTICCERIA PINTAURO, VIA ROMA 275**

Famous for its Sfogliatelle.

MARTINA FRANCA – **(PUGLIA) SFORNATUTTO, VIA LANUCARA**

One of the best bread shops in southern Italy.

ALGHERO – **(SARDINIA) CASA DEL FORMAGGIO, VIA MAZZINI 43**

If you like sheep's cheeses, this shop will delight your palate.

EATING HABITS

HERE I HAVE TO REPEAT THE BASIC TRUTH that Italians prefer to eat local food and specialities. The Emiliani will buy far more fresh egg-pasta, the local speciality, than the people of Puglia or Sicily. In the south, dried pasta made with flour from the durum wheat grown there reigns supreme. That said, nowadays dried pasta is the norm also in northern Italy for the simple reason that it is far more reliable. Very few housewives make pasta at home these days, although as a treat, fresh pasta may be bought in specialist shops; hardly ever in supermarkets.

The sauces are usually homemade; only if very pressed for time would any Italian lower themselves to buy a jar or can of pasta sauce. This in spite of the fact that sauces sold in Italy are all made in Italy and hence are far better than those made abroad, because of the quality of the ingredients and the knowledge of the makers.

Cakes, biscuits (cookies) and desserts – referred to as *dolci* – are not everyday food, mostly made for festive or formal occasions. Meals usually end with cheese and fruit.

Even children are not given many sweet things; they eat the same food as their parents and at the same time. Restaurants and trattorias do not have special food for children: you simply ask for smaller portions.

Italians do not eat out very often and eat only two meals a day. *Colazione* – breakfast – is not a meal, only a brioche and a cup of caffè e latte or an espresso at the next-door bar; anything quick and easy. *Pranzo* – lunch – in cities is now mostly eaten in a place near the office. In smaller towns and in the country people still go home for lunch, as all children do from school. This used to be the most important meal of the day, but now *Cena* – dinner – has become the main meal when all the family is round the table. The table is still the most important piece of furniture in an Italian home. The television might well be blasting away, but the family sits round the table and shares the dishes placed in the middle, with chunks of bread scattered around and the bottles of wine and water.

If you are lucky you might be asked to join a family for a meal. This happens more often in the country and in the South where people are more hospitable. Then you can really appreciate the love, care and importance that most Italians give to their food. And you might well eat dishes that never appear on a restaurant menu. It is one of the best experiences you can have.

EATING PLACES

Ristoranti – *These are the smartest places to eat out. Prices and quality vary as in other countries.*

Trattorie – *These are less formal and the food is usually more "casalingo" – familiar. Often there is no menu; the owner or waiter will recite and suggest the dishes.*

Pizzerie – *Ideal for a smaller meal, not necessarily smaller in quantity as in choice. Go where you see "Forno a Legna" – wood-fired oven – and remember that in the country pizzerie are usually only open in the evening.*

Tavola Calda & Tavola Fredda – *These are the sitting-down-to-eat part of a bar, offering hot dishes at the "Tavola Calda" and cold dishes at the "Tavola Fredda". Good places for a quick, cheap meal.*

Caffès and Bars – *where you drink a coffee or some sort or a drink, standing at the bar. They all serve "tramezzini" – sandwiches, panini and various tarts, brioches etc.*

Rosticcerie & Friggitorie – *Food is roasted in the first and fried in the second. Both are excellent providers of fast food that you can take home "da asporto" or eat there. The Friggitorie specialize in fish, while in a Rosticceria you can buy meat or poultry.*

the
Regions
of Italy

ABRUZZO

SPECIALITIES

Ventricina – *a salami flavoured with chilli, fennel and orange zest*

Maccheroni alla chitarra – *square homemade spaghetti with lamb ragù*

Agnello cacio e uova – *lamb fricassée*

Scamorza – *pear-shaped cow's cheese*

Cassata di Sulmona – *sponge cake layered with custard, chocolate and praline*

WINES
Montepulciano d'Abruzzo, Trebbiano

ALTHOUGH SITUATED between northern and southern Italy, the cooking of Abruzzo belongs to the south and consists of two distinct cuisines: the coastal one based on fish and that of the hinterland based on pork and lamb.

The Abruzzese version of brodetto* **, the fish soup made along the length of the Adriatic coast, is unlike others in that it contains no saffron, which is surprising since the crocus from which saffron is extracted is extensively cultivated near the capital of the region, L'Aquila. In fact saffron appears in only one local dish, scapece* (pickled fried fish). Chillies, however, appear in abundance. Small squid are eaten raw,

seasoned with chilli, octopus is cooked with chilli and the best known local pasta dish, maccheroni alla chitarra*, is doused with it, as is the succulent 'ndocca 'ndocca*, an offal (variety meat) stew.

Pasta-making was once a craft in the region, but is now a large-scale industry, with local brands in strong competition with those from Naples. It is that tradition, as well as the high-quality durum wheat grown locally, that has made the modern product so successful.

Excellent vegetables abound in the region. They are especially good in a rich minestrone* called le virtù, made in the spring with dried pulses (legumes), pasta and the new vegetables.

Some of the many pork products include prosciutto d'Aquila, similar to the Spanish jamón serrano, and ventricina, a sausage made with pork, chilli, wild fennel and orange zest. As in all other mountainous regions, lamb is prepared by the shepherds just as it was hundreds of years ago. It might be cooked "a catturo" (in a large copper pan in the open air) with basil, onion, sage and chilli, or with cheese and egg, or all'arrabbiata, which is alive with chilli.

Cheeses are of great importance in the regional diet, pecorino* being the favourite. The local caciocavallo* is made from buffalo's milk, and is spiced with chilli. Mozzarella* is made from cow's milk, as is scamorza*, which is sometimes grilled on a spit.

The locals have a sweet tooth, too, and enjoy finishing their meal with a pudding. Although desserts are served only on special occasions, the variety available is remarkable. Some are simple, others are elaborate, like the nocci attorrati – a version of almond praline, and the soft confetti*.

The most important produce of this region is the spice saffron, which is said to be even better quality than the best Spanish saffron.

BASILICATA

SPECIALITIES
Capocollo and other salami

Luganega – *sausage*

Lagane con lenticchie – *wide tagliatelle with lentils*

Agnello e cardoncelli – *lamb with local mushrooms*

Scapice – *fried anchovies or sardines flavoured with mint*

Burrata and burrini – *soft cheeses*

WINE
Aglianico del Vulture

THIS SMALL SOUTHERN region, also know by its Latin name of Lucania, is the poorest in Italy and its food reflects its poverty. First comes the pig, king of the table in all poor homes and raised by nearly every rural family in Basilicata. From the beloved animal comes salsiccia*, salami*, capocollo*, prosciutto* and salted pork fat, the last also being preserved with chilli and spread on toasted bread. The locals have been making excellent pork

products since Roman times. Luganega* was first made there, as can be seen from a reference by Varro and a recipe by Apicius. Lamb and kid are also popular, as they are in the neighbouring regions, with which Basilicata shares most of its dishes.

Bread is made with durum wheat and is similar to the bread of Puglia. The traditional shape, called panella, can be as large as a cartwheel, and keeps for up to one week. All homemade pasta is also made with durum wheat flour and water, in the same shapes as in Puglia. The traditional dressing for pasta is a ragù containing small pieces of pork or lamb called 'ntruppic, meaning obstacles. The final touch is given by hot peppers fried in olive oil, and a generous grating of hard salted ricotta*, the local speciality.

Vegetables make handsome dishes in their own right, such as ciammotta – a mixed dish of fried vegetables, and the interesting mandorlata di peperoni, combining (bell) peppers with almonds. Pulses (legumes) are also important, and they are prepared in a wide variety of imaginative ways, of which lagane e lenticchie (large tagliatelle and lentils) is the oldest.

The fish dishes from the two stretches of coast, the Ionio and the Tirreno, are the same as in Puglia and Calabria respectively. But the Lucani created their own special recipe for baccalà*, baked salt cod layered with potatoes, dressed with olive oil, oregano, garlic and the ubiquitous chilli.

Burrata*, burrini* and mozzarella* are the local cow's milk cheeses.

The desserts are rich with almonds. Particularly interesting are panzarotti* – sweet ravioli filled with puréed chick peas (garbanzo beans) flavoured with chocolate, sugar and cinnamon.

CALABRIA

SPECIALITIES

Capocollo, 'ndugghia, soppressata – *all salami flavoured with chilli*

Mustica – *sun-dried anchovies*

Ovotarica – *dried tuna roes*

Sagne chine – *a rich lasagne dish*

Fresh tuna

Scamorza, provolone and caciocavallo – *cow's milk cheeses*

Fichi alla sibarita – *stuffed dried figs*

ALTHOUGH CALABRIA IS TODAY one of Italy's poorest regions, Calabrese food has its origins in the region's great past. Greeks, Arabs, Normans, French and Spaniards have all influenced the cooking, which excels in vegetable dishes. Aubergines (eggplants) are especially popular and are cooked in an endless variety of ways from sweet-and-sour and the richest parmigiana**, to a type of fried aubergine sandwich that is filled with provolone and 'ndugghia, a pork sausage derived from the French andouille.

Fresh meat is a rarity, but all sorts of salami* are produced, of which capocollo, a salami made from the neck of the pig, soppressata, made with pig's blood and 'ndugghia are the most popular. These salami are flavoured with chilli, the traditional Calabrese spice. In winter, kitchens are festooned with chilli peppers that earlier in the year had framed south-facing front doors and windows.

The region is rich in fungi that grow on the Sila, a 3000-metre-high (9800-foot-high) plateau where the vegetation is similar to that which grows on the distant Alps. Chestnuts, too, are abundant on this fertile plateau.

Pasta is still made at home with durum wheat flour and water by women who shape lagane, ricci di donne (ladies' curls), capieddi é previti (priests' hats) and maccheroni (made with a knitting needle!). Pasta is usually combined with a vegetable sauce or with pulses (legumes). The richest pasta dish is sagne chine, lasagne layered with pork, peas, mozzarella, artichokes, cheese and tomato sauce.

Along the Mediterranean and Ionian coasts fish is the staple food. In the southernmost tip swordfish is quite common and is prepared in the same ways as in nearby Sicily: in pizzaiola* (tomato, oregano and mozzarella) or braised in white wine, or in bundles stuffed with olives and capers, all recipes containing the ubiquitous peperoncino (chilli). Anchovies are also popular (see recipe for baked fresh anchovies on page 98* **), as are sardines and tuna, mostly cooked with tomatoes. The local delicacies are mustica, also called rosamarina (salted anchovies layered with chilli) and ovotarica (dried tuna roes).

All the southern Italian cheeses are produced in Calabria, mozzarella*, provolone and caciocavallo from cow's milk, and also pecorino and some goat's cheeses.

Desserts are only prepared on special occasions, and most of them have strong connections with those of Sicily, with which they share the exotic Middle Eastern flavours. Dried figs, almonds, candied fruits, raisins and sultanas (golden raisins) feature in many of them – often chopped small and fried. A lovely nougat from Reggio Calabria is torrone gelato, which is a mixture of chopped candied fruit and almonds held together in a sausage shape in melted multi-coloured sugar.

Dried figs are another speciality of this region; they are stuffed with nuts — almonds or hazelnuts — and flavoured cinnamon and are sometimes coated with chocolate.

Two citrus fruits native to this region are citron and bergamot. The skin of the citron is candied and used in cakes and sweets. The bergamot, a type of mandarin, is prized for its aromatic oil that is used for flavouring liqueurs and Earl Grey tea and goes into the making of eau de Cologne and other cosmetic products. It is not edible as a fruit, because it is unpleasantly bitter, but if you are lucky you might come across bergamot marmalade, an exquisite, aromatic preserve, made on a small scale locally and rarely exported.

The other prized product is the local olive oil — it has a fruity depth with undertones of almond, and a peppery aftertaste.

CAMPANIA

SPECIALITIES

Pizza

Gattò di patate — *potato cake filled with salami and cheese*

Mozzarella in carrozza — *fried mozzarella sandwich*

Stuffed vegetables

All sorts of dried pasta dishes, mainly based on tomatoes

Fritto misto — *mixed fried fish*

Polpo alla Luciana — *stewed octopus*

Gelati — *ice creams and sorbets (sherbets)*

Sfogliatelle — *little pastries*

Mozzarella — *made from buffalo's milk*

Scamorza, provolone, caciocavallo — *cow's milk cheeses*

WINES

Greco di Tufo, Sant' Agata dei Goti, Taurasi

THE COOKING of Campania reflects the temperament of its inhabitants; cheerful, gutsy and inventive. It is what foreigners used to think of as typical Italian food. Spaghetti with tomatoes, pizza, mozzarella, stuffed or grilled (broiled or barbecued) (bell) peppers and aubergines (eggplant)... all these familiar dishes were born in or around Naples and went to the United States with the massive emigration of Neapolitans at the end of the nineteenth and beginning of the twentieth centuries. Fish and seafood are also popular now in Campania, they are usually served grilled, roasted or in the lightest fritto misto*.

Excellent vegetables and fruit grow here in abundance thanks to the volcanic soil and the ideal climate. The ingenuity of the locals and the sophisticated experience of the great chefs of the noble families, most of them trained in France, have created an array of vegetable main course dishes. The gattò di patate**, the parmigiana di melanzane** and the peperoni ripieni di pasta** are just a few examples.

The English aristocrats appreciated Neapolitan life during their Grand Tours. They enjoyed spaghetti alla pommarola (with tomato sauce) and fritto misto, eaten from the street stalls, as much as the extravagant cooking of the court and the aristocracy. These are the two extremes of a cuisine that is diverse, but nonetheless is always based on the quality of the ingredients and the creativity of the cook.

Dried pasta is the staple of Campania. It was born in Naples and it was here that the perfect marriage of spaghetti and tomato took place around the end of the eighteenth century, the tomatoes being the excellent ones that grow around

Vesuvius. Then the Neapolitans added clams and other seafood to the pasta, or used it to mop up the juices of their succulent ragù*.

Rice only appears in sartù*, an elaborate dish resulting from the union of French haute cuisine and Neapolitan earthiness. Sartù, when cut or eaten, drips ivory filaments of buffalo mozzarella*, the other great Neapolitan product that has infiltrated all corners of the globe. Mozzarella goes in the classic pizza, in calzoni*, and in stuffed vegetables. Other local cheeses of note are scamorza*, provolone* and caciocavallo*, all used both at the table and in cooking.

Neapolitan cakes are extravagantly rich, based on ricotta, nuts and citrus fruits. At Easter, pastiera* appears in every patisserie, while the cheerful pyramid of struffoli* is triumphantly placed on the table at Christmas and the dreamy sfogliatelle* delight all year round. And then there is the wide range of iced desserts, from granita* to spumone*, all benefiting from the excellent local fruit. When you have tasted one of these gelati you will agree the famous motto "See Naples and die" should be "Eat Neapolitan gelato and die!".

EMILIA-ROMAGNA

SPECIALITIES

Prosciutto di Parma, culatello, salame Felino, mortadella and other cured pork products

Cappellacci, anolini, tortellini, tagliatelle, lasagne and other stuffed pasta

Faraona all' aceto balsamico — *guinea fowl with balsamic vinegar*

Zampone with lentils

Parmigiano reggiano

Squacquerone — *a very soft cow's milk cheese*

Aceto balsamico

WINES
Albana, Lambrusco, Sangiovese

THIS REGION EMBRACES two different areas, Emilia, the western part, and Romagna to the east along the Adriatic. The cooking of these two sub-regions is different, yet many general characteristics are shared. It is always full-flavoured cooking created by people, and for people, who are deeply involved with what they eat.

The local housewives are experts in making pasta. Shapes and stuffings vary, but the quality is always the best. The imaginative creativity in matching shapes with different sauces is unequalled.

The Emiliani have also been able to create masterpieces from pork and milk. From the pig come as many kinds of salami and prosciutto as there are towns in the region. Piacenza excels in its coppa* and pancetta*, and Parma in its world-famous prosciutto* and culatello*. Reggio-Emilia is well-known for its large sausages, such as cotechino* and cappello del prete. The mortadella of Bologna, the zampone* of Modena and the salama da sugo* of Ferrara should be sought out in each city by any food lover.

Milk is the vital ingredient for the third most important product of the region — Parmesan cheese. Grana padano* and the more valuable Parmigiano-Reggiano* are a must for pasta sauces, for baked pasta dishes and for some meat and vegetables dishes known as alla parmigiana. Parmesan is even used in a fish dish, sogliole all'Emiliana, where sole are baked in wine and stock and sprinkled with the cheese.

Romagna, thanks to its coastline, offers many fish dishes. From sole to eels there is a wide choice of fish and they are usually cooked more elaborately here than elsewhere. And the Romagnoli's love for fish finds its apotheosis in brodetto* (fish soup), which is more full of flavour than most other fish soups up and down the coast.

Being great gourmets and hearty eaters, the Emiliani and Romagnoli could hardly ignore the delights of sweet eating. The almondy and crunchy torta sbrisolona**, the honeyed and spiced spongata*, the rice cakes sometimes in a pastry shell, Torta di Riso** and the tagliatelle cake are just a few that can be bought in the superb patisseries, all of which – like all other food shops – sell outstanding products. Shopping for food in Bologna, Parma or Ferrara is as rewarding as shopping for clothes in Milan or Florence.

The diversity of this rich cuisine has always been the cause of great rivalry among the seven provinces which compete in offering some of the finest dishes within the vast repertoire of Italian cooking. And a final word for yet another outstanding local product of the region: aceto balsamico* (balsamic vinegar), which is becoming increasingly popular all over Europe and beyond.

FRIULI-VENEZIA GIULIA

SPECIALITIES
Prosciutto di San Daniele
Cialzons – *ravioli with a variety of fillings – from potatoes to dried figs*
Jota – *cabbage soup*
Fish soup from Grado
Stinco arrosto o in umido – *roast or braised shin of pork or veal (ham hock or veal shank)*
Montasio – *cow's milk cheese*
Formaggio di malga – *fresh cheese made in the highest mountains*

Gubana – *a cake filled with nuts and sultanas (golden raisins)*
Strudel made with apple and/or ricotta

WINE
Collio

THIS SMALL REGION on the border with Austria and Slovenia is in a world of its own. Rich in history and art, it offers the gastronome unending surprises, in a way that is typical of a frontier country influenced by the cooking of neighbouring states. These influences – Austrian, Hungarian, Slav and Balkan – have been assimilated into the local cooking, which also has much in common with the cooking of the inland part of Veneto. While the basic ingredients are those of the Po Valley and the Alps, the spices, the aromas and the flavourings are definitely foreign.

This juxtaposition of cuisines is more evident in Venezia Giulia, while the cooking of the mountainous area of Friuli is deeply rooted to the land and its products. This is a poor cuisine based on beans, polenta* and soups. Notable among the vegetables are the white turnips with which the Friulani make broade, which are traditionally served with boiled pork.

A local pork product of great renown is prosciutto di San Daniele*, a prosciutto rightly considered to be on a par with prosciutto di Parma*. Pork also features in toc de purcit, where the meat is stewed in wine with a suitable quantity of spices. In Trieste goulash is a favourite; it is less fiery than its Hungarian counterpart and, in keeping with foreign customs, it is often served with tagliatelle or bigoli*.

Bigoli, Venetian by origin, are also served with fresh sardines. Another traditional pasta is cialzons, half-moon shaped ravioli; the stuffings, unlike other ravioli, contain an extraordinary variety of ingredients, from rye bread, potatoes and spinach to chocolate, lemon rind and candied citron. The traditional recipe calls for up to 40 different fillings. The dressing is the simplest – melted butter and freshly grated Parmesan. Another notable dish to look out for is potato gnocchi containing plums.

The cooks in this region excel in making soups, including bean and barley soup, cabbage and pork soup and the delicate paparot*.

Among the vegetables grown in the region, the asparagus of Aquilea and of Sant'Andrea near Gorizia are famous. Also abundant is the delicious radicchietto nano di Gorizia (dwarf chicory/endive). It is delicate, with a pleasantly bitter flavour and the small velvety leaves are ready in the spring when grown under glass and later when grown out-of-doors.

The sea along the coast from Grado, east of Venice, to Trieste is dotted with mussel and oyster farms. Seafood and risotti are a speciality here, as are the various fish soups. Montasio is the best local cheese and it is the essential ingredient of frico*, served at most Friulani parties.

The foreign influences become even more evident in the desserts, with a type of baked orange custard called koch, and strucolo*, the local strudel, both of Austrian origin. Another strudel, presnitz*, the traditional Easter sweet stuffed with candied fruits and spices, came from the east, while from Venice the local cooking has adopted the fritole*, which is eaten at carnival time.

LAZIO

SPECIALITIES

Carciofi alla giudea and all other kinds of artichoke dishes

Pinzimonio – *an olive oil dip*

Spaghetti alla carbonara

Saltimbocca – *sautéed veal escalopes (scallops) with sage and prosciutto*

Porchetta

Pecorino romano – *mature ewe's cheese*

Ricotta

WINE
Frascati

EVERYTHING IN THE region centres around the capital city, Rome, which simply brims over with lustful *joie-de-vivre*, whether it's for love, food, shopping or clothes. For this reason the cooking of Lazio seems to identify itself with the cooking of Rome, just as it did over 2000 years ago when Roman banquets were a wonderful gastronomic and spectacular theatrical experience.

In later centuries, cardinals and popes were happy to revel in the pleasures of life, among which good food ranked high. Great chefs were in charge of their meals, some of which recalled the banquets of Imperial Rome in their lavishness, if not their licentiousness! A dish that is still prepared at carnival time, and which better than most illustrates the richness of the baroque cuisine of papal Rome, is the pasticcio di maccheroni. Its filling consists of macaroni dressed with meat juices, layered with chicken livers, tiny rissoles and pieces of sausage. A layer of crème patissière is spread on top of the macaroni before sealing with a lid of sweet pastry dough.

However, in spite of all this extravagance the cooking of Rome is essentially simple and down to earth. In the past, as still today, the best-loved foods of the ordinary Romans were bread, cheese, lamb, olives, fresh vegetables (particularly wild greens), all locally produced.

The Roman countryside, with its volcanic soil, is ideally suited to the cultivation of vegetables. Remarkable for their excellence, the vegetables in Rome are extremely fresh and very varied. Globe artichokes are the quintessential Roman vegetable; they are used in numerous preparations, of which carciofi alla giudea* is the best known. Also popular in the region is pinzimonio* – a variety of raw vegetables are set on the table to be eaten with a dip of olive oil, lemon juice, salt and pepper – hardly worth mentioning but for the superb quality of the vegetables. Misticanza*, a mixture of wild salads, with wild asparagus and its cousin wild hop, appears on the tables in great abundance as soon as spring arrives.

The Romans are masters at making succulent dishes from simple ingredients. Gnocchi di semolino**, for instance, which Escoffier codified in his *Guide Culinaire* as "gnoki à la romaine" are made simply from semolina, milk and egg. In the hands of the Romans, however, they become "a dream of succulent lightness" as Waverley Root describes them in *The Food of Italy*. The same combination of utter simplicity and exquisite delicacy is found in stracciatella*, the best-known Roman soup. Roman frittate* contain vegetables or cheeses such as ricotta*, buffalo mozzarella* or pecorino*.

The Romans also have a talent for creating appetizing dishes from offal (variety meats), like coratella d'agnello* – lamb's offal – or the delicate pagliata, which is the upper intestine of a milk-fed calf or lamb made into a ragù* or simply grilled (broiled) or cooked on the barbecue.

Along the coast all sorts of fish end up on the table, as do the eels of Lake Bolsena. When I lunched at an unpretentious trattoria in Marta, on the shores of the lake, I could choose between five different ways my eel could be cooked: arrosto, alla cacciatora*, in sweet-and-sour sauce, on the spit or sautéed with bay leaves. Which, I wonder, was the favourite recipe of the thirteenth-century French Pope Martino IV, who had the eels immersed in Vernaccia wine, with fatal results for the fish, but which caused the flavour of the wine to infuse the raw flesh of the eels.

Even down to the desserts, the cuisine of the region has not changed much through the centuries. In the local trattorie they still serve maritozzi* and budino di ricotta (ricotta pudding), which were the usual fare served in the inns way back in the fifteenth century. And at carnival time, Rome has its frappe*, just as Milan has its chiacchiere* and Venice its galani*.

LIGURIA

SPECIALITIES

Trenette or gnocchi al pesto

Focaccia – *local bread*

Farinata – *chick pea (garbanzo bean) cake*

Pansoti con preboggion – *ravioli filled with wild herbs*

Cima alla genovese – *stuffed breast of veal*

Torta pasqualina – *artichoke and egg pie*

Candied fruits, marrons glacés

WINE

Cinqueterre

THE LIGURIANS LIVE between the sea and the mountains that rise steeply a few kilometres inland, and in this narrow strip they have created one of the most luscious vegetable gardens of Europe. They are helped by a temperate climate and the beneficial effect of the sea air on the plants.

It is these fruits of the Ligurian soil that have always taken pride of place in the local cooking. Meat and cereals were imported from Piedmont and Provence; on the peasant's table the only meat that appeared was rabbit. Still now, if you go for a walk up the peaceful green hills behind the over-crowded Riviera, you will see a row of rabbit hutches next to virtually every house. Nearby there will be bushes of rosemary and sage growing strongly and smelling sweet in the sun, and it is not difficult to anticipate how these fresh ingredients will soon be combined in the kitchen.

In the western Riviera olive trees are abundant, and the oil produced from their fruit – the local cooking fat – has a delicate sweet flavour that blends with every dish.

Focaccia* ** provides a good example of the quality of the cooking. It is simply bread dough, covered with sliced onion, stuffed with soft cheese or sprinkled with herbs. Simple it may be, but in Liguria focaccia reaches perfection. This quality of "just right-ness" is achieved by finding the perfect balance between one flavour and another, and the precise use of ingredients. The supreme example of this is pesto* **, which is the simplest of all sauces, yet is only really perfect when made with the local fresh basil and the right proportion of the remaining ingredients. Other examples of this perfect balance are found in the preboggion*, a mixture of local herbs used for stuffing ravioli, and in stuffings for vegetables.

Oddly enough, the cooking of a region with such a long coastline is not strong on fish, which is usually cooked very simply, as indeed fresh fish should always be. The Ligurian sea yields a poor harvest, but the Genoese, who are traditionally thrifty and hard-working people, have learned to make the best of what the sea offers them. They have created excellent dishes, such as mackerel with peas, out of second class fish. Their ciuppin, a fish soup, is often puréed in order to eliminate the mass of bones from the poorer fish. There are many molluscs, especially in the Gulf of La Spezia, where there are also extensive mussel farms. And there are a variety of recipes for salted and dried cod, of which the Genoese are particularly fond.

In Liguria even the puddings are based on local ingredients. The spices which the Genoese brought to Europe on their ships never touched their food. When at home, they made use of fresh, locally grown fruits, and they learnt from the Arabs how to crystallize them. They became such experts that during the nineteenth century European royal houses kept a purveyor of candied fruits in Genoa. Crystallized fruits, sultanas (golden raisins) and pine nuts, all local products, appear in most of their desserts, from the rich dome-shaped pandolce* to the delicate fried ravioli stuffed with marrow (large zucchini), candied pumpkin and orange and citron peels.

Apart from pesto, Ligurian specialities have not travelled much beyond the frontier; you must really visit the region to experience and enjoy the delicacies of the cooking.

LOMBARDIA (LOMBARDY)

SPECIALITIES

Bresaola − *air-dried fillet of beef (beef tenderloin)*

All types of risotti

Pizzoccheri − *buckwheat pasta with Savoy cabbage and potatoes*

Cassoeula − *pork and cabbage stew*

Ossobuco − *a casserole made with veal shin (shank) with the bone marrow left in*

Grana padano, gorgonzola, mascarpone, taleggio

Mostarda di Cremona − *preserved candied fruits in syrup flavoured with mustard*

Torrone − *nougat*

Panettone − *a rich dough-based fruit cake*

WINES

Franciacorta, Lugana, Valtellina

THE GREAT EXPANSE of this region covers the Valle Padana (the Po Valley), where the land is rich and the people are hard working. Yet the food on everybody's table reflects the past when the majority of the people ate humbly. Polenta, especially in the mountain areas, is the staple accompaniment to most meat, and the evening meal starts with an ample bowl of minestra* (soup). We owe the now world-famous minestrone* ** soup to the resourcefulness of the region's housewives, who added pork rind and rice to the usual beans and seasonal vegetables.

Pasta arrived relatively late in Lombardy, hence only a handful of recipes are traditional, the best known being tortelli di zucca* (pumpkin ravioli) from Mantova, and pizzoccheri** from Valtellina. The differences between these two dishes, the first rich and opulent like the

Renaissance which created it, the other as poor and humble as the forgotten northern valleys where it originated, typifies the complexity of the Lombard cuisine.

There are several styles of regional cooking, but certain common elements link these cuisines together. Meat is braised or stewed rather than grilled (broiled) or roasted, and butter is the cooking fat. Milk is used in soups and desserts, and cream appears in many Milanese dishes, partly as the result of a strong link with French cooking. Lately there has been a rediscovery of traditional dishes in some Milanese restaurants: ossobuco* **, served with a creamy risotto giallo made with marrow bone, is cooked without tomatoes and with a well-balanced gremolada*; crisp and juicy costolette* ** with l'oss (the bone in Milanese dialect); and vitello tonnato* made without mayonnaise (as in the original recipe) are but a few examples.

To the east of Milan, towards Veneto, polenta reigns supreme as the accompaniment to succulent meat and fish dishes, served with sauces which the polenta absorbs, and softens to become part of the sauce. Along Lake Garda the climate changes, as does the gastronomic scene. The cooking becomes lighter and fresher, and the countryside is dotted with the sparkling green of the lemon and citron groves, as well as the silvery green of the olive trees. The oil of Lake Garda, produced in very small quantities, is one of the local gems.

Of all Lombard towns, it is Mantova which best fulfils the expectations of its visitors. Standing apart from the usual tourist route, set on a romantic and misty plane, Mantova is rich in art and in local dishes. Both have the same origin − the court of the Gonzagas.

The white truffles found on the banks of the Po enrich the ravioli* stuffed with capon, opulent timballi* and risotto with wild duck, said to have been first made for a papal visit to the city in 1543.

In Pavia the most famous risotto* is, again, linked to the clergy; it is the risotto alla Certosina (in Carthusian style), which uses freshwater prawns (shrimp) from the nearby rivers. Frogs from the marshy planes around Pavia are nowadays served in guazzetto* in special trattorias just as they were served to the German emperor Frederico Barbarossa way back in the twelfth century.

I have left to the end this region's most important contribution to the gastronomy of Italy, the cheeses, of which there are a great number. Besides the world-famous gorgonzola, there are crescenza*, quartirolo*, bitto, taleggio, caprini and mascarpone.

MARCHE (THE MARCHES)

SPECIALITIES

Olive ascolane – *stuffed olives, breaded and deep-fried*

Truffles

Vincisgrassi – *a type of lasagne*

Porchetta – *roast pork*

Coniglio in porchetta – *roast rabbit*

Formaggio di Fossa – *special pecorino*

Caciotta – *cheese made from ewe's and cow's milk*

Frustingolo – *Christmas cake from Ascoli Piceno*

WINES

Rosso Conero, Verdicchio

THE SERENE AND PEACEFUL aura of this too-little-known region seems to pervade its cooking. There are two main kinds of cuisine in the region, the coastal cooking which is based on fish, and the inland cooking which is divided between the vegetable and poultry dishes of the hills and the shepherd dishes of the mountains.

The variety of fish and seafood is extensive. It culminates in the richest brodetto* (the fish soup of the Adriatic), which here contains up to 13 different kinds of fish. It is flavoured with wine vinegar and occasionally with saffron. Fish is cooked simply, mainly grilled (broiled), the creativity of the locals showing itself in the ravioli of ricotta and parsley dressed with a sole and tomato sauce, and in the cooking of stoccafisso*, of which the most characteristic recipe is in potacchio*. This is a sauce highly flavoured with rosemary and garlic, used mostly with chicken and rabbit. The latter, a popular meat, is also cooked in porchetta (roast pork), so called because, like the porchetta* which triumphs on stalls on market days, it contains wild fennel.

In the pasta repertoire I must mention the maccheroni di Campofilone, thin tagliatelle made with eggs and durum wheat flour and dressed with a delicious ragù of pork, veal and fresh tomatoes, and the superb vincisgrassi* **.

Truffles, both white and black, are another of the riches of this region; alas they are far too often exported to Alba or Norcia where they are sold for a higher price. And all other wild fungi are found in abundance in the woods on the slopes of the Apennines.

Elaborate cooking goes into the preparation of vegetable dishes, which become a course in their own right. Courgettes (zucchini) are sautéed with pancetta, onion and garlic and then stewed with tomatoes. Cauliflowers, popular all over Italy, are coated in a light batter of egg, flour and dry white wine, to which some cooks add a tablespoonful of mistra (a local liqueur made with aniseed) and then fried.

Cheese always appears on the table at the end of the meal, the most popular being pecorino*, which is sometimes served wrapped in walnut leaves. Other specialities include formaggio di fossa (pecorino aged in special caves) and casciotta, which is two-thirds sheep's and one-third cow's milk.

Cakes are more like sweet bread, apart from frustingolo, the Christmas cake of Ascoli Piceno, which is similar to the better-known panforte* of Siena.

A final mention must be made of the superb olives, which in southern Marche are stuffed with minced (ground) meat and fried – olive all'Ascolana – a perfect antipasto.

MOLISE

SPECIALITIES

Capocollo, soppressata – *salami*

Lamb, grilled (broiled) and roasted, and all lamb offal (variety meats)

Thick fish soup

Scamorza – *cow's milk cheese, often grilled (broiled)*

Calciuni – *fried sweet ravioli*

Ciambelline – *ring-shaped biscuits (cookies)*

THIS LITTLE-KNOWN region was, until recently, part of the combined region Abruzzo-Molise. Its basic food is based on the cooking of the shepherds and of the contadino (the small farmer). In the autumn (fall) the shepherds still take their flocks down to the lowlands of Puglia in an annual emigration known as the transumanza, only to return to the mountains in the spring in a journey whose origins date from pre-Roman times. Their food is whatever is to be found by the roadside, simply cooked on a wood fire.

The contadino owns small plots of land in which he manages to grow excellent vegetables in often unyielding soil. His basic diet usually consists of these home-grown vegetables, plus bread and oil, salami and salsiccie, the legacy of the beloved pig which still today is owned by nearly every family.

In addition, pasta is the staple and is produced in many shapes, some shared with Abruzzo to the north – taccozze, sagne, laganelle* and fusilli* – others with Puglia to the south – recchiettelle and cavatelli. The northern staple, polenta, is eaten in Molise more than in other southern regions; it is combined with fried vegetables in a dish called polenta* a tordiglioni, and, in another dish, with sausage, just as it is in the north. Soups also reflect the poverty of the locals in mixtures of dried beans, pasta and pig's trotters (feet) and nettles. A thick broth of celery and potatoes, layered in earthenware dishes, is similar to the tielle* of Puglia but without the fish.

Fish is prepared along the short coastline, either grilled (broiled) or fried, and in soups usually containing tomatoes and chilli, here given the delightful name of diavolillo (little devil).

Meat is rarely eaten, with the exception of offal (variety meats). Molise has the largest repertoire of tripe dishes in Italy, the tripe being mostly of lamb and kid. A delicious tripe dish which is especially good in this region is alla combusciana (boiled ox tripe dressed with a vinaigrette and served with celery).

In a society dedicated to stock breeding, cheeses – caciocavallo*, scamorza*, pecorino* – are important products.

They are mostly still made locally. Worth mentioning is a soft cheese, called burrino, originally from Campania, which can be eaten fresh and creamy when just made, or four to five weeks old when slightly tangy.

Desserts often contain lovely ewe's milk ricotta*, such as calciuni (fried ravioli stuffed with chestnuts, almonds and spices, and traditionally eaten at Christmas), and frittelle di ricotta (a type of fried, sweet ravioli but with only the stuffing and no pasta around it). As in the rest of southern Italy, most desserts are small nuggets of delight, more often fried than baked. This is the usual way of cooking sweets, since in the old days few households had an oven while they all had a frying pan (skillet) and plenty of good-quality olive oil – the superb condiment of Molisano food.

PIEMONTE (PIEDMONT)

SPECIALITIES
White truffles
Grissini – *breadsticks*
Bagna caôda – *garlicky anchovy dip for vegetables*
Carne all'albese – *raw meat, similar to Carpaccio*
Gnocchi alla bava – *potato dumplings with melted cheese*
Most risotti
Bollito misto – *mixed boiled meats*
Brasato al Barolo – *beef or veal braised in Barolo*
Castelmagno – *cow's milk cheese, one of the best in Italy*
Toma – *a group of cow's milk cheeses, also made in Lombardy*
Baci di dama – *almond biscuits (cookies)*
Pere cotte al vino – *pears stewed in wine*
Cioccolatini – *all sorts of chocolates*
Gianduiotti – *hazelnut chocolates*

WINES
Asti Spumante, Barbaresco, Barolo, Gattinara, Gavi, Roero

FRENCH COOKING HAS influenced the cuisine of this northern region of Italy. Here the cooking is elegant and yet still tied to the land, thanks to the pride the locals have in their produce and products. As a result of this dichotomy the local cooking is best described as cucina borghese (the cuisine of the bourgeoisie).

Another interesting aspect of Piedmontese cooking is that it seems to correspond to all the requirements of a healthy diet. Garlic is an important seasoning, which is not the case in the other northern regions. Rice and vegetables – some of the best in Italy – are eaten in abundance: the asparagus of Santena, the onions of Ivrea, the cardoons of Chieri and the (bell) peppers of Asti.

These vegetables, and others, come into their own in the best known of all Piedmontese antipasti, bagna caôda* **. Antipasti are certainly a highlight of the Piedmontese cuisine; perhaps only in Puglia is the array so formidable.

Then, of course, there are the white truffles of Alba, the jewel in Piedmont's crown, far superior to the black truffles of Périgord. A salad of ovuli* fungi and white truffles, a bruschetta* of truffle cream and anchovy fillets layered with truffle are musts during the truffle season.

Piedmont is one of the most important rice growing regions of Italy. The quality of this rice was already recognized and appreciated in the eighteenth century when the American president Thomas Jefferson smuggled two bags of rice out of Piedmont so that he could plant it in his estate in Virginia. There are many recipes for risotti: with cardoons, with artichokes, with Barolo• and the rustic paniscia** (risotto with sausage, beans and various vegetables). Then there is the delicate riso con la fonduta* and, of course, risotto with truffles.

Pasta is not of great importance in Piedmontese cuisine. The two original pasta dishes from this area are agnolotti* (a kind of meat ravioli whose delicate stuffing contains spinach), dressed with butter and truffles when in season, and tajarin (thin tagliatelle, see recipe page 68 for Tajarin all'albese**).

Meat and game dishes abound. Bollito misto* is the classic boiled meat dish, which should contain at least five different cuts of meat. Sanato* is the most prized Italian veal; it is also used raw, thinly cut, in carne all'albese. A sprinkling, or even a shower, of truffles can make this one of the great gastronomic experiences.

Cheeses are excellent and still mostly produced artisanally. These include the tangy-flavoured bra, a cow's milk cheese to which ewe's milk is sometimes added, and castelmagno*, a powerful-tasting cow's milk cheese, which was a favourite of many kings from Charlemagne to Vittorio Emanuele II and the soft, ubiquitous, yet outstanding toma*.

Desserts, sweets (candies), cakes and chocolates play an important part in the cuisine and the life of the locals. Zabaione*, pesche ripiene**, panna cotta*, the nutty-chocolaty flavoured torta gianduia, the pretty baci di dama* ** (lady's kisses) and, by way of contrast, the brutti ma buoni (ugly but good) are just a few. These, and many others, are what the Piedmontese love to eat at the many cafés that are so much part of their social life.

PUGLIA

SPECIALITIES

Incapriata − *cooked chicory (endive) and broad (fava) bean purée*
Tarantello − *salted tuna*
Capocollo − *cured ham flavoured with wine*
Ciceri e tria − *strips of fried pasta and chick peas*
Tielle di pesce − *baked fish dishes*
Polipetti − *tiny octopus*
Burrata − *mozzarella cheese stuffed with cream*
Cotognata − *quince cheese*
All kinds of bread
Lampascioni − *wild muscary bulbs in oil*

WINES

Castel del Monte, Copertino, Locorotondo, Primitivo di Manduria, Salice Salentino

PUGLIA HAS SHORT, mild winters, long sun-drenched summers and a rich fertile soil where everything grows in abundance. Given these blessings of nature, it is no wonder that vegetables are an important part of the local cuisine, supported by fish and pasta − a wholesome trio. Tomatoes, artichokes, fennel, chicory (endive), onions are all eaten raw, dipped in the fruity local olive oil as part of the magnificent array of antipasti*. The large bowls of broad (fava) bean purée with blanched wild chicory − incapriata*, and bowls of chick peas (garbanzo beans), reflect the strong links with Greek cuisine.

Since antiquity Puglia has had close ties with the countries of the eastern Mediterranean, particularly Greece. It is the region where the influence of Greece is strongest, and where the people seem to be more similar to their neighbours across the sea than to their compatriots on the other side of the Apennines.

In Bari, fishermen can still be seen carrying out a time-honoured procedure: they put small octopus, just caught, in a flat basket which they twirl with a rhythmic movement to make the tentacles of the octopus curl around. These curly octopus are eaten raw with lemon juice and olive oil, or fried. The Pugliesi love to eat their fish raw, provided they know where they were caught. The tielle di pesce** (fish pies) are the most satisfying fish dishes ever invented. Layers of fish or mussels, potatoes and/or rice, onions and/or courgettes (zucchini), are impregnated with the unforgettable taste of the local olive oil.

Pugliese olive oil competes with Tuscan and Ligurian oils for first place in the quality stakes, and there is no question of the quantity that is produced being challenged. The extra virgin olive oil is exported worldwide, while much of it is mixed with less good grades to produce pure olive oil.

Puglia's other important product is cheese. Whether fresh or aged, dried or smoked, it is all farm-made from cow's and ewe's milk, and all excellent. There are scamorze*, mozzarelle*, burrini*, and the fabulous burrata*, produced only in Puglia (which was allegedly exported by personal jet to the Shah of Iran's table in Teheran).

Vegetables and cheeses often form part of a meal that has pasta as the centrepiece. The types of pasta are more numerous in Puglia than anywhere else in Italy. The most popular of these, apart from the usual maccaroni and spaghetti, are cavatieddi (shells), laganelle (small lasagne), minuicchi (tiny gnocchi) and orecchiette (little ears). The fact that these lovely names are all affectionately bestowed diminutives confirms the fondness of the Pugliese for this food.

Pasta used to be, and sometimes still is, homemade, using durum wheat semolina, plain (all-purpose) flour and water, but it is much harder than the northern dough made with flour and eggs. The various shapes are paired with the right sauce, orecchiette (little ears), for instance, with rucola* (rocket/arugula), turnip tops (greens) or other wild plants.

The favourite meats of the Pugliesi are lamb and kid. The usual way of cooking the meat, which is often larded, is by grilling (broiling) or cooking on the barbecue, flavoured with rosemary and sage. This was the only way for the nomadic shepherds who, with their huge flocks, used to return home from the mountains of Abruzzo to the plateaus of Puglia before winter set in. This ancient voyage, which takes place twice a year, is called transumanza (see page 38).

Above all, bread marks Puglia as a region with ancient traditions. Pugliese housewives are proud of their bread, and the tradition of making it at home is still alive. Once a week, huge round shapes of bread dough are prepared, using some dough from the previous batch as a starter in place of fresh yeast, the leavened loaves being taken to the village bakery for baking. Of all these breads the most famous, and by far the best, is the pane di Altamura*.

In everything you see and touch, Puglia retains the feeling, and dignity, of a very ancient and civilized region. It was in Puglia that one of the most erudite and talented of men, Frederic II of Swabia, nicknamed Stupor Mundi, chose to live. He is said to have declared: "It is clear that the God of the Jews did not know Puglia, or he would not have given his people Palestine as the Promised Land".

SARDEGNA (SARDINIA)

SPECIALITIES

Malloreddus – *tiny gnocchi flavoured with saffron*

Pane carasau – *very thin crisp bread*

Pane frattau – *soaked Pane Carasau layered with tomatoes and pecorino and topped with a fried egg*

Porceddu – *spit-roasted piglet*

Burrida – *fried chunks of fish dressed with a sauce containing pine nuts and garlic*

Bottarga – *cured roe of grey mullet or tuna*

Pecorino and salted ricotta

Seadas – *fried ravioli filled with fresh pecorino and dressed with honey*

WINES

Cannonau, Cerasuolo di Vittoria, Vermentino, Vernaccia di Oristano

OVER THE CENTURIES Sardinia has suffered many invasions, but the invaders never ventured beyond the coast into the interior of the island; as a result there are two cuisines, one of the coastal areas and the other of the mountainous interior.

Recipes for fish that have been adopted from the invaders by the coastal people include cassola, a fish and sea-food stew of Spanish origin, and burrida*, a direct descendant of the Genoese buridda*, while the Sicilians taught them how to make bottarga* from grey mullet and tuna roes. All kinds of fish are caught around the coast, even lobster and spiny lobster (see recipe on page 96). Fish is usually grilled (broiled), roasted or poached and tossed with local olive oil and lemon juice.

The Sardinians are not people of the sea; the traditional food is based on products of the land – milk, cheese and roast meat, all accompanied by bread.

The traditional bread keeps well, such as the large civraxiu and the unleavened carta da musica* or pane carasau.

Traditionally the women are the bread makers, while the men cook the meat outdoors just as they have done for centuries. Whether kid, lamb or the succulent porceddu* (piglet), the animal is usually roasted on a spit or occasionally "in caraxiu" (in a pit dug in the earth), a method originally evolved so as to conceal the cooking of a stolen animal. All these roasts are flavoured with local herbs. For special occasions the most elaborate of roasts is made – pastu mistu consists of a large animal stuffed with a smaller one, which contains another, and so on.

The island is also rich in game. From wild boar, roebuck and partridge down to quail, thrushes and blackbirds, they all end up on the spit with rosemary and other herbs. Pork is not only roasted, it is used to make salami*, of which the most highly prized is prosciutto* made from wild boar. Sausages are spiced with wild fennel and chilli, and flavoured with the local strong vinegar and/or with garlic.

The Sardinians learnt the craft of pasta making from the Genoese, but their dough is made with hard wheat semolina and water and it often contains a pinch of saffron. The local malloreddus* are so popular that their shape has now been reproduced in commercial dried pasta, known as gnocchetti sardi. Culurzones*, or culurgiones, are ravioli* filled with potatoes, ricotta* and mint (the ancient recipe) or with Swiss chard and very fresh pecorino (the modern one).

The local cheeses, all made from ewe's milk, have a place of great importance in such a pastoral community. The pecorino sardo* is deservedly extremely well-known throughout Italy, as well as being exported. Pecorino Romano* is also produced in Sardinia, and fiore sardo is a one-year-old pecorino used a lot in cooking. Ricotta* is fresh, or salted for grating or smoked; goat's cheese can be fresh or seasoned.

Sardinian dolci are small, and usually eaten at the end of the meal with a glass or two of sweet wine. Most of them contain ricotta or other cheeses, cooked must and the local honey, which is reputedly the best in Italy. The most popular is seadas (fried ravioli filled with fresh pecorino and covered with honey).

SICILIA (SICILY)

SPECIALITIES

Arancine – *fried rice balls*
Sarde a beccafico – *baked fresh sardines*
Pasta con le sarde – *pasta with fresh sardines, wild fennel and other ingredients*
Pesce spada alla griglia – *grilled (broiled or barbecued) swordfish*
Salmoriglio – *vinegary sauce for fish*
Caponata – *aubergine (eggplant) stew*
Gelati – *many ice creams and sorbets (sherbets)*
Cassata – *ice cream cake*
Pasta reale – *almond paste*

WINES

Contessa Entellina, Marsala, Moscato di Pantelleria

SICILY, AN ALLURING and fascinating island, has had a chequered history. From the time when it was colonized by the Greeks, it has had to live under the rule of many occupying powers. Yet from each of these – Greeks, Saracens and Normans – the Sicilians acquired new learning and new skills, often adapting and improving them, whether in architecture, philosophy or cooking.

They learnt the ways of Greek cooking so well that the rich Athenians used to employ Sicilian cooks. In fact, the foundations of Sicilian cooking, which in its turn has greatly influenced all Italian cooking, are Greek. It is based on simple local food: fish, with innumerable fish soups, and vegetables.

Over a millennium later, another great civilization overtook the island. This was the period of Arab domination, during which many new foods and new methods of cooking were introduced. The Saracens brought aubergines (eggplant), spinach, bitter oranges, almonds, rice, apricots, sugar and spices. They taught the Sicilians how to dry fruits and how to make the delicious dolci for which Sicily is still famous. It is also from the Saracens that the Sicilians learnt the basic techniques of making sorbet (sherbet). And last but not least, the Arabs introduced to Sicily the art of distillation, the very word alcohol being a corruption of the Arabic *al-kohl*.

Next came the Normans, who brought to Sicily their own recipes from the north, their northern methods of cooking, and of preserving fish and meat. It was in the twelfth century, during the Norman domination, that the first reference to spaghetti appeared. King Roger II commissioned an Arab geographer to explore Sicily, and in his writings there is a reference to people making flour and water into strings which they called *itryah*. In Sicily and southern Italy, spaghetti is still called *trii* in some recipes.

To this day the Sicilians' favourite food is pasta. In brodo or asciutta (in stock or not), pasta appears at least once a day on the Sicilian table. The dish of pasta is dressed with a rich sauce, to be finally showered with grated local pecorino* or with salted ricotta*, a local speciality. Fish and pasta is a Sicilian culinary marriage, and from the many recipes I can only mention pasta with fresh sardines**, which is made all over the island in endless variations, the constants being the pasta, the sardines and the wild fennel.

The other favourite way to serve pasta is with vegetables, especially with aubergines. A popular recipe is pasta alla Norma, with aubergine, tomato and salted ricotta, named after Bellini's masterpiece, which in Catania (birthplace of Bellini and of this dish) is synonymous with perfection.

Fish is plentiful. A visit to the market in Palermo – Vucciria – reveals the richness of the Sicilian sea. Fierce swordfish and sinister-looking octopus lie next to cheerful red mullet, and crawly crustaceans next to silvery blue sardines and anchovies. The varieties of fish and seafood may be innumerable, but the manner of cooking is limited. This is because the Sicilians like to eat fish that is simply cooked, so as to enhance the taste of the fish itself, a rule written by the Syracusan Archestratus, whose fourth-century BC culinary notes are the earliest to be known in the Western world.

A characteristic of Sicilian cooking is that most dishes are based on simple ingredients, which are then embellished and enriched to make the end result a fantastic and almost baroque achievement. An example is the caponata**, which, starting with fried aubergine and onion, can end gloriously with a lobster on the top.

But the food in which the Sicilians particularly excel are the dolci*, an Arab legacy, and the sorbets. Sicilian sorbets and ice creams are paragons of excellence, owing as much to the Sicilian expertise as to the excellent fruit with which they are often made.

TOSCANA (TUSCANY)

SPECIALITIES

Crostini – *rounds of toast with a selection of savoury toppings*
Finocchiona – *fennel-flavoured salami*
Ribollita – *vegetable soup*
Pappardelle con la lepre – *large tagliatelle with hare*
Cacciucco – *fish soup*
Fagioli all'uccelletto – *stewed cannellini beans*
Pecorino delle crete senesi Marzolino – *excellent pecorinos*
Panforte – *a dense cake flavoured with cloves and cinnamon*
Ricciarelli – *sweet treats made from ground almonds, honey and orange zest*

WINES

Bolgheri, Brunello di Montalcino, Chianti, Nobile di Montepulciano, Vernaccia di San Gimignano, vin santo

TUSCAN COOKING has often been described as the best "cucina povera" (poor) in the whole of Italy, povera in this context meaning lacking elaboration and based totally on the quality of the ingredients. Although the city-states of Tuscany were torn apart by fierce and bitter clashes all through the Middle Ages, they remained unified in their cooking. The elements and ingredients are the same throughout the region, even though in the north they have a certain affinity with the cooking of Liguria and Emilia-Romagna, and in the south with that of Rome. One of the main elements common to all Tuscan cooking, apart from its simplicity and the excellence of the primary ingredients, is the wide use of herbs. Thyme, sage, rosemary and tarragon, the last seldom found elsewhere, are added to soups, meat and fish. Spices are common in Tuscan cooking, fennel seeds and chilli being popular. Chilli is called "zenzero" in Tuscany, a word that elsewhere in Italy means ginger.

The Tuscan olive oil is what makes the region's food so unmistakably Tuscan. Rather than a dressing, it is the main character in the gastronomic scenario of the Tuscan table. Food is sautéed and fried in it, soups are benedette by it (given a last minute benediction by spooning some oil into them), and every vegetable is made tastier with a couple of tablespoons of it. Olive oil is also used in the preparation of dolci*, as in castagnaccio* and in all types of fritters, in which the local cooking is particularly rich.

A traditional Tuscan meal should start with a soup. Thick and nourishing, full of vegetables, beans, herbs and olive oil, it will be ladled over the local pan sciocco (unsalted bread). The ribollita* ** of Siena and Florence rival in variety the acquacotta* of the Maremma, made with local vegetables and seasoned with the creativity of the cook. Traditionally pasta is not a Tuscan forte, although nowadays you can eat a good dish of pasta in most restaurants. There are, however, two pasta dishes that are Tuscan through and through: pappardelle con la lepre** and pici*.

Meat, chicken and pig are all superb – roasted on the spit or grilled (barbecued), they are eaten as they are, no sauces and no trimmings. All kinds of game are popular, from roebucks and boars to thrushes and skylarks, not only for their gastronomic value but also because of the Tuscan passion for shooting almost anything that moves.

Pork meat is cured to make the soppressata* of Siena, the biroldo of

Pistoia, sausages with chilli, fennel-flavoured finocchiona* and all the prosciutti*. The prosciutti from Tuscany, sometimes smoked, are much smaller and leaner than the more famous ones from Parma, but they have a stronger taste. Salumi* made from wild boar are also a local speciality.

The other great love is the bean. Not for nothing have the Tuscans been nicknamed mangia fagioli (bean eaters). They invented the best way to cook fagioli*, namely in a flask, to retain the taste of the white cannellini*. The modern equivalent of that method is to stew the beans in a cone-shaped earthenware pot. Beans are served as an accompaniment to pork, as in arista** or with grilled (broiled) chops and fegatelli* (grilled liver wrapped in caul fat).

Along the Tuscan coast the most traditional dishes are based on fish. The cacciucco*, a soup, and triglie (red mullet) alla Livornese** are the best-known dishes from the northern stretch of coast, while further south the catch is grey mullet, which is usually grilled, as well as cuttlefish, flying squid and octopus. Another speciality found only in Tuscany are the cieche* or ce'e (tiny baby eels) caught at the mouth of the Arno near Pisa. They are thrown alive into hot olive oil flavoured with sage and garlic.

Tuscany offers the best pecorini*, made with ewe's milk, of which the ones from the Crete Senesi and from Pienza are the most highly prized. Also famous is the marzolino* del Chianti, which Caterina de' Medici loved so much that she had it sent regularly to France. The usual, and the best, way to end a meal is with pecorino, which, in April, is accompanied by young raw broad (fava) beans.

TRENTINO-ALTO ADIGE

SPECIALITIES

Biroldo — *blood sausage*
Polenta e funghi — *polenta and wild mushrooms*
Canederli — *bread gnocchi*
Speck — *smoked prosciutto*
Ravioli alla pusterese — *ravioli filled with sauerkraut or spinach*
Vezzena — *cow's milk cheese*
Zelten — *Christmas cake of rye flour (Alto Adige) or wheat flour (Trentino)*
Apfel strudel — *apple strudel*

WINES

Caldaro, Santa Maddalena, Teroldego

THE COOKING OF these two northern areas, which are joined together for administrative reasons, is very different. In Trentino the influence of the cooking of Veneto is total, while — in gastronomic terms — Alto Adige could reasonably be described as an Austrian province, albeit with a powerful Italian influence.

In Trentino, as in Veneto, polenta* is a staple. It is made with either maize flour (cornmeal) or buckwheat flour (known as polenta nera because of the dark colour of the buckwheat) or a mixture of the two, and sometimes potato flour. It is eaten with pork meats of any kind, with cheeses or with stockfish.

Polenta is also eaten with a stew of mixed mushrooms, in which the Dolomites are particularly rich. The harvest of wild mushrooms includes ceps, chanterelles, chiodini* and russole*, plus many other species which only grow in this area. The largest fungi market in Italy is Trento, where on some days as many as 250 different species have been counted.

Cheeses, nearly all made from cow's milk, are an important product of Trentino, the best being vezzena*. Apples are grown in great quantity, and their quality is first class. Some local restaurants having created savoury recipes based on these fruits; one such is a risotto alla renetta (with renette apples), in which you can detect the influence, however slight, of German cooking.

In Alto Adige the cooking is whole-heartedly and unashamedly Austrian. It is cooked by people who are originally Austrian for tourists who are mainly of German descent. The food, in restaurants as much as in homes, is truly traditional. Oddly enough, while many dishes from Alto Adige have been incorporated into the cooking of Trentino, none from Trentino has made the slightest impression on the chauvinistic inhabitants of Alto Adige, even pasta having been almost entirely excluded. The one dish the two regions have in common is known as knödel in Alto Adige and canederli* in Trentino. It consists of bread gnocchi* containing speck*, salami* or liver, which after being boiled, are dressed with butter and cheese.

The pig is king of the table, pork often being accompanied by sauer-kraut. It is boiled, roasted or made into salumi*, usually smoked, of which speck is the best known.

The only traditional pasta dish is ravioli alla pusterese, the pasta being made with rye and wheat flour. The stuffing is either spinach and ricotta* or sauerkraut, in which case the ravioli are fried rather than boiled. Bread is brown, and also made with wheat and rye flours; the rye is grown in the local valleys.

The desserts and sweets (candies) are as Austrian as their names.

Kastanientorte is made with chestnut purée mixed with butter, flour, sugar and eggs; the cake, when baked, is covered with whipped cream. The local strudel contains seasonal fruit and egg custard and is flavoured with poppy seeds. Zelten, made with a yeast dough of rye flour, is studded with dried figs, sultanas (golden raisins), dates, pine nuts and walnuts. Zelten is one of the many preparations to have been adopted by the Trentini who, like their neighbours to the north, make it for Christmas. But in its journey south, zelten has shed the rye flour for wheat flour and gained some eggs, and as a result has become white, and lighter, giving it the Italian flavour and appearance that is totally lacking in the cooking of Alto Adige. After all, this area (also known as Süd Tirol) only became part of Italy in 1918.

UMBRIA

SPECIALITIES
Wild boar salami and prosciutti
Spaghetti alla nursina – *spaghetti with black truffles*
Lenticchie – *local lentils*
Palombacci – *roast squabs and all other feathered game*
Porchetta – *spit-roasted piglet*
Anguilla – *eel from Lake Trasimeno*
Attorta – *cake in the shape of a snake*
Pinoccate – *Christmas biscuits (cookies) made with pine nuts*

WINES
Orvieto, Sagrantino di Montefalco, Torgiano

UMBRIA IS A SMALL land-locked region of central Italy, straddling the Apennines between Tuscany to the west, Marche to the east and Lazio to the south. It is here, in Umbria, that the craft of slaughtering a pig and preparing the various cuts, performed by the norcini* (pork butchers) is at its best. The meat of the Umbrian black pigs is particularly tasty because the animals live in the mountains and feed on wild plants and herbs, and even truffles.

Pork products – salami*, sausages, cured and smoked meat and prosciutti*, appear as the *pièces de resistance* on every restaurant's antipasto* trolley. Then there is the splendid porchetta*, roasted on the spit and served whole, a dish born in Umbria, and now popular all over central Italy.

Beef is good, too, especially when it comes from cattle bred near the border with Tuscany, where the Umbrian breed has been crossed with the famous Chianina breed. The sheep and goats reared on the hills, the variety of game in the mountains and the farm birds and rabbits all go to make Umbria a paradise for the meat lover. This meat is often cooked on wood fires, the smell of which is irresistible at lunchtime around the countryside.

The pasta repertoire includes three local specialities: strascinati* and umbrici, both kinds of long thick spaghetti, and ciriole, fairly thick tagliatelle, all made with a dough using durum wheat semolina, eggs and water. During the autumn (fall) the black truffles enhance many dishes, from pasta sauces to rabbit and pigeon.

Another speciality of the region is chocolate, which has made Perugia, the region's capital, a famous name all over the world. The well-known company, Perugina, is based here, and makes the cleverly named chocolates, Baci* (kisses). These are modern sweets (candies), but I particularly like the creativity of the Umbrians with their traditional dolci*, many of which are linked to ancient superstitions. A cake called attorta is made in the shape of a large coiled snake, and eating it is said to protect you from snake bites.

VALLE D'AOSTA (VAL D'AOSTA)

SPECIALITIES

Mocetta – *cured wild goat thigh, chamois or beef*
Lardo d'Arnad – *salt pork fat with herbs*
Zuppa di castagne – *chestnut and rice soup*
Carbonade – *preserved beef stew*
Game dishes
Fontina cheese
Robiola – *soft cow's milk cheese*
Montebianco – *chestnut and cream pudding*

MOUNTAINS AND MORE mountains are the feature of this small region in the extreme north-west of the country. Yet the land is widely cultivated even at high altitudes, and its cooking reflects the topography. The most important elements are polenta, bread made traditionally from a mixture of rye and wheat flour, and soup, in which bread is usually present.

The soups are all based on good stock. In local kitchens the stockpot is always on the fire – an earthenware pot, is usually used, the older the better. Traditionally the Valdostani breed cattle mainly for cheese, and do not kill the animals until they are too old for milk or for work. Hence the meat is perfect for stock. It is boiled for several hours with all the vegetables. Once the stock is made, the meat is sometimes salted and put in barrels in layers with herbs and garlic, and this preserved meat is used all the year round. The classic local meat dish, carbonade**, used to be made with this meat.

Game is not as abundant as it was in the past. Venison, hare, pheasant, partridge and occasionally grouse and wild goat can be enjoyed during the season. But the most characteristic local game is marmot.

The other main pillar of the Valdostana cuisine is cheese, the excellence of which results from the rich pastures at high altitudes where the cattle spend their summers. The valleys around Aosta, the region's capital, account for the main production of fontina*, which is among the best cheeses of Italy. It is used a lot in cooking, notably in the Piedmontese fonduta*, and in the polenta côncia (polenta layered with fontina and butter and then baked). Tomini*, small cheeses made with cow's milk, are dressed with olive oil and lemon juice and served as part of the antipasto*.

The antipasti of this region can be as gargantuan as those of Piedmont – mocetta* (smoked roe deer), ham, dried sausages and boudin (a type of black pudding/blood sausage), fungi dishes when in season, the lovely tomini and the convivial fonduta are just a few.

In this rustic cooking there are two traditional desserts that are worthy of the high tables. One is montebianco*, a chestnut and cream pudding, and the other is the fiandolein, which consists of a runny crème anglaise poured over a bed of thinly sliced rye bread.

Fruit is not abundant, but there is usually a good harvest of chestnuts and fine wild strawberries, blueberries and raspberries. The pear variety, Martin Sec, grows only in this region and is always served poached in red wine.

Mention must be made of the excellent local honey, the best from the Valle di Cogne, where the beehives are situated high on the slopes of the Gran Paradiso.

VENETO

SPECIALITIES

Bigoli in salsa – *wholemeal (whole-wheat) spaghetti with anchovy sauce*

Pasta e fagioli – *pasta and bean soup*

Risi e bisi – *rice with peas*

Grilled (broiled) Treviso radicchio

All seafood and seafood risotti

Baccalà alla vicentina – *stockfish poached in milk*

Tiramisù – *coffee soaked sponge and mascarpone*

Zaleti – *maize biscuits (cornmeal cookies)*

Asiago – *cow's milk cheese*

WINES

Bianco di Custoza, Prosecco, Soave, Valpolicella Amarone, Recioto della Valpolicella

WITHIN THIS rich region there is considerable variety, yet the main elements of the cooking are similar throughout. These facets of the Veneto cuisine result from the time when the Republic of the Serenissima held sway over the entire region, and yet allowed the local communities to keep their separate customs and traditions.

The Venetians have a love of refinement. It was in Venice that the first fork was used in the eleventh century, for example. New food, too, travelled from Venice to the rest of Italy. One such was maize flour (cornmeal), which, in the seventeenth century, became the golden thread running through the cooking of northern Italy. The locals began to cook this new flour as they had cooked the others – buckwheat, chick pea (garbanzo bean) or millet – for centuries. They adopted it wholeheartedly, and polenta, plain, grilled (broiled) or fried, became the accompaniment to meat, fish or game.

The Venetians also popularized rice. It was first grown in Lombardy, but it was the Venetians, with their voyages to the Middle East, who saw its potential. They matched rice with their other favourite foods, fish and vegetables. They say they have a different risotto for each day of the year!

There is very little tradition of pasta in Veneto except for pasta e fagioli (pasta and beans). This thick soup, made everywhere in Italy, achieves perfection in Veneto thanks partly to the excellent local beans. One other pasta of Veneto is bigoli* (a kind of handmade thick spaghetti), sometimes made with whole-wheat flour.

Treviso is world famous for its radicchio rosso* and it adorns the stalls of the Rialto market in autumn (fall). In the spring wild and cultivated salads are displayed in all shades of green. Nearby the large white asparagus of Bassano testify to the excellent produce of the mainland. Peas and little artichokes come from the islands around the lagoon.

The other basic food of Venice and the lagoon is fish, and this also can be appreciated at Rialto. The selection is always bewildering. Away from the coast, stoccafisso* (dried cod) was adopted instead. In Veneto stoccafisso is wrongly called baccalà*, and recipes abound, such as baccalà alla vicentina and baccalà mantecato.

Inland there are a few meat dishes, all of the slow-cooking type but the favourite is poultry. Interesting recipes are turkey with pomegranates, bigoli* with duck and guinea fowl with an ancient piquant sauce called peverada*.

The sweet preparations are mainly simple biscuits (cookies) or sweet focaccie*. Baicoli*, zaleti* and other biscuits are eaten with a glass of wine.

the
Recipes

Bagna Caôda
Hot Garlic and Anchovy Dip

Piedmontese cuisine is one of the richest in antipasti, and bagna caôda is one of the most popular. Made in the area close to Liguria, where the sweet oil with which it is made comes from, it should be served in an earthenware pot placed over a spirit lamp or a nightlight in the middle of the table, as for a Swiss fondue. The raw or blanched vegetables to dip into it can be anything seasonal.

SERVES 6–8

50 g/2 oz/4 tbsp unsalted (sweet) butter

4 garlic cloves, very finely sliced

5 salted anchovies, boned and rinsed, or 10 canned or bottled anchovy fillets, drained

200 ml/7 fl oz/scant 1 cup extra virgin olive oil, preferably Ligurian or another mild variety

MELT THE BUTTER in a small deep earthenware pot or a very heavy-bottomed saucepan over the lowest heat. As soon as the butter has melted, add the garlic and sauté for a few seconds. The garlic should not colour.

Add the anchovies to the pot and pour in the olive oil very gradually, stirring the whole time. Cook for about 10 minutes, always on the lowest possible heat and stirring constantly.

Serve the dip when all the ingredients are well blended and smooth.

Frittata al Formaggio
Cheese Frittata

This is probably the most commonly made frittata* in an Italian kitchen (there is always some Parmesan and eggs), but every kind of frittata — cheese, vegetable or spaghetti* — is versatile; perfect as a starter (appetizer), it is also good as a light main course after a soup, or to take on a picnic.

SERVES 4

7 large (extra-large) free-range (farm-fresh) eggs

salt and freshly ground black pepper

50 g/2 oz/⅔ cup freshly grated Parmesan cheese

25 g/1 oz/2 tbsp grated Gruyère (Swiss) cheese

40 g/1½ oz/3 tbsp unsalted (sweet) butter

BEAT THE EGGS LIGHTLY in a bowl to blend the yolks and the whites. Season with salt and pepper and add the grated Parmesan and Gruyère (Swiss) cheeses, beating well.

Melt the butter in a 25 cm/10 in non-stick frying pan (skillet). When the butter begins to foam, pour in the egg mixture and turn the heat down as low as possible. Cook for about 10 minutes until the eggs have set and only the top surface is still runny. While the frittata is cooking, heat the grill (broiler).

Now place the frittata under the preheated grill and cook until the top is set. When done the frittata should be set, but still soft.

Loosen the frittata with a palette knife or metal spatula and gently slide it onto a round serving dish or plate. Serve the frittata hot, or warm or leave to cool to room temperature.

Mozzarella in Carrozza
Fried Mozzarella Sandwich

A classic snack from Campania. Its name literally means "mozzarella in a carriage", the bread being the carriage. You can also use a ciabatta* cut into thick slices.

SERVES 4

400 g/14 oz Italian mozzarella cheese,
    2-days old cut into 5 mm/¼ in slices
8 large slices of white bread
salt and freshly ground black pepper
225 ml/8 fl oz/1 cup milk
2 free-range (farm-fresh) eggs
75 g/2½ oz/generous ½ cup flour
vegetable oil, for frying

NOTE: In Campania, buffalo's mozzarella is used. Here you could use cow's mozzarella, although the result will not be quite as good. Use 2-day old mozzarella which will have shed some of its whey.

DIVIDE THE MOZZARELLA into 8 equal portions. Don't worry if it crumbles a little. Cut each slice of bread in half and then lay a portion of mozzarella on each piece of bread. Sprinkle with salt and pepper and cover with another piece of bread.

Pour the milk into a soup plate, while in another soup plate, beat the eggs together with a little salt and pepper. Spread the flour out on a board or a plate.

Pour enough oil into a frying pan (skillet) to come 1 cm/½ in up the side of the pan. Heat the oil quickly until it is very hot but not smoking.

While the oil is heating, dip one of the sandwiches into the milk very quickly, coat lightly with flour and then dip into the egg, letting any excess egg flow back into the soup plate.

By this time the oil should be hot enough, so carefully slip the sandwich into the pan using a spatula if necessary. Repeat with the remaining sandwiches, keeping them in a single layer. Fry the sandwiches until they are a deep golden brown on each side. Drain on kitchen paper (paper towels) and serve.

Salviata
Sage Pudding

This ancient Tuscan dish consists of a baked savoury custard highly flavoured with sage. The sage must be fresh and young, when it is sweet and aromatic.

SERVES 4

6 free-range (farm-fresh) eggs
2 tsp plain (all-purpose) flour
20 g/¾ oz/⅓ cup fresh sage
    leaves, chopped
½ garlic clove, finely chopped
40 g/1½ oz/½ cup freshly grated
    Parmesan cheese
2 tbsp double (heavy) cream
salt and freshly ground black pepper
1 tbsp olive oil

HEAT THE OVEN to 170°C/325°F/ Gas Mark 3. Lightly beat the eggs, add the flour and beat well to incorporate. Don't worry if there are some lumps, they will disappear in cooking. Blend in all the other ingredients except the oil.

Grease a 15 cm/6 in round ovenproof dish with the oil. Pour the egg mixture into the dish and bake in the preheated oven for about 30 minutes, until well risen and set but still soft.

Cozze Ripiene

Stuffed Mussels

The Italian love of stuffed food is well demonstrated in this excellent recipe.

SERVES 6

1.25–1.5 kg/2½–3¼ lb mussels in
    their shells
10 tbsp dried breadcrumbs
10 tbsp chopped fresh flat-leaf parsley
2 garlic cloves, finely chopped
freshly ground black pepper
7 tbsp olive oil
salt
2 tbsp grated mature (sharp)pecorino or
    Parmesan cheese

TO CLEAN THE MUSSELS, put them in a sink and scrub them thoroughly with a hard brush, scraping off any barnacles with a knife and tugging off the beards. Make sure that you discard any mussel that remains open after you tap it on a hard surface and put the rest in cold water. Rinse until the water is clear, changing the water as many times as necessary. Most mussels are farmed now and quite clean.

Heat the oven to 230°C/450°F/ Gas Mark 8.

When the mussels are cleaned, put them in a large saucepan. Cover and cook, in their own liquid, over a high heat for about 4 minutes until the mussels are open, shaking the pan occasionally. Shell the mussels, reserving one half of each empty shell.

Strain the mussel liquid through a sieve (strainer) lined with cheesecloth or muslin. Mix together the breadcrumbs, parsley, garlic and plenty of pepper, then add the olive oil and 4 tablespoons of the mussel liquid. Combine well together. Taste and adjust the seasonings.

Place the mussels in their shells on 2 baking (cookie) sheets. With your fingers, pick up a good pinch of the breadcrumb mixture and press it down on each mussel, covering it well and filling the shell. Sprinkle with the grated pecorino or Parmesan cheese. Bake in the preheated oven for 10 minutes, swapping the baking sheets from top to bottom halfway through the cooking time if necessary.

Crostini alla Chiantigiana

Chicken Liver Pâté on Crostini

These, the most traditional of all crostini*, are made throughout Tuscany. In this version from Chianti a little tomato paste is usually added to the pâté mixture to help counteract the sweetness of the livers.

SERVES 8

225 g/8 oz chicken livers
4 tbsp extra virgin olive oil
25 g/1 oz/2 tbsp unsalted
    (sweet) butter
½ celery stalk, very finely chopped
½ carrot, very finely chopped
1 small onion, very finely chopped
3 tbsp dry white wine
1½ tsp tomato paste diluted with 4 tbsp
    warm water
salt and freshly ground black pepper
1 tbsp capers, preferably in salt, rinsed
    and chopped
1 small garlic clove, chopped
1 salted anchovy, boned, rinsed, and
    chopped, or 2 canned or bottled
    anchovy fillets, drained and chopped
slices of toasted ciabatta bread, to serve

CLEAN THE CHICKEN LIVERS and cut them into very small pieces. Put the olive oil and half the butter in a saucepan. When the butter has melted, add the celery, carrot and onion. Cook for 10 minutes, stirring frequently.

Turn down the heat, add the chicken livers and cook until they have lost their raw colour. Raise the heat, pour the wine over and boil briskly until the wine has almost evaporated. Now add the diluted tomato paste and a little salt. Cover the pan and continue to cook over a low heat for 5 minutes.

Take the pan off the heat and mix in some pepper, the capers, garlic, anchovies and remaining butter. When the butter has melted, chop the mixture or work it in a food processor for a few seconds until smooth. Return the mixture to the pan and cook for a further 3 minutes or so, stirring constantly.

The pâté is now ready to spread over toasted bread, which should be good country bread, preferably ciabatta. The crostini can be served warm or cold.

Panzanella
Bread and Vegetable Salad

This is a rustic bread salad made in central Italy, which varies according to the vegetables available and the mood of the cook. What the dish must have is good country bread — two or three days old and preferably unsalted, like Tuscan bread. The vegetables must also be good, especially the tomatoes. This is the popular Tuscan version. It is best made two or three hours in advance.

SERVES 6
½ red onion
salt
6 tbsp extra virgin olive oil, preferably Tuscan
2 garlic cloves, bruised

2 fresh red chillies, split and de-seeded
1 yellow (bell) pepper
2 large ripe, firm tomatoes
½ cucumber
2 handfuls of fresh basil leaves, torn
1 tbsp capers, preferably in salt, rinsed
about 2 tbsp red wine vinegar
200 g/7 oz/about 7 slices best country bread (see introduction), crust removed

AT LEAST 1 HOUR (but preferably 2–3 hours) before you want to serve panzanella, slice the onion into very thin rings, put the rings in a bowl with 1 teaspoon salt and cover with cold water. Leave to soak. This is not necessary if the onion is really mild or you don't mind the strong flavour of raw onion. Put the olive oil, garlic and chillies in a bowl and leave to infuse for the same length of time.

Trim, core and quarter the yellow (bell) pepper and cut it into small cubes. Rinse the tomatoes, cut in half and squeeze out the seeds. Cut the tomato flesh into small cubes. Do this on a plate to collect the juice. Peel the cucumber and cut it in half, scrape out the seeds if necessary, then slice it. Put all these ingredients in a bowl, with the tomato juice from the plate, the basil and capers.

Drain and dry the onion and add it to the bowl. Remove the garlic and chillies from the oil. Beat 2 tablespoons vinegar into the oil to form an emulsion and pour over the vegetables. Season with salt.

Slice the bread and cut into 2 cm/ ¾ in pieces. Add the bread to the salad and immediately start mixing until everything is thoroughly combined. Taste and adjust the quantities of salt and vinegar.

Serve the salad cold, but not chilled.

Tonno e Fagioli in Insalata
Tuna and Bean Salad

Now that red onions are readily available, this traditional Tuscan salad has become much more pleasant than when made with stronger varieties of onion.

SERVES 4

½–1 red onion, according to size
salt
2 x 400 g/14 oz cans cannellini beans
5 tbsp olive oil
freshly ground black pepper
200 g/7 oz can Italian or Spanish tuna in olive oil, drained

SLICE THE ONION very thinly and put it in a bowl. Pour in cold water to cover, add 1 teaspoon salt and set the bowl aside for at least 1 hour. This will make the onion sweeter and more digestible.

Rinse the beans under cold water and drain well. Turn them into a bowl and dress them with half the oil and salt and pepper to taste. Toss thoroughly but gently and pile the beans into a dish or bowl. Flake the tuna and put it on top of the beans.

Drain the onion slices and pat them dry with kitchen paper. Sprinkle the onions on top of the tuna. Pour over the rest of the oil and season to taste with salt and pepper.

Pancotto
Bread Soup

Made in most regions of Italy, pancotto comes in as many versions as there are cooks. This is one of my pancotti*. Make it with good country bread such as Pugliese or pain rustique, not with sliced loaf or sandwich bread, which will make it gluey, thick and unpleasant.

SERVES 4

175 g/6 oz/about 4 slices stale crustless white bread (see introduction)
5 tbsp extra virgin olive oil
½–1 tsp crushed dried chillies
3 garlic cloves, chopped
2 tbsp chopped fresh flat-leaf parsley
1.5 litres/3 pints/1⅔ quarts hot light meat or chicken stock, or best bouillon cubes dissolved in the same quantity of water
salt and freshly ground black pepper
freshly grated pecorino cheese, to serve

CUT THE BREAD into very small pieces and process in a food processor for a few seconds, or chop coarsely.

Put the olive oil, chillies, garlic and parsley in a pan and sauté for 30 seconds. Add the bread and cook, stirring frequently, for 3 or 4 minutes, until the bread begins to turn pale golden brown. Add the heated stock and simmer for 30 minutes in a covered pan.

Taste and check the seasonings before serving. Serve the soup with grated pecorino cheese on the side.

La Ribollita

Tuscan Bean Soup

I was taught to cook La Ribollita by my neighbours in Chianti. If you cannot find cavolo nero*, replace it with more Savoy cabbage. Soak the beans for twelve hours and prepare the soup a day in advance to allow the flavours to develop.

SERVES 6–8

225 g/8 oz/1¼ cups dried
    cannellini beans
5 tbsp extra virgin olive oil
1 Spanish (Bermuda) onion, sliced
½–1 tsp crushed dried chillies
salt
2 ripe fresh tomatoes, peeled, de-seeded
    and coarsely chopped
1 tbsp tomato paste
3 potatoes, cut into small cubes
2 carrots, cut into small cubes
1 small leek, both white and green parts,
    cut into small pieces
3 celery stalks, cut into small pieces
250 g/9 oz/3 cups shredded cavolo nero
    (see introduction)
200 g/7 oz/2½ cups shredded
    Savoy cabbage
2 garlic cloves, sliced
3 or 4 sprigs of fresh thyme
freshly ground black pepper

FOR COOKING THE BEANS

1 onion, cut into quarters
1 small celery stalk, cut into pieces
sprigs of fresh sage, rosemary
    and parsley
3 garlic cloves, sliced

TO SERVE

1 or 2 Spanish (Bermuda) onions
6–8 slices of country-type bread,
    such as Pugliese
2 garlic cloves, cut in half
2 tbsp extra virgin olive oil

SOAK THE BEANS in cold water for 12 hours, then drain and rinse them.

Put the beans in a large stockpot with all the ingredients for cooking the beans. Pour in enough cold water to cover the beans by about 5 cm/2 in. Bring slowly to the boil. Cover and cook gently until the beans are well done, about 1½ hours.

Lift all the beans out of the liquid with a slotted spoon. Purée three-quarters of the beans into a bowl using a food mill with the large-hole disc fitted. Alternatively, purée them coarsely in a food processor, then turn them into a bowl. Leave the remaining beans whole and strain the cooking liquid into another bowl, discarding the herbs and vegetables.

Put the olive oil into the pot in which the beans were cooked. Add the onion and chillies and sprinkle with a pinch of salt. Sauté for about 10 minutes. Add the tomatoes and tomato paste and cook for 2 or 3 minutes, then mix in the bean purée. Let it take up the flavour for a couple of minutes while you stir it, then add all the other vegetables, the garlic and thyme.

Measure the bean liquid and add enough water to make it up to about 1.5 litres/3 pints/1⅔ quarts. Add it to the pot, together with salt, and bring to the boil. Cook over the lowest possible heat for about 2 hours. Add pepper and check seasoning. Leave overnight.

The next day, heat the oven to 180°C/350°F/Gas Mark 4.

Mix the whole beans into the soup. Slice the onion very finely and arrange in a thin layer all over the surface of the soup. Put the pot in the preheated oven and cook until the onion is tender. This will take about 1 hour.

Rub the bread with the halved garlic cloves, then toast under the grill (broiler). Put the bread into individual soup bowls. Ladle the soup over it, drizzle a little oil over each bowl and serve.

Minestrone alla Milanese

Milanese Vegetable Soup

You can add small tubular pasta to this soup instead of rice, although the classic Milanese version is always made with rice.

SERVES 6–8

150 g/5 oz/¾ cup dried borlotti beans
50 g/2 oz/4 tbsp unsalted (sweet) butter
50 g/2 oz pancetta, chopped
3 onions, sliced
4 carrots, diced
2 celery stalks, diced
2 courgettes (zucchini), diced
100 g/3½ oz/⅔ cup French (green) beans, diced
100 g/3½ oz/scant 1 cup shelled fresh peas
200 g/7 oz/2½ cups Savoy cabbage, shredded
1.5–2 litres/3–4 pints/1⅔ -2¼ quarts meat stock, or 3 best bouillon cubes dissolved in the same quantity of water
350 g/12 oz floury (mealy) potatoes, such as Idaho or Russet, cut in half
225 g/8 oz ripe fresh tomatoes, skinned, or canned plum tomatoes, drained
salt and freshly ground black pepper
175 g/6 oz/¾ cup + 2 tbsp Italian rice, preferably Vialone Nano
75 g/2½ oz/scant 1 cup freshly grated Parmesan cheese

SOAK THE BEANS in cold water for 12 hours, then drain and rinse them.

Melt the butter in a large, heavy pot, preferably flameproof earthenware, and add the pancetta and onions. Sauté gently for 5 minutes or so and then add the diced carrots and celery. After 2 or 3 minutes, add the borlotti beans. Sauté for a further 5 minutes, stirring frequently, then add the diced courgettes (zucchini) and French (green) beans and peas. After 5 minutes or so, mix in the cabbage. Stir everything together for about 5 minutes to coat in the fat.

Add the stock, potatoes, tomatoes, salt and pepper to taste. Bring the soup to the boil, cover the pan and simmer over a very low heat for about 3 hours.

Lift out the potatoes with a slotted spoon, mash them with a fork, then return them to the soup. Taste and adjust the seasoning.

Add the rice and cook the soup for about another 10 minutes, until al dente. Stir in 4 tablespoons of the grated Parmesan and serve the remaining cheese separately.

Cook's tip

Homemade stock is invariably the best choice for making soup. However, some good-quality brands of ready-made stock can be found in the chiller cabinets in supermarkets. If you are buying ready-made stock or stock (bouillon) cubes, always check the ingredients carefully, keeping an especially sharp eye on the salt content.

Minestra di Pomodori alla Calabrese

Tomato Soup

A recipe from Calabria in southern Italy, where excellent tomatoes grow. Make it only when you can get hold of really good tomatoes.

SERVES 4–5
6 tbsp extra virgin olive oil
2 garlic cloves, finely chopped
5 ripe fresh tomatoes, peeled and
   coarsely chopped
1 onion, thinly sliced
2 tbsp chopped fresh flat-leaf parsley
salt and freshly ground black pepper
140 g/4½ oz/1 cup ditalini or other
   small tubular pasta
freshly grated mature (sharp) pecorino
   cheese, to serve

HEAT THE OLIVE OIL in a pan, preferably earthenware, and add the garlic, tomatoes, onion and half the chopped parsley. Sauté for about 10 minutes, stirring frequently.

Add 1.5 litres/3 pints/1⅔ quarts water, salt and pepper. Bring to the boil and cook, uncovered, over very low heat for about 20 minutes.

Raise the heat and drop in the pasta. Cook the pasta until al dente. Add the remaining parsley before serving.

Serve the pecorino in a bowl for sprinkling over the soup.

Jota

Bean and Barley Soup

This version is from Venezia Giulia, where sauerkraut is used instead of brovade (macerated turnips), which is traditionally used in Friuli.

SERVES 4
100 g/3½ oz/½ cup dried borlotti beans
25 g/1 oz/2 tbsp unsalted
   (sweet) butter
2 tbsp olive oil
150 g/5 oz smoked pancetta, cubed
1 garlic clove, chopped
1 small onion, chopped
2 tbsp chopped fresh flat-leaf parsley
1 tbsp chopped fresh sage
1 litre/1¾ pints/1 quart meat stock, or
   best bouillon cubes dissolved in the
   same quantity of water
100 g/3½ oz/½ cup pearl barley, rinsed
2 tbsp extra virgin olive oil
150 g/5 oz/¾ cup sauerkraut
salt

SOAK THE BEANS in cold water for about 12 hours, then drain and rinse them.

Melt the butter with the olive oil in a stockpot and add the pancetta, garlic, onion and herbs. Sauté for 10 minutes, then add the beans and stir to coat them in the fat. Pour in the stock, cover the pot and simmer for about 1 hour.

Add the barley and continue to simmer for a further hour, until the barley and beans are tender.

Heat the extra virgin olive oil in a saucepan and sauté the sauerkraut for about 10 minutes, then add it to the soup, together with some hot water if the soup is too thick. Don't add too much water though, because this type of soup should be thick. Add salt to taste; no pepper is added in the traditional recipe. Cook for a further 15 minutes and then serve.

Paniscia

Bean and Vegetable Soup

I have chosen this recipe from Novara in north-eastern Piedmont as an example of the creativity of "cucina povera". The dish is a nourishing, thick risotto*-style soup, a perfect all-in-one meal.

SERVES 4–6

200 g/7 oz/1 cup dried borlotti beans
1 knuckle of unsmoked bacon or ham (fresh ham hock)
1 bay leaf
1½ onions [1 sliced, ½ finely chopped]
1 carrot, diced
1 celery stalk, diced
2 or 3 cabbage leaves, shredded
75 g/2½ oz unsmoked pancetta, cut into cubes
40 g/1½ oz/3 tbsp unsalted (sweet) butter
2 garlic cloves, finely chopped
2 sprigs of fresh rosemary, chopped
100 g/3½ oz luganega or other mild pure pork sausage
225 g/8 oz/1 heaped cup Italian risotto rice
1 tbsp tomato paste
120 ml/4 fl oz/½ cup red wine
salt and freshly ground black pepper

SOAK THE BEANS in cold water for 12 hours, then drain and rinse them.

Put the soaked beans, bacon or ham knuckle (ham hock), bay leaf, sliced onion, carrot, celery and cabbage in a heavy saucepan. Cover with about 2 litres/4 pints/2¼ quarts cold water and bring slowly to the boil. Simmer, covered, for about 3 hours.

Leaving the soup to simmer, lift out the knuckle and remove the meat from the bone. Cut the meat into small pieces and reserve. Remove the bay leaf from the soup and discard.

Put the pancetta, butter, garlic, rosemary, luganega and the finely chopped onion into a clean saucepan and fry gently for 10 minutes, stirring frequently. Add the rice and mix thoroughly to coat all the grains. Mix in the pieces of meat from the knuckle and the tomato paste, then cook, stirring, for 1 minute. Pour over the wine and boil briskly for a couple of minutes.

Add 200 ml/7 fl oz/scant 1 cup of the simmering soup and stir. When the rice has absorbed nearly all the liquid, add another 150 ml/5 fl oz/⅔ cup of the soup. Keep stirring the rice and adding more soup as the rice dries out, but do not add too much soup at one time. The rice should cook over medium heat.

When the rice is cooked, strain the remaining soup and add any beans or pieces of vegetable to the soup, but do not add any more liquid. Give the soup a good stir and then taste and season with salt and pepper.

Zuppa di Farro e Fagioli

Farro and Bean Soup

There are many different zuppe di farro, but they all work on the same principle: the farro cooks in a bean purée. In its original version this recipe contains the fat of a prosciutto* knuckle or hock instead of pancetta*.

SERVES 6
200 g/7 oz/1 cup dried borlotti beans
vegetable stock, as necessary
1 celery stalk
2 garlic cloves
½ onion
100 g/3½ oz unsmoked pancetta, cut into cubes
about 6 fresh sage leaves
1 sprig of fresh rosemary, needles only
a handful of fresh marjoram
1 tbsp olive oil
1 tbsp tomato paste
salt and freshly ground black pepper
a pinch of ground cloves
2 pinches of ground cinnamon
¼ tsp grated nutmeg
150 g/5 oz/¾ cup pearl farro (see page 234)
extra virgin olive oil, to serve

SOAK THE BEANS in cold water for about 12 hours, then drain and rinse them and put them in a stockpot, preferably earthenware.

Pour over enough water to cover the beans by about 5 cm/2 in. Bring to the boil, then cook at a very low simmer for 2–3 hours until the beans are very tender.

Lift the beans out of the cooking liquid with a slotted spoon and purée them in a food mill, if available, or in a food processor until smooth.

Measure the bean liquid and add enough vegetable stock to make up to 1 litre/1¾ pints/1 quart.

Chop or process the celery, garlic, onion, pancetta and herbs to a pounded mixture. Put into the pot in which the beans were cooked, together with the olive oil. Sauté for 5 minutes, stirring occasionally, then mix in the tomato paste and sauté for 1 minute. Add the bean purée and turn it over and over for 5 minutes or so to take up the flavour of the soffritto*. Add the measured liquid, stirring constantly, and bring to the boil. Season with salt and pepper and add the spices.

Rinse the pearl farro and add to the pot. Cook until it is tender, which will take about 40 minutes.

Serve the soup in individual bowls with a generous drizzle of extra virgin olive oil.

Cook's tip
Keep a note of the "use by" date on all dried pulses (legumes) — and check it from time to time. In any case, they should always be eaten within a year of being harvested. Otherwise they will become hard and wrinkly and no amount of cooking will make them tender.

Brodo di Carne

Meat Stock

Italian brodo* di carne is much more delicate than English or French meat stock. This is the meat stock I have used in testing the recipes in this book, but if you don't have the time or inclination to make it I recommend you use a good-quality bouillon cube or powder dissolved in the same quantity of water as the stock.

MAKES 1.5–2 LITRES/
3–4 PINTS/1⅔–2¼ QUARTS
1.5 kg/3¼ lb assorted beef, veal and
   chicken, cut into large pieces
1 onion, halved and stuck with 3 cloves
1 or 2 carrots, cut into pieces
2 celery stalks, cut into pieces
1 fennel stalk or a few feathery
   fennel tops
1 leek, cut into pieces
a handful of mushroom peelings
   or stalks
6 parsley stalks
1 bay leaf
1 garlic clove, peeled
1 ripe fresh tomato, quartered
6 peppercorns
1 tsp salt

PUT ALL THE INGREDIENTS in a stockpot. Add about 3 litres/5 pints/3½ quarts cold water, or enough to cover everything, and bring to the boil. The water must be cold to start with, so that the meat and vegetables can slowly release their juices. Set the lid very slightly askew for the steam to escape and turn the heat down to the minimum for the stock to simmer. The best stock is made from liquid that cooks at 80°C/175°F, rather than 100°C/210°F (boiling point). Using a slotted spoon, skim off the scum that comes to the surface during the first 15 minutes of cooking. Cook for about 3 hours.

Strain the stock through a large sieve (strainer) lined with muslin or cheesecloth. Leave to cool and then put in the refrigerator.

Remove any fat that has solidified on the surface. When there are only a few specks of fat left, heat the stock and drag a piece of kitchen paper (paper towel) gently across the surface. The fat will stick to the paper.

Taste the stock. If it is too mild, reduce over a high heat until the required taste is obtained. Cover with clingfilm (plastic wrap) and keep in the refrigerator for up to 3 days, or in the freezer for up to 3 months.

Cook's tip

A frugal – and indeed sensible – Italian housewife will cut the meat off the bones after making the stock and serve it as part of a meal with some freshly cooked potatoes. You can use any combination of beef, veal and chicken for this stock, but avoid lamb and pork.

Brodetto Abruzzese

Fish Soup from Abruzzo

Brodetto* is the fish soup of the Adriatic, and there are as many versions as there are ports. Of all the brodetti, this is one of the very best.

SERVES 4–5

1.5 kg/3¼ lb assorted fish, such as monkfish, rascasse (scorpion fish), red and grey mullet, John Dory or hake, but not salmon or any blue fish (mackerel, pilchard, herring, sardine etc)

1 onion, sliced

4 tbsp red wine vinegar

1 bay leaf

500 g/1 lb small cuttlefish or squid

7 tbsp extra virgin olive oil

3 garlic cloves, finely sliced

1 dried red chilli (or more depending on strength), crumbled

400 g/14 oz canned plum tomatoes, with their juice, chopped

1½ tsp tomato paste

salt

1 kg/2 lb 2 oz mussels, well scrubbed and tightly closed

150 ml/5 fl oz/⅔ cup dry white wine

slices of toasted ciabatta or Pugliese bread, rubbed with garlic

REMOVE THE HEADS and tails from the fish, then remove and discard the gills. Put the heads and tails in a saucepan with the onion, wine vinegar and bay leaf to make fish stock. Cover with cold water, bring slowly to the boil and simmer for 30 minutes. Strain and discard the heads and tails.

Meanwhile, cut the fish into bite-sized pieces and set aside. Clean the cuttlefish or squid and cut into strips. Put the olive oil, garlic and chilli in a heavy pan and sauté over low heat until the garlic is just coloured. Add the chopped tomatoes and juice and the tomato paste and cook for 5 minutes, stirring frequently. Add the cuttlefish or squid and some salt and cook until they are tender – about 40 minutes to 1 hour, depending on their size.

Now choose an earthenware pot, the sort that can be put straight on the heat and is large enough to hold all the ingredients. Put some of the cuttlefish and tomato sauce at the bottom, cover with a layer of raw fish and a few mussels and then add some more cuttlefish and tomato sauce. Repeat the layers until all the ingredients are used.

Pour over the wine and enough fish stock to come to about 2.5 cm/1 in above the level of the fish. If necessary, make up the level of the liquid with some hot water. Cook over a medium heat for 15 minutes or so, shaking the pot occasionally, but without stirring, which would break the fish.

Serve very hot, with the toasted bread rubbed with garlic.

Cook's tip

Fish stock is ready much more rapidly than meat stock. Not only is there no advantage in cooking it for longer than 30 minutes, doing so is likely to spoil the flavour.

PASTA

Pasta al Tonno
Pasta with Tuna

This dish exists in many forms — here is the classic version. Use best canned tuna, not skipjack tuna, which is less good.

SERVES 4 AS A FIRST COURSE

2 garlic cloves, chopped
6 tbsp olive oil
a bunch of fresh flat-leaf
    parsley, chopped
a small piece of dried chilli
2 salted anchovies, boned, rinsed and
    chopped, or 4 canned or bottled
    anchovy fillets, drained and chopped
200 g/7 oz best canned tuna, yellowfin
    if possible, in olive oil, drained
    and flaked
salt and freshly ground black pepper
350 g/12 oz spaghetti
12 black olives

PUT THE GARLIC, olive oil, parsley and chilli in a large frying pan (skillet) and sauté gently for 1 minute. Add the anchovies and tuna, stir gently and cook for 10 minutes. Taste and add salt if necessary, and plenty of freshly ground black pepper.

Meanwhile, cook the spaghetti according to the packet instructions. Drain when very al dente and turn it quickly into the frying pan. Stir-fry for a minute or so, mixing constantly to coat the pasta with the sauce.

Scatter the pasta with the olives and serve at once.

Spaghetti alla Puttanesca
Spaghetti in a Chilli and Anchovy Sauce

Not the most elegant of names — puttana is a prostitute — but surely one of the most delicious of pasta sauces. The sauce is allegedly from the slums of Rome; it is quick to make, piquant and gutsy like the locals themselves, and is now made all over Italy. This recipe is a classic version.

SERVES 4 AS A FIRST COURSE

350 g/12 oz spaghetti
6 tbsp olive oil
2.5 cm/1 in piece of fresh red chilli,
    seeded and finely chopped
3 salted anchovies, boned, rinsed and
    chopped, or 6 canned or bottled
    anchovy fillets, drained and chopped
2 garlic cloves, very finely sliced
500 g/1 lb/2½ cups ripe fresh
    tomatoes, peeled, de-seeded and cut
    into thin strips
100 g/3½ oz/scant 1 cup large black
    olives, pitted and sliced
1 tbsp capers, preferably in salt, rinsed
1 tbsp chopped fresh flat-leaf parsley

COOK THE SPAGHETTI according to the packet instructions. While the pasta is cooking, put the olive oil, chilli, anchovies and garlic in a large frying pan (skillet) and cook for 1 minute, mashing the anchovies to a paste with a fork. Add the tomatoes, olives and capers and cook for a further 5 minutes, stirring frequently.

Drain the spaghetti, turn it into the frying pan and add the parsley. Fry for 1 minute, tossing the pasta all the time.

Serve the pasta at once, straight from the pan.

Pasta con la Mollica

Pasta with Breadcrumbs, Tomatoes, Parsley and Anchovies

In the poor regions of southern Italy, toasted breadcrumbs were, and often still are, used instead of Parmesan or pecorino cheese. The result is different, but I find it just as good.

SERVES 4 AS A FIRST COURSE
250 g/9 oz ripe fresh tomatoes, peeled
2 garlic cloves, finely sliced
1 tsp crushed dried chillies
1 tbsp chopped fresh flat-leaf parsley
6 tbsp extra virgin olive oil
350 g/12 oz spaghetti or linguine
salt
4 salted anchovies, boned and rinsed,
    or 8 canned or bottled anchovy
    fillets, drained
1 tsp dried oregano
6 tbsp dried breadcrumbs

HALVE THE TOMATOES, squeeze out some of their seeds and chop the flesh. Put the garlic, chillies, parsley and half the olive oil in a large frying pan (skillet) and sauté for 1 minute. Add the tomatoes and cook over medium heat for 5 minutes, stirring frequently. Meanwhile, cook the pasta in boiling salted water according to the packet instructions.

Chop the anchovy fillets and add them to a small frying pan with the rest of the oil. Cook, mashing them against the bottom of the pan, for about a minute and then scoop them with their juices into the tomato sauce. Add the oregano and cook for 1 minute. Taste and check the salt. Withdraw the pan from the heat until the pasta is ready.

Drain the pasta and add to the frying pan. Stir, sprinkle with the breadcrumbs and stir-fry for a further minute.

Spaghetti alla Nursina

Spaghetti with Black Truffles

The black truffle of Norcia in Umbria is used in this recipe to give a majestic flavour to a dish of humble spaghetti*.

SERVES 4 AS A FIRST COURSE
75 g/2½ oz black truffles
7 tbsp olive oil
1 garlic clove, crushed
2 salted anchovies, boned, rinsed and
    chopped, or 4 canned or bottled
    anchovy fillets, drained and chopped
salt and freshly ground black pepper
350 g/12 oz thin spaghetti

SCRUB THE TRUFFLES gently under cold water and then pat them dry with kitchen paper (paper towels). Grate the truffles through the smallest holes of a cheese grater.

Put the truffles with half the olive oil in a small saucepan and cook over a very low heat for 1 minute. Take off the heat, add the garlic and anchovies and mash and pound the mixture with a fork. Return to the heat and cook very gently for a further 5 minutes, stirring the whole time. The heat must be very low – on no account should the sauce be allowed to boil. Taste and add salt if necessary, and a generous amount of pepper.

Cook the spaghetti according to packet instructions. Toss with the remaining olive oil in a heated serving dish and spoon over the truffle sauce. Serve immediately.

Pasta con le Sarde
Pasta with Fresh Sardines

Possibly the most famous Sicilian pasta dish, and said by many to be the best.

SERVES 4

50 g/2 oz/⅓ cup sultanas
 (golden raisins)
50 g/2 oz/½ cup pine nuts
5 tbsp olive oil
I onion, very finely sliced
salt
75 g/2½ oz/7 tbsp fennel leaf tops (the
 feathery fronds)
2 salted anchovies, boned and rinsed, or
 4 canned or bottled anchovy fillets,
 drained
500 g/I lb fresh sardines, filleted
I tsp fennel seeds
freshly ground black pepper
350 g/12 oz penne or rigatoni

NOTE: In Italy this recipe is made with wild fennel, which is slightly different from the cultivated bulb fennel and has thick and plentiful fronds. If you can't get enough of the feathery leaf tops, make up the quantity with a mixture of finely chopped fennel bulb and fresh flat-leaf parsley.

SOAK THE SULTANAS (golden raisins) in warm water for IO minutes. Drain and dry well with kitchen paper (paper towels). Dry-fry the pine nuts in a cast-iron frying pan (skillet) for 3–4 minutes to release the aroma.

Put 3 tablespoons of the olive oil in a frying pan. Add the onion and a little salt and sauté gently, stirring frequently, for IO minutes until soft. Mix in the sultanas and pine nuts and continue cooking for a further 2 minutes.

Meanwhile, blanch the fennel in a large saucepan of salted boiling water for I minute. Lift the fennel out of the water with a slotted spoon, drain and dry with kitchen paper. Reserve the cooking water. Chop the fennel and add to the onion mixture. Cook slowly for IO–I5 minutes, adding a couple of tablespoons of the fennel water whenever the mixture appears dry.

Heat the oven to 200°C/400°F/ Gas Mark 6.

Chop the anchovies and about half the sardines and add to the pan with the fennel seeds and a generous grinding of pepper. Cook for IO minutes, stirring frequently and adding more fennel water whenever necessary. Taste and adjust the seasoning.

While the sauce is cooking, cook the pasta in the remaining fennel water until very al dente. Add more water if necessary. Drain, return the pasta to the pan and dress immediately with the sardine sauce.

Grease a deep ovenproof dish with a little oil and turn the pasta into it. Lay the remaining sardines over the pasta, drizzle with the rest of the oil and cover with foil. Bake for I5 minutes.

Orecchiette con i Broccoli

Orecchiette with Broccoli

The use of anchovies, sultanas (golden raisins) and pine nuts is a feature of the cooking of southern Italy, in this case Puglia. Here the sauce dresses the local pasta.

SERVES 4 AS A FIRST COURSE

3 tbsp sultanas (golden raisins)
500 g/1 lb broccoli
salt
1 onion, sliced
6 tbsp extra virgin olive oil
2 salted anchovies, boned, rinsed and chopped, or 4 canned or bottled anchovy fillets, drained and chopped
25 g/1 oz/¼ cup pine nuts
freshly ground black pepper
350 g/12 oz orecchiette, shells or any medium-sized pasta shapes
50 g/2 oz/⅔ cup freshly grated pecorino cheese

SOAK THE SULTANAS (golden raisins) in a cup of warm water. Wash the broccoli. Cut the thicker stalks into rounds and divide the heads into small florets. Cook the florets and the stalks in boiling salted water for 3 minutes after the water has come back to the boil. Drain and set aside.

Sauté the onion in 4 tablespoons of the oil in a fairly large sauté or frying pan (skillet) until soft. Meanwhile, heat the rest of the oil in a small saucepan, mix in the anchovies and cook over a really low heat for 1 minute, pressing the anchovies down to reduce to a pulp. Set aside. Drain the sultanas and mix into the onion together with the broccoli and pine nuts. Stir very gently,

taking care not to break up the florets, and cook over low heat for 10 minutes or so. Add the anchovy sauce and salt and pepper to taste.

Cook the pasta in plenty of boiling salted water according to the packet instructions. Drain and turn into the frying pan, then gently toss over the heat for a minute or two.

Add the pecorino, toss well and serve immediately, preferably straight from the pan.

Linguine all'Aglio, Olio e Peperoncino

Linguine with Garlic, Oil and Chilli

One of the best possible ways to serve linguine* – or spaghetti* – is with this simplest of all dressings which takes just a few minutes to prepare.

SERVES 4 AS A FIRST COURSE

350 g/12 oz linguine or spaghetti
salt
5 tbsp extra virgin olive oil
3 garlic cloves, sliced
½–1 tsp crushed dried chillies

COOK THE PASTA in plenty of boiling salted water. Meanwhile, heat the oil, garlic and chillies in a large heavy frying pan (skillet) and sauté for 1 minute.

Drain the pasta, then immediately turn it into the frying pan. Stir-fry for about 1 minute, then serve.

Tajarin all'Albese

Tagliatelle with White Truffles

The best resting place for a white truffle is on a plain risotto* (see page 80) or on a dish of tagliatelle*, as they serve it in Alba in Piedmont, centre of the white truffle hunting area. The tagliatelle used there are called tajarin*.

SERVES 4

75 g/2½ oz/5 tbsp unsalted
   (sweet) butter
4 tbsp dry white wine
a pinch of grated nutmeg
salt and freshly ground black pepper
Tagliatelle made with 300 g/10 oz/
   1½ cups Italian 00 flour and 3 large
   (extra-large) free-range (farm-fresh)
   eggs (see page 70), or 500 g/1 lb
   fresh tagliatelle or 350 g/12 oz dried
   egg pasta
50 g/2 oz/⅔ cup freshly grated
   Parmesan cheese
1 white truffle, about 50 g/2 oz, cleaned

MELT THE BUTTER and then pour in the wine. Boil briskly to reduce by half, which will take 4 or 5 seconds. Season with nutmeg, salt and pepper.

Cook the tagliatelle according to packet instructions. Drain and transfer immediately to a heated serving bowl. Pour the butter sauce over the pasta, mix in the Parmesan, then slice the truffle over the top with a truffle slicer or a small knife. Serve immediately.

Pasta e Fagioli alla Veneta

Venetian Pasta with Beans

A popular soup in most regions, the Pasta e Fagioli of Veneto is the best known.

SERVES 4

200 g/7 oz/1 cup dried borlotti beans
50 g/2 oz unsmoked pancetta, chopped
4 tbsp olive oil
1 garlic clove, chopped
1 small carrot, chopped
1 small celery stalk, chopped
1 small onion, chopped
a few needles of fresh rosemary, chopped
1 knuckle of unsmoked bacon or ham
   (fresh ham hock)
1.5 litres/3 pints/1⅔ quarts meat stock
175 g/6 oz/1½ cups small soup pasta
salt and freshly ground black pepper
freshly grated Parmesan cheese, to serve

SOAK THE BEANS in cold water for 12 hours, then drain and rinse them.

Put the pancetta and the olive oil in a stockpot and sauté for 1 minute. Add the garlic, carrot, celery, onion and rosemary and sauté gently until soft. Add the beans and bacon or ham knuckle, cover with stock and simmer, covered, until the beans are tender. This takes about 2 hours.

Lift out the knuckle (hock). Remove the meat from the bone and cut it into strips. Lift out half the beans using a slotted spoon and purée them in a food mill or food processor. Return the purée and meat to the pan and, when the soup returns to the boil, add the pasta, salt and pepper. You may need to add some water before you add the pasta. Mix and simmer until the pasta is cooked.

Pasta 'Ncasciata

Pasta Pie

A Sicilian pasta pie, the pasta being encased ('ncasciata) in the fried aubergines (eggplant). This is a stunning and tasty dish, full of different flavours.

SERVES 6

2 aubergines (eggplant), weighing about
   700 g/1½ lb in total
salt
1½ quantities Tomato Sauce 2 (see
   page 176)
vegetable oil, for frying
400 g/14 oz penne or rigatoni
50 g/2 oz/⅔ cup freshly grated
   Parmesan cheese
1 tbsp dried oregano
freshly ground black pepper
2 hard-boiled, free-range (hard-cooked,
   farm-fresh) eggs, sliced
150 g/5 oz Italian salami, thickly sliced
   and cut into strips
200 g/7 oz Italian mozzarella
   cheese, sliced
50 g/2 oz caciocavallo
   cheese, sliced
2 tbsp dried breadcrumbs
2 tbsp extra virgin olive oil

CUT THE AUBERGINES (eggplant) lengthways into thin slices. Place the slices in a colander, sprinkling salt between the layers. Leave to drain for about 1 hour.

While the aubergines are draining, make the tomato sauce.

Rinse the salted aubergines thoroughly and pat each slice dry, then fry them in plenty of hot vegetable oil. Do not fry too many at a time. When they are golden brown on both sides, remove the slices and put on kitchen paper (paper towels) to drain.

Heat the oven to 190°C/375°F/ Gas Mark 5.

Cook the pasta according to the packet instructions, then drain when very al dente and immediately dress with the tomato sauce. Add the Parmesan and oregano, mix well and then taste and check seasonings.

Line the bottom and sides of a 20 cm/8 in springform cake tin (pan) with aubergine slices. Cover the bottom with a layer of pasta and then with sliced eggs, salami strips, aubergine slices, mozzarella and caciocavallo slices. Repeat these layers until all the ingredients are used, finishing with a layer of pasta. Sprinkle with the dried breadcrumbs and drizzle with the olive oil.

Put in the preheated oven and bake for about 20 minutes or, until the dish is heated right through.

Remove the pie from the oven, then run a spatula around between the pie and the inside of the pan. Place a round serving dish upside down over the pan and invert the pan onto it. Leave the pie to stand for a few minutes, then unclip the side of the pan and carefully remove it. Remove the base of the pan and serve immediately.

Pasta all'Uovo

Egg Pasta

Pasta is made in different ways in many of the regions, but the most popular Pasta all'Uovo is the one made in Emilia, for which this is the traditional recipe.

MAKES ENOUGH FOR 4 AS A FIRST COURSE, 3 AS A MAIN COURSE

300 g/10 oz/2 cups Italian 00 flour
a pinch of salt
3 large (extra-large) free-range (farm-fresh) eggs
extra flour, for dusting

PUT THE FLOUR on the work surface (countertop) and make a well in the middle. Add the salt and the eggs. With a fork or your fingers, mix the eggs and draw in the flour gradually. Work quickly until it forms a mass. Scrape the work surface clean and wash your hands.

If you prefer, you can use a food processor instead. Put in the flour and salt, switch on the machine and drop in the cracked eggs through the funnel. Process until a ball of dough is formed. Transfer the dough to a lightly floured work surface.

Knead the dough for 5 to7 minutes. Wrap in clingfilm (plastic wrap) and allow to rest for at least 30 minutes. You can leave it for 3 or 4 hours.

Unwrap the dough and knead on a lightly floured surface for 2–3 minutes, then divide into 4 equal parts. Take one piece of dough and keep the remainder wrapped in clingfilm. Roll out the dough by hand, or by machine following the manufacturer's directions.

If you are making lasagne, or any type of stuffed pasta, proceed to the cutting and stuffing. If you are making long pasta, before you cut it, allow the dough to dry until it is no longer sticky. Feed each strip of dough through the broad cutters of the pasta machine for tagliatelle or fettuccine, or through the narrow cutters for tagliolini. For tonnarelli, stretch the dough out only to the fourth setting of the machine. When dry, feed the sheet through the narrow cutter to achieve a sort of square spaghetti.

Pasticcio di Penne con Formaggi e Funghi

Baked Penne with Cheese and Mushrooms

A pasticcio* is a type of Italian pie, often without a pastry case. Use fresh porcini when they are in season instead of the dried ones.

SERVES 4

20 g/¾ oz/⅓ cup dried porcini, soaked, drained and chopped
500 g/1 lb/7 cups fresh cultivated mushrooms, thinly sliced
1 garlic clove
50 g/2 oz/4 tbsp unsalted (sweet) butter
salt and freshly ground black pepper
300 g/10 oz penne
butter for the dish
150 g/5 oz Bel Paese cheese, thinly sliced
150 g/5 oz fontina cheese, thinly sliced
75 g/2½ oz/scant 1 cup freshly grated Parmesan cheese
200 ml/7 fl oz/scant 1 cup double (heavy) cream

HEAT THE OVEN to 200°C/400°F/ Gas Mark 6. Sauté the porcini and fresh mushrooms with the whole garlic clove in 25 g/1 oz/2 tbsp of the butter over a high heat. Add salt and pepper, lower the heat and cook for 3 minutes. Discard the garlic.

Cook the pasta according to the packet instructions. Drain and dress with the remaining butter.

Butter an ovenproof dish and cover the bottom with a layer of pasta. Distribute about a quarter of the mushrooms and sliced cheeses evenly over the pasta layer and sprinkle with 1 tablespoon of the Parmesan. Add another layer of pasta and cover with mushrooms and cheese as before. Repeat until you have used all the ingredients, finishing with a layer of sliced cheeses. Pour over the cream and sprinkle with salt and pepper.

Cover the dish with foil and bake in the preheated oven for 10 minutes. Remove the foil and bake uncovered for a further 10 minutes, or until a light crust has formed on the top. Remove from the oven and allow to settle for 5 minutes before serving.

Maccheroni alla Chitarra

Macaroni with Lamb Ragù

A chitarra is the instrument used to make homemade pasta, consisting of a wooden frame with taut metal wires, giving this recipe its odd name — guitar-style maccaroni. A chitarra makes square spaghetti known as tonnarelli*.

SERVES 3–4
50 g/2 oz salted pork back fat (lardo*) or unsmoked fatty pancetta, chopped
300 g/10 oz lamb fillets (boneless neck of lamb), trimmed and diced
½–1 tsp crushed dried chillies
1½ tsp dried oregano
1 garlic clove, chopped
salt

4 tbsp olive oil
100 g/3½ oz/1½ cups mushrooms, chopped
1 small onion, finely chopped
4 tbsp red wine
3 tbsp red wine vinegar
1½ tbsp tomato paste diluted with 4 tbsp warm water
1 tbsp flour
Tonnarelli made with 300 g/10 oz/ 2 cups Italian 00 flour and 3 large (extra-large) free-range (farm-fresh) eggs (see page 70), or 500 g/1 lb fresh tagliatelle or 350 g/12 oz dried egg pasta
2 tbsp chopped fresh flat-leaf parsley

PUT THE PORK BACK FAT or pancetta in a sauté pan and heat until hot. Add the lamb, season with the chillies, oregano and garlic and brown well on all sides. Sprinkle with salt, cook for about 30 seconds and then lift the meat out with a slotted spoon and set aside.

Add the oil to the pan and heat. Sauté the mushrooms for 5 minutes. Lift them out and set aside with the lamb. Put the onion into the pan and sauté gently until soft. Pour in the wine and vinegar and boil briskly until the liquid has nearly all evaporated.

Add the diluted tomato paste to the pan with the flour. Cook, stirring constantly, for 2 minutes. Sprinkle with some salt. Return the lamb and the mushrooms to the pan and cook, covered, until the lamb is very tender, about 45 minutes. Taste and check salt.

Cook the pasta in plenty of boiling salted water. Drain as soon as it is al dente, which will only take some 30 seconds if you are using homemade tonnarelli. Do not overdrain the pasta. Turn the pasta into a heated bowl, toss with the sauce and sprinkle with the flat-leaf parsley. Serve at once.

Timballo di Maccheroni del Gattopardo

Pasta Pie in a Sweet Crust

The sensuous description of the timballo* served at a nineteenth-century banquet in The Leopard *by Giovanni Tomasi di Lampedusa, inspired me to try and recreate that fabulous dish. It is a lengthy and complicated performance, but the excellence and the beauty of the dish is worth the time and effort involved. The use of sweet pastry (dough) to envelope savoury ingredients is a characteristic trait of past centuries.*

SERVES 6–8

FOR THE SWEET PASTRY (DOUGH)

250 g/9 oz/1⅔ cups flour, preferably Italian 00

140 g/4½ oz/1¾ sticks unsalted (sweet) butter, cut into small pieces

1 large (extra-large) free-range (farm-fresh) egg

1 free-range (farm-fresh) egg yolk

115 g/4 oz/½ cup + 2 tbsp caster (superfine) sugar

a pinch of salt

FOR THE FILLING

140 g/4½ oz/1¾ cups unsalted (sweet) butter

150 g/5 oz luganega, skinned and crumbled

150 g/5 oz skinless, boneless chicken breast (breast half), cut into thin strips

100 g/3½ oz chicken livers, trimmed and cut into small pieces

100 ml/3½ fl oz/scant ½ cup dry white wine

4 or 5 tbsp passata (strained, puréed tomatoes)

salt and freshly ground black pepper

100–150 ml/3½–5 fl oz/½–⅔ cup strong meat stock

100 g/3½ oz prosciutto, thickly sliced and then cut into thin strips

100 g/3½ oz black truffle, grated, or 2 tsp truffle paste

250 g/9 oz/2¼ cups maccheroncini or pennette, or small tubular pasta

75 g/2½ oz/scant 1 cup freshly grated Parmesan cheese

2 tbsp dried breadcrumbs

2 hard-boiled, free-range (hard-cooked, farm-fresh) eggs, cut into wedges

FOR THE GLAZE

1 free-range (farm-fresh) egg yolk

2 tbsp milk

2 pinches of salt

FIRST PREPARE THE SWEET PASTRY (see method on page 155). Dust the dough lightly with flour, wrap it in clingfilm (plastic wrap) and chill.

Next make the filling. Heat 50 g/ 2 oz/4 tbsp of the butter in a small saucepan and when it begins to sizzle, add the luganega and cook for a minute or two, stirring very frequently. Add the chicken portion and cook for 5 minutes over medium heat, then add the chicken livers. As soon as they have lost their raw colour, splash with the wine and boil briskly until the wine has nearly all evaporated. Mix in the passata (strained, puréed tomatoes) and season with salt and pepper to taste. Lower the heat and cook very gently for a further 10 minutes or so, adding a couple of tablespoons of the stock when the mixture becomes too dry. Transfer to a bowl and mix in the prosciutto and truffle or truffle paste.

Heat the oven to 220°C/425°F/ Gas Mark 7.

Cook the pasta until very al dente. Drain well and slide it into the bowl with the meat mixture. Add half the Parmesan and the remaining butter and mix very well (hands are the best tool). Add a little more stock if the pasta seems too dry.

Butter a 20 cm/8 in springform cake tin (pan) or raised pie mould. Roll about one-third of the pastry (dough) into a round large enough to cover the bottom of the pan. Place the round of pastry on the bottom of the pan. Roll out half the remaining pastry into a side strip and use it to line the sides of the pan. Seal the joins with cold water. Sprinkle the remaining Parmesan and the breadcrumbs over the bottom. Pile half the pasta into the mould and then place the hard-boiled (hard-cooked) eggs here and there, handling them very gently or they will break. Add the remaining pasta and level the top.

Roll out the remaining pastry into a round and place it on top of the pasta. Seal the pastry lid to the side strip. Gently beat together the ingredients for the glaze and paint the top of the pie with it. Make a few decorations with the pastry trimmings and brush with glaze before fixing to the top of the pie.

Bake in the preheated oven for about 10 minutes. Turn the heat down to 180°C/350°F/Gas Mark 4 and continue baking for a further 20 minutes, until the pastry is beautifully golden all over.

Let the timballo cool down in the tin for about 10 minutes, then unmould it onto a round dish and serve.

Pasta e Ceci
Pasta and Chick Peas

Chick peas (garbanzo beans) tend to be best eaten within a year of being harvested, so it is best to always try to buy them from a store with a rapid turnover.

SERVES 4

200 g/7 oz/scant 1 cup dried chick peas
   (garbanzo beans)
1.5 litres/3 pints/1⅔ quarts vegetable
   stock or water
2 sprigs of fresh rosemary
4 garlic cloves, chopped
5 tbsp extra virgin olive oil
225 g/8 oz ripe fresh tomatoes,
   peeled and chopped, or canned
   tomatoes, chopped
salt and freshly ground black pepper
150 g/5 oz/1¼ cups small tubular
   pasta, such as ditalini
freshly grated Parmesan cheese,
   to serve (optional)

SOAK THE CHICK PEAS (garbanzo beans) in cold water for about 12 hours, then drain and rinse them and put them in a heavy stockpot, preferably flameproof earthenware. Add the stock or water. Tie the rosemary sprigs in a muslin or cheesecloth bag and add to the pot. Add the garlic and pour in half the olive oil. Bring to the boil, cover the pot tightly and cook at the lowest simmer until the chick peas are tender, which can take from 2 to 4 hours. Do not add salt until the chick peas are nearly ready or it will harden their skins.

When the chick peas are nearly done, purée the tomatoes and add to the soup. Remove and discard the rosemary bundle. Stir well, add salt and pepper to taste and cook for about 10 minutes.

Check that there is enough liquid in the pan, as you may have to add some boiling water. Add the pasta and cook until al dente. Ladle the soup into individual bowls and drizzle a little of the remaining oil into each. Parmesan can be passed separately.

Anolini alla Piacentina

Anolini Stuffed with Braised Beef

Anolini are one of the many types of stuffed pasta of Emilia-Romagna and they originate from Piacenza. They are small, half-moon shaped ravioli*, traditionally served in meat stock. They are also served asciutti* — drained and dressed with butter and grated Parmesan cheese — or with a ragù* of chicken livers and mushrooms, a complement to the stuffing itself.

SERVES 4–6

75 g/2½ oz/5 tbsp unsalted
    (sweet) butter
2 tbsp vegetable oil
350 g/12 oz braising steak, in one piece
1 onion, finely chopped
1 celery stalk, finely chopped
1 small carrot, finely chopped
150 ml/5 fl oz/⅔ cup dry white wine
1 tbsp tomato paste
200 ml/7 fl oz/scant 1 cup meat stock
salt and freshly ground black pepper
4 tbsp freshly grated Parmesan cheese,
    plus extra to serve
50 g/2 oz/1 cup fresh breadcrumbs
a pinch of grated nutmeg
2 large (extra-large) free-range (farm-
    fresh) eggs
Egg Pasta made with 300 g/10 oz/
    2 cups Italian 00 flour and 3 large
    (extra-large) free-range (farm-fresh)
    eggs (see page 70)

HEAT 25 G/1 OZ/2 TBSP of the butter with the oil in a saucepan. Add the braising steak and brown very well on all sides.

Lift the meat out of the pan and set aside. Add the onion, celery and carrot to the pan and sauté until soft, stirring frequently. Return the meat to the pan and then pour over the wine. Boil briskly until reduced by three-quarters.

Dilute the tomato paste with the stock and add to the pan with salt and pepper to taste. Cook over very low heat, with the lid on the pan, for about 3 hours, turning the meat over from time to time and adding a little warm water if necessary. The juices should be thick by the end of the cooking time.

In a bowl, mix together 2 tablespoons of the Parmesan cheese with the breadcrumbs. Spoon over about half the cooking juices from the meat and stir well.

Cut the meat into pieces, then chop finely or work to a coarse mixture in a food processor. Add to the cheese and breadcrumbs with the grated nutmeg, taste and adjust the seasoning. Mix in the eggs.

Prepare the pasta. Working with about one-third at a time and keeping the rest covered with a cloth, roll it out and cut it into rounds with a fluted 5 cm/2 in biscuit (cookie) cutter. Place a small spoonful of the meat mixture in the middle of each round, lightly moisten the edge of the pasta with cold water and fold the round over the stuffing in a half-moon shape. Press firmly around the edge.

Drop the anolini into a large saucepan of boiling salted water and cook until ready, which will take from 5 to 10 minutes, depending on how dry they are. Lift them out of the water into a colander with a slotted spoon and transfer them to a heated bowl.

Melt the remaining butter, pour it over the anolini and sprinkle with the remaining Parmesan cheese. Serve immediately, with extra grated Parmesan at the table.

Pizzoccheri

Buckwheat Pasta with Potato and Cabbage

Pasta made with buckwheat is called pizzoccheri, but it is also the name of this rustic but excellent dish from the Alpine valley of Valtellina. If you cannot find pizzoccheri, or you are not inclined to make them, use whole-wheat spaghetti instead.

SERVES 6

FOR THE PASTA

200 g/7 oz/scant 2 cups buckwheat flour

100 g/3½ oz/⅔ cup flour, preferably Italian 00

1 tsp salt

1 large (extra-large) free-range (farm-fresh) egg

about 120 ml/4 fl oz/½ cup warm milk

FOR THE DRESSING

225 g/8 oz potatoes, cut into cubes

salt and freshly ground black pepper

300 g/10 oz Savoy cabbage, cut into 1 cm/½ in strips

75 g/2½ oz/5 tbsp unsalted (sweet) butter

1 small onion, very finely chopped

1 garlic clove, very finely chopped

6 fresh sage leaves, torn into pieces

a little butter for the dish

150 g/5 oz fontina cheese, cut into slivers

75 g/2½ oz/scant 1 cup freshly grated Parmesan cheese

FIRST MAKE THE DOUGH for the pasta. Mix together the two flours and the salt on the work surface (countertop). Make a well in the middle and break the egg into it. Using a fork, begin to bring in the flour from the edge, while slowly adding the milk. Gradually add the milk, since you may not need all of it. Alternatively, you may need to add a little warm water or a couple tablespoons of white flour. The dough should be soft and elastic, although it is much stickier and wetter than dough made with only white flour and eggs. Knead for 5 minutes, and then wrap the dough in kitchen paper (paper towel) or clingfilm (plastic wrap) and let it rest for at least 1 hour.

Roll out the dough to a thickness of about 3 mm/⅛ in. Cut the rolled-out pasta into noodles, about 2 x 10 cm/ ¾ x 4 in. Lay the strips out on clean cloths, without letting them touch.

Heat the oven to 180°C/350°F/ Gas Mark 4.

Put a large saucepan containing about 4 litres/7 pints/4½ quarts water on the heat. Add 1½ tbsp salt and the potato and bring to the boil. After about 10 minutes, when the potato cubes begin to soften at the edges, add the cabbage and continue cooking for about 5 minutes, until the cabbage has lost its crunchiness. Slide in the pizzoccheri, mix well. Bring back to the boil and cook for 5 minutes.

Meanwhile, put the butter, onion, garlic and sage in a small heavy-based pan and cook gently, stirring very often, until the onion becomes pale gold. Remove the sage.

Butter a shallow ovenproof dish. When the pizzoccheri are cooked, drain the whole mixture in a colander. Spoon a ladleful or two of the pasta mixture over the bottom of the dish and add a little of the two cheeses, a little of the onion-butter sauce and plenty of pepper. Add more pasta and dress it again in the same way until the whole lot is dressed. Toss thoroughly.

Cover with foil and put in the preheated oven for 5 minutes, until the cheese has melted. Serve straightaway.

Vincisgrassi

Rich Lasagne with Prosciutto, Mushrooms and Sweetbreads

A baked pasta dish from Marche. Its odd name has been attributed to the dish having been created for Prince Windischgratz, the general in charge of the Austrian forces during the Napoleonic wars. However, a similar dish called Pringsgras was mentioned in an eighteenth-century book. Whatever its origin, the dish is superb, though rather complicated. This is the original recipe. Nowadays the pasta is usually made without wine, and the brains and sweetbreads are often replaced by minced (ground) veal.

SERVES 8

100 g/3½ oz/7 tbsp unsalted (sweet) butter

50 g/2 oz/⅓ cup chopped prosciutto

I medium onion, cut in half

I medium carrot, cut in half

250 g/9 oz fresh chicken livers, trimmed, cleaned and cut into small pieces

50 ml/2 fl oz/¼ cup dry white wine

I tbsp tomato paste diluted with 100 ml/3½ fl oz/scant ½ cup warm meat stock

20 g/¾ oz/⅓ cup dried porcini

100 g/3½ oz/1½ cups brown mushrooms, cleaned and sliced

I garlic clove, bruised with the flat side of a knife

2 tbsp olive oil

250 g/9 oz mixed calf's brains and sweetbreads, cleaned and blanched

100 ml/3½ fl oz/scant ½ cup single (light) cream

½ tsp freshly grated nutmeg

¼ tsp ground cinnamon

salt and freshly ground black pepper

Béchamel Sauce made with 100 g/3½ oz/7 tbsp butter, 75 g/2½ oz/generous ½ cup flour and I litre/1¾ pints/I quart milk (see page 179)

25 g/1 oz/2 tbsp unsalted (sweet) butter

50 g/2 oz/⅔ cup freshly grated Parmesan cheese

FOR THE LASAGNE

400 g/14 oz/4 cups Italian 00 flour

200 g/7 oz/1⅓ cups fine semolina (semolina flour)

4 large (extra-large) free-range (farm-fresh) eggs

40 g/1½ oz/3 tbsp unsalted (sweet) butter, at room temperature

4 tbsp vin santo or Marsala

I tsp salt

I tbsp vegetable or olive oil

PUT 75 G/2½ OZ/5 TBSP of the butter, the prosciutto, onion and carrot in a saucepan over low heat and let the vegetables cook gently to flavour the butter. Lift out the vegetables and discard. Add the chicken livers and sauté for about I minute. Pour in the wine and reduce briskly until it has evaporated. Add the diluted tomato paste, mix well and and bring the sauce to the boil. Lower the heat and simmer very gently for 30 minutes. Add a little water during the cooking if the liquid dries out.

While the chicken livers are cooking, soak the dried porcini in 50 ml/2 fl oz/¼ cup warm water for 20 minutes. Drain, reserving the liquid. Sauté the brown mushrooms with the garlic in the olive oil for 5 minutes. Remove the garlic and discard.

Strain the porcini liquid through a sieve (strainer) lined with muslin or cheesecloth. Chop the porcini and put them into the chicken liver sauce with the fresh mushrooms and the porcini liquid. Finely chop the brains and sweetbreads and add to the sauce with the cream and spices. Taste, check seasoning and continue cooking for 10 minutes.

Make the béchamel sauce and cover with clingfilm (plastic wrap) to prevent a skin from forming.

For the lasagne, mix the flour and semolina on a work surface (countertop), make a well in the middle and drop in the eggs, butter, vin santo and salt. Mix and knead, following the instructions on page 70.

Butter a 28 x 20 cm/11 x 8 in lasagne dish. Cut the pasta into 28 cm/11 in strips 10 cm/4 in wide. Cook 3 or 4 lasagne at a time in plenty of salted boiling water to which 1 tablespoon oil has been added.

Mix three-quarters of the Parmesan into the béchamel and spread 3 tablespoons over the bottom of the dish and cover with a layer of lasagne. Spoon over 3–4 tablespoons of the chicken liver sauce and the same amount of béchamel. Cover with layer of lasagne, and repeat until all ingredients are used up, finishing with a layer of lasagne and béchamel. Allow to stand for 4 hours for the flavours to combine.

Heat the oven to 200°C/400°F/ Gas Mark 6 and bake the vincisgrassi for about 25 minutes. Sprinkle with the remaining Parmesan. Melt the remaining butter, pour it over the top and leave to stand for about 5 minutes before serving.

Tagliatelle al Limone e Erbe Odorose

Tagliatelle with a Lemon and Herb Dressing

This is based on an old Piedmontese recipe. The herbs can be any you have to hand, as long as there is a good selection.

SERVES 4 AS A FIRST COURSE
40 g/1½ oz/4 tbsp unsalted (sweet) butter
grated rind and juice of 1 lemon, preferably organic or unwaxed
3 tbsp chopped mixed fresh herbs, such as parsley, sage, rosemary and chives
150 ml/5 fl oz/⅔ cup double (heavy) cream
salt and freshly ground black pepper
Tagliatelle made with 300 g/10 oz/2 cups Italian 00 flour and 3 large (extra-large) free-range (farm-fresh) eggs, or 500 g/1 lb fresh tagliatelle or 350 g/12 oz dried egg pasta
50 g/2 oz/⅔ cup freshly grated Parmesan cheese

MELT THE BUTTER in a small, heavy pan. Add the lemon rind, herbs, cream, salt and pepper. Bring slowly to the boil and simmer, stirring constantly, for 2 minutes. Add the lemon juice to the pan and bring back to the boil, take the pan off the heat and keep warm.

Cook the tagliatelle in plenty of boiling salted water according to the packet instructions until it is al dente. Drain, but do not overdrain, and then transfer to a heated bowl.

Dress the pasta with the sauce and a sprinkling of Parmesan cheese. Toss very well and serve at once, with the remaining cheese passed at the table.

Ziti alla Palermitana

Ziti in a Tuna Fish Sauce

Two of the most traditional Sicilian ingredients — ziti* and tuna — are put together in this simple but delicious pasta dish. If you cannot find ziti, use bucatini or any small tubular pasta.

SERVES 4 AS A FIRST COURSE
I small onion, finely chopped
salt and freshly ground black pepper
5 tbsp extra virgin olive oil
2 garlic cloves, finely chopped
2 salted anchovies, boned, rinsed and
    chopped, or 4 canned or bottled
    anchovy fillets, drained and chopped
350 g/12 oz ripe fresh tomatoes, peeled,
    de-seeded and coarsely chopped
2 tsp dried oregano
75 g/2½ oz best canned tuna, yellowfin
    if possible, in olive oil, drained
    and flaked
350 g/12 oz/3 cups ziti
50 g/2 ½ cup grated caciocavallo cheese

IN A LARGE SAUCEPAN, gently sauté the onion with 2 pinches of salt in the olive oil for 7 minutes on low heat, stirring frequently.

Mix in the garlic and continue cooking for a further 2 minutes. Mix in the chopped anchovies, pounding them against the bottom of the pan with a spoon. After I minute or so, throw in the tomatoes and oregano. Cook the sauce for about 30 minutes.

Add the flaked tuna and cook for a further 10 minutes. Add salt to taste if necessary, and plenty of black pepper.

Cook the ziti, or other type of pasta, according to the packet instructions, in plenty of boiling salted water. Drain well (tubular pasta has a tendency to retain some water). Dress the pasta with the sauce and cover with grated caciocavallo.

Lasagne al Forno

Baked Lasagne

I find that commercially-made fresh pasta is not good, and this applies even more to lasagne. I prefer to buy a good Italian brand of dried lasagne or, of course and much better, to make my own.

SERVES 4–6
Bolognese Meat Sauce (see page 174)
Béchamel Sauce made with 750 ml/
    1¼ pints/3⅓ cups milk, 75 g/
    2½ oz/7½ tbsp butter, 50 g/2 oz/
    ⅓ cup flour and 2 pinches of grated
    nutmeg (see page 179)
Egg Pasta made with 300 g/10 oz/
    2 cups Italian 00 flour and 3 large
    (extra-large) free-range (farm-fresh)
    eggs (see page 70)
I tbsp salt
I tbsp vegetable or olive oil
75 g/2½ oz/scant I cup freshly grated
    Parmesan cheese
25 g/I oz/2 tbsp unsalted
    (sweet) butter

FIRST MAKE the Bolognese meat sauce. While it is cooking, make the béchamel sauce.

Prepare the pasta, roll it out and cut into 12 x 8 cm/5 x 3 in rectangles, without letting the pasta dry. Lay the rectangles out, separate from each other, on clean kitchen towels.

Fill a large sauté pan with water, add the salt and oil and bring to the boil. When the water is boiling, slide in 5 or 6 lasagne sheets at a time. Cook for 1–2 minutes, depending on the thickness of the dough, moving the pieces around with a wooden fork or spoon to stop them from sticking to each other. When they are cooked, lift them out with a fish slice (pancake turner) and plunge them into a bowl of cold water. Lift out, lay on clean cloths and gently pat dry with kitchen paper (paper towels).

Heat the oven to 220°C/425°F/ Gas Mark 7.

Butter a 30 x 20 cm/12 x 8 in ovenproof dish. Spread 2 tablespoons of the Bolognese sauce on the bottom. Cover with a layer of lasagne, spread over 2 tablespoons of the Bolognese and the same of the béchamel. Sprinkle with a little Parmesan and repeat, building up the dish in thin layers until you have used up all the ingredients. The top layer must be béchamel.

Dot with the butter and bake in the preheated oven for 20 minutes. Remove from the oven and leave to stand for at least 5 minutes before serving, to allow the flavours to develop.

NOTE: If you don't want to make your own pasta, you can use 500 g/1 lb dried lasagne in this recipe instead.

RICE, POLENTA AND GNOCCHI

Risotto alla Milanese
Risotto with Saffron

In the old days beef marrow was used to add flavour to Risotto alla Milanese. It has a delicate yet deeply rich flavour that is particularly well suited here. You can use white wine instead of red if you prefer; the colour will be less deep and the flavour lighter. This is my family's recipe.

SERVES 4 AS A FIRST COURSE

1 litre/1¾ pints/1 quart homemade
  meat stock or chicken and meat stock
1 shallot or ½ small onion,
  finely chopped
90 g/3 oz/6 tbsp unsalted
  (sweet) butter
350 g/12 oz/1¾ cups Italian rice,
  preferably Carnaroli
6 tbsp red wine
1 sachet (envelope) of saffron powder or
  ½ tsp saffron threads, pounded
salt and freshly ground black pepper
50 g/2 oz/⅔ cup freshly grated
  Parmesan cheese

BRING THE STOCK to simmering point and keep it at a very low simmer.

Put the shallot and 50 g/2 oz/4 tbsp of the butter in a saucepan, sauté until soft and translucent, and then add the rice and stir until well coated with fat. Pour in the wine, boil for 2 minutes, stirring constantly, and then pour in 200 ml/7 fl oz/scant 1 cup of the hot stock. Cook until nearly all the stock has been absorbed and then add another 150 ml/5 fl oz/⅔ cup of the simmering stock. The risotto should cook at a steady, lively simmer.

About halfway through cooking (risotto takes about 15–18 minutes to cook), add the saffron dissolved in a little stock. When the rice is ready – it should be soft and creamy, not mushy or runny – taste and adjust the seasoning.

Take off the heat and mix in the rest of the butter and 2 tablespoons of the Parmesan. Serve immediately, with the rest of the Parmesan handed separately.

Risi e Bisi

Rice and Peas

This classic dish from Venice should be made with very young peas. Since these are almost impossible to find in the market, I use sugar snap peas.

SERVES 4 AS A FIRST COURSE

900 g/2 lb young fresh petits pois (baby peas) or sugar snap peas

salt

25 g/1 oz/2 tbsp unsalted (sweet) butter

2 tbsp mild extra virgin olive oil

1 small onion, very finely chopped

3 tbsp chopped fresh flat-leaf parsley

225 g/8 oz/1 heaped cup Italian rice, preferably Vialone Nano

½–1 tbsp fennel seeds, according to taste, crushed

freshly ground black pepper

50 g/2 oz/⅔ cup freshly grated Parmesan cheese

TRIM AND SHELL the peas, keeping the pods and peas separate. Discard any blemished pods and wash the others. Put the pods in a saucepan and add 1.5 litres/3 pints/1⅔ quarts water and 2 teaspoons salt. Boil until the pods are very tender. Drain, reserving the liquid, and purée the pods in a food processor or blender until smooth. If the purée is stringy, press it through a sieve (strainer). Put the purée in a saucepan, add 1 litre/1¾ pints/1 quart of the cooking liquid and bring slowly to the boil, keep the stock on a gentle simmer.

Meanwhile, put the butter, oil, onion and 1 tablespoon of the parsley in a stockpot. Sauté very gently for 5 minutes or so. Add the shelled peas and cook, stirring all the time, for 2 minutes. Stir in the rice. When the rice grains are coated in the butter and oil, pour in the simmering pod stock. Mix well and bring to the boil.

Add the fennel seeds and pepper and then boil, covered, for 15–20 minutes or until the rice is cooked. Turn off the heat and mix in the Parmesan and the remaining parsley. Ladle the risotto into soup bowls and serve immediately.

Risotto in Bianco

Basic Risotto

Slivers of white truffle are showered on this risotto when they are in season, which traditionally accompanies Ossobuco Milanese (see page 122) and Costolette alla Milanese (see page 125).

SERVES 4 AS A FIRST COURSE

1.2 litres/2 pints/1⅓ quarts light meat or vegetable stock

1 small onion, very finely chopped

50 g/2 oz/4 tbsp unsalted (sweet) butter

300 g/10 oz/1½ cups Italian rice, preferably Arborio or Carnaroli (see note)

50 g/2 oz/½ cup freshly grated Parmesan cheese

salt

freshly ground black pepper (optional)

BRING THE STOCK to a gentle simmer. Put the onion in a fairly large, heavy saucepan with half the butter. Sauté for about 15 minutes, stirring very frequently and adding a little water so that the onion does not brown.

Add the rice to the pan and stir until well coated with the butter. Cook, stirring constantly with a wooden spoon, until the outside of the grains becomes translucent and the rice begins to stick to the bottom of the pan.

Now pour over about 150 ml/5 fl oz/⅔ cup of the stock. Let the rice absorb it and then add another ladleful. Continue to add stock gradually and in small quantities, so that the rice always cooks in liquid but is never drowned by it. Stir constantly at first; after that you need to stir frequently but not all the time. The heat should be medium, so that the rice cooks steadily at a lively simmer. If you run out of stock before the rice is cooked, add a little boiling water in the same way.

When the rice is cooked (good rice takes about 18 minutes), take the pan off the heat. Taste and add salt, and pepper if you like. Add the rest of the butter, cut into small pieces, and the Parmesan. Put the lid firmly on the pan and leave for 1–2 minutes until the butter and the Parmesan have melted.

Give the risotto a vigorous stir and serve at once, with more Parmesan handed separately in a bowl.

NOTE: This is the most versatile of all risotti. It is excellent by itself, but it can also have vegetables, fish or sausages added to it, thus changing its flavour and appearance. The variety of rice used should vary according to the recipe, and so should the stock. For a vegetable risotto use Vialone Nano rice and vegetable stock; if you want a fish risotto, use Carnaroli rice and fish stock; while for a risotto alla Milanese or a risotto with sausage or meat, you can use Arborio or Carnaroli.

Risotto al Branzino

Risotto with Sea Bass

Of all the modern risotti, Risotto al Branzino is one of the most successful. The sea bass gives it a delicate but delicious fish flavour.

SERVES 3

2 tbsp extra virgin olive oil
1 garlic clove, bruised
100 g/3½ oz skinless sea bass fillet, cut into small pieces
salt and freshly ground black pepper
1 tsp sweet paprika
5 tbsp dry sherry
5 tbsp brandy
1 litre/1¾ pints/1 quart fish stock
4 tsp olive oil
50 g/2 oz/4 tbsp unsalted (sweet) butter
½ onion, sliced
250 g/9 oz/1¼ cups Italian rice, preferably Carnaroli
2 tbsp dry white wine
a few leaves of fresh flat-leaf parsley

HEAT THE EXTRA VIRGIN olive oil with the garlic in a frying pan (skillet) and add the fish. Season with salt, pepper and paprika, splash with the sherry and brandy and add a couple of tablespoons of the fish stock. Stir, remove the garlic and set aside.

Place the fish stock in a saucepan, bring to the boil and keep it covered at the lowest simmer.

Heat the olive oil, half the butter and the onion in a heavy saucepan. Sauté gently for a few minutes until the onion is soft but not brown, then mix in the rice and cook over a lively heat until you can hear it make a ringing noise on the side of the pan. Add the wine and let it evaporate. Continue cooking the rice by adding the hot stock a little at a time.

After the rice has been cooking for 12 minutes, stir in the fish with its sauce. When the rice is done (after about 15–18 minutes), take the pan off the heat and leave for a few moments, then mix in the remaining butter.

Garnish with the flat-leaf parsley and serve immediately.

Risotto alla Paesana

Risotto with Vegetables

All seasonal vegetables are used in this recipe, which is also known as risotto primavera. You can add asparagus spears or green beans, depending on the season.

SERVES 4 AS A FIRST COURSE

I litre/I¾ pints/I quart homemade chicken or vegetable stock

75 g/2½ oz/5 tbsp unsalted (sweet) butter

I tbsp olive oil

I medium onion, finely sliced

250 g/9 oz/I¼ cups Arborio or Vialone Nano rice

I medium carrot, diced small

2 celery stalks, cut into thin slices

100 g/3½ oz/scant I cup shelled fresh peas

2 ripe fresh tomatoes, peeled, de-seeded and coarsely chopped

I medium courgette (zucchini), diced small

75 g/2½ oz/¾ cup freshly grated Parmesan cheese

salt and freshly ground black pepper

BRING THE STOCK to simmering point. Put 50 g/2 oz/4 tbsp of the butter, the oil and onion into a heavy pan and sauté gently until the onion is soft and translucent. Add the rice and cook for I minute, stirring constantly so that the rice is coated with the fat. Pour over about 200 ml/7 fl oz/scant I cup of the stock and cook, stirring constantly, until nearly all the stock has been absorbed. Then add another 150 ml/5 fl oz/⅔ cup of the simmering stock and continue stirring. Adjust the heat so that the rice cooks steadily at a lively simmer.

When the rice has been cooking for about 10 minutes, add the carrot, celery, peas and tomatoes. Mix, and keep adding small amounts of stock as soon as the rice begins to look dry.

After a further 5 minutes, add the courgette (zucchini). Cook, stirring and adding more simmering stock as necessary. Do not add too much stock in one go – when the rice is nearly done, add no more than 4 tbsp at a time. The risotto should be ready in about 20 minutes.

When the rice is tender but al dente, take the pan off the heat and mix in the remaining butter and half the Parmesan. Taste and add salt if necessary, and pepper. Allow the butter to melt, stir thoroughly and turn the risotto into a heated dish.

Serve at once, with the rest of the Parmesan in a bowl on the side.

Cook's tip

To peel tomatoes place them in a bowl and pour in boiling water to completely cover them. Leave for 15–30 seconds, depending on how ripe they are, then lift them out with a slotted spoon and place in a bowl of cold water to refresh. The skins should now slip off easily.

Riso Arrosto alla Genovese

Rice Baked with Pork and Dried Porcini

This is my adaptation of a recipe in Cuciniera Genovese, *a book that is still considered to be the bible of Genoese cooking, by the nineteenth-century writers GB and Giovanni Ratto. It is the only traditional Italian rice dish that is cooked in the oven. In the original recipe the meat is veal and heifer's elder (udder), a great delicacy that has now, alas, disappeared. It is suggested that sausage can be used instead, but it must not be spicy or herby, another great difficulty. All things considered, I suggest using minced pork (ground). I make Riso Arrosto in a flameproof baking dish.*

SERVES 3

20 g/¾ oz/⅓ cup dried porcini
I small onion, finely chopped
a lovely bunch of fresh flat-leaf
    parsley, chopped
salt
50 g/2 oz/4 tbsp unsalted
    (sweet) butter
I garlic clove, chopped
300 g/10 oz lean minced (ground) pork
600 ml/I pint/2½ cups homemade
    strong meat stock
300 g/10 oz/1½ cups Arborio rice
40 g/1½ oz/6 tbsp freshly grated
    Parmesan cheese
6 tbsp red wine
freshly ground black pepper

HEAT THE OVEN to 200°C/400°F/ Gas Mark 6. Soak the dried porcini in 100 ml/3½ fl oz/scant I cup hot water for about 30 minutes. Remove the porcini from the water and, if there is still some grit, rinse them under cold water. Pat dry and chop them. Filter the liquid of the porcini through a sieve (strainer) lined with a piece of muslin or cheesecloth. This may not be necessary if you pour the liquid very gently so that any sand is left at the bottom of the bowl.

Gently sauté the onion and parsley with ½ teaspoon salt in the butter until soft. Add the garlic and cook for 2 minutes, stirring frequently. Add the porcini, sauté for a minute or two, then mix in the pork and brown well. Pour in 4–5 tablespoons of the stock and cook over very gentle heat for 5 minutes, stirring frequently.

Meanwhile, bring the remaining stock and the porcini liquid to the boil in another pan.

Stir the rice and 1½ tablespoons of the Parmesan into the pan with the meat mixture. Add the wine and cook for about 2 minutes, stirring constantly. Pour in the boiling stock, add pepper to taste and mix well. Cover the pan, transfer to the preheated oven and cook until the rice is done and a lovely crust has formed on top, 10–15 minutes.

Serve with the rest of the Parmesan on the side.

Polenta

This is the old-fashioned way to make polenta. It is made with traditional polenta flour, not instant polenta.

SERVES 6
2 tsp salt
300 g/10 oz/2 cups coarse-ground
polenta flour (coarse cornmeal)

Choose a large, deep, heavy saucepan and fill it with 1.8 litres/3½ pints/2 quarts water. When the water comes to the boil, add the salt. Remove the pan from the heat and add the polenta flour (cornmeal) in a very thin stream, letting it fall through the nearly closed fist of one hand while the other stirs constantly with a long-handled wooden spoon. Now cook the polenta for at least 40 minutes, stirring constantly for the first 10 minutes and then every minute or so.

When ready, transfer the polenta to a bowl, previously moistened with cold water. Leave it to rest for a few minutes and then turn the bowl upside down on to a large round platter or a wooden board covered with a white napkin. The polenta will fall on to it and look, as it should, like a golden mound.

Polenta Made in the Oven

This is a modern and easy variation of the above method, which does not require stirring.

Heat the oven to 190°C/375°F/Gas Mark 5. Bring 1.8 litres/3½ pints/2 quarts water to simmering point. Remove the pan from the heat and add 2 teaspoons salt, then gradually add 350 g/12 oz/2⅓ cups polenta flour (cornmeal) in a very thin stream, letting it fall through the nearly closed fist of one hand while the other stirs constantly with a long-handled wooden spoon. Return the pan to the heat and bring slowly to the boil, stirring constantly in the same direction. Boil for 5 minutes, still stirring. Now transfer the polenta to a buttered ovenproof dish and cover with buttered foil.

Cook in the preheated oven for 1 hour.

Cook's tip

Polenta was originally cooked in a round-based, unlined copper vessel called a paiolo, which hung over the fire. Nowadays, a large saucepan is required. However, it is possible to buy an electrically operated polenta "paddle". This can be set to the required time and takes much of the hard work out of making polenta the traditional way.

Polenta Pasticciata

Baked Polenta with Meat and Dried Porcini

There are many versions of polenta pasticciata — here is one of the most popular.

SERVES 4–6

FOR THE POLENTA

300 g/10 oz/2 cups coarse-ground
    polenta flour (coarse cornmeal)
2 tbsp salt

FOR THE SAUCE

25 g/1 oz/½ cup dried porcini
3 tbsp olive oil
25 g/1 oz/2 tbsp unsalted
    (sweet) butter
I small onion, finely chopped
I small carrot, finely chopped
½ celery stalk, finely chopped
350 g/12 oz lean minced (ground) beef
I bay leaf
salt and freshly ground black pepper
2 tbsp tomato paste diluted with
    100 ml/3½ fl oz/scant ½ cup
    meat stock
butter for the dish
6 tbsp freshly grated Parmesan cheese

FIRST MAKE THE POLENTA following one or other of the instructions on page 84. Pour the hot polenta onto a wet surface — marble, plastic or similar, but not wood — and spread it out to a thickness of about 2.5 cm/1 in. Leave to cool.

Soak the dried porcini in 100 ml/ 3½ fl oz/scant ½ cup warm water for 30 minutes. Lift them out gently, wash under cold water, squeeze and dry. Chop them coarsely. Strain the soaking liquid through a sieve (strainer) lined with muslin or cheesecloth and set aside.

Heat the oven to 200°C/400°F/ Gas Mark 6.

Put the oil, butter and onion in a heatproof earthenware pot and sauté until the onion is soft. Mix in the porcini, carrot and celery and sauté for a further few minutes. Add the minced (ground) beef and cook until it has lost its raw colour, then add the bay leaf and salt and pepper to taste. Turn the heat down to low and pour in the diluted tomato paste and the liquid in which the mushrooms have soaked. When the sauce is boiling, turn the heat down as low as possible and cook, uncovered, for about 2 hours.

Taste and check seasoning and remove the bay leaf.

Grease a shallow 20 x 15 cm/8 x 6 in ovenproof dish generously with butter. Cut the polenta into 1 cm/½ in slices and cover the bottom of the dish with a layer of polenta. Spoon over about one-third of the sauce and sprinkle with 2 tablespoons of the Parmesan. Repeat the layers of polenta, sauce and Parmesan until all the ingredients are used, then bake in the preheated oven for about 30 minutes.

Allow to stand for a good 5 minutes before serving.

NOTE: This recipe is made with traditional polenta flour, not instant polenta. You can use instant polenta instead — it only takes 5 minutes to cook. It's not as good, but it does save time and effort.

Rotolo di Patate e Spinaci

Potato and Spinach Roll

I have always found that my mother's recipe for Rotolo di Spinaci made with potato dough is much nicer and easier than the traditional method, which uses homemade pasta. Instead of dressing it with butter and Parmesan before browning it in the oven, you may prefer to cover it with a thin béchamel sauce (see page 179) flavoured with plenty of Parmesan and a grating of nutmeg.

SERVES 6

500 g/1 lb floury (mealy) potatoes, such as Idaho or Russet

salt

1 onion, very finely chopped

1 tbsp olive oil

1 kg/2 lb 2 oz spinach, cooked and chopped, or 500 g/1 lb/5⅓ cups frozen chopped spinach, thawed and well drained

100 g/3½ oz/scant ½ cup ricotta

100 g/3½ oz/generous 1 cup freshly grated Parmesan cheese

pinch of grated nutmeg

1 large (extra-large) free-range (farm-fresh) egg yolk

freshly ground black pepper

1 large (extra-large) free-range (farm-fresh) egg

1 tsp baking powder

200 g/7 oz/1⅓ cups flour, preferably Italian 00

200 g/7 oz best ham, thinly sliced

75 g/2½ oz/5 tbsp unsalted (sweet) butter

SCRUB THE POTATOES and boil them in their skins in plenty of lightly salted water for about 20 minutes, until they are tender.

Meanwhile, heat the oven to 200°C/400°F/Gas Mark 6 and prepare the filling. Sauté the onion in the olive oil for 2–3 minutes until soft. Add the spinach and cook for 2 minutes, stirring frequently. Transfer the spinach to a bowl and add the ricotta, half the Parmesan, the nutmeg, egg yolk and salt and pepper. Mix very thoroughly.

Drain the potatoes, peel them as soon as they are cool enough to handle, then push them through a food mill or potato ricer straight on to the work surface (countertop). Make a well in the middle of the potatoes, drop the whole egg into it and add a little salt, the baking powder and most of the flour. Knead, adding more flour if necessary, for about 5 minutes. The dough should be soft, smooth and slightly sticky. Shape it into a ball.

Roll out the potato dough into a 35 x 25 cm/14 x 10 in rectangle. Cover it with the ham and then spread the spinach filling over it to cover all but a 1 cm/½ in border all around. Roll the potato dough up into a large salami shape and then wrap the roll tightly in muslin or cheesecloth and tie both ends securely with a piece of string.

Fill a fish kettle, or another long deep pan that can hold the rotolo, with water. Add 1 tablespoon salt and bring to the boil, then gently lower the roll into the water. Return the water to the boil and cook, partially covered, for 30 minutes.

Lift the roll out, being careful not to break it, unwrap it and leave to cool.

Cut the roll into 2 cm/¾ in thick slices, and place them slightly overlapping on a heated ovenproof dish. Melt the butter, pour it over the slices and sprinkle with the remaining Parmesan. Bake in the preheated oven for about 15 minutes, until golden.

Gnocchi alla Romana

Semolina Gnocchi

Also called gnocchi di semolina, these are the easiest gnocchi to prepare. If possible, buy Italian semolina, which is more coarsely ground than other semolinas. If you prefer, these gnocchi can be dressed with a thin béchamel sauce (see page 179) or with cream and Parmesan.

SERVES 4

I litre/1¾ pints/1 quart milk
salt
225 g/8 oz/1½ cups + 2 tbsp coarse-
   ground semolina (semolina flour)
3 large (extra-large) free-range (farm-
   fresh) egg yolks
75 g/2½ oz/scant 1 cup freshly grated
   Parmesan cheese
¼ tsp grated nutmeg
75 g/2½ oz/5 tbsp unsalted
   (sweet) butter
a little butter for the dish

HEAT THE MILK with a little salt in a heavy saucepan. When it begins to simmer, add the semolina in a very thin stream, beating quickly to prevent lumps forming. Cook for about 15 minutes, beating constantly until the semolina has formed a thick paste and comes away from the side of the pan.

Take the pan off the heat. As soon as the semolina has cooled a little, add the egg yolks one at a time. When all the eggs have been thoroughly mixed in, add all but 4 tablespoons of the Parmesan, then add the nutmeg, 25 g/1 oz/2 tbsp of the butter and salt to taste. Incorporate everything thoroughly and then turn the mixture out onto a slab of marble or the work surface (countertop), having previously moistened it with cold water. Spread the semolina mixture to a thickness of

1 cm/½ in and then leave to cool completely. This will take about 2 hours.

Heat the oven to 230°C/450°F/ Gas Mark 8.

Cut the semolina into 4 cm/1½ in rounds. Place a layer of the rounds in the bottom of a buttered ovenproof dish, put the cut pieces in between and then cover with another layer of the gnocchi rounds, slightly overlapping.

Melt the remaining butter and pour it over the gnocchi. Sprinkle with the remaining Parmesan and bake in the preheated oven for about 15 minutes, until the gnocchi are heated through. Remove from the oven and allow to cool for a few minutes before serving.

NOTE: The whole dish can be prepared in advance and then simply baked just before serving.

Gnocchi di Patate

Potato Gnocchi

These are the gnocchi of Lazio and Veneto, easier to make than those of Piedmont, which do not contain any egg.

SERVES 4

1 kg/2 lb 2 oz floury (mealy)
   potatoes, scrubbed
1 tsp salt
300 g/10 oz/1½ cups flour, preferably
   Italian 00
1 large (extra-large) free-range (farm-
   fresh) egg, beaten
75 g/2½ oz/5 tbsp unsalted
   (sweet) butter
2 garlic cloves, lightly crushed
3 or 4 fresh sage leaves, torn
75 g/2½ oz/scant 1 cup freshly grated
   Parmesan cheese

BOIL THE SCRUBBED POTATOES in plenty of water. Drain and peel while still hot. Sieve the potatoes, using a food mill or a potato ricer, on to the work surface (countertop).

Sprinkle the salt on to the flour in a bowl and mix well.

Add the beaten egg and half the flour to the potatoes. Knead, gradually adding more flour, until the mixture is soft, smooth and slightly sticky. Shape the mixture into rolls, about 2.5 cm/1 in in diameter, and then cut into 2 cm/¾ in pieces.

To shape the gnocchi, take a fork and hold it with the prongs resting on the work surface at an angle of about 45°. Take each piece of dough and dust it with flour, then press it lightly with the thumb of your other hand against the inner curve of the prongs and, with a quick down-wards movement, flip it towards the end of the prongs. The gnocchi should be concave on the thumb side, and convex with ridges on the fork side.

Bring 5 litres/8 pints/5½ quarts water to the boil in a large saucepan. Do not put salt in the water as this tends to make the gnocchi stick together.

Meanwhile, make the sauce. Put the butter, garlic and sage in a small heavy saucepan and cook slowly. The sauce is ready when the foam has disappeared and the butter is light golden. Discard the garlic and keep the sauce warm.

Drop the gnocchi into the boiling water, about 30 at a time. Cook for 20 seconds after they come to the surface, then lift out with a slotted spoon, pat dry with kitchen paper (paper towels) and transfer to a heated dish. Pour over a little sauce, sprinkle with some Parmesan and keep warm. Repeat until all the gnocchi are cooked. Pour the remaining sauce over and sprinkle with Parmesan.

Gnocchi di Zucca

Butternut Squash Gnocchi

Butternut or kabocha squash mixed with sweet potatoes come close to the spicy sweetness and moist texture of a northern Italian pumpkin. These gnocchi are a traditional speciality of Veneto and southern Lombardy. The first dressing is the classic dressing from Veneto, while the second one from Lombardy is the one that is mostly used everywhere else.

SERVES 4–5

I tbsp vegetable oil

500 g/I lb butternut or kabocha squash

500 g/I lb orange-fleshed
   sweet potatoes

200 g/7 oz/I½ cups flour, preferably
   Italian 00

2 tsp baking powder

salt

2 large (extra-large) free-range (farm-
   fresh) eggs

4 tbsp freshly grated Parmesan cheese

a generous grating of nutmeg

DRESSING I

75 g/2½ oz/5 tbsp unsalted
   (sweet) butter

25 g/I oz/⅓ cup freshly grated
   Parmesan cheese

I tbsp sugar

I tsp ground cinnamon

DRESSING 2

75 g/2½ oz/5 tbsp unsalted
   (sweet) butter

6 fresh sage leaves, snipped

50 g/2 oz/½ cup freshly grated
   Parmesan cheese

HEAT THE OVEN to 180°C/350°F/ Gas Mark 4. Line a baking tray (cookie sheet) with foil and then brush the foil with oil. Wipe the squash and cut it in half. Scoop out and discard the seeds and fibres and place the squash, cut side down, on the foil. Pierce the sweet potatoes with a skewer and place them on the foil with the squash. Bake for about I hour, until both vegetables can be pierced easily with a fork.

Peel the sweet potatoes and scoop the flesh out of the skin of the squash. Purée both vegetables through a food mill or a potato ricer into a bowl. Mix in the flour, baking powder and salt and then break in the eggs. Mix very well to incorporate, then add the Parmesan and season with nutmeg and salt.

Bring a large saucepan of salted water to the boil. I find it easiest to make the gnocchi with a piping (pastry) bag and a plain large nozzle (tip), but you may prefer to make the gnocchi by shaping small balls with floury hands.

To pipe the gnocchi, fill the bag with the squash mixture and hold it over the saucepan, squeezing it with one hand and cutting the mixture as it comes out of the nozzle with the other. Cut short shapes about 2 cm/¾ in long, letting them drop straight into the simmering water. Don't cook all the gnocchi together, but do it in 3 batches. Cook them for I or 2 minutes after they have come to the surface of the water. Lift out each batch with a slotted spoon and place in a shallow, large ovenproof dish. Dress each batch separately and keep the dish in a low oven.

For the first dressing, melt the butter in a bain-marie or double boiler. Pour it over each batch of gnocchi and sprinkle with Parmesan, sugar and cinnamon.

For the second dressing, put the butter and sage leaves in a small saucepan and let the butter melt and begin to foam. Spoon over each batch of gnocchi and sprinkle with the grated Parmesan.

Malfatti

Spinach and Ricotta Gnocchi

Malfatti means badly made, an appropriate name for these rustic gnocchi, which are often different shapes and sizes. Use the green leaves of Swiss chard if you can find them, as in the original recipe from Emilia.

SERVES 4

500 g/1 lb cooked or frozen leaf
    spinach, thawed
salt
2 large (extra-large) free-range (farm-
    fresh) eggs
200 g/7 oz/scant 1 cup ricotta
200 g/7 oz/1⅓ cups flour, preferably
    Italian 00
½ tsp grated nutmeg
100 g/3½ oz/generous 1 cup freshly
    grated Parmesan cheese
freshly ground black pepper
100 g/3½ oz/7 tbsp unsalted
    (sweet) butter

SQUEEZE ALL THE water out of the spinach with your hands. Chop the spinach very finely or pass it through the coarsest setting of a food mill.

In a bowl, beat the eggs together and mix in the ricotta. Beat again. Mix in the flour, spinach, nutmeg and half the Parmesan. Taste and adjust the seasoning.

Dust your hands with flour and form the mixture into balls the size of large marbles. Place them on a tray and chill in the refrigerator for about 30 minutes.

To cook the gnocchi, bring 5 litres/8 pints/5½ quarts salted water to the boil in a very large saucepan. Add the gnocchi, a dozen at a time, and cook them for 3–4 minutes after the water returns to the boil. Lift them out with a slotted spoon and transfer them to a dish. Dot with a little butter, sprinkle over a little Parmesan and keep them warm while you are cooking the remaining mixture.

Meanwhile, melt the remaining butter in a small saucepan. Just before serving, spoon the butter over the cooked gnocchi, sprinkle with the remaining Parmesan and serve at once.

Cook's tip

Nutmeg should always be freshly grated — and that means at the very last moment. The oils which give nutmeg its characteristic flavour and aroma are extremely volatile and evaporate quickly. Store whole nutmeg in an airtight container.

Dentice al Sale

Dentex Baked in a Crust of Salt

Dentex is part of the extensive bream family and this is an excellent way to cook it — the crust of salt preserves the full flavour of the fish. Any member of the bream family, porgy or any fairly large white fish such a sea bass can be cooked in the same way. This is my translation of a recipe in La Cucina d'Oro, *edited by Giovanni Nuvoletti in association with the Accademia Italiana della Cucina.*

SERVES 4
I dentex (with head and tail left on),
   about I kg/2 lb 2 oz
3 kg/6½ lb coarse sea salt

HEAT THE OVEN to 200°C/400°F/ Gas Mark 6. Spread a 2 cm/¾ in layer of salt on the bottom of a roasting pan. Lay the fish over it and cover with the rest of the salt, patting it well into the fish with your hands.

Bake in the preheated oven for at least I hour. To test if the fish is cooked, break a little bit of the salt crust along the spine of the fish and pull out a fin. If the fin comes away easily with its bones, then the fish is ready.

Serve the fish in its salt crust at the table and break it open there. The scales will come away together with the salt. Serve only with mild extra virgin olive oil and lemon juice as accompaniments, which are more than enough.

Nasello alla Palermitana

Breaded Hake with Anchovies

Ideally you should use a whole fish, which looks more attractive. If you cannot find it, you can simply use a fillet of hake, or cod or whiting.

SERVES 4
1.25 kg/2½ lb hake, cleaned but with
   head and tail left on
5 tbsp olive oil
salt and freshly ground black pepper
3 or 4 sprigs of fresh rosemary
I garlic clove, finely chopped
3 salted anchovies, boned and rinsed,
   or 6 canned or bottled anchovy
   fillets, drained
4 tbsp dried breadcrumbs
juice of ½ lemon, preferably organic or
   unwaxed

HEAT THE OVEN to 180°C/350°F/ Gas Mark 4. Brush the inside of the fish with a little of the olive oil and season with salt and pepper. Put the rosemary sprigs in the cavity and secure with one or more wooden toothpicks.

Heat the remaining oil in a small frying pan (skillet) and sauté the garlic for 30 seconds or so over low heat. Take off the heat and mash in the anchovies. Rub the fish all over with the anchovy mixture and then spread with the breadcrumbs.

Place the fish in an oiled ovenproof dish, preferably metal, and bake in the preheated oven for about 30 minutes, or until the fish is cooked right through. Five minutes before the fish is ready, sprinkle with the lemon juice.

A golden crust should form all around the fish, but if it appears to be dry, baste with the cooking juices and some oil.

Spigola al Forno
Baked Sea Bass

This recipe comes from Mediterranean Seafood *by Alan Davidson. In his introduction he writes, "Success depends on having in the first place a really fresh fish."*

SERVES 6
1 sea bass, about 1.5 kg/3¼ lb
1 garlic clove, chopped
lots of fresh herbs (rosemary, thyme
    and marjoram are all suitable),
    coarsely chopped
lots of fresh flat-leaf parsley,
    coarsely chopped
salt
1 tbsp dried breadcrumbs
1 wine glass olive oil
1 tsp lemon juice

HEAT THE OVEN to 200°C/400°F/ Gas Mark 6. Scale, wash and gut the fish. Put the chopped garlic, herbs and parsley into the gut cavity and the gills.

Place the fish in an oiled shallow ovenproof dish, salt it lightly, sprinkle with breadcrumbs and pour over the olive oil into which you have previously beaten the lemon juice. Cook for 25–30 minutes in the preheated oven.

Branzino alla Rivierasca coi Carciofi
Sea Bass with Artichokes

This superb and easy recipe from the Ligurian Riviera combines two of the favourite local foods. This version comes from Marcella Hazan's The Second Classic Italian Cookbook.

SERVES 4
4–6 medium globe artichokes
½ lemon
4 tbsp olive oil
3 tbsp lemon juice
salt and freshly ground pepper
1 sea bass, about 900 g/2 lb , cleaned
    and scaled, but with head and tail on,
    and rinsed in cold water
1 tsp rosemary needles

HEAT THE OVEN to 220°C/425°F/ Gas Mark 7. Trim and prepare the artichokes, keeping only the tender leaves and the heart. Rub the artichoke with the half lemon each time you cut it, to prevent it turning black. Cut each artichoke in quarters lengthways, remove the soft purply curling leaves with prickly tips and cut away the fuzzy "choke" beneath them. Slice the artichoke quarters lengthways into the thinnest possible slices and sprinkle a few drops of lemon juice over them.

Mix the olive oil, lemon juice, salt and pepper in a small bowl and set aside.

Pat the fish dry with kitchen paper (paper towels) and place it in a rectangular ovenproof dish just large enough to contain it. Add the sliced artichokes and three-quarters of the oil and lemon juice mixture. Sprinkle the rosemary over the fish. Turn the artichoke slices so they are all coated with juice and stuff some of the artichokes into the fish's cavity. Coat the fish with the remaining oil and lemon mixture and place it in the upper third of the preheated oven. After 20 minutes cooking, baste the fish and stir the artichokes. Bake for another 15–20 minutes, then transfer the fish to a heated serving dish. This has to be done very carefully, otherwise the fish will break. The best way is to lift it with two spatulas, one in each hand.

Spread the artichokes around the fish, pour over it all the juices from the dish and serve immediately.

Triglie alla Livornese
Red Mullet in Tomato Sauce

A favourite of the Italians, red mullet is cooked in a number of ways, of which this recipe from Livorno is the best known. The heads of the fish must be left on because they give flavour to the dish, and also because the fish look better this way. Where red mullet isn't available, try red snapper or grey mullet, although the flavour isn't as fine.

SERVES 4
4 red mullet, about 250 g/9 oz each
4 tbsp flour
6 tbsp extra virgin olive oil
I garlic clove, very finely chopped
I small onion, finely chopped
I bay leaf
½ tbsp chopped fresh thyme
a small piece of dried chilli
salt and freshly ground black pepper
400 g/14 oz canned chopped
    tomatoes, drained
2 tbsp chopped fresh flat-leaf parsley

ASK YOUR FISHMONGER to clean the fish, scale it well and remove the gills. The liver of red mullet should be left in the cavity. Wash the fish under cold running water and dry thoroughly. Coat the fish with flour.

Heat the olive oil in a large frying pan (skillet) over a medium heat. Slide in the fish and sauté for about 2 minutes on each side.

Add all the other ingredients and turn down the heat. Cook gently for about 10 minutes, basting the fish occasionally and turning it over once.

Taste and check the amount of seasoning before serving.

Orata alla Pugliese
Baked Gilt-head Bream and Potatoes

A traditional way to cook fish in Puglia is to bake it with potatoes. I prefer to parboil the potatoes first, so that they will be ready at the same time as the fish. Gilt-head bream is the best of the bream family, but if you can't get one, you can use any other member of that family or snapper.

SERVES 6
6–8 waxy potatoes
I gilt-head bream, about 1.5–1.8 kg/
    3¼–4 lb, cleaned
salt
a bunch of fresh flat-leaf parsley
I garlic clove
150 ml/5 fl oz/⅔ cup extra virgin olive oil
100 g/3½ oz/generous I cup grated
    mature (sharp) pecorino cheese
freshly ground black pepper

BOIL THE POTATOES for 5 minutes, then drain, peel them and set them aside. When cold, slice them thinly. Season the cavity and the outside of the fish with a little salt.

Heat the oven to 200°C/400°F/Gas Mark 6.

Chop the parsley and garlic. Pour 4 tablespoons of the olive oil into an ovenproof dish (I use a metal lasagne pan) and cover the bottom with half the potatoes, half the parsley and garlic mixture and half the cheese. Season with a little salt and plenty of pepper. Drizzle with a little of the oil and lay the fish over this. Spread over the other half of the parsley and garlic, potatoes, and cheese, in that order, season as before, and drizzle with the rest of the oil.

Bake in the preheated oven for 25 minutes.

Cefalo con le Zucchine

Grey Mullet with Courgettes

The sweetness of the courgettes (zucchini) is a good foil for the grey mullet.

SERVES 4

500 g/1 lb courgettes (zucchini)
salt
1 garlic clove, chopped
2 tbsp chopped fresh flat-leaf parsley
freshly ground black pepper
1 fresh grey mullet, about 1 kg/2 lb 2 oz, cleaned, scaled and gutted, but with head and tail on
150 ml/5 fl oz/⅔ cup extra virgin olive oil

CUT THE COURGETTES (ZUCCHINI) into rounds, put them in a colander and sprinkle lightly with salt. Leave for about 30 minutes. This will bring out the excess water. Drain and dry them and then mix in the garlic, parsley and pepper.

Heat the oven to 190°C/375°F/ Gas Mark 5.

Season the fish inside and out with salt and pepper and sprinkle 1 tablespoon of the oil inside. Lay the fish in a large ovenproof dish or a roasting pan and spoon the courgettes around it. Pour over the rest of the oil and mix with the courgettes.

Cover the dish with foil and bake in the preheated oven for 20 minutes. Remove the foil, stir the courgettes and spoon some of the cooking liquid over the fish. Cook for a further 15 minutes or so, until the fish is ready.

Sogliole al Basilico e ai Pinoli

Sole with Basil and Pine Nuts

An old recipe from the town of Caorle, east of Venice, from a splendid book, Antica Cucina Veneziana, by the great food historian Massimo Alberini. The recipes have been adapted from the originals by Romana Bosco, a leading contemporary cookery teacher who runs the school Il Melograno in Turin. This is my adaptation.

SERVES 4

4 sole, about 300 g/10 oz each, gutted and skinned
1 tbsp extra virgin olive oil
2 tbsp pine nuts, coarsely chopped
5 or 6 fresh basil leaves

FOR THE MARINADE

4 tbsp olive oil
3 tbsp lemon juice
1 tbsp chopped fresh basil
salt and freshly ground black pepper

WASH THE FISH, dry thoroughly and lay them on a dish.

Prepare the marinade. Put the olive oil in a bowl, beat in the lemon juice until emulsified, then the basil, salt and pepper. Spoon the marinade over the sole and leave to marinate for an hour or so.

Heat the oven to 200°C/400°F/ Gas Mark 6.

Lift the sole out of the marinade. Grease a shallow, large ovenproof dish with the olive oil and lay the fish in it. Place the dish in the preheated oven and cook for about 10 minutes.

Heat the marinade and add the pine nuts. When the liquid boils, pour it over the sole and cook in the oven for a further 5 minutes or so. Sprinkle with basil leaves before serving.

Sogliole in Saor

Sole Fillets in a Sweet-and-Sour Sauce

This is served as an antipasto* in Venice, but it makes a good main course too. You can use plaice (or flounder) fillets instead of sole, or sardines, which must be boned but left in one piece, butterfly-fashion, not divided into two.

SERVES 6–8

50 g/2 oz/⅓ cup sultanas
   (golden raisins)
flour for dusting
salt
700 g/1½ lb sole fillets
oil for deep-frying
2 tbsp olive oil
225 g/8 oz mild onions, thinly sliced
2 tsp sugar
120 ml/4 fl oz/½ cup good
   wine vinegar
4 bay leaves
50 g/2 oz/½ cup pine nuts
2 or 3 pinches of ground cinnamon
2 cloves
12 black peppercorns, lightly crushed

SOAK THE SULTANAS (golden raisins) in a little warm water to plump them. Meanwhile, spread some flour on a board and season with salt, then coat the fish lightly in the flour.

Heat the oil for deep-frying in a wok or a frying pan (skillet). When the oil is very hot but not smoking, slide in the sole fillets, a few at a time. Fry gently for about 3 minutes on each side until a golden crust has formed. With a fish slice (pancake turner), transfer the fish to a plate lined with kitchen paper (paper towels), to drain.

Heat the olive oil and onions in a small frying pan. Add a pinch of salt and the sugar. Cook the onions gently, stirring frequently, until golden. Turn the heat up and pour in the wine vinegar, then boil briskly until the liquid is reduced by half.

Lay the fish neatly in a shallow dish. Pour over the onion sauce and put the bay leaves on top. Drain the sultanas (golden raisins) and scatter them on top of the dish together with the pine nuts, spices and peppercorns. Cover the dish with clingfilm (plastic wrap) and leave to marinate in the refrigerator for at least 24 hours or, even better, for 48 hours.

Remove from the refrigerator about 2 hours before serving to bring the dish back to room temperature.

Cook's tip

There are several varieties of sole of which Dover sole is the best known. It is also said to have the finest flavour and texture. Lemon sole is also well known but it is actually a fish from the group known as dabs and not a true sole.

Trance di Pesce alla Casalinga

Fish Steaks in Tomato Sauce

You can cook almost any white fish steaks in this popular way. My favourite is cod, because of its texture, but hake, haddock or even skate wings are suitable. This dish is better made with canned tomatoes, rather than fresh ones, because they have more juice, which is needed for the sauce. If you like saffron with fish, add a pinch of pulverized saffron threads just before you add the fish.

SERVES 4

4 large white fish steaks
(see introduction)
salt and freshly ground black pepper
5 tbsp extra virgin olive oil
½ mild onion, finely chopped
a bunch of fresh flat-leaf parsley, chopped
1 dried red chilli, chopped
1 garlic clove, chopped
400 g/14 oz canned peeled tomatoes,
with their juice

WASH AND DRY THE fish steaks and press a little salt and pepper into them on both sides.

Choose a sauté pan or frying pan (skillet) that is large enough for the fish steaks to fit in a single layer. Heat the oil and onion in the pan and sauté for about 7 minutes. Add half the parsley, chilli and garlic to the onion and sauté for a couple of minutes, moving the mixture around quite often.

Pour in the tomatoes with their juice. With a wooden spoon, break the tomatoes into smallish pieces. Season with salt and cook for 10 minutes.

Add the fish, laying one steak next to the other. Spoon some of the juice over the fish and cover the pan. Cook over a low heat for 10–15 minutes (depending on the thickness of the fish), turning the steaks over halfway through cooking.

Before serving, check seasoning and sprinkle with a mixture of the remaining parsley, chilli and garlic.

Aragosta al Forno

Roasted Spiny Lobster

You can use large langoustines, Dublin Bay prawns (jumbo shrimp) or a small lobster instead of spiny or rock lobster.

SERVES 2

4 tbsp olive oil
900 g–1.25 kg/2–2½ lb spiny or rock
lobster, preferably uncooked
salt and freshly ground black pepper
juice of 3 lemons, preferably organic
or unwaxed
2 tbsp dried white breadcrumbs
2 tbsp chopped fresh flat-leaf parsley

HEAT THE OVEN to 180°C/350°F/ Gas Mark 4 and grease a roasting pan with a little of the olive oil.

Split the lobster in half lengthways. Detach and discard the head (or use it for soup) and detach the claws. Remove the tail meat from the shell using poultry shears. Make a shallow incision along the tail and flatten the meat slightly with a cleaver or rolling pin. Lay it in the prepared pan together with the claws.

Sprinkle with salt, half the lemon juice, the breadcrumbs, parsley, half the olive oil and some pepper. Bake in the preheated oven for about 15 minutes, then allow to cool for 5 minutes.

Whisk the remaining lemon juice and oil together with salt and a generous grinding of pepper and serve separately.

Pesce Spada alla Trapanese

Swordfish in a Tomato, Olive and Cornichon Sauce

This is my adaptation of a recipe translated from Il Gastronomo Educato *by Denti di Pirajno, a twentieth-century Sicilian writer and a great gastronome. Try to buy steaks from the belly of the fish, which have the most delicate flavour.*

SERVES 4

I onion, chopped
2 tbsp extra virgin olive oil
4 cornichons (sweet dill pickles)
6 black olives, pitted
2 tbsp capers, preferably in salt, rinsed
I celery stalk
salt and freshly ground black pepper
2 tbsp tomato paste
600 g/I¼ lb swordfish, thinly sliced
about I tbsp lemon juice

PUT THE ONION in a large sauté pan and cover with 100 ml/3½ fl oz/scant I cup water. Bring to the boil and simmer, covered, for a couple of minutes. Turn up the heat, add the olive oil and continue cooking until the water has evaporated and the onion is golden. You must stir frequently at the end of cooking so that all the bits of onion are golden without sticking to the botttom of the pan.

Meanwhile, chop the cornichons (sweet dill pickles), olives, capers and celery and mix them all together. When the onion is golden, add the chopped mixture and season with salt and plenty of pepper. Cook over gentle heat for 5–6 minutes.

Dilute the tomato paste with 200 ml/7 fl oz/scant I cup boiling water and then pour into the pan. Cook, stirring frequently, until the sauce begins to thicken, this will take a further 5–7 minutes.

Now add the fish and cook for about 5 minutes, turning it over once. The length of the cooking time depends on the thickness of the steaks. It is better to undercook swordfish rather than overcook it.

Put the fish and its sauce on a heated serving dish, pour over the lemon juice and serve at once.

Cook's tip

Cornichons are small gherkins (sweet dill pickles). Their name means "little horns". The best and most flavoursome varieties are pickled in white wine vinegar rather than spirit vinegar.

Acciughe alla Moda di Reggio Calabria

Baked Fresh Anchovies

You can use sardines or sprats in this recipe instead of anchovies. They are less delicate in flavour than fresh anchovies, but they are more readily available. This applies particularly to sprats, a good fish and always sold very fresh. (In the United States, sprats, similar to herring, are also sold salted, smoked or in oil. Do not use these. Use fresh herring, if necessary.) Freshness should always be the top priority.

SERVES 4
700 g/1½ lb fresh anchovies
   (see introduction)
4 tbsp olive oil
5 tbsp fresh breadcrumbs
I tbsp capers, preferably in salt, rinsed
2 garlic cloves, crushed
½ dried red chilli, chopped
I tbsp chopped fresh marjoram
salt
a little oil for the dish

PULL THE HEAD OFF THE BODY of each anchovy with a sharp movement. This should also remove the central bone and the inside. Wash the anchovies thoroughly under cold water and pat them dry.

Heat the oven to 200°C/400°F/ Gas Mark 6.

Mix together all the other ingredients. Grease a shallow ovenproof dish with a little oil and cover the bottom with a layer of anchovies. Spread half the breadcrumb mixture over the fish, cover with another layer of anchovies and then with the rest of the crumbs.

Bake in the preheated oven for 20 minutes. Serve hot, but not straight from the oven, or at room temperature.

Sarde a Beccaficu

Baked Sardines

You can also make this dish with sprats (see left), which are often sold fresher in the market than sardines. They are, after all, from the same family – the Clupeidae.

SERVES 4
25 g/I oz/2 tbsp sultanas
   (golden raisins)
I kg/2 lb 2 oz fresh sardines
5 tbsp olive oil
100 g/3½ oz/1¾ cups soft
   white breadcrumbs
25 g/I oz/¼ cup pine nuts
2 garlic cloves, chopped
2 tbsp capers, preferably in salt, rinsed
   and chopped
2 tbsp chopped fresh flat-leaf parsley
2 tbsp freshly grated pecorino cheese
salt and freshly ground black pepper
2 tbsp orange juice
4 or 5 bay leaves, torn

HEAT THE OVEN to 200°C/400°F/ Gas Mark 6. Soak the sultanas (golden raisins) in some hot water while you prepare the fish.

Cut off the heads of the sardines, split them open underneath and clean them. Lay them open side down on a wooden board and press the backbone down gently. Cut the backbone at the tail end and remove it. Wash and dry the sardines.

Heat 3 tablespoons of the olive oil in a frying pan (skillet) and add the breadcrumbs. Fry them gently until golden and then add the pine nuts, garlic, capers, parsley and the drained sultanas. Mix well and cook for I or 2 minutes. Transfer the mixture to a bowl and mix in the pecorino and season with salt and pepper to taste.

Sprinkle the sardines on both sides with a little salt and a generous grinding of pepper. Spread a little stuffing on the inside of each fish, roll up from the head end and secure with a wooden toothpick. Place in a greased ovenproof dish with their tails sticking up.

Drizzle the rest of the oil over the sardines and sprinkle with the orange juice. Stick the bay leaves here and there, cover with foil and bake in the preheated oven for 20 minutes.

Polpo alla Luciana

Stewed Octopus

A classic Neapolitan dish, and one of the best ways to cook an octopus, Polpo alla Luciana is usually eaten only with bread.

SERVES 4
1 kg/2 lb 2 oz octopus
3 ripe fresh tomatoes, peeled and
    chopped, or 3 canned tomatoes,
    drained and chopped
7 tbsp olive oil
2 garlic cloves, chopped
½–I tsp crushed dried chillies
2 tbsp chopped fresh flat-leaf parsley
salt and freshly ground black pepper

PREPARE THE OCTOPUS by cleaning and beating it, or ask your fishmonger to do this. Wash it and place it in a deep pot, preferably flameproof earthenware.

Add all the other ingredients, tie a double sheet of foil around the pot and cover with a tight lid. Cook at the lowest possible simmer for 2 hours, without ever removing the lid.

Let the octopus cool for 30 minutes in the covered pot before you take it to the table. Serve it straight from the pot, cutting out a piece of this delectable monster for each person.

Sgombri con le Cipolle

Mackerel with Onion

In eastern Liguria, where this dish comes from, it is usually served at room temperature, never chilled. It should be eaten no sooner than the day after it has been made. This is so that the onion can become sweeter in the wine and vinegar marinade, and to allow the flavour of the sauce to penetrate the fish.

SERVES 4
400–500 g/14 oz–I lb onions,
    preferably Spanish (Bermuda) or
    white, very finely sliced
2 large mackerel, filleted
200 ml/7 fl oz/scant I cup dry
    white wine
100 ml/3½ fl oz/scant ½ cup wine
    vinegar, preferably white
8–10 juniper berries, crushed
salt and freshly ground black pepper
3 sprigs of fresh thyme
2 or 3 bay leaves

HEAT THE OVEN to 180°C/350°F/ Gas Mark 4. Spread out half the onion slices in an ovenproof dish large enough to contain the fish in a single layer. (I use a metal lasagne pan.) Lay the fish on top and then cover with the rest of the onion.

Put the wine, vinegar and juniper berries in a bowl and mix in salt and pepper to taste. Pour over the fish and onions and tuck the herbs here and there under the onion.

Bake in the preheated oven for about 15 minutes. Leave to cool, then chill the dish for at least 24 hours. Bring the dish back to room temperature before serving. This will take about 2 hours.

Trance di Tonno in Salsa Rinascimentale

Tuna Steaks in a Sweet-and-Sour Sauce

Nowadays tuna steaks are usually simply grilled (broiled), and very good they are too. For a change, try this recipe, which is my adaptation of a sixteenth-century recipe by Bartolomeo Scappi. The sweet-and-sour sauce tempers the oiliness of the fish.

SERVES 4
12 pitted prunes
100 ml/3½ fl oz/scant ½ cup dry
    white wine
4 tbsp olive oil
4 fresh tuna steaks, no more than
    2 cm/¾ in thick
I shallot, very finely sliced
I½ tbsp balsamic vinegar
½ tsp grated nutmeg
¾ tsp ground cloves
¼ tsp ground cinnamon
salt and freshly ground black pepper
½ tsp powdered saffron or I tsp
    saffron threads
100 ml/3½ fl oz/scant ½ cup meat
    stock

SOAK THE PRUNES in the wine for about an hour. Grease a shallow roasting pan with I tablespoon of the olive oil and lay the tuna steaks in it.

Put the remaining oil, the shallot, balsamic vinegar, nutmeg, cloves, cinnamon, salt and pepper into a pan and bring to the boil.

Lift the prunes out of the wine and add the wine to the saucepan. If you are using saffron threads, put them in a metal tablespoon and squash them with a smaller spoon. Heat the stock, dissolve the saffron in it, then add the saffron liquid or powder to the pan with all the other ingredients. Stir well and cook for about 15 minutes.

Meanwhile, heat the oven to 200°C/400°F/Gas Mark 6. Cut the prunes into strips and scatter over the fish.

Taste and adjust the seasoning of the sauce, then spoon it over the fish. Bake in the preheated oven for 15 minutes, until the fish is cooked through. Baste twice during cooking.

Polpettone di Tonno

Tuna Roll

An easy dish to make, and a good one to eat as long as you use best quality tuna canned in olive oil.

SERVES 3–4
200 g/7 oz best canned tuna in olive
    oil, drained
2 large (extra-large) free-range (farm-
    fresh) eggs
I hard-boiled, free-range (hard-cooked,
    farm-fresh) egg, coarsely chopped
2 tbsp chopped fresh flat-leaf parsley
50 g/2 oz/⅔ cup freshly grated
    Parmesan cheese
a pinch of grated nutmeg
salt and freshly ground black pepper
100 ml/3½ fl oz/scant ½ cup wine
    vinegar
100 ml/3½ fl oz/scant ½ cup dry
    white wine
4 or 5 parsley stalks
I small onion, sliced
salt

TO SERVE
4–5 tbsp extra virgin olive oil
I tsp lemon juice
capers, preferably in salt, rinsed
black olives
lemon slices

USING A FORK, flake the tuna in a bowl. Add the raw eggs, chopped hard-boiled egg, parsley, Parmesan, nutmeg and plenty of pepper. Mix thoroughly with your hands. Moisten a piece of muslin or cheesecloth, wring it out and lay it out flat. Place the tuna mixture on the cloth and roll it into an 8 cm/3 in diameter log shape. Wrap the cloth around it and tie both ends with string.

Place the roll in a shallow oval sauté pan or roasting pan into which it just fits. Add the vinegar, wine, parsley stalks, onion and a little salt, then pour in enough water to cover the roll by about 1 cm/½ in. Cover the pan with a lid and bring to the boil, then cook over a very low heat for 45 minutes.

Lift the tuna roll out of the liquid and transfer it to a board. Place a plate over it and put a weight on top of the plate. Leave to cool for at least 2 hours.

TO SERVE: When the roll is cold, unwrap it carefully and it cut into 1 cm/½ in slices. Arrange the slices on a dish so that they slightly overlap with each other. Beat together the oil, lemon juice and a pinch of salt until emulsified, then spoon this dressing over the slices. Scatter the capers and olives here and there and garnish with the lemon slices.

Baccalà alla Vicentina

Salt Cod Cooked in Milk

This recipe comes from Vicenza, where stockfish (stoccafisso) is used, not salt cod (baccalà). I always make the dish with salt cod, and it works well, because I can't buy stockfish in England.

SERVES 4
500 g/1 lb salt cod

200 g/7 oz onions, very finely sliced
150 ml/5 fl oz/⅔ cup olive oil
a small bunch of fresh flat-leaf parsley, chopped
2 garlic cloves, chopped
2 salted anchovies, boned, rinsed and chopped, or 4 canned or bottled anchovy fillets, drained and chopped
500 ml/18 fl oz/1¼ cups milk
2–3 tbsp flour
½ tsp ground cinnamon
salt and freshly ground black pepper
4 tbsp freshly grated Parmesan cheese

SOAK THE SALT COD in a large bowl of cold water for a minimum of 24 hours, changing the water 4 or 5 times a day. If you can, it is best to soak it for 48 hours.

Heat the oven to 150°C/300°F/Gas Mark 2.

Skin the salt cod and cut it into thick slices. Sauté the onion in the olive oil in a saucepan over a low heat until soft. Add the chopped parsley, garlic and anchovies and cook over a very low heat for no more than 1 minute, stirring constantly. Pour in the milk and bring to the boil. Stir well and boil for a couple of minutes, then take the pan off the heat.

Mix the flour with the cinnamon and a little salt and pepper and dip the fish pieces in it until they are covered. Place the fish in a flameproof earthenware pot in which the slices will fit tightly in a single layer. Add the cheese and cover with the milk mixture. Bring slowly to the boil, cover the pot and continue cooking in the oven until all the liquid has been absorbed. The liquid should only occasionally bubble during cooking, it should never boil. It should be ready in about 2–2½ hours, and is always traditionally eaten with polenta.

Scampi all'Abruzzese

Langoustines in a Hot Tomato Sauce

You can use uncooked Dublin Bay prawns or tiger prawns (jumbo shrimp) if you can't get langoustines. All crustaceans must be eaten very fresh, so I prefer to buy frozen, uncooked ones. Unfortunately they will have a softer texture and a less intense sea flavour, but at least they are safe to eat. I use Italian anchovy paste that comes in a tube; if you can't get it, use four anchovy fillets, chopped and mashed.

SERVES 4

24 raw langoustines
a large bunch of fresh flat-leaf parsley, stalks removed
3 garlic cloves
1 or 2 dried red chillies, depending on how strong they are and how hot you like your food
6 tbsp extra virgin olive oil
2 tsp anchovy paste (see introduction)
500 g/1 lb very ripe, fresh tomatoes, peeled, de-seeded and chopped
120 ml/4 fl oz/½ cup dry white wine
salt and freshly ground black pepper

NOTE: If you have any leftovers at the end of the meal, chop the langoustines and use them to dress a dish of pasta, adding a little more olive oil if necessary.

RINSE THE LANGOUSTINES well, remove the heads and shell them by cutting the carapace along each side where the upper shell meets the undershell. (The heads and the claws can be used to make a delicate stock for a fish risotto.)

Chop the parsley, garlic and chilli and sauté them gently in a frying pan (skillet) with the olive oil for about 1 minute. Mix in the anchovy paste and continue cooking gently for a further 30 seconds or so, stirring the whole time.

Now throw in the langoustines and let them take up the flavours of the oil for a minute before adding the tomatoes. Turn everything over in the pan once or twice and then add the wine. Cook at a higher heat for about 3 minutes. Season with salt and pepper to taste. Serve at once, preferably from the same pan.

Calamari Ripieni

Stuffed Squid

To serve the squid you can either cut each one in half and give two opened halves per person, or you can slice the squid into 2-cm/¾-in slices and spoon them and the tomato sauce onto a bed of boiled rice.

SERVES 4

4 squid, about 20 cm/8 in long
2 tbsp chopped fresh flat-leaf parsley
1 tbsp chopped fresh marjoram
1 small, mild dried chilli, crumbled
3 garlic cloves, chopped
7 tbsp extra virgin olive oil
2 salted anchovies, boned, rinsed and chopped, or 4 canned or bottled anchovy fillets, drained and chopped
50 g/2 oz/1 cup fresh breadcrumbs
salt and freshly ground black pepper
1 small onion, finely chopped
4 tbsp dry white wine
400 g/14 oz canned plum tomatoes, drained and chopped

HEAT THE OVEN to 200°C/400°F/ Gas Mark 6. Clean the squid, leaving the sacs whole. Wash them very well. Detach the wings and the tentacles and chop them.

Sauté the parsley, marjoram, chilli and garlic in a frying pan (skillet) with 3 tablespoons of the oil for 1 minute, then add the chopped wings and tentacles and cook for 5 minutes. Add the anchovies and after 30 seconds or so, stir in the breadcrumbs. Cook until they begin to get crisp and golden. Season to taste and then put the mixture into the squid sacs. The sacs should only be two-thirds full or they will burst during cooking. Pin each top closed by threading with a wooden toothpick.

Pour the remaining oil into a roasting pan and heat until hot. Add the onion and sauté until soft. Add the squid and cook for 5 minutes over gentle heat, turning them over slowly. Pour over the wine and tomatoes, season to taste and bring slowly to the boil. Boil for 5 minutes. Cover the pan with foil, place in the preheated oven and cook for 1 hour.

Seppie in Zimino

Cuttlefish with Swiss Chard

This is a traditional way of cooking cuttlefish in eastern Liguria and Versilia in Tuscany. If you can't find cuttlefish, use squid. If you can't get Swiss chard you can use spinach, but not the young sort that lacks flavour and is only suitable for eating raw in salads, nor beet spinach.

SERVES 4

700 g/1½ lb cuttlefish
5 tbsp olive oil
1 onion, finely chopped
2 garlic cloves, finely chopped
1 tbsp finely chopped celery leaves
1½ tbsp tomato paste
salt and freshly ground black pepper
500 g/1 lb Swiss chard

PREPARE AND wash the cuttlefish under cold running water. Cut the body into 1 cm/½ in strips and chop

the tentacles. Dry with kitchen paper (paper towels).

Put the olive oil, onion, garlic and celery leaves into a heavy pot, flame-proof earthenware if possible, and sauté gently for 10 minutes or so. Stir in the cuttlefish and continue cooking for 5 minutes, turning it over and over. Add the tomato paste and sauté for a further minute.

Add 4–5 tablespoons hot water and salt to taste. Mix well, cover the pan and cook until the cuttlefish are tender, about 45 minutes.

Meanwhile, remove the white stalks from the Swiss chard (you can keep them for another dish) and wash the leaves. Drain and dry the leaves as you would with salad leaves and throw them into the pot. Cover the pot and cook for 10 minutes. Season with plenty of pepper and salt to taste.

Serve straight from the pot.

POULTRY AND GAME

Pollo Tonnato
Chicken with Tuna Fish Sauce

This is a variation on the classic recipe for Vitello Tonnato. Here, in the original recipe from Lombardy there is no mayonnaise, although it has become a popular addition in many modern versions. The dish can be served hot or cold.

SERVES 4–6

200 ml/7 fl oz/scant I cup chicken stock

200 ml/7 fl oz/scant I cup dry white wine

I carrot

I celery stalk

I onion stuck with 2 cloves

I garlic clove

I bay leaf

12 black peppercorns, crushed

salt

I organic or free-range chicken, about 1.5 kg/3¼ lb

200 g/7 oz canned best tuna in olive oil, drained

2 salted anchovies, boned and rinsed, or 4 canned or bottled anchovy fillets, drained

4 tbsp crème fraîche, soured (sour) cream or double (heavy) cream

juice of ½ lemon, preferably organic or unwaxed, or more to taste

2–3 tbsp extra virgin olive oil

2 tbsp chopped fresh flat-leaf parsley, to serve

PUT THE STOCK, wine, carrot, celery, onion, garlic, bay leaf, peppercorns and salt in a flameproof casserole and bring to the boil. Lower the chicken, breast side up, into the casserole. Cover with the lid and cook at a very low simmer until the chicken is tender, which will take about I hour.

Leave the chicken to cool in the casserole and then lift it out and place it on a board. Strain the stock and reserve the vegetables. Remove and discard the bay leaf.

Put the tuna and anchovies and the vegetables from the stock in the bowl of a food processor. Whiz to a purée. Add the crème fraîche or cream, lemon juice and olive oil and whiz again. Add enough of the chicken stock for the sauce to be thick like single (light) cream. Taste and adjust seasoning and lemon juice.

Cut the chicken into pieces or carve it and remove the bones. Place it on a serving dish and coat with the tuna sauce. Sprinkle with the parsley before serving to garnish.

NOTE: Both hot and cold versions of this dish are good served on a bed of cold or hot boiled rice, dressed with some extra virgin olive oil. If you want to serve the dish hot, make the sauce as soon as the chicken is cooked

Pollo alla Cacciatora

Chicken with Vinegar

There are an endless number of recipes for Pollo alla Cacciatora, most of which contain tomatoes and mushrooms. This one, from Marche, is typical of central Italy. Without tomatoes or mushrooms, it is a fresh dish with a more modern slant, yet its flavour is equally full. If you prefer, you can just use chicken leg portions.

SERVES 4

I organic or free-range chicken, about
   1.25–1.5 kg/2½–3¼ lb, cut into
   6–8 portions
I lemon, preferably organic or unwaxed,
   cut in half
salt and freshly ground black pepper
4 tbsp good red wine vinegar
2 garlic cloves
I small dried red chilli
3 sprigs of fresh rosemary, about
   10 cm/4 in long
4 tbsp extra virgin olive oil

WASH AND THOROUGHLY DRY the chicken pieces and rub them with the lemon halves. Rub a little salt and pepper over each piece.

Put the vinegar, I garlic clove, the chilli, I rosemary sprig, ½ tsp salt and a little pepper in a dish. Add the pared rind of the lemon and lay the chicken in the dish, turning the pieces over to coat them. Leave to marinate for 2 hours or longer.

Heat the oil with the remaining garlic and rosemary in a large sauté pan and sauté for I minute. Remove and discard the garlic. Add the chicken pieces, laying them down in a single layer, and brown them very well on all sides. Turn the heat down and, after about 7 minutes, add a couple of tablespoons of the marinade and a couple of tablespoons of hot water. Continue cooking and pouring over small amounts of marinade and hot water until the thighs feel tender when pricked with a fork. If you finish the marinade, add only hot water. When cooked, remove the breast pieces and keep them warm while the legs finish cooking. The chicken will be cooked in about 20–25 minutes.

Transfer the chicken pieces to a heated dish and keep warm. Turn the heat up to high, add a couple of tablespoons of water and bring to the boil while loosening the cooking residues from the bottom of the pan. Pour the pan juices over the chicken and serve immediately.

Cook's tip

Lemons are described as having been waxed when they have been treated with an ethylene gas called diphenyl. This is used to keep their skins bright yellow and fresh looking. It is difficult to wash off completely, so organic or unwaxed lemons are preferable, especially for recipes using the rind.

Pollo Arrosto

Roast Chicken

When it comes to cooking a whole chicken, pot roasting is more common than oven roasting in Italy. Cuts of veal and pork are also roasted in the same way.

SERVES 4–6
50 g/2 oz/4 tbsp unsalted
   (sweet) butter
1 sprig of fresh rosemary
4–6 fresh sage leaves
1 garlic clove
salt and freshly ground black pepper
1 organic or free-range chicken, about
   1.5 kg/3¼ lb
1 lemon, preferably organic or unwaxed,
   cut in half
2 tbsp olive oil
150 ml/5 fl oz/⅔ cup dry white wine

PUT A KNOB (PAT) OF BUTTER, the herbs, garlic, 1 teaspoon salt and a generous grinding of pepper into the cavity of the bird, then rub it all over with one of the lemon halves and sprinkle with salt and pepper.

Heat half the remaining butter and the olive oil in an oval flameproof casserole and brown the chicken on all sides. Pour over the wine, boil briskly for 1 minute and then cook slowly, with the lid slightly askew so that the steam can escape. Turn the chicken over halfway through cooking and add a little boiling water if there is no liquid left at the bottom of the casserole. The chicken should be cooked in about 1¼–1½ hours. Test to see whether it is ready by pricking the thickest part of a thigh: the juice that runs out should be clear.

When cooked, transfer the chicken to a board and cover with foil. Squeeze the juice from the remaining lemon half into the casserole, add the remaining butter and 4–5 tablespoons hot water. Boil for 2–3 minutes, stirring constantly and scraping up the cooking residue from the bottom of the pan. Uncover the chicken, carve and serve with the cooking juices.

Petti di Pollo al Ragù di Porcini

Chicken Breasts in a Mushroom Sauce

This unpretentious dish is typically Italian. I translated this recipe from the book Cucina Creativa all'Italiana *by the great chef, Angelo Paracucchi.*

SERVES 4
5 tbsp olive oil
4 boneless chicken breasts (breast halves)
5 tbsp meat stock
salt and freshly ground black pepper
1 onion, finely chopped
150 g/5 oz/2 cups fresh porcini,
   cleaned and sliced
5 tbsp dry white wine
300 g/10 oz tomatoes, peeled, de-seeded
   and diced

HEAT 3 tablespoons of the oil in a sauté pan. Add the chicken breasts (breast halves) and fry them on both sides until brown. Reduce the heat, add the stock and salt and pepper, and cook for 7–8 minutes or until the chicken is cooked through.

Meanwhile, sauté the onion in the rest of the oil in a saucepan. Add the porcini and sauté them for 1 minute, then pour the wine over them and cook until it has evaporated. Add the tomatoes and continue to simmer until the sauce begins to thicken. Taste and adjust the seasoning.

Cut the chicken breasts in half lengthways and place them on a warmed serving dish. Spoon the porcini sauce over them and serve.

NOTE: When fresh porcini are not available, use 15 g/½ oz/¼ cup dried porcini and soak them in just enough warm water to cover for 10 minutes. Drain and strain the soaking liquid through muslin (cheesecloth), then add it to the sauce with 2 extra tomatoes.

Petti di Pollo al Prosciutto

Chicken Breasts with Prosciutto and Mozzarella

A dish of great ease and simplicity, relying solely — as so many Italian dishes do — on the quality of the ingredients.

SERVES 4
4 boned organic or free-range chicken
  breasts (breast halves)
salt and freshly ground black pepper
25 g/1 oz/2 tbsp unsalted
  (sweet) butter
2 tbsp olive oil
200 g/7 oz Italian mozzarella cheese
4 fresh sage leaves
100–115 g/3½–4 oz prosciutto di
  Parma, preferably thickly sliced
150 ml/5 fl oz/⅔ cup dry
  white wine

HEAT THE OVEN to 180°C/350°F/ Gas Mark 4. Cover the chicken breasts (breast halves) with clingfilm (plastic wrap) and lightly flatten them with a meat mallet (bat). Uncover, and then season all over with salt and pepper.

Heat the butter and the olive oil in a large frying pan (skillet). When the foam subsides, slide in the chicken breasts, skin side down, and sauté until brown. Turn the breasts over and sauté for a further 5–6 minutes. Transfer them to an ovenproof dish.

Slice the mozzarella and place a quarter of it over each chicken breast. Put 1 sage leaf on top of the mozzarella and cover with a slice of prosciutto, cut to the size of the breast. If your prosciutto is sliced thinly, cover with 2 slices.

Pour the wine into the frying pan and boil rapidly to reduce by half. Pour the reduced wine over the chicken. Cover the dish with foil and cook in the preheated oven for about 10 minutes or until the mozzarella begins to ooze out. Serve immediately.

Cook's tip

A meat mallet (bat) is also known as a tenderizer and may be made from wood or metal. One side of the head is usually notched and is used for breaking down the fibres of red meats, while the other side is smooth for pounding flat. It is the smooth side that you require for poultry and even then, you should only beat it lightly. If you do not have a meat mallet, use the side of a rolling pin.

Tacchino Ripieno alla Lombarda

Turkey Stuffed with Meat, Chestnuts and Fresh Fruits

It may be presumptuous of me to call this recipe "alla Lombarda" as there is no traditional recipe for a turkey à la lombarde. However, this is how it was made in my home in Milan, from a recipe by my paternal grandmother, who came from Voghera in south-west Lombardy. The original recipe did not use olive oil, but salted pork fat, which is more suitable — but difficult to find outside Italy.

SERVES 12

I bronze hen turkey, about 5–6 kg/
    10–13 lb, with giblets
200 g/7 oz unsmoked pancetta
2 tbsp olive oil
150 g/5 oz/1¼ sticks unsalted
    (sweet) butter
100 g/3½ oz luganega or other coarse-
    grained, mild continental sausage,
    skinned and crumbled
50 g/2 oz/½ cup minced
    (ground) veal
½ tsp grated nutmeg
¼ tsp ground cinnamon
salt and freshly ground black pepper
100 g/3½ oz/scant ½ cup pitted
    prunes, soaked
2 dessert apples, peeled, cored
    and diced
2 pears, peeled, cored and diced
300 g/10 oz chestnuts, peeled
50 g/2 oz/½ cup shelled walnuts
100 ml/3½ fl oz/scant ½ cup dry
    Marsala
I onion, sliced
I sprig of fresh rosemary
I sprig of fresh sage
150 ml/5 fl oz/⅔ cup dry white wine
I tbsp flour

FOR THE STOCK

I small carrot
I onion
I celery stalk
I bay leaf
4 or 5 parsley stalks
6 black peppercorns, crushed
I tsp salt
150 ml/5 fl oz/⅔ cup red wine

FIRST MAKE THE STOCK. Put the neck, gizzard and heart (reserve the liver) from the turkey giblets into a saucepan and add all the other ingredients for the stock. Add enough water so that the level comes 5 cm/2 in above the ingredients, bring to the boil and then simmer for about 2 hours. Strain.

Heat the oven to 180°C/350°F/Gas Mark 4.

Chop half the pancetta and put it in a small pan with the olive oil and 50 g/2 oz/4 tbsp of the butter. Add the luganega and veal and the chopped liver from the turkey. Sauté for 2–3 minutes and then add the spices and salt and pepper. Transfer to a bowl and add all the fruits, nuts and Marsala. Mix very thoroughly, then taste and adjust seasoning.

Rub the turkey with salt and pepper inside and out and push the stuffing into its cavity. Sew the opening closed with a needle and coarse cotton thread. Put the bird in a roasting pan and cover its breast with the remaining pancetta, sliced. Tie it in place with string. Set aside about 25 g/1 oz/2 tbsp of the butter and add the rest, cut into pieces, to the roasting pan together with the onion, rosemary and sage.

Put the pan in the preheated oven for 30 minutes and then add the wine and enough stock to come about 2–3 cm/¾–1¼ in up the sides of the pan. Cook, basting very often, until the bird is done, this will take a further 3–3½ hours. About 30 minutes before the end of cooking, remove the pancetta covering the breast, turn the heat up to 200°C/400°F/Gas Mark 6 and let the turkey breast become brown and shiny. Test to see if the bird is done by piercing the thickest part of a thigh: the juices should run clear.

Transfer the bird to a heated dish and make the sauce. Strain the cooking juices into a pan and add the remaining butter blended with the flour, bit by bit, stirring vigorously and swirling the pan. If you want a bit more gravy, add some stock. Bring to a simmer and boil gently to cook the flour. Transfer to a heated sauceboat and serve.

NOTE: If you are worried about stuffing the cavity of the bird, halve the quantities of the stuffing ingredients and stuff only the neck. Sprinkle some herbs and salt and pepper in the cavity.

Fagiano alla Milanese

Milanese Pheasant

Pheasant is popular in Lombardy, as it is in Tuscany, where all game is a favourite due to the passion for hunting in the region. In Tuscany the pheasant is usually oven-roasted in oil and pancetta* and flavoured with sage and/or rosemary. In Lombardy, recipes such as this one are more elaborate, influenced by French cuisine.

SERVES 2–3
1 hen pheasant, trussed
salt and freshly ground black pepper
50 g/2 oz/4 tbsp unsalted (sweet) butter
25 g/1 oz unsmoked pancetta, cut into cubes or strips
100 g/3½ oz lean pork, coarsely minced (ground)

1 shallot, stuck with 2 cloves
¼ tsp ground cinnamon
½ tsp grated nutmeg
150 ml/5 fl oz/⅔ cup meat stock
150 ml/5 fl oz/⅔ cup dry white wine
100 ml/3½ fl oz/scant ½ cup double (heavy) cream

SEASON THE PHEASANT inside and out with salt and pepper. Heat the butter and the pancetta in a heavy, oval flameproof casserole. Add the pheasant and fry on all sides for about 10 minutes. Add the liver from the pheasant, the pork, shallot, spices and salt and pepper. Pour over the stock and wine and bring to the boil. Cover the pan and cook at a low simmer for about 1 hour or until the bird is tender.

Remove the pheasant from the pan and keep warm.

Purée the sauce and transfer it to a clean pan. Bring to the boil and, if it is too thin, reduce rapidly over high heat. Turn the heat down, stir in the cream and cook for a further 5 minutes, stirring constantly.

Cut the pheasant into neat portions and lay it on a heated serving dish. Coat with a little of the sauce and serve the rest separately in a bowl.

Anatra all'Apicio

A Duck Recipe from Apicius

The Romans loved duck, judging by the number of recipes in Apicius' *book* De Re Coquinaria. *As with the cooking of most meats in Roman times, the duck is plunged into boiling water before it is roasted. This rids the bird of some of its fat.*

SERVES 3

1 sprig of fresh dill
1 bay leaf
salt
1 duck, preferably a Barbary or
   Gressingham, with giblets
150 ml/5 fl oz/⅔ cup strong
   red wine
1 sprig of fresh rue (optional)
5 garlic cloves, unpeeled and bruised
1 onion stuck with 2 cloves
1 celery stalk
1 carrot
3 or 4 parsley stalks
1 tbsp olive oil

FOR THE SAUCE
a bunch of fresh coriander (cilantro)
1 sprig of fresh lovage or celery leaves
1 tsp cumin seeds
6 black peppercorns
1 tbsp dried oregano
1 tbsp golden unrefined sugar
sea salt
1 tbsp wine vinegar
15 g/½ oz/1 tbsp unsalted
   (sweet) butter
1 tbsp flour

BRING A SAUCEPAN OF WATER to the boil. Add the dill, bay leaf, a little salt and the duck and bring slowly back to the boil. Simmer for 15 minutes and then lift the duck out of the stock. Reserve the stock.

Remove the legs and the breast from the carcass and remove and discard the skin. Cut the breast into diagonal slices. Marinate these parts in the wine with the optional rue, the garlic and salt for 2–3 hours at room temperature.

Put the carcass, with the neck and gizzard, into the stock in which the duck has cooked. Add the onion, celery, carrot and parsley stalks and simmer for about 1 hour. With a metal spoon, remove as much as you can of the fat which has risen to the surface.

Meanwhile, prepare the sauce. In a mortar, pound together the coriander (cilantro), lovage, cumin seeds, peppercorns, oregano, sugar, sea salt and the chopped duck liver, moistening with the vinegar. (You can use a food processor, of course.) Melt the butter in a saucepan and blend in the flour, stirring vigorously, then remove the pan from the heat. Gradually add 300 ml/ 10 fl oz/1¼ cups of the strained duck stock, stirring until it has been completely absorbed. Stir in the pounded ingredients and cook very gently for 10 minutes, stirring very often. Taste and adjust seasoning. Remove from the heat and keep warm.

Lift the duck legs and breast slices out of the marinade and dry thoroughly. Strain the marinade. Heat the olive oil in a non-stick frying pan (skillet) and, when it is really hot, fry the duck legs for about 8 minutes. Add the breast slices and fry for 2 minutes. Remove from the pan and keep warm. Pour the marinade into the frying pan and reduce over high heat until there is only about 3 tablespoons left. Pour this over the duck and then serve, with the sauce.

Quaglie all'Aceto Balsamico

Roast Quail with Balsamic Vinegar

Balsamic vinegar is used here to flavour quail, a common practice in the provinces of Modena and Reggio-Emilia, where it is also popular as a flavouring for roast guinea fowl and roast rabbit.

SERVES 2–4 DEPENDING ON SIZE

4 quail
salt and freshly ground black pepper
2 tbsp olive oil
100 ml/3½ fl oz/scant ½ cup strong homemade meat stock or stock made with a good-quality meat bouillon cube
3 tbsp balsamic vinegar
25 g/1 oz/2 tbsp unsalted (sweet) butter

HEAT THE OVEN to 200°C/400°F/ Gas Mark 6. Clean and wipe the quail thoroughly and rub them inside and out with salt and pepper.

Heat the olive oil in a heavy-based ovenproof pan and fry the quail over medium-high heat, turning them over on all sides. This will take no longer than 5 minutes. Add half the stock and place the pan in the preheated oven. Roast for 10–15 minutes, basting twice. Halfway through cooking, drizzle 1 tablespoon of the balsamic vinegar over the birds. When they are cooked, transfer them to a heated dish and keep warm.

Deglaze the pan with the remaining vinegar, then add the remaining stock. Bring slowly to the boil and boil for 1–2 minutes.

Cut up the butter and add it little by little to the sauce, stirring vigorously and constantly. Taste and adjust the seasoning. As soon as the butter has melted, spoon a litttle over the quail and serve the rest in a heated serving bowl or jug (pitcher).

Faraona al Mascarpone

Guinea Fowl with Mascarpone Stuffing

A recipe from southern Lombardy, the birthplace of mascarpone. This dish is best served with mashed potatoes.

SERVES 3

1 guinea fowl, about 1.6 kg/3½ lb
100 g/3½ oz/scant ½ cup mascarpone
salt and freshly ground black pepper
2 tbsp vegetable or olive oil
100 g/3½ oz/7 tbsp unsalted (sweet) butter
1 small celery stalk, chopped
1 small carrot, chopped
2 shallots, chopped
150 ml/5 fl oz/⅔ cup dry white wine
5–6 tbsp milk

CLEAN AND WIPE the guinea fowl and put the mascarpone inside it together with some salt and pepper.

Put the oil, butter, celery, carrot and shallots in a flameproof pot into which the guinea fowl will fit snugly. Place the bird on the vegetables, add the chopped giblets (if you have them) and put the pot on the heat. Pour over the wine and season with salt and pepper. Cover the pot and simmer gently for 1¼–1½ hours or until the bird is cooked. Keep an eye on the pot and add a couple of tablespoons of hot milk if it starts to run dry.

Remove the bird from the heat and keep hot. Purée the cooking liquid, then reheat and serve in a sauceboat.

Coniglio ai Peperoni
Rabbit with (Bell) Peppers

This is my version of a recipe published in La Cucina d'Oro, *a book of 1482 recipes edited by Count Giovanni Nuvoletti in cooperation with the Accademia Italiana della Cucina. The recipe suggests the use of suet, which indicates its ancient origin. Nowadays, oil is more commonly used. If you want to use a wild, rather than a domestic, rabbit, cook it for 10 minutes longer at the beginning.*

SERVES 4

1 rabbit, about 1 kg/2 lb 2 oz, cut
   into pieces
50 g/2 oz/¼ cup suet, or
   3 tbsp olive oil
50 g/2 oz/4 tbsp unsalted
   (sweet) butter
1 tbsp rosemary needles
1 bay leaf
100 ml/3½ fl oz/scant ½ cup meat
   stock
3 yellow (bell) peppers
2 tbsp extra virgin olive oil
3 salted anchovies, boned, rinsed and
   chopped, or 6 canned or bottled
   anchovy fillets, drained and chopped
2 garlic cloves, chopped
salt and freshly ground black pepper
1 tbsp wine vinegar

WASH AND DRY the rabbit pieces. Chop the suet and heat it (or the oil) in a flameproof casserole with half the butter and the rosemary. Add the rabbit and the bay leaf and brown on all sides. Pour over half the stock and let the rabbit cook, uncovered, over low heat for about 20 minutes, adding a little more stock when necessary.

Meanwhile, wash and dry the (bell) peppers. Discard the seeds and ribs and cut the peppers into thin strips.

In another pan, heat the remaining butter with the extra virgin olive oil and the anchovies. Cook slowly until the anchovies become a mush and then add the garlic and the peppers. Season with salt and plenty of pepper. Cook for 5 minutes and then mix in the vinegar. Continue cooking for a further 10 minutes, stirring frequently.

Add the pepper mixture and finish cooking the whole thing together, about a further 20 minutes, turning the pieces of rabbit over two or three times.

Cook's tip

Ask your butcher to prepare the rabbit for you if you are unsure how to do it yourself. Make sure you avoid using imported frozen rabbit which lacks the flavour of fresh and has a drier texture.

Lepre in Salmì

Jugged Hare

In my Milanese home, a little grated chocolate was always added to this quintessentially Lombard dish, which should also contain the liver, heart, lungs and blood of the hare. If you cannot get these, pig's liver can be used instead.

SERVES 6

I hare (jack rabbit), about
    2–2.5 kg/4½–5½ lb, cut into
    smallish pieces
75 g/2½ oz/5 tbsp unsalted
    (sweet) butter
50 g/2 oz unsmoked pancetta, cubed
I onion, very finely chopped
I tbsp flour
the liver, heart, lungs and blood of the
    hare (jack rabbit), chopped, or
    200 g/7 oz pig's liver, chopped
25 g/I oz bitter plain (bittersweet)
    chocolate, grated
salt and freshly ground black pepper
200 ml/7 fl oz/scant I cup double
    (heavy) cream

FOR THE MARINADE

I bottle of Barbera or other strong red
    Piedmontese wine
2 sprigs of fresh thyme
2 sprigs of fresh rosemary
I large onion, cut into pieces
2 garlic cloves, cut into pieces
I celery stalk, cut into pieces
4 bay leaves
6 fresh sage leaves
2 cloves
a pinch of grated nutmeg
I cinnamon stick
5 juniper berries, bruised
I tsp coarse sea salt
6 black peppercorns, crushed

WASH THE PIECES of hare (jack rabbit) thoroughly and dry them. Put the pieces in a large bowl and add the wine and all the other marinade ingredients. Leave in a cold place, but not in the refrigerator, covered, for about 24 hours.

Remove the hare from the marinade; reserve the marinade. Dry the hare pieces thoroughly. Heat the butter and pancetta in a heavy pan. Add the onion and sauté until golden. Add the hare and brown very well on all sides, then sprinkle the flour over it and cook for about 5 minutes, turning the pieces over and over (fry in batches if your pan is not big enough). Cover with the marinade and add the chopped offal (variety meats) and the blood or the chopped pig's liver, the grated chocolate and salt and pepper to taste.

Cover the pot and cook slowly, either over a very low heat or in a preheated oven at 170°C/325°F/Gas Mark 3, until the meat is tender. This could take 2 hours for a young animal, but as long as 4 hours for an older one. Transfer the hare to a heated serving dish add keep warm.

Remove the cinnamon and woody bits of herbs from the sauce and purée the sauce through a food mill or in a food processor. Return it to the pan and mix in the cream, then return the hare to the pan and cook gently for 5 minutes for a final blending of the flavours.

Serve with soft polenta, perfect for the rich, gamy juices.

Spezzatino di Cinghiale

Wild Boar Stew

In Chianti they eat a lot of wild boar, which they shoot during the season and freeze part of it for the rest of the year. This recipe is ideally suited for the cheaper cuts of the animal — the long, slow cooking makes it tender and succulent. Serve with polenta*.

SERVES 6

1.3–1.5 kg/3–3¼ lb wild boar, cut into
  pieces
6 sprigs each of fresh rosemary and sage
12 garlic cloves
salt and freshly ground black pepper
½–1 tsp crushed dried chillies
1 tbsp fennel seeds
150 ml/5 fl oz/⅔ cup olive oil
500 ml/18 fl oz/1¼ cups red wine,
  preferably Chianti
a generous grating of nutmeg
2 tbsp tomato paste
400 g/14 oz canned chopped tomatoes,
  with their juice

WASH THE MEAT and put it in a single layer in a large, shallow pan. Add 2 or 3 of the sprigs of rosemary and sage, half the garlic cloves and salt and pepper. Cover the pan tightly and simmer very gently for 30–40 minutes without any added liquid. Drain the meat and pat it dry; remove and throw away the herbs and garlic.

Chop the remaining herbs and garlic and mix in the chillies and fennel seeds.

Heat the oven to 150°C/300°F/ Gas Mark 2.

Cover the bottom of a large frying pan (skillet) with about half the oil. Turn the heat up to high and, when the oil is very hot, add the meat and fry until it is a good deep brown. Splash with about 150 ml/5 fl oz/⅔ cup of the red wine and let it bubble away completely.

Remove the meat to a flameproof casserole or, better still, an earthenware pot. Season with salt and pepper and the nutmeg.

Wipe the frying pan clean and pour the rest of the oil into it. When hot, add the chopped mixture and sauté for 3 minutes or so, then stir in the tomato paste. Cook for a further 3 minutes, add the chopped tomatoes and their juice and bring to the boil. Simmer for 5 minutes, then pour in the remaining wine. Bring back to the boil, simmer again for about 5 minutes and then pour this sauce over the meat. Cover the dish tightly — use a piece of foil if you haven't got a tight-fitting lid – and cook in the preheated oven for 3 hours, stirring occasionally. The meat is ready when very tender.

Taste and adjust the seasoning before serving.

Cook's tip

Although wild boar can still be found in some parts of the European mainland, notably Italy, it is not, strictly speaking, game — a creature to hunt — in the UK or US, although it has been reintroduced to parts of Britain. It is not the same as American feral hogs. However, it is increasingly popular as a farmed animal.

Capriolo alla Alto Atesina

Stewed Venison

In the Tyrol the meat used is roebuck, which is often from farmed animals – their meat has less flavour, but needs to be hung for a shorter period. In England I have made the dish with venison, which is usually the meat of red deer.

SERVES 6

1.5 kg/3¼ lb boneless venison
4 tbsp olive oil
2 tbsp flour
50 g/2 oz smoked pancetta, diced
50 g/2 oz/⅓ cup salted pork fat, diced, or 4 tbsp olive oil
1 or 2 Spanish onions, about 225 g/ 8 oz/2 cups, very thinly sliced
salt and freshly ground black pepper
¼ tsp ground cinnamon
¼ tsp ground cloves
300 ml/10 fl oz/1¼ cups soured (sour) cream

FOR THE MARINADE

1 carrot, cut into pieces
1½ onions, coarsely sliced
1 celery stalk, cut into pieces
1 tbsp rock salt (coarse sea salt)
12 juniper berries, bruised
8 black peppercorns, crushed
3 cloves
1 sprig of fresh rosemary
2 or 3 sprigs of fresh thyme
1 sprig of fresh sage
3 tbsp olive oil
3 bay leaves
3 garlic cloves
1 bottle of good full-bodied red wine

HEAT ALL THE INGREDIENTS for the marinade until just boiling. Allow to cool.

Cut the venison into pieces about 5 cm/2 in thick. Put them in a bowl and add the marinade. Cover the bowl and leave for 2 days, preferably in a cool place other than the refrigerator.

Lift the meat from the marinade and pat dry with kitchen paper (paper towels). Strain the marinade, saving only the liquid.

Heat the oven to 170°C/325°F/ Gas Mark 3.

Heat 2 tablespoons of the olive oil in a large cast-iron frying pan (skillet). Add the meat and brown very thoroughly on all sides. Fry in 2 batches so that it browns properly. Transfer to a plate.

Add the flour to the frying pan and cook until brown, stirring and scraping the bottom of the pan with a metal spoon. Add about half the marinade liquid and bring to the boil, stirring constantly and breaking down any lumps of flour with the back of the spoon.

Put the rest of the oil, the pancetta and pork fat in a flameproof casserole and cook for 5 minutes. Add the onion slices and a pinch of salt and continue cooking until the onion is really soft. Add a couple of tablespoons of hot water to prevent the onion from burning.

Now add the meat with all the juice that has leaked out, the thickened marinade from the frying pan and about 150 ml/5 fl oz/⅔ cup of the remaining marinade to the casserole. Season with salt, pepper and the spices and bring slowly to the boil. Cover the casserole and place in the preheated oven. Cook for about 1 hour, adding a little marinade twice during cooking.

Heat the soured (sour) cream in a small pan and add to the casserole. Return the casserole to the oven and cook for 30 minutes or until the meat is very tender. The cooking time depends on the quality and age of the animal.

MEAT DISHES

Coda alla Vaccinara
Braised Oxtail

The freshness of the celery counteracts the rich heaviness of the oxtail. Some recipes omit the preliminary blanching of the oxtail. Coda alla Vaccinara is best made one or two days in advance to allow the flavours to develop.

SERVES 4
1.25 kg/2½ lb oxtail
225 g/8 oz pork rind
50 g/2 oz pancetta or unsmoked streaky (fatty) bacon, cut in one thick slice, chopped
3 tbsp olive oil
25 g/1 oz/2 tbsp pork fat or lard
1 tbsp chopped fresh flat-leaf parsley
1 or 2 garlic cloves, chopped
1 onion, finely chopped
1 carrot, finely chopped
200 ml/7 fl oz/scant 1 cup dry white wine
2 tbsp tomato paste diluted with 225 ml/8 fl oz/1 cup meat stock
salt and freshly ground black pepper
225 g/8 oz/2 cups thickly sliced celery

HEAT THE OVEN to 170°C/325°F/ Gas Mark 3. Blanch the oxtail and pork rind for 5 minutes in boiling water. Drain and refresh under cold water. Cut the rind into strips.

Put the pancetta, olive oil, pork fat, parsley, garlic, onion and carrot into a heavy flameproof casserole and sauté until soft. Add the oxtail and pork rind and fry gently for a further few minutes. Splash with the wine and boil rapidly to reduce, turning the meat over a few times. Add the diluted tomato paste and salt to taste. Cover the pan and place the casserole in the preheated oven. Cook for about 2 hours until the meat is tender, turning it over 2 or 3 times. Remove the casserole from the oven and leave to cool completely, then put it in the refrigerator until required.

On the day you are serving the dish, remove and discard the solidified fat from the surface. Put the casserole on top of the stove and bring to the boil, then add the celery and cook, covered, for a further 20 minutes. Add a generous grinding of pepper, taste and check salt before serving. Alternatively, you can reheat the dish in the oven. Bring it to the boil on top of the stove, add the celery and cover the pan, then place in the oven preheated to 200°C/400°F/Gas Mark 6. It will take 30 minutes to reheat.

Bistecca alla Fiorentina
Grilled Steak

The steak used in Florence for this famous dish comes from the Chiana cattle, a breed that produces very tasty meat in ample quantities, even from an animal no more than 2 years old. Buy the best meat, and you will eat something similar to the original steak from Florence. La Fiorentina is always cooked on a charcoal or wood fire.

SERVES 2 OR 3
1 T-bone steak at least 2.5 cm/1 in thick, about 600 g/1¼ lb
salt and freshly ground black pepper
olive oil or lemon juice

SEASON THE STEAK with freshly ground black pepper on both sides, rubbing it into the meat with your fingers. Grill the steak over a charcoal or wood fire. When one side is done (the steak must be served rare), turn the steak over and sprinkle the cooked side lightly with salt, then grill the other side and sprinkle lightly with salt. Each side takes about 3–4 minutes to cook.

Some cooks drizzle a little extra virgin olive oil over the meat just before serving, while others prefer lemon juice.

Brasato alla Lombarda

Beef Braised with Vegetables and Spices

Less known than the brasati from Piedmont, this brasato† is spiced with what used to be called the four Lombard spices: cloves, cinnamon, pepper and nutmeg.

SERVES 6

2 tbsp vegetable oil

1 kg/2 lb 2 oz boneless beef in one piece, such as topside or chuck steak (rump or chuck roast), neatly tied

1 large onion, quartered

2 carrots, cut into big chunks

2 celery stalks, cut into pieces

2 cloves

a generous grating of nutmeg

2 bay leaves

½ tsp ground cinnamon

50 g/2 oz/4 tbsp unsalted (sweet) butter

1 tbsp olive oil

200 ml/7 fl oz/scant 1 cup red wine

7 tbsp strong meat stock, or ¼ bouillon cube dissolved in 7 tbsp water

salt and freshly ground black pepper

HEAT THE OVEN to 150°C/300°F/ Gas Mark 2. Heat the vegetable oil in a frying pan (skillet). When it is hot, brown the meat very well on all sides to sear. Place the meat on a plate.

In a flameproof casserole with a tight-fitting lid, put the onion, carrots, celery, cloves, nutmeg, bay leaves, cinnamon, butter and olive oil. Place the seared meat on top of the vegetables and spices.

Put the frying pan back on the heat, pour in the wine and boil briskly for 20 seconds, scraping the bottom of the pan with a metal spoon. Pour the contents of the pan over the meat and vegetables and add the stock and salt and pepper. Cover the casserole with foil and place the lid on tightly.

Cook in the preheated oven for about 3 hours, turning the meat over every 30 minutes. The meat is cooked when it can be pricked easily with a fork. Transfer it to a board and leave it to cool a little.

Skim the fat from the cooking liquid and discard the bay leaves. Purée the sauce using a food processor or food mill, then taste and adjust the seasoning and keep warm.

Carve the meat into 1 cm/½ in slices and arrange them on a heated dish. Cover with some of the sauce and serve the rest separately.

Carbonade

Beef Casserole

A traditional recipe from Val d'Aosta, the region just to the east of the Alps from France, where the food has strong French and Swiss influences. Originally the dish used to be made — in the long winter months — with preserved meat. Carbonade is always served with polenta*.

SERVES 4

800 g/1¾ lb beef in a single piece, from the shoulder (chuck steak or chuck roast) if possible
50 g/2 oz/4 tbsp unsalted (sweet) butter
1 tbsp vegetable or olive oil
700 g/1½ lb onions, finely sliced
salt
1 tbsp flour
500 ml/18 fl oz/2¼ cups strong red wine
freshly ground black pepper
½ tsp grated nutmeg

CUT THE MEAT into thin slices. Heat the butter and the oil in a heavy flameproof casserole, add the meat and fry on all sides. Add the meat in batches so that it will fry in a single layer, putting it on a side plate after frying each batch.

Add the onions to the casserole and season with a little salt, which will help them soften without browning. When the onions are soft, return the meat to the pan and add the flour. Fry for a minute or so, stirring constantly, then pour in about a ladleful of the wine. Bring to the boil, then cover and cook for a couple of hours over a very low heat, adding half a ladleful of wine whenever the meat becomes too dry.

When the meat is tender, add pepper and the nutmeg and continue cooking for a further 10 minutes or so.

Spezzatino di Manzo alla Bolzanese

Beef Stew with Paprika and Sage

I love this recipe from Alto Adige. It shows how to make a basic spezzatino that you can vary by changing the herbs, eliminating the paprika, or introducing other spices or vegetables. The recipe also works well with stewing veal or pork.

SERVES 4–6

2 Spanish (Bermuda) onions, sliced
25 g/1 oz/2 tbsp unsalted (sweet) butter
2 tbsp olive oil
about 20 fresh sage leaves
900 g/2 lb stewing steak, cut into cubes
1 tsp paprika
250 ml/9 fl oz/generous 1 cup red wine
1½ tbsp flour
400 g/14 oz tomato passata (strained, puréed tomatoes)
salt and freshly ground black pepper

SAUTÉ THE ONIONS in a large saucepan in the butter and oil until soft, about 7–10 minutes. Add the sage and sauté for 1 minute, then add the meat and brown well on all sides. Mix in the paprika and add the red wine. Turn up the heat and boil briskly to reduce, stirring constantly. Sprinkle with the flour and cook for 1 minute. Add the tomato passata (strained puréed tomatoes) and season with salt and pepper to taste.

Bring the sauce to the boil, cover and cook very gently for about 2 hours, until the meat is tender. Turn the meat over occasionally and check that it isn't sticking to the bottom of the pan, add a little hot water if necessary.

Stufato alla Napoletana

Beef Braised in Tomato Sauce

In Naples most of the sauce is used to dress a dish of maccheroni* – served before (not with) the stufato. The secret of a good stufato is that it must cook at a very gentle simmer for at least 4 hours.

SERVES 6–8

1.25–1.5 kg/2½–3¼ lb chuck steak or eye of silverside (chuck roast or rump), in one piece

1 garlic clove, chopped

1 tsp dried oregano

salt and freshly ground black pepper

50 g/2 oz unsmoked pancetta, cut into strips or cubes

2 tbsp olive oil

2 tbsp tomato paste

400 g/14 oz canned chopped tomatoes, with their juice

FOR THE MARINADE

300 ml/10 fl oz/1¼ cups light red wine

2 tbsp olive oil

1 small onion, thickly sliced

1 celery stalk. cut into pieces

4 or 5 garlic cloves, unpeeled and crushed

1 bay leaf

2 or 3 parsley stalks

a handful of fresh basil leaves

2 cloves

¾ tsp grated nutmeg

¼ tsp ground cinnamon

5 black peppercorns, crushed

1 tbsp coarse sea salt

PLACE THE MEAT IN A BOWL. Mix all the ingredients for the marinade and spoon over the meat. Leave in a cool place (not the refrigerator unless the weather is hot) for 12 hours, turning the meat over whenever you remember.

Heat the oven to 170°C/325°F/ Gas Mark 3. Lift the meat out of the marinade and dry thoroughly.

Mix together the garlic, oregano, salt and pepper and coat the pancetta in the mixture.

If you have a larding needle, use it to lard the meat with strips of dressed pancetta; if not, make incisions in the meat following the direction of the grain and push in cubes or strips of pancetta with a chopstick or the handle of a small wooden spoon. Push well down. Whichever method you use, work from one end of the meat to the middle, then repeat from the other end.

Heat the olive oil in a large frying pan (skillet) and sear the meat until brown on all sides. Transfer to a heavy flameproof pot just large enough to hold the meat snugly. Strain the marinade and pour over the meat.

Add the tomato paste to the frying pan, stir and sauté for no more than 30 seconds. Add the tomatoes and their juice and season with salt and pepper, bring to the boil and then pour over the meat. Bring to the boil again, cover the pot with a piece of foil and a lid and place in the preheated oven. Cook for about 4–4½ hours until the meat is so tender that it can be cut with a spoon. Turn the meat over every 30–45 minutes.

When the meat is ready, transfer it to a wooden board and leave it to rest for 10 minutes or so, then carve into slices at least 5 mm/¼ in thick (an electric knife is ideal for this). Lay the slices on a heated dish, spoon over the juices and serve at once.

Polpette alla Casalinga

Homemade Meatballs

To get good-quality lean minced (ground) beef, I buy chuck steak (chuck roast) from the butcher and have it minced after the fat has been removed.

SERVES 5–6

50 g/2 oz crustless white bread
   (about 2 slices of best country bread)
milk
500 g/1 lb very lean minced
   (ground) beef
1 garlic clove
a small bunch of fresh flat-leaf parsley
50 g/2 oz mortadella, chopped
4 tbsp freshly grated Parmesan cheese
a pinch of grated nutmeg
salt and freshly ground black pepper
3 free-range (farm-fresh) eggs
2 tbsp flour
50 g/2 oz/¾ cup dried breadcrumbs
25 g/1 oz/2 tbsp unsalted
   (sweet) butter
2 tbsp olive oil

TO FINISH
150 ml/5 fl oz/⅔ cup meat stock or
   600 ml/1 pint/2½ cup Tomato
   Sauce I (see page 176)

SOAK THE BREAD in enough milk to cover it. After about 5 minutes, squeeze it dry and place in a large bowl with the beef. Chop the garlic and parsley and add to the beef along with the mortadella, Parmesan, nutmeg and salt and pepper to taste.

Lightly beat the eggs with a pinch of salt and mix half into the meat mixture. Mix very thoroughly with your hands, then shape the mixture into squashed balls the size of mandarins. Lightly coat with flour and then with the remaining egg.

Dredge each polpetta in breadcrumbs, patting the crumbs into the meat with the palm of your hand. Put in the refrigerator for at least 1 hour. If you have time, you can leave them for much longer to chill.

Fry the polpette gently on each side in butter and oil. When they are brown all over, add the meat stock or tomato sauce and cook, covered, for about 10 minutes.

NOTE: Instead of the meat stock or tomato sauce, I sometimes finish these polpette with a lemon sauce. For this, I mix 2 free-range (farm-fresh) egg yolks with the juice of 1 lemon (preferably organic) and 250 ml/9 fl oz/1 cup plus 2 tbsp hot meat stock. I add this just before I turn the heat off.

Polpettone Freddo
Cold Meat Loaf

This is my favourite way of making a polpettone*: cooking it in the oven avoids the nuisance of having to turn it over in the frying pan (skillet). It can be eaten hot, but I prefer it cold, lightly moistened with extra virgin olive oil and served with Salsa Verde (see page 180) on the side.

SERVES 6

50 g/2 oz crustless white bread
  (about 2 slices best country bread)
4 tbsp milk
500 g/1 lb/4 cups lean minced
  (ground) beef
50 g/2 oz Italian salami,
  minced (ground)
1 free-range (farm-fresh) egg
2 tbsp freshly grated Parmesan cheese
3 tbsp chopped mixed fresh herbs, such
  as parsley, rosemary, sage and basil
1 tbsp very finely chopped onion
1 garlic clove, very finely chopped
grated rind of 1 lemon, preferably
  organic or unwaxed
salt and freshly ground black pepper
2 tbsp extra virgin olive oil

HEAT THE OVEN to 200°C/400°F/ Gas Mark 6. Put the bread in a bowl, cover with the milk and leave to soak for 10–15 minutes.

Meanwhile, put the minced (ground) beef, salami, egg, Parmesan, herbs, onion, garlic and lemon rind in a large bowl and mix thoroughly.

Squeeze the bread and add to the meat mixture. Add salt and pepper and mix again. Grease a 500 g/1 lb loaf tin (8½ x 4½ in bread pan) with oil and fill it with the mixture. Press down well and bang the tin on the work surface (countertop) once or twice to release any air bubbles. Brush the top with a little olive oil.

Place the tin in the oven and cook for about 35 minutes. The polpettone is cooked when it has shrunk from the sides of the pan.

Remove the pan from the oven and pour away the fat from around the meat. Allow the polpettone to cool in the tin and then transfer to a carving board. Carve when completely cold and lay the slices, slightly overlapping, on a dish. Brush lightly with oil to serve.

Nodini
Veal Noisettes

Nodini is a classic dish from Milan, where veal is the most popular meat. You can use noisettes of spring lamb instead of veal if you prefer, as they might be more readily available.

SERVES 4

4 noisettes of veal, at least 3 cm/
  1¼ in thick
1 sprig of fresh sage
50 g/2 oz/4 tbsp unsalted
  (sweet) butter
3 tbsp flour
5 tbsp dry white wine
salt

TIE THE NOISETTES into a round shape with thread, or secure them with wooden toothpicks.

Sauté the sage in the butter in a large pan and add the noisettes, lightly coated with flour. Turn the heat up and fry gently on both sides, being careful not to prick the noisettes when you turn them.

Add the wine and sprinkle with salt. Cover and cook over a low heat for about 20 minutes, until the wine has evaporated and the meat is glazed.

Ossobuco alla Milanese

Milanese Ossobuco

The Milanese recipe for ossobuco* does not contain tomatoes. Here it is, in the original version. Buy ossobuchi all the same size, so they take the same amount of time to cook.

SERVES 4

4 ossobuchi, about 250 g/9 oz each
flour for dusting
salt and freshly ground black pepper
2 tbsp olive oil
40 g/1½ oz/3 tbsp unsalted (sweet) butter
I small onion, finely chopped
½ celery stalk, finely chopped
150 ml/5 fl oz/⅔ cup dry white wine
300 ml/10 fl oz/1¼ cups meat stock

FOR THE GREMOLADA
I tsp grated rind from an organic or unwaxed lemon
½ garlic clove, very finely chopped
2 tbsp chopped fresh flat-leaf parsley

TIE THE OSSOBUCHI around and across with string as you would a parcel and then lightly coat them in flour mixed with I teaspoon of salt.

Heat the olive oil in a heavy sauté pan which has a tight-fitting lid and is large enough to hold the ossobuchi in a single layer. Add the ossobuchi and brown them on both sides in the hot oil. Remove them to a side dish.

Add 25 g/I oz/2 tbsp of the butter to the sauté pan together with the onion and celery. Sprinkle with a little salt, which will help the onion release its liquid and soften without browning. After about 10 minutes, when the vegetables are soft, return the meat to the pan together with the juice that has accumulated.

Heat the wine in a saucepan and pour it over the meat. Turn up the heat and boil to reduce by half, scraping the bottom of the pan with a metal spoon.

Heat the stock in the saucepan used for heating the wine and pour about half over the ossobuchi. Turn the heat down to very low and cover the pan. Cook the ossobuchi for 1½–2 hours, until the meat has begun to come away from the bone. Carefully turn the ossobuchi over every 20 minutes or so, taking care not to damage the marrow in the bone. If necessary, add more stock during cooking, but very gradually – no more than 3 or 4 tablespoons at a time. If by the time the meat is cooked the sauce is too thin, remove the meat from the pan and reduce the liquid by boiling briskly.

Transfer the ossobuchi to a heated dish and remove the string. Keep warm in a cool oven.

Cut the remaining butter into 3 or 4 pieces and gradually add them to the sauce. As soon as the butter has melted, remove the pan from the heat. The sauce should not boil. The addition of the butter will give the sauce a glossy shine and a delicate taste.

Mix the ingredients for the gremolada together, stir into the sauce and leave for I or 2 minutes. After that, just spoon the sauce over the ossobuchi and serve immediately.

Tomaxelle

Stuffed Veal Rolls

Tomaxelle were created in Liguria to use up leftover meat. The Ligurians are masters of stuffed food. In fact every Ligurian dish seems to contain another dish that is equally good. The original recipe includes chopped cow elder (udder), an ingredient that is largely unavailable nowadays. I have replaced it with sweetbreads; calf's brains are also a perfectly good substitute.

SERVES 4

500 g/1 lb veal escalopes (scallops)

flour for dusting

50 g/2 oz/4 tbsp unsalted (sweet) butter

1 tbsp olive oil

4 tbsp dry white wine

1 tbsp tomato paste

200 ml/7 fl oz/scant 1 cup meat stock

FOR THE STUFFING

20 g/¾ oz/⅓ cup dried porcini

100 g/3½ oz calf's or lamb's sweetbreads

1 tbsp white wine vinegar

100 g/3½ oz lean stewing veal

25 g/1 oz/½ cup fresh white breadcrumbs

100 ml/3½ fl oz/scant ½ cup meat stock

salt and freshly ground black pepper

1 tbsp pine nuts, chopped

1 tbsp chopped fresh marjoram

1 tbsp freshly grated pecorino or Parmesan cheese

a pinch of grated nutmeg

a pinch of ground cloves

1 free-range (farm-fresh) egg

1 garlic clove, very finely chopped

FIRST PREPARE THE STUFFING. Soak the porcini in a cupful of warm water for at least 30 minutes. Lift out, rinse under cold water and dry very thoroughly. Blanch the sweetbreads in some boiling water to which you have added the wine vinegar for 2 minutes. Drain and pat dry with kitchen paper (paper towels). Remove the blood and lumps of fat and as much of the covering thin membrane as you can. Chop the sweetbreads together with the veal and porcini. Soak the breadcrumbs in the stock, squeeze out and put in a bowl with the remaining ingredients for the stuffing. Add the meat mixture and salt and pepper to taste and mix very thoroughly together.

Cut the escalopes (scallops) into pieces about 10–12 cm/4–5 in long. Spread the stuffing evenly over each slice and then roll up the slices as for beef olives (beef rollups). Tie with securely thread and coat the rolls lightly with flour.

Heat the butter and oil in a large sauté pan or frying pan (skillet). When the butter begins to colour, add the tomaxelle and brown on all sides. Add the wine and reduce for one minute, then add the tomato paste. Cook, stirring, for 30 seconds, then mix in about 100 ml/3½ fl oz/scant ½ cup of the stock. Bring to the boil and cook gently for 15–20 minutes, turning the tomaxelle over from time to time. Whenever the liquid dries out too quickly, add a couple of tablespoons of stock. Likewise, if the liquid appears too thin at the end of cooking, transfer the tomaxelle to a serving dish and reduce the cooking juices until they are nice and thick.

Cima alla Genovese

Genoese Stuffed Breast of Veal

A splendid "cucina povera" dish of Liguria. It is always served cold.

SERVES 8

1 kg/2 lb 2 oz boned breast of veal
1 onion
1 celery stalk
1 carrot
1 bay leaf
4 black peppercorns
2 litres/4 pints/2¼ quarts meat stock

FOR THE STUFFING
50 g/2 oz white bread, crust removed
   (about 2 slices best country bread)
100 ml/3½ fl oz/scant ½ cup milk
1 small onion, finely chopped
25 g/1 oz/2 tbsp unsalted
   (sweet) butter
100 g/3½ oz stewing veal, cubed
100 g/3½ oz calf's or lamb's
   sweetbreads, cleaned, blanched
   and diced
salt and freshly ground black pepper
2 tbsp pistachio nuts, skinned
1 tsp chopped fresh marjoram
1 free-range (farm-fresh) egg
75 g/2½ oz/generous ½ cup cooked
   peas
3 tbsp freshly grated Parmesan cheese

FIRST PREPARE THE STUFFING. Soak the bread in the milk for 10 minutes or so. Sauté the onion in the butter until soft and then add the stewing veal and cook for 10 minutes, stirring frequently. Mix in the sweetbreads and cook for a further 5 minutes. Season with salt and pepper and take the pan off the heat.

Finely chop the cooked veal and sweetbreads. Add 1 tablespoon hot water to the pan and boil for 1 minute, scraping the bottom of the pan with a metal spoon. Pour the pan juices into a bowl and add the remaining stuffing ingredients. Squeeze the milk out of the bread and add the bread to the bowl. Mix thoroughly and season to taste.

Make a horizontal cut in the breast of veal along one of the long sides. Put the stuffing into this pocket, not too tightly because it will swell while it cooks. Sew up the cut, shaping the meat into a neat roll.

Chop the onion, celery and carrot into chunks and place in a flameproof oval casserole with the bay leaf and peppercorns. Add the stock and bring to the boil. When the stock is boiling, gently lower the meat into it. Turn the heat down to low and cook for 2 hours.

Lift out the meat and put it between two plates with a weight on top. Allow to cool completely before carving it into 1 cm/½ in slices.

Saltimbocca alla Romana

Veal Rolls

Originally saltimbocca were always made rolled up, but nowadays you can find them unrolled, with the prosciutto* and sage simply laid flat on the slices of veal.

SERVES 4
150 g/5 oz prosciutto, very thinly sliced
8 veal escalopes (scallops), total weight
   500 g/1 lb
8 fresh sage leaves
flour, for dusting
salt and freshly ground black pepper
50 g/2 oz/4 tbsp unsalted
   (sweet) butter
1 tbsp olive oil
100 ml/3½ fl oz/scant ½ cup dry
   white wine

PLACE A SLICE OF PROSCIUTTO over each escalope (scallop) – the prosciutto should be a little smaller than the veal. Put 1 or 2 sage leaves in the middle and roll the veal in a sausage shape. Secure with a wooden toothpick, threading it along the length of the roll. Dredge in flour mixed with salt and pepper.

Heat half the butter and all the olive oil in a large frying pan (skillet). As soon as the foam begins to subside, put in the meat rolls. Brown on all sides until quite golden, not pale beige.

Heat the wine in a separate saucepan and pour over the saltimbocca. Turn the heat up, bubble the wine for 1 minute, and cook for a further 3 to 4 minutes. Transfer the saltimbocca to a heated dish, remove the toothpicks and keep the meat warm.

Add a couple of tablespoons of boiling water to the pan, then add the remaining butter a little at a time, swirling the pan around and stirring constantly. Taste and check seasoning.

Pour the sauce over the meat and serve at once.

Costolette alla Milanese

Milanese Veal Chops

This is my translation of Ada Boni's classic recipe published in her book Cucina Regionale Italiana.

SERVES 6
6 veal chops
2 large (extra-large) free-range (farm-
   fresh) eggs, lightly beaten
150–200 g/5–7 oz/2–2¾ cups dried
   white breadcrumbs
150 g/5 oz/1¼ sticks unsalted
   (sweet) butter
salt
lemon wedges, to garnish

TO PREPARE THE CHOPS, trim them at the point where the rib meets the backbone. Flatten them a little and make small cuts all around them so that they will not shrink in cooking. Coat the chops in the beaten egg, then in the breadcrumbs, pressing the crumbs hard into the meat with your hands.

Heat the butter in a frying pan (skillet) that is large enough to hold the chops in a single layer. When the butter begins to colour, add the chops and cook at a lively heat until a crust is formed on the underside – about 3 minutes. Turn them over, turn the heat down and cook for 5 minutes. Now season with salt and transfer the chops to a heated serving dish. Garnish with lemon wedges to serve.

Scaloppine alla Perugina

Veal Escalopes with Prosciutto and Chicken Livers

Alla perugina means "in the style of Perugia", but in fact this dish could be from any central Italian town. You can use turkey escalopes (scallops) instead of veal; they are a good substitute. To look pretty, the escalopes should be thinly sliced and smallish in size. If they are more than 5 mm/¼ in thick, beat them thin with a meat pounder.

SERVES 4

2 salted anchovies, boned and rinsed, or 4 canned or bottled anchovy fillets, drained

I garlic clove

100 g/3½ oz chicken livers, cleaned and rinsed

I tbsp capers, preferably in salt, rinsed

75 g/2½ oz prosciutto

rind of ½ lemon, preferably organic or unwaxed

6 fresh sage leaves

4 tbsp extra virgin olive oil

500 g/I lb veal escalopes (scallops), see introduction

I tbsp lemon juice

salt and freshly ground black pepper

CHOP TOGETHER the anchovies, garlic, chicken livers, capers, prosciutto, lemon rind and sage. I find this is best done in the food processor.

Heat the olive oil in a large frying pan (skillet). Slide in the escalopes (scallops) and brown well on both sides. Lower the heat, sprinkle with the lemon juice, a little salt and a lot of pepper. Cook them until done, which depends on their thickness – if they have been sliced thinly they should take 2–3 minutes. When done, transfer them to a heated dish, cover with foil and keep warm.

Now spoon the chopped chicken liver mixture into the pan and cook over a lively heat for about 3 minutes. Turn the mixture over frequently.

Place a little mound of the chicken liver mixture on top of each escalope. Deglaze the cooking juices in the empty pan with 2–3 tablespoons hot water. Boil it up, scraping the bottom of the pan to loosen any cooking residue.

Pour the pan juices over the scaloppine and serve at once.

Cook's tip

A chicken liver consists of two lobes joined together by a sinewy membrane. Trim off the membranes with a sharp knife before rinsing the livers under cold running water. Pat dry with kitchen paper (paper towels).

Costolettine a Scottadito

Barbecued Baby Lamb Chops

Scottadito means "burns the finger", which implies these chops should be eaten very hot straight from the fire, with the fingers. It is a country dish from the Apennines east of Rome, where the lambs are slaughtered very young, usually while still milk-fed. So try to get very young lamb — the chops should be small and the fat must be white.

SERVES 4

I tbsp chopped fresh marjoram
½ tbsp chopped fresh mint
I tbsp chopped fresh thyme
I garlic clove, finely chopped
freshly ground black pepper
8 or 12 lamb chops, depending on size
juice of I lemon, preferably organic
  or unwaxed
½ tsp Dijon mustard
4 tbsp extra virgin olive oil
salt

MIX THE CHOPPED HERBS, the garlic and pepper together and coat the chops with this, pressing the mixture hard with your hands into both sides of the meat. Place the chops in a greased dish and leave for at least I hour to marinate.

Light the barbecue and let the charcoal get very hot.

Meanwhile, strain the lemon juice into a small bowl. Add the mustard, then gradually add the olive oil, beating constantly. The sauce will become quite thick when well beaten. Taste and season.

When the charcoal is very hot, place the chops on the grill. Cooking time depends on the heat of the fire and the thickness of the meat. As a rough guide, allow 3 minutes each side if you like your lamb pink, longer if you want it more cooked. When the chops are cooked, sprinkle with salt. Serve the lemon sauce separately.

Agnello, Cacio e Uova

Lamb Fricassée

Lamb is the most popular meat in central Italy. In this recipe from Abruzzo it is finished off with a sauce of egg and pecorino* sharpened with lemon juice, the Italian version of the French fricassée.

SERVES 4

I tbsp olive oil
1.3 kg/3 lb leg of lamb, boned and cut
  into 2.5 cm/I in cubes
2 tbsp olive oil
1 onion, very finely sliced
I tsp chopped fresh thyme
150 ml/5 fl oz/⅔ cup dry white wine
salt and freshly ground black pepper
3 large (extra-large) free-range (farm-
  fresh) egg yolks
3 tbsp grated mature pecorino cheese
15 g/½ oz/¼ cup fresh white breadcrumbs
juice of I lemon, preferably organic
  or unwaxed

HEAT THE OLIVE OIL in a large non-stick frying pan (skillet). When hot, add the meat and brown well on all sides. Remove the meat to a side plate.

Put the olive oil and the onion in a flameproof casserole and sauté until soft. Add the meat and the thyme, mix well and then pour over the wine. Bring to the boil and season with salt and pepper. Cover and cook until ready, about 45 minutes.

Beat the egg yolks with the cheese, breadcrumbs and lemon juice, add a good grinding of pepper and mix into the lamb. Cook for a further 5 minutes, until the egg sauce has thickened. Taste and adjust the seasonings before serving.

Agnello alla Cacciatora con le Patate

Lamb and Potato Stew

The term "alla cacciatora" is applied to a number of dishes which are usually rustic and made with seasonal ingredients. (Cacciatora means "hunter".) In this recipe from Liguria, potatoes and porcini are cooked with lamb. When fresh porcini are not in season, you can use cultivated brown mushrooms instead.

SERVES 6

20 g/¾ oz/⅓ cup dried porcini

4 tbsp olive oil

1 kg/2 lb 2 oz shoulder of lamb, boned and cut into 5 cm/2 in cubes

1 small onion, finely chopped

250 g/9 oz/3½ cups fresh porcini, sliced

2 tbsp tomato paste

750 g/1 lb 10 oz waxy potatoes, cut into chunks

1 bay leaf

salt and freshly ground black pepper

6–8 tbsp meat stock

2 tbsp chopped fresh flat-leaf parsley

SOAK THE DRIED PORCINI in 250 ml/8 fl oz/1 cup hot water for at least 30 minutes and then drain, reserving the liquid.

Heat the olive oil in a flameproof casserole and brown the meat well on all sides. Lift the meat out and set aside. Add the onion and the dried and fresh porcini to the casserole and cook for 10 minutes until tender, stirring frequently. Return the meat to the casserole and add the tomato paste, potatoes and bay leaf. Strain the porcini liquid through a sieve (strainer) lined with muslin or cheesecloth and add to the pan. Season the stew to taste.

Cover and simmer very gently for about 1½ hours. If necessary, add a few tablespoons of warm stock or water to the sauce during cooking. Sprinkle with the parsley before serving.

NOTE: If you prefer, you can cook this dish in the oven preheated to 170°C/ 325°F/Gas Mark 3.

Cosciotto di Agnello Arrosto con le Cipolline

Roast Leg of Lamb with Tiny Onions

This is one of the very few recipes for lamb which originated in Northern Italy. It it my adaptation of a recipe from a nineteenth century book, il Cuoco Milanese, a book which I rate highly.

SERVES 8

25 g/1 oz pancetta or unsmoked streaky (fatty) bacon

4 garlic cloves

2.25-2.75 kg/5-6 lb leg of lamb

300 ml/10 fl oz/1¼ cups good, but light red wine

500 g/1 lb small white onions

1 tsp sugar

the juice of 1 orange

the juice of lemon

50 g/2 oz/4 tbsp unsalted (sweet) butter

FOR THE MARINADE

½ tbsp coarse sea salt

6 peppercorns, bruised

a selections of fresh herbs, such as parsley, celery leaves, rosemary, sage, thyme, and marjoran

4 tbsp olive oil

FINELY CHOP THE PANCETTA and the garlic. Make a few deep slits in the lamb and push little pellets of the mixture into the slits with the help of a chopstick.

Rub the leg with the coarse salt and place it in an overnproof dish with the peppercorns and herbs. Pour over the oil and leave to marinate for 24 hours or so, turning the meat over as often as you remember.

Heat the oven to 180°C/350°F/ Gas Mark 4.

Pour the wine over the lamb and roast for 1 hour, basting the meat twice.

Put the onions into a saucepan and cover with cold water. Bring to the boil and then drain. Peel the onions, taking care to leave the roots on. Now add the onions to the lamb and bake for another hour, basting the whole lot every 20 minutes or so.

Remove the leg to a board, cover it with foil and leave it to rest while you make the sauce.

Lift out the onions with a slotted spoon, transfer to a dish and keep hot.

Strain the cooking juices into a saucepan. Skim off as much fat as you possibly can.

Mix in the sugar and the citrus juices and then taste and adjust the seasoning.

When the sauce is simmering add the butter in little pieces and let it melt slowly, while you stir the whole time.

Carve the lamb in thick slices and serve with the onions and the sauce.

Rostisciana
A Pork and Onion Dish

La Lombardia in Cucina by Ottorina Perna Bozzi is the best book on Lombard food. This recipe is my adaptation of a recipe from that book. The sausage should be luganega, available in Italian delis. A good coarsely ground pork sausage with a 90% meat content, neither herby nor spiced, would do instead.

SERVES 4

500 g/1 lb onions, finely sliced
40 g/1½ oz/3 tbsp unsalted
   (sweet) butter
salt
500 g/1 lb luganega, cut into chunks
1 tbsp olive oil
200 g/7 oz pork steak from the
   shoulder or leg, thickly cut
100 ml/3½ fl oz/scant ½ cup dry
   red wine
freshly ground black pepper

COOK THE ONIONS in the butter with 1 teaspoon of salt over a gentle heat for about 30 minutes, until they soften and begin to turn gold. Stir very often and add a tablespoon of water if necessary, to prevent burning.

Meanwhile, in a cast-iron frying pan (skillet), fry the sausages quickly in the olive oil until well browned all over. Remove the sausages to a board. Add the steak to the pan and fry for 2 minutes on each side.

Now cut the sausages and pork into chunks and then return them all to the pan. Pour over the wine and let it bubble away for 1 or 2 minutes.

Transfer the sausages and pork to the onion pan. Pour about 6 tablespoons water into the frying pan in which the meat was cooked and boil for 30 seconds to deglaze, stirring and scraping the bottom of the pan to release the bits. Spoon the cooking juices over the onion and the sausage mixture and let everything cook together very gently, with a lid on, for 10 minutes.

Add pepper and check the salt before serving. Serve very hot.

Maiale al Latte

Loin of Pork Braised in Milk

Many regions claim to have invented this excellent dish. This recipe is particularly suitable for today's less flavoursome pork.

SERVES 6

I kg/2 lb 2 oz boned loin of pork, rindless but with a thin layer of fat, tied in several places
4 tbsp vegetable oil
3 cloves
a pinch of ground cinnamon
I sprig of fresh rosemary
2 garlic cloves, bruised
I tsp coarse sea salt
4 or 5 black peppercorns, crushed
I bay leaf
25 g/I oz/2 tbsp unsalted (sweet) butter
300 ml/I0 fl oz/I¼ cups milk
salt and freshly ground black pepper

PUT THE PORK IN A DISH and add half the oil, the cloves, cinnamon, rosemary, garlic, salt, peppercorns and bay leaf. Coat the pork all over in the marinade and leave for about 8 hours in a cool place (not in the refrigerator unless it is very hot). Turn occasionally.

Pat the meat dry. Heat the butter and the rest of the oil in a heavy flameproof casserole into which the pork will fit snugly. When the foam begins to subside, add the meat and brown well on all sides.

Heat the milk to boiling point, then pour it slowly over the meat. Sprinkle with salt and pepper, place the lid slightly askew on the pan and cook for about 2 hours at a steady, low simmer. Turn the meat over and baste every 20 minutes or so. By the end of cooking the milk should be a rich dark golden colour, and quite thick. If it is too pale by the time the meat is done, boil briskly without the lid until it darkens and thickens.

Transfer the meat to a wooden board and leave for I0 minutes or so, covered with foil.

Skim as much fat as you can from the surface of the sauce, add 2 tablespoons hot water and boil over a high heat for about 2 minutes, scraping the bottom of the pan with a metal spoon. Taste and adjust the seasoning.

Remove the string, carve the pork into I cm/½ in slices and arrange the slices on a heated serving dish. Spoon the sauce over the pork, or spoon over only a little of the sauce and serve the rest separately in a heated sauceboat.

Arista alla Fiorentina

Florentine Roast Pork

This is one of the most popular Tuscan roasts, usually served cold, accompanied by cannellini beans. Ask your butcher for the bones from the pork and put them around the meat in the roasting pan They make the juices tastier.

SERVES 6

2 garlic cloves, finely sliced
2 sprigs of fresh rosemary, about 10 cm/4 in long
salt and freshly ground black pepper
I kg/2 lb 2 oz boned loin of pork, without rind
2 cloves
3 tbsp olive oil

CHOP THE GARLIC and rosemary needles together, add salt and pepper and mix well. Make small incisions in the pork and push a little of the rosemary mixture into the meat. Pat the rest of the mixture all over the meat, stud the meat with the cloves and then rub with half the olive oil. Leave the meat to stand in a cool place for a few hours to absorb all the flavourings.

Heat the oven to 180°C/350°F/ Gas Mark 4.

Put the rest of the oil and the meat in a roasting pan and place the pan in the preheated oven. Roast for about 2 hours, basting and turning the meat every 20 minutes or so and turning the oven up to 220°C/425°F/ Gas Mark 7 for the last 10 minutes to brown the meat. When tender, transfer it to a wooden board and leave it to rest for 10 minutes or so.

Remove as much fat from the cooking liquid as you possibly can. Add 4 tablespoons hot water to the pan and boil briskly, stirring vigorously to loosen the residue at the bottom of the pan.

Carve the meat and spoon over the cooking juices. The pork is equally succulent and delicious whether served hot or cold.

Gulasch alla Triestina

Goulash from Trieste

This is the type of goulash made in Venezia Giulia, the region around Trieste which was under the Austro-Hungarian empire until the Great War. There it is often served with tagliatelle as it is indeed served in Austria.

SERVES 4
50 g/2 oz smoked pancetta or smoked streaky (fatty) bacon
50 g/2 oz/4 tbsp unsalted (sweet) butter

2 large sweet onions
750 g/1½ lb boned pork shoulder, cut into 2.5 cm/1 in pieces
2 tsp paprika, or more depending on strength and taste
1 tbsp flour
1 tbsp tomato purée
1 tsp grated lemon rind
salt and freshly ground black pepper
120 ml/4 fl oz/½ cup red wine
2 large yellow or red peppers
2 large ripe tomatoes, skinned and roughly chopped
300ml/10 fl oz/1¼ cups meat stock

HEAT THE PANCETTA and half the butter in a saucepan. Add the onions and sauté until soft, but not brown. Add the meat and brown well on all sides.

Mix in the paprika, flour and tomato purée and cook for 1 to 2 minutes, stirring constantly. Add the lemon rind, salt and pepper.

Pour the wine over the meat and reduce by boiling rapidly for 2 minutes. Add the peppers and the tomatoes and mix well. Cover with the stock and simmer, tightly covered, for about 1½ hour.

Just before serving, uncover the goulash and reduce it over a high heat. The sauce should thicken and become velvety. Taste and add more paprika if necessary.

Filetto di Maiale alla Cavalcanti

Pork Fillet with Elderberries, Almonds and Balsamic Vinegar

The Neapolitan haute cuisine of the eighteenth and nineteenth centuries was very sophisticated, often using sweet ingredients in savoury dishes. This recipe is by Ippolito Cavalcanti, a nineteenth-century aristocrat and cookery writer.

SERVES 4

600 g/1¼ lb pork fillets (tenderloin)
40 g/1½ oz/3 tbsp unsalted
   (sweet) butter
2 tbsp olive oil
120 ml/4 fl oz/½ cup good red wine
salt and freshly ground black pepper
4 tsp sugar
a pinch of ground cinnamon
2 tbsp balsamic vinegar
1 tbsp very finely ground almonds
2 tbsp elderberries
1 tbsp capers, preferably in salt, rinsed

TRIM THE FAT OFF the pork fillets (tenderloin) and cut them in half, if necessary, so they will fit into a large sauté pan.

Heat half the butter and the olive oil in the pan and add the pork. Sauté until brown on all sides.

Bring the wine to the boil in a separate small pan and pour over the meat with 2 tablespoons hot water. When the liquid has come back to the boil, add salt and pepper. Turn the heat down so that the liquid will just simmer, cover the pan tightly and cook for 10 minutes, or until the pork is done. Remove the meat from the pan and keep warm.

Add the sugar and cinnamon, the balsamic vinegar, almonds, elderberries and capers to the pan and cook, stirring constantly, for 2 minutes. Break the remaining butter into small pieces and add gradually to the sauce while gently stirring and swirling the pan.

Slice the meat (not too thinly), and return it to the pan for 2 minutes to absorb the flavour of the sauce, then serve immediately.

Cook's tip

Elderberries are not widely available commercially but do grow wild all over the countryside throughout Europe. Do not pick them from the roadside as they may be polluted by traffic fumes. Use them as soon as possible after gathering. Blueberries are a good substitute and American readers could also use huckleberries.

Braciole di Maiale alla Pizzaiola

Pork Steaks with Mozzarella and Oregano

The word pizzaiola indicates a dish containing the ingredients used in the topping of a Neapolitan pizza. All "alla pizzaiola" dishes are of Neapolitan origin.

SERVES 4

500 g/1 lb pork steaks, thinly cut
salt and freshly ground black pepper
2 or 3 sprigs of fresh marjoram
150 ml/5 fl oz/⅔ cup red wine
225 g/8 oz canned plum
   tomatoes, drained
3 tbsp olive oil
1 garlic clove, crushed
4 tbsp flour
25 g/1 oz/2 tbsp unsalted
   (sweet) butter
4 tbsp meat stock
100 g/3½ oz Italian mozzarella cheese,
   cut into very thin slices
1 tbsp dried oregano

PUT THE PORK STEAKS in a dish and sprinkle with salt, pepper and the sprigs of marjoram. Pour over the red wine and leave to marinate for about 1 hour.

Heat the oven to 200°C/400°F/ Gas Mark 6.

Purée the tomatoes through a food mill or sieve (strainer) directly into a saucepan. Add 1 tablespoon of the olive oil, the garlic and salt and pepper to taste. Cook over a lively heat without the lid, for 5 minutes.

Lift the steaks out of the marinade (reserve the liquid) and pat dry with kitchen paper (paper towels). Turn the steaks over in the flour, coating both sides well. Shake off any excess flour.

Heat the rest of the oil and the butter in a large frying pan (skillet). When the foam has nearly disappeared, slide in the steaks and fry briskly to sear both sides. Pour over the strained liquid from the marinade and let it bubble for about 30 seconds, then add the stock and salt and pepper and bring the liquid to the boil. Lower the heat and cook, covered, for 5–7 minutes.

When the meat is cooked, transfer it to an ovenproof dish.

Deglaze the frying pan with a little water and reduce it to only 3 or 4 tablespoonfuls. Spoon the mixture over the steaks.

Cover each steak with a layer of cheese and place a spoonful of tomato sauce in the middle. Sprinkle with oregano, salt and black pepper. Pop the dish into the preheated oven for about 5 minutes to allow the cheese to melt.

Stinco in Umido con le Patate

Stewed Shin of Pork with Potatoes

You can make this recipe with veal, pork or even lamb shins (shanks). Veal shins are rather small and will only serve 2 or 3 people, but one shin from a continental calf will do for 4 to 6 people. One pork shin can usually serve 3 or 4 people. Served with potatoes and accompanied by some spinach or steamed broccoli, this makes a delicious and nourishing winter meal.

SERVES 3–4

1 shin of pork (fresh ham hock), about
   1 kg/2 lb 2 oz
1 mild onion, finely sliced
4 garlic cloves, chopped
salt and freshly ground black pepper
4 tbsp olive oil
200 ml/7 fl oz/scant 1 cup red wine
2 tbsp chopped fresh rosemary, sage
   and thyme
400 g/14 oz canned chopped tomatoes
about 150 ml/5 fl oz/⅔ cup meat stock
800 g/1¾ lb/5⅓ cups waxy potatoes,
   cut into chunks

HEAT THE OVEN to 180°C/350°F/ Gas Mark 4. Singe any coarse hair from the shin of pork (ham hock). Now sprinkle it with 1 teaspoon salt and a good grinding of pepper and pat the seasoning into the rind.

Put the onion, garlic, 1 teaspoon salt and the olive oil in a flameproof casserole and sauté gently for 3 or 4 minutes. Add 3 or 4 tablespoons of water and continue cooking over a low heat until the onions are soft; this will take about 15 minutes.

Push the onion and garlic to one side of the pan, lay the pork in the empty side and turn the heat up a little. Brown the pork on all sides and then pour over the wine and boil for 2–3 minutes. Add the herbs, then mix in the tomatoes with their juice and half the stock. Cover the casserole with a tight-fitting lid and cook in the oven for 2 hours, until the meat falls easily from the bone. If necessary, add a little more stock during cooking and turn the shin over. Check the seasoning of the cooking juices, which should be rich and savoury.

Meanwhile, parboil the potatoes. When nearly cooked, add them to the casserole, about 15 minutes before the cooking time of the meat is up, with a little more stock if the cooking juices are too dry. Turn the potatoes over in the sauce and put the casserole back in the oven.

Let the meat rest for about 5 minutes and then cut it into chunks. Serve the meat surrounded by the potatoes.

Cassoeula

Pork Casserole with Cabbage

This is an adaptation of my mother's recipe for this ancient Lombard dish. Like all traditional dishes it is the subject of passionate controversy. Should it be eaten the day after it is made? Should it contain tomato paste? Should the Savoy cabbage be al dente or mushy? Whatever it is, a genuine cassoeula should contain different cuts of pork and it should be served with polenta. I always make it one or two days in advance, chill it and remove some of the fat, then reheat it before serving.

SERVES 8

2 pig's trotters (feet), cut into
    4 pieces
1 pig's tail, cut into pieces (optional)
250 g/9 oz pork rind
1 tbsp vegetable oil
50 g/2 oz/4 tbsp pure pork lard
1 large onion, coarsely chopped
2 carrots, sliced
2 or 3 celery stalks, diced
500 g/1 lb boneless belly of pork (fresh
    pork side), cut into cubes
salt and freshly ground black pepper
500 g/1 lb mild pure pork sausage,
    diced
2 kg/4¼ lb Savoy cabbage, shredded

COVER THE TROTTERS (FEET) and the tail with cold water, bring to the boil and simmer for 30 minutes. Add the pork rind and cook for a further 5 minutes. Remove the meat from the saucepan and cut the rind into 5 cm/2 in squares.

Allow the stock to cool and then refrigerate. When the fat has solidified on the surface, remove and discard it. Put the oil, lard and onion in a large, heavy flameproof casserole (Dutch oven) and sauté until soft. Add the carrots and celery and fry gently for 5 minutes, stirring frequently.

Increase the heat, mix in the trotters, the rind and the tail, if you have used, and fry for 2 minutes. Add the pork and fry for 5 minutes longer, mixing frequently. The meat must not stick to the bottom of the pan or it will give a slightly bitter taste to the whole dish.

Add the reserved stock and more water to cover the meat.

Sprinkle with the seasoning, cover with a lid and cook over the gentlest heat for 2 hours. Add the sausage and the Savoy cabbage, mix well and cook for 20 minutes. Taste and adjust the seasoning before serving.

Animelle Fritte

Fried Sweetbreads

In Milan, many famous ingredients, including the famous costolette*, are cooked in this way. Brains and sweetbreads are well suited to this type of cooking, where their delicacy is enveloped in a golden buttery crust. The sweetbreads should be calf's, but I find lamb's are quite good too.

SERVES 3–4
600 g/1¼ lb sweetbreads
½ lemon, preferably organic or unwaxed
1 large (extra-large) free-range (farm-fresh) egg
salt and freshly ground black pepper
3 tbsp flour
6 tbsp dried breadcrumbs
40 g/1½ oz/3 tbsp unsalted (sweet) butter
3 tbsp olive or vegetable oil
lemon wedges, to serve

RINSE THE SWEETBREADS under cold water and put them in a saucepan of cold water with the lemon. Bring to the boil and simmer for 8–10 minutes. Drain, then cool them pressed between 2 plates. When they are cold, remove the lumps of fat and the skiny. Cut the sweetbreads into neat pieces.

Lightly beat the egg with some salt and pepper. Spread the flour on a plate and dredge the nuggets of sweetbread very lightly in the flour. Coat them in the egg and then the breadcrumbs, pressing the crumbs firmly into the meat.

Heat the butter and oil in a large frying pan (skillet): the ideal size is 25 cm/10 in. When the fat is beginning to become golden, slide in the sweetbread nuggets. Fry on both sides until a lovely deep golden crust has formed and then turn down the heat and cook for a further 5 minutes.

Transfer the sweetbreads to a heated dish, pour over the sizzling butter and serve at once, with the lemon wedges.

Fegato alla Veneziana

Calf's Liver with Onions

The liver can either be sliced thinly or cut into strips. Some versions add the liver to the onion, but I prefer to remove the onion so that the liver can spread out better, and the cooking is easier to control.

SERVES 4
50 g/2 oz/4 tbsp unsalted (sweet) butter
4 tbsp vegetable oil
700 g/1½ lb onions, very finely sliced
salt
700 g/1½ lb calf's liver, very finely sliced
freshly ground black pepper
1 tbsp chopped fresh flat-leaf parsley

HEAT HALF THE BUTTER and the oil in a frying pan (skillet) large enough to hold the liver in a single layer. When the foam subsides, add the onions and a pinch of salt to the pan, mix well and cook very gently for 30 minutes. The onion should be very soft and just coloured. Stir occasionally during cooking, pressing the onions against the sides of the pan to release the juices.

When the onions are cooked, lift them out of the pan with a slotted spoon and set aside. Add the remaining butter to the pan and turn up the heat. When the foam begins to subside, add the liver and fry for 2 minutes on each side. Do not overcook: the liver should be pink inside.

Return the onions to the pan, season with salt and pepper and give a good stir. Sprinkle with the parsley and serve at once.

Coppa di Testa

Pig's Head Brawn

A dish from Umbria and Marche, made at home and also sold in norcinerie – local delis. The flavour of coppa is similar to that of French rillettes, but more spicy.

SERVES 8–10

½ pig's head, chopped into 4 pieces
4 tbsp coarse sea salt
3 bay leaves
1 onion, unpeeled and stuck with
   2 cloves
1 large celery stalk
1 carrot
1 cm/½ in piece of cinnamon stick
7 black peppercorns
¼ nutmeg, grated
2 cloves
1 dried chilli
2 garlic cloves, peeled
1 tsp sugar
4 tbsp balsamic vinegar
salt
pared rind of 1 orange, preferably
   organic or unwaxed
25 g/1 oz/¼ cup pine nuts, toasted
25 g/1 oz/¼ cup fresh pistachio nuts,
   blanched and peeled

SCRAPE THE RIND AND BURN all the hairs from the pig's head. Pat the head all over with the coarse salt. Put it in a bowl and lay 2 of the bay leaves over it. Cover and set aside in the refrigerator for 24 hours.

Remove the bay leaves. Put the head in a large stockpot, cover with cold water and bring to the boil, then blanch for 5 minutes. Drain and add the onion, celery, carrot and remaining bay leaf. Cover with fresh cold water and simmer steadily for about 3½–4 hours, until the meat comes away easily from the bones.

Drain the contents of the stockpot and put the solids in a bowl. (Keep the liquid for a bean soup or an earthy risotto.) When the meat is cool, remove all the bones from the head, cut the meat into small pieces and transfer to a bowl. Throw away the boiled vegetables. In a mortar, pound together the cinnamon, peppercorns, nutmeg, cloves, chilli, garlic and sugar, moistening the mixture with the vinegar, and mix into the meat. Add a generous quantity of salt, remembering that any food eaten cold needs more seasoning. Cut the orange rind into little pieces and add to the bowl together with the pine nuts and pistachios. Mix thoroughly with your hands and add 4 or 5 tablespoons of the reserved liquid. Taste and adjust the seasoning.

Lay a kitchen cloth (dish-towel) on the work surface (countertop) and place the meat mixture on it. Roll up like a Swiss (jelly) roll with the help of the cloth. Tie both ends and put on a wooden board. Place another board and a weight over it and leave until cold. Chill for at least 1 day – the brawn (head cheese) keeps well for up to 4 or 5 days – and then slice thinly and serve with a light salsa verde (see page 180).

Fagottini di Verza

Stuffed Cabbage Parcels

Many traditional meat dishes from Milan, like this one, contain Savoy cabbage. In the older versions of this recipe the parcels (cabbage rolls) are finished off only in stock, the tomato paste being a nineteenth-century addition.

SERVES 4

400–500 g/14 oz–1 lb Savoy cabbage
salt and freshly ground black pepper
250 g/9 oz lean minced (ground) beef
100 g/3½ oz luganega sausage, skinned
  and crumbled
3 tbsp freshly grated Parmesan cheese
1 free-range (farm-fresh) egg
a pinch of grated nutmeg
25 g/1 oz good-quality white bread,
  with the crust removed (about 1 slice)
5 tbsp milk
1 clove
1 garlic clove, peeled
1 tbsp tomato paste diluted with 4 tbsp
  hot meat stock
25 g/1 oz/2 tbsp unsalted
  (sweet) butter
olive oil for the dish

REMOVE AND DISCARD the tough outside leaves of the cabbage. Peel off the inner leaves. This is easily done by cutting them off at the core end and unfolding them gently. Wash the leaves.

Bring a large pan of salted water to the boil. Add the cabbage leaves and blanch for 3 minutes after the water has come back to the boil. Lift them out with a slotted spoon and place on a double thickness of kitchen paper (paper towels).

Put the beef, luganega, Parmesan and egg into a mixing bowl and combine everything together. Add salt, pepper and nutmeg. Mix well.

Put the bread, milk and clove in a small saucepan and place the pan over low heat. Cook, stirring, until all the milk has been absorbed and the bread is mushy. Remove the clove, add the bread to the meat mixture and mix well. Add seasoning to taste.

Heat the oven to 190°C/375°F/ Gas Mark 5.

Pat the cabbage leaves dry. Divide the large leaves in two and remove the central stalk. Remove the core end of the stalk from the smaller leaves. Place a heaped tablespoon of the stuffing in the middle of the leaves and roll the leaves up into little bundles, tucking under the ends of the leaves and tying them up with shredded leeks.

Choose a shallow ovenproof dish that will hold the bundles in a single layer. Rub the dish with the garlic and grease with a little oil. Place the cabbage bundles very close to each other in the dish, pour over the hot stock and tomato paste mixture and dot with the butter.

Cover the dish with foil and bake for 25 minutes.

Bollito Misto

Mixed Boiled Meats

The original bollito misto* also includes 1 small fresh calf's tongue. If you can buy one, cook it separately for about an hour, then peel it and add it to the stockpot with the veal. If you are using a pre-cooked cotechino*, follow the manufacturer's directions. If the cotechino is uncooked, soak it in cold water for 4 to 5 hours, then prick it all over with a needle, wrap it in a piece of muslin or cheesecloth and tie both ends with string. Place the cotechino in a saucepan, cover with water and simmer for 2 to 2½ hours. Both kinds of cotechino are cooked separately.

SERVES 10–12

1 large onion, stuck with 1 clove
2 celery stalks
1 leek
2 carrots
1 kg/2 lb 2 oz beef flank or brisket, in
   one piece
3 ripe fresh tomatoes, quartered
5 or 6 black peppercorns, lightly crushed
a few parsley stalks
salt
500 g/1 lb shoulder of veal, in one
   piece, or 2 large ossibuchi
½ a fresh chicken, preferably a
   boiling hen
1 cotechino, about 500 g/1 lb

PUT THE ONION, CELERY, leek and carrots in a very large saucepan, cover with cold water and bring to the boil. Add the beef and bring back to the boil. Lower the heat – the stock should be just simmering. Remove the scum that comes to the surface during the first few minutes of cooking. Add the tomatoes, peppercorns, parsley and some salt. Cover the pan and simmer for 1½ hours.

Add the veal and simmer for a further hour.

Put the chicken in and cook for 1–2 hours, depending on whether the bird is a roaster or a boiler.

When you serve the bollito, transfer the cooked cotechino to the pan with all the other meats, then lift one piece of meat at a time out of the stock and carve only as much as you need to go round for the first helping. Keep the rest of the meat in the stock, as this prevents the meat from getting dry.

Put the carved meat on a heated large platter and bring it to the table, with dishes of boiled potatoes, carrots, onions and any other seasonal roots, all cooked separately. Other traditional accompaniments are little bowls of Salsa Verde (see page 180) and/or Bagnet Ross (see page 173), and mostarda di Cremona*.

Cook's tip

Boiling fowl are larger and fatter than orasters, weighing 2.25–3.25 kg/5–7 lb. They are not usually seen in supermarkets, but good butchers can provide them.

Rognoncini Trifolati all'Acciuga e Limone

Lamb's Kidneys with Anchovies and Lemon

The kidneys usually used in Italy are calf's kidneys, which do not need any preliminary treatment to rid them of too strong a taste. But if you use lamb's or pig's kidneys you must first soak them in acidulated water or blanch them. I prefer lamb's kidneys.

SERVES 4
500 g/I lb lamb's kidneys
2 tbsp wine vinegar
40 g/I½ oz/3 tbsp unsalted
  (sweet) butter
I tbsp flour
2 salted anchovies, boned, rinsed and
  chopped, or 4 canned or bottled
  anchovy fillets, drained and chopped
3 tbsp extra virgin olive oil
I garlic clove, finely chopped
salt and freshly ground black pepper
I tbsp chopped fresh flat-leaf parsley
2 tsp lemon juice

SPLIT THE KIDNEYS in half and remove and discard the cores. Rinse the kidneys briefly, then put them in a bowl and cover with cold water. Mix in the vinegar and leave to soak for at least 30 minutes. Drain. Blend the butter, flour and anchovies. Set aside.

Heat the olive oil with the garlic in a frying pan (skillet). Add the kidneys and sauté until they begin to change colour; this takes only a few minutes. They will become tough if overcooked. Lower the heat and add the anchovy mixture gradually, stirring constantly. Taste and add seasoning. Cook for I minute. Turn off the heat, add the parsley and lemon juice and serve.

Finocchi al Latte

Fennel Braised in Milk

A recipe from Vincenzo Corrado's book Il Cuoco Galante. *I have added the quantities for the ingredients, which are not specified in his recipes. It is an ideal accompaniment to a roast chicken and it also makes a good antipasto*.*

SERVES 4
900 g/2 lb fennel bulbs
salt
¼ tsp ground cinnamon
¼ tsp grated nutmeg
freshly ground black pepper
200 ml/7 fl oz/scant I cup full-fat
  (whole) milk
120 ml/4 fl oz/½ cup double
  (heavy) cream
I tsp sugar

CLEAN THE FENNEL by removing any bruised parts and the stalks. Blanch for 3 minutes in boiling salted water. Drain and cut into segments about 2.5 cm/ I in thick.

Put the spices, pepper and 150 ml/ 5 fl oz/⅔ cup of the milk in a large sauté pan and add the fennel. Cover and cook over gentle heat until tender, about 15–20 minutes. Turn the fennel over every now and then and add a little more milk whenever the fennel looks too dry. At the end of cooking there should be no liquid left and the fennel should just stick to the bottom of the pan.

Pour over the cream and sprinkle with the sugar. Stir gently and cook for a further 5 minutes.

Sformato di Finocchi

Fennel Mould

Of all the sformati, this is one of the tastiest and "one of the most gentle" writes the great Artusi. He suggests serving it as an accompaniment to boiled capon, or by itself with a garnish of chicken giblets and sweetbreads.

SERVES 6–8

700 g/1½ lb fennel bulbs
50 g/2 oz/4 tbsp unsalted
  (sweet) butter
salt
300 ml/10 fl oz/1¼ cups full-fat
  (whole) milk
3 tbsp flour
2 pinches of grated nutmeg
freshly ground pepper,
  preferably white
3 large (extra-large) free-range (farm-
  fresh) eggs
4 tbsp freshly grated Parmesan cheese
3 tbsp dried breadcrumbs

CUT AWAY THE GREEN TOPS, stalks and any bruised or brown parts from the outside of the fennel. Reserve a handful of the green tops.

Cut the fennel bulbs into vertical slices about 5 mm/¼ in thick. Wash the slices and the reserved fennel tops and dry them.

Melt half the butter in a frying pan (skillet). When the butter begins to foam, add the fennel and cook for 5 minutes. Add salt and half the milk. Cover the pan and cook very gently until the fennel is tender, this will take about 20 minutes. Keep a watch on the fennel and add a little water if it becomes too dry.

Chop the fennel to a very coarse purée, either by hand or in a food processor. Transfer to a bowl.

Heat the oven to 190°C/375°F/ Gas Mark 5.

Make a fairly thick béchamel sauce with the remaining butter, the flour and the rest of the milk (see page 179). Flavour with the grated nutmeg and some pepper and then add to the fennel in the bowl.

Beat the eggs together lightly with a fork and add to the fennel mixture with the Parmesan. Mix very thoroughly, then check the seasoning.

Grease a 1.2 litre/1¾ pint/1 quart ring mould very generously with butter. If you are worried about unmoulding the sformato, line the bottom of the ring with greaseproof (waxed) paper and butter the paper. Sprinkle the mould with the breadcrumbs and then shake off the excess crumbs.

Spoon the mixture into the prepared mould. Place the mould in an ovenproof dish and fill the dish with very hot water to come two-thirds of the way up the side of the mould. Place in the preheated oven and cook for about 45 minutes, until a thin skewer or a toothpick inserted into the middle of the sformato comes out dry.

Allow to stand for 5 minutes. Loosen the sides of the sformato with a metal spatula and place a round dish over it. Turn the dish and the mould over, shake the mould lightly and lift it off. Remove the lining paper, if used, and serve, garnished with the fennel fronds if desired.

Porri alla Milanese

Leeks and Eggs with Butter and Parmesan

In Milan the "poor man's asparagus" (the leek) is served in the same way as real asparagus, and it is just as good. With the addition of some potatoes, this is a perfect all-in-one vegetarian meal.

SERVES 4

8–12 thin leeks
salt
4 tbsp freshly grated Parmesan cheese
75 g/2½ oz/5 tbsp unsalted
    (sweet) butter
6–8 free-range (farm-fresh) eggs
freshly ground black pepper

HEAT THE OVEN to 170°C/325°F/ Gas Mark 3. Trim and thoroughly wash the leeks, leaving some of the best green tops attached. Cook in plenty of boiling salted water for about 5–7 minutes, until they are cooked through but still firm and compact. Drain thoroughly and gently squeeze out all the water with your hands. Pat dry with kitchen paper (paper towels).

Butter an oval ovenproof dish and lay the leeks in it. Sprinkle with some of the Parmesan and dot with a little of the butter. Place the dish in the preheated oven while you cook the eggs.

Heat the remaining butter in a large frying pan (skillet) and break as many eggs into it as you wish – but no more than eight. Sprinkle the whites, but not the yolks, with salt. (Salt hardens the surface of egg yolks.) When the eggs are cooked, slide them gently over the leeks. Pour over all the butter from the pan, then sprinkle with the remaining grated Parmesan and a generous grinding of pepper.

Cipolline in Agrodolce

Onions in a Sweet-and-Sour Sauce

There are many versions of this dish. This one, made with butter and flavoured with tomato paste, is characteristic of Emilia.

SERVES 4

700 g/1½ lb small white (pearl) onions
50 g/2 oz/4 tbsp unsalted
    (sweet) butter
1 tbsp tomato paste diluted with 2 tbsp
    warm water
1 tbsp sugar
2 tbsp wine vinegar
salt and freshly ground black pepper

TO PEEL THE ONIONS, plunge them into boiling water for a few seconds. It will then be quite easy to remove the skins. Do not remove the roots or the onions will fall apart during cooking.

Put the peeled onions and the butter in a large sauté pan with the diluted tomato paste and about 300 ml/10 fl oz/1¼ cups warm water. Cook, uncovered, over a medium heat for about 30 minutes, stirring frequently but very gently.

Add the sugar, vinegar, salt and pepper. Mix well, turn the heat down to low and continue cooking for about 1 hour. Add more water if necessary during cooking. At the end of cooking, the onions should be a rich brown colour and soft but still whole.

Allow to cool, then serve the onions at room temperature.

Cavolfiore in Umido

Cauliflower with Tomato Sauce

A variety of vegetables, most commonly potatoes and green beans, are also cooked in this way. The cauliflower must be very tender, not crunchy.

SERVES 4

3 tbsp olive oil
2 tbsp chopped fresh flat-leaf parsley
I garlic clove, chopped
I tbsp tomato paste
I head of cauliflower, about 500 g/I lb, divided into florets
200 ml/7 fl oz/scant I cup meat or vegetable stock
salt and freshly ground black pepper

PUT THE OLIVE OIL, parsley and garlic in a heavy saucepan and fry gently for I minute. Add the tomato paste and cook, stirring, for a few seconds, then add the cauliflower florets.

Sauté for 5–I0 minutes, turning the florets over gently to coat them in the oil and tomato mixture. Pour in the stock, season with a little salt and pepper and then cook, covered, for I0–I5 minutes until the cauliflower is tender.

Remove the florets and reduce the juice until rich and full of flavour. Pour over the florets and serve.

Sedano alla Moda del '700

Celery with Cream

The eighteenth-century cookery writer Vincenzo Corrado wrote some of the best recipes for vegetables, of which this is one. ('700 means eighteenth century.) I have adapted it from his book Il Cuoco Galante.

SERVES 4

2 large heads of celery, about 500 g/I lb in total, trimmed and washed, with outer hard stalks and strings removed
100 ml/3½ fl oz/scant ½ cup milk
salt
150 ml/5 fl oz/⅔ cup double (heavy) cream
5 tbsp freshly grated Parmesan cheese
½ tsp grated nutmeg
freshly ground pepper, preferably white
2 large (extra-large) free-range (farm-fresh) egg yolks

HEAT THE OVEN to I90°C/375°F/ Gas Mark 5.

Cut the celery into 5–6 cm/2–2½ in pieces and put them in a sauté pan. Pour over the milk and add salt. Cover and cook slowly until the celery is tender but still al dente, about I0 minutes.

Butter an ovenproof dish and transfer the celery to it. Heat the cream to boiling point in a small saucepan. Draw off the heat and add the Parmesan, nutmeg, pepper, a pinch of salt and the egg yolks. Beat well and spoon over the celery. Cook in the preheated oven for I5 minutes.

Serve at once.

Asparagi alla Parmigiana

Asparagus with Melted Butter and Cheese

No pepper is added in this simple and delicious traditional recipe from Parma.

SERVES 4

900 g/2 lb asparagus
50 g/2 oz/½ cup freshly grated
  Parmesan cheese
75 g/2½ oz/5 tbsp unsalted
  (sweet) butter
salt

TRIM THE ASPARAGUS SPEARS as usual and wash under cold water. Tie them in bundles and steam or boil them until they are thoroughly cooked, not crunchy. Transfer the bundles to an oval flameproof dish, remove the string and sprinkle with some of the Parmesan. Keep warm in the oven. Preheat the grill (broiler).

Melt the butter and pour over the asparagus. Sprinkle with the rest of the Parmesan and a little salt. Place under the grill for a few minutes until a light golden crust forms.

Carciofi coi Piselli

Artichokes with Peas

There are more recipes for artichokes in Rome than anywhere else in Italy. This tasty dish is one of the best.

SERVES 4

4 tender young artichokes
lemon juice
2 shallots or 1 small onion
50 g/2 oz prosciutto
3 tbsp olive oil
15 g/½ oz/1 tbsp unsalted
  (sweet) butter
150 ml/5 fl oz/⅔ cup meat stock
300 g/10 oz/2½ cups shelled fresh
  garden peas, or frozen petits pois (baby peas), thawed
salt and freshly ground black pepper

PREPARE THE ARTICHOKES by discarding the tough outer leaves, cutting off about 2 cm/¾ in from the tops and removing the stalks. Plunge the artichokes into acidulated water (water to which 1 tbsp of wine vinegar has been added) to prevent them from turning black.

Finely chop the shallots or onion and prosciutto and put in a heavy saucepan or flameproof earthenware pot with the olive oil and butter. Sauté gently while you cut the artichokes in half (removing the furry chokes if necessary) and then into quarters. Dry them and add to the pan. Cook the artichokes over a medium heat for about 5 minutes, turning them over in the fat.

Pour the stock over the artichokes, add the fresh peas and season with a little salt and plenty of pepper. Cook until the artichokes and peas are tender – you might have to add a couple of tablespoons of water during cooking if the dish seems too dry. If you are using frozen peas, add them about halfway through cooking the artichokes.

Gattò di Patate

Potato Cake filled with Mozzarella and Prosciutto

You can serve this cake hot or warm as a first course, or as a second course after a soup. It is always a popular choice.

SERVES 4

850 g/1 lb 14 oz floury (mealy) potatoes, such as Idaho or Russet
100 ml/3½ fl oz/scant ½ cup milk
75 g/2½ oz/5 tbsp unsalted (sweet) butter
salt and freshly ground black pepper
a small grating of nutmeg
50 g/2 oz/⅔ cup freshly grated Parmesan cheese
2 large (extra-large) free-range (farm-fresh) eggs
1 large (extra-large) free-range (farm-fresh) egg yolk
175 g/6 oz Italian mozzarella cheese, cut into slices
75 g/2½ oz prosciutto, not too thinly sliced
75 g/2½ oz mortadella or salami

FOR THE PAN AND TOPPING
20 g/¾ oz/4 tbsp unsalted (sweet) butter
4 or 5 tbsp dried breadcrumbs

SCRUB THE POTATOES and cook them in their skins in plenty of boiling water until you can easily pierce through to their middles with the point of a small knife.

Meanwhile, heat the oven to 200°C/400°F/Gas Mark 6.

Drain the potatoes and peel them as soon as they are cool enough to handle. Pass them through a food mill or potato ricer to make a purée, letting it fall into the pan in which the potatoes were cooked.

Heat the milk and add to the purée with the butter. Beat well and then add ½ teaspoon salt, pepper, nutmeg and the Parmesan. Mix well, add the eggs and egg yolk and mix again very thoroughly.

Butter a 20 cm/8 in springform cake tin (pan) and cover the buttered surface with breadcrumbs. Spoon half the potato mixture into the pan, cover with the mozzarella, prosciutto and mortadella or salami, then spoon the rest of the purée over the top. Dot with the remaining butter and sprinkle very lightly with some breadcrumbs.

Bake in the preheated oven for 20–30 minutes, until the gattò is brown on top and hot in the middle (test by inserting a small knife into the middle and then bringing it to your lip – it should feel hot). If it is still a bit pale, flash it under the grill (broiler).

Allow the gattò to stand for 10 minutes before serving.

Cook's tip

Most of the minerals and vitamins in potatoes are located just beneath the skin, so cooking them before peeling them preserves more of these nutrients. It also enables you to peel them more thinly than you would be able to when they are raw.

Patate in Umido

Stewed Potatoes

These potatoes are an ideal accompaniment to grilled (broiled or barbecued) sausages and chops, sautéed chicken or an omelette. If you leave out the pancetta, they are also good for a vegetarian supper.

SERVES 4
700 g/1½ lb waxy potatoes
salt
25 g/1 oz/2 tbsp unsalted
  (sweet) butter
2 tbsp olive oil
50 g/2 oz/⅓ cup pancetta, cut
  into cubes
1 onion, finely chopped
1 garlic clove, finely chopped
1 tbsp fresh marjoram or ½ tbsp
  dried marjoram
1 tbsp tomato paste diluted with
  7 tbsp hot stock
freshly ground black pepper

PEEL THE POTATOES and cut them into 2.5 cm/1 in cubes. Boil in lightly salted water for 5 minutes.

While the potatoes are cooking, put the butter, olive oil and pancetta in a heavy saucepan and cook for 1 minute. Add the onion and garlic and sauté gently for 5 minutes. Drain the parboiled potatoes and add them to the pan, turning them over very gently but thoroughly to coat them in the fat. Cook for 3–4 minutes.

Add the marjoram and diluted tomato paste and season with some salt and pepper. Stir well and cook, covered, until the potatoes are tender, turning them over frequently. Use a fork to turn the potatoes over, as this is less likely to break them up than using a spoon. However, if some pieces do break off, you can console yourself with the thought that this dish is also known as patate alla contadina – potatoes cooked the peasant's way. Taste, adjust the seasoning and serve.

Spinaci alla Romana

Spinach Sautéed with Sultanas and Pine Nuts

A Roman way – and an excellent one – to cook spinach.

SERVES 4
1 kg/2 lb 2 oz fresh spinach
salt
25 g/1 oz/2 tbsp sultanas
  (golden raisins)
½ garlic clove, finely chopped
4 tbsp olive oil
25 g/1 oz/2 tbsp unsalted
  (sweet) butter
25 g/1 oz/¼ cup pine nuts, toasted
freshly ground black pepper

TRIM THE SPINACH and wash in a few changes of cold water until there is no sand at the bottom of the sink. Put it in a large saucepan with 1 teaspoon salt and cook until tender, about 3 minutes. Drain the spinach and leave until cool enough to handle, then squeeze out all the moisture with your hands.

While the spinach is cooking and cooling, soak the sultanas (golden raisins) in warm water for 10 minutes. Drain and dry.

Sauté the garlic in the olive oil and butter for 30 seconds and then add the spinach, sultanas and pine nuts. Fry gently for 5 minutes, turning frequently. Season well to taste.

Timballini di Spinaci

Spinach Timbales

Instead of individual, small timbales, you can use an 1 litre / 1¼ pint / 1 quart ring mould for this recipe and bake it for 40 minutes. You can spoon a little tomato sauce into the hole and serve the rest of the sauce in a sauceboat.

SERVES 8

600 g / 1¼ lb cooked spinach or frozen leaf spinach, thawed

25 g / 1 oz / 2 tbsp unsalted (sweet) butter

1 tbsp finely chopped onion

2 free-range (farm-fresh) eggs

100 g / 3½ oz / generous 1 cup freshly grated Parmesan cheese

200 ml / 7 fl oz / scant 1 cup double (heavy) cream

3 tbsp freshly squeezed orange juice, preferably from an organic or unwaxed fruit

grated nutmeg

salt and freshly ground black pepper

butter and dried breadcrumbs for the moulds

Tomato Sauce 2 (see page 176), to serve

HEAT THE OVEN to 190°C/375°F/ Gas Mark 5. Thoroughly squeeze the liquid out of the spinach. Heat the butter and the onion and sauté gently until the onion is soft. Add the spinach and sauté for about 5 minutes to let it take up the flavour. Transfer to a food processor and blend to a very coarse purée, or chop well by hand. Put the mixture in a bowl. In another bowl, lightly beat the eggs with the Parmesan. Add the cream and orange juice with nutmeg, salt and pepper to taste, then mix in the spinach very thoroughly.

Grease eight 150 ml / 5 fl oz / ⅔ cup moulds or ramekins very generously with butter. Check that the bottoms are really well covered with butter and then sprinkle with dried breadcrumbs. Shake off the excess crumbs and then fill the moulds with the spinach mixture.

Put the moulds in a roasting pan and pour enough boiling water into the pan to come two-thirds of the way up the sides of the moulds. Place in the preheated oven and bake until set, about 20 minutes.

When the timballini are ready, loosen them with a small spatula and turn the moulds over on to heated plates. Serve at once, spooning some tomato sauce around them.

Radicchio Rosso alla Trevisana

Grilled Red Radicchio

Although this dish is better made with the more flavourful radicchio rosso di Treviso, the round radicchio di Chioggia that is available everywhere is quite a good substitute.

SERVES 4

4 radicchio heads, about 1 kg / 2 lb 2 oz

6 tbsp extra virgin olive oil

salt and freshly ground black pepper

HEAT THE GRILL (BROILER). Discard the bruised outside leaves of the radicchio heads, then cut the heads into quarters and wash and dry them thoroughly. If small, leave the heads whole.

Place the radicchio in the grill (broiler) pan, spoon over the olive oil and season with salt and a generous amount of pepper. Cook under the preheated grill for 10 minutes, taking care to turn the pieces of radicchio so that they do not burn. Transfer to a dish and spoon over the juice from the grill pan. Serve hot or cold.

Funghi Trifolati

Sautéed Mushrooms with Parsley and Garlic

Fresh porcini are the best fungi to prepare in this way, but the dish is also good as I have described it here, with a mixture of both wild and cultivated mushrooms and a handful of dried porcini to boost the flavour.

SERVES 4

25 g/1 oz/½ cup dried porcini
500 g/1 lb fresh mushrooms, wild
    and cultivated
2 shallots
4 tbsp extra virgin olive oil
15 g/½ oz/1 tbsp unsalted
    (sweet) butter
1 garlic clove, finely chopped
4 tbsp chopped fresh flat-leaf parsley
salt and freshly ground black pepper

PUT THE DRIED PORCINI in a bowl, cover with hot water and leave for about 30 minutes.

Meanwhile, clean the fresh mushrooms. Unless they are very dirty, wipe them with damp kitchen paper (paper towels) rather than washing them. Cut them into thick slices.

Lift the porcini out of the water. Wash them under cold running water if you find some grit still attached. Cut them into small pieces.

Finely chop the shallots, put them in a large sauté pan and sauté with the olive oil and butter until soft. Add the garlic, half the parsley, a little salt and plenty of pepper. Cook, stirring constantly, for 1 minute and then add the porcini. Cook for 5 minutes or so and then throw in the fresh mushrooms and some parsley. Cook over a lively heat for about 10 minutes, turning the mushrooms over very quickly so that they do not stick to the bottom of the pan. There should be very little liquid left by the end of cooking.

Sprinkle with the rest of the parsley before serving.

Cappelle di Porcini alla Graticola

Grilled Cep Caps

You can also prepare large brown mushroom caps this way but, of course, they will never taste quite as good as porcini.

SERVES 4

700 g/1½ lb fresh porcini
salt
6 tbsp extra virgin olive oil
freshly ground black pepper
1 garlic clove, chopped
4 tbsp chopped fresh flat-leaf parsley

DETACH THE STALKS from the porcini caps and keep the stalks for a sauce or soup. Wipe the caps clean with kitchen paper (paper towels) and put them on a board. Sprinkle with salt and leave for half an hour or so to rid them of some of the liquid.

Gently pat the caps dry and put them, gill side down, on a grill (broiler) pan. Drizzle them with half the olive oil, season with pepper and cook under a hot grill for 2 minutes.

Turn the caps over gently. Sprinkle the garlic and parsley all over the gill side and drizzle with the remaining oil. Grill for about 2 minutes.

They are delicious served hot, warm or cold.

Parmigiana di Melanzane

Baked Aubergines

Many regions from north to south have claimed the origins of this popular dish. The ingredients are, however, so typically Neapolitan that Naples must be its birthplace. There are many versions, and nowadays some cooks prefer to grill (broil), rather than fry, the aubergines (eggplant). I find the result less good. Parmigiana di melanzane should be eaten warm, not hot and it is at its best at room temperature.

SERVES 4–5

1.5 kg/3¼ lb aubergines (eggplant)

salt

5 tbsp olive oil

400 g/14 oz canned plum
   tomatoes, drained

1 garlic clove, bruised

a few fresh basil leaves, torn

freshly ground black pepper

vegetable oil for frying

300 g/10 oz Italian mozzarella cheese

50 g/2 oz/⅔ cup freshly grated
   Parmesan cheese

2 hard-boiled, free-range (hard-cooked,
   farm-fresh) eggs, sliced

CUT THE AUBERGINES (EGGPLANT) lengthways into slices about 5 mm/ ¼ in thick. Sprinkle generously with salt, put in a colander and leave them to drain for 1 hour or longer.

Rinse the aubergine slices under cold water and pat thoroughly dry with kitchen paper (paper towels).

Heat the oven to 200°C/400°F/ Gas Mark 6.

Put 2 tablespoons of the olive oil in a small saucepan with the tomatoes, garlic and basil. Season and cook for 10 minutes.

Purée the mixture in a food processor or food mill to make a sauce.

Put enough vegetable oil into a deep frying pan (skillet) to come 2.5 cm/ 1 in up the side of the pan and heat until very hot. Test the temperature by immersing the corner of an aubergine slice in the oil – it should sizzle. Put in as many aubergine slices as will fit in a single layer. Fry until golden brown on both sides, then lift them out and drain on kitchen paper. Repeat until all the slices are fried.

Grease the bottom of a shallow oven-proof dish with 1 tablespoon of the remaining olive oil. Cover with a layer of aubergine slices, then spread over a little tomato sauce and some mozzarella slices. Sprinkle with a little salt, a lot of pepper and some Parmesan. Spread over a few slices of hard-boiled (hard-cooked) egg and cover with another layer of aubergines. Repeat the layers until all the ingredients are used up, finishing with a layer of aubergines and a sprinkling of Parmesan. Pour over the remaining olive oil and cook in the preheated oven for about 30 minutes.

Allow to stand for at least 10 minutes before serving.

Caponata

Aubergines in a Sweet-and-Sour Sauce

Caponata, a Sicilian creation, appears in many different versions throughout the island. The dish can be garnished with tiny boiled octopus, with a small lobster, with prawns or shrimp, or with bottarga* (the dried roe of the grey mullet or tuna fish) a speciality of Sicily and Sardinia.

SERVES 4

750 g/1 lb 10 oz aubergines (eggplant)
vegetable oil, for frying
salt
the inner stalks of 1 celery head, coarse
   strings removed
7 tbsp olive oil
1 onion, very finely sliced
225 g/8 oz/1⅓ cups canned plum
   tomatoes, drained and chopped
freshly ground black pepper
1 tbsp granulated sugar
6 tbsp white wine vinegar
1 tbsp grated continental bitter
   (bittersweet) chocolate (minimum
   70% cocoa solids)
4 tbsp capers, preferably in salt, rinsed
50 g/2 oz/⅓ cup large green olives,
   pitted and quartered
2 hard-boiled, free-range (hard-cooked,
   farm-fresh) eggs, to serve

CUT THE AUBERGINES (EGGPLANTS) into 1 cm/½ in cubes. Heat 2.5 cm/1 in vegetable oil in a frying pan (skillet). When the oil is hot, add a layer of aubergines and fry until golden brown on all sides. Drain on kitchen paper (paper towels), sprinkling each batch lightly with salt. Repeat until all the aubergines are cooked.

Wash and dry the celery and cut into pieces the same size as the aubergines. Fry in the oil in which the aubergines were cooked, until golden and crisp. Drain on kitchen paper.

Pour the olive oil into a clean frying pan and add the onion. Sauté gently for about 10 minutes until softened. Add the tomatoes and cook, stirring frequently, over a medium heat for about 15 minutes. Season with salt and pepper.

While the sauce is cooking, heat the sugar and vinegar in a small saucepan. Add the chocolate, capers and olives and simmer the mixture gently until the chocolate has melted. Add to the tomato sauce and cook for a further 5 minutes.

Mix the aubergines and celery into the tomato sauce. Stir and cook for 20 minutes, so that the flavours of the ingredients can blend together. Pour the caponata into a serving dish and allow to cool.

Before serving, cover the caponata with the hard-boiled (hard-cooked) eggs which have been passed through the smallest holes of a food mill, or pushed through a metal sieve (strainer).

Peperonata

Peppers and Onion Stewed in Tomato Sauce

To turn this classic peperonata into a more modern dish, simply spice it up with 1 or 2 dried red chillies, finely chopped, and a few drops of Tabasco sauce.

SERVES 4

1 kg/2 lb 2 oz mixed red, yellow and
    green (bell) peppers
300 g/10 oz mild onions, finely sliced
5 tbsp extra virgin olive oil
2 garlic cloves, sliced
salt
500 g/1 lb ripe fresh tomatoes, peeled
    and chopped
freshly ground black pepper
2 tbsp chopped fresh flat-leaf parsley

WASH AND DRY the (bell) peppers. Cut them into quarters and remove the cores, seeds and ribs. Cut each pepper quarter lengthways into strips.

Sauté the onion in the olive oil in a heavy pan over a medium heat until softened. Add the garlic, peppers and salt. Cook for a further 10 minutes, stirring frequently.

Mix in the tomatoes and bring to a simmer. Turn the heat down and cook for about 25 minutes, stirring occasionally. Add pepper to taste and sprinkle with parsley. Cook for a further minute or two before serving.

Peperoni Ripieni di Pasta

Peppers Stuffed with Pasta

This is an attractive-looking, modern antipasto*. You can use small ditalini or pennette instead of spaghetti. Whatever pasta you use, remember to drain it when it is still slightly undercooked.

SERVES 4

4 large yellow (bell) peppers
100 g/3½ oz/scant 1 cup black olives,
    pitted and chopped
2 tbsp chopped fresh flat-leaf parsley
1 garlic clove, chopped
1 salted anchovy, boned, rinsed and
    chopped, or 2 canned or bottled
    anchovy fillets drained and chopped
1 tbsp capers, preferably in salt, rinsed
½–1 tsp crushed dried chillies
salt and freshly ground black pepper
5 tbsp extra virgin olive oil
300 g/10 oz spaghetti
2 tbsp dried breadcrumbs

GRILL (BROIL) the (bell) peppers until the skin is charred all over. When they are cool enough to handle remove the skins with a small knife. Halve, remove the cores, seeds and ribs and wipe clean.

Combine the olives, parsley, garlic, anchovies, capers, chillies, salt and pepper and half the olive oil in a bowl.

Cook the spaghetti and drain when slightly undercooked. Transfer to the bowl with the chopped ingredients and mix thoroughly. Adjust the seasoning.

Heat the oven to 220°C/425°F/ Gas Mark 7.

Brush a roasting pan with oil. Place the pepper halves in the pan and fill with the pasta mixture. Sprinkle with crumbs and oil. Bake for 10 minutes until a light crust has formed.

Peperoni in Agrodolce
Sweet-and-Sour Fried Peppers

The original recipe for this dish comes from the excellent book I Sapori del Sud *by Mariano and Rita Pane. The vinegar here must be top quality, otherwise do not attempt this recipe.*

SERVES 3–4
4 large (bell) peppers (2 yellow, 2 red)
vegetable oil for frying
salt and freshly ground black pepper
3 tbsp best red wine vinegar
1½ tbsp soft brown sugar

WASH AND DRY the (bell) peppers and cut them in half. Remove the cores, stalks and seeds. Now cut each pepper half into strips about 3–4 cm/1¼–1½ in wide.

Pour enough vegetable oil into a wok or deep frying pan (skillet) to come 2–3 cm/¾–1¼ in up the side of the pan. (A wok is more economical than a frying pan, and I never recycle oil, so I use a little oil in the pan and fry in 3 batches.) Heat the oil over a high heat until it is very hot, but not smoking, then slide in as many strips of peppers as will fit loosely in the pan and fry them on both sides until tinged a light golden brown.

Transfer the peppers to a board or a plate lined with kitchen paper (paper towels). I use tongs for this job, because I find them the best tool to let the oil drip back into the pan. Pat the peppers dry with kitchen paper and then lay them on a serving dish. Sprinkle with salt and pepper.

Put the vinegar and sugar in a small pan and dissolve the sugar over a gentle heat. After that, pour the mixture over the peppers and let the dish cool completely. Serve at room temperature.

Best eaten at least 24 hours later.

Peperoni Arrostiti
Grilled Peppers

A classic antipasto* from Piedmont, now popular all over Italy. I like the (bell) peppers dressed with a little sauce, as described here.

SERVES 4
4 beautiful red or yellow (bell) peppers
3 salted anchovies, boned and rinsed,
    or 6 canned or bottled anchovy
    fillets, drained
3 garlic cloves
2 tbsp chopped fresh flat-leaf parsley
½–1 tsp crushed dried chillies
5 tbsp extra virgin olive oil

PLACE THE (BELL) PEPPERS on a thick wire mesh disc set over the flame of a burner, or on an open wood fire. Alternatively, put them under a hot grill (broiler). Turn the peppers until they are charred all over, including the tops and bottoms.

Let the peppers cool and then remove the skin with a small knife and a piece of kitchen paper (paper towels); it will come off very easily as long as the peppers have been well charred. Do not rinse the peppers: water will certainly remove the papery skin, but it will remove the taste as well. Cut the peppers in half, remove the stalks and seeds and then cut them lengthways into strips. Put them on a dish.

Pound the anchovies with the garlic, parsley and chillies in a mortar, or chop very finely. Put the olive oil and the anchovy mixture in a very heavy pan and heat very slowly, stirring and pounding the whole time until the mixture is mashed. Spoon over the peppers and leave to marinate for at least 4 hours. The longer you leave them – up to a week in the refrigerator – the better they will get.

Piselli al Prosciutto

Peas with Parma Ham

I have translated the recipe for this traditional Roman dish from Ada Boni's Cucina Regionale Italiana. *"The dish," she writes, "which can be a gastronomic experience, is a true Roman creation. Roman peas are deliciously sweet and tender."*

SERVES 4

1.5–1.6 kg/3¼–3½ lb fresh peas
50 g/2 oz/4 tbsp unsalted
   (sweet) butter
1 small onion, finely chopped
salt and freshly ground black pepper
150 ml/5 fl oz/⅔ cup hot stock or water
pinch of sugar (optional)
75–100 g/2½–3½ oz prosciutto,
   cut into strips
triangles of bread fried in butter,
   to serve (optional)

SHELL THE PEAS. Melt the butter and sauté the onion over low heat until it begins to change colour. Add the peas, season with salt and pepper, and moisten with stock. Cook over a brisk heat for 10 minutes if cooking fresh young peas, or until tender with older ones. No sugar is required with Roman peas – but some peas may require a little sugar to sweeten them. Two minutes before the peas are ready, add the prosciutto and stir gently.

The dish can be served accompanied with triangles of crisply fried bread, if you like.

Fagioli all'Uccelletto

Cannellini Beans with Garlic, Sage and Oil

The name of this Tuscan recipe, meaning "in the bird's style", has always been a cause of dissension. Artusi holds that they are called this because they are cooked with sage, the essential flavouring for small birds. Other writers maintain it is because these beans are the traditional accompaniment to birds.

SERVES 4

5 tbsp extra virgin olive oil
a sprig of fresh sage
2 garlic cloves, unpeeled and bruised
250 g/9 oz ripe fresh tomatoes, peeled
   and chopped, or canned chopped
   tomatoes, drained (see notes)
800 g/1¾ lb/generous 5½ cups cooked
   and drained cannellini beans
   (see notes)
salt and freshly ground black pepper

HEAT THE OLIVE OIL in a flameproof earthenware pot. Throw in the sage sprig and garlic cloves and sauté for 1 minute. Add the tomatoes and cook for 20–25 minutes until the oil separates from the tomato juices.

Mix in the cannellini beans. Season with salt and pepper and continue cooking for 15 minutes or so.

These beans are good served hot, warm or cold, but never chilled.

NOTES: The beans can be stewed with or without the tomatoes. Instead of the tomatoes and add a little water or stock.

To prepare the beans, soak 300 g/ 10 oz/1½ cups dried cannellini beans in cold water overnight, drain, rinse, then boil them in water with ½ onion, 2 or 3 fresh sage leaves, 1 bay leaf and 1 garlic clove for 1–1½ hours or until tender.

Polpettone di Fagiolini

Green Bean and Potato Pie

As with all other Ligurian vegetable pies, this one is equally good hot or cold, but it should not be eaten straight from the oven or chilled.

SERVES 6

20 g/¾ oz/⅓ cup dried porcini
250 g/9 oz floury (mealy) potatoes
500 g/1 lb/3 cups French
　(green) beans
2 free-range (farm-fresh) eggs
75 g/2½ oz/scant 1 cup freshly grated
　Parmesan cheese
salt and freshly ground black pepper
1 tsp chopped fresh marjoram
3 tbsp extra virgin olive oil
dried breadcrumbs

SOAK THE DRIED PORCINI in 250 ml/8 fl oz/1 cup hot water for about 30 minutes. Lift them out, rinse them if they are still gritty and pat dry with kitchen paper (paper towels). Chop coarsely and put in a large bowl.

Scrub the potatoes and cook them in their skins in plenty of boiling water. Drain and peel, then purée them in a food mill or potato ricer and then add to the porcini.

Heat the oven to 180°C/350°F/ Gas Mark 4.

Trim the beans, wash them and cook in boiling water until soft, not crunchy. This may take from 5–10 minutes, depending on how fresh or old the beans are. Drain, dry with kitchen paper and chop. Add to the porcini and potato mixture.

Lightly beat the eggs with the Parmesan, salt, pepper and marjoram. Fold into the porcini, potato and bean mixture. Mix in 1 tablespoon of the olive oil and taste and adjust seasoning.

Grease a 20 cm/8 in ovenproof dish with 1 tablespoon of the remaining olive oil and sprinkle some dried breadcrumbs all over the inside of the dish. Shake off the excess crumbs. Spoon the vegetable mixture into the dish, smooth the top with a spatula and then sprinkle lightly with breadcrumbs. Drizzle the rest of the oil evenly all over the top and bake in the preheated oven for about 1 hour, until a light golden brown crust has formed.

Remove the pie from the oven and allow to stand for at least 5 minutes before serving.

Fave col Guanciale

Broad Beans with Pancetta

Guanciale, traditional in this recipe, is the cured jowl of a pig — which is still sold in Italy — but if you cannot find it, use pancetta*, as here.

SERVES 4

200 g/7 oz pancetta, cut into cubes
1 small onion, chopped
4 tbsp extra virgin olive oil
2 kg/4½ lb fresh young broad (fava)
　beans (1 kg/2 lb 2 oz/6⅔ cups
　shelled)
about 150 ml/5 fl oz/⅔ cup vegetable
　stock or water
salt and freshly ground black pepper

FRY THE PANCETTA with the onion in the olive oil for a good 10 minutes, stirring very frequently.

Add the broad (fava) beans and coat them in the fat for 2–3 minutes and then add 100 ml/3½ fl oz/scant ½ cup stock or water.

Cover and cook over low heat until the beans are tender but still whole, about 10 minutes. You may need to add a little more stock during cooking.

Lenticchie in Umido

Stewed Lentils

Buy Umbrian or Puy lentils for this recipe, if you can find them. They stay whole during cooking, they cook in a shorter time than other green or brown lentils.

SERVES 4

2 tbsp olive oil

50 g/2 oz/⅓ cup unsmoked
   pancetta, diced

I small onion, very finely chopped

4 or 5 fresh sage leaves or ¼ tsp dried sage

350 g/12 oz/1½ cups small Italian or
   French lentils (see introduction)

salt and freshly ground black pepper

PUT THE OLIVE OIL and pancetta in a heavy saucepan and heat for 2 minutes. Add the onion and sage and sauté for 5 minutes.

Add the lentils and as soon as they are well coated with fat, pour over about I litre/1¾ pints/1 quart boiling water. Cover and simmer for about I hour, or until the lentils are soft but still whole, and nearly all the liquid has been absorbed. Add salt and pepper to taste.

DESSERTS, CAKES AND BISCUITS (COOKIES)

Pasta Frolla dell'Artusi
Artusi's Sweet Pastry Dough

I use this excellent recipe when I make sweet pastry dough. It is my adapted translation from Pellegrino Artusi's ever popular book La Scienza in Cucina e l'Arte di Mangiar Bene, *first published in 1891. If you wish to roll out the dough without going mad, use icing (confectioners') sugar; or pound caster (superfine) sugar very finely.*

MAKES ENOUGH FOR I PIE

100 g/3½ oz/¾ cup + 4 tbsp icing
   (confectioners') sugar, or 100 g/
   3½ oz/½ cup caster (superfine) sugar

250 g/9 oz/1⅔ cups Italian 00 flour

140 g/4½ oz/9 tbsp + I tsp
   unsalted (sweet) butter

I large (extra-large) free-range (farm-
   fresh) egg

I large (extra-large) free-range (farm-
   fresh) egg yolk

IF CONVENIENT, PREPARE this pastry a day in advance – this will make it crisper when cooked. Mix the sugar with the flour. If the butter is not malleable, then knead it with a wet hand on the work surface (countertop). Rub in the butter, then add the eggs and extra yolk, using a knife blade at the beginning in order to knead it as little as possible.

NOTE: To knead it more easily, mix the last crumbs with a drop of white wine or Marsala•, which makes the pastry more friable.

Pesche Ripiene alla Piemontese

Stuffed Peaches

A classic recipe from Piedmont, where often a few of the kernels from the cracked peach stones (pits) are ground and mixed into the filling to give it a stronger almond flavour.

SERVES 4

4 large freestone peaches, halved and
    stoned (pitted)
40 g/1½ oz/about 12 amaretti
15 g/½ oz/2 tbsp almonds in their
    skins, blanched and peeled (see note)
40 g/1½ oz/3 tbsp caster
    (superfine) sugar
2 tsp unsweetened cocoa powder
150 ml/5 fl oz/⅔ cup Moscato wine
25 g/1 oz/2 tbsp unsalted
    (sweet) butter

HEAT THE OVEN to 200°C/400°F/ Gas Mark 6. Scoop out some of the flesh from the peaches to make large cavities. Chop and mash the flesh and place in a bowl. Crumble the amaretti and add to the bowl. Coarsely grind the almonds, then add to the bowl with most of the sugar, the cocoa and just enough wine to moisten the mixture. Mix well to combine.

Place the peaches in a buttered ovenproof dish and fill them with the mixture. Dot each half with a knob (pat) of butter. Pour the rest of the wine around the peaches and sprinkle with the rest of the sugar. Bake in the preheated oven for 20–25 minutes. Serve at room temperature.

NOTE: To blanch and peel the almonds, drop them into a pan of boiling water. Boil the almonds for 30 seconds after the water has come back to the boil. Drain well, and remove the skins by gently squeezing the almonds between your fingers.

Arance Caramellate

Caramelized Oranges

The usual practice is to serve these oranges whole, but I find it easier to serve them sliced. It is a classic, and perfect, end to a meal.

SERVES 4

6 blood oranges, preferably organic
    or unwaxed
175 g/6 oz/¾ cup + 2 tbsp caster
    (superfine) sugar
2 tbsp lemon juice, preferably from an
    organic or unwaxed fruit
2–3 tbsp Grand Marnier

SCRUB 2 OF THE ORANGES very thoroughly and remove the peel with a swivel-action potato peeler, trying not to remove the pith. Cut this peel into thin batons. Plunge the batons of peel into boiling water and boil them for 6–7 minutes to rid them of their bitterness. Drain them and set aside.

Peel all the oranges completely (don't leave any pith on them), then slice them and put the slices in a bowl.

Put the sugar, lemon juice and 2 tablespoons water in a small saucepan. Heat gently until the sugar dissolves, then boil to make a pale caramel. Do not stir the syrup, just let it become golden. Then mix in 150 ml/ 5 fl oz/⅔ cup boiling water, then add the sliced peel. Cook for 5 minutes or so and add the Grand Marnier.

Pour the caramel over the oranges, leave until cold, then cover the bowl with clingfilm (plastic wrap) and chill until ready to serve.

Budino di Ricotta alla Romana

Ricotta Pudding

This is one of the many ricotta* dishes from central Italy. It is far better made with fresh ricotta, rather than the heat-treated kind sold in tubs.

SERVES 6–8

50 g/2 oz/⅓ cup sultanas (golden raisins)

4 tbsp white rum

250 g/9 oz/1 cup + 2 tbsp fresh ricotta

2 heaped (heaping) tbsp crème fraîche or double (heavy) cream

3 large (extra-large) free-range (farm-fresh) eggs, separated

200 g/7 oz/1 cup caster (superfine) sugar

3 tbsp flour, preferably Italian 00

½ tsp ground cinnamon

25 g/1 oz/2 tbsp mixed candied peel, chopped

grated rind of 1 lemon, preferably organic or unwaxed

1 tsp lemon juice

unsalted (sweet) butter and dried breadcrumbs for the pan

icing (confectioners') sugar, to decorate

PUT THE SULTANAS (golden raisins) in a bowl. Pour over the rum and leave until the sultanas are plump.

Heat the oven to 180°C/350°F/Gas Mark 4.

Pass the ricotta through a food mill or sieve (strainer) into a bowl to aerate it (a food processor cannot be used for this) and then mix in the crème fraîche lightly but thoroughly. Mix in the egg yolks one at a time, then the sugar, flour, cinnamon, candied peel, sultanas and rum and the lemon rind. Mix thoroughly.

Whisk the egg whites with the lemon juice until stiff and fold lightly into the mixture.

Grease a deep 20 cm/8 in cake pan or 1 litre/1¾ pint/1 quart metal mould very generously with butter and then cover the buttered surface with breadcrumbs. Shake off excess crumbs and spoon the mixture into the pan. Bake for 40–50 minutes, until a skewer inserted in the middle comes out dry. Unmould immediately on to a round dish and sprinkle lavishly with icing (confectioners') sugar before serving.

This pudding should be eaten warm or cool, but not straight from the oven or chilled.

Cook's tip

The bowl used for whisking egg whites must be free of all traces of grease or the whites will not foam. Plastic is not suitable as it is easily scratched so it is difficult to make sure that it is grease-free. Glass or metal, particularly copper, are ideal.

Tiramisù

Mascarpone Pudding

This relatively modern pudding from Treviso can be made in endless versions. Every cook can add his or her touch. This is my version. I like to sprinkle grated chocolate over, rather than cocoa powder, and to put pieces of chocolate inside too.

SERVES 6

150 ml/5 fl oz/⅔ cup strong
   espresso coffee
3 tbsp brandy
50 g/2 oz continental bitter
   (bittersweet) chocolate (minimum
   70% cocoa solids)
3 large (extra-large) free-range (farm-
   fresh) egg yolks
4 tbsp caster (superfine) sugar
250 g/9 oz/1 cup + 2 tbsp mascarpone
2 large (extra-large) free-range (farm-
   fresh) egg whites
about 18 Savoiardi biscuits (cookies)
chocolate-coated coffee beans,
   to decorate

NOTE: Savoiardi are similar to sponge fingers (ladyfingers), but less sweet and more absorbent. They can be bought in Italian food stores and good supermarkets.

MIX THE COFFEE and brandy together. Grate about a quarter of the chocolate and set aside. Cut the rest of the chocolate into small pieces.

Beat the egg yolks with the sugar until pale and forming soft peaks. Fold in the mascarpone a tablespoon at a time and then whisk very thoroughly until the mixture is very smooth and without any lumps.

Whisk the egg whites until stiff and fold gradually into the mascarpone and egg mixture. Mix well but lightly.

Dip the biscuits (cookies) one at a time into the coffee and brandy mixture. Turn them over once or twice until they become pale brown, but do not let them soak up too much liquid. Lay about 6 or 7 biscuits on an oval dish, to make a base. Spread over about a quarter of the mascarpone cream and scatter with some chocolate pieces. Dip more biscuits into the coffee mixture and make another layer. Spread with another quarter of the cream and scatter with chocolate pieces. Cover with the last layer of moistened biscuits and spread with half the remaining cream. I make the second layer one or two biscuits smaller than the base, and the top layer smaller still.

Cover the dessert with clingfilm (plastic wrap) and put it, with the reserved cream, in the refrigerator for about 6 hours.

Before serving, remove the clingfilm and spread the reserved cream over the top, smoothing it down neatly with a spatula. Sprinkle the grated chocolate all over the top and decorate with the coffee beans.

Torta di Riso

Rice Cake

A cake not a pudding, originally from Tuscany and Emilia-Romagna, torta di riso is always eaten cold and should be made one or two days in advance. The many recipes for it fall into two categories — with or without a pastry shell. My recipe here is without.

SERVES 6–8

750 ml/1¼ pints/3⅓ cups full-fat (whole) milk
175 g/6 oz/¾ cup + 2 tbsp caster (superfine) sugar
1 strip of lemon peel, yellow part only, preferably organic or unwaxed
a 2.5 cm/1 in piece of vanilla pod (bean), split in half
a 5 cm/2 in piece of cinnamon stick
a pinch of salt
150 g/5 oz/¾ cup Arborio rice
125 g/4½ oz/¾ cup almonds in their skins, blanched and peeled (see page 156)
50 g/2 oz/½ cup pine nuts
4 free-range (farm-fresh) eggs, separated
25 g/1 oz/2 tbsp candied orange, lemon and citron peels, chopped
the grated rind of ½ lemon, preferably organic or unwaxed
3 tbsp rum
unsalted (sweet) butter and dried breadcrumbs for the tin (pan)
icing (confectioners') sugar, to decorate

PUT THE MILK, 2 tbsp of the sugar, the lemon peel, vanilla, cinnamon and salt in a saucepan and bring to the boil.

Add the rice and stir well with a wooden spoon. Cook, uncovered, over very low heat for about 40 minutes, until the rice has absorbed the milk and is soft and creamy. Stir frequently during cooking. Set aside to cool.

While the rice is cooling, heat the oven to 180°C/350°F/Gas Mark 4.

Spread the almonds and pine nuts on a baking tray (cookie sheet) and toast them in the preheated oven for about 10 minutes, shaking the tray once or twice to prevent them burning. Remove them from the oven (leaving the oven on at the same temperature) and let them cool a little before chopping them coarsely by hand or in a food processor. Do not reduce them to powder.

Remove the lemon peel, vanilla pod (bean) and cinnamon stick from the rice and spoon the rice into a mixing bowl. Incorporate one egg yolk at a time into the rice, mixing well after each addition. Add the remaining caster (superfine) sugar, the toasted and chopped nuts, candied peel, grated lemon rind and rum to the rice and egg mixture and combine everything together thoroughly.

Whisk the egg whites stiffly and fold into the rice mixture.

Butter a 25 cm/10 in springform cake tin (pan), line the bottom with parchment paper and butter the paper. Sprinkle all over with breadcrumbs and shake off the excess.

Spoon the rice mixture into the prepared tin and bake in the oven for about 45 minutes, until the cake has shrunk away from the side of the tin. Insert a thin skewer or toothpick into the middle of the cake — it should come out moist, but clean.

Leave the cake to cool completely in the tin and then remove the clipped band and turn the cake over on to a dish. Remove the base of the pan and the lining paper, place a round serving dish over the cake and turn it over again. To decorate, sprinkle lavishly with sifted icing (confectioners') sugar before serving.

Torta di Mele all'Olio

Apple Cake made with Oil

Of all the apple cakes, this is my favourite. It is a moist cake, particularly good at the end of a meal with a spoonful of cream. It is also one of the few cakes made with oil instead of butter. Use a mild Ligurian extra virgin olive oil if you can but ordinary olive oil will do just as well.

SERVES 8–10
115 g/4 oz/¾ cup sultanas
    (golden raisins)
150 ml/5 fl oz/⅔ cup olive oil
200 g/7 oz/1 cup golden caster
    (superfine) sugar
2 large (extra-large) free-range (farm-
    fresh) eggs
350 g/12 oz/2⅓ cups Italian 00 flour
1 tsp ground cinnamon
1½ tsp bicarbonate of soda (baking soda)
½ tsp cream of tartar
½ tsp salt
500 g/1 lb dessert apples, peeled and
    diced small
grated rind of 1 lemon, preferably
    organic or unwaxed

SOAK THE SULTANAS (golden raisins) in warm water for 20 minutes.

Meanwhile, heat the oven to 180°C/350°F/Gas Mark 4. Pour the olive oil into a bowl, add the golden caster (superfine) sugar and beat until the sugar and oil become homogenized. Add the eggs one at a time and beat until the mixture has increased in volume and looks like thin mayonnaise.

Sift together the flour, cinnamon, bicarbonate of soda (baking soda), cream of tartar and salt. Add the dry ingredients gradually to the oil and sugar mixture, folding them in with a metal spoon. Mix thoroughly and then add the diced apples and lemon rind.

Drain and dry the sultanas and add to the mixture. Mix very thoroughly. The mixture will be quite stiff at this stage.

Butter and flour a 20 cm/8 in springform cake tine (pan). Spoon the mixture (batter) into the tin and bake for at least 1 hour, until a toothpick inserted in the middle of the cake comes out dry. Remove the cake from the pan and cool on a wire rack.

Zabaione

Zabaglione

This famous dessert was said to have been created in the seventeenth century as a result of a mistake by the chef of the Duke Carlo Emanuele the 1st of Savoy. He accidentally poured some fortified wine into an egg custard. It soon became the pudding served by the Piedmontese aristocracy.

SERVES 4
5 large (extra-large) free-range (farm-
    fresh) egg yolks
7 tbsp caster (superfine) sugar
a pinch of ground cinnamon
5 tbsp dry Marsala
5 tbsp white wine

PUT THE EGG YOLK with the sugar in the top of a double boiler or in a round, heavy-based saucepan and beat with a wire whisk or an electric mixer until pale yellow and creamy. Beat in the cinnamon.

Place the top of the double boiler or the saucepan over a pot of simmering (not boiling) water. Add the Marsala• and then the wine, whisking constantly. The zabaione will swell into a light frothy mass and then it will begin to form soft mounds. Remove from the heat immediately and spoon into wine glasses or small bowls. Zabaione should be served hot. If you want to serve it cold, pipe with whipped cream.

Torta di Mandorle

Almond Cake

Of the many Italian cakes, those made with almonds are among the most popular, and rightly so. This gluten-free cake is perfect served with soft fruit or fruit sorbets (sherbets).

SERVES 6–8

3 large (extra-large) free-range (farm-fresh) eggs, separated

150 g/5 oz/¾ cup caster (superfine) sugar

50 g/2 oz/6 tbsp potato flour

150 g/5 oz/1¼ cups ground almonds

2–3 drops pure almond essence (extract)

1½ oranges, preferably organic or unwaxed

icing (confectioners') sugar, to decorate

HEAT THE OVEN to 180°C/350°F/ Gas Mark 4. Beat the egg yolks with the caster (superfine) sugar until pale and thick. Add the potato flour and then the ground almonds. Incorporate well. Add the almond essence (extract), grated rind (peel) of one of the oranges and the strained juice of 1½ oranges. Whisk the egg whites until they form stiff peaks and fold gently into the mixture.

Grease a 20 cm/8 in springform cake tin (pan) generously with butter. Fill with the mixture (batter) and bake in the pre-heated oven for 45 minutes, or until a toothpick inserted in the middle of the cake comes out dry.

Leave to cool in the tin for 5 minutes and then unmould the cake. When cold sprinkle with icing (confectioners') sugar before serving.

Ricotta alla Mentuccia

Ricotta with Mint

The original idea for this simple and quick dessert comes from my late friend and mentor Massimo Alberini, arguably the greatest Italian food historian. The combination of ricotta* and mint may sound odd, but it works very well, as long as you use the mint sparingly. Mint varies in strength depending on the variety and the time of year. Taste it first and add just enough to give the ricotta a subtle minty flavour. Do not use the heat-treated ricotta in tubs, it is not good enough for this dish.

SERVES 4

300 g/10 oz/1¼ cups best fresh ricotta (see introduction)

3 tbsp demerara (raw) sugar

1½ tsp ground ginger

¾ tsp ground cinnamon

about 1 handful fresh mint leaves

PUT THE RICOTTA in the freezer for 15 minutes to harden it. Cut the ricotta into slices about 2 cm/¾ in thick. Lay them all on a dish and put the dish in the refrigerator for 2 hours.

Mix the sugar, ginger and cinnamon together and cover each ricotta slice with a layer of this mixture, patting it lightly into the ricotta. Put the dish back in the refrigerator and leave it for at least 3 hours – the sugar will have partly dissolved and penetrated the ricotta.

If the mint leaves are large, tear them a little. Scatter the mint over the ricotta and serve.

Torta Sbrisolona

Crumbly Almond and Polenta Cake

Mantova in southern Lombardy boasts many specialities, of which this is one. Its name comes from sbriciolare, meaning "to crumble", because the cake breaks into lots of delectable nutty crumbs when it is cut. In Mantova it is eaten with sweet wine.

SERVES 6

115 g/4 oz/1 cup almonds in their skins, blanched and peeled (see page 156)

115 g/4 oz/½ cup + 2 tbsp granulated or caster (superfine) sugar

150 g/5 oz/1 cup flour, preferably Italian 00 flour

115 g/4 oz/¾ cup coarse polenta flour (coarse cornmeal)

grated rind of 1 lemon, preferably organic or unwaxed

a pinch of salt

2 large (extra-large) free-range (farm-fresh) egg yolks

115 g/4 oz/1 stick unsalted (sweet) butter, at room temperature, plus extra for the tin (pan)

icing (confectioners') sugar, to decorate

HEAT THE OVEN to 200°C/400°F/ Gas Mark 6.

Spread the almonds on a baking tray (cookie sheet) and toast them in the preheated oven for 7 minutes or until golden brown.

Remove the almonds from the oven and turn the heat down to 180°C/ 350°F/Gas Mark 4.

Put the almonds in a food processor with 2 tablespoons of the sugar and process until they are reduced to a coarse powder.

In a bowl, mix the flour, polenta (cornmeal), the remaining sugar, the lemon rind, ground almonds and salt. Add the egg yolks and work with your hands until the mixture is crumbly. Add the butter to the crumbly mixture and work again to incorporate it thoroughly, until the dough sticks together in a crumbly mass.

Grease a shallow 20 cm/8 in round cake tin (pan) generously with butter and line the bottom with baking parchment. Spread the mixture (batter) evenly in the pan, pressing it down with your hands. Bake for 40–45 minutes, or until the cake is golden brown and a skewer inserted in the middle comes out dry.

Turn the cake out onto a wire rack and peel off the paper. Leave to cool. Before serving, sift icing (confectioners') sugar over the cake.

Torta di Pane

Bread Cake

One of the many bread cakes, made all over the peninsula to use up old bread. This version should be made one day in advance to allow all the flavours to blend. Use a Pugliese loaf or French country bread.

SERVES 8

5 slices country-type white bread (see introduction), 1 day old

75 g/2½ oz/5 tbsp unsalted (sweet) butter

200 ml/7 fl oz/scant 1 cup milk

300 ml/10 fl oz/1¼ cups single (light) cream

40 g/1½ oz/⅓ cup sultanas (golden raisins)

3 tbsp rum

115 g/4 oz/½ cup + 2 tbsp caster (superfine) sugar

grated rind (peel) of 1 lemon, preferably organic or unwaxed

a pinch of ground cloves

½ tsp ground cinnamon

a pinch of ground ginger

a pinch of powdered saffron

25 g/1 oz/2 tbsp candied peel, chopped

25 g/1 oz/¼ cup pine nuts

3 large (extra-large) free-range (farm-fresh) eggs, separated

icing (confectioners') sugar, to decorate

unsalted (sweet) butter for the tin (pan)

HEAT THE OVEN to 190°C/375°F/Gas Mark 5.

Remove the crust, chop the bread coarsely and toast it in the preheated oven for 5 minutes. Transfer to a bowl and add the unsalted (sweet) butter. Bring the milk and cream to the boil in a small pan and pour over the bread and butter. Beat well and leave to cool.

Meanwhile, soak the sultanas (golden raisins) in the rum for 15 minutes. When the bread and milk mixture is cool, beat it with a fork until soft and mushy. Add the sugar, sultanas and rum, the lemon rind, spices, candied peel and pine nuts and mix very well.

Lightly beat the egg yolks and add to the bread mixture. Whisk the egg whites until they form stiff peaks but are not dry, and fold them gently into the bread and fruit mixture.

Line a buttered deep 18 cm/7 in cake tin (pan) with baking parchment, butter the paper and spoon the mixture (batter) into the tin. Bake in the preheated oven for about 1 hour, then turn the oven down to 150°C/300°F/Gas Mark 2 and bake for a further 20 minutes, or until a skewer inserted into the middle of the cake comes out dry.

Allow to cool completely in the tin then unmould and peel off the paper. Put the cake on a pretty dish and sprinkle lavishly with icing (confectioners') sugar.

Panforte

Fruit and Spice Cake

This ancient cake is the Christmas cake of Siena. It is now, with panettone*, very popular abroad, and can be found around Christmas in supermarkets and Italian shops. Unlike panettone*, panforte is easy to make at home.

SERVES 8–10

225 g/8 oz/1½ cups almonds in their skins, blanched and peeled (see page 156)

100 g/3½ oz/scant 1 cup walnuts

50 g/2 oz/½ cup hazelnuts

100 g/3½ oz/generous ½ cup candied orange and lemon peels, cut into small pieces

1 tsp ground cinnamon

a generous pinch of ground coriander

a generous pinch of freshly ground white pepper

a generous pinch of freshly ground mace

100 g/3½ oz/⅔ cup flour, preferably Italian 00

175 ml/6 fl oz/¾ cup honey

75 g/2½ oz/5 tbsp granulated sugar

rice paper, to line the pan

TO SERVE

2 tbsp icing (confectioners') sugar

1 tsp ground cinnamon

WITH A MEZZALUNA, finely chop the almonds, walnuts and hazelnuts. You can use a food processor, but be careful not to reduce the mixture to a paste. It must be very grainy. Put these ingredients into a large bowl. Add the orange and lemon peels, half the cinnamon, the coriander, white pepper and the mace. Mix with a wooden spoon until all the ingredients are well blended and then add 75 g/2½ oz/ ½ cup of the flour.

Pour the honey into a lined copper or stainless steel saucepan and place it over a medium heat. Add the sugar and stir until the honey is completely melted and the sugar incorporated. Do not allow the mixture to boil.

Remove the saucepan from the heat and transfer the contents to the bowl with the nuts, candied peel and spices. Using a wooden spoon, mix well but gently, until all the ingredients are thoroughly blended.

Heat the oven to 180°C/350°F/ Gas Mark 4.

Line the bottom and sides of a loose-based 20 cm/8 in tart or quiche tin (pan) or shallow cake tin with rice paper. Spoon in the mixture (batter), smoothing it out in the tin. Mix the remaining flour and cinnamon together and sift this mixture evenly over the top. Place in the preheated oven and bake for about 35 minutes.

Remove from the oven and cool in the tin for about 10 minutes. Remove the sides and the bottom of the tin and transfer the panforte to a wire rack to cool completely – about 8 hours.

Wrap tightly in foil to store (see note).

Before serving, transfer the panforte to a serving plate and sprinkle over the icing (confectioners') sugar mixed with the cinnamon.

NOTE: Panforte is better eaten at least one week after it has been made. Wrapped in foil, it keeps well for 2–3 months.

Budino di Panettone

Panettone Pudding

There are now a number of recipes to use up any leftover panettone*, and this is one of them — for the original panettone pudding as it was made years ago in my home. Another simple way to serve any leftover panettone is to toast it and spread with mascarpone — this is an old favourite!

SERVES 4–6

200 g/7 oz/about 7 slices panettone

2 tbsp rum

I tbsp Marsala

300 ml/10 fl oz/1¼ cups single (light) cream

300 ml/10 fl oz/1¼ cups full-fat (whole) milk

¼ tsp ground cinnamon

grated rind of I small lemon, preferably organic or unwaxed

100 g/3½ oz/½ cup caster (superfine) sugar

3 large (extra-large) free-range (farm-fresh) eggs

unsalted (sweet) butter for the basin (bowl)

HEAT THE OVEN to 170°C/325°F/ Gas Mark 3.

Cut the panettone into thin slices. It doesn't matter if it crumbles. Sprinkle with the rum and Marsala•.

Bring the cream and milk slowly to the boil with the cinnamon, lemon rind and sugar. Turn off the heat and set aside to cool.

Beat the eggs very lightly together and then pour in the milk mixture, beating constantly.

Butter a pudding basin (heatproof bowl) or other dome-shaped mixing bowl or mould which will hold no more than I litre/1¾ pints/I quart. Put the panettone into it and pour over the custard mixture, then put the basin in a roasting pan and pour in enough boiling water to come about two-thirds of the way up the sides of the basin. Place in the preheated oven and bake for I–1¼ hours, until set.

Remove the basin from the roasting pan, allow the pudding to cool and then chill until you are ready to serve. Ease the pudding away from the inside of the basin with a spatula and then invert the basin onto a round dish. Tap the basin and give the dish a shake or two: the pudding should gently unmould.

NOTE: For a finishing touch you can decorate the pudding with a sprinkling of grated chocolate or chopped almonds and serve it with pouring cream. Or you can spread whipped cream over the top.

Certosino

Spiced Fruit Cake

Far lesser known than panettone*, the Christmas cake from Milan, certosino originates from Bologna. It is similar to an English fruit cake in that it contains dried fruits and nuts, but the result is a lighter cake, which becomes more mellow and rich on keeping.

SERVES

75 g/2½ oz/½ cup seedless raisins

2 tbsp sweet Marsala or sherry

7 tbsp tsp clear honey

150 g/5 oz/¾ cup caster (superfine) sugar

40 g/1½ oz/3 tbsp unsalted (sweet) butter

1 tbsp aniseed

1 tsp ground cinnamon

350 g/12 oz/3 cups flour, preferably Italian 00

150 g/5 oz/⅔ cup apple purée, slightly sweetened

150 g/5 oz/1¼ cup blanched almonds, coarsely chopped

50 g/2 oz/½ cup pine nuts

75 g/2½ oz continental bitter (bittersweet) chocolate (minimum 70% cocoa solids), chopped

140 g/4½ oz/scant 1 cup candied orange and lemon peels, chopped

½ tbsp bicarbonate of soda (baking soda)

a little butter for the pan

4 tbsp apricot jam

crystallized fruits and blanched almonds, to decorate

SOAK THE RAISINS in the Marsala• or sherry for 20 minutes.

Meanwhile, heat the oven to 180°C/350°F/Gas Mark 4.

Gently heat the honey, sugar, butter and 3 tablespoons water until the sugar has dissolved. Add the aniseed and cinnamon. Slowly pour this over the flour, mixing thoroughly.

Mix in the soaked raisins, apple purée, blanched almonds, pine nuts, chopped chocolate and chopped candied peel. Dissolve the bicarbonate of soda (baking soda) in a little warm water and add to the cake mixture (batter). Mix the ingredients very gently, but thoroughly.

Butter a shallow, loose-bottomed 25 cm/10 in cake tin (pan) and spoon the mixture into it. Bake in the preheated oven for about 1¼–1½ hours and then turn out onto a wire rack.

Gently warm the apricot jam and brush it over the top of the cooled cake. Stud with crystallized fruit and/or blanched almonds. Brush more jam over the fruit and leave to dry, then wrap in clingfilm (plastic wrap). Store the cake in an airtight container for 2–3 months.

Baci di Dama

Lady's Kisses

The name of these biscuits (cookies) comes from their shape, which suggests the pouting of a lady's lips. Originally from Piedmont, they are now made commercially everywhere, but they are far better homemade.

MAKES ABOUT 35–40

140 g/4½ oz/1 cup best almonds in their skins, blanched and peeled (see page 156)

140 g/4½ oz/¾ cup caster (superfine) sugar

140 g/4½ oz/9 tbsp + 1 tsp unsalted (sweet) butter, at room temperature

1 tsp pure vanilla essence (extract)

a pinch of salt

140 g/4½ oz/scant 1 cup flour, preferably Italian 00

a little butter for the baking tray (cookie sheet)

175 g/6 oz continental bitter (bittersweet) chocolate (minimum 70% cocoa solids)

HEAT THE OVEN to 180°C/350°F/ Gas Mark 4.

Put the almonds on a baking tray (cookie sheet) and dry in the preheated oven for 5 minutes.

Put the almonds in a food processor. Add 1–2 tablespoons of the sugar and process to a powder. Add the butter, vanilla and salt. Process again until the mixture is creamy. Transfer to a bowl.

Sift the flour, letting it fall over the almond mixture. Fold in the flour very thoroughly with your hands.

Break off pieces of the dough the size of cherries, and roll them into balls. Place them on a buttered baking tray, about 2 cm/¾ in apart. Bake for 15 minutes, or until golden brown

Leave to cool on the tray and then transfer to a wire rack.

Melt the chocolate in a bain-marie or microwave oven. When the biscuits are cold, spread a little melted chocolate over the flat side of one biscuit, then stick the flat side of another to it. Repeat with the remainder.

Cantucci di Prato
Almond Biscuits

Many cooks have their own way of making cantucci. I find this recipe a good one, the cantucci having just the right crunchy hardness.

MAKES ABOUT 40
a pinch of saffron threads
½ tsp fennel seeds
100 g/3½ oz/scant 1 cup almonds in their skins
40 g/1½ oz/⅓ cup pine nuts
250 g/9 oz/⅔ cup flour, preferably Italian 00
225 g/8 oz/1 cup + 2 tbps caster (superfine) sugar
a generous ¼ tsp baking powder
2 large (extra-large) free-range (farm-fresh) eggs
unsalted (sweet) butter for the baking tray (cookie sheet)

HEAT THE OVEN to 200°C/400°F/Gas Mark 6.

Reduce the saffron threads to a powder by crushing them between 2 metal spoons, pour on 1 teaspoon boiling water and leave to infuse. Bruise the fennel seeds. Put the almonds and pine nuts on a baking tray (cookie sheet) and lightly toast in the preheated oven for 5 minutes. Remove from the oven (leaving the oven on at the same temperature), then chop each almond in half if large.

Sift the flour, sugar and baking powder onto the work surface (countertop). Stir to mix and make a well in the middle. Beat the eggs lightly with the fennel and saffron. Pour the mixture into the well and work it gradually into the dry ingredients, adding the nuts at the end. When everything is well mixed,

divide in half and pat and roll each piece with well floured hands to a 30 cm/12 in long sausage. Lay them, well apart, on a greased and floured baking tray and bake in the oven for 15–18 minutes.

Take the tray out of the oven and reduce the temperature to 150°C/300°F/Gas Mark 2 or a little less. Cool the cantucci for 10 minutes, then cut them diagonally into 1 cm/½ in slices. Lay the slices side by side on the tray and return to the oven for the second baking – for 45 minutes or so, until well dried out.

Cool completely before storing in an airtight container. They will keep for up to 2–3 months.

Panna Cotta
Cooked Cream Dessert

This is the classic recipe for the now famous Piedmontese dessert. Originally served by itself it is now usually accompanied by fresh or stewed fruit.

SERVES 6
10 g/⅓ oz gelatine leaves
450 ml/15 fl oz/scant 2 cups double (heavy) cream
150 ml/5 fl oz/⅔ cup full fat (whole) milk
150 g/5 oz/¾ cup caster (superfine) sugar
1 tsp pure vanilla extract
4 tbsp white rum

PUT THE GELATINE LEAVES in a bowl and fill with cold water. As soon as the leaves soften, bend them so that they are all submerged in water. Leave for 10 minutes or so. Squeeze the leaves out and put them in a small saucepan with 4 tbsp of water. Dissolve over the low heat while stirring constantly.

Mix the cream and milk together in a saucepan, add the sugar and bring very slowly to the simmer, stirring constantly. Stir in the rum and the vanilla extract and then draw the pan off the heat and stir in the dissolved gelatine. Mix very thoroughly.

Brush six 150 ml/5 fl oz/⅔ cup ramekins with a little flavourless oil and pour the panna cotta into them. Leave to cool, cover with clingfilm (plastic wrap) and chill for at least 4 hours.

To unmould, place the ramekins in a sink of hot water for about 20 seconds. Run a palette knife (spatula) around the sides of the ramekins, place a dessert plate over the top and turn the plate and the ramekin upside down. Give a knock or two to the bottom of the ramekin and then lift it away. It should come away easily, but if the dessert is still stuck, put the ramekin back into the hot water for a few seconds. Put the unmoulded desserts back into the fridge.

Zaleti

Polenta Biscuits

Venetian biscuits (cookies) with a name that means "the little yellow ones" in the local dialect. They are mostly eaten dunked into a glass of sweet wine.

MAKES ABOUT 40
75 g/2½ oz/½ cup sultanas
    (golden raisins)
4 tbsp dark rum
250 g/9 oz/⅔ cup finely ground
    polenta flour (fine cornmeal), or
    instant polenta
100 g/3½ oz/⅔ cup flour
1 tsp baking powder
a pinch of salt

115 g/4 oz/½ cup + 2 tbsp caster
    (superfine) sugar
150–200 ml/5–7 fl oz/⅔ cup–scant
    1 cup full-fat (whole) milk
100 g/3½ oz/7 tbsp unsalted
    (sweet) butter
grated rind of ½ lemon, preferably
    organic or unwaxed
unsalted (sweet) butter for the baking
    trays (cookie sheets)
icing (confectioners') sugar, to decorate

HEAT THE OVEN to 180°C/350°F/ Gas Mark 4.

Put the sultanas (golden raisins) in a bowl and add the rum. Let them plump up for at least 30 minutes. Drain and pat them dry.

Sift the two flours together into a bowl with the baking powder and salt, and then add the sugar. Now take a small saucepan and pour into it 150 ml/5 fl oz/⅔ cup of the milk. Add the butter and heat gently until it melts. Pour this liquid into the bowl gradually with one hand, while you work it into the flour mixture with the other. Mix in the sultanas and the lemon rind. The dough should be soft, but not so soft that you cannot shape the zaleti. If necessary, gradually add a little more milk.

Prepare 2 baking trays (cookie sheets) by buttering them generously. With floured hands, pinch off a piece of the mixture about the size of a walnut and then roll it between the palms of your hands to a shape similar to a tiny baguette. Place on the baking trays, leaving space between the zaleti as they will spread out during baking. Bake for about 10–12 minutes, but check after 8 minutes. They are ready when they turn deep yellow and are browning at the edges. Let them cool on a wire rack and serve sprinkled with icing (confectioners') sugar.

Torrone Molle

Soft Nougat

This is one of the traditional desserts of northern Italian families, as indeed Elizabeth David wrote in her Italian Food. *This recipe is from my family home. It must be made with the best unsweetened cocoa powder.*

SERVES 8

115 g/4 oz/1 cup almonds in their skins,
  blanched and peeled (see page 156)
200 g/7 oz/¾ stick unsalted
  (sweet) butter
200 g/7 oz/1 cup granulated sugar
115 g/4 oz/1 cup best unsweetened
  cocoa powder
1 large (extra-large) free-range (farm-
  fresh) egg
1 large (extra-large) free-range (farm-
  fresh) egg yolk
115 g/4 oz plain biscuits (cookies), such
  as digestives (graham crackers)
2 tbsp dark rum
candied flowers and blanched or sugared
  almonds, to decorate

HEAT THE OVEN to 180°C/350°F/ Gas Mark 4. Spread the almonds on a baking tray (cookie sheet) and bake for 7–10 minutes until they turn golden. Grind coarsely in a food processor.

Cream together the butter and sugar until light and fluffy. Add the cocoa a spoonful at a time and beat hard until it has been completely incorporated. This takes a little time and some beating; it can be done in a food processor. Now mix in the ground almonds.

Lightly beat together the whole egg and the egg yolk and add to the butter mixture, stirring until well blended.

Crush the biscuits (cookies) with a rolling pin and add to the mixture (dough) with the rum. Mix thoroughly.

Line an 8½ x 4½ in loaft tin (bread pan) with clingfilm (plastic wrap) and spoon in the mixture. Press it down well to eliminate any air pockets and level the top with a spatula. Cover with clingfilm and chill for at least 4 hours.

Decorate with candied flowers, such as violets or rose petals, and blanched or sugared almonds.

Sorbetto di Limone al Basilico

Lemon Sorbet with Basil

The flavour of the lemon in this sorbet (sherbet) is immediately apparent, but the basil blends in so perfectly that is seems only to add a rather mysterious taste to the sorbet. It is extremely attractive to look at in its pale green coat speckled with the dark green spots of the basil. Use young, sweet basil, not an old pungent plant. An ice cream machine is essential for making a good sorbet.

SERVES 4–6

8 lemons, preferably organic or unwaxed
2 oranges, preferably organic or unwaxed
350 g/12 oz/1¾ cups caster
  (superfine) sugar
2 dozen large fresh basil leaves, chopped

SCRUB AND DRY THE FRUIT. Remove the rind, without chipping into the white pith, and put it in a saucepan. Add 600 ml/1 pint/2½ cups water and the sugar. Bring slowly to the boil and simmer until the sugar has dissolved. Turn up the heat to medium and boil rapidly for 3–4 minutes. Take off the heat and allow to cool completely.

Remove the rind from the cold syrup. Squeeze the lemons and oranges, strain the juice and add to the syrup with the basil leaves. Freeze the mixture in an ice cream machine.

Gelato di Crema

Custard Ice Cream

Italian ice cream is usually made with an egg custard, rather than with just cream. The custard makes the ice cream lighter and easier to blend with other flavourings, such as fruit juices. This is the standard recipe which serves as a base.

SERVES 8–10

I litre/I¾ pints/I quart full-fat
    (whole) milk, or 500 ml/18 fl oz/
    2¼ cups milk and 500 ml/
    18 fl oz/2¼ cups double
    (heavy) cream
300 g/10 oz/2¼ cups caster
    (superfine) sugar
the rind of I lemon, preferably organic
    or unwaxed
8 large (extra-large) free-range (farm-
    fresh) egg yolks

PUT THE MILK or milk and cream in a saucepan with half the sugar and the lemon rind and bring to the boil. Take off the heat and leave to cool.

Whisk the egg yolks with the rest of the sugar until frothy and pale. Remove the lemon rind from the milk and slowly add the milk mixture to the egg mixture, beating constantly with a wooden spoon. Heat the mixture either over a very low heat or in a bain-marie, until the custard is thick and coats the back of a spoon. Immediately put the pan in a bowl of cold water and allow to cool. Stir constantly for the first minute, and then you can leave it.

Pour the mixture into the bowl of an ice cream machine and follow the manufacturer's instructions.

If you don't have an ice cream machine, transfer the cream to a bowl, preferably a metal one, and place it in the freezer. Stir it with a fork every 20 minutes during the first 2 hours to prevent crystals from forming. After that you can leave it alone. It will be ready in about 6 hours.

Granita al Caffè

Coffee Granita

The Italian ice concoction par excellence. It is usually eaten sitting at a pavement café, just watching the world go by.

SERVES 4

600 ml/I pint/2½ cups freshly brewed
    espresso coffee
about 4 tbsp caster (superfine) sugar
120 ml/4 fl oz/½ cup whipping cream
I tbsp icing (confectioners') sugar

HEAT THE COFFEE, add 4 tablespoons sugar and stir to dissolve. Taste, and add a little more sugar if you prefer. Pour the coffee into a freezing tray and leave until cold, then freeze until solid.

Plunge the bottom of the tray into a bowl of hot water for a few seconds, break up the coffee ice into chunks and then process in a food processor until it forms small crystals. Return to the tray and place back in the freezer.

Before serving, place 4 long-stemmed wine glasses in the refrigerator to chill. Whip the cream and then stir in the icing (confectioners') sugar to sweeten slightly.

Remove the granita from the freezer. If too solid, process again for a few seconds just before serving. Spoon the granita into the chilled glasses and top with the whipped cream.

Cassata di Sulmona

Praline and Chocolate Cassata

Less famous than Sicilian cassata*, but arguably better, this is from Sulmona, Abruzzo.

SERVES 6–8

FOR THE PRALINE

2 tbsp granulated sugar

1 tsp lemon juice

25 g/1 oz/2 tbsp almonds in their skins, blanched and peeled (see page 156)

FOR THE CASSATA

75 g/2½ oz/⅓ cup caster (superfine) sugar

100 g/3½ oz/7 tbsp unsalted (sweet) butter, at room temperature

3 large (extra-large) free-range (farm-fresh) egg yolks

25 g/1 oz/¼ cup hazelnuts, toasted, skinned and coarsely chopped

25 g/1 oz continental bitter (bittersweet) chocolate (minimum 70% cocoa solids), broken into tiny pieces

1 tbsp unsweetened cocoa powder, sifted

350 g/12 oz Madeira cake (or pound cake), sliced

5 tbsp Centerbe, Strega or Chartreuse or any other herb liqueur

icing (confectioners') sugar, chocolate flakes and ground hazelnuts, to decorate

PREPARE THE PRALINE. Heat the sugar and the lemon juice with ½ tablespoon water over low heat until the sugar has completely dissoved. Turn up the heat and boil rapidly until the syrup is golden, not brown. Remove from the heat and mix in the almonds.

Pour onto a greased baking tray (cookie sheet) and leave to set.

When the praline is cold, put it between 2 sheets of greaseproof (waxed) paper and crush with a rolling pin. Alternatively, crush the praline in a food processor. Set aside.

Prepare the cassata. Put the sugar and butter in a bowl and beat until creamy, then beat in the egg yolks one at a time. Now divide the mixture (batter) into 3 parts and add the praline to one part, the hazelnuts and chocolate to the second and the cocoa to the third.

Line a 900 g/2 lb 9 x 5 in loaf tin (bread pan) with clingfilm (plastic wrap). Cover the bottom with a layer of cake, moisten with liqueur and spread over the praline mixture. Cover with more cake moistened with liqueur and spread over the chocolate and hazelnut mixture. Now place the last layer of cake, moisten with liqueur and spread over the cocoa mixture. Cover with clingfilm (plastic wrap) and place in the refrigerator for at least 6 hours or overnight. To serve, unmould the cassata on to a dish and decorate with icing (confectioners') sugar, chocolate flakes and/or ground hazelnuts.

Spumone al Caffè

Coffee-flavoured Iced Mousse

Sometimes this spumone* can separate, with the coffee cream falling to the bottom. This happens when the coffee is not very well pulverized, but it tastes just as good.

SERVES 6–8

2 tbsp very finely ground espresso coffee

4 large (extra-large) free-range (farm-fresh) egg yolks

115 g/4 oz/½ cup + 2 tbsp caster
(superfine) sugar

¼ tsp ground cinnamon

300 ml/10 fl oz/1¼ cups single (light)
cream

2 tbsp brandy

300 ml/10 fl oz/1¼ cups double
(heavy) cream

2 large (extra-large) free-range (farm-
fresh) egg whites

CRUSH THE COFFEE with a rolling pin until it is powdery. Put the egg yolks, sugar, coffee and cinnamon in a bowl and beat until well blended.

Heat a saucepan half full of water and when little bubbles form on the bottom of the pan, place the bowl containing the egg mixture over it. Beat until the mixture has reached the consistency of a mousse and has more than doubled its volume. Keep the water just below simmering point.

Heat the single (light) cream. When it is warm, pour it over the egg mixture, beating constantly. Take off the heat, add the brandy and continue beating until the mixture is cool.

Whip the double (heavy) cream until soft peaks form and then fold it gently into the egg mixture. Whisk the two egg whites until hard peaks form and then fold them gently into the mixture.

Line a 1 litre/1¾ pint/1 quart loaf tin (bread pan) with clingfilm (plastic wrap) and spoon in the mixture. Freeze for at least 3 hours until firm, stirring the mixture twice during this time.

SAUCES

Bagnet Ross

This tomato sauce is traditionally served in Piedmont with their gran bollito misto*. So too is Salsa Verde (see page 180).

ENOUGH FOR 6 SERVINGS

700 g/1½ lb/4 cups ripe fresh
tomatoes, peeled and chopped

1 small onion, thickly sliced

1 carrot, cut into rounds

1 celery stalk, cut into pieces

2 fresh sage leaves, torn into pieces

1 small sprig of fresh rosemary

2 garlic cloves, peeled

a small bunch of fresh flat-leaf parsley

a few fresh marjoram leaves

1 small dried red chilli

1 tsp tomato paste

salt

7 tbsp wine vinegar

1 tbsp sugar

a pinch of ground cinnamon

PUT THE FIRST 12 ingredients in a saucepan and cook over a very low heat for 30 minutes. Purée through a food mill or sieve (strainer) and return to the pan.

Mix in the vinegar, sugar and cinnamon and cook for about 20 minutes, until the sauce is thick. Taste and adjust seasoning.

Serve warm or cold.

Ragù alla Bolognese

Bolognese Meat Sauce

Every Italian cook must have their own favourite version of Ragù alla Bolognese. This is mine, which is my mother's recipe and maybe my grandmother's as well.

ENOUGH FOR 4 HELPINGS OF PASTA

50 g/2 oz/4 tbsp unsalted
(sweet) butter
2 tbsp olive oil
100 g/3½ oz unsmoked pancetta,
finely chopped
I small onion, very finely chopped
I small carrot, very finely chopped
I small celery stalk, very finely chopped
350 g/12 oz lean braising steak,
minced (ground)
5 tbsp red wine
I½ tbsp tomato paste
100 ml/3½ fl oz/scant ½ cup hot
meat stock
salt and freshly ground black pepper
5 tbsp milk

HEAT THE BUTTER and olive oil with the pancetta in a deep, heavy-based saucepan. Fry gently for 2–3 minutes and then add the chopped vegetables. Fry over a medium heat until the vegetables are soft, stirring frequently.

Add the minced (ground) beef and cook until it has lost its raw colour. Pour over the red wine and boil briskly for 2–3 minutes until the liquid has almost evaporated.

Dilute the tomato paste with the stock and add to the pan. Season to taste and cook for 5 minutes, stirring frequently. Bring the milk to simmering point in a separate small pan.

Pour the milk over the meat (the liquid should just come level with it) and stir thoroughly. Cook, uncovered, over the lowest heat for at least 2 hours. The ragù should not boil, but just break a few bubbles on the surface. Stir it occasionally during cooking and taste and adjust the seasoning at the end.

Ragù alla Napoletana

Neapolitan Meat Sauce

This ragù* is far lesser known than the Bolognese ragù. The sauce is used to dress the pasta (ziti* or maccheroni*) as a first course and then the meat is eaten as the second course, served with a little of the sauce. You should cook this dish at the lowest possible simmer for a very long time. In Naples it is put on the heat first thing in the morning, to be ready for lunch.

ENOUGH FOR 6–8 HELPINGS OF PASTA

I kg/2 lb 2 oz lean boneless pork or
beef rump, in one piece
50 g/2 oz/⅓ cup unsmoked
pancetta, diced
6 tbsp olive oil
salt
½ garlic clove, finely chopped
3 onions, finely chopped
2 carrots, finely chopped
I celery stalk, finely chopped
150 ml/5 fl oz/⅔ cup red wine
I tbsp tomato paste
300 ml/10 fl oz/I¼ cups hot
meat stock
300 ml/10 fl oz/I¼ cups tomato sauce
(see note)

WIPE THE MEAT with a damp cloth and make a few incisions in it with the point of a sharp knife. Push a small piece of pancetta into each incision. Heat the olive oil in a flameproof casserole, add the meat and brown it all over. Sprinkle with salt and add the chopped garlic, onions, carrots and celery. Cook slowly until the vegetables are lightly browned. Add the red wine, bring to the boil and let it evaporate.

Dilute the tomato paste with 150 ml/5 fl oz/⅔ cup of the hot stock. Add to the pan and simmer for 30 minutes.

Add the remaining hot stock and the tomato sauce and continue cooking over a very low heat for at least 3 hours. Turn the meat over every half an hour or so and add a few tablespoons of hot water whenever necessary.

NOTE: For the tomato sauce, I use my recipe for Tomato Sauce I on page 176.

Salsa di Noci

Walnut Sauce

This is the traditional Ligurian dressing for pansotti (the local ravioli) and other local pasta. Be careful when you buy shelled walnuts. They must be eaten soon after they are harvested or they will be rancid and ruin any dish you add them to. I buy a lot in their shells at Christmas, shell them and freeze them.

ENOUGH FOR 4 HELPINGS OF PASTA
25 g/1 oz/1 slice good-quality country-style bread
100 g/3½ oz/scant 1 cup shelled walnuts, preferably blanched and skinned
1 garlic clove, peeled
3 tbsp freshly grated Parmesan cheese
3 tbsp extra virgin olive oil
4 tbsp double (heavy) cream
salt

SOAK THE BREAD in warm water for about 5 minutes and then squeeze dry. Pound the bread, walnuts and garlic in a mortar (or blend in a food processor) and then add the Parmesan cheese, olive oil, cream and salt to taste.

Salsa allo Speck

Speck Sauce

Of all pasta shapes, I find tagliatelle* goes best with a dressing of this creamy, smoky sauce.

ENOUGH FOR 4 HELPINGS OF PASTA
40 g/1½ oz/3 tbsp unsalted (sweet) butter
200 g/7 oz speck, in julienne strips
100 ml/3½ fl oz/scant ½ cup dry white wine
a generous pinch of powdered saffron or ½ tsp saffron threads
freshly ground black pepper
150 ml/5 fl oz/⅔ cup double (heavy) cream
salt
6 tbsp freshly grated Parmesan cheese, plus extra for the table

HEAT THE BUTTER in a frying pan (skillet) large enough to hold the pasta later. When the butter is sizzling, add the speck and sauté for 5 minutes. Add the white wine and cook briskly until the wine has nearly all evaporated.

If you are using saffron threads, place them in a metal spoon and crush them with a teaspoon. Add the saffron and pepper to the frying pan and stir well. After about 1 minute, pour in the cream and bring to the boil, stirring constantly. Taste and add salt if necessary. Take off the heat.

When the pasta is cooked, drain it and transfer to the pan of sauce. Stir-fry for 1 minute and then add the cheese. Serve at once, handing round extra Parmesan in a bowl.

Sugo di Pomodoro 1

Tomato Sauce 1

A rich tomato sauce, which I like to use for dressing a bowl of penne*, or to add to some polpette*, leftover boiled meat or poached chicken.

MAKES 600 ML / 1 PINT /
2½ CUPS
800 g / 1¾ lb canned plum tomatoes
2 tsp tomato paste
1 tsp sugar
2 onions, chopped
2 celery stalks, chopped
5 tbsp extra virgin olive oil
salt and freshly ground black pepper
4 tbsp good red wine
25 g / 1 oz / 2 tbsp unsalted
    (sweet) butter

CHOP THE TOMATOES COARSELY. This is best done by cutting the tomatoes with kitchen scissors while they are still in the can, having first poured a little of the liquid into a heavy-based saucepan.

Put the chopped tomatoes in the saucepan, together with the rest of their liquid, the tomato paste, sugar, onions, celery, olive oil, salt and pepper. Cook for 15 minutes or so, and then purée the sauce through a food mill, or in a food processor or blender.

Return the sauce to the pan and add the wine. Continue cooking for a further 40 minutes. Mix in the butter, taste and check seasoning.

Sugo di Pomodoro 2

Tomato Sauce 2

A quicker and more southern-tasting tomato sauce than Tomato Sauce 1, and suitable for spaghetti*, gnocchi* or fish.

MAKES 600 ML / 1 PINT /
2½ CUPS
1 garlic clove
1 small onion or 2 shallots
1 tsp sugar
about 2 tbsp vegetable stock
750 g / 1 lb 10 oz ripe fresh tomatoes,
    peeled and chopped
salt and freshly ground black pepper
6 fresh basil leaves, torn
4 tbsp extra virgin olive oil

CHOP THE GARLIC and onion together. Put them in a pan with the sugar and 2 tablespoons stock. Cover and cook very gently, stirring every now and again, for 15–20 minutes, adding a little more stock or water if necessary. At the end of cooking the onion will be soft and the stock will have more or less evaporated.

Add the tomatoes to the pan, season with salt and pepper and cook for no longer than 5 minutes after the sauce has come to the boil. Add the basil and the oil, just before serving.

La Peverada

Pepper Sauce

A sauce that accompanies roast birds in Treviso and bollito misto* in Verona, now made with variations all over northern Italy. The essential ingredient is pepper in abundance. It is an ancient sauce that can be traced back to the fifteenth century, when pepper was a symbol of wealth.

ENOUGH FOR 4 SERVINGS

50 g/2 oz/4 tbsp unsalted
  (sweet) butter
2 garlic cloves, bruised
1 clove
3 tbsp dried breadcrumbs
300 ml/10 fl oz/1¼ cups meat stock
salt and freshly ground black pepper

PUT THE BUTTER, garlic and clove in a small saucepan, or preferably an earthenware pot. Sauté these ingredients until the garlic begins to colour, then remove and discard the garlic and clove.

Add the breadcrumbs and sauté for a minute or two, turning them over and over in the fat. Add about 100 ml/3½ fl oz/scant ½ cup of the stock and cook over a low heat until the sauce thickens. Add salt to taste and a very generous quantity of pepper.

Continue cooking for about 30 minutes, stirring frequently and adding a little more stock whenever necessary. The sauce should have a thickish consistency. Taste and adjust the seasonings.

Amatriciana

Pancetta and Tomato Sauce

Amaticiana is traditionally made with pork jowl and flavoured with a lot of dried chilli and grated pecorino* to counterbalance the fattiness of the meat. The grated pecorino is handed round separately. Bucatini* is the traditional pasta to serve with it; spaghetti* is a good alternative.

ENOUGH FOR 4–6 HELPINGS OF PASTA

450 ml/16 fl oz/2 cups tomato sauce
  (see method)
350 g/12 oz unsmoked pancetta, cut
  into 1 cm/½ in cubes
1 tbsp olive oil
1 small onion, very finely chopped
salt
1 garlic clove, finely chopped
1 dried chilli, finely chopped
120 ml/4 fl oz/½ cup dry white wine
freshly ground black pepper

FIRST PREPARE the tomato sauce, either your favourite or using the recipe for Tomato Sauce 1 on page 176.

Put the unsmoked pancetta cubes and olive oil in a non-stick frying pan (skillet) and sauté until the fat has run out of the pancetta and it is crisp and brown. Stir frequently.

Add the onion and a pinch of salt to the frying pan and sauté for about 10 minutes. Mix in the garlic and chilli. Cook for a further minute or so and then add the white wine. Turn up the heat and let the wine bubble away to reduce it by half.

Pour in the tomato sauce and simmer for 15 minutes for the flavours to combine. Taste and season.

Salsa ai Quattro Formaggi

Four cheeses sauce

Farfalle is the best shape of pasta for this sauce, but penne, more easily available, are good too.

ENOUGH FOR 3/4 HELPINGS OF PASTA

50 g/2 oz/4 tbsp (sweet) unsalted butter
50 g/2 oz taleggio, cut into small pieces
50 g/2 oz Gorgonzola, cut into small pieces
cayenne pepper
50 g/2 oz/⅔ cup freshly grated Parmesan cheese
100 g/3½ oz/scant 1 cup coarsely grated mozzarella

MELT HALF THE BUTTER in a small saucepan on a very low heat and then add the taleggio and the Gorgonzola and season with two or three pinches of cayenne. Let them melt slowly, while you stir occasionally.

Cook the pasta in plenty of boiling salted water, drain and turn it into a lightly buttered shallow ovenproof dish smeared with butter. Toss with the remaining butter and half the parmesan and then spoon it in the cheese sauce and mix thoroughly.

Sprinkle the mozzarella and the remaining Parmesan over the top and bake in a hot oven, 200°C/400°F/Gas Mark 6 for about 5 minutes until the mozzarella is just melted.

Fonduta

Piedmontese Fondue

The main ingredient of this great Piedmontese sauce is one of the great Piedmontese cheeses — fontina*. During the autumn (fall), it is showered with slivers of white truffle. The sauce isn't too difficult to make, but you must take care when incorporating the egg yolks with the milk. The end result should be velvety smooth, without lumps or threads, and for this a double boiler is essential. Fonduta is an unassuming sauce of perfectly balanced, complex flavours. It is served with polenta*, boiled rice or crostini*.

SERVES 4

300 g/10 oz Italian fontina cheese
about 250 ml/9 fl oz/generous 1 cup milk
50 g/2 oz/4 tbsp unsalted (sweet) butter
1 tbsp flour
3 large (extra-large) free-range (farm-fresh) egg yolks
freshly ground pepper

ABOUT 6 HOURS before you want to serve the fonduta, dice the cheese. Put it in a bowl and add milk to just cover it.

When you are ready to serve, put the butter in the top half of a double boiler, add the fontina cheese with the milk and set over simmering water.

Beat the flour into the egg yolks and add this mixture to the cheese and milk mixture, beating constantly with a wire whisk. Continue cooking and stirring until the fontina has melted and the sauce is very smooth, creamy and shiny. Add freshly ground black pepper; salt is not necessary because the cheese provides the salt. Do not cook any longer or the cheese will become stringy.

Serve in a heated bowl, which should be earthenware so that the fonduta remains hot and fluid.

Salsa di Funghi Secchi

Dried Porcini Sauce

This sauce is for spaghetti* or tagliatelle*, but I also love it with a bowl of boiled rice.

ENOUGH FOR 3 HELPINGS
OF PASTA

25 g/1 oz/½ cup dried porcini
50 g/2 oz/4 tbsp unsalted
   (sweet) butter
2 tbsp chopped fresh flat-leaf parsley
I garlic clove, very finely chopped
salt and freshly ground black pepper
150 ml/5 fl oz/⅔ cup single
   (light) cream

SOAK THE PORCINI in 250 ml/8 fl oz/1 cup hot water for about 30 minutes. Lift out the porcini and strain the soaking liquid through a sieve (strainer) lined with muslin or cheesecloth. Rinse the porcini to remove any grit, then pat dry and chop coarsely.

In a frying pan (skillet) large enough to hold the pasta later, heat the butter with the parsley and garlic. Add the porcini and cook for about 10 minutes, adding 3–4 tablespoons of the soaking liquid. Sprinkle with salt and freshly ground black pepper.

When the pasta is nearly done, add the cream to the sauce and stir well. Transfer the drained pasta to the frying pan and stir-fry for 1 minute, adding more of the porcini liquid if the dish seems too dry.

Besciamella

Béchamel Sauce

This is the Italian version of the classic French sauce béchamel.

MAKES ABOUT 450 ML/
16 FL OZ/2 CUPS

600 ml/1 pint/2½ cups hot milk
50 g/2 oz/4 tbsp unsalted
   (sweet) butter
40 g/1½ oz/4 tbsp flour, preferably
   Italian 00
salt and freshly ground pepper,
   preferably white
grated nutmeg

HEAT THE MILK until it just begins to bubble at the edge. Meanwhile, melt the butter in a heavy-bottomed saucepan over a low heat. Blend in the flour, stirring vigorously. Remove the pan from the heat and add the hot milk, just a few tablespoons at a time. You must let the flour mixture absorb each addition of milk thoroughly before adding any more.

When all the milk has been absorbed, return the pan to the heat. Season with salt, pepper and nutmeg and bring to the boil. Cook over the gentlest heat for at least 10 minutes, stirring constantly.

Salsa di Mascarpone

Mascarpone Sauce

Ada Boni(is probably the most famous Italian cookery writer of the twentieth century. In her recipe for fettuccine con mascarpone, from the book Il Talismano della Felicità, *she mixes in some prosciutto*, thus achieving a perfect result. This is my adapted translation of that recipe. Nowadays, even in Italy, pasta is dressed with more sauce than it used to be. This sauce can be used to dress fettuccine* or tagliatelle*.*

ENOUGH FOR 3 HELPINGS OF PASTA

150 g/5 oz/⅔ cup mascarpone
2 organic egg yolks
100 g/3½ oz prosciutto, cut into very thin strips
50 g/2 oz/⅔ cup freshly grated Parmesan cheese

COOK THE CHOSEN PASTA according to the packet instructions and drain, reserving the cooking water. In a heated serving bowl, dilute the mascarpone with a few tablespoons of the pasta water. Add the egg yolks, beating them in gently but thoroughly with a wooden spoon. Then mix in the prosciutto and half the grated cheese.

Transfer the drained pasta to the bowl and toss very thoroughly. Serve, handing round the rest of the cheese.

Salsa Verde

Green Sauce

I make a different Salsa Verde acccording to what it has to accompany and what is best in my herb border — rocket (arugula) or mint, dill or tarragon. Sometimes I substitute a boiled potato for the bread, or I may omit the hard-boiled (hard-cooked) egg and add a raw egg yolk instead. This recipe is a guide, beyond which you can discover your own favourite version, always bearing in mind that a Salsa Verde made with lemon is best for fish, while for meat — such as a bollito* — it should contain vinegar. Garlic is not used in the old, traditional Salsa Verde, but I like a little bit of it.

ENOUGH FOR 4–6 SERVINGS

25 g/1 oz/½ cup fresh white breadcrumbs
1–1½ tsp red wine vinegar
1 small garlic clove
40 g/1½ oz/¾ cup fresh flat-leaf parsley
2 tbsp capers, preferably in salt, rinsed
6 cornichons (sweet dill pickles): if unobtainable, use an extra 1 tbsp capers
1 hard-boiled, free-range (hard-cooked, farm-fresh) egg
3 salted anchovies, boned and rinsed, or 6 canned or bottled anchovy fillets, drained
2 tsp Dijon mustard
150 ml/5 fl oz/⅔ cup extra virgin olive oil
freshly ground black pepper
salt

PUT THE BREADCRUMBS in a bowl and pour the wine vinegar over them. Set aside.

Peel and halve the garlic, then remove the hard central core if necessary. The core is pungent rather than sweet.

Put the parsley, capers, cornichons (sweet dill pickles), hard-boiled (hard-cooked) egg, anchovies and garlic together on a board and chop them very finely. Put this mixture into another bowl.

Squeeze out the vinegar from the bread and add the bread to the mixture in the bowl, working it in with a fork. Add the mustard and then gradually add the olive oil, beating the whole time. Season with a good deal of pepper. Taste and add salt if necessary: the anchovies and capers may have given enough salt to the sauce. You might like to add a little more vinegar — it depends on the strength of your vinegar and how you like the sauce.

NOTE: The sauce can be made in a food processor, but do not overprocess it — the parsley should be in small pieces.

Pesto

This is the traditional pesto recipe of the western Riviera. You can vary it, but whatever you do, use a mild extra virgin olive oil, not a peppery one.

ENOUGH FOR 4 HELPINGS OF PASTA OR GNOCCHI

20 g/¾ oz/2½ tbsp pine nuts
50 g/2 oz/2 cups fresh basil leaves
1 garlic clove, peeled
a pinch of coarse sea salt
4 tbsp freshly grated Parmesan cheese
2 tbsp freshly grated mature (sharp)
   pecorino cheese
120 ml/4 fl oz/½ cup extra virgin olive
   oil, preferably Ligurian

HEAT THE OVEN to 180°C/350°F/ Gas Mark 4. Spread the pine nuts on a baking tray (cookie) and put the tray in the preheated oven for 3–4 minutes. I do this because toasting releases the aroma of the nuts.

Put the basil leaves, garlic, pine nuts and salt in a mortar. Grind with the pestle, crushing all the ingredients against the side of the mortar until the mixture has become a paste. You can use a food processor or a blender.

Mix in the grated cheeses and pour over the oil very gradually, beating with a wooden spoon.

Salsa di Fiori di Zucchine

Courgette Flower Sauce

I have dressed a bowl of pasta with this delicate sauce, as they do in Umbria, but I have also used it to accompany a roast fish. It is just perfect. If you grow courgettes (zucchini) or other summer squash, you will have your own flowers to use. If not, you can sometimes buy bunches of them during the season in specialist Italian food stores.

ENOUGH FOR 4 HELPINGS OF PASTA

12 courgette (zucchini) flowers
I small onion, chopped
a bunch of fresh flat-leaf parsley
4 tbsp extra virgin olive oil
a pinch of powdered saffron or a few
   saffron threads
4 tbsp hot light vegetable stock
salt and freshly ground black pepper
I large (extra large) free-range (farm-
   fresh) egg yolk
75 g/2½ oz/scant I cup freshly grated
   pecorino cheese

WASH THE FLOWERS and chop them very finely with the onion and parsley.

Put half the olive oil and the chopped ingredients in a saucepan and sauté very gently for about 10 minutes, stirring frequently.

Meanwhile, dissolve the saffron in the hot stock and add to the pan. Stir well and cook for a further 10 minutes. Add salt and pepper to taste and then purée the sauce through a food mill, or in a food processor or blender.

When your pasta is cooked, drain, turn into a heated bowl and toss at once with the rest of the oil. Mix the egg yolk and the pecorino into the sauce, pour the sauce over the pasta and serve.

Focaccia

Focaccia* is a pre-prandial snack eaten at home, in the street, in bars, anywhere. This recipe makes a soft focaccia — the traditional Focaccia alla Genovese from Genoa. It can be topped with rosemary or thin slices of sweet onion before cooking if desired.

SERVES 6–8

500 g/I lb/4 cups Italian 00 flour
I½ tsp easy-blend (rapid-rise)
   dried yeast
I heaped (heaping) tsp fine salt
6 tbsp extra virgin olive oil
I tsp coarse sea salt

PUT THE FLOUR IN a bowl. Sprinkle with the yeast and the fine salt and pour in about 4 tablespoons of the oil. Mix very quickly and then gradually add about 300–350 ml/10–12 floz/ I–I½ cups warm water (it should be blood temperature). Mix again quickly and stop as soon as the dough is blended.

Put the dough on a floured work surface (countertop) and knead quickly for I–2 minutes. The dough will be very damp. Wash the bowl and dry it, then oil it lightly. Return the dough to the bowl, cover the bowl with a folded damp cloth, and leave in a warm corner of the kitchen (out of any draughts) until doubled in size (about 2 hours).

Knock back (punch down) the dough. Turn it over and over, punching it all over. Put it into a 30 x 23 cm/12 x 9 in baking tray (cookie sheet) and press out in an even layer. Cover and leave in a warm place for a further hour or so, until the dough is soft and light.

Heat the oven to 240°C/475°F/ Gas Mark 9.

Mix the remaining oil with a little water. Dip your fingers into this mixture and press down into the focaccia to form hollows. Sprinkle with the coarse sea salt and brush the top with with the remaining oil and water mixture. (The water mixed with the oil keeps the surface soft during baking.)

Turn the heat down to 220°C/ 425°F/ Gas Mark 7 (you only need a blast of heat at first) and bake the focaccia until golden brown, about 20 minutes. Turn the focaccia out on to a wire rack and eat while still warm. Otherwise, reheat it in a low oven before eating.

Focaccia Dolce

Sweet Focaccia

Also called Fugazza di Casa (its Venetian name), this is a characteristic sweet bread from northern Italy. The focaccia* here is my adaptation of a recipe from the late Giuseppe Maffioli, an authority on the cooking of Veneto. It looks like a cake but it has a similar texture to country bread, with a most delicate and well-balanced flavour of rum and lemon. I find it a perfect accompaniment to stewed fruit, a glass of vino di Cipro or vin santo•, a cup of tea, coffee or even hot chocolate. A great all-rounder.

SERVES 6
300 g/10 oz/2 cups strong white flour (bread flour)
1 tsp bicarbonate of soda (baking soda)
2 tsp cream of tartar
a pinch of salt
3 large (extra-large) free-range (farm-fresh) eggs, separated
100 g/3½ oz/½ cup caster (superfine) sugar
100 g/3½ oz/7 tbsp unsalted (sweet) butter, at room temperature

4 tbsp milk, preferably full-fat (whole)
2 tbsp dark rum
the grated rind of 1 lemon, preferably organic or unwaxed
unsalted (sweet) butter and dried breadcrumbs for the tin (pan)

FOR THE TOPPING
1 free-range (farm-fresh) egg yolk mixed with 2 tbsp milk
sugar crystals

HEAT THE OVEN to 180°C/350°F/ Gas Mark 4.

Sift the flour, bicarbonate of soda (baking soda), cream of tartar and salt into a large bowl. Add the egg yolks, incorporating them one by one, and then the sugar, unsalted (sweet) butter, milk, rum and lemon rind. Mix very hard and thoroughly.

Whisk the egg whites until stiff and then fold them into the mixture (batter) with a light upward movement.

Grease an 18 cm/7 in cake tin (pan) generously with butter and sprinkle the entire inside with dried breadcrumbs. Shake off the excess crumbs and spoon the mixture into the tin. Brush the top with the egg yolk and milk mixture and then scatter some sugar crystals all over.

Place the pan in the preheated oven and bake for about 1 hour. When a toothpick inserted in the middle of the cake comes out dry, unmould the cake and leave it to cool on a wire rack.

Pugliese

Bread Loaf from Puglia

This round loaf is quite easy to make at home. Use fruity olive oil if you can buy it, preferably from Puglia.

MAKES I LOAF

15 g/½ oz fresh yeast (I cake
   compressed fresh yeast)
½ tsp sugar
750 g/I lb 10 oz/5 cups unbleached
   strong flour (bread flour)
I tbsp salt
4 tbsp extra virgin olive oil

CRUMBLE THE YEAST in a bowl, add the sugar and 2 tablespoons lukewarm water. Stir to a smooth cream and then let it stand for 5 minutes or so, until it starts to become frothy.

Put the flour on the work surface (countertop) and mix in the salt. Make a well in the middle and pour the yeast into the well. Pour in the oil and gradually add 400 ml/14 fl oz/ I¾ cups warm water (it should be blood temperature). Mix together by gathering the flour from the wall of the well as you pour the water. Add more water if necessary – you might need a further 50 ml/2 fl oz/¼ cup or so. The dough should be soft but not sticky.

Knead for 10 minutes and then shape the dough into a ball and put it into a bowl that has been lightly greased with oil. Turn the ball over so that it becomes lightly coated with oil. Cover with a damp kitchen cloth (dish towel) and leave to rise in a warm place (out of any draughts) until it has doubled its size, about 3–3½ hours.

Transfer the dough to a baking tray (cookie sheet). Pull out the sides of the dough and then push them under the dough. Turn it around through 90° and do the same again. Go on doing this several times – it is equivalent to knocking back (punching down). Cover with a damp cloth and let it rise for a further I–I½ hours.

Heat the oven to 230°C/450°F/ Gas Mark 8.

Lightly dust the loaf with flour and put the tray in the preheated oven. Bake for 10 minutes, then turn the heat down to 200°C/ 400°F/Gas Mark 6 and bake for a further 30 minutes, until the loaf sounds hollow when tapped underneath. Cool on a wire rack.

Cook's tip

Fresh yeast is obtainable from bakery suppliers and some health-food stores, but is not generally found in supermarkets. Store it in a plastic container in the refrigerator for up to 10 days. Punch a few holes in the lid of the container to prevent condensation. Fresh yeast should be a light beige colour and smooth in texture. If it turns grey and crumbly, it is no longer fit for use. If you are unable to obtain fresh yeast, you can substitute dried yeast, but as it is more concentrated you should halve the quantity. Dried yeast will also take longer to activate at the beginning of the recipe. After adding it to the lukewarm water and sugar, leave to stand for about 10 minutes until frothy, then stir to a creamy consistency and proceed according to the recipe.

Grissini

Bread Sticks

This is the traditional recipe for Grissini di Torino. If you add 2 tablespoons extra virgin olive oil, they become Grissini all'Olio.

15 g/½ oz fresh yeast (1 cake compressed fresh yeast)
475 g/15 oz/3⅓ cups unbleached strong flour (bread flour)
1 tsp salt
fine semolina, for dusting
olive oil for the tray

CRUMBLE THE YEAST and dissolve it in 4 tablespoons warm water. Then add enough of the flour to make a soft dough. Cover and leave to rise in a warm corner of the kitchen for about 30 minutes. This is the biga, or first starter.

Make a well with the rest of the flour on the work surface (countertop), add the salt and about 275–325 ml/9–11 fl oz/1–1½ cups warm water. (It should be blood temperature. If the water is too hot, it will kill the yeast when you add the biga.) Knead to a soft dough and then knead in the biga. Add enough water for the dough to come easily together. Knead for about 10 minutes until the dough is soft, velvety and elastic. Some tiny bubbles should appear on the surface.

Transfer the dough to a greased bowl, turn it around to coat with the oil and cover with a damp cloth. Leave to rise in a warm place (out of any draughts) until doubled in size, about 1 hour.

Sprinkle the dough and your hands with semolina. Break off a large piece of dough and roll it out between your hands or against the work surface into a long thin roll. Cut the roll into breadstick lengths (about 30 cm/12 in) and place the little sticks on a baking tray (cookie sheet) lightly greased with oil. Repeat with the remaining dough, then cover the grissini with a damp cloth (dish towel) and leave to rest in a warm place for 1 hour.

Heat the oven to 220°C/425°F/Gas Mark 7.

When the oven is hot, bake the grissini for 5 minutes, checking after 3 minutes to see if they are already done. Cool on a wire rack.

Pasta per Pizza

Pizza Dough

**MAKES TWO 30 CM/12 IN
PIZZAS**
**500 g/1 lb/3¼ cups strong white flour
(bread flour)**
**1 sachet easy-blend dried yeast
(1 envelope rapid-rise dried yeast)**
1 tbsp salt
1 tbsp olive oil
a little extra virgin olive oil, to finish

PLACE THE FLOUR on the work surface (countertop), mix in the yeast and salt and make a well in the middle. (In Italy we start all bread doughs on the work surface, not in a bowl.)

Pour the oil into the well, together with 200 ml/7 fl oz/scant 1 cup warm water (it should be blood temperature). Begin to knead by gathering flour from the side of the inner wall of the well. Gradually incorporate more warm water (350–400 ml/12–14 fl oz/ 1¼–1¾ cups in all) until a thick dough is formed.

Knead for about 10 minutes and then divide the dough into 2 balls. Place them in 2 greased bowls covered with a damp cloth (dish towel) and then leave them to rise in a warm place (out of any draughts) until they have doubled in size, about 2½ hours.

Lightly flour 2 square baking trays (cookie sheets) and heat the oven to its hottest temperature.

Knock back (punch down) one of the balls and stretch and roll it into a round about 5 mm/¼ in thick. The dough will want to spring back at first, but eventually it will do what you want. Leave a thicker rim all around the round. Do the same with the other ball

of dough. Place the rounds on the prepared baking trays and add your chosen topping (see The Classic Toppings on the following pages).

Bake in the preheated oven for about 12–15 minutes, until the pizzas are brown at the edges. When still hot, brush the rims with a little extra virgin olive oil.

Cook's tip
Easy-blend (rapid rise) dried yeast is widely available from supermarkets and does exactly what it says on the label. It comes in small sachets (envelopes) – about 6–7 g – and should be stored in a cool dry place. Keep an eye on the "use-by" date. Stale yeast is unusable and will not foam sufficiently to enable to the dough to rise.

THE CLASSIC PIZZA TOPPINGS:

Pizza alla Marinara

This is the original pizza and it is also the simplest to make.

700 g/1½ lb ripe fresh tomatoes, peeled
4 tbsp extra virgin olive oil
2 garlic cloves, very finely sliced
2 tsp dried oregano
salt and freshly ground black pepper

CUT THE TOMATOES in half, squeeze out some of the juice and coarsely chop the flesh.

Spread the tomatoes over the pizza dough bases (crusts), drizzle with the olive oil and sprinkle with the garlic, oregano, some salt and plenty of pepper. Bake as instructed on page 186.

Pizza Margherita

The topping was created to honour the visit of Queen Margherita to Naples in the nineteenth century. It has the three colours of the Italian flag: green (basil leaves); white (mozzarella cheese); red (tomato).

200 g/7 oz Italian buffalo mozzarella
4 tbsp extra virgin olive oil
salt and freshly ground black pepper
500 g/1 lb ripe fresh tomatoes,
    de-seeded and chopped
12 fresh basil leaves
1 tbsp freshly grated Parmesan cheese

GRATE THE MOZZARELLA coarsely into a bowl and add 2 tablespoons of the olive oil and season with plenty of pepper. Leave to stand for 1 hour or so.

Spread the grated mozzarella and the chopped tomatoes evenly over the pizza dough bases (crusts), sprinkle with the basil leaves and grated Parmesan and drizzle with the remaining olive oil. Bake as instructed on page 186.

Pizza Aglio, Olio e Peperoncino

A pizza without tomatoes, which is probably the predecessor of all pizzas.

SERVES 4
7–8 tbsp extra virgin olive oil
4 garlic cloves, very finely sliced
2 tsp dried oregano
salt and freshly ground black pepper
½–1 tsp crushed dried chillies

DRIZZLE THE OLIVE OIL over the pizza dough bases (crusts) and then sprinkle with the garlic, oregano, some salt and pepper and the crushed chillies. Bake as instructed on page 186.

Pizza Rustica

Sausage, Prosciutto and Cheese Pie

A country pie from Abruzzo in central Italy. It has nothing to do with the pizza from Naples – it consists of a pastry case out of which a myriad different luscious morsels cascades when cut.

SERVES 4–6

150 g/5 oz luganega or mild pure pork
   sausage, skinned and crumbled

1 tbsp olive oil

140 g/4½ oz Italian mozzarella

250 g/9 oz/generous 1 cup fresh ricotta

50 g/2 oz/⅓ cup smoked provola, diced

50 g/2 oz/⅔ cup freshly grated
   Parmesan cheese

½ garlic clove, chopped

2 tbsp chopped fresh flat-leaf parsley

2 pinches of chilli powder or crushed
   dried chillies

100 g/3½ oz prosciutto, chopped

100 g/3½ oz mortadella, chopped

2 free-range (farm-fresh) eggs,
   lightly beaten

freshly ground black pepper

1½ tbsp dried breadcrumbs

a little butter for the tin (pan)

FOR THE PASTRY

250 g/9 oz/2½ cups flour, preferably
   Italian 00

140 g/4½ oz/9 tbsp unsalted
   (sweet) butter

2 free-range (farm-fresh) egg yolks

1½ tsp salt

1 tbsp caster (superfine) sugar

2 tbsp cold water

TO GLAZE

1 free-range (farm-fresh) egg yolk

2 tbsp milk

a pinch of salt

FIRST MAKE THE PASTRY DOUGH, either by hand or in a food processor. Divide it into 2 balls, one larger than the other. Wrap them in clingfilm (plastic wrap) and chill.

Meanwhile, put the sausage and olive oil in a small frying pan (skillet) and sauté quickly for 5 minutes, turning it over and over. Transfer to a bowl and let it cool.

Crumble the mozzarella and add with all the other ingredients, except the breadcrumbs, to the bowl and mix very thoroughly – hands are best for this. Chill.

Heat the oven to 200°C/400°F/ Gas Mark 6. Grease a 20 cm/8 in springform cake tin (pan) with butter.

Take the pastry dough out of the refrigerator. As soon as it is malleable, roll out the larger ball and cover the bottom and sides of the tin. Sprinkle the dough in the tin with breadcrumbs and then spoon in the filling. Roll out the smaller ball of dough to make a lid and place it over the filling. Turn the edges over to form a border and press together with the prongs of a fork.

Just before you bake the pie, mix the ingredients for the glaze together and brush over the lid. Make some holes here and there with a fork. Bake in the preheated oven for 10 minutes and then turn the oven temperature down to 180°C/350°F/Gas Mark 4 and bake for a further 45 minutes.

Do not serve the pie straight from the oven, let it cool for at least 10 minutes. It is also excellent served at room temperature.

NOTE: Try to buy fresh ricotta if you can, not the heat-treated kind sold in tubs. If you can't find smoked provola, buy a mildly smoked cheese, such as smoked Caerphilly from Wales.

Pissaladeira

Also called Sardenaira, this is a kind of pizza from the western Riviera more akin to its French namesake pissaladière than to its compatriot in Naples. Some recipes have tomato in the topping as well.

SERVES 6

I quantity pizza dough
   (see page 186)
I kg/2 lb 2 oz red or white
   sweet onion, finely sliced
6 tbsp olive oil
I tsp sugar
salt
6 salted anchovies, boned, rinsed
   and chopped, or 12 canned or
   bottled anchovy fillets, drained
   and chopped
I garlic clove, very finely sliced
freshly ground black pepper
a little olive oil for the tin
2 tsp dried oregano
12 small black olives, pitted

MAKE THE PIZZA DOUGH and leave it to rise in a single piece. Prepare the topping while the dough is rising.

Put the onions, olive oil, sugar and a little salt in a large sauté pan or heavy-based frying pan (skillet). Cover and cook over a very low heat for about 45 minutes, or until the onions are soft and golden. Stir occasionally and add 2 tablespoons water if the onions begin to burn.

Add the anchovies and garlic to the onions and cook, uncovered, over a very low heat for a further 5 minutes, pounding the anchovies to a paste with a fork. Add pepper, then taste the mixture and add salt if necessary.

Heat the oven to 220°C/425°F/Gas Mark 7. Brush a 25 cm/10 in tart or quiche tin (pan) with olive oil.

Roll out the pizza dough to a thickness of about 5 mm/¼ in and large enough to line the tin. Press the dough into the tin and slightly up the sides. Spoon the onion and anchovy topping over the dough, spreading it out evenly. Sprinkle with the oregano and dot with the olives.

Bake in the preheated oven for 15 minutes, then reduce the oven temperature to 190°C/375°F/Gas Mark 5 and bake for a further 5 minutes. Remove from the oven and allow to stand until warm.

Serve the Pissaladeira at room temperature.

190

the A-Z of Ingredients

ABBACCHIO *Baby lamb*

The meat of a young lamb, which should have been slaughtered when still milk-fed. Nowadays, however, some baby lambs are killed when they begin to eat grass. If properly butchered, abbacchio is a very pale meat, with a tender and delicate flavour, subtley suggesting the flavour of an older lamb.

Abbacchio is one of the great specialities of Rome, where it is cooked in several different ways. It is often roasted in the oven or on the spit, served brodettato† or alla cacciatora†.

ACCIUGA *Anchovy*

A small sea fish, also known as alice, caught around the coasts of Italy, although now becoming scarce as a result of to the overfishing of the 1960s and 1970s. When fresh, its back, void of scales, is a lovely blue-green colour and its sides silvery grey. It is easy to tell if an anchovy is fresh, since its back turns deep blue or black when it has been out of the sea for too long. It is smaller than the sardine, and has the distinguishing feature of a projecting upper jaw.

Most of the anchovies caught are preserved, either in salt: acciughe sotto sale or in oil: filetti di acciuga sott'olio. When preserved in salt, the headless fish are placed in small barrels and layered with sea salt. Before being used they are washed in cold water and the bone removed. Anchovies preserved in salt are usually larger than the canned filleted ones, and they retain their flavour better. The other advantage of buying salted anchovies is that you can see what you are buying.

Filetti di acciuga sott'olio are anchovy fillets that are preserved in oil in cans. The principal manufacturers are in Marche, Puglia and Sicily.

Acciughe sotto sale and filetti di acciughe are used extensively in Italian cooking, imparting their characteristic flavour to many sauces and dishes. A wide variety of pasta sauces are made from mashed anchovies, the best known of these being the one used in Venice to dress bigoli*, a kind of whole-wheat spaghetti. Anchovies are also used in many stuffings for baked vegetables, they are mashed into oil-based sauces to accompany boiled vegetables, especially spinach and cauliflower, and they are used to decorate the toppings of many types of pizzas, from the traditional to the modern.

Pasta d'Acciuga is anchovy paste sold in a tube and is a mixture of preserved anchovies and olive or vegetable oil. It is full of flavour and is often a more useful ingredient than preserved anchovies, as you can regulate the flavour easily.

ACETO *Vinegar*

In Italy this term usually refers to wine vinegar. It is produced by the oxidation of the alcohol in wine, which gives acetic acid. Traditionally, vinegar is coloured by enocyanin, a natural colouring contained in wine, but the use of flavourings is not allowed except in aromatic examples.

Both red and white wine vinegar are used in Italian cuisine, the red being made from black grapes and the white from white grapes. Good white wine vinegar should be clear, transparent and a pale pinkish-yellow colour; good red wine vinegar should also be clear, and the colour varies from pale pink to dark ruby. The colour of red wine vinegar has no bearing on its quality.

Wine vinegar is mainly used in salad dressings. It is also used in sweet-and-sour sauces for vegetables and fish, for pickling vegetables, for marinating meat or fish and to sharpen the flavour of the cooking juices of meat and fish.

ACETO BALSAMICO
Balsamic vinegar

This is the only vinegar not made from wine, but from the cooked and concentrated must of the white grapes of the Trebbiano vine. Balsamic vinegar is aged in kegs made of different woods: oak, cherry, chestnut, mulberry and ash, one for each year of maturing. When the new grapes arrive in the autumn (fall) some must from the first year is syphoned into the next barrel, some of this into the third year barrel, and so on. The result of this complicated process is a nectar with a well-balanced flavour and a rich velvety-brown colour.

By law, vinegar that is labelled "aceto balsamico tradizionale" must be at least ten years old and, in fact, it is sometimes 50 years old or more. It is a full-bodied, rich vinegar with a dark brown colour glinting with gold, and is very aromatic, with a peculiarly delicious flavour all of its own.

There also exists a commercial version, called simply "aceto balsamico", which cannot be sold as "tradizionale". It has a similar flavour, but has not been aged for so long. The flavour is sometimes obtained by adding a little caramel to a good-quality white wine vinegar.

Balsamic vinegar is produced in the province of Modena in Emilia-

Romagna, and also, by a slightly different method, in the province of Reggio-Emilia. Up until the 1980s it was almost unknown outside the region, but now it is a popular ingredient in many dishes. Good balsamic vinegar is used to dress strawberries, to sharpen a vanilla ice cream, to flavour consommé and for special marinades. It seems odd, but aceto balsamic tradizionale also makes an excellent thirst-quenching drink diluted with ice and sweetened with a little sugar.

ACQUACOTTA *Vegetable soup*

A traditional soup from the Tuscan Maremma region, now made all over Tuscany. As its name, "cooked water", implies it is the humblest of all soups, its flavour depending entirely on the excellence of the vegetables. It varies from one place to another, but consists basically of onion, tomato and celery sautéed in the best Tuscan olive oil and then covered with water. Acquacotta is poured over toast made from the local unsalted bread and topped with eggs, which are poached in the soup.

AFFETTATO *Literally, "sliced"*

A dish of sliced raw pork meats, a feast to the eye and a joy to the palate. Affettato must include prosciutto*, two or three kinds of salami*, coppa* and mortadella*, plus some local specialities, all spread out on a large dish and, in northern Italy, sometimes scattered with small curls of butter. It is the only dish with which butter is served, and, of course, lots of crusty white bread. Salad is not served with it, although pickled vegetables sometimes are.

Traditionally, affettato was served as an antipasto* at lunch. Now it might take the place of the first course, or be served as the main course of an informal lunch.

AGLIATA

Garlicky breadcrumb or herb sauce

There are two sauces with this name. The Ligurian version is of Provençal origin: breadcrumbs that have been soaked in vinegar are pounded with lots of garlic, then a good quantity of olive oil is slowly added. It is served with boiled fish.

The Piedmontese agliata consists of chopped parsley, celery, basil and garlic mixed with soft local cheese and dressed with olive oil and lemon juice. It is served with hot toast dripping with olive oil.

Agliata is one of the oldest sauces and features in *Libro per Cuoco*, which was written by Anonimo Veneziano(in the fourteenth century.

AGLIO *Garlic*

Garlic, an important ingredient in Italian cooking, although never a principal component except in such sauces as agliata* or, to a minor extent, bagna caôda* and with chilli in a sauce for spaghetti*. Garlic is widely used as a flavouring in many dishes, either as a basic element or as an ingredient in larding or in marinating etc. Italian cooking is not as garlicky as foreigners think. Often, and especially in northern Italian cooking, the clove of garlic is used whole and discarded before the dish is served. Fresh garlic, available in late spring and in summer, is sweeter than dried garlic. In Piedmont garlic is often steeped in milk for some hours (aglio dolce) so it imparts only a mellow flavour.

AGNELLO *Lamb*

Meat from a very young, milk-fed lamb is called agnellino da latte or, in Rome, abbacchio*. Lamb is the traditional Easter fare everywhere in Italy. The best recipes come from central Italy, where very young lamb is roasted on a spit, with rosemary and other herbs.

If the lamb is a little older, the leg or shoulder is pan-roasted with a little wine, or cut in pieces and stewed with various sauces, usually containing tomatoes. Vinegar, lemon juice and anchovy fillets are often used in lamb dishes. In Venezia-Giulia horseradish is added to a lamb stew at the end of the cooking time for a flavouring hardly ever found elsewhere in Italian cooking. It is an excellent recipe which originates from Austrian cuisine. The recipe given on page 128 is the traditional one from central Italy.

AGONE *Freshwater fish*

A freshwater fish that lives in the waters of the Alpine lakes. Its flesh is not very highly regarded. It is usually eaten fresh, deep-fried in olive oil, or grilled (broiled). It is best in the spring and autumn (fall). On Lake Como agone is dry-cured, when it is known as missoltit*.

AGRODOLCE *Sweet-and-sour sauce*

A dressing made with vinegar and sugar to which bay leaf, onion, garlic, herbs and spices are added. Sultanas (golden raisins) and pine nuts or tomatoes are also often added. Agrodolce is usually made with balsamic vinegar, and is served with fish, game and vegetable dishes, especially those containing onions and aubergines (eggplant).

AGUGLIA *A type of fish*

A beautifully slender fish, measuring from 40–80 cm/15–30 in in length, this is known as garfish, gar, greenbone and needlefish in English. It has a solid and tasty flesh which is particularly popular in Venice. Once common on the north Adriatic coast, it is now comparatively rare. It comes close to the shore during spring, when it is caught. However it is at its best during the autumn (fall) when it is found only in the high seas.

Small aguglie are cut into chunks and fried in a tomato sauce – in the same way as eel.

ALBESE, CARNE ALL'
A beef dish

In this traditional dish, originally from Alba, a town in Piedmont, beef is finely sliced as for a carpaccio*. The slices of beef are dressed with extra virgin olive oil, lemon juice, salt and pepper and slivers of the best Parmigiano-Reggiano, plus white truffle or raw ceps when they are in season.

ALBICOCCA *Apricot*

Cultivated in all the temperate areas of Italy, apricots flourish in the same climatic conditions as the almond to which they are related. The tree flowers early, just after the almond, and the fruits are ready to pick in June. Like figs, albicocche should ideally be picked off the tree, still warm from the sun, and popped straight into one's mouth – Italians usually prefer to eat apricots raw.

Apricots are also used to make jam, which goes into a variety of desserts. They are also often stewed in a white wine and cinnamon syrup or preserved in alcohol.

In the south albicocche are also dried at home by placing them, split in half, in the sun for a few days. A traditional family pudding from northern Italy is made with rice boiled in milk, sweetened with a little sugar, and then baked in layers with poached dried apricots flavoured with cinnamon.

ALLORO *Another name for lauro or bay see* LAURO

AMARETTI
Almond biscuits (cookies)

Biscuits (cookies) made of ground almonds, egg white and sugar, prepared in most regions of Italy. Some are soft, like the amarettus of Sardinia, others are crunchy like the well-known Amaretti di Saronno in Lombardy, sold in their characteristic wrapping. The latter also contain some bitter almond or almond essence (extract).

Amaretti are eaten as an accompaniment to various mousses and creams. They are the main ingredient of a Piedmontese pudding, bônet*, and they occasionally appear in a few savoury dishes.

ANATRA DOMESTICA
Domestic duck

This bird, which was not very popular in Italy up to World War II, is now widely bred in northern Italy. The most common is the anatra comune and the muschiata, so called because of its musky smell.

A rather special Venetian recipe is called bigoli co'l'anara – the duck is boiled with carrot, onion and celery, then removed and a kind of spaghetti called bigoli* is cooked in the strained stock. The bigoli are dressed with a ragù* made with the duck's liver and heart, and are served as a first course. The duck itself follows, accompanied by the piquant peverada* sauce.

The other splendid recipe from Venice is anara col pien, a traditional dish served on the day of the Festa del Redentore, on the third Sunday in July. The boned duck is stuffed with some minced (ground) veal or chicken,

the bird's liver and some soppressa* (a soft Venetian salami*), and bread soaked in Marsala.

And then, of course, there is the anatra all'arancia – duck with orange, or rather paparo all'arancia as it is called in Tuscany, where it originated. Although the French would hotly contest the Tuscan origin of this dish, the Tuscans say that it arrived in France with Caterina de' Medici and her courtiers.

ANATRA SELVATICA
Wild duck

The many species of wild duck available vary in size, plumage and colour. The best species for the table are Germano (the French Colvert) or Mestolone (Canard Souchet).

Wild duck is drawn straight away, plucked after one day and then hung for up to two days. It is roasted on the spit, in the oven or pan-roasted or braised in the same way as the domestic duck, but for longer.

ANGUILLA *Eel*

Common eels vary in length up to a maximum of 1.5 m/1½ yards in the female fish. The wild eels from the Comacchio lagoon and those of the

Po delta, caught on their way back to the Sargasso sea, are supposedly among the tastiest available. Nowadays eels are also farmed in *valli*, fenced waters where the catch is controlled according to market demand.

Eels should be bought when they are still alive, since their flesh deteriorates very rapidly once they are dead (they can live for a surprisingly long time out of the water). It is a delicious fish, quite rich but delicate, which was appreciated by the Romans, great connoisseurs of fish, and often served at Renaissance banquets.

Eels are often stewed in wine. Other classic dishes are either alla griglia, where unskinned grilled (broiled) eel chunks are threaded onto skewers with bay leaves or stewed in tomato sauce and vinegar, or fritta – the floured chunks being fried in olive oil. The fried pieces can also be marinated and kept in vinegar with other flavourings.

ANICE *Anise*
A tall herb, native to the Middle East, with pretty white flowers, similar to wild fennel. It was introduced to Sicily by the Arabs. The aromatic fruit contains the oil-bearing seeds called semi di anice (aniseed), for which the plant is cultivated. In Tuscany aniseed is used in salads and to flavour grilled (broiled) fish. But its main use is in patisserie. Biscuits (cookies) and focacce* are frequently flavoured with aniseed, or with liqueurs based on the plant.

ANICINI *Aniseed biscuits (cookies)*
Although made all over Italy, the best-known anicini are those from Sardinia, where they are served with a glass of Vernaccia, the full-bodied local wine.

ANIMELLE *Sweetbreads*
The thymus gland of a calf or lamb, which disappears in the adult animal is a popular ingredient in Italian cuisine. In Italy animelle are usually blanched, then coated in egg and breadcrumbs and fried, or they are sautéed in butter and sprinkled with lemon juice. Because they lack a pronounced taste, animelle are ideal for stuffings or for thickening sauces.

The Romans, who are the best offal (variety meats) cooks, use sweetbreads and peas to stuff very young artichokes, which are then coated in a light batter and fried.

ANTIPASTO *Hors d'oeuvre*
Literally, "before the meal" and not "before the pasta" as it is so often taken to mean. The sight of an antipasto counter, which greets you as you enter a restaurant, is both a joy to the eye and a promise of the mouthwatering delights to come. The counter is loaded with a range of appetizing dishes, some traditional, some the creation of the chef.

Antipasti can be cold, as they mostly are, or hot. Among the cold you can choose between an antipasto misto, an affettato* or an antipasto di pesce. The antipasto misto will usually include a delicious array of tuna fish and beans, hard-boiled (hard-cooked) eggs with various fillings, arancini, olives from

Gaeta (round and blackish), a selection of grilled (broiled) (bell) peppers, various vegetables stewed in tomato sauce or in a sweet-and-sour sauce and stuffed vegetables.

The affettato consists of sliced pork products such as prosciutto* and salami*. From the antipasto di pesce you could choose stuffed mussels, raw anchovies marinated in olive oil and lemon juice, fish marinated in a sweet-and-sour sauce or a seafood salad.

The hot antipasto could include a slice or two of cotechino* or zampone*, a dish of snails, a few fish or chicken croquettes or small meat balls, or a slice of vegetable torte. However, hot antipasti usually take the place of a first course nowadays.

ARAGOSTA *Spiny lobster*
This delicious crustacean differs from the true lobster in that it is smaller (up to 50 cm/20 in) and has no claws. Although it is to be found around the coasts of Sardinia and Sicily, the aragosta has otherwise become rare in the seas around Italy. This is partly because its inflated price has encouraged over-fishing.

In Italy aragosta is usually eaten cold with olive oil and lemon juice, or split in half and grilled (broiled). The recipe given on page 96 comes from Sardinia. Many modern recipes combine long pasta with lobster, often using head, roes and other bits usually discarded, to which wine and tomatoes are added. The sauce is then puréed and is flavoured with garlic, chilli and parsley.

ARANCIA *Orange*
The pride of the citrus family. The arancia amara (bitter orange) was brought to Sicily by the Saracens around AD 1000 and was cultivated on the island with great success. Bitter oranges were grown as a flavouring, rather than for making preserves or marmalade.

The arancia dolce (common orange) is widely cultivated in southern Italy, especially in Sicily and in the fertile area of Calabria around Reggio. Many different varieties of orange are grown, so that the supply of fresh oranges can extend from November to March. Among the blood orange varieties, the moro and the tarocco are the earliest ripening types, followed by the ruby-red sanguinello, while the blond calabrese, like the Spanish Valencia, comes as late as May.

A traditional dish that is still very popular in Sicily is a salad made with orange slices, onion, olive oil, salt and pepper. Oranges are mainly used in dessert making, either as a flavouring or as a base ingredient, or they are, of course, eaten just as they are.

ARANCINI *Croquettes*
The literal translation is "little oranges" but these are, in fact, little rice croquettes stuffed with various ingredients. They are made with risotto or boiled rice dressed with butter and grated cheese. Coated in egg and breadcrumbs, they are fried in butter, strutto* or oil. The four traditional stuffings are meat and tomatoes, chicken livers and tomatoes, mozzarella* and tomatoes and a ragù* of ham and peas.

Arancini are originally from Sicily, and are the best known of the very few traditional rice dishes from that island. In the traditional Sicilian recipe arancini are made with boiled rice dressed with eggs and pecorino* and stuffed with meat juice and young pecorino. In Rome, arancini are made with a plain risotto and stuffed with a

Bolognese sauce or a mushroom ragù. Arancini have now been adopted by Italians up and down the entire country who love to eat them in bars with aperitifs.

AROMI *Herbs*

A general term used to describe various herbs, such as rosemary, sage, thyme, oregano etc. Aromatic vegetables, such as celery and onion are also called aromi. The term is used when no specific herbs are mentioned, the choice being left to the discretion and knowledge of the cook, as in *un po' di aromi* (a few aromatic herbs).

ARROSTO *Roast(ed)*

The word can be a noun and refer to a dish, as in arrosto morto or arrosto di manzo (roasted beef), or it can be an adjective as in pollo arrosto** (roast chicken). For the method of preparing an arrosto, see arrostire†.

ASIAGO *A type of cheese*

A controlled denomination half-fat cheese made from cow's milk, named after the area in Veneto, near Vicenza, where it is made. The large meadowlands of this plateau enjoy a mild, dry climate suitable for the production of a cheese which cannot be made commercially, as the process requires continuous care. Asiago is greatly prized in Veneto, as indeed it is all over Italy and also abroad.

There are two kinds of asiago: asiago d'allevo and asiago pressato. Asiago d'allevo is a table cheese when it is young and freshly made, or a grating cheese after twelve to eighteen months. Asiago pressato is a young hard cheese, tangy but delicate, excellent for the table. It is made from full (whole) cow's milk, and aged for about a

month. Both types of asiago are ideal for cooking.

ASPARAGI *Asparagus*

Asparagus is one of the most highly regarded vegetables in Italy. There are many varieties of cultivated asparagi, from thin to fat and from white to green or purple. The asparagi of Bassano, a town in Veneto, are considered to be the best; they are fat and white because they have been picked while still buried in sand. Veneto asparagi are traditionally served with an oil and lemon juice mixture into which the yolks of hard-boiled (hard-cooked) eggs have been pounded. The asparagus of Pescia, in Tuscany, are also excellent, as are the Napolitano, which are a beautiful purple colour.

Asparagus is usually eaten cold with olive oil and lemon juice, or hot with butter. The recipe given on page 144 is for asparagi alla Parmigiana, which is another traditional way of serving it in Italy. This is also a favourite in France, where it is called à la Milanaise, while in Italy asparagi alla Milanese is asparagus dressed with butter and Parmesan and served with fried eggs. Asparagus can also be part of a fritto misto*, when the raw tips are coated in batter and deep-fried in oil.

Asparagi di campo (wild asparagus) are still found along sandy roads in central Italy. They are thin and green, and very tasty.

ASTICE *Lobster*

The largest crustacean, also called elefante di mare, is a lovely dark blue colour. It is rare in the seas around Italy, but a few are caught off the coast of Sardinia, where a pasta sauce has been created for the benefit of the Costa Smeralda set. It is made with the meat from the lobster claws, and mushrooms sautéed in butter. A grating of white truffle is added to give the dish an even more exotic flavour.

B

BABÁ *Rum baba*

A dessert first made in Naples, according to tradition; it was probably brought by French chefs employed by grand households. It is made with a sweet yeast dough, which is baked to a rich golden colour in a tall mould with a hole. Removed from the mould, it is then soaked in a syrup strongly laced with rum, thin icing (frosting) is poured on and slivered almonds sprinkled over. Babá is served with a hot sauce made with local sweet wine.

BACCALÀ *Salt cod*

The repertoire of Italian specialities would be greatly diminished without baccalà, a name that in Veneto refers to stoccafisso* (stockfish), thus causing endless confusion. The difference between baccalà and stoccafisso is in the curing process, not in the type of fish. Baccalà is cod that has been salted at sea, then dried on land. It consists of large chunks, or a side of fish only lightly dried. It needs soaking in milk or water for no less than 24 hours before cooking. In Italy it is also sold ready to cook.

Several regions of Italy offer excellent recipes for baccalà. In Liguria it is traditionally cooked with spinach – baccalà in zimino – or fried and served with a sauce made from fresh breadcrumbs and chopped garlic. Baccalà alla Fiorentina is shallow fried and stewed in tomato sauce, while in Rome the baccalà is coated in a light batter to which whipped egg white has been added, and then deep-fried. One of the tastiest dishes comes from Abruzzo e Molise and combines baccalà with celery, pine nuts, sultanas (golden raisins), olives and tomatoes. Of the two traditional recipes from Naples, one is similar to that from Abruzzo, while the other adds grilled (broiled) (bell) peppers to the fried fish.

BACI *Small sweets (candies)*

Literally, "kisses". The best known baci are the chocolatey Baci Perugina. Others are Baci di Dama, small almond and chocolate biscuits (cookies), whose name (lady's kisses) expresses their quality. See the recipe on page 167.

BAICOLI *Biscuits (cookies)*

The most popular of Venetian biscuits (cookies), baicoli are made with flour, butter, sugar, egg white and fresh yeast. The dough is baked in a roll about

30 cm/12 in long and then put aside for 48 hours. The roll is cut into thin slices and the slices are baked again. Baicoli are sold in cans of a traditional design, which include wording in praise of the biscuits in Venetian dialect. The Venetians like eat baicoli dipped in sweet white wine, hot chocolate or zabaione*.

BAGNA CAÔDA *A type of sauce*

This hot, garlicky sauce is made with oil and butter, anchovy fillets and garlic (often first soaked in milk – aglio dolce). See recipe on page 52. The name means hot bath, since this sauce from Piedmont must be kept hot when it's at the table, usually in an earthenware pot over a spirit flame. Raw (bell) peppers, cardoons, cabbage, celery and fennel are dipped into it. In some localities boiled vegetables such as onion, carrots, potatoes and turnips are dipped when cooked. Then, when there is only a little of the sauce left, eggs are broken into it and scrambled. As with many dishes from Piedmont, bagna caôda is a very convivial dish, shared by everyone at the table.

BARBABIETOLA *Beetroot (beet)*

This under-rated root is popular in northern Italy, where it is usually sold already cooked – either boiled or baked. The latter is the more traditional method and the one that gives a better result because it allows the root to retain a more pronounced flavour.

The season for beetroots (beets) is early autumn (fall) when you can find them on the stalls of every street market, alongside baked onions. These two vegetables are used together in a salad dressed only with salt, the best olive oil and perhaps red wine vinegar. Beetroots are also served in a salad combined with potatoes and leeks or cauliflower – all typical winter vegetables.

BARBA DI FRATE

A green vegetable

The name of this small plant (meaning "friar's beard"), is owing to its appearance – like long, thick chives. It grows wild wherever the soil is damp and sandy. It is cultivated in northern and central Italy, where it is also called agretto. Barba di frate tastes like samphire and, when it is very young, is eaten raw in salad. When older it is boiled like spinach, and either dressed with olive oil and lemon juice or sautéed in olive oil with garlic.

BASILICO *Basil*

The word comes from the Greek word *basilikos*, meaning royal. Basil is the herb which everyone links with Italy. Originally from Judea, it quickly became popular all over Italy and especially in Liguria, the region which popularised it in pesto*. The Ligurian variety of basil, called Genovese, has a particularly strong flavour. The Napoletano variety has a larger leaf and a more delicate scent and is better suited to drying. However, basil does not dry well and its flavour changes considerably. The best way to keep basil is to layer the leaves with olive oil in a sterilized jar, or to freeze the leaves.

Apart from in pesto, basil is used in salads and tomato sauces. It also gives an extra dimension to a minestrone* or a vegetable soup.

BECCACCIA *Woodcock*

This migratory bird is shot in the winter in the woods of central and southern Italy and in Sicily. Woodcock are hung unplucked for three or four days, and when plucked can either be cooked undrawn, as with all small birds, or drawn, as is more customary nowadays.

Its being so rare, there are not many Italian recipes for woodcock. In Arezzo they are drawn and stuffed with their chopped entrails mixed with stewed and boned thrushes, pancetta*, black truffle and vin santo•. The bird is then roasted in the oven or on the spit. In Basilicata the drawn woodcock is cooked on the hob (stove top) with a little white wine. The finely chopped entrails are sautéed with capers and salted anchovies in olive oil, moistened with Marsala• and spread on grilled (toasted) bread. The simpler method, and perhaps the most successful, is to roast a drawn bird wrapped in pancetta or prosciutto*. The liver and heart are mashed in the cooking juices with some anchovy fillets.

BECCACCINO *Snipe*

The snipe is one of the most difficult birds to shoot because of the sudden start of its flight. In Italy it appears between September and November, and February and April. There is disagreement as to whether snipe should be cooked drawn or undrawn. They must be drawn only when the weather is warm and damp. Snipe are roasted in the oven or on the spit, or pot-roasted, then always served on a crouton, which must be of white bread.

BEL PAESE *A type of cheese*

This cheese (its name means "beautiful country") was christened by its creator, Egidio Galbani. He began to manufacture Bel Paese in 1906 on his return from a voyage through France, where he had learnt the secret of making Port Salut, a similar cheese. Bel Paese, made from cow's milk, is good to use at the table and, as it melts easily, also for cooking. It can replace mozzarella, whose quality is less good outside Italy.

BESCIAMELLA *Béchamel sauce***

A French sauce, although some food historians say it has been made in Italy for centuries, and by a simpler method than the French béchamel. Besciamella is an integral part of most oven-baked pasta dishes. It is also used a lot with vegetables for gratin dishes or for stuffing, as well as for binding ingredients in polpette* and crocchette*.

BIANCHETTI
Anchovy or sardine fry

Bianchetti are also called gianchetti in Liguria, and many other names in various dialects. They look like a whitish grey mass and can be bought boiled and dressed with olive oil and lemon juice from delicatessens. In Italy they are also available uncooked from good fishmongers, in which case they must not have been out of the sea any longer than a day, and should be boiled in sea water.

BIETA *or* BIETOLA *Swiss chard*

This has always been a popular vegetable throughout Italy. There are two varieties. The first, colloquially known as erbette, has a thin greenish stalk. Erbette are often boiled with herbs and dressed with olive oil. It is also used in stuffings, especially for pasta. Ravioli, for instance, are always stuffed with this variety of Swiss chard rather than spinach, as it is sweeter.

The other variety, which is also found in Britain and the United States, has a thick white stalk. The leaves must be torn from the stalks and prepared separately. The leaves can be cooked in the same way as erbette, while the stalks are dressed with butter and Parmesan or baked in a cheese sauce.

BIGNÈ *Profiteroles*
Bignè is the Italianization of the French beignet. They are made with choux pastry, baked and filled with crema pasticcera*, chocolate custard or Chantilly cream. They are seldom made at home, but are bought in pasticcerie* together with other small rich cakes.

There are a few savoury bignè, most often filled with different cheeses.

BISCOTTO *Biscuit (cookie)*
Biscotto (literally, "cooked twice") is a biscuit (cookie), but the word is also used to describe an unleavened cake or bread – pan biscotto. Biscotti are sweet unless otherwise specified. Many towns have their own special biscuits that are often made for feast days or other special occasions.

Biscotti began to appear at the table in various forms during the sixteenth century, usually served with fruit, jellies and other sweet things at the beginning of a meal. It was only in the nineteenth century that they began to be produced commercially and therefore became widely popular at the time when drinking coffee and chocolate became fashionable. Biscotti can still be served with these drinks, as well as with tea. Biscotti are also served, as in the past, with sweet wines into which they are dunked. Some biscuits

also accompany ice creams, mousses or custards.

BISTECCA *Steak*
A phonetic rendition of "beefsteak". A bistecca is a thick slice of beef cut from the fillet (tenderloin) or rump (round). It can also mean a chop, as in bistecca alla Fiorentina, a thin slice of beef, a slice or chop of veal or a pork steak. In these cases, however, the kind of steak would be specified, eg bistecca di vitello or di maiale. A classic recipe is bistecca all' arrabbiata; a thin slice of beef sautéed in oil and flavoured with plenty of chilli in the same way as the pasta dish.

BITTO *A Lombard cheese*
A cow's milk cheese from the province of Sondrio in Lombardy, where it is made by the shepherds in the Alpine valley of Valtellina. Although little-known outside Lombardy, it is regarded within the region as one of the great Lombard cheeses. Fresh bitto, creamy in taste and aromatic, is a table cheese, while the seasoned cheese, which looks like grana*, is tangy and is for grating. It is also added to some local dishes like pizzoccheri* and polenta taragna (buckwheat polenta).

BOCCONCINI
A "mouthful" of food

The word is a diminutive of boccone ("mouthful"), and refers to food that can be eaten in one mouthful. There are three main types of bocconcini. One is a stew consisting of small chunks of veal cooked in a tomato and white wine sauce. Then there are the bocconcini di mozzarella*, small balls of buffalo or cow's milk mozzarella, very popular outside Italy. Thirdly there are the small balls of flavoured ricotta* coated in breadcrumbs and fried, a speciality of central Italy and Emilia – fresh ricotta must be used and not the UHT (ultra heat-treated) ricotta in tubs.

BOERI *Cherry liqueur chocolates*

Boeri are round plain (semisweet) chocolates containing a cherry floating in a liqueur or eau de vie in which it has been preserved.

BOLLITO MISTO
A mixture of boiled meats

The particular mixture of meats in this well-known dish varies with the locality. In Piedmont and Lombardy beef is the main ingredient, while in Emilia-Romagna pork products – cotechino* and zampone* – take first place. A classic bollito misto should include beef, veal, chicken, tongue, a cotechino and half a calf's head. The meats are lowered into boiling water at different times, according to how long they take to cook.

Bollito misto is made in large quantities for at least eight people. Restaurants that offer bollito misto (and only the best still do) serve it on special trolleys with the meats in different compartments full of piping hot stock. The meat is removed from the stock and carved especially for each customer, so that it never gets dry. It is accompanied by different sauces, depending on the region. The two most common are salsa verde* (a parsley sauce), and salsa rossa* (a tomato sauce, sometimes sweet-and-sour). The best known bollito is the Piedmontese gran bui*, which is served with at least three sauces, the green and red, as above, plus saussa d'avie*. In Veneto bollito is accompanied by la peverada, while in Lombardy a bowl brimming with mostarda di Cremona* is put on the table together with salsa verde.

BOMBOLONI *A type of doughnut*

These doughnuts without jam are a speciality of Tuscany. They are made with a yeast and egg dough, fried and sprinkled with sugar.

BÔNET *A pudding from Piedmont*

A pudding, named after the bonnet-shaped copper mould in which it is traditionally cooked. It is a Piedmontese speciality made with crushed amaretti*, eggs, sugar, milk, cocoa and rum. It is cooked in a bain-marie.

BORRAGINE *or* BORRANA *Borage*

A sturdy annual herb, native to the Mediterranean, which grows wild on the hillsides close to the sea. Always eaten cooked, it is especially popular in Campania and Liguria, where it is added to the stuffing of local ravioli*.

BOTTARGA
Dried roe of grey mullet or tuna

The roe, removed immediately after the fish is caught, is pressed hard and then salted and dried in the sun. It resembles a lovely brown square sausage. This delicate preparation is served as an antipasto*, cut into thin slices and marinated in olive oil and lemon juice. It is also grated to make an excellent pasta sauce. Another recipe from Oristano, in Sardinia where the fattest grey mullet are caught, suggests sautéeing bottarga in olive oil and mixing cooked spaghetti into it. Bottarga is an artisanal product mostly made in Sardinia and sold all over Italy and abroad in the best delicatessens.

Bottarga can also be made from dried tuna roe. This has a grey colour, a stronger, saltier flavour and is made mainly in Sicily.

BRACIOLA *A cut of meat*

As happens so often with Italian culinary terms, this word is used in different regions to describe different kinds, or cuts, of meat. In most regions a braciola is a chop or a steak of different animals, usually cooked alla brace (grilled/broiled), hence its name.

In southern Italy a braciola is a dish in which a slice of meat is covered with different ingredients, then rolled up, tied and cooked. In Puglia some of the cooking juices, made with concentrated tomato and red wine, are used to dress pasta as a first course, while the braciole are served as a second course – never together! In braciola Napoletana the stuffing consists of chopped prosciutto*, sultanas (golden raisins) and pine nuts, and the pork rolls are cooked for a long time in white wine. Braciola can also refer to a steak of a large fish, such as swordfish.

BRANZINO *or* SPIGOLA
Sea bass

This fish is one of the most highly prized in Italy, with firm white flesh and no lateral bones. Sea bass are now extensively farmed in Puglia and in the Po delta. The farmed fish is easily recognizable not only by its price but also by its colour; they do not show the shimmering shades from grey-black on the back to the pale silver at the sides of the wild species. All farmed fish come more or less in the same size, from 250–350 g/9–12 oz, which is the quantity most restaurants want per portion. As is the case with farmed salmon, it is inferior in taste and texture to the wild fish.

Sea bass, like all good fish, are best cooked simply. Small bass are grilled (broiled), while the bigger fish are boiled in a court bouillon and served with lemon juice and olive oil. Although this is the best dressing, more elaborate sauces are sometimes offered. Branzino is also good boned and stuffed. The usual stuffing is seafood, but I have come across an interesting recipe in which the sea bass, boned from the back, is stuffed with kidneys, calf sweetbreads, prosciutto*, Swiss chard, truffles and spices. It is cooked in meat juices and then served with veal juices.

BRESAOLA *Raw beef*

This raw fillet of beef (beef tenderloin) that has been salted and air-dried, ready to eat within two to three-and-a-half months is a speciality of Valtellina, an alpine Lombard valley. Here it is always served as an antipasto* at important dinners. Its taste is more delicate, yet a little sharper, than prosciutto* di Parma.

Mature bresaola is served thinly sliced and dressed with a little good olive oil, a few drops of lemon juice and freshly ground black pepper. A young bresaola, which these days is more common, should be eaten by itself, very thinly sliced.

BROCCOLO *or* BROCCOLETTO *Broccoli*

There are two main varieties of this vegetable from the cabbage family. One is the common variety found outside Italy, showing large stalks and flowery heads coming from a single stalk, called calabrese as it comes from Calabria. The other variety has a single large head varying in colour from greenish white to purple-green, with a similar appearance to cauliflower. In Sicily and other southern regions the name broccolo is also applied to cauliflower, thus giving rise to much confusion.

All the recipes for broccoli come from the south. It is usually blanched and then cooked in olive oil, garlic and chilli, to which soft breadcrumbs and cheese may be added. Broccoli strascinati† can also be cooked without having been previously blanched. A recipe from Calabria puts all the above ingredients in layers in an ovenproof dish, and bakes them for 30 minutes in a hot oven. Stewed broccoli makes excellent pasta sauces, sometimes containing sultanas (golden raisins), pine nuts and/or anchovy fillets, the best known being the Sicilian arriminata.

BRODETTO

An assortment of steamed fish or meat

Two different dishes come under this name. The best known is a fish soup which has almost as many variations as there are ports in Italy, from Trieste in the north to Abruzzo in the south. This soup usually comprises an assortment of fish and other seafood, some of which, such as rascasse – also known as scorpion fish – grey mullet, scampi (jumbo shrimp) and cuttlefish or squid, are indispensable. The fish is usually stewed complete with its head.

Some regional variations are that the traditional brodetto from Venice contains no tomato, brodetto in Romagna is flavoured with vinegar, the brodetto marchigiano has saffron added halfway through the cooking, while in Abruzzo this is replaced by lots of chilli (see recipe on page 63).

The speciality of Lazio, brodetto pasquale (Easter brodetto) does not contain fish – instead an assortment of beef and lamb, herbs, onion and other flavourings is simmered for hours. The strained stock is then thickened with egg yolks and Parmesan cheese flavoured with lemon juice and poured over toasted bread as a first course. The meat is served as the second course.

BRODO *Stock*

Three kinds of stock are used in Italian cooking, brodo di carne (meat stock, see recipe on page 62), brodo di pollo (chicken stock) and brodo vegetale (vegetable stock).

Brodo di carne is a vital ingredient for a wide variety of dishes, including clear soups, risottos, braised meats or vegetables and some sauces. It is light and freshly flavoured, unlike the concentrated, full-bodied stock of France or Britain. A good brodo di carne must be made with a selection of meat and bones from beef and veal (never pork or lamb, as these would give the stock too strong a flavour), and the usual flavourings of vegetables and herbs.

Some cooks add half a boiling fowl or capon to the meat stock. However for a brodo di pollo, these cuts are mainly used by themselves, with the usual flavourings. Chicken stock is especially popular for soups containing small stuffed pasta such as tortellini.

Vegetable stock is made with a combination of any of the following: potatoes, carrots, onions, leeks, turnips, green celery, parsley and dried or cultivated mushrooms. After long, slow cooking, the strained liquid is usually used in vegetable soups and fish soups or sauces. For a richer stock, the vegetables are first sautéed in butter and then cooked at length in water.

BROSS *A Piedmontese cheese*

This cheese from Piedmont is made only in small quantities, and yet it is quite well known. Its manufacture is complicated, not to say ritualistic. A fresh cheese, usually a robiola* but sometimes a goat's or ewe's milk cheese, is cut up and placed in an earthenware pot to ferment with grappa*, white wine, vinegar, oil, pepper and chilli. When ready, it is spread on hot toast or hot slices of polenta. The first mouthful is like fire, but after a time you may get used to its fierce flavour!

BRUSCANDOLI *Shoots*

The name in the Veneto dialect for two kinds of shoots – from hops and holly. They are both used to make excellent risotti, with hops in Padova and with holly in Verona. In Rome a soup is made with hop shoots, and my childhood memories are of delicious dishes of hop shoots in Brianza, the area between Milan and Como, where the blanched shoots are dressed with plenty of melted butter and showers of grated Parmesan.

BRUSCHETTA
Grilled (toasted) bread

The beginning of many a Roman meal, bruschetta consists of thick slices cut from a large round loaf of bread, grilled over charcoal, rubbed with garlic and then dressed with peppery extra virgin olive oil. Although born in Lazio and Abruzzo, bruschetta is now popular all over Italy and abroad, and appears with many different toppings (the traditional of which are chopped tomatoes in Lazio, chopped wild fennel in Tuscany and cannellini beans in Umbria). Everything, of course, is dressed with the best local olive oil before serving.

BRUTTI MA BUONI
Hazelnut biscuits (cookies)

These knobbly biscuits (cookies) from Piedmont are made with the famous hazelnuts of that region. Their name, meaning "ugly but good", describes them aptly.

BUDINO *A type of pudding*

Though hard to define, the word budino refers to a preparation similar to the old-fashioned moulded English pudding, round in shape, with a soft texture and a trembling consistency, cooked in a bain-marie. Hot budini can be served in the pudding basin (heatproof bowl) or unmoulded. Cold budini are always served unmoulded. Budini are sometimes accompanied by a sweet sauce, such as a chocolate or jam or an egg custard.

Budini are most likely to be sweet and are made with endless variations up and down the country, such as the budini di riso, di semolina and di ricotta**. In Friuli there are three different types of budino. In budino di avena, oats are cooked in milk and then mixed with eggs and sugar and poured into a mould, which is chilled before serving. The second budino is a sweet béchamel held together by eggs and strongly laced with Marsala•. Finally there is an interesting budino di patate (potato pudding) – mashed potatoes are mixed with butter, sugar, cream and eggs, some sultanas (golden raisins) and pine nuts are added, and the pudding is baked and served hot. There are also some savoury budini, of which budino alla Genovese is the best known, made with chicken and prosciutto* and bound with eggs and béchamel**.

BURIDDA *A fish soup*

This traditional soup from Liguria is made with dogfish, rascasse, cuttlefish or squid, and prawns (shrimp). Some pieces of stoccafisso*, previously soaked, are sometimes added. All the ingredients are stewed in an earthenware pot in layers with onions, tomatoes, wild mushrooms, pine nuts and salted anchovies, covered with some olive oil and dry white wine. Although the name derives from the Provençal soup bourride, the two are quite different, but both contain local fish.

BURRATA *A soft cheese from Puglia*

This soft cheese, made from full-fat (whole) cow's milk, is one of the best specialities of Puglia.

The making of burrata is a difficult and interesting craft. The milk of the previous evening is heated to a low temperature, and rennet is added. When the milk has coagulated, it is broken up thoroughly to release the whey. The small curdled bits are then plunged into boiling water and, through a laborious mixing process, they take the shape of long square strings, called lucini. At this point the dairy man from Puglia has to practise the same art as his northern compatriot in Murano does when he is blowing glass. He blows inside one lucino which swells up, forming a little balloon-shaped casing into which some flaked lucini are pushed, together with some cream. The neck of the blown lucino is tied up, and the burrata is made.

This delicate cheese has no equal, and in my opinion it merits a long detour. Burrata cannot travel, however, so you must go to it, although I have found it in Milan in highly specialized salumerie†.

BURRIDA *A Sardinian fish dish*

This fish dish from Sardinia is not the same as Genoese buridda (note the slightly different spelling). Although the Genoese brought their fish soup to Sardinia when they occupied the island, the Sardinians made a new dish out of it. The Sardinia burrida is made with only one type of fish, usually dogfish, which is poached and then covered with a garlicky sauce containing finely chopped walnuts or pine nuts.

BURRO *Butter*

Butter is mainly used in northern Italy because, unlike the more arid southern regions, the lush Po Valley and lower

Alps are rich in pasture, and thus are excellent cattle-breeding areas.

Butter is the cooking fat for the classic costoletta alla Milanese, and it is used a lot, whether raw or melted, sometimes flavoured with fresh sage and garlic, to dress all types of ravioli, gnoccchi and tagliatelle. This combination, with grated Parmigiano-Rieggiano, is unbeatable. Butter is also important in the making of the more sophisticated traditional cakes and pastry. Italian butter is, by tradition, unsalted (sweet), although salted butter is becoming more easily available in some specialist shops. In Italy, butter is never put on the table.

BUSSOLAI *Biscuits (cookies)*

These are ring-shaped biscuits (cookies), made in northeast Italy with a dough into which eggs, sugar, butter and a liqueur called rosolio are mixed. In Friuli, they are eaten dipped in wine. Bussolai used to be given to a child by its godparents on the day of Confirmation. After the ceremony, the children would parade around the streets with their bussolai tied together with ribbons of every colour.

CACAO *Cocoa*

Unsweetened cocoa powder is used instead of chocolate in some desserts and a few savoury dishes, as in jugged hare or sweet-and-sour dishes, usually of Sicilian origin, such as caponata di melanzane* **. A northern Italian dessert called torrone molle** (soft nougat) is made with cocoa powder, which must be very good quality.

CACCIATORE *A small salami*

Originally from Lombardy and Piedmont, the cacciatore mixture is similar to that of a salame Milano, the lean and fat pork meat being ground to the size of grains of rice. Cacciatori weigh around 150 g/5 oz, and are eaten after maturing for about four months. Cacciatori are seldom served as part of an antipasto*, but are cut in chunks about 2–3 cm/¾-1¼ in thick and eaten with bread, at any time of the day, as a snack. The name, meaning "hunter", points to the fact that this small salame is the ideal size to fit in the hunter's bag.

CACCIUCCO *A type of fish soup*

Originally from Livorno, this soup is now made in every town along the coast of Versilia in Tuscany. The Livornesi claim it is the oldest Italian fish soup, and that they learnt the recipe from the Turks, with whom they had traded since the early days. It is, in fact, a stew rather than a soup, thick, rich and black. It traditionally contains chilli, and should be made with at least five different kinds of fish – one for each of the c's in cacciucco.

CACIO *Cheese*

A less common word for cheese than formaggio*, still in use in central and southern Italy.

CACIOCAVALLO *A semi-soft cheese from southern Italy*

This cow's milk cheese can be eaten fresh, when its crust is pale yellow and its flavour mellow, or it can be aged for up to six months. By then it will be piquant and suitable for grating. Fresh caciocavallo is also used in cooking, as it melts beautifully. In Sicily it is sliced and fried quickly in olive oil, then lightly sprinkled with wine vinegar, oregano and a generous grinding of black pepper.

Its name, literally "horse-cheese", is said to derive from the Turkish *qasqawal*, the name of a similar cheese.

CACIOTTA *Small, flat cheeses*
This name refers to several small, flat cheeses, weighing no more than 1 kg/ 2lb 2 oz. Caciotta can be made with cow's, ewe's or goat's milk, or a mixture of all three, and can vary from white and mellow to buff yellow and piquant. When made with cow's milk it has a delicate flavour, while it is pleasingly pungent when made with ewe's or goat's milk. A typical farm cheese of central Italy, caciotta is nowadays also made commercially and is extremely popular.

CAFFÈ *Coffee*
Caffè espresso, black and strong, has become one of the hallmarks of Italy, but there are many variations, all made in a machine that forces steam through the finely ground coffee. Caffè macchiato is espresso with a dash of cold milk; caffè corretto is espresso with grappa*. Caffè ristretto is an even stronger espresso, while caffè lungo is a weaker brew served in a bigger cup, the steam being pushed through for longer.

Cappuccino, so called because its colour resembles that of the habit of the Capucine friars, is caffè lungo with hot whisked milk, often topped with grated chocolate. Cappuccino senza spuma is similar, but the hot milk is added without whisking. Then there is caffè e latte, half coffee and half hot milk, and caffè con latte, which is a caffè lungo with more than a dash of cold milk. Caffè con panna is caffè lungo topped with sweetened, whipped cream. In the summer, popular drinks are caffè freddo (cold coffee), and granita di caffè, which is halfway between a sorbet (sherbet) and a drink.

Coffee is used a lot as a flavouring in sweet preparations, such as tiramisu, or as a main ingredient, as in coffee ice creams, semifreddi* or granite* **.

CALAMARI *Squid*
A favourite food everywhere in Italy, with many methods of preparation. Small squid (calamaretti) are best fried, either by themselves or in a fritto misto di pesce*, to which they add a delicate sweet taste and texture. The other popular cooking method is to grill (broil or barbecue) them, threaded on skewers (their having previously been marinated in oil and pepper), and then dress them with lemon juice and chopped parsley. In a recipe from Naples, tiny squid are stewed in a tomato sauce enriched with sultanas (golden raisins), pine nuts and olives.

Medium-sized squid are usually stuffed with breadcrumbs (soft or dried), parsley, garlic and pepper, plus the chopped tentacles, then everything is lightly sautéed in olive oil. In other recipes the basis of the stuffing is boiled rice. When stuffed, the squid are sewn up and cooked in white wine, tomato sauce, or both, either in the oven or directly on the heat (see recipe on page 102).

Large squid are generally stewed. Although they have a less rich flavour and a more chewy consistency than cuttlefish, they share the same recipes. Cleaned and cut into pieces, they are cooked in tomato sauce and wine, to which onions, garlic and other flavourings are added.

In Liguria the squid is called totano*, which is the Italian name for flying squid, a different and less superior species, while in Tuscany cuttlefish are sometimes called calamari – a confusion of names which is typical of Italian gastronomy!

CALZONE *A folded-over pizza*

To make calzone, pizza dough is rolled out to an oval, and one half is covered with ingredients that differ according to the locality, the whim of the cook, or the food in the larder (pantry). The other half is folded over to form a large half-moon shape (rather than a "trouser", which is what calzone means) and sealed. It is then baked. Calzone Napoletano is stuffed with salami* or prosciutto*, mozzarella*, ricotta* and Parmesan*. Calzone Pugliese contains onion, tomatoes, salted anchovies and capers. The third calzone of note comes from Basilicata and is made with Swiss chard and flavoured with chilli. In Puglia the same stuffing is used for calzoneddi (small calzoni), which are deep-fried in olive oil, and make a superb snack.

CAMOSCIO *Roe deer*

An inhabitant of the Alps and the higher peaks of the Apennines, where its meat is considered to be better than that of all other deer (see Daino page 230). Roe deer must be marinated, and is then cooked in chunks with lots of onion (alla Alto Atesino**). Or, a leg is larded with smoked pancetta and pot-roasted.

CANEDERLI *A dumpling*

This is the gnocchi* of the Trentino region, similar to the Austrian *knödel*, from which their name derives. Canederli are made with stale bread (usually rye bread), soaked in milk, and mixed with eggs and a little flour. To this speck*, onion, parsley and marjoram, all finely chopped, are added. Canederli can be as large as oranges or as small as walnuts. The smaller ones are usually served in a clear soup or tossed in melted butter or in the juices of a roast; the larger type is usually an accompaniment to a stew.

CANESTRELLO *Small scallops*

Canestrelli are small scallops (known as queens in Britain). They are quite common in the Mediterranean, and especially in the northern Adriatic. In Venice they are used to make risotto, while further south along the coast in Romagna you might find them in a pasta sauce. In the simplest recipes, though, the scallops are briefly sautéed in oil with breadcrumbs, chilli and parsley and finished off with a splash of white wine. The most popular method is to fry them and serve them as part of a fritto misto di pesce* or boiled as part of a seafood salad.

CANNELLA *Cinnamon*

Cinnamon is a popular flavouring, especially in northern Italy. It is added mostly to sweet preparations, but also to a few meat dishes, such as stews, game casseroles and braised joints.

CANNELLONI *A type of pasta*

There are two kinds of cannelloni – one known only in Piedmont, and the other known all over the world. Cannelloni alla Piemontese, or alla barbaroux, are made with pancake (crêpe) batter rather than with pasta dough. The more familiar cannelloni are made with lasagne which have been boiled for a very short time. In the original recipe for these (cannelloni alla Napoletana) the cannelloni are filled with tomato sauce and mozzarella* and covered with more tomato sauce and Parmesan. However, the cannelloni that have become one of the mainstays of Italian-type food all over the world are filled with a meat ragù* and covered with a béchamel sauce.

CANNOLO *A dessert*

Cannolo is one of the two dishes that have been described as "the two unshakeable rocks of Sicilian desserts", the other being cassata*. It consists of tubes of pastry made with melted pork fat and flavoured with cocoa. These are fried in oil and, when cold, stuffed with sweetened ricotta studded with candied peel, pistachio nuts and pieces of chocolate, all flavoured with orange water. Nowadays, cannoli may also be filled with crema pasticcera* or chocolate cream.

CANNONCINO *A small cake*

One of the small paste* (cakes) bought in a pasticceria*, consisting of a spiral shape of puff pastry, filled with crema pasticcera*, whipped cream or rich chocolate.

CANOCCHIA *or* SPANOCCHIA *Mantis shrimp*

Also called cicala in Tuscany and Liguria, canocchia is a small crustacean found especially on flat sandy beaches from Venice down to Marche.

Canocchie are blanched for three minutes in a court bouillon. Left until cool, they are either served as they are, so that guests can peel them at the table, or added to fish soups. They can also be shelled, coated with flour, dipped in egg and breadcrumbs and fried, or sautéed in olive oil, garlic and white wine with some breadcrumbs mixed in at the end. In Venice they are also used in a risotto.

CAPITONE *Large eel*

The capitone is a very long (up to 1.5 m/5 ft) and fat eel. The best capitoni are caught at the mouth of the Po. They are eaten fresh, in the same ways as smaller eels, or preserved in oil. This latter method provides the traditional food on Christmas Eve in Rome and Milan.

CAPOCOLLO *A cured cut of pork*

The boned and rolled shoulder and neck of a pig aged four to six months, eaten thinly sliced. It is a salume* characteristic of central and southern Italy, and is flavoured differently according to the region where it is made. In Puglia capocollo is also lightly smoked.

CAPONE *or* CAPPONE *Gurnard*

A most attractive fish which can vary in size and colour. It has firm, excellent white flesh and is comparatively free from bones. Recipes suggest baking the fish in the oven with white wine, or boiling it, and dressing it with a light lemony and oil sauce.

CAPPASANTA *Scallop*

Cappasanta is the Venetian name for scallop. In other regions, it is called ventaglio, pettine maggiore or conchiglia di San Giacomo. They are extremely rare around the coasts of Italy, and it is only in Venice, on the fish market stalls of the Pescheria, that these molluscs, with their shiny ivory and coral colour, are to be found.

The Venetians also have the only authentic Italian recipes. In one, cappesante gratinate, the cappasanta are lightly coated in flour and sautéed in butter. A little dry white wine is then added, with a few sprigs of chopped tarragon, and salt and pepper. They are placed in pairs on one shell and browned in a preheated oven or under a grill (broiler).

CAPPELLO DEL PRETE
A type of sausage
This sausage, a speciality of Parma, is in the shape of a priest's triangular hat. The meat is the same as that in a zampone* and it is served, after long cooking, with the same accompaniment as zampone, that is, potato purée, stewed lentils and spinach. It is now produced commercially and often pre-cooked.

CAPPERO *Caper*
Italian capers are supposedly the best and grow on walls and rocks along the coasts of southern Italy and of all the islands. Those grown on the island of Pantelleria where the volcanic soil and hot, dry climate provide ideal conditions are particularly good. The best capers are the smallest ones.

It is the buds of the flowers that are eaten. They are preserved layered with sea salt, in wine vinegar or in brine, the best being those preserved in salt. Capers are one of the trademarks of Mediterranean dishes, added to a pasta

sauce, a pizza topping or a fish dish, but always at the last minute, since they should not be cooked.

CAPPON MAGRO
A Genoese salad
This is an elaborate fish and vegetable salad from Genoa. The fish (various types) are boiled, layered with boiled vegetables and crackers in a pyramid shape. The dressing is a salsa verde containing soft breadcrumbs, hard-boiled (hard-cooked) eggs, pine nuts and capers.

CAPPONE *Capon*
A neutered male which grows to be larger than a cock (rooster) and has a more delicate flavour. Nowadays they are raised commercially, although some raised on farms can still be found.

The usual method of cooking capon is to boil it. In all Renaissance recipes, ravioli* and maccheroni* were cooked in capon stock and the flesh was used for stuffing the pasta. This is still the case today with cappelletti* or anolini*. Capon is also roasted, sometimes with a finely sliced truffle pushed under its skin. It is, with turkey, the traditional bird eaten, in the north, at Christmas.

CAPRESE *A mozzarella salad*
A combination of tomatoes, mozzarella* and basil dressed with olive oil, salt and pepper. There is also a sauce called caprese for dressing gnocchi* or ravioli*. It is made with the same ingredients that are briefly cooked so as to keep their fresh flavour.

CAPRETTO *Kid*
Kid is still a traditional dish in central and southern Italy. It is similar to young lamb but has a more pungent smell and flavour. In spite, or perhaps

because of that, connoisseurs consider it a better meat than lamb. All recipes for lamb can be used for kid.

Stuffed kid is a traditional peasant dish from Calabria. The kid is boned and then stuffed with vermicelli*, dressed with a tomato sauce containing chicken giblets and the offal (variety meats) of the kid. The kid is roasted in the oven, then brought to the table whole, surrounded by new potatoes and small onions.

CAPRINO *A type of cheese*
A cheese that, judging by its name (capra means "goat") should be made with goat's milk. In fact, only a few farm-made caprini are made entirely with goat's milk. Most of the caprini on the market are made commercially with a mixture of goat's and cow's milk, or just cow's milk. The best are made in Lombardy with cow's milk that has been skilfully processed to obtain a high fat content. They are kept in olive oil and eaten dressed with the best olive oil and plenty of pepper.

CAPRIOLO *Roebuck*
Caprioli are now farmed while the wild animal is protected because it is very rare. A young roebuck is excellent roasted on the spit, the best part being the saddle. If the capriolo is older, it is marinated in wine with onion, celery, carrot, parsley, juniper berries, pepper and salt before cooking. It is then roasted on the spit or in a large oven and basted frequently with wine to keep the meat moist and succulent during cooking. Capriolo can also be stewed.

CARBONARA
A creamy pasta sauce
This sauce for bucatini or spaghetti is originally from Lazio and Abruzzo.

It takes its name from the carbonari (charcoal burners), once a familiar sight in the mountain forests of those regions, where the simple ingredients with which the sauce is made were available. Pasta alla carbonara gained international fame through the soldiers of the Allied armies, who brought it back from Rome to their native countries after the end of the Second World War. They found in the sauce the familiar foods of their homeland, eggs and a kind of bacon, successfully combined with their new love, spaghetti.

The sauce is made by dressing the pasta, as soon as it is al dente†, with cured pork jowl that has been sautéed in olive oil, and then pouring over it a mixture of eggs and Parmesan. The eggs should hardly curdle, and the pasta and should remain slippery and light. Some cooks add a little onion or garlic or herbs to the pork jowl, others like to cut its fatiness by adding a couple of tablespoons of white wine. Pork jowl is often replaced by unsmoked pancetta*.

CARCIOFO *Globe artichoke*
Artichokes grow in fields called carciofaie all over central and southern Italy. There are many varieties of artichoke, some with thorns and some without. Very small carciofi are usually preserved in olive oil in jars and served as part of a mixed antipasto*. Young artichokes with thorns are eaten raw, dipped in olive oil. With older specimens the tough outer leaves and the beard near the heart have to be removed; they are then sliced and cooked in different ways.

In Liguria the local variety with thorns, Spinoso di Liguria, is the main ingredient in their torta pasqualina*. However, Rome supplies the best recipes. Here the local variety is the thornless one, called Romanesco, similar to the Breton found in Britain, but smaller. Carciofi alla giudea is a recipe from the Jewish quarter of the city. The artichokes, opened up like a rose, are gently fried whole in olive oil. In carciofi alla Romana the artichokes are stuffed with parsley, local mint, breadcrumbs and garlic and cooked in the oven in oil and water. In Venice there are the excellent yellow Canarino and the early Castraure, which are simply cooked in the oven with oil, parsley, garlic and water.

Artichoke hearts, called fondi di carciofo, are sold in cans, preserved in brine, but they are also found fresh in some shops during the spring. Artichoke hearts are stewed in olive oil with a sprinkling of finely chopped garlic and herbs. They can be eaten raw, finely sliced, or blanched and stuffed with various ingredients such as chicken, tuna or prosciutto*.

CARDO *Cardoon*
In central Italy the cardo is also known as "gobbo" (hunchback) because of the way that the plant curves during blanching. This vegetable, which is cultivated for its leaf-stalks, is a spectacular Mediterranean thistle like the globe artichoke. It is the blanched stem that is eaten, not the flower bud. In its method of cultivation and cooking, it is more similar to celery than the artichoke, while its flavour is reminiscent of the artichoke, though slightly sweeter.

When young, cardoons are eaten raw, as they are when they are dipped in the traditional Piedmontese sauce bagna caôda* **, of which they are the principal vegetable. They can also be cooked in a little water, flavoured with

olive oil, garlic and parsley and finished off with a light sauce of egg yolk and lemon.

CARNE *Meat*
While pork is popular throughout Italy, beef and veal are the favourites in the north, lamb and, to a lesser extent kid, being the meats of central and southern Italy. Chicken is eaten everywhere, but the stronghold of chicken dishes is Tuscany, famous for the free-range birds of the Valdarno. Tuscany also produces the best beef in Italy, from the Chianina breed. Other meats eaten in Italy are rabbit, hare, horse, donkey, game (including almost anything that flies), frogs and snails. These last two are considered great delicacies.

Large cuts of meat are roasted in the oven, on the spit or pot-roasted, this last method being the most popular. A favourite method for less tender cuts is stewing for a long time or braising in stock and/or wine, especially in northern Italy. Slices of meat are grilled (broiled or barbecued) or fried, often coated in egg and breadcrumbs, or sautéed in butter or oil, and sauced at the end with lemon, wine etc, as in scaloppine al Marsala.

CAROTA *Carrot*
Carrots grow all over Italy and are widely cultivated in the north and in Marche. There are many different varieties and colours of carrot, from white to purplish red, but the most common are the familiar orange-coloured ones which are either short and fat, or long and thin. They are harvested all year around.

Carrots are used primarily as a flavouring for soups, stocks, marinades and soffritti* – the basis of so many dishes. When young they are also eaten in salads, simply dressed with olive oil and lemon juice. When not so young, carrots are cut into sticks or rounds and braised in stock, or sautéed slowly in butter and/or oil. They are often flavoured with Parmesan, with oregano or parsley, and in one of the very few recipes from southern Italy, a couple of tablespoons of Marsala• are added at the end.

Boiled carrots are one of the classic accompaniments to bollito misto*. They can also be coated in flour and fried in olive oil. Grated carrots make a good sauce for roast or boiled meat: they are first sautéed with onions in olive oil and butter, and then cooked in stock and vinegar with some tomato paste and a little sugar.

CARPA *Carp*

The male carp with the soft roe is better than the female specimen. The best variety of carp is the carpa a specchi, which has large scales and a golden green colour. Unfortunately much carp is now farmed, and they have a muddy flavour – one of the reasons why carp is no longer appreciated in Italy as it was in past centuries. The best wild carp are caught in Lake Trasimeno in Umbria. The traditional way of cooking it is to bake it with pancetta and tomatoes.

CARPACCIO *Thinly sliced beef*

This is a relatively new dish which, in just a few years, has become a favourite the world over.

Carpaccio was created in 1961 by Giuseppe Cipriani of Harry's Bar in Venice for an aristocratic Venetian lady who was on a strict diet. He named the dish after the famous painter Vittore Carpaccio (1450–1522), because there was an exhibition of his paintings in Venice at the time, and "because the

colours of the dish remind me of the reds that Carpaccio used".

Carpaccio, or filetto al Carpaccio to give it its proper name, is very thinly sliced fillet of beef (beef tenderloin), dressed with a small amount of mayonnaise, to which is added a touch of mustard, a drop of brandy and Tabasco sauce, plus enough cream to make the sauce of a fluid consistency. Sometimes a teaspoonful of thick tomato sauce is added.

Many cooks mistakenly use the name Carpaccio to describe what is in fact carne all'albese*. And I have recently seen recipes named Carpaccio that have nothing in common with the original. They are called Carpaccio simply because they are made with any raw meat, dressed with any sort of dressing. Unfortunately, there is no copyright on the names of recipes.

CARPIONE
Freshwater fish and a fish dish

This rare freshwater fish, found in Lake Garda, is from the same family as salmon. However it is more similar to trout, but more highly regarded. Carpione is usually simply boiled and dressed with oil and lemon juice, or a delicate salsa verde – with no garlic.

Carpione is also the name of a sweet-and-sour preparation of fresh water fish previously fried and then marinated in a vinegary sauce. It is a popular northern Italian antipasto*.

CASSATA *Three different desserts*

The oldest type of cassata is the Cassata Siciliana, a concoction consisting of an outer layer of Madeira cake containing a mixture of sweetened ricotta* flavoured with vanilla, chocolate or cinnamon, sometimes studded with candied peel or pumpkin and/or pieces of chocolate. The cake is covered with almond paste, traditionally green, or with sugar icing (frosting) and decorated with candied fruit or fruits made of marzipan.

A second cassata is that from Sulmona in Abruzzo for which the recipe is on page 172. The third type of cassata is the popular iced cassata, cassata gelata, a modern recipe for iced cake.

CASTAGNA *Chestnut*
This beautiful, shiny nut has been one of the staple foods of the mountain regions for centuries, especially of the Apennines. Chestnuts come in many varieties, of which marroni is the best, usually with a single large nut in each prickly shell. Marroni are light brown, sometimes striped with white, and the thin inner skin is easily peeled. Other varieties have two or even three nuts per shell.

There are many savoury and sweet recipes for chestnuts, all from northern Italy. The exception is one from Marche called castagne dei morti (because it is made on All Souls' Day, 2 November). The cooked and peeled chestnuts are sprinkled with sugar and grappa*, which is then flamed.

Chestnuts are roasted, boiled in milk or stock and then eaten or used in other preparations. Apart from the now universal chestnut stuffing for turkey, a similar stuffing is used in Lombardy for rabbit. A recipe from Piedmont suggests roasted chestnuts and baked onions as an accompaniment to pot-roasted beef, in the juice of which they receive a final cooking. Again in Lombardy, an ancient dish called busecchina is made with chestnuts, previously boiled and skinned, and then cooked in milk and white wine. When

nearly all the liquid has been absorbed, the chestnuts are served covered with cream. The first prize for all chestnut preparations must go to monte bianco*, the dessert from Val d'Aosta. But the best-known sweet made with chestnuts is marrons glacés. These are extensively made commercially or artisanally in Piedmont and Lombardy, and are quite comparable to the better-known French variety.

Chestnuts are also dried in Italy (castagne secche) and can then be eaten all the year around. To reconstitute, they are soaked in warm water for several hours and then boiled in milk to which a bay leaf is usually added. They can be used in savoury or sweet dishes. But, when dried, chestnuts lose their richness and are definitely inferior in flavour to the fresh variety.

There is also a flour, farina di castagne, made with ground, dried chestnuts. It is used to make castagnaccio* and fritters. Farina di castagne is also mixed with white flour to make tagliatelle, an excellent pasta when dressed with a gamy sauce.

CASTAGNACCIO
A flat bread made from chestnut flour
This bread made with chestnut flour was originally from Tuscany and is now found all over Italy. The basic ingredients of castagnaccio are chestnut flour and oil, to which sultanas (golden raisins), pine nuts, walnuts and fennel seeds are added. The mixture, bound together with water, is baked in large, flat copper pans.

CASTRATO *Mutton*
Castrato is eaten in central Italy, although less so than it used to be since many people now prefer the sweeter taste of lamb to the stronger, fuller

flavour of a castrato. Castrato is a red meat and, when still quite young, is excellent roasted or grilled (broiled or barbecued), and eaten slightly underdone, like beef. The meat of older animals is suitable for making ragù* or stews.

CAVALLO *Horse*

Horse meat is still eaten in Italy, although less than it used to be prior to, and during, the last war. It is tougher than beef, though more nourishing and digestible, and has a sweetish taste which some people find objectionable. Until the last war, horse meat, being cheaper than beef or other meats, was often bought to save money; nowadays prices are much the same and it is bought simply by those who prefer it. Horse-meat butchers make sausages and salami* from horse, donkey or mule meat. They are all slightly different and all very good.

CAVOLFIORE *Cauliflower*

Cauliflower is a popular vegetable, particularly in the north. In southern Italy, broccoli is sometimes called cavolfiore, which can be confusing.

Boiled cauliflower florets are often dressed with olive oil and vinegar. Salted anchovies, previously pounded, are sometimes added. Another popular way to serve cauliflower is to sauté the blanched florets gently in butter and cover them with Parmesan before bringing to the table. The sformato* di cavolfiore is an elegant dish that can be served as a first course. As with many other vegetables, cauliflower can also be breaded and fried and then served as an accompaniment to meat, or as part of a fritto misto*. It is also the main ingredient of a Neapolitan dish called insalata di rinforzo. Here, the boiled florets are dressed with anchovy fillets, green and black olives, olive oil, vinegar, capers, garlic and salt. The florets are traditionally served in a dome-shaped mound.

CAVOLINI DI BRUXELLES *Brussels sprouts*

There are no traditional recipes for Brussels sprouts, although they are grown in northern Italy and are becoming more popular. They are always blanched and then sautéed in butter and sometimes covered with Parmesan-flavoured béchamel and baked or gently fried with pancetta*. A modern pasta sauce combines shredded Brussels sprouts sautéed in oil with smoked pancetta and chilli, to which a few tablespoons of cream and grated Parmesan are added at the end with the pasta for a final toss.

CAVOLO *Cabbage*

There are three main types of cabbage: cavolo cappuccio (which includes primo, Dutch and red cabbage), cavolo verza (Savoy cabbage) and cavolo nero (Tuscan cabbage).

Cabbage, including primo and Savoy, is now less popular in Italy than it used to be. But there are still some well-liked recipes such as the Milanese cassoeula**

or the involtini di verza. Savoy cabbage is often used in soups, particularly minestrone* **. It is also stewed at length with white wine or vinegar in a classic dish from the Veneto region, verze soffegae.

Cavolo nero, meaning black cabbage, is the characteristic Tuscan cabbage. It has no head, only curly deep green leaves, rather than black, and it has a slightly more bitter and less cabbagey flavour than ordinary varieties. It apppears in many Tuscan soups, of which la ribollita* ** is the best known, and in pork stews. There is a traditional sweet tart from Lucca in which the cavolo nero is laid on crema pasticcera*.

CECI *Chick peas (garbanzo beans)*

Chick peas (garbanzo beans) are excellent served on their own, as well as mixed with other flavours. They are eaten all over Italy, though more in the south, where they are widely cultivated. Here they are often cooked with pasta. Among the many pasta and chick pea dishes is a recipe from Puglia (see page 73), originally made with large local tagliatelle, called tria. One of the oldest chick pea dishes, however, has its origins in the north. It is ceci con la tempia, a rich stew of chick peas, loin of pork and the pig's temple and is the traditional fare in Milanese homes on All Souls' Day.

Chick peas are never eaten fresh; they are always dried, and for this reason they must be soaked for at least twelve hours before cooking. Chick pea flour is used to make two of the oldest Ligurian dishes, farinata*, similar to the Provençal socca, and panissa*.

CEDRO *Citron*

A fruit of the citrus family that grows plentifully in Calabria and Sicily. It resembles a lemon in colour, but a large quince in shape, and has a thick skin. It is seldom eaten fresh, and is mainly cultivated for the thick and aromatic rind (peel) which is candied and used in many sweet preparations.

CEFALO *Grey mullet*

Also called muggine*, there are many species of this fish, the best being the golden grey mullet. When caught in clean water, grey mullet is an excellent fish with rather fatty firm white flesh and very few bones. But the fish's flavour can be changed for the worse if it has lived in muddy water or waters close to industrial waste. It must be eaten very fresh and be cleaned thoroughly. Grey mullet is grilled (broiled), boiled, cooked in cartoccio† with herbs and olive oil, or baked as in the dish from Marche (see recipe on page 94). Like sea bass and red mullet, it is also good baked on a bed of fennel or, better still, of wild fennel leaves. A great delicacy, called bottarga*, is made from the dried roe of the female fish.

CENCI *Fritters*

Literally meaning "rags", these lozenge-shaped fritters are made with a batter of flour, butter, sugar and eggs, rolled out very thin. They are the carnival fritters of Tuscany.

CERNIA *Grouper*

This Mediterranean fish, of which there are many species, can be as long as 1 m/1 yd. In spite of its rather ugly appearance, grouper has an excellent flavour, is free from lateral bones and lends itself to many different methods of cooking. The whole fish is delicious roasted with herbs, or boiled and served with a thin salsa verde. The steaks can be grilled (broiled) or stewed in tomato sauce. Alan Davidson, in *Mediterranean Seafood*, gives an interesting recipe cernia ripiena, in which the grouper is stuffed with prawns (shrimp), dried porcini and Parmesan, all bound with eggs, and then baked with butter and white wine.

CERVELLO *Brains*

Because of their creamy texture, melting consistency and delicate flavour, brains are one of the most highly regarded, popular foods of Italy, as indeed of all continental Europe. Calves' brains are eaten in Lombardy and Tuscany, while baby lambs' brains are a favourite of the Romans and Neapolitans. Cervello alla Napoletana is made with baked lambs' brains scattered with black olives, capers, dried breadcrumbs and olive oil. The other traditional recipe is cervello fritto alla Milanese.

CERVO *Red deer*

Generally, the loin is roasted, while the leg should be pot-roasted in the same way as a leg of wild boar. In which case it is marinated, and cooked, in wine. Most recipes for buck and roe deer are suitable for red deer. Nowadays red deer is no longer wild but farmed in huge fenced-off reserves, especially in Sardinia, and its meat has lost some of the gamy flavour.

CETRIOLO *Cucumber*

Cetrioli are in fact smaller than British cucumbers and are traditionally eaten raw. They are usually peeled and sliced very thinly, then sprinkled with salt and left for 30 minutes to dégorge. This makes them less bitter and more digestible (although it is hardly necessary now that the commercially produced cetriolo has lost much of its charac-teristic flavour). They are then drained, dried and dressed with olive oil, vinegar, salt and pepper, and mixed with tomatoes and (bell) peppers. Bigger cetrioli are cut in cubes or batons, so that the central part containing the seeds can be removed.

There is also a smaller variety of cetrioli called cetriolini used for preserving in vinegar. Cetriolini are used as a garnish for cold dishes such as vitello tonnato; they are also used in vinegary sauces like salsa verde* to accompany meat rather than fish.

CHIACCHIERE *Sweet fritters*

No food is more reminiscent of carnival week in Milan than these sweet fritters, a kind of fried sweet pastry, flavoured with Marsala•. Big trays of them are displayed in every bakery and pasticceria†. To make Chiacchiere, the dough is rolled out very thinly, then cut into rectangles. Two cuts are then made in each piece to make the chiacchiere lighter when cooked. Nowadays chiacchiere are baked as well as fried; they are then sprinkled with icing (confectioners') sugar.

CHIODI DI GAROFANO
Cloves

Cloves are one of the essential spices in Italian cooking. One or two cloves are stuck in an onion to flavour a stock, or they are added to braised meat and to marinades. But they are always used with great discretion. Cloves are also available in powdered form. They were known as one of the four sweet (or Lombard) spices, the others being cinnamon, nutmeg and white pepper.

CHIZZE *Savoury bread snacks*

These little pillows of bread dough are stuffed with prosciutto*, Swiss chard and young Parmesan, or sometimes with other stuffings; they are then fried in strutto*. They are the traditional snack food of Reggio-Emilia, always there at country festivities or as a pre-prandial snack.

CIAMBELLA *A ring-shaped cake*

A cake, originally from Marche and Emilia-Romagna, made in the shape of a large ring. It is a very homely confection – every housewife has her own version. The dough is made from flour, butter, eggs and sugar, with various flavourings added. Ciambella, served with crema pasticcera* can be eaten at the end of a meal. It is also eaten at breakfast dipped in caffè latte (coffee and milk), or at any time of the day with sweet wine.

There are many traditional ring-shaped cakes in regional Italian cooking and they take different names in each region. In some places you can also find savoury ciambelle, made with cheese and/or salami*, sometimes in small individual sizes.

CIAUSCOLO

A soft salami from Marche

A soft salami* from Marche, made with minced (ground) pork meat and fat. Flavoured with garlic, it is one of the few salami that is eaten spread on bread instead of sliced.

CICCIOLI

Pork or goose crackling (cracklings)

These succulent tiny morsels of crackling are formed when the fatty parts of the pig or goose are melted to obtain fresh lard. Ciccioli are best eaten as soon as the liquified fat is poured away, when they are still light and hot. In Emilia-Romagna pork ciccioli are mixed with the dough of the local flatbread, or spread over a leavened bread of Piacenza, while in Lazio they are eaten as an antipasto*. The flatbread that is baked with ciccioli is now made commercially.

CICORIA *or* RADICCHIO

Chicory (Endive)

Many plants, wild and cultivated, make up this large family, which includes the popular red radicchio*, the long bunchy catalogna and the Roman puntarelle*. All these cultivated varieties are best in autumn (fall) and winter, their proper season. They have a pleasingly bitter flavour and can be eaten raw or cooked. Raw chicory is dressed, usually cut into thin strips, with olive oil and vinegar. In the provinces of Modena and Reggio-Emilia this is usually balsamic vinegar, whose sweetness counteracts the bitterness of the plant. In Emilia it is also dressed with pancetta*, sautéed with garlic in oil, with a little vinegar added at the end. Young chicory is excellent grilled (broiled), and all chicory can be boiled and then dressed, or finished off in other ways.

The wild variety of cicoria, of which the dandelion is the most common, is usually referred to as cicorino. It is more bitter than the cultivated variety and, when eaten raw, it should be very young. In Puglia it is used in incapriata*.

CILIEGIA *Cherry*

This cheerful fruit, whose rich shades of red replace the delicate whiteness of its blossom, is only available in late spring and early summer. Ciliegia is a member of the large genus of *Prunus*, and it is a hybrid derived from two species, *Prunus cerasus*, the morello cherry, and *Prunus avium*, the sweet cherry. There are two main groups of cherries, tenerine (ones with soft pulp) and duracine (those with hard pulp), the latter being paler in colour and larger. The best Italian cherries come from Campania, Puglia, Veneto and, notably, Emilia-Romagna, where, in the orchards around Modena, the famous di Vignola cherries are grown.

In present-day Italy cherries are normally eaten fresh. They are also candied or preserved in alcohol after being dried in the sun for at least a day. These cherries are used a lot in cakes and sweets (candies).

CIME DI RAPA

Turnip tops (greens)

Turnip tops (greens) are a popular vegetable, especially in Tuscany, Rome and southern Italy, where they are also known as broccoletti. They are boiled and eaten in salad, or parboiled and then sautéed in oil with garlic and chilli, or tomatoes, as in Tuscany. They can also be cooked in a saucepan, with only the water attached to their leaves in a slow stewing method, which retains the pronounced flavour of the vegetable. In Puglia, turnip tops are often cooked with pasta and eaten with it, dressed with olive oil and chopped garlic.

CINGHIALE *Wild boar*

Wild boars are still to be found in the mountains of central and southern Italy, but they are now mainly raised semi-wild in large fenced-off reserves in forests or on hills.

Wild boar is a favourite meat in Lazio and Tuscany, where it is some-times found fresh in the markets. The most appetizing recipe, cinghiale in agrodolce (in a sweet-and-sour sauce) comes from the borders of Tuscany and Lazio. Here the boar, previously marinated in wine and various flavourings for 48 hours, is cooked

slowly in oil. Towards the end, onion, grated chocolate, prunes, pine nuts, raisins, candied citron and orange peel, as well as the marinade, are added. The dish is served with toasted bread. A young boar is good grilled (broiled or barbecued), either whole or in steaks, and the meat should be slightly underdone; it can also be cooked as pork in any recipe. One of my favourite recipes from Chianti is on page 114.

Wild boar is mainly used to make salami*, prosciutti* and coppa*. In Tuscany and Umbria there are a number of food shops that sell these products, made on nearby farms. Some coppa and prosciutti taste of truffle because the boars eat truffles whenever they can find them. Most of these products are, in fact, made with the meat of a meticcio, a hybrid cross between a pig and a wild boar. Meticci are reared in farms but retain their wild characteristics.

CIOCCOLATA *Hot chocolate*

Unsweetened cocoa powder is dissolved in hot milk, or water, with sugar added to make hot chocolate – which became very popular in Italy in the eighteenth century, somewhat later than in the rest of Europe. Like coffee, it was at first the drink of the aristocracy, usually accompanied by dry biscuits (cookies). Today, cioccolata has lost popularity. However, when you are in Venice, a cup of hot chocolate at Florian's on the Piazza is still the most pleasurable drink to sip while listening to the orchestra.

CIOCCOLATO
Chocolate

Chocolate is used less in patisserie in Italy than in other parts of Europe. Its main use is as a flavouring or a decoration. Chocolate is also used to flavour savoury dishes, as in the recipe for hare** (page 113). A Florentine recipe flavours tagliatelle with cocoa powder and dresses it with a sweet-and-sour sauce. Sicily's well-known caponata** is often flavoured with grated chocolate.

CIPOLLA *Onion*

Throughout history, onions have been an indispensable ingredient in almost every country's cooking. There are many varieties of onions, from the tiny white ones to the large specimens of a beautiful purple colour. The onions of Brianza have been appreciated for centuries for their delicate flavour, and for the way they keep their pretty shape all through the cooking. They are often stewed whole in butter and meat stock. The tastiest and mildest onions are grown in Piedmont, where the high mineral content of the soil provides favourable conditions.

Some recipes call for a special variety. The red onions of Tropea in Calabria are used in a salad because they are sweet and the little white ones are ideal in a sweet-and-sour sauce (see recipe on page 142). Onions are often stuffed in Italy, the best-known recipes being from Piedmont. An unusal dish from the borders of Piedmont and Lombardy mixes amaretti* and mostarda di Cremona* in the stuffing, while another from Liguria contains tuna. And, finely chopped, onions are one of the basic elements of most soffritti† .

A common sight in the market towns of northern Italy for centuries is that of people keeping warm on freezing winter mornings by standing near large braziers. The onions are being roasted in them with their skins on. These are taken home, peeled and sliced, and eaten with olive oil and salt.

COCOMERO *Watermelon*

Known as anguria in northern Italy where, in the summer, they can be seen stacked in pyramids by the roadside, like cannon balls on the ramparts of medieval castles.

It is *the* summer fruit, popular all over the peninsula and cultivated mostly in Lazio and Puglia. The large watermelon with its green striped skin is the favourite in Italy because of its stronger flavour. In Sicily a sorbet (sherbet) called "jelu i muluni" is a delicious mixture of watermelon juice and sugar, studded with candied pumpkin and chocolate pieces and flavoured with cinnamon. Other sorbets are made with watermelon, usually sharpened by lemon juice or flavoured with coffee. The Sicilians serve these refreshing desserts decoratively on a bed of lemon or vine (grape) leaves.

CODA DI BUE *Oxtail*

A favourite cut of meat of the Romans, who have the best recipes for it (see coda alla vacccinara**, page 116). Pig's tail, called codino, is also eaten in pork stews together with other cuts of pork.

CODA DI ROSPO *Monkfish*

A large fish with a grotesque head that lives at the bottom of the sea and is quite common in the Adriatic. Although ugly to look at it is good to eat with its firm and elastic flesh, similar to lobster.

Monkfish is usually sold without the head, but the head is worth buying, when available, because it makes excellent fish stock. Monkfish is a highly prized fish, especially in Venice where it is split in half and simply grilled (broiled). A good recipe from Romagna suggests frying the monkfish, cut into steaks, and then baking it covered with a mixture of chopped hard-boiled (hard-cooked) egg yolks, dried breadcrumbs, parsley and garlic, all moistened by the oil in which the fish has been cooked. Another recipe from the coast further south finishes off the fried fish in a tomato sauce flavoured with oregano, anchovy fillets and garlic.

COLLA DI PESCE

Leaf gelatine (gelatin)

The best colla di pesce, the culinary gelatine (gelatin) commonly used in Italy, is made from the dried bladder of a sturgeon. However it is also made from fish waste or seaweed. It dissolves easily and evenly, has no flavour whatsoever and gives the preparation in which it is used a less gluey consistency than powdered gelatine.

COLOMBA *A traditional Easter cake*

If you walk past a pasticceria† or a bakery in any town in Lombardy during Holy Week you will be tempted by a most delicious smell. It is the smell of the colomba pasquale (literally the "Easter dove"), which is in fact a cake

shaped like a dove. The Colomba is made with a light and very buttery dough similar to that used for the Milanese panettone*, and it is covered with sugar crystals and almonds. It contains a lot of candied peel, but no sultanas (golden raisins). A modern colomba may be covered with chocolate or with marzipan. Colomba is now popular all over northern Italy and has begun to cross the Alps.

CONCENTRATO DI POMODORO *Tomato paste*

There are three varieties of concentrato di pomodoro, a light variety, which is the most common, and two stronger varieties – these are doppio concentrato, 100 g/3½ oz/⅓ cup of which equates to 500 g/ 1 lb of fresh tomato, and triplo concentrato, 100 g/3½ oz/⅓ cup of which is the equivalent of 600 g/1¼ lb of fresh tomato. All varieties, and particularly the strong ones, should be used sparingly and allowed to cook in the sauce for some time to reduce their acidity. A small amount of sugar helps the process.

In southern Italy and Sicily, tomato paste is made at home and is called strattù. It can only be made in the summer, when the tomatoes and the sun are at their best. The tomatoes, cut in half and sprinkled with sea salt, are spread out in large baskets in the sun. After four or five days they are puréed, and again placed in the sun until the liquid evaporates and the purée takes on a reddish brown colour. Oil is then added and the paste is spooned into jars and sealed. It then keeps well through the winter.

CONCHIGLIA DI SAN GIACOMO *Scallop*

See CAPPASANTA

CONFETTI
Confetti or sugared almonds

There are two different kinds of confetti, the soft and the hard. The soft, made by hand on a small scale, consist of a paste, usually almond, covered with a layer of sugar. Hard confetti (sugared almonds) are made with a whole almond which is then coated in sugar. Hard white confetti are given by the newly weds to their family and friends; they are also part of the buffet at first Communion parties, while at Christenings they are coloured blue for a boy and pink for a girl.

CONFETTURA *Jam*

After years of confusion regarding the usage of the two words, confettura and marmellata, a recent official decree stated that confettura is jam and marmellata is marmalade – simple! All sorts of jam are made in the country: pumpkin, tomato and even rose petal, but the most popular are apricot, plum and peach. Jams are the most common topping for crostate* (tarts).

CONIGLIO *Rabbit*

Rabbit has never been *haute cuisine* food, but its meat is excellent and healthy, with a high protein and a low cholesterol and fat content.

There are two breeds of rabbit, wild and farmed, the former almost unobtainable in Italy, but cooked as hare (jack rabbit) when available. Domestic rabbit, on the other hand, is popular, especially in Liguria and Veneto, where there are several rabbit farms. The quality of the domestic rabbit depends on its diet, breeding and age. It lends itself to many preparations, most of them also suitable for chicken. The usual method of cooking it is alla cacciatora†. The best domestic rabbit I ever ate was a coniglio in porchetta, a speciality of Marche, when the rabbit was cooked like a suckling pig – porchetta. The recipe on page 112 is for rabbit with (bell) peppers, a traditional dish from Tuscany, where rabbit is also prepared as in the recipe for lepre in salmì**.

CONSERVA *Preserve*

The favourite Italian conserva is that of tomato, so much so that tomato preserve is simply called conserva in southern Italy. The most popular way of making tomato preserve is to bottle the purée and boil it in the bottle. *A macchina per i pomodori* (tomato machine) still goes around from village to village in August to prepare the purée for all the locals. The most commonly used conserva di pomodoro these days is made commercially and preserved in cans. The first such conserva was made in 1875 in Parma by Francesco Cirio, and not, as is often stated, in Naples.

Other vegetables are preserved in oil, wine vinegar or al naturale†, which means the vegetable is parboiled and bottled with water. Some fruit is preserved in alcohol, including apricots, cherries, grapes and peaches.

Traditionally fish and meat were also preserved, but this is dying out due to the availability of frozen products. In Calabria meat is preserved in salt with chilli and fennel seeds and aged for a few months. When ready for use, it is soaked overnight and then cooked with broad (fava) beans in soup or with tomatoes to serve with pasta. In some farms in northern Italy, goose is still preserved in oil and salt and flavoured with spices, to be enjoyed during the long winter months.

CONTORNO *Accompaniments*

This term includes vegetables, and/or other ingredients that accompany a main dish. The contorno can be served on the same plate or on a separate plate, but at the same time. The contorno is never an integral part of the main dish. Thus a roast will often be surrounded by small roasted or sautéed potatoes; braised peas or French (green) beans are an accepted contorno to costolette alla Milanese* ** or fricandò*. Spinach sautéed in olive oil is frequently the contorno to saltimbocca alla romana* **, while the contorno de rigueur to a roast, but only to a roast, is a fresh green salad, especially in the spring when many different leaves are available in the market.

It is rare for more than one vegetable to be served as a contorno. Pasta and risotti are never referred to as contorni, nor are they served with contorni, with the exception of risotto* with ossobuco* or with costoletta*.

COPPA
A cured cut of pork or brawn (head cheese)
In northern Italy a coppa is the pig's raw boned shoulder, rolled and cured in saltpetre, salt, pepper and nutmeg. Put into pig casing, it is aged for about 3 months. A perfect coppa should be made of equal parts of lean and fat meat. When well prepared, coppa tastes similar to prosciutto*, although more earthy and vigorous. It should be sliced thinly, but not be wafer thin.

In central Italy coppa is a brawn made from pig's head. It is called coppa di testa** or, occasionally, coppa d'inverno (winter coppa) because pigs are slaughtered in the winter and it must be eaten soon after it is made.

CORATELLA
A type of offal (variety meat)
Coratella is a mixture of the heart, lights and liver of a young lamb, or more rarely of a kid. This offal is a delicacy of central Italy, especially Rome, and also of Calabria and Sardinia. In Rome it is cooked with the local artichokes or with masses of onions, while in Sardinia the offal is cooked with peas and plenty of basil.

COSTATA *A cut of beef*
An entrecôte or T-bone steak. A costata is usually 4–6 cm/1½–2½ in thick and weighs about 450 g/1 lb. However in some regions costata means a boneless steak, but always of beef. The best way to cook a costata is to grill (broil) it, as in bistecca alla Fiorentina*. Costata is usually served with roast or fried potatoes, but it goes very well with a spring salad or a salad of tender French (green) beans.

Costata alla pizzaiola*, a recipe from Naples, is fried and then finished off in a tomato sauce flavoured with anchovy fillets and capers, reminiscent of a pizza topping.

COSTA see BIETA

COSTOLETTA *Chop*
This can be a chop of veal, lamb or pork, but not beef. The best known is the costoletta alla Milanese**, a veal chop which must have a bone, and should be 1–1½ cm/½–⅝ in thick. Some cooks marinate the chops in milk to produce a more delicate flavour and a whiter colour.

The costolette alla valdostana are stuffed with Fontina and then coated and fried as the "Milanese". When in season, a few slices of white truffle can be added to the Fontina. Lamb costolette are eaten mainly in central and southern Italy where they are sautéed and served with a tomato and peppers sauce. In Tuscany these costolette are breaded and fried like the Milanese.

A Roman recipe for grilled lamb chops is on page 127.

The most lavish recipe for both veal and lamb costolette is written by Artusi¢, who suggests that the fried costolette should be covered by slices of white truffle and Parmesan or Gruyère "but both must be sliced as thin as possible," he writes, and then they are placed in the oven with a little stock or meat juice and finished off with a sprinkling of lemon juice.

COTECHINO
A pork sausage

This large sausage is sold all over the peninsula, although it is less popular in the south. It is made with pork rind mixed with lean pork meat and back fat; the coarsely chopped mixture is then flavoured with salt, pepper, cloves and cinnamon and pushed into pig casing. Although it is easy to make this sausage, it is difficult to make it well; cotechini are often too dry or too salty, or the mixture is chopped too coarsely or too finely. Cotechino is ready to eat two or three weeks after being made, and it should be eaten within three months. Nowadays they are usually produced commercially, on a large scale, but they are also made in small quantities by pork butchers. These cotechini should be soaked in cold water for about three hours, pierced all over with a thick needle and then cooked for a long time wrapped in a cloth. Most of the cotechini sold outside Italy are pre-cooked. Although easier to prepare, they are certainly not as good.

Cotechino is traditional food in northern Italy, where it is usually served with either lentils, polenta* (coarse cornmeal), stewed Savoy cabbage or as part of a bollito misto*. In a recipe from Modena cotechino is parboiled and then, with its skin removed, wrapped in prosciutto* and a slice of beef. It is then cooked with onion in Lambrusco, the local sparkling red wine. In Cremona dried porcini are used instead of prosciutto, and the cotechino is sautéed with an onion and then cooked in stock. In Bergamo, sliced cooked cotechino is further cooked in a rich tomato sauce for extra flavour, and it is then baked in the oven in layers with polenta and grated Parmesan cheese; the dish is called polenta e codeghin.

COTENNA DI MAIALE
Pork rind

Pork rind is used to make salami*, cotechini* and other pork sausages. It is also used by itself, previously blanched, to give flavour to soups, as in a bean soup from Abruzzo to which a trotter (foot) is also added. The other cotenna used in soups, or in pasta sauces, is that of prosciutto*, which must be previously blanched or soaked.

COTOGNA *Quince*

This is the golden apple of classical Greece that Paris gave to Aphrodite. Quinces, originally from Iran, were already popular in Roman times, and in the famous book by Apicius¢ there is a recipe for preserving them. "Pick perfect quinces with stems and leaves. Place them in a vessel, pour over honey and new wine and you will preserve them for a long time." In modern Italy quinces are used to make jams, jellies and cotognata*.

COTOGNATA *Quince cheese*

Quince cheese is a popular dessert all over Italy, although its birthplace is

Sicily, where it is still made according to family tradition. The recipe, together with the attractive pottery moulds in which the cotognata is dried, are handed down from one generation to the next. Cotognata is preserved, covered with sugar and then cut into squares.

But the best cotognata is said to be made in Genoa, renowned for its candied fruits and fruit jellies. A preparation containing quinces, must and walnuts is made in Emilia-Romagna and Piedmont, and served with a soft polenta.

COZZE or MITILI *Mussels*

Although these are the correct Italian names, mussels are also called peoci* in Venice, muscioli in Marche and muscoli in some other regions. As this variety of regional names suggests, they are the popular molluscs. Nowadays mussels are nearly always cooked; they are put in fish soups and used in pasta sauces, sometimes containing tomatoes. They are also stuffed with breadcrumbs, parsley, garlic, tomatoes, grated pecorino* and eggs – or any combination of these ingredients**. Doused with the best olive oil, they are baked for about 15 minutes. In Taranto in Puglia, where the mussels grow large and fat in the Mare Piccolo, a saltwater lagoon, a dish called teglia di cozze is popular. This is a delicious combination of potatoes, courgettes (zucchini), tomatoes and mussels. In a traditional dish from Chioggia, the port at the south end of the Venetian lagoon, shelled mussels are added to diced potatoes and gently stewed in fish stock. The dish is finished with a drizzle of the best olive oil.

CREMA *Creams*

This term includes butter creams, custard sauces and, rarely, smooth soups. They are all of French origin, brought to Italy after the seventeenth century, when French gastronomy took the lead.

CREMA FRITTA *Fried cream*

Popular in northern Italy, this dish consists of a thick, cold crema pasticcera* cut into pieces, coated in egg and breadcrumbs and fried. In Veneto and Liguria it is served as a dessert, while in Emilia-Romagna it is an indispensable part of fritto misto*.

CREMA INGLESE
English custard

An Italianization of crème anglaise, a French preparation, originating in English custard (custard sauce). Of all the sweet creams, this custard is the most popular; it is used with stewed fruits or cakes such as panettone* or colomba*. It is also the basis of most ice creams.

CREMA PASTICCERA
Crème pâtissière

This custard is the one used most often in Italian patisserie. It is a mixture of eggs and milk, thickened by flour. Crema pasticcera is the basis of zuppa inglese*, it forms the filling of many desserts and is served by itself with Marsala•, chocolate and other flavourings.

CRESCENTINA
A type of bread

Crescentina is a mixture of flour and water plus lard or crackling (cracklings). It may be leavened and baked or cut into diamond shapes and fried. In Bologna, it is cut into rounds, and pieces of prosciutto* are often kneaded into the dough before frying. In Romagna, a few kilometres east, the same thing is known as piadina*.

CRESCENZA
A type of cheese from Lombardy

A traditional cow's milk cheese of the stracchino* family, made in Lombardy, where it is also called stracchino. It is now made commercially and is popular in the north.

The cheese is made with milk taken from cows in the evening when they are tired after grazing in rich pastures all day. It is made from pasteurized milk and it must be eaten within one week of being made, or it tastes acidic.

Crescenza has a delicate, though rich, flavour and is a pure white colour.

CRESPELLE *Pancakes (Crepes)*

Crespelle are particularly popular in Tuscany, with the well-known recipe crespelle alla fiorentina, stuffed with spinach and ricotta and covered with béchamel. There is only one traditional recipe: scrippelle 'mbusse, a soup from Abruzzo in which the batter contains parsley and the pancakes (crepes) are stuffed with pecorino* and covered with chicken stock.

An alternative way of making crespelle is to fold them like a little bag, rather than rolling them up. They are filled with a meat stuffing, and are known as fazzoletti (handkerchiefs). Crespelle are also known as cannelloni*.

CROCCANTE *A "crunchy" nougat*

Croccante is a sweet preparation made in most regions with almonds or hazelnuts, caramelized sugar and flavourings. In Piedmont and Veneto it is made with roasted hazelnuts. In southern Italy the nut mixture is flavoured with orange zest, in Lazio with vanilla and in Liguria usually with lemon.

CROCCHETTE *Croquettes*

These are made with mashed potato, minced (ground) meat, poultry, fish or risotto, and bound with béchamel and/or egg. Crocchette are usually oval in shape and are always coated in egg and breadcrumbs and then fried in butter and/or oil. Crocchette are often made from leftovers which, mixed with egg, Parmesan and other flavourings become a good dish in their own right.

CROSTACEI *Crustaceans*

Although difficult to classify because of their diversity, the characteristic they have in common is that their bodies are protected by a horny outer layer. The most popular crostacei in Italy are gamberi*, scampi*, granchi*, mazzancolle* and canocchie*. All crostacei should be bought live and killed by plunging into boiling water. Their freshness is detected, as with other sea creatures, by their smell, which should be sweet, and by their quick reaction when touched.

CROSTATA *Tart*
Crostate are always sweet, and usually made with a sweet pastry. Although there are only three traditional tarts (of ricotta* from Rome, of jam from Emilia and of marzipan from Sicily), a look in the window of any pasticceria† will show that they can be made with many different fillings today.

CROSTINI *Bread-based products*
Crostini can be croûtons, or slices of country bread, lightly oiled or buttered or moistened with vin santo• or stock and then toasted. Crostini alla Napoletana are similar to pizza, the bread being covered with a slice of mozzarella*, a piece of anchovy fillet and a morsel of tomato, and then baked. Crostini di mare consist of thick slices of bread hollowed out, buttered and toasted in the oven, and then filled with seafood, breadcrumbs, parsley, garlic and olive oil. The best known crostini are those from Tuscany, topped with chicken or game livers**.

CULATELLO *A pork product*
This is made from the fillet of a pig's thigh, aged for about a year in the area between Parma and the river Po. It looks like an oversized egg, weighs about 3 kg /6½ lb, has a soft, melt-in-the-mouth texture and a flavour similar to prosciutto*, but

more defined. It is eaten cold, as an antipasto*, thinly sliced, with bread. It is also made commercially at Christmas when it is traditional fare in northern Italy.

CUORE *Heart*
The most popular is the heart of a calf, which is usually marinated in slices in olive oil, garlic, chilli and lemon and then grilled (broiled) or pan-fried. It is also baked whole wrapped in pork caul, stuffed with pancetta*, soft bread-crumbs and flavourings. Lamb's heart is eaten with all the other offal (variety meats) in the coratella*. Chicken and other birds' hearts are part of the giblets and, with the liver, make excellent sauces for pasta or risotto*, or to accompany sformati*.

CUSCUSU *Couscous dishes*
There are two dishes with this name, one from Trapani in western Sicily, made from couscous mixed with various fish, octopus and other seafood. The other cuscusu is made in Livorno and is a couscous mixed with stewed cabbage and tiny meat balls cooked in a tomato sauce. Both these ports had a thriving trade with North Africa, hence the use of couscous.

DADO *Bouillon or stock cube*
Even for the best cooks, dadi are an important standby. This may be because the stock cubes you buy in Italy

have a genuine taste; they are full of flavour and yet delicate. (Italian bouillon cubes are available from delicatessens in other countries.) They are used in soups, added to sauces and savoury dishes, and used in some risotti*. Dadi would not be used, however, in very delicate risotti such as risotto alla Milanese** or the Venetian risi e bisi**. Some cubes are flavoured with porcini (see funghi) and these, with the addition of fresh mushrooms, make a good risotto.

DAINO *Roe deer*

A large inhabitant of the Alps, where its meat is considered to be better than that of the red deer. Roe deer is first marinated, and it is then cooked alla Alto Atesino (see Stewed Venison recipe on page 115), or a leg is larded with smoked pancetta and pot-roasted.

DATTERO DI MARE

Literally, "date-shell"

The extraordinary property of this mollusc, which looks like a date, is that it erodes the rock to make a lodging place for itself. Its scientific name is, in fact, *lithophaga* (stone eater). It achieves this feat by emitting an acid which makes a hole in which it nests. Datteri di mare are found in the gulf of La Spezia and in Puglia, although they have recently become quite rare. They are hard to gather, and their fishermen have to use special boats.

Datteri di mare are a highly prized mollusc, usually cooked in the shell. Because of their delicate flavour they are best simply cooked, such as in a soffritto* of oil, garlic and parsley, into which they are thrown to open up. They are also eaten raw, but in this case they must only be caught where the water is known to be clean.

DENTICE *Mediterranean dentex*

This is an excellent specimen of the large sea bream family, the Sparidae. It can be as long as 1 m/1 yd, but the average length is about 30–40 cm/12–16 in. Dentice are found all around the coasts of Italy.

It is usually cooked by grilling (broiling) or roasting, and often accompanied by a sauce made with olive oil, lemon juice and mashed, salted anchovies. The larger specimens are cut into steaks and then grilled, or pan-fried in olive oil.

Dentice like sea bass can be cooked in a crust of salt**, ideal for sealing in its flavour.

DIAVOLICCHIO *Chilli*

This diminutive of diavolo ("devil") is the name given to chilli in Abruzzo and Basilicata. Chilli is the most popular flavouring of these two regions, where it is used lavishly. It is put in salami* and sausages, in fish soup (the brodetto of Abruzzo** is characterized by it), in pasta sauces and with sweet (bell) peppers.

Diavolicchio can be used both fresh and dried. The drying takes place in the sun – in the countryside in the summer you can still see doorways and balconies festooned with chains of scarlet diavolicchio.

DOLCE *Sweet*

A range of sweet preparations are covered by this term, although strictly speaking dolce is the course served at the end of a meal. When dolce is part of a dessert it always follows cheese and precedes fruit, although nowadays fruit might be omitted after a dolce.

A dolce is not an everyday part of a meal; it is reserved for special occasions or public feasts, all of which have their special regional dolce. As they are eaten on feast days, dolci are even more regional than other types of cooking. Patron saints, as well, have their own special dolci, in every town in Italy.

The dolci of the north are often little more than sweet breads, the panettone* Milanese being the prime example. The dolci of central Italy are richer, with lots of spices, nuts, candied peel and honey, as in the panforte* **from Siena or the certosino ** from Bologna. Also in this part we see the birth of the dolce al cucchiaio† – a dessert that can be eaten with a spoon, such as zuppa inglese*. In southern Italy the main ingredients of dolci are almonds and candied fruits, a heritage from Arab cooking. There are many exceptions to this rule. After all, the birthplace of zabaglione*, the dolce al cucchiaio par excellence, is Piedmont, while a ciambella* (sweet ring-shaped bread) is a traditional dolce of Puglia.

The making of some dolci was a prerogative of the nuns. Alberto Denti di Pirajno, in his *I Siciliani a Tavola*, suggests that the reason for this is that when the Arab harems were dismantled by the Normans, some of the inhabitants – all passionate sweet-eaters and makers – took refuge in convents. There they occupied themselves with making sweets, and it was from them that the nuns learned the craft, which they carried on and perfected.

DOLCELATTE
A creamy, blue cheese
This mild gorgonzola* was created by the firm of Galbani, the company that created Bel Paese*, for the British market. It is made in round shapes of about 12 kg/26½ lb, and aged for two months. Dolcelatte is virtually un-known in Italy.

DRAGONCELLO *Tarragon*
Also called serpentaria or estragone, this culinary herb has a distinctive aroma, strong yet at the same time subtle. It is used very little in Italy except in Siena. In fact it is also known as erba di Siena, where a salsa al dragoncello is made to go with boiled meats, the tarragon replacing the parsley of salsa verde*.

ERBE AROMATICHE *Herbs*
There has lately been a resurgence in the use of herbs, although the number of different herbs used is smaller. Parsley is the most popular Italian herb, followed by rosemary, bay leaf, marjoram, sage, thyme, oregano and basil, with mint, tarragon, borage, chives and wild fennel used less frequently.

There are always one or two parti-cular herbs that enhance the basic characteristics of a certain type of food or a dish, while at the same time complementing its flavour with their own. For instance a rabbit should always be cooked with thyme; the herb to go with veal escalopes (scallops) is sage or parsley, while an arrosto (roast meat or poultry) would never be cooked without a sprig or two of fresh rosemary. Wild fennel goes in the porchetta* (roasted pig) of central Italy, in the Tuscan arista* and in the famous Sicilian pasta with fresh sardines. Nor would the Tuscan fagioli all'uccelletto* be what it is without the sage leaves gently sautéed in rich oil.

Herbs are preserved in many ways. Some can be successfully dried hanging in bunches in a dry and well-aired room, or they can be dried in a very low oven. Salt is a good preservative – the clean herbs, whole or chopped, are put in jars in layers with sea salt. Thyme, bay leaves, basil, wild fennel and rosemary can be preserved in oil. The simplest and most modern method of preserving herbs is freezing. Some herbs, such as sage, should be frozen whole, while others, parsley for instance, are better chopped first. That said, there is no doubt that fresh herbs are far more aromatic and sweeter, and should always be used in preference to herbs that have been preserved by whatever method.

ERBE SELVATICHE
Wild herbs and plants
This term is refers to all edible wild herbs and plants. Restaurant and home cooks alike now recognize the culinary value of these simple, unpretentious plants. On the hillsides behind the fashionable Italian riviera, cooks and gardeners are out at dawn on a spring morning gathering wild herbs for the stuffing of pansotti* (Genoese ravioli).

In Emilia these plants are dressed with pieces of pancetta* sautéed in oil and poured hot on salad, enriched by a touch of balsamic vinegar.

ESTRATTO
Extract, a concentrated flavouring
The two estratti are di carne, that is beef extract, and di pomodoro, that is tomato extract.

The estratti di carne, universally used in Italy, are commercially produced and sold in jars and tubes.

The estratto di pomodoro is home-made and is a speciality of Sicily and southern Italy. It is called strattù* in Sicily and concentrato di pomodoro* in other parts of Italy.

FAGIANO *Pheasant*
Its meat is excellent, that of the female being superior in taste and tendernesss. (The plucked female is easily recognized by a smaller body and a shorter tail.) Pheasant must be hung before it is drawn and plucked. Most gastronomes agree that the period of hanging should be between five and fifteen days, depending on the sex and age of the bird and the climate.

The Italian methods of cooking pheasant are similar to the French, although Italian recipes tend to be simpler. A male bird is usually covered with pancetta and pot-roasted. Older birds are braised in wine, and young hens are roasted in the oven. An old Venetian recipe suggests a rich stuffing made with hard cheese, egg yolk, garlic, fennel, sultanas (golden raisins), spices, herbs, sugar and Morello cherries. The pheasant is then pot-roasted. The recipe on page 109 shows the French influence on Milanese cooking.

FAGIOLINO *or* CORNETTO *French or green bean*
These names refer to a type of bean with an edible pod. There are many varieties of this vegetable: the roundish

white Bobis, the flat yellow Meraviglia di Venezia, the purplish Trionfo Violetto and the attractive marbled green Anellino di Trento. Another delicious variety is fagiolini di Sant' Anna, which is grown mainly in Tuscany.

French beans are boiled in plenty of salted water. They must cook fast and without a lid. Once properly cooked, they are thoroughly drained, after which some recipes recommend rinsing under cold water to help retain their colour. Unless served cool as a salad – a common dish – French beans undergo a second cooking, alla Genovese† (sautéed in butter or oil, with garlic and anchovies), alla Milanese† (with cream and Parmesan) or alla Fiorentina (in a tomato sauce flavoured with fennel seeds). When they are young, fresh and of the best quality, fagiolini can be cooked in a tomato sauce without any pre-cooking.

FAGIOLO *Bean*

The humble bean, the seed of a leguminous plant, and its cousin the broad (fava) bean have for centuries been called "la carne dei poveri" ("poor man's meat"). This is because these pulses (legumes) are highly nutritious, yet cost very little. Dried beans in fact contain a little more protein than an equal weight of meat, and they are also quite rich in vitamins.

Beans that are to be dried are harvested in the late summer, while fresh beans are harvested in early summer. They are eaten in soups and in salads, mashed and stewed, with pasta and with meat, flavoured with sage or rosemary, garlic or onion.

It is in Veneto that the top quality of beans grow – fagioli di Lamon. They are large with a tender skin, a velvety texture and a full flavour, and are the best for the famous local pasta e fagioli**, in which the beans are combined with pork rind, pig's trotters (feet) and even chunks of cotechino*, all flavoured with rosemary.

The most popular variety of bean is the borlotti, pale pink with red speckles, perfect for soups and stews because of its consistency. The best borlotti come from the country around Vigevano, a town south of Milan as well known for its beans as for its fifteenth-century square. Borlottini are a small type of borlotti and they are used for the same dishes. The Tuscan varieties are the cannellini and the toscanelli, both white beans, usually eaten sautéed or in salads. The Tuscans, not for nothing called mangia-fagioli ("bean eaters"), have a vast repertoire of bean recipes. One good recipe is fagioli all'uccelletto, for which you can find my recipe on page 153. In Umbria the same dish is made without the addition of the tomatoes. The Tuscan tonno e fagioli** (beans and tuna) sprinkled with sweet red onion, is a popular antipasto. In contrast to the Venetian pasta e fagioli, the Tuscan zuppa di fagioli is made with beans and black cabbage (the Tuscan variety) and at the end the soup is poured over stale bread. Every region, in fact, has its bean dishes, all good and nourishing.

When they are in season fresh beans are not dried, but used as they are. Dried beans, which are the ones most commonly used outside Italy, need some soaking and/or pre-cooking. Beans should be cooked until they are soft, which we Italians consider to take a minimum of two hours. Al dente† beans are simply uneatable. Many of the cooked canned beans that are convenient to use and are now on the market are of excellent quality.

FAGOTTINI *Literally, "small faggots"*

Fagottini consist of an outside layer of dough wrapped around various stuffings. The dough can be a leavened pizza dough or a shortcrust pastry (pie dough) made with olive oil and/or strutto* – pure melted lard.

Fagottini used to be fried, but now that cooks have become more conscious of diet and health, they are often baked. Another sort of fagottini are fagottini di verza** , a dish from Milan – also called involtini di verza – where a meat stuffing is wrapped in blanched Savoy cabbage leaves.

FARAONA *Guinea fowl*

In Tuscany guinea fowl is usually roasted, when it forms part of arrosto misto (mixed roast meats). In Veneto it is stuffed with onions and cloves and cooked in an earthenware pot, faraona in tecia. But possibly the most succulent result comes from an old recipe (see page III) from the Lombardy region.

Guinea fowl are mostly farmed, a fact that makes it very important to buy them from a good supplier. Farmed guinea fowl has sadly lost that slight gamy flavour, which made it more like pheasant than chicken.

FARINA *Flour*

When the word is used by itself it means the flour made from soft wheat. This is the flour from which bread and cakes are made.

In Italy flour is divided into five different grades according to the proportion of husk and whole grain it contains. The grades go from 00, the whitest and silkiest, to Integrale, which is produced from the whole grain. Most bakers most commonly use 00 flour nowadays for cakes, some kinds of egg pasta and luxury types of bread. It

is also used in homes for delicate preparations, sauces and egg pasta. If you make your own pasta I recommend Italian 00 flour, available in the best supermarkets and Italian delis.

FARINATA
A type of pancake

This thick pancake is made with chick pea (garbanzo bean) flour. It is a speciality of Liguria, and is similar to the Niçoise socca. To make farinata, the chick pea flour is mixed with water to a thinnish paste, lots of olive oil is added and the mixture is then poured into a large, round, flat copper pan. It is baked in a wood oven, and is ready when a light crust has formed on the top.

Farinata is hardly ever made, or eaten, at home: its place is in the street, where it is bought from stalls while shopping at the market, or in a bar, to be eaten with a glass of white wine. Farinata is the sort of food that can only be fully appreciated when eaten in its native habitat.

FARRO *Emmer wheat*

This was the precursor of durum wheat, and the Italian word farina* (flour) is derived from its name. Farro was the staple of the poor throughout the ages. Nowadays it is cultivated mainly in Tuscany, and also in Umbria and Lazio. Elsewhere it can be bought in most Italian delis and from mail-order firms. The farro on the market is usually pearl (the outside skin having been removed) and it does not need soaking.

Farro is often used in soups thickened by beans, as in the traditional soup on page 61. Due to the resurgence of traditional regional cooking, and the interest in healthy food, farro is used now by the greatest restaurateurs.

FARSUMAGRU *or* FARSUMAURU *Stuffed meat*

A celebrated Sicilian dish, now well known throughout Italy. Farsumagru consists of a lean piece of beef or veal, stuffed with many rich ingredients.

FAVA *Broad bean*

This familiar pulse (legume) grows easily everywhere in Italy. Being nutritious it is a staple food for poorer people in central and southern Italy. In Tuscany broad (fava) beans, when young, are eaten raw at the end of the meal, served in their pods, together with a piece of pecorino* – a perfect ending to any meal.

Southern Italian cooking is rich in recipes for broad beans, which are used fresh in the spring and dried all year around. The oldest of these recipes is for a purée of broad beans which is made today as it was in ancient Egypt, where it originated. The dish is called incapriata* in Puglia and macco* in Sicily, and it consists of dried broad beans, previously soaked, peeled and boiled until soft enough to be mashed. This delicate purée is served dressed with olive oil, with wild fennel mixed in (Sicily) and with boiled wild chicory or turnip tops (greens). Unless very young, broad beans, both fresh and dried, should be peeled. It is a lengthy job, but a necessary one. Dried broad beans can often be found already peeled in health-food shops, and they are delicious. They must be soaked for at least eight hours.

FAVE DEI MORTI
Literally, "broad beans of the dead"

These little biscuits (cookies), made in Lombardy and Lazio, are so called because they are about the size of broad (fava) beans, and they are prepared on All Souls' Day, 2 November. They are made with flour, sugar, almonds and pine nuts, bound together with egg white and baked.

FECOLA DI PATATE
Potato flour

An important attribute of this potato flour is that it is gluten-free. It has a very delicate, yet distinctive, flavour, and is used to replace some or all of the flour in certain cakes. A little potato flour is often used in sauces as a thickening agent, dissolved in a little cold water.

FEGATELLI DI MAIALE
A pig's liver dish

This pig's liver is wrapped in caul fat and grilled (broiled) or fried. It is one of the great specialities of Tuscany and Lazio. Fegatelli alla Fiorentina are coated with a mixture of wild fennel, garlic, breadcrumbs and other spices, then wrapped in caul fat and threaded on skewers. They are grilled on charcoal or cooked in the oven. In a recipe from

Arezzo the fegatelli, dressed with wild fennel, salt and pepper, are threaded on skewers alternately with pieces of lamb and then grilled. In Lazio fegatelli are flavoured with bay leaves.

FEGATINI
Chicken livers

These are sold fresh in pollerie – poultry shops – and in some butchers' shops. Tuscany is the best region for them – Tuscan chickens tend to grow quickly, so that large livers can be obtained from young birds, thus avoiding the unpleasant flavour found in chicken livers from older birds.

The Tuscans produce the dish that makes the best use of chicken liver, crostini alla toscana**. Fegatini are also used in a risotto from Padova, risotto con i rovinassi (which is the dialect word for chicken livers), and in a Venetian spaghetti sauce, bigoli* coi rovinassi. In this dish the chicken livers are sautéed in butter and oil, flavoured with sage and then splashed with dry white wine. Another use of chicken livers is in sauces to accompany sformati* and risotti*, often in combination with sweetbreads, brains, prosciutto* etc.

FEGATO *Liver*

Liver is widely eaten all over the peninsula. The best known of all liver dishes is fegato alla Veneziana**. Another delicious way to prepare fegato is alla Milanese† (calf's liver coated in egg and breadcrumbs and fried in butter). Nearly all other recipes for calf's liver are from northern Italy, while in central and southern Italy pig's liver is a favourite. However, a good recipe for pig's liver from northern Italy is fegato alla lodigiana, in which the liver, cut into chunks and highly flavoured with wild fennel, is wrapped in prosciutto* and then in caul fat. It is then fried in butter, as is nearly all Lombard food. But the main use of pig's liver is in the production of all kinds of salumi* and salami, mostly uncooked, such as the mortadella di fegato made around Lake Orta in Piedmont. Lamb's liver is mainly eaten in combination with other lamb's offal (variety meats), as in the Roman coratella di abbacchio*.

Liver must be bought and eaten while it is very fresh.

FESA *A cut of meat*

A cut from the thigh of a calf, or of an older animal, more or less equivalent to the end of the rump. Animals are cut differently on the Continent, so there is no British or American equivalent. Fesa is used for scaloppine* (escalopes/scallops) of veal or beef. Fesa of beef is the best cut for carpaccio*. Fesa of veal is the best cut for an arrosto morto* or a vitello tonnato*.

FETTINE *Thin slices of meat*

Meaning literally "small slices", fettine are thinly cut slices of beef, veal or pork. They are bought pre-sliced and are then cooked in many different ways. Often they are simply shallow fried in butter and olive oil, but they can be used for more elaborate preparations. Veal fettine are used for frittura piccata*, for saltimbocca* or messicani*, pizzaiola*, uccellini scappati* or involtini*.

When simply sautéed, fettine are the modern food for busy or, perhaps, lazy cooks, some of whom even serve them every day! They are the Italian answer to the French steak or the American hamburger.

FICO *Fig*

Once ripe, figs perish quickly, so those eaten straight from the tree are far superior to those you buy in shops. Shop-bought figs are usually picked before they are ripe and thus have very little taste.

The fig is the only fruit that is formed, not from the flower, but with the flowers inside its covering of skin. There are two main varieties. One fruits twice a year, in July and in the late summer. The early figs, called fiorone, are large and rather tasteless. The later crop, which is the only crop for the other variety, is the luscious fruit that is so highly prized. These two main varieties can have fruit with black or green skin.

Figs are eaten as fruit and also with prosciutto* or salami*. They are also used as a filling for tarts or they are stewed in honeyed and spiced wine and served with egg custard. Fig jam is one of the best and most popular Italian preserves.

When dried, the figs are known as fichi secchi. They are popular throughout Italy, and especially so in Calabria where they are dried in the sun on bamboo trellises. Then they are minced (ground) and put in cakes, or stuffed with a mixture of almonds and walnuts, orange peel and a little honey and served as dessert.

FICO D'INDIA *Prickly pear*

The Italian name means Indian fig, but these fruits are neither pears nor figs, being the fruit of an opunta, a cactus. Prickly pears grow wild in Sicily and southern Italy, but the best species, the bastardona, is achieved with the intervention of man. The farmer removes the first fruits as soon as they begin to take shape. The next growth then produces fruits which are harder and tastier. Prickly pears are best eaten raw with a squeeze of lemon juice, but it is not a fruit that I rate very highly.

FINANZIERA
A traditional offal (variety meat) dish

An elaborate creation of Piedmontese origin, made with a selection of white meat and offal (variety meat), cooked in butter and flavoured with dried porcini or Marsala•. Finanziera can be served by itself, as an accompaniment to a plain risotto or as a rich sauce for a sformato*.

FINOCCHIETTO *or* FINOCCHIELLO SELVATICO *Fennel (herb)*

A perennial herb, with feathery foliage, which grows wild in hot climates. The fronds make a delicious stuffing for fish when finely chopped and mixed with other herbs and breadcrumbs. It is an important ingredient in the Sicilian dish, pasta with sardines**. It is also used with pork. The Florentine arista* **(roast loin of pork) is flavoured with finocchietto, as is porchetta*.

FINOCCHIO *Fennel (vegetable)*

The bulbous part at the base of this plant's stalk is one of the most popular vegetables in Italy. Fennel is a native of the Mediterranean, and it seems to be sweeter and more aromatic in Italy than elsewhere.

In Tuscany wedges of fennel are placed on the table at the end of the meal with apples and oranges. But it is mostly eaten as a vegetable or in a salad; in fact because of its versatility it is the most commonly prepared winter vegetable.

As a salad – raw, thinly sliced, dressed with lemon juice and olive oil – it is most refreshing, while it makes a perfect fresh, light antipasto mixed with some flakes of a good grana* or with some crumbled ricotta and lots of pepper. A Sicilian salad mixes fennel with oranges, chicory (Belgian endive) and black olives. Another traditional way of eating fennel is pinzimonio*.

To prepare fennel the stalks must be cut away and the thick outer leaves and brown parts removed. Fennel should always be dressed very lightly, olive oil and a pinch of salt being all it needs.

There are many recipes for cooked finocchio, of which the following is a selection. Finocchi fritti: fennel bulbs are cut lengthwise into wedges and blanched for five minutes, then coated in egg and breadcrumbs and fried. Finocchi al burro e formaggio: fennel is slowly stewed in butter and a little water for about 30 minutes and then sprinkled with Parmesan. Finocchi in tegame: the fennel is sautéed in oil flavoured with garlic for ten minutes, then half-covered with water and stewed until it is tender and the water is absorbed. Finocchi gratinati: fennel bulbs are cut into wedges, boiled until al dente† and then gently sautéed in butter for a few minutes. They are then covered with a thin béchamel flavoured with nutmeg and baked in the oven for 20 minutes. Finocchio is also used in soups, and to make sformati* **, see page 141.

Semi di finocchio are the seeds of some varieties of fennel, usually wild, which are better than the cultivated varieties. They are used to flavour fegatelli*, arista* **, the superb Tuscan salami called finocchiona*, as well as a score of lesser known dishes.

FINOCCHIONA
A type of salami
The most typical of Tuscan pork products, finocchiona is a large coarse-grained salami* made with pure pork meat plus some fat from the belly. It is flavoured with pepper, garlic and wild fennel seeds, and aged for between seven and twelve months.

FIOR DI LATTE
Cow's milk mozzarella
Made with cow's milk, this cheese is made in the same way as buffalo mozzarella*. Nowadays fior di latte is often called mozzarella. It is produced commercially and is used a lot on pizzas and other preparations.

FIORE DI ZUCCA
Courgette (zucchini) flower
The yellow flowers of courgette (zucchini) and pumpkin are a delicacy. The flower that sprouts in June and July from the long, thin undeveloped stem – the male shoot – is used. The stamen inside the flower, and the stalk, must be removed before cooking. The classic way to cook fiori di zucca is to fry them, coated in a light batter. In Lazio they are stuffed with grated Parmesan or mozzarella*, breadcrumbs, a piece of anchovy fillet and parsley.

In Abruzzo there is a pasta sauce made with fiori di zucca and saffron. There is also a risotto recipe with courgette flowers – they are cooked separately in oil with a little parsley and basil and then added to the rice at the end of the cooking (see recipe on page 182).

FOCACCIA *A type of bread*

Focaccia can be savoury or sweet and can be flavoured with various ingredients. It is like a thick pizza, but with a texture more like bread. The basic recipe for focaccia is simply flour, salt and yeast, kneaded with water. After being set aside to rise, focaccia is baked in a hot oven.

They are many different kinds of focaccia from all over Italy. Liguria and the southern regions offer the greatest variety. Focaccia alla Genovese is the basic dough dripping with the local olive oil. Focaccia con le cipolle, or sardenaria (with onions) is another local speciality, the sliced onions are scattered on the top and liberally doused with oil. Recco, a village between Genoa and Santa Margherita, has its own focaccia, which is two layers of dough, the top rolled out so thin as to be transparent, containing formaggetta, a local soft cow's milk cheese. This melts during baking to permeate the focaccia.

The focacce of Puglia and Calabria are like thick pizzas stuffed with different ingredients, such as batavia, salt cod, tomatoes and mozzarella*. In Naples the local focaccia is called tortano* and it is baked in the shape of a ring. Another rich Neapolitan focaccia is casatiello – eggs in their shells are gently pushed into the ring-shaped leavened dough before it is baked. In a more modern version, the eggs are broken into a hollow in the dough and then covered with more dough.

There are also some sweet focacce, such as the ancient Venetian fugassa**.

The focaccia Vicentina from Vicenza is made with a dough similar to its Venetian cousin. It is baked in small shapes, often like doves, enveloping hard-boiled eggs. The focaccia di Castelnuovo, a town near La Spezia, is made at Easter with polenta flour, pine nuts and olive oil.

FONTAL *A semi-soft cheese*

A relatively new cheese, fontal was created in Trentino after the Second World War. It is made commercially from pasteurized cow's milk, and aged for three months. It has a pleasingly sweet flavour and a semi-soft texture. Fontal is a good table cheese, as well as an excellent cooking cheese and can be used in toasted sandwiches, savoury pies etc. It is also used to make fonduta instead of fontina*, which it resembles.

FONTINA *A type of cheese*

If there is a cheese that really melts in your mouth, fontina is it. This semi-soft cheese from Val d'Aosta is made from cow's milk in large round shapes weighing from 5–10 kg/11–22 lb. Fontina is ready to eat in four or five months. It is a buff-coloured cheese that has a few small holes and a thin crust. Fontina is, with Parmesan, the best cooking cheese, and its characteristic taste combines beautifully with many dishes. Possibly the most important of these is fonduta, which is a soup although it can be used as a sauce. Gnocchi alla bava, (literally, "dribbling gnocchi"!), is another excellent dish in which fontina plays an important part. The cooked potato gnocchi are lavishly covered with fontina and then baked for five minutes to allow the cheese to melt.

It is difficult to find real fontina outside Italy, or indeed outside good cheese shops in northern Italy. Judging by my experience, the fontina that is exported is not suitable for making fonduta** (see recipe on page 178).

FORMAGGIO *Cheese*

There are said to be about 450 Italian cheeses, mostly made in northern Italy. Nobody has been able to classify them, but they have been divided into groups according to the milk used in their making: cow, ewe, goat, buffalo, or a mixture of two or more of them. The cheeses are classed as fresh when they must be eaten as soon as they are made (mozzarella* and mascarpone* among them); semi-soft, which must be eaten within two months (Bel Paese* and Gorgonzola*); semi-hard, ready within six months of ageing, and hard, such as Parmesan, which are only sold after at least six months of ageing.

Most of the cheeses made in southern Italy are "a pasta filata" ("plastic curd cheeses"). This means that the soured curd is cut up, then covered with boiling water and worked with a wooden stick until it begins to form a thread. The cheese is then kneaded by hand until it holds its shape. The best known formaggi a pasta filata are mozzarella, provolone* and caciocavallo*.

Cheeses can be divided into table, grating and cooking cheeses. Some grating cheeses and cooking cheeses are interchangeable, and quite a few table cheeses can be used in cooking. Gorgonzola, for example, a typical table cheese, is used in many sauces for pasta, gnocchi and polenta, and to make a risotto*. Fontina* is a cooking cheese, but it is equally good as a table cheese, as is buffalo mozzarella. Parmesan is the grating cheese *par excellence*, but it is a superb table cheese as well.

Cheese is always eaten before fruit, and also before desserts, if served, the order being cheese, dessert and fruit. While some people have endorsed the English habit of eating cheese with only a knife, in most families a knife and fork are used. Cheese is eaten with bread, but never with butter. In the country, Parmigiano and pecorino* are often eaten with pears or with young broad (fava) beans, the favourite beginning or end of a spring meal in Tuscany and Lazio.

FRAGOLA *Strawberry*

Strawberries are grown mainly in northern Italy, which has the right combination of sun and rain. Among the many varieties the most popular is the gorella – they are intensely red, with a firm flesh. The fragola with the most fragrant scent is the fragolina di bosco. This species is the cultivated plant of the wild strawberry, the *Fragaria vesca*. It is a small fruit of a vivid red colour and is used in a sottobosco*. Another popular species is the fragola ananassa, a hybrid originating from two American species, of a paler colour and medium size. Also quite popular are fragoloni – meaning large strawberries.

The Italians, with their choice of good local fruits, are less keen on strawberries than the British and Americans. The most common way to eat them is simply sprinkled with sugar and dressed with lemon and/or orange juice, or with red or white wine. The large fruits are cut in half or even into quarters for the flesh to absorb the dressing. A custom from Emilia-Romagna is to dress strawberries with balsamic vinegar. Strawberries are also used as a topping for tarts, and in sorbets (sherbets).

FRAGOLINO *A type of fish*

A member of the bream family, this the French pageot rouge, very similar to the red bream of northern waters. Its pretty name derives from fragola* (strawberry) because of the pinkish-red colour of its skin. Not a very common fish, fragolino has a tasty meat and is usually grilled (broiled), brushed with olive oil and lemon juice.

FRATTAGLIE *Offal (Variety meats)*

The word is also applied to the extremities, and refers to the offal (variety meats) of animals, but not birds (see rigaglie*). Frattaglie are a favourite food of the Italians, who are not squeamish about eating the brains, tails or ears of any animal.

FRICANDÒ *A braised cut of veal*

This refers to a cut of veal braised in a manner deriving, as does its name, from the French fricandeau. In modern recipes the veal is larded with prosciutto* and then browned in butter and cooked slowly with a little Marsala• for about two hours.

FRICASSEA *A creamy meat dish*

The name of a dish to which egg yolks, beaten with lemon juice, are added at the end of the cooking. The main ingredient is usually lamb, chicken or rabbit. In Liguria the egg yolks are added when the meat is still on the heat, so that they will be scrambled, while in Tuscany they are mixed into the chicken or lamb off the heat, so the egg yolks will only thicken, not scramble. The meat is sautéed in butter with onion and herbs; mushrooms are also added in Tuscany, and pine nuts in Liguria. It is then cooked in a little stock.

FRICO *Cheese fritters*

These wafer-thin cheese fritters are made in Friuli, where they say that "all the aromas of the pastures are to be found in these fritters". They are *the* most traditional dish in a cuisine particularly rich in traditional dishes.

Frico is made with the local montasio* cheese that has been aged for about six months. Sliced very thin, montasio is spread in a non-stick frying pan (skillet) containing melted butter or lard and cooked slowly like a pancake (crepe). Potatoes can be added to the cheese (a slow-cooking dish, still made in the country, which I find irresistible) or – in an old recipe redolent of Austro-Hungarian cooking – frico can be made with onions and Reinette apples.

FRITOLE *Fritters*

A Venetian speciality, made with flour, sultanas (golden raisins) and candied peel. They are associated with Carnival in Venice, so much so that "fare le fritole" is synonymous with enjoying oneself. There is a Venetian saying: "Le fritole xe come le done; se no le xe tonde e un poco grassote, no le xe bone" (fritole are like women; if they are not round and a little fat, they are not good).

FRITTATA *A type of omelette*

This is the Italian omelette, closer to a Spanish tortilla or a Middle-Eastern eggah than to a French omelette. It is a flat round omelette, and one in which the eggs should be completely set, although still moist. Other ingredients can be added to the eggs: grated cheese for a frittata al formaggio* **, sweated onions for a frittata con le cipolle, chopped prosciutto* for a frittata al prosciutto, or indeed any suitable vegetable or any leftovers from the day before. Leftover spaghetti can make an excellent frittata, as can peperonata*.

In Sicily a delicious frittata is prepared with ricotta salata*, while Liguria boasts a frittata with courgettes (zucchini), one with artichokes and another with bianchetti*. Ligurian frittate are always seasoned with herbs.

FRITTATINE *A small omelette*
Frittatine are made like pancakes (crepes) but the mixture is usually made entirely with eggs, no milk, water or flour. Frittatine can be stuffed as pancakes, or they can be piled one on top of the other in layers with tomato sauce and mozzarella*, or with béchamel, mushroom and ham sauce, or spinach and ricotta*. This impressive-looking combination, for which each writer or cook seems to have a different name, is then heated in the oven.

FRITTEDDA
A Sicilian vegetable stew
This is a traditional dish from Sicily consisting of a stew of peas, artichokes and broad (fava) beans.

FRITTELLE *Fritters*
A broad term which in the main is applied to small pieces of sweet or savoury food coated in batter and deep-fried. Some frittelle are common to the whole of Italy. These include: apple fritters, anchovy fritters and rice fritters. Others are regional specialities.

In Alto Adige they make frittelle of buckwheat flour and milk fried in melted lard. The Sicilian frittelle are made with cut-up fruit, coated in Marsala•-flavoured batter and sprinkled with sugar. In Sardinia the frittelle are made with wild fennel – the mountain fennel, which is so aromatic and sweet, is boiled, chopped and mixed into an egg batter. The mixture is spooned into hot oil.

It is not only the filling, but also the batter that varies according to the region or the main ingredient. This can be made with egg, water and flour, with egg, milk and flour or with egg whites and flour. It may contain yeast, Marsala or other wines. Some frittelle do not even have a batter, like the frittelle of potatoes made in Puglia.

Sweet frittelle, such as the Venetian fritole* are a Carnival treat. Another time for frittelle is the feast of San Giuseppe, on 19 March. The frittelle made for this occasion are similar to the Venetian fritole but are a speciality of Tuscany and southern Lombardy.

FRITTO *Fried food*
The word is used as a noun, either accompanied by an attribute – as in fritto di pesce – or by an adjective as in fritto misto. See Friggere in the Terms and Techniques section (page 351).

FRITTO MISTO
A selection of fried morsels
Every visitor to Italy must be familiar with that delectable assortment of fried morsels, of every size and flavour, known as a fritto misto. There are many different versions of the dish, but the best known are the Piemontese, the Bolognese and the Napoletano.

The fritto misto Piemontese contains small veal escalopes (scallops), thin slivers of calf's liver, sweetbreads, brains and croquettes of chicken. It also includes seasonal blanched vegetables, such as courgette (zucchini) and aubergine (eggplant) slices, cauliflower florets, artichoke wedges, celery chunks and mushroom caps. The Piedmontese crown their fritto misto with fried amaretti*, fried apple rings and semolina rounds. The cooking fat used is olive oil and butter.

The fritto misto Bolognese is the grandest and the most lavish, and is an entire meal in itself. The usual ingredients are accompanied by the stecchi Bolognesi*, mortadella*, Parmesan and bread, and in addition there are sweet custard fritters and apple fritters. Everything is coated in batter, or egg and breadcrumbs, and fried in butter and strutto*. It is known as il grande fritto misto.

The Neapolitan fritto misto is called frienno magnanno, ("frying and eating"). This describes the way it should be served: the cook fries while the family eat, since fried food loses its crispness if kept hot. Apart from the usual slices of liver and sweetbread, it contains panzarotti*, rice and potato croquettes, slices of mozzarella* and hard-boiled (hard-cooked) egg yolks coated in béchamel. There are also all the seasonal vegetables and wedges of local tomatoes with their lovely fragrance. These are deep-fried in olive oil, leaving intact the natural flavour and texture of the food, inside a crisp, light crust.

A fritto misto that stands apart from the others is fritto misto di pesce (of fish), of which the Neapolitans are masters. Liguria, too, has excellent recipes for fritto misto di mare. In a fritto misto di pesce the selection may include small sole, anchovies, small octopus, calamari* cut into rings and small red mullet... in fact any small fish and shelled crustaceans, as long as they are fresh. The fish and seafood are lightly coated in flour, and immersed in a pan of sizzling olive oil.

FRITTURA *A dish of fried food*
The most common use of the word is in frittura di pesce, which is another name for fritto misto* di mare (mixed fried fish). A classic Milanese dish is frittura piccata. Thin floured slices of veal are simply sautéed in butter, splashed with a little lemon juice and showered with plenty of freshly chopped parsley. At the end of the cooking time, for good measure, a little more butter is swirled into the sauce to give it a smooth shine.

FRUMENTO *Wheat*
Wheat is broadly divided into soft wheat and durum wheat. Bread is made with soft wheat, while commercially made pasta must, by law, only be made with durum wheat. Both wheats grow in Italy, durum wheat in the south because it needs hotter sun to ripen, and soft wheat in the north. For this reason pasta originated in the south, where durum wheat bound with water is also used to make pasta at home. In the north, tagliatelle and lasagne are made with soft wheat bound with eggs.

FRUTTA *Fruit*
It is rare in Italy to finish a meal without fruit, although nowadays, if there is a dessert, fruit may not be served.

Every region has its own fruit. We speak of the pears and Reinette apples of Val d'Aosta, and of its sottobosco* (strawberries, raspberries and blue-berries), of the cherries of Romagna, the peaches and plums of Marche, the figs of Liguria and Tuscany, the raspberries of Lombardy and the oranges and lemons of Sicily and Calabria. Then we have the walnuts of Sorrento and the hazelnuts of Avellino and Piedmont, the Tuscan chestnuts, the Sicilian almonds and black and white grapes nearly everywhere, but mostly in Puglia.

Fruit is also used to make desserts, the most popular being the macedonia di frutta* – fruit salad. Apples and pears are sometimes stewed in red or white wine, peaches are steeped in wine, strawberries served with peaches or oranges make a great combination, and all of them are used to produce ice cream, sorbets (sherbets) and granite*.

FRUTTA CANDITA
Candied fruit

The fruits most commonly candied are mandarins, figs, plums, pears and apricots. Candied fruits, particularly the candied peel of lemon, orange and citron add appeal and flavour to most sweet preparations, from panettone* to cassata siciliana*. They are also used for decoration, chopped or cut into squares. Some flowers are also candied for decoration, the best known being Parma violets, small violets especially grown at the edges of woods around Parma.

The Sicilians claim to make the best candied fruits which preserve the flavour of the fresh fruits. Elsewhere in Italy one of the best-known firms making candied fruits is Romanengo of Genoa, who have been manufacturers of candied fruits since 1780 and have served most European royal families.

FRUTTA DI MARTURANA *A type of sweet*

These sweets are made with almond paste and shaped to resemble various fruits. They were originally made by the nuns of the Convent of Martorana in Palermo and in the old days the Palermitani used to go to the convent on Sunday morning after Mass to buy them from the nuns. Nowadays they are also made commercially, and every pasticceria on the island, and elsewhere, sells them.

FRUTTA SECCA *Dried fruit*

Dried fruit, including all nuts, which dry naturally, and the fruits that are artificially dried, such as apricots, prunes etc. Regional dishes are made with dried figs (see fico*). In Lombardy stoned (pitted) prunes, dates and apricots are stuffed with sweetened mascarpone*.

FRUTTI DI MARE *Seafood*

All marine creatures that are not actually fish or cephalopods come under this collective name, which means, literally, fruits of the sea. A visit to a fish market in any Italian coastal town will reveal an array of these creatures, which will vary according to the local sea and the season. Any fish market is a paradise to the fish lover; the air is full of a salty tang, and there is the chance to chat with the stallholders about how to cook this fish, or what to do with that mollusc, while the woman next to you joins in and gives you her own recipe.

In recent years many establishments in which frutti di mare are farmed have been set up along the coasts. The biggest and best of these are in the gulf of Trieste, and along the coast from there all the way to Grado, east of Venice. The frutti di mare that are most successfully farmed are mussels, which are exported all over Europe, and oysters. In the farms the larvae of the molluscs are attached to ribbons of nylon net which are tied round buoys. Once the molluscs have reached a good size they are then placed in large pools of filtered sea water to rid them of any impurities.

FUGAZZA**
A sweet bread

This is a type of Venetian focaccia*, although it is not the usual savoury focaccia, but a sweet bread prepared at Easter. At Easter, Venice seems to exude the smell of freshly baked fugazza (see recipe on page 183), and its characteristic domed shape takes pride of place in the windows of every baker's shop and pasticceria.

FUNGHI
Wild and cultivated mushrooms

When the fungi season begins in August or September, the Italians' passion for the hunt is unleashed. At dawn they start for the woods with their baskets (never plastic bags) and small knives. The basket allows the spores of the picked fungi to fall to the ground and produce more fungi again next year. Nobody will ever tell you where his hunting ground is. People hide behind trees or pretend to have found nothing on the very spot where they have just picked a basketful of ceps or chanterelles.

Wild mushrooms are plentiful in the Dolomites, the Ligurian Apennines and the Sila in Calabria, and many different species are found in the local markets. The species for sale vary according to the area, and the local health authority usually specifies which species are permitted. They are likely to include only the most common ones, such as ceps and other boletus, chanterelles, some species of russula and lactaris, and the parasol. In the market at Trento, the best for mushrooms in Italy, some 250 species have been counted on the stalls in the autumn (fall).

There are only very few places where you can gather unlimited quantities of wild mushrooms; the maximum weight is usually 2 kg/4½ lb per basket.

There are many recipes for fungi in contemporary cooking. In the most common recipe boleti are cooked in oil with garlic and parsley, sometimes sprinkled with lemon juice – trifolati†. In Friuli they splash their funghi trifolati with the local Tocai wine instead of lemon juice. In Tuscany they make a good dish by sautéeing a mixture of wild mushrooms, chicken livers and sage leaves. The caps of the larger species are delicious "a cotoletta" (coated in egg and breadcrumbs and fried in butter). The recipes for stuffed fungi are also excellent, the large caps being filled with different stuffing, all including the chopped stems, and then baked. The most popular recipe is from Liguria, with salted anchovies, marjoram and soft breadcrumbs. A risotto with wild mushrooms is better than most risotti, and a dish of tagliatelle or taglierini dressed with a mushroom sauce is utterly mouth-watering. Some species, *Amanita caesaria*, *Boletus edulis* and *Caprinus comatus*, when very young, are quite delicious raw, dressed simply with lemon juice and olive oil.

Mushrooms are cultivated commercially on a large scale. There are two or three species of cultivated fungi usually found in the shops, the best being the *Agaricus hortensis* (the horse mushroom). It is organically cultivated on horse manure and is better than the usual cultivated mushroom.

Wild mushrooms can be preserved in different ways, but they must be young and in perfect condition. The best-known method is by drying (see funghi secchi*). Salting is another technique, suitable for all mushrooms except the fragile species with a delicate taste. Many species, such as chanterelles, boletus, russulas and field (portabello) mushrooms, can be preserved in oil, as long as they are very young. There are many ways to prepare them, but basically the fungi are sautéed in oil, sometimes with some flavourings, splashed with wine vinegar and pressed into sterilized jars which are then sealed. Raw wild mushrooms can be frozen, although this is only suitable for a few species, and then they must be cooked from frozen.

The recipe for cappelle di porcini alla graticola on page 148 comes from *The Mushroom Book* (published by Dorling Kindersley) by Thomas Lassoe, mycologist at the University of Copenhagen, to which I contributed the recipe section.

In Italy, as in some other countries in continental Europe where there is a continuing tradition of picking wild mushrooms, identifying the species gathered is not usually a problem as expert help is widely available. It is essential that any wild fungi should be properly and fully identified before anyone eats them, especially as some edible and toxic species may look almost identical.

Described below are four of the most popular species of fungi found in Italy.

Cantarello This is the French chanterelle, one of the most delicious of all wild fungi. It grows in deciduous woods from spring to autumn (fall). A chanterelle looks like a small apricot-coloured trumpet and smells of apricot.

Chiodino This is the name given to two types of wild fungus, one of which, the honey fungus, grows on trees, and the other which grows on the ground. The chiodini that grow on trees are one of the most common fungi that people gather in the woods.

Porcino: Boletus edulis, the cep or penny bun, the king of fungi. In Italy, porcini

begin to appear in the spring, sometimes as early as the end of March, and they can be found up to the end of July. Then in the autumn there is another, larger crop, from September to November. This is the period when a professional cercatore (picker) can bring back 30–40 kg/66–88 lb of porcini a day, some for sale and some for drying. See recipe for Cappelle di Porcini alla Graticola on page 148.

Prataiolo is both the field and the cultivated mushroom. The field mushroom is not highly prized, its flavour not being very pronounced.

FUNGHI SECCHI
Dried wild mushrooms

This is the most satisfactory way to preserve some species of fungi, because their flavour is concentrated by the drying process. Porcini (ceps) are the best of all dried mushrooms. They are sold in packets in many delis and large supermarkets, usually of 10–20 g/ ¼–¾ oz. Although that seems a very small quantity for the price one has to pay, it only takes 10 g/¼ oz/2 tbsp to give a risotto or a sauce a distinctive mushroomy flavour. I like to add a small amount of dried porcini to any dish of cultivated mushrooms to give them a strong flavour.

G

GALANI *A Venetian carnival fritter*

Galano is the Venetian dialect word for a bow, and these are the carnival fritters of Venice. The dough, made with butter, egg, sugar and flour, is flavoured with grappa, wine from Cyprus or Marsala•.

GALANTINA *Galantine*

Galantine is made with a boned bird, or veal, cut in small pieces and mixed with prosciutto*, tongue, pistachio nuts and truffles. The meat is sometimes marinated in Marsala•. The galantina is enclosed in the skin of a turkey or in a cloth which is simmered in stock for about two hours. When cold, it is thinly sliced and surrounded with diced jelly made with the stock.

GALLETTE

Dry biscuits (crackers or toasts)

Gallette enjoyed a brief spell in fashion in the 1960s, but with the revival of traditional foods Italians have returned to their beloved bread. Various kinds of pâté are occasionally spread on gallette, but the only place they hold in traditional cooking is as an ingredient in the Genoese cappon magro*. Sweet gallette are also available made of sweetened shortcrust pastry (pie dough).

GALLETTO *A young rooster*

A galletto is no more than 500 g/1 lb in weight and is never a battery (intensively raised) chicken. In Tuscany it is still served in country trattorie cooked on the spit.

GALLINA *A hen*

A two-year-old hen that is still laying eggs, but whose output has slightly diminished with age. Its meat is very tasty, tastier than a younger bird, although a bit tougher. This hen will take much longer to cook – up to four hours – and will be leathery to eat, but the stock will make the most delicate yet tasty, soups and very delicious sauces.

The chicken used in a bollito misto* should be a gallina. In a recipe from Lombardy the hen is stuffed with a mixture of breadcrumbs, saffron, Parmesan, eggs, chopped Savoy cabbage, garlic and sage. But the most interesting recipe comes from Sardinia. The hen, stuffed with sultanas (golden raisins), walnuts, saffron, sugar, cinnamon, eggs and breadcrumbs, is boiled with vegetables. Then when it is cooked it is wrapped in myrtle leaves, pressed between two plates, and left to stand for two or three days to allow the aromatic flavour of the leaves to penetrate the meat. It is then served cut into portions and garnished with the stuffing.

GAMBERETTO *Shrimp*

Gamberetti are small, no more than 10 cm/ 4 in, and pink or grey in colour. The grey shrimp is also called gambero della sabbia, because it burrows in muddy sand. It is popular in Venice, where it is boiled in salted water containing a slice of lemon. Another favourite Venetian way to prepare gamberetti is, after blanching and shelling them, to sauté them in plenty of olive oil, parsley and garlic. They are served with the white Venetian polenta.

Both pink and grey shrimp are fried in their shells as part of a fritto misto di pesce*. They are also used in a classic Venetian risotto.

GAMBERO

A Mediterranean prawn (shrimp)

This includes many different species. They are large, measuring up to 20 cm/ 8 in, varying in colour from pink to deep red. The best are caught in deep waters, but they are also farmed. One species, the Mazzancolla, also know as Gambero Imperiale, can be as long as 22 cm/9 in. They are mainly caught in the Tyrrenian sea for the pleasure of the Romans, who flock to the nearby coast to enjoy them. The Venetians, creators of the best seafood risotti, have a splendid risotto coi gamberi in which prawn heads and carapaces are boiled in court-bouillon and lightly beaten to extract the juices, which are added to the rice. This gives the risotto a delicate pinkish tinge and the sweet taste of the sea. Unusually for a fish risotto, this usually contains Parmesan, added at the end of cooking, not at the table.

Apart from being grilled or simply boiled and eaten as they are with olive oil and a touch of lemon juice, prawns are often served "in umido"†. Shelled, they are shallow-fried in olive oil with garlic and parsley and finished off with capers and lemon juice. Sometimes, one or two chopped fresh tomatoes are thrown in as well.

GELATINA

Gelatine (Gelatin), jelly or aspic jelly

The best gelatina is made without gelatine (gelatin), but only with calf's foot, pig's trotter (foot) and pork rind. Gelatina is used in many cold meat and cold chicken dishes, all of French origin, or in dishes like galantines.

Southern Italian cooking excels in fruit jellies. In Sicily, the gelatina d'arancie, one of their specialities, is made with their best oranges, orange flower water, leaf gelatine, sugar and white rum. Another kind of gelatina is the preserve made with fruit flesh, fruit juice and sugar. There are also the small fruit jellies, favourites of children and old people alike.

GELATO

Ice creams and sorbets (sherbets)

This word, the literal meaning of which is "frozen", is rather confusingly used for both ice creams and sorbets (sherbets). Strictly speaking, however, a gelato is an ice cream, that is a mixture of egg custard, sugar and other flavourings, while the correct word for a sorbet is sorbetto.

The manufacture of gelati is controlled by stringent regulations, which do not allow more than two per cent of additives. Also, the sweetness must be given by natural rather than synthetic sugars. Many gelaterie in Italy show a sign saying produzione propria, meaning that the gelati are made on the premises, and these are the ones to look for. There will be sorbets and ice creams, and the choice is so extensive that it is bewildering. It covers the whole range from thick, rich gelati laced with liqueur, such as Tiramisù and Malaga, to those made only with the purest and freshest fruit juices. A characteristic of the best gelati, and especially of those made in Naples or Palermo, is the addition of an extra flavour that brings out the aroma of the main ingredient. There may be a drop or two of orange in the strawberry sorbet, a suspicion of pistachio in the egg custard or a pinch of cinnamon in the chocolate.

GHIOTTA

A pan, or an Umbrian game dish

A ghiotta was originally the dripping pan in which the cooking juices collected. The word is now applied to an Umbrian dish of game, served with a sauce made with local red wine, chopped prosciutto*, sage, rosemary, garlic, juniper berries, lemon juice, vinegar and olive oil. When this mixture is well-reduced, the chopped liver of the roasting animal or bird is mixed into it. Another traditional dish is the ghiotta di pescespada (swordfish), a recipe from eastern Sicily. The fish steaks are first fried in oil and then tomatoes, pine nuts, sultanas (golden raisins), olives, onions, celery and capers are added to make a sauce. The fish finishes cooking in the oven, covered with the sauce. Also from the south is ghiotta della Vigilia (for Christmas Eve). This is made with stockfish and cauliflower cooked in a ghiotta of onions, tomatoes, green olives and pears. The traditional ghiotta from Abruzzo consists of a variety of vegetables, including sliced potatoes, tomatoes, (bell) peppers and courgettes (zucchini), all layered with olive oil, salt and pepper in an earthenware pot and cooked, covered, in the oven. On modern restaurant menus alla ghiotta is used to describe tasty, gutsy dishes.

GHIOZZO *Goby*

A fish prized by the Venetians (known as gô in Venetian dialect). All the recipes come from around Venice. Because goby is bony it is used in fish soups, sometimes with eel, sometimes alone accompanied by a soft polenta. There are also risotti* of goby and a rice dish containing goby and borlotti beans, a speciality of Murano.

GIANDUIA *A rich chocolate cake*

This elaborate cake from Turin takes its name from gianduiotti* because its flavour is similar. It comprises a fatless sponge, made with ten eggs and 200 g/7 oz/1⅓ cups of flour, moistened with Cognac and maraschino, filled with a rich chocolate and hazelnut cream and covered with chocolate glaze. It is is sold in most good patisseries – few people ever make it at home.

GIANDUIOTTI

A type of chocolate

A speciality of Piedmont, gianduiotti were created in 1865 by Caffarel and Prochet of Turin, who gave them their name becuse they were originally shaped like the hat of Gianduia, the Turinese character in traditional pantomime. The chocolates, a mixture of best chocolate, toasted hazelnuts from the Langhe, vanilla and sugar, are wrapped in gold foil. Although they are now made commercially, there are still a

Gianduiotti
Cioccolatini alle Nocciole Gianduia

200 g ℮   7.00 OZ

Bonbons au chocolat et noisettes   Milk-hazelnut chocolates handful of craftsmen who produce them by hand, and these are one of the very best chocolates in the world.

GIARDINIERA
A vegetable garnish

Preserved vegetables are used to make giardiniera including button (white) mushrooms, celery, onion, cornichons (sweet dill pickles), long green (bell) peppers, cauliflower florets and carrots. They are blanched for five minutes in water and vinegar and then placed in sterilized jars and covered with a mixture of wine vinegar, olive oil, a little salt and sugar. Most people buy giardiniera ready-made, and serve it with nervetti* – brawn (head cheese) – or cold meats.

GINEPRO *Juniper*

A bushy plant, with prickly leaves, of which only the berries are used in cooking. They are small, with a scent reminiscent of pine.

The principal use of juniper berries is for making gin, while the poor-quality berries are pressed to extract the oil and used in cosmetics and perfumery. The fattest and most handsome blue berries are kept for culinary use. They are often used to flavour game, stews, pork and pâté. They are also added, lightly crushed, to wine vinegar that is used for agro-dolce* (sweet-and-sour) dishes.

GIRASOLE *Sunflower*

These are extensively cultivated for their oil, which is used for certain kinds of frying, although not for deep-frying. The sunflower seeds are eaten toasted and salted; in some parts of Italy children buy them in packets and they are still one of the Sicilians' favourite snacks.

GNOCCHI *Small dumplings*

Gnocchi can be made with potatoes, semolina, maize (cornmeal), ricotta and flour, bread or other ingredients. They are nourishing and unpretentious, but they can be harder to produce than many more sophisticated dishes. The difficulty lies in making the mixture light, yet tough enough not to disintegrate in boiling water.

All northern regions have their special gnocchi. Many of these are made with puréed potatoes, with or without egg, and dressed with fontina* and butter or with melted butter and sage, one of the most common ways. Gnocchi alla cadorina from Veneto, made with potatoes, are succulent with butter and smoked ricotta or with melted butter and ground cinnamon. Gnocchi all'ossolana are from northern Lombardy; they are made only with flour, eggs, Parmesan and nutmeg and served with plenty of melted butter and fresh sage. Gnocchi di zucca (pumpkin gnocchi see recipe on page 89) are made in the provinces of Brescia and Mantua, in Lombardy. The cooked pumpkin is puréed and mixed with flour, egg whites and some spices. Some cooks add two or three amaretti* to the dough. The yellow dumplings are boiled in water and dressed with butter flavoured with garlic and rosemary.

Although gnocchi di polenta, cut into shapes rather than rolled, are less popular than potato gnocchi, they make a very appetizing dish, dressed with plenty of cheese and butter or a thin béchamel. They also provide an excellent way to use leftover polenta. Another kind of gnocchi to make use of leftovers is gnocchi di riso, a speciality of Reggio-Emilia. The cooked rice is mixed with eggs and breadcrumbs into balls the size of a walnut, which are then simmered in hot stock and dressed with butter and more Parmesan cheese.

For gnocchi alla Parigina (à la Parisienne) choux pastry, usually made with half milk and half water, is piped through a piping (pastry) bag and cut while dropping into simmering water or stock. When cooked, the gnocchi are dressed with plenty of butter and Parmesan, or covered with a thin creamy cheese sauce. In either case the gnocchi are baked in the oven until a golden crust has formed.

Venezia Giulia makes one of only two kinds of sweet gnocchi. They are potato gnocchi containing a plum or an apricot, dressed with butter, spices and sugar. In spite of being sweet they are served as a first course. The other sweet gnocchi, from Marche, are made with the odd combination of pecorino* and sugar. Egg yolks are mixed with milk and potato flour. The mixture is brought to the boil and then spread on a marble table. When cold it is cut into squares which are then piled in a dish, in layers, and sprinkled with sugar, cinnamon, butter and the local fresh pecorino. Baked in the oven, these gnocchi are quite special. And finally there are the semolina gnocchi** from Rome (see page 87) and malfatti** (see page 90).

GNOCCO FRITTO
Bread fritters

These bread fritters are from Emilia-Romagna. The gnocco is made with bread dough containing about 50 g/ 2 oz/4 tbsp of pure melted lard. When leavened, the dough is cut into lozenges and deep-fried in oil or strutto*. Eaten hot, in place of bread, with salami* or other pork products and with soft cheese, gnocco fritto is one of the tastiest foods of the splendid Emilian cuisine. Gnocco fritto is the name given to these fritters in Modena and Reggio Emilia. In Bologna the same fritters are called crescentine*, and in Romagna piadine*.

GORGONZOLA
A creamy blue cheese

This blue-veined cheese is named after its place of origin, an area that is now part of the eastern suburbs of Milan. It is made with pasteurized cow's milk in small blocks of 25–30 cm/10–12 in, weighing about 10 kg/22 lb with a minimum fat content of 48%. It ripens in two to three months. The blue veins are produced by pricking the cheese with long metal needles that expose the cheese to the air at different points, helping to form the mould. In farm-made Gorgonzola, the ageing of the cheese still takes place, as it has through the centuries, in natural caves in the Alpine valleys of Valsassina and Val Brembana. Commercially produced Gorgonzola is aged in store rooms where the climatic characteristics of the caves are reproduced. When ready, the cheese is stamped with its place of origin (similar to the DOC applied to wines) and wrapped in special foil.

GRANA *A group of hard cheeses*

This is the generic name for hard, grainy cheeses (hence the name), the best known being Parmigiano-Reggiano*.

The other popular grana is the grana Padano, a DOC cheese made in 27 provinces of the Po Valley, with a good flavour ranging from mellow to piquant, depending on its age. Grana Padano is made in large blocks — around 30 kg/66 lb — from the partially skimmed unpasteurized milk of cows aged from 18 to 24 months. The cheeses that have been granted the stamp of quality by the Consortium have grana Padano stamped within a lozenge all over their dry yellow crust. Although a pleasant table cheese, especially when young, grana Padano's main role is in the kitchen, where it can be used to replace its better-known, more expensive, and undeniably superior cousin, Parmigiano-Reggiano.

Among the other grana cheeses are grana Lodigiano and grana Piacentino. These have all but disappeared, although you may be able to find some made on a small scale by local cheese-makers.

GRANCEVOLA or GRANCEOLA or GRANSEOLA Spider crab

A highly regarded crustacean of the northern Adriatic. The grancevola is a large crab with hairy legs and a knobbly (knobby) shell. The flavour of the meat is sweet and delicate, and never has the heavy quality of the Atlantic crab. The smaller female grancevola is more rewarding because it contains more meat, especially during the winter months when it carries the eggs. However the male specimen, called granzon in Venetian dialect, has a tastier meat.

Spider crabs must be first boiled, to open them; the meat and coral is then extracted from the shell, chopped, and served back in the shell, dressed with olive oil and lemon juice. In Venice there is a risotto di granseola, similar to a shrimp risotto, finished off with a mantecatura of knobs (pats) of butter, Parmesan, brandy and parsley.

GRANCHIO COMUNE

Shore crab

These smallish crabs, about 7 cm/2¾ in long, can be found on many sandy beaches in Italy, especially in the areas around Venice and the northern Adriatic.

Female granchi are the best for eating. In a risotto recipe, the boiled meat and the lower shells are pounded in a mortar until smooth, then added to the rice.

You can see Venetians catching shore crabs in the sand on the Lido, but there is usually very little meat left once the shell is removed.

GRANCIPORRO

A type of crab

This large crab (up to 30 cm/12 in) can be found, albeit rarely, close to the shore of the Venetian lagoon. It is cooked in a court bouillon and served with melted butter and flavoured with parsley and plenty of garlic, with garlicky crostini*, or simply boiled and dressed with a mild extra virgin olive oil and lemon juice or vinegar.

GRANELLI Fries (testicles)

Unfortunately this offal (variety meat) is hard to find these days, owing presumably to squeamishness or perhaps prudery. Granelli are delicious, with a taste halfway between sweet-breads and brains. They can be cooked like sweetbreads. A recipe from Tuscany is used when various animals, including calves, lambs or horses, are castrated. The blanched and peeled fries are coated in flour and egg and fried in olive oil.

GRANITA An iced drink

This refreshing drink should consist only of fruit juice or coffee and sugar, these being frozen and then crushed to obtain an icy, finely ground mush. Granite made with good-quality fruit juices or excellent coffee are regaining the popularity they once enjoyed. The most popular is granita di caffè**, which is often served with a spoonful of whipped cream on top, and granita di limone, the most refreshing of all drinks.

GRANO *Wheat*

Grano is another word for frumento (wheat). Strictly speaking, however, grano is a grain of cereal.

GRANO SARACENO
Buckwheat

Buckwheat grows at high altitudes, and all the dishes based on it come from the Alpine regions. In Lombardy a kind of pasta (pizzoccheri**) is made with its flour, as well as a dark polenta, called polenta taragna. In Friuli, buckwheat flour is used in a soup, dressed with milk and melted butter, while the cooking of Alto Adige, rich in superb sweet preparations, offers a cake made with buckwheat flour and filled with blackcurrant jelly – an interesting combination of flavours.

GRANOTURCO *or* MAIS
Maize (Corn)

Maize (corn) arrived in Italy from the New World in the sixteenth century. This yellow grain was christened granoturco (Turkish grain) because at the time so many things of foreign origin came, or were thought to come, from Turkey, so the term "turco" became synonymous with anything from abroad.

Maize established itself well in northern Italy. It was ground into farina gialla (yellow flour), and polenta* (coarse cornmeal) began to be made, soon becoming the staple diet of much of northern Italy. Nutritionally, however, maize is not as adequate as wheat, barley or oats, as it is lacking in vitamin B, and a deficiency in this causes the chronic illness pellagra. This disease, in fact, killed a horrendous number of poor country people in the Lombardy and Veneto regions during the nineteenth century.

Maize is mainly used for flour. Corn cobs were sometimes roasted and eaten in the countryside of Veneto, but they were not considered proper food for people. Now that people are better off, much of the extensive production of maize is for animals.

Farina di Granoturco *or* Farina Gialla, can be ground fine, medium or coarse, the three grades being used for different dishes, the choice depending also on the locality. As well as polenta, biscuits (cookies) and cakes are also made with this flour, especially in northern Italy.

GRAPPA
Italian brandy

Distilled from the fermented residue of pressed grapes.

GRASSO *Fat*

In a culinary context grasso refers to vegetable oils as well as animal fats. Nowadays the fat most commonly used in cooking is olive oil (not necessarily extra virgin), because it is regarded as healthier, but in the past the particular fat used was a defining characteristic of the regional cuisine. Thus the cooking of northern Italy was based on butter and pork fat, olive oil only used, occasionally, on salads.

In the other regions, from Liguria and Tuscany southwards, the cooking was, and still is, based on olive oil, plus lard or other pork fats.

The modern tendency for the health-conscious to replace animal fat with olive oil can alter the flavour of some dishes for the worse, or at best give a different result.

GRIGLIATA MISTA
A mixed grill (broil)

This term refers to a platter of different kinds of meat or fish, grilled (broiled or chargrilled) on direct heat. Grigliate are the restaurant dishes *par excellence* because they need so many ingredients. A fish grigliata in Venice, for instance, will have one or two small sole, a few small cuttlefish, a scampi (jumbo shrimp) or two and maybe a piece of monkfish – the best local fish.

A grigliata di carne (mixed meat grill) is made up of a minute steak, a piece of veal kidney, one or two slices of pancetta*, a sausage and a slice of liver, or a selection of any of these.

There are some restaurants that now serve only grigliate, a sure sign that it is very much in fashion. This is no doubt also owing to the absence, or near absence, of cooking fat, the speed with which it can be prepared and the minimum expertise required. A grigliata is often, however, a disappointing dish because of the difficulty of cooking all the different components for the right length of time.

GRISSINI *Breadsticks*

These little breadsticks appear, usually wrapped in cellophane, on every table in every Italian restaurant inside or outside Italy. These are the unremarkable, and often not very good, factory-made grissini, but many bakeries in Italy, and especially in Turin, still make the authentic article by hand, and the result is another thing altogether. However they are made, grissini are always fun to eat and an ideal food to quieten hunger before a meal. Grissini are not easy to make at home, but I have managed to make them following the recipe on page 185.

There is now a new kind of grissini that come from Veneto. These grissini, all made in small bakeries, are short and stubby. The dough always contains oil, and it is proved – set aside to rise – for 20 hours, giving the grissini a fragrant flavour and a beautifully friable texture. They are sold under a variety of names, including Bibanesi, made in the town of Bibano, Pan del Conte and Prosecchini, which contain a little must from the grapes used to make Prosecco wine. They are excellent, and I urge you to look out for them.

GRONGO *Conger eel*

Conger eel is a saltwater fish which can be as long as 2 m/2 yd, varying in colour from pale purple to nearly black. Conger eel can be caught all year around, often quite close to the mouth of a river, which – unlike its close cousin, the freshwater eel – it never actually enters.

Its firm, close-textured meat has a strong, distinctive flavour, greatly appreciated by some, while others consider it too fatty. It needs long, slow cooking, usually done in tomato sauce and/or wine. It is one of the tastiest fish to include in a fish soup, and it should always be part of the Tuscan dish, cacciucco*.

GUANCIALE
A cured pig's jowl

In culinary terms, guanciale (which otherwise means "pillow") is the jowl of a pig. It is salted and cured in the same way as the more common pancetta*, which it resembles in appearance and taste, although guanciale is always coated with a sprinkling of coarsely ground black pepper.

Guanciale is a speciality of central Italy, especially Lazio, where it is the main ingredient in spaghetti all'amatriciana* **. However, both salt pork and pancetta are adequate substitutes for guanciale if you are unable to find it.

GUBANA
A strudel

This strudel from Friuli is traditionally eaten at Easter. It is either made with sweetened bread dough or puff pastry, rolled around a filling of raisins, candied peel, sultanas (golden raisins), chocolate, dried figs and prunes etc. The strudel is then formed into a spiral shape before baking.

GULASCH
Goulash

From Hungary gulasch spread to all parts of the Austrio-Hungarian Empire, and it soon became a popular dish of Venezia Giulia. It has now been adopted by birrerie (pubs or bars) and is served all over Italy. The gulasch from Venezia Giulia is less spicy than the original version, and it is sometimes Italianized by the addition of tomatoes.

Gulasch is served with polenta, potatoes, or nowadays with the more fashionable tagliatelle* – the traditional Austrian style of serving gulasch is with egg noodles.

I

IMPANADA *or* IMPANATA
A pie

A Sardinian and Sicilian dish consisting of two rounds of bread dough stuffed with vegetables, ricotta and sometimes minced (ground) lamb or pork. The baked pie can be served hot or cold.

INCAPRIATA
A vegetable dish

This vegetable dish from Puglia consists of a purée of dried broad (fava) beans and boiled wild chicory. The two vegetables are served on the same plate, but kept separate. They are dressed by each person on his or her plate with olive oil, and they are eaten together by putting a blob of purée on the fork and then forking a leaf of chicory.

INDIVIA
Endive (Chicory)

There are two main varieties of indivia; riccia (curly), and scarola (batavia or round, crisp lettuce). Both are used raw and in cooking. A recipe from Sicily combines indivia with oranges and fennel. In an interesting recipe from the cuisine of the Roman ghetto the blanched leaves of the curly endive (chicory) are sautéed and then baked covered with fresh anchovies and flavoured with mixture of garlic, parsley and dried breadcrumbs. In another recipe from Rome, batavia is braised for 15 minutes in an oil-based tomato sauce with salted anchovies and garlic. The indivia belga a close cousin, is far less popular and, being a recent import, does not have any place in traditional cooking.

INSALATE *Salad*

The usual dressing for salads is olive oil, wine vinegar or lemon juice and salt. The proportion of vinegar to oil depends on the fruitiness of the oil and the acidity of the vinegar. As a guide, the dressing for four portions of insalata should be 4 tablespoons of oil and 1–2 tablespoons of vinegar. The olive oil must be extra virgin and the vinegar wine vinegar, usually red. Garlic is a rare adddition, present only in particular salads. Artichokes, fennel and plum tomatoes are best dressed only with olive oil and salt. A gentle shower of basil, some parsley, a few rings of red onion or a sprinkling of oregano are all optional additions to the basic dressing. In Italy, a green salad is hardly ever served with mayonnaise, but it is never eaten "dry", that is without any dressing.

INTEGRALE *Whole-wheat*

This refers to whole-wheat flour, and to the products made with whole-wheat flour. Thus, grissini* integrali, pane* integrale or pasta* integrale, which is usually spaghetti.

INTINGOLO *A ragù*

This is a ragù of meat, or in southern Italy, of fish. The meat – usually lamb, kid or, in Rome, hare, or fish as in swordfish in Calabria and tuna in Sicily – is cut up into small pieces (never minced/ground). These pieces are cooked slowly in wine and stock, with prosciutto*, onion, celery and other flavourings. The dish is served with fried or toasted bread to mop it up.

INVOLTINI
Literally, "small parcels"

These are rolls of meat, prosciutto* or vegetables containing various stuffings. The meat is usually thinly cut veal. The stuffing is often ham and/or chicken bound with béchamel and/or egg, Parmesan and other flavourings. The involtini are sautéed in butter and splashed with white wine or Marsala•. A stuffing from Naples is made with tomato sauce and mozzarella*, while involtini alla Modenese contain prosciutto*, luganega* and sage. The involtini di prosciutto usually contain a mixture of ricotta* and béchamel.

Modern involtini are made with thin slices of pink roast beef containing blanched vegetables dressed with a tartare sauce or a mayonnaise. A modern addition is the involtini of swordfish (see Pesce Spada).

ITALICO *A soft, mild cheese*

A mild cheese, with a sweet taste, a soft creamy texture and good melting properties. Italico is similar to the better-known Bel Paese.

KNOEDEL *A type of dumpling*

Similar to the canederli* from Trentino, these are bread gnocchi made in Alto Adige. A version of knoedel made only in Alto Adige are the schwartzplentene knoedel. These are made with rye and buckwheat bread mixed with smoked pancetta*.

They are boiled and served with sauerkraut and tomato sauce.

KRAPFEN or CRAFEN
Doughnuts

These doughnuts are a speciality of Alto Adige, Venezia Giulia and Friuli, the regions that were Austrian up to 1918. Krapfen are now quite popular all over Italy.

L

LAMPASCIONI *Edible bulbs*

These are the bulbs of a muscary plant (grape hyacinth). They grow wild everywhere in southern Italy and are now cultivated in Puglia. They are similar to small onions, which they also resemble in taste. Although they are bitter, their bitterness can be removed before cooking by soaking them for up to 48 hours in cold water or by blanching. The most common way to prepare lampascioni is to bake or boil them and then eat them in salad. They are also stewed with wine and tomatoes. A purée of lampascioni is eaten, spread on thick slices of local bread. They can be bought roasted and preserved in oil.

LAMPONE *Raspberry*

Not typical Italian fruit, raspberries grow mostly in Piedmont and Lombardy, where the climate is suitable, and they are also found wild in Alpine woods. These wild lamponi are deliciously fragrant, and are used as part of the fashionable sottobosco*.

LAMPREDA *Sea lamprey*

Primitive eel-like creatures, with a slimy yellowish skin. They have no jaws, but a round sucking mouth and a grating tongue with which they suck blood from their prey. Despite their unpleasant appearance and habits, the flesh of the lamprey is extremely delicate, although fatty and somewhat indigestible. When preparing it, the blood should be kept for adding to the sauce. It is rarely obtainable these days, but as the late British food writer Alan Davidson says "there is a certain special sensation which its consumption affords to the imaginative diner who is aware of its habits and antiquity".

LARDELLI *Strips of meat*

These are long strips of salted pork fat or pancetta*, used to lard a joint.

LARDO *Pork fat*

This is the layer of hard fat nearest to the skin of a pig's back and not melted pork fat as in British or American lard. It is cured by salting or, more rarely, smoking. Lardo was once one of the basic cooking fats in most regions, especially where there are no olive trees. Nowadays lardo has almost disappeared from everyday cooking because of worries about health. However, a battuto† of lardo, with the usual other flavourings, remains one of the indispensable ingredients for giving a traditional dish its authentic taste. The best lardo, always eaten very finely sliced as an antipasto, is that of Arnad in Val d'Aosta and of Colonnata in Tuscany.

LATTE *Milk*

Italians are not great milk-drinkers, nor are there many Italian dishes based on milk. The most common milk recipe is for a soup, a peasant dish from Lombardy and Piedmont. The most unusual of the recipes using milk is maiale al latte** (pork cooked in milk). Rice is sometimes cooked in milk and butter is added at the end, sometimes with a flavouring of cinnamon and grated nutmeg.

Milk is also used for a number of puddings, although nowadays it is often replaced partly or wholly by cream.

LATTEMIELE *Sweetened cream*
Literally, milk and honey, but actually whipped sweetened cream. The milk in the southern part of Lombardy used to be so thick that, when shaken, it quickly became like whipped cream. In the old days, honey and cinnamon were added, although now sugar has replaced the honey.

LATTUGA *Lettuce*
The three main varieties grown in Italy today are Romana (Cos), lattuga a cappuccio (round) and ricciolina or lollo, from Lollobrigida, thanks to the curvaceous leaves (curly lettuce). Romana is the most popular type and is the crispest – the best for salads.

Lettuce is also used in cooking, and soups are made with it. Lattuga ripiena (stuffed lettuce) is a traditional dish still made in Liguria. A recipe from Rome combines lettuces with beans. The dried beans, previously soaked and boiled, are sautéed in olive oil with the lettuce, and then tomatoes are added.

LAURO or ALLORO *Bay*
The leaves of the sweet lauro, a native of the Mediterranean, are used to flavour meat dishes, broths, fish soups, stews and many other dishes. In Sicily a dish is made with mild sausages lying on a bed of branches of bay. This is baked in the oven for ten minutes or so, then a layer of

sliced oranges is placed on top and the baking is continued for a further 15 minutes. In Umbria a traditional tomato sauce for pasta contains a dozen bay leaves and a good pinch of ground cinnamon.

LAVARELLO or COREGONE *A freshwater fish*
This freshwater fish lives in the deepest waters of some lakes. It is found wild in Lake Como and Lake Bolsena, but it is now also farmed. Lavarello has a very delicate meat, similar to wild trout, and in central Italy it is cooked in the oven with garlic, wild fennel or rosemary, chilli and dried breadcrumbs. In Lombardy the favourite local dressing of melted butter and sage is used.

LEGUMI *Pulses (Legumes)*
The most common pulses (legumes) are peas, beans, lentils, chick peas (garbanzo beans) and vetches. The union of pulses with pasta, fairly common in northern Italy, occurs mostly in soups, while in the south it appears in pasta dishes. In a dish from Veneto borlotti beans are used with polenta and a few anchovies are added to tickle the palate. All pulses should be eaten within one year of being harvested.

LENTICCHIA *Lentil*
This popular pulse (legume) is enjoyed by everyone, in all regions of Italy. Continental lentils, which keep their shape when cooked, are grown in many regions of Italy, although the best come from Abruzzo and Umbria. The lentils from Castelluccio, a small hill-town east of Spoleto, are the best. They are tiny, beige-green lentils that have a sweeter, yet fuller flavour than others. Unlike all other pulses, lenticchie do not need soaking unless they have been stored for too long.

There are many different ways to cook lentils, whether in soups or as vegetables. One of the most popular ways to cook them is "in umido"† (see the recipe on page 155).

LEPRE *Hare*

Hare is popular in northern and central Italy. In the north it is usually stewed in wine and in the blood of the animal, in a recipe called lepre in salmì**, following the local tradition of slow cooking. In central Italy a hare, which must be young, is roasted on the spit or in the oven. The Tuscans have one of the best recipes, lepre in dolce-forte (literally, "in sweet and strong"). The jointed hare is stewed in wine with onion, celery, carrot, herbs, garlic and tomatoes. A sauce made with reduced vinegar and water, to which sultanas (golden raisins), orange and citron peel, pine nuts and grated chocolate are added, is poured over at the end. Recipes for braised hare, in salmì or in civet, call for the blood to be added to the cooking juices.

LIEVITO *Raising agent*

There are three types of lievito: lievito naturale, also called madre or biga – starter – for making country bread; lievito di birra – yeast – for more refined bread and rustic cakes and lievito chimico – baking powder – for cakes and biscuits (cookies).

LIMONE *Lemon*

Lemons play an important role in many sweet and savoury dishes. Among these are pollo al limone (chicken with a lemon pushed inside), vitello tonnato*, ossobuchi* and frittura piccata*. Fish dishes cry out for lemon juice, and, even though purists object, fritto misto di pesce* is better with lemon.

Risotto al limone is a most successful recipe. The rice, cooked in stock with the usual soffritto*, is flavoured half-way through with chopped sage and rosemary. At the end of the cooking a soupçon of grated lemon rind (peel), an egg yolk and the juice of half a lemon are added. The risotto is finished with Parmesan and butter. A favourite recipe of mine is tagliatelle al limone, an old recipe from Piedmont in which pasta is dressed with melted butter flavoured with lemon juice, cream and Parmesan cheese.

Sweets (candies), cakes and pastries all benefit from a hint of grated lemon rind. On a hot summer's day, a gelato* al limone is the best ice cream there is, and a spremuta* di limone (pure lemon juice) is the most thirst-quenching drink. A granita* di limone (frozen lemon juice crushed into small crystals) is a successful combination of gelato and spremuta.

LINGUA *Tongue*

Both fresh and pickled, tongue is a familiar food in the northern regions of Italy. If fresh, the tongue is that of a pig, or more often a calf, while lingua salmistrata (pickled) is always that of a young ox, a vitellone*. Pickled tongue is cured with saltpetre and spices and then boiled; this is the lingua sold in many delis, and in grocers' shops and supermarkets in vacuum packs. The best tongue is sold not curled and pressed but left in its original shape, with all the root removed.

Pickled tongue can also be bought raw, and boiled at home, and many people still do this. The root is removed and used by the thrifty cook to make stuffings and rissoles. The tongue is served hot with salsa verde* or other sauces, or it is left to cool in its original shape, never rolled, and served with salad. A whole tongue is more often bought and served fresh than pickled. It can be cooked in many ways. In some places in Piedmont one can still find sheep's tongues, cut into slices, coated in batter and fried.

It is the tongue of a calf, however, that is most frequently cooked at home. The most popular use of a calf's tongue, or in this case usually half a tongue, is in a bollito misto**.

In Tuscany, Emilia and Umbria you can sometimes find on the market wild boar's tongues which have been smoked. It is a delicacy not to be overlooked.

LOMBATA *A cut of meat*

This is the back of a calf or an ox from its shoulders to its haunch, with or without the bone. It is a term that covers many different cuts. Fillet (tenderloin), cutlets, sirloin etc are all part of a lombata, and recipes are written for the individual cuts. That said, because of the various regional names of dishes, there are often references to lombata as a dish cooked in a special way, rather than meaning a butcher's cut.

LOMBATINE
Boneless veal or pork cutlets or steaks

These steaks or cutlets are prepared in many ways — veal in a butter-based sauce and pork in a tomato sauce, for example. In Naples, pork lombatine are also cooked with grilled (broiled) and peeled (bell) peppers.

LONZA *(1) A type of salami*

A regional name for a salted and air-cured salami* made from the leg of a pig. It is found only in Marche and Umbria, where it is made in a small artisan way for family consumption.

LONZA *(2) A loin of pork*

Also called lombo, lombata and, in northern Italy, carré, lonza is a loin of pork. It is usually sold rindless. The best known lonza dish is the Tuscan arista**. Another great lonza dish, maiale al latte**, originally from Pesaro is now popular all over northern Italy.

LUCCIO *Pike*

Pike is a freshwater fish, but can sometimes be found in the sea at river mouths. It is savage and devours any other fish in sight. It even manages to grab ducks by swimming on the surface; indeed, their remains have been found in its stomach. The best pikes are found in the rivers and lakes of Umbria, Lazio and Lombardy. The recipes from Lombardy are straightforward, and rather less original than those from central Italy, the pike being served with a hot piquant sauce based on capers and anchovies.

LUGANEGA *A mild sausage*

This mild sausage has a delicate flavour. Pork meat, both lean and fat flavoured with salt, pepper and other spices, is coarsely ground and then encased in a narrow casing made from a pig's gut. It is sold fresh and, in country shops, great lengths are coiled up so that it is also called salsiccia a metro (sausage by the metre). Luganega is also sold in supermarkets in vacuum packs. Milan, and all Lombardy, is famous for its luganega, and vies with Veneto for having the largest production and consumption. The luganega of Lombardy is reputedly the best, where the top award should go to Monza, the suburb of Milan more famous for its Grand Prix race than for its sausage. In and around Monza luganega is still made to order — grated Parmesan is added, and the mixture is moistened with dry white wine instead of water.

LUMACA *Snails*

In Rome small snails are eaten for the feast day of St John, 24 June, in a dish known as lumache di San Giovanni. The snails are cooked in oil with garlic, onion, chilli, mint and tomatoes. These snails are the very small ones known as grigette di vigna ("small grey ones of the vineyard"), being so small they are rather a bore to eat. The same applies to those found in Venice, bovoletti*, which appear on the stalls in the fish market in June. The Venetians adore them and, once they have been blanched, they dress them with garlic and oil. Small snails are also the favourites of the Palermitani, who eat them in July for the saint's day of Santa Rosalia, the city's patron saint, where they are sold on the street from smoking cauldrons. The small snails are sautéed in oil with chopped garlic and fresh parsley and then sucked out of their shells. In Pavia, snails are the main ingredients in a gourmet dish: they are cooked in oil, garlic and parsley, with boned frogs' legs and dry white wine, the whole thing topped by slivers of white truffle. The best big snails are called 'da vigna'. They are large and have light hazelnut coloured shells. Lumache have been appreciated from Roman to modern times, so much so that they are now farmed. Apart from eating them à la Bourguignonne, the most popular Italian recipe is from Piedmont. The snails, boiled in stock, are finished off for 10 minutes on a bed of stewed onion and seasoned with plenty of pepper.

LUPPOLO *Hops*

Hops are also called bruscandolo in Veneto and lovertis in Lombardy. The part that is eaten is the young shoot, before it flowers. It has a flavour similar to wild asparagus, and is prepared in the same way – boiled and dressed, usually, with olive oil and lemon juice. Hop shoots are eaten a lot in central Italy, and in Rome where an excellent soup, zuppa di lupari, is made by stewing the hop shoots in olive oil flavoured with garlic. Prosciutto*, cut into strips, is added and the soup is thickened with egg yolks and ladled over crostini*.

MACCO *A bean soup*

This traditional soup, made in Sardinia, Calabria and Sicily, is eaten on Saint Joseph's day, 19 March, when the dried pulses (legumes) of the previous year are finished off, before the new ones are harvested. It differs from region to region, but basically consists of a thick soup of broad (fava) beans, mixed with wild plants (wild fennel in Sicily) or tomatoes, to which other pulses or pasta can be added. It is dressed with local olive oil, black pepper and pecorino*.

MACEDONIA DI FRUTTA *Fruit salad*

Macedonia is so called by analogy with the country of the same name, which is inhabited by a mixture of people. Macedonia is a favourite summer dessert both in restaurants and in homes. It usually contains bananas, apples and pears, in addition to which it should include a good variety of seasonal fruits plus some tropical fruit

– a fairly recent development. The fruit, cut into small cubes, sprinkled with sugar and dressed with orange and lemon juices, is steeped for at least two hours and served chilled, without cream.

There is also a winter macedonia which is made with all sorts of dried fruits. These are first soaked in sweet white wine and water and then poached in the liquid, to which sugar and spices have been added.

MAGGIORANA *Marjoram*

A perennial herb that grows on the Mediterranean coast. It has a sweet flavour, and is used in many local cuisines. Above all, marjoram is the trade mark of the cooking of Liguria, a region famous for its herbs. In Liguria it is added to vegetable torte*, to stuffed vegetables and to the stuffing of pansoti*, Ligurian ravioli.

MAIALE *Pork*

The word means both pig, the animal, and pork, its meat. Maiale is the most popular provider of food throughout the peninsula. Thanks to the pig the larder is replenished with all sorts of food for the rest of the year. When I was young we lived on a farm in Emilia for a few years, and I can still remember the terrified scream of the poor pig, who knew what was going to happen. All through that day, the farm was buzzing with frenetic activity. The norcino (the butcher who specialized in making pork products), came to the farm to kill and bleed the pig, to sort out the different cuts, to salt, mince (grind), flavour, smoke them and cook them to make prosciutti*, salami*, cotechini* and salsiccie*. The leftover meat was chopped up and put into a large earthenware pot for a ragù*.

By the evening the screams were forgotten as we dived into dishes of hot ciccioli*. Huge copper saucepans, full of fat, were spluttering on the heat for hours, until all the fat was rendered to make strutto*. The crackling ciccioli were then retrieved and eaten with focaccia*. And the following day, any bits and pieces left over were stewed in wine and tomatoes, and served with a golden mound of piping hot polenta*.

Most country families still keep or share a pig, and the maialatura (slaughtering of the maiale) is traditionally something of a feast day. In some remote villages in southern Italy the maialatura has ritualistic overtones that go far back into history.

Nowadays maiale are big business, suppling the important salumi* industry with its raw material. Many piggeries are situated near dairy farms, and the pigs are fed with whey, a by-product of the cheese making. These pigs produce the sweetest and fattest prosciutti. They are, however, considered rather too large and fat by the purists, who prefer the lean meat of the mountain pigs, such as those of Umbria or Abruzzo, where their meat tastes of the berries and herbs on which they feed. Many local products are made on a small scale with this type of pig, and their taste is much stronger and more earthy.

Recipes for pork meat are similar throughout the country, although every region claims to have its own special one. The great recipe claimed by both Marche and Emilia is maiale al latte**. Another winner is arista alla Fiorentina* ** and, also from Tuscany, scottiglia*. Milan has its famous cassoeula* **, Italy's most comforting and nourishing feast of pork meats. Also from Milan comes a simple dish of pork chops cooked at length with tomatoes in butter and sage. Ten minutes before serving, a small piece of luganega* is placed on top of each chop for a different texture and a more intense flavour.

MALFATTI *A green gnocchi*
Also called gnocchi* verdi, these are green gnocchi, made in Lombardy with spinach and ricotta (see page 90).

MALLOREDDUS
A type of gnocchi
A Sardinian type of very small gnocchi made with durum wheat semolina and water, and flavoured with saffron. They are usually served with a tasty ragù* made from local sausage and fresh tomatoes. There is now a dried pasta called gnocchetti sardi on the market, which is the commercial version.

MANDARINO *Mandarin*
This citrus fuit is very much associated with Italy, although mandarins have been partly superseded by tangerines, clementines and satsumas, all hybrids, some better and some less good. At Christmas, when local oranges are not yet in season, a bowl of mandarins makes a most decorative sight, and at Epiphany mandarins are put in children's stockings. Mandarins are used to make sorbets (sherbets) and bavarois, and to decorate fruit tarts.

MANDORLA *Almond*
There are two varieties of almond tree and they look identical, but one produces sweet almonds and the other bitter almonds. Sweet almonds are used to make the pasta di mandorle or pasta reale*, as well as marzapane*. And all over Italy they are one of the favourite ingredients in sweets (candies), cakes

and desserts. Among the best-known preparations made with almonds are amaretti*, ricciarelli* di Siena and torrone*. Almonds are also eaten salted and toasted or coated with sugar (confetti*) or with caramelized sugar (mandorle pralinate). Almonds are also popular in some traditional southern Italian pasta sauces, which might also contain sultanas (golden raisins), and basil or other herbs, and/or tomatoes.

Ermelline (bitter almonds) are toxic. However, the prussic acid they contain is volatile, and evaporates on heating. Three or four bitter almonds are mixed with 200 g/7 oz/1¼ cups of sweet almonds to make amaretti di Saronno; they give the biscuits (cookies) their peculiar bitter flavour. A few bitter almonds are often added to sweet almonds in other preparations to emphasize the almond taste, which they do far better than almond extract.

MANDORLATO *A type of nougat*
This kind of nougat is made in Veneto. It is made with honey, which is slowly heated. Whisked egg whites are folded into this, and then almonds and a good measure of cinnamon. The mixture is then cooled between sheets of rice paper. Nowadays mandorlato is made commercially, when it also contains candied citron.

MANZO *A young ox and its meat*
Manzo is eaten more in northern Italy than elsewhere, because the fertile pastures of the Po Valley and the foothills of the Alps are excellent breeding grounds for cattle. Another locality to supply excellent beef is the Val di Chiana in Tuscany, where the cattle grow large when they are still young, so that their meat becomes tasty when it is still lean.

Manzo is often bought either sliced, when it is known as fettine*, minced (ground) to make polpette* or in a piece for roasting or braising. The shin (shank) is used for stews, and the fillet (tenderloin) for steaks or for roasting. The offal (variety meat) is prepared in many different ways, although it is not as popular as calf's offal.

Manzo is also boiled, either as part of a bollito misto* or by itself, when it is known as il lesso* or manzo lesso, a staple dish in virtually every Lombard household.

MARICONDE *A small dumpling*

These small balls the size of hazelnuts are made from selected ground almonds, a mixture of breadcrumbs, Parmesan, butter and egg, and cooked and served in good meat stock. Sometimes minced (ground) boiled chicken is added too. It is a typical example of the delicate soups of Lombardy.

MARITOZZI *A sweet bun*

These bread rolls studded with pine nuts, sultanas (golden raisins) and orange and citron peels, and thickly covered with icing (confectioners') sugar, are a speciality of Rome. They are sometimes cut in half and filled with whipped cream.

MARMELLATA *Marmalade*

A fruit preserve most commonly made with sweet oranges, mandarins and other citrus fruits, but never with bitter oranges as elsewhere.

MARRONE *see* CASTAGNA

MARZAPANE *Marzipan*

Marzapane is a mixture of sugar, ground almonds and eggs, with which almond biscuits (cookies), such as petits fours, are made. It is the same mixture as the English and American marzipan. In Italy marzapane is often flavoured with cinnamon or lemon rind.

MARZOLINO *A Tuscan cheese*

A type of Tuscan pecorino*, made from ewe's milk in a cylindrical shape, in the provinces of Siena and Arezzo. Its name comes from Marzo (March), the month during which it is prepared. It is then either eaten fresh or left to age, when it becomes hard and slightly piquant.

MASCARPONE

A creamy cheese

This creamy soft cheese, originally from Lombardy, is now produced commercially all over northern Italy. It is made with the cream of very fresh milk from cows that have been fed on fresh or naturally dried fodder, rather than fodder dried in silos; so the aroma of the flowers and herbs is preserved.

Mascarpone is now exported in tubs bearing an expiry date. This mascarpone is certainly not as good as the farm product wrapped in muslin (cheese-cloth), as sold in some cheese shops in northern Italy, but it is good enough for making some special desserts and sauces. Of these the best known is the relatively modern tiramisù* **, originally from Treviso, but now popular all over the world. An older type of dessert is the crema mascarpone, which is mascarpone beaten with sugar, egg yolks and rum.

Mascarpone can also be used to make a savoury cream, by combining it with caviar, truffles, smoked trout etc, and for one of the most delectable pasta sauces when mixed with egg yolks. Another use of mascarpone in a savoury preparation is a layered cheese made with mascarpone and gorgonzola, a modern creation popular in Britian and the United States.

MAZZAFEGATI
Pig's liver sausage

These sausages are made in Umbria and Marche. The Umbrian mazzafegati are quite sweet, as they are made with a mixture of pig's liver, sugar, sultanas (golden raisins) and pine nuts. The mazzafegati from Marche are a mixture of minced (ground) liver and lights of the pig, flavoured with spices and pushed into pig casing.

MAZZETTO ODOROSO
or AROMATICO *Bouquet garni*

Consisting of parsley, rosemary, sage, thyme, bay leaf and, sometimes, marjoram, bouquets garnis can be found in greengrocers' shops, but they are not as much a part of the Italian culinary scene as they are in France.

MEASCIA *A bread pudding*

This is the Lombard bread and butter pudding. The bread, cut into cubes, is soaked in milk and then mixed with eggs, lemon rind, slices of apple and pear, sultanas (golden raisins), sugar, white flour and polenta flour (coarse cornmeal). After baking, the cake is sprinkled lavishly with chopped fresh rosemary, which gives meascia its characteristic and unusual flavour.

MELA *Apple*

Less popular in Italy than in other European countries, the many varieties of apple available are nearly all foreign, apart from the Mantovana, from Mantua, and the Limoncella. The best areas of cultivation are all in northern Italy, except for a small area south of Naples, where the excellent Annurca grows, an apple that is now becoming very popular.

The only characteristic Italian use of the apple is when, sliced and coated with batter, it is fried and served as part of a fritto misto*. It also appears in quite a few simple cakes and desserts, of which the best known are a charlotte from Lombardy and an apple pudding from Trentino. (You will find a recipe for an apple cake made with olive oil on page 160.)

MELAGRANA *Pomegranate*

This is the fruit of the beautiful shiny green tree, with its vermilion flowers, you can see dotted around lovely gardens in central and southern Italy. Pomegranate is eaten, albeit rarely, in fruit salads, or used to make a pleasant drink called granatina. There is a recipe for roast turkey from Venice in which pomegranate juice is added to give bite to the livers of the bird which are sautéed separately to make the sauce. Some pomegranate seeds are scattered over the turkey at the end.

MELANZANA
Aubergine (eggplant)

Aubergines (eggplant) have become very popular, especially in southern Italy where they grow. Several varieties are grown that vary in size, colour and shape, but as long as they are hard and have a beautiful shiny skin, they all taste the same.

The many recipes for aubergines are mainly from southern Italy and Sicily, where they have been enjoyed for much longer than in the north. The two best known are caponata* ** from Sicily, and parmigiana di melanzane* ** from Naples. Aubergines mix well with pasta, as in pasta alla Norma* or the elaborate pasta 'ncasciata**, a Sicilian pie. At the other extreme, few dishes are as simple and good as grilled (broiled or barbecued) or roast aubergines.

Aubergines lend themselves to being stuffed and they are also well suited to being preserved. This can be done by first blanching aubergine cubes in vinegar, packing them in jars, covering them in olive oil flavoured with oregano and garlic and sealing. The jars are then sterilized in boiling water for 30 to 40 minutes.

MELONE *Melon*

Also called popone in southern Italy, melon is mainly served with prosciutto*, thus being almost the only fruit that is eaten at the beginning of the meal. It is also used in fruit salads. Of the many varieties of melon, two are particularly connected with Italy, the Napoletano, with its oval shape, bright orange flesh and green or yellow skin, and the Cantalupo, which was first cultivated in the garden of the papal residence at Cantalupo, near Rome. The melons were so highly esteemed that they were given by the popes as gifts.

MENTA *Mint*

There are three main varieties of mint in Italian cooking.

Mentuccia (also called nepitella) – Corsican mint, is sweeter and more aromatic than the other varieties. It is used in quite a few dishes from central and southern Italy, and also in custards and ice cream.

Menta romana – spearmint, is the characteristic flavouring added to a dish of Roman tripe, its pronounced piquancy beautifully counteracting the sweetness of the tripe.

Menta piperita – peppermint, which is used in the production of liqueurs and the manufacture of confectionery.

MERINGA *Meringue*

There is a Swiss and an Italian version of meringue. Both are made with whisked egg whites and sugar, but the method is different.

Swiss meringues are made without any heating, simply by adding sugar to the whisked whites, while the Italian meringue mixture is made by beating a hot sugar syrup into the whisked egg whites. The Italian meringue is not as light as the Swiss meringue and, having a tougher, more resilient texture, is better suited for small patisseries. It is not often made at home.

MERLUZZO *Cod*

This is not a Mediterranean fish, and it is only found dried (stoccafisso*), salted (baccalà*) or frozen, in supermarkets. The nearest Mediterranean equivalent to fresh cod is nasello* (hake), an unrelated fish.

MESCIUA *A bean soup*

In local dialect, mesciua means "a mixture". This soup used to be the nourishment of the poorest people; now it is served in chic restaurants in the province of La Spezia in Liguria, its motherland. It is a mixture of cannellini beans, chick peas (garbanzo beans) and emmer wheat or whole wheat grains, cooked until soft and then simply dressed with Ligurian olive oil and pepper.

MESSICANI *A veal dish*

These veal bundles, oddly named "Mexicans", consist of thin slices of veal wrapped around a mixture of sausage, Parmesan, eggs and nutmeg. The bundles, stuck through in pairs on to wooden sticks, are then sautéed in butter that has been flavoured with sage. A splash of Marsala• is the final addition to this delicate and tasty dish from Milan, which, like ossobuco* **, is traditionally served with risotto alla Milanese* **.

MIDOLLO *Beef marrow*

There is enough marrow in one bone for a risotto alla Milanese* **, for which it is the traditional fat, or for a sauce. Marrow is also used in passatelli*, and in various stuffings such as that for sweet fried ravioli, when it is mixed with candied fruits and pinenuts. In ossobuchi* ** the bone marrow is the tastiest part.

MIELE *Honey*

Honey is produced in all the regions of Italy. Among those which merit a special mention are the honey of Vesuvius, which comes from mountain flora, and the honey of Calabria and Sicily, made from orange blossom. But, as so often, it is Sicily which offers the most highly prized varieties: the honey from zagara (the flower of the lemon tree), from thyme and from thyme and mint from Trapani are the best. Tuscan and Sardinian honey from strawberry plants has a bitter flavour and a light golden colour tinged with green, while the honey from lavender, from Liguria, is delicate and has the characteristic aroma of the lavender flowers. Some Sicilian sweets are made with honey rather than sugar.

MIGLIACCIO

A polenta-based cake

A cake made with polenta* flour (coarse cornmeal). In Emilia-Romagna the flour is mixed with pig's blood and sugar. In Tuscany, however, migliaccio is a polenta or focaccia containing sultanas (golden raisins).

MILLECOSEDDE

A Calabrian bean soup

A soup from Calabria whose name means "a thousand little things". It is made with all the dried beans available, plus cabbage, onion, celery and wild fungi, cooked together for several hours in an earthenware pot. Some short tubular pasta is boiled separately and then mixed with the vegetables and the soup is dressed with olive oil and grated pecorino* before serving.

MILZA *Spleen*

The spleen of oxen, calves and pigs is used in some traditional recipes. It tastes like liver, and has the same texture. In Tuscany, calf's spleen is used with chicken liver to make the best known crostini* **, while in Rome, ox spleen is blanched and then cut into thin slices. It is sautéed in olive oil and lard with garlic and sage for a few minutes and is then flavoured with pounded salted anchovies.

MINESTRA *Soup*

In minestra the various elements, whether cubes of vegetables, grains of rice or pasta shapes, are quite separate and distinct, and are distinguishable from the stock in which they cook. This is what differentiates it from a zuppa*, which is a thicker mixture, that is often ladled on to the slices of bread.

Some minestre are light and delicate, such as stracciatella*, minestra di passatelli* or minestra paradiso*. These are made with the best homemade stock into which other ingredients, such as cheese, minced (ground) white meat and breadcrumbs, bound with egg, have been cooked. There are also the thicker minestre, of peasant origin, based on one or more vegetables cut into cubes and cooked in water or stock, usually with pasta or rice added at the end. This category is vast and includes such classics as minestra di pasta e fagioli** (pasta and bean soup), minestre of other pulses (legumes), of Savoy cabbage and rice and of milk and rice.

Northern Italy has a large repertoire of thick soups, which is what the climate demands, while in central and southern Italy they are lighter. This can be seen when you compare how, for instance, a bean soup is made in different regions. In Veneto, which boasts the original recipe, a soffritto* is made with pancetta*, and a ham bone is added to it, while the Neapolitan version is made with water, tomatoes and herbs, and dressed with olive oil. The recipe on page 59 is for a soup that is simplicity itself, minestra coi pomodori (with tomatoes).

Minestra is still served at the evening meal as a first course in many homes. Recently, however, it has lost ground to more popular pasta or risotto dishes.

MINESTRA MARICONDA *A type of soup*

This soup from Lombardy consists of soft breadcrumbs soaked in milk, bound with eggs and flavoured with Parmesan and nutmeg. The mixture is dropped, a teaspoonful at a time, into simmering homemade stock.

MINESTRA MARITATA
A baked savoury dish

There are three versions of minestra maritata, from Naples, Calabria and Puglia, and they all contain different vegetables that go well together. The versions from Calabria and Puglia contain chicory, wild fennel, bulb fennel, celery and batavia. The vegetables are blanched and then layered with olive oil

and pecorino*, covered with soft bread-crumbs and baked in the oven. The resulting dish is more like a vegetable pie than a soup. In the Neapolitan version pork rind, sausage etc are also added to the layered vegetables.

MINESTRA PARADISO
A light soup

A speciality of Emilia, this soup is light and delicate, ideal to have in the evening after the large, heavy lunch that is characteristic of the region. Eggs, mixed with Parmesan and bread-crumbs, are beaten into the stock.

MINESTRINA *A thin soup*

This thin soup is made with best chicken stock or a light meat stock, containing either pastina* (small pasta shapes), barley or semolina, which have been cooked in the stock. Minestrina is rather out of fashion, and now tends to be regarded as food for invalids.

MINESTRONE *A vegetable soup*

A thick vegetable soup, the many different versions of which have one thing in common: the cut-up vegetables are simmered for a long time in water and/or stock. The remarkable thing about this slow cooking is that each piece of vegetable retains its shape and does not become mushy, while the soup acquires the taste of all the

vegetables that have been cooked in it. Minestroni are soups of northern Italy, and can be divided into two broad categories according to the method of cooking: minestrone col soffritto* and minestrone a crudo*.

In minestrone col soffritto the chopped vegetables are sautéed in either butter, pork fat, oil or lard, or in a mixture of any of these, together with pancetta* and/or pork rind. The vegetables go into the saucepan in order according to how long they take to cook. They are then covered with water or stock and cooked for a long time. At the end rice, or sometimes small tubular pasta such as ditalini*, is added.

In minestroni a crudo the raw vegetables are put into the water or stock together, without being first sautéed. Best olive oil is added towards the end of the slow cooking. Sometimes the olive oil is heated with garlic and chopped herbs and then added to the soup at the end. This type of minestrone is usually made with pasta rather than rice. The Tuscan version is the classic example of this type of soup.

Any vegetable can go into a minestrone, but there are some that are essential. These are onion, celery, carrots, potatoes, beans and tomatoes. The other frequently used vegetables are courgettes (zucchini), cabbage, peas, French (green) beans and leeks. In winter, canned tomatoes are used instead of fresh, and dried beans replace fresh beans, which are only in season for a short period in the spring.

Minestrone is nicer when it is made a day in advance. It can be served cold in the summer, but never chilled.

MISSOLTIT *Preserved fish*
This fish preparation is a speciality of Lake Como. Agoni*, small freshwater fish caught in the spring, are air-dried hanging by their heads, the tiny silvery fish waving and shimmering in the wind and sun. They are then put in layers in special barrels called missolte, from which the preserved fish takes its name. Missoltit, now a rarity, are only to be found locally.

MISTICANZA *Mixed salad leaves*
A mixture of wild salad leaves which are picked in the fields and along the banks of the ditches in the area of Lazio called Castelli-Romani. According to Roman gastronomes, misticanza should contain 21 different kinds of wild salad. Even if this is a little excessive, a good misticanza must include a selection of rocket (arugula), wild chicory, wild fennel, sorrel, mint, dandelion and lamb's lettuce (corn salad).

MOCETTA *Cured goat*
This boned and cured thigh of a chamois, wild goat or domestic goat is a speciality of the Val d'Aosta. The boned thigh, flavoured with garlic, herbs, juniper berries and pepper, is first salted like a prosciutto*, and then hung in a dry cellar for three or four months. It is traditionally eaten with brown bread spread with butter, and sometimes also with honey.

MOLECA *A soft crab*
This crab is a speciality of the Venetian lagoon, where it has been bred for over two centuries. In their natural habitat, male crabs lose their carapace in the spring and autumn (fall), when they are ready to mate. This development can be induced in special baskets, called *vieri*, which are kept under strange-looking platforms in the Venetian lagoon between Chioggia and Pellestrina.

The Venetians love them, and to achieve gastronomic perfection they put live moleche in a bowl containing beaten eggs, in which, having devoured much of the eggs, they drown. They are then coated in flour and fried in olive oil, and the Venetians have their treasured moleche col pien (moleche with stuffing), the stuffing being the egg. Another way to eat them is, once fried, to cut them up and mix them with eggs in a frittata*.

MOLLICA *Fresh breadcrumbs*
Mollica is used a great deal in Italian cooking, as a binder in polpette* and polpettoni*, in fillings for ravioli and other pasta shapes and in stuffings for vegetables, fish etc. In Calabria, slightly dried mollica is the main ingredient in many pasta sauces, a classic recipe for which is given on page 65.

MONTEBIANCO
A chestnut dessert
This is a sweet concoction of puréed chestnuts, previously cooked in milk flavoured with vanilla, rum and cocoa or grated chocolate and covered with whipped cream to resemble the peak of Mont Blanc (hence its name).

MONDEGHILI *Meatballs*
A poor man's dish of meatballs made in Lombardy from the leftover meat of a boiled or roast cut. The meat is minced (ground) and mixed with eggs, bread soaked in milk, a little mortadella* or salami*, chopped parsley, grated lemon rind and grated nutmeg. The mixture is made into little balls and then coated in breadcrumbs and fried in butter.

MONTASIO *A type of cheese*
Originally from an Alpine valley of the same name in Friuli, the production of this cheese is now limited to the three provinces of Belluno, Treviso and Udine.

Montasio is a semi-soft or hard buff-yellow coloured cheese with a compact texture and tiny holes. It is made with unpasteurized milk. After two months it is eaten as a table cheese, when its flavour is milky and sweet. After one or two more months it becomes pleasantly strong and is also suitable for cooking. After ageing for more than a year montasio becomes slightly piquant and similar to pecorino*, and is also used for grating.

MONTONE *Ram or mutton*
The word refers both to the animal — ram, and its meat — mutton. Nowadays the meat usually comes from a castrated animal, when it is called castrato*.

MORA DI GELSO *Mulberry*
The gelsi (mulberry trees) most commonly found in Italy are those producing white berries. The trees producing black more di gelso, which are the best kind to eat, are much less common.

MORA DI ROVO *or* SELVATICA *Blackberry*
These berries grow wild in most parts of northern Italy, and on the mountains in the rest of the country. They are not cultivated as a crop. Blackberries are often used to make jams and jellies, and they are also eaten fresh by themselves, splashed with lemon or orange juice or added to a fruit salad or a sottobosco* (wild fruit salad).

MORMORA *Striped bream*
This is a fine fish, which usually measures about 12 cm/5 in in length.

Mormora has a flat body, silver in colour, with characteristic dark grey vertical stripes. It is more commonly found in the Adriatic than in the other Italian seas. It can be roasted or grilled (broiled or barbecued), or cooked in any of the ways used for its most famous cousin, the orata*.

MORSEDDU *A pork dish*

This is a breakfast dish from Calabria, the only region in Italy where that meal is taken seriously. Morseddu is a mixture of pig's offal (variety meat) and pork meat, stewed in red wine and tomatoes spiced with chilli and herbs. It is eaten in trattorie, scooped into a pitta*, a roll like the Greek equivalent.

MORTADELLA *A type of sausage*

Mortadella consists of pork meat or a mixture of pork and sometimes beef, plus egg whites and spices. It may also contain pistachios, wine and sugar. Of the meat, 70% is lean – shoulder, pieces of leg, end of loin – while the rest is fat, consisting of the jowl. The best mortadella have a lovely pink colour and are very large – they can weigh up to 50 kg/110 lb. Mortadella keeps well but, once sliced, should be eaten as quickly as possible. It should not be cut as thin as prosciutto* – a mistake that is often made outside Italy.

Mortadella is chiefly made in the provinces of Bologna, Reggio-Emilia and Modena, although some mortadelle are also produced in Lombardy, Veneto and Marche. The reputation of the mortadella from Bologna is so high, and its association with that city so strong, that in Milan mortadella used to be known as bologna, while in the United States it is often called boloney.

Apart from being served as part of an affettato*, mortadella goes into a number of stuffings for pasta and into the mixture for polpette* (rissoles) and polpettoni*. It also lends itself to cutting into cubes, to be served with drinks before a meal.

MORTADELLA DI FEGATO *A type of sausage*

This type of mortadella* contains pig's liver mixed with lean and fat pork meat, pork rind and pancetta*, moistened with red wine. It is usually served as part of the antipasto*.

MOSCARDINO or MUGHETTO or, in Venice, POLPETTO *Small octopus*

These are small octopus with curled tentacles; the smaller they are, the more highly prized. There is a similar kind of moscardino, the moscardino bianco, which is less highly regarded because its meat is tougher and it does not have the smell of musk which is the characteristic of the proper specimen. Moscardini are usually fried and eaten as part of a fritto di pesce*.

MOSCIAME *Preserved fish fillet*

To preserve it the dolphin fillet is cut into strips, salted and dried in the sun. The word is also applied to the fillet of a tuna or swordfish, similarly treated. It is a speciality of Liguria, where it is added to cappon magro*. When sliced very thinly and dressed with olive oil and lemon juice, mosciame is a delicious antipasto*.

MOSTACCIOLI *Small cakes*

These small cakes are made in Abruzzo, Calabria and other regions of Italy. The mostaccioli Abruzzesi and Calabresi use similar ingredients and are prepared in much the same way. The dough is made from a mixture of honey, chopped almonds, flour, orange peel, sugar and spices, moistened in Abruzzo with cooked must, and in Calabria with a splash of white wine. Mostaccioli are also popular in Lombardy and they have links with Assisi; St Francis, on his death bed, is said to have asked for a local widow to come to him with almonds and honey, to prepare for him for the last time his favourite sweets – mostaccioli.

MOSTARDA *A condiment*

There are three different kinds of mostarda used in Italy.

The best known is the mostarda di Cremona, or mostarda di frutta, which is served in Lombardy as the classic accompaniment to boiled meats. It comprises various candied fruits, whole or cut into pieces, which are covered with a thick honey and white wine syrup, highly flavoured with spices and mustard. Its taste is a combination of sweet and hot, rather than sweet and sour.

Mostarda di Venezia is made with minced (ground) quince, powdered mustard and sugar, and it can be bought in shops or made at home.

Mostarda tout-court is a Sicilian sweet made with grape must, sultanas (golden raisins), almonds and pine nuts. The mixture is poured into various small moulds, and dried in the sun.

MOSTO *Must*

This is the juice from grapes before it is made into wine by fermentation. In Puglia, mosto is a common drink and in all southern regions it is combined with other ingredients to make sweets.

MOZZARELLA
A type of cheese

In theory this name should apply only to mozzarella made from buffalo milk; the correct name for mozzarella made with cow's milk being fior di latte*. Buffalo mozzarella should be eaten within 24 hours of being made, dripping with its own buttermilk. It is pure white with a wonderful taste all of its own – delicate, fresh and fragrant, and it squeaks when you cut it. It is far tastier and has more body than mozzarella made from cow's milk.

Mozzarella is a low-fat cheese and is very digestible. The best way to eat a buffalo mozzarella is on its own, or with tomatoes and olives, in insalata caprese*. Mozzarella is used a lot in cooking, when it is better to use a day-old cheese that has been cut into slices and left to drain for a few hours. For this purpose, cow's milk mozzarella is an acceptable alternative to buffalo mozzarella.

Mozzarella is used in many pizza toppings, in some pasta dishes in combination with tomatoes and in some meat dishes. A well-known dish made with mozzarella is mozzarella in carrozza**. Mozzarella can also be smoked over straw and wood chips.

MUGGINE
Grey mullet

Another name for cefalo* (grey mullet); the name is used mainly on the Tyrrenian coast.

MUSCOLI
Mussels

Another name for cozze* (mussels).

MUSETTO *A spicy sausage*

This spicy sausage is made in Friuli and Venezia Giulia. It consists of a mixture of pork meat from the snout and rind, spiced with black pepper, cloves, nutmeg, cinnamon and chilli, plus fresh coriander (cilantro), a rarity in Italian cooking. Local white wine is added, and the mixture is pushed into a casing made of ox gut. It is boiled in the same way as a cotechino* and traditionally served hot with broade* (pickled turnips), which, with their sweet-and-sour flavour, temper the fattiness of the spicy sausage.

NASELLO *Hake*

This fish is plentiful in the Mediterranean and its flesh is delicate in flavour. Of the many recipes, nasello alla Marchigiana and nasello alla Palermitana (see page 91) are the best known. For nasello alla Marchigiana the fish is marinated for up to two hours in oil flavoured with onion, garlic, salt and pepper, then coated with breadcrumbs, grilled (broiled) and served with anchovy sauce.

Nasello is excellent simply baked and served with an oil and lemon sauce, or baked in white wine flavoured with onion and served with its reduced cooking juices, to which some lemon juice and a grating of lemon zest are added. A large fish can also be cooked "in umido"† – popular in the south.

NECCI *Chestnut flour pancake (crepe)*

These are a particular speciality of the mountainous parts of the provinces of Lucca and Pistoia. They are made with chestnut flour, olive oil, water and salt and are cooked in hot embers using a special, ancient instrument called testi, which are long-handled tongs with iron discs at the end. Necci are eaten warm, stuffed with ricotta* or fresh pecorino*. They are so popular that there is even an annual sagra (festival) dei necci from 15-16 August in the pretty town of Bagni di Lucca.

NERO DI SEPPIA
Cephalopod ink

The black ink of cephalopods is used to colour risotto or spaghetti. In risotto cuttlefish ink usually is used – it has a stronger flavour than the octopus ink used with spaghetti in Naples. You can buy sachets of cuttlefish ink from any good fishmonger.

NERVETTI
A type of brawn (head cheese)

Similar in substance to brawn (head cheese), but brawn is made with pork meat and pork jelly, nervetti is made with the cartilages of the shin (shank) and knee of a calf. And unlike brawn, nervetti contains no fat. Nervetti is one of the traditional dishes that is on show in all the best salumerie† of Milan.

NESPOLA *A type of fruit*

Two fruits share this name, the nespola del Giappone (Japanese medlar or loquat), and the nespola comune (medlar).

The nespola del Giappone, which used to be the fruit of as a purely ornamental tree in many gardens, is now cultivated and is a popular fruit in early summer. The fruit has a sharp yet pleasant taste.

The other variety, the medlar, has a fruit that is inedible until it has fermented, after a period of natural decay. They are not the most delectable of fruits.

NOCCIOLA *Hazelnut*

Hazel trees grow everywhere in Italy, but the best nuts are from Piedmont. The nuts are eaten by themselves and they are also used widely in confectionery, of which the Gianduiotti* and the Torta Gianduia*, both from Turin, and the torrone* are the best known.

NOCE *Walnut*

The main cultivation of walnut trees is in Campania. The nuts are best from September to the spring. Walnuts are eaten by themselves at the end of a meal, with fruit. They are also used in cooking, mixed with other ingredients, for sweets, sauces and stuffings.

The best-known sauce is salsa di noci* ** from Liguria, which is served with pansôti*, the local ravioli*, or with tagliatelle. An interesting stuffing for roast pheasant from Piedmont contains walnuts, soft local cheese, lemon and grape juice, a glass of port, butter and spices. Another excellent stuffing created by Salumeria Peck of Milan mixes walnuts with cream, minced (ground) veal, Parmesan cheese, egg and nutmeg, and is used to stuff chicken thighs which are then cooked in foil in the oven. Walnuts are also important in the making of cakes and desserts.

NOCE MOSCATA *Nutmeg*

This is a popular spice, especially in northern Italy; a pinch of freshly grated nutmeg appears in the list of ingredients of many recipes. It brings out the taste in spinach, it makes a béchamel and vegetable sformato* more lively, it enhances the flavour of fungi and is a must in the stuffing for ravioli*. Nutmeg also goes well in ragù*, stews and fish soups, as well as in fruit poached in wine and in traditional fruit cakes.

NODINI *Veal noisettes*

Unlike other European countries, in Italy noisettes are always of veal, and it is only in Lombardy that they are a traditional dish. Nodini are cut from the lower part of the loin and have a short bone, with hardly any fat. (See recipe on page 121.)

OCA *Goose*

The accepted way to cook goose is to roast it with a stuffing that contains roast chestnuts, apples, luganega* and a few crumbled amaretti*. Goose is also preserved, oca in pignatto being a speciality of Veneto.

Italian-Jewish cooking has many recipes for goose. Two recipes from the Venetian-Jewish cuisine are for salami* and prosciutto* made from goose meat.

OLI VARI *Various oils*

The consumption of oils in Italy, other than olive oil, is small, although it has increased recently. This is partly because of the rising cost of olive oil and partly because of the emphasis on lighter ingredients.

The oils that are becoming increasingly popular in Italian cooking are groundnut (peanut) and sunflower, both used for frying. These oils are also occasionally used together with olive oil or butter as cooking fat.

OLIO D'OLIVA *Olive oil*

Although it is now the prime cooking fat of Italian cuisine, the use of olive oil only became widespread in northern Italy after the Second World War; prior to that it was just used in salads, never in cooking.

The olives for making oil are harvested in November, December and January, before they are ripe. They are collected by pickers, either with large wicker baskets, or by spreading large nets around the base of each tree and shaking it.

As soon as they are harvested, the olives are taken to the frantoio (mill), where the oil must be extracted within a week – the best oil is produced from olives processed within one or two days of picking. The olives are cleaned and washed in cold water, and then crushed. The kneaded pulp is layered on fibrous mats then pressed between huge stones or metal plates. The whole process takes place without using any heat or chemicals.

The first oil extracted from this pressed pulp is known as the first pressing. Most of this is marketed in various grades under the name of virgin olive oil. The remainder of the oil, which may not comply with regulations because of an over-pronounced taste or smell, or if the colour is too dark, or it is too acidic, is known as refined and is usually blended with virgin oil and sold simply as olive oil. Outside Italy there are only two grades: extra virgin olive oil and olive oil.

Which region's oil to choose is to a certain extent a matter of taste. Liguria produces a pale golden oil which is sweet and delicate, suitable for most dishes and palates. The oil from Chianti is fruity and peppery, with tinges of green. From the south, which accounts for 80% of the national production, comes the oil from Puglia, which has a detectable almond flavour, a taste that can also be savoured in oils from Calabria. Most people choose according to their taste and purse. Extra virgin oil is used for salads and for any dish that requires the addition of uncooked oil; virgin oil or pure oil are used for cooking. The simpler the dish, the greater the need to use the best quality oil.

Olive oil should be consumed within the year; it does not keep for more than 18 months even in the best conditions. It is at its best between six months and one year from the time it was produced. It should be stored in an opaque container, earthenware being ideal, at a moderate and stable temperature and in a dry atmosphere.

OLIVA *Olive*

Olives for making oil are harvested in the winter (see Olio d'Oliva), while those for the table are harvested at different times. Green olives are harvested at the end of the summer, and black olives in winter, when they are fully ripe. After being harvested, olives are subjected to any one of a number of different processes, depending on their variety. The best green olives are the small ones from Calabria and the large ones from Ascoli Piceno and Puglia, while among the black olives, those from Gaeta and the small ones from Liguria, Taggiasca, are the connoisseurs' favourites.

There is a traditional Sicilian recipe for stuffed olives in which the stuffing is a mixture of anchovy fillets and capers. In Olive all'Ascolana, a recipe from Ascoli Piceno, in Marche, large, stoned (pitted), olives are stuffed with minced (ground) pork, prosciutto*, Parmesan and other flavourings, all bound with egg. They are then coated with egg and breadcrumbs and fried.

The olives that are added to pasta sauces such as puttanesca* **, and to fish dishes, are usually black, while green olives are used in a few rabbit and chicken dishes.

OMBRINA
A delicate-flavoured Mediterranean fish
This fish is quite common in the Mediterranean, found mainly in rocky waters. Ombrina has a delicate white meat, and it can be cooked in the same way as sea bass, which it resembles. It is excellent grilled (broiled) or baked.

ORATA *A type of sea bream*
This is the French daurade, a beautiful fish which tastes excellent. Steaming or grilling (broiling) are the best methods of cooking orata, but always with a minimum of flavouring, to allow its superb flavour to be appreciated.

ORIGANO *Oregano*
Oregano is a herb that grows wild in dry and sunny parts of Italy, mostly in central and southern regions. It is usually sold already dried; it is the only herb that is better dried than fresh. Of all herbs, oregano, with basil, is the one most closely associated with Italian food; mention of oregano immediately calls to mind pizza, tomato and aubergine (eggplant) dishes.

ORTICA *Nettle*
Only the young tops of the nettle are eaten as a vegetable or in soups. The stinging hairs on the leaves are destroyed by boiling.

Nettles have been an ingredient of peasant cooking for centuries. They have a sweet flavour that goes particularly well in soup with rice. Among the many recipes my favourite is a risotto* in which the nettle leaves are used in the same way as spinach.

ORZO *Barley*
Barley is mainly grown in northern Italy. The barley on the market today is always pearl barley, in which the

husked berry has been polished. It is made into soup in Val d'Aosta, Alto Adige and Friuli. These regions have dishes of German and Austrian origin, where barley is more popular than in Italy. A new dish, orzotto, has recently appeared on the culinary scene; it is a risotto made with barley instead of rice. It has the great advantage over risotto that it never overcooks, that you can prepare it beforehand and even freeze it.

OSSOBUCO *A cut of veal*

Literally, "bone with a hole", ossobuco is obtained by cutting across the hind shin (shank) of a milk-fed calf. Inside the circle of meat is the bone, and inside the bone the marrow, this being the essence of the dish.

Ossobuchi are first tied into neat parcels and then, traditionally, cooked "alla Milanese"† (see the recipe on page 122). In my opinion, although there is some disagreement, ossobuco alla Milanese should not include tomatoes. An ossobuco made with tomatoes is, however, a traditional dish of Emilia-Romagna.

OSTRICA *Oyster*

The oysters of Venice are grown in farms situated along the coast between Venice and Trieste. They are also farmed in the Gulf of Taranto. There the larvae are fixed to bundles of lentisk twigs that are lowered into the Mar Grande, the larger of the two seas of Taranto. After two months the bundles are fished out and the lentisk twigs are embedded in the Mar Piccolo (the small sea). Here the oysters thrive, thanks to some freshwater springs on the sea bed. (Oysters grow best in waters that are not very salty, which is why Atlantic oysters are better than their Mediterranean cousins.)

Oysters are usually served raw with a squeeze of lemon and perhaps a touch of cayenne. In Puglia, however, the famous Taranto oysters are baked for a few minutes with olive oil, freshly ground black pepper and a sprinkling of breadcrumbs mixed with chopped fresh parsley.

P

PAGELLO *A type of sea bream*

This tasty sea bream has lovely firm white flesh. It lends itself to being cooked in the simplest way, such as grilling (broiling), brushing with olive oil and roasting in the oven or cooking "in padella"†, with or without tomatoes.

PAGRO *A type of sea bream*

A beautiful fish, of the family of sea breams. It is similar to the dentice*, but less delicate. The best way to cook a pagro is to bake it, stuffed with herbs and breadcrumbs, although any recipe for a dentice or orata* is suitable.

PALOMBACCIO or COLOMBACCIO *Wood pigeon*

Originally wild, wood pigeons are now bred in captivity. They are very popular in Umbria, where the best recipes come from, but they are also found in Tuscany and Lazio.

The best-known recipe for wood pigeon is palombaccio alla ghiotta. The bird, traditionally undrawn and well-oiled, is wrapped with prosciutto* and

cooked on the spit. The leccarda†
placed under the spit, is filled with salsa
ghiotta* (a sauce made with wine and
herbs) and the rotating palombaccio is
brushed regularly with the sauce.
Halfway through the cooking the
giblets are removed, chopped and added
to the sauce. When the palombaccio is
cooked, it is cut into pieces and placed
in the leccarda with one or two
anchovy fillets. Older palombacci are
cooked in salmì† (jugged) or made
into pâtés and terrines.

PALOMBO *Dogfish*

One of the least vicious members of
the shark family, palombo can reach a
length of 1.5 m/1½ yds. This is the fish
one can see cut into huge chunks on the
stalls of the Mercato del Pesce in
Venice, where it is euphemistically
called vitella di mare (sea veal). It is not,
from the culinary point of view, a
particularly great fish.

PAMPEPATO *A sweet, peppery bread*

This is an ancient kind of very peppery
sweet bread. There are two forms of
pampepato, one made in Ferrara and
the other in Umbria and Marche. The
Ferrarese pampepato is ring-shaped,
containing almonds and pine nuts and
is often coated with chocolate icing
(frosting). It is the local Christmas
cake. The pampepato from central Italy
is made into the shape of rolls, studded
with almonds, walnuts, pieces of
chocolate, sultanas (golden raisins) and
candied fruit.

PANATA *or* PANADA
A bread soup

A bread soup from Veneto and Emilia,
panata is made by cooking stale bread
in stock, dressing it with oil and
Parmesan, and flavouring with nutmeg.

PANCETTA *Cured pork*

Pancetta is exactly the same cut of
meat as streaky (fatty) bacon, namely
the belly of a pig, although it is
differently cured. There are two kinds
of pancetta: pancetta tesa, which is left
in it natural state, like bacon, and
pancetta arrotolata (rolled pancetta).
Pancetta tesa is cured for about 20
days. Pancetta arrotolata is made from
very fatty pancetta, and shows only
two or three streaks of lean meat. It is
flavoured with cloves and pepper,
rolled up, sewn and tied up. Pancetta
tesa can also be smoked and is a
speciality of Alto Adige, Friuli and
Val d'Aosta.

Pancetta tesa is one of the most
important elements in a soffritto*, the
starting point for so many dishes, in
pasta sauces such as carbonara* or as a
component in all kinds of spiedini*
(kebabs), whether of meat, liver or
fish. Pancetta arrotolata is also used in
stuffing or served with other salumi*.

PANCOTTO *Bread soup*

This means literally, "cooked bread"
but could best be described as bread
soup. It is the most widespread of all
peasant soups, and must be made
with good country bread, plus a
combination of local ingredients. In a
typical northern Italian version these
added ingredients are butter and
onion, and the soup, made with meat
stock, is sprinkled with Parmesan. In
Liguria, herbs and grated pecorino* are
the flavouring, while in the south
tomatoes are a classic addition. The
pappa col pomodoro* of Tuscany is
pancotto by another name. In a version
from Puglia the pancotto is made with
rocket (arugula) and potatoes, and the
bread is added to the soup at the end.
My recipe is on page 56.

PAN DI SPAGNA

A sponge cake

Literally, "Spanish bread". A fatless sponge cake, similar to Madeira cake, used in dessert recipes such as zuppa inglese*.

PANDOLCE

Genoese Christmas cake

Pandolce is shaped like a rather flat dome and has trianglar cuts in the top. The dough is compact and stuffed with zibibbo* (a kind of raisin), pine nuts, candied pumpkin and candied citron, and it is flavoured with orange flower water, fennel seeds and various spices. When the cake is brought to the table a sprig of bay is placed in the top, and traditionally the youngest member of the party cuts the cake.

PANDORO *Veronese Christmas cake*

This is the Christmas cake of Verona, with the delightful name of "golden bread" because of its colour. The cake comprises flour, eggs, butter and yeast. Pandoro is baked in a star-shaped mould, and lavishly covered with icing (confectioners') sugar. It has a light texture and a buttery taste. Pandoro is hardly ever made at home. It is now widely available outside Italy.

PANE *Bread*

In Italy, pane has always been the food of life. There are a number of sayings in which bread stands for food, or nourishment. A saying that expresses Italians' regard for bread is "é buono come il pane", used to describe a kind, generous, warm-hearted person. Many loaves have a cross impressed into the dough before it goes into the oven, while in the country some old people still make the sign of the cross before cutting into a new loaf. Regional loaves have symbolic shapes for special occasions such as christenings or weddings, especially in the south, where tradition has not yet been swept away by progress.

Bakeries are so good today that there is no reason for Italians to bake bread at home – most of the bread is still baked where it is sold, and people know that bread is far better made by experts and baked in a proper bread oven. Only in some remote parts of southern Italy, or in some sophisticated kitchens in "Chiantishire", are private bread ovens still in use.

There are more than 1000 different shapes of bread, some only made locally, others produced all over Italy. The latter are mainly small rolls of white bread weighing about 25 g/1 oz, of which the michetta* and the biovetta* are the most common. These are the traditional shapes of the north. In central Italy the loaves are larger and suitable for long keeping, eg the unsalted Tuscan and Abruzzese bread, with loaves weighing about 450 g/1 lb. In southern Italy traditional loaves are large enough to last a week, such as the schiacciato of Puglia which weigh 2 kg/4½ lb each, even this being smaller than the civraxiu loaves of Sardinia, which are made with potatoes in the east of the island. And in Sardinia there is also the thinnest bread, the carta da musica, round paper-thin sheets made from a mixture of soft flour and durum wheat flour. Other special breads are rye bread, buckwheat bread and those containing milk, oil, nuts etc. Lastly there are the numerous breads produced at religious festivals in ancient symbolic shapes.

In Italy a meal would not be called a meal without bread, which is automatically put on the table. No wonder that the consumption of bread in Italy is among the highest in the European Union.

PANE
Types of bread

BIOVA *and* BIOVETTA
Large loaves and small rolls from Piedmont, very light and soft inside, with a lovely golden crispy crust.

CARTA DA MUSICA *(literally, "music paper")* also known as PANE CARASAU
This Sardinian bread is made with unleavened dough, rolled out into rounds so thin that they develop cracks on the surface. Pane carasau is now made commercially and sold all over Italy, and also abroad. With it a dish called pane fratau is prepared in Sardinia. The blanched discs of the bread are covered with chopped tomatoes and grated pecorino* and a poached egg is laid on the top.

CIABATTA
A relatively modern shaped loaf, originally from Lake Como but now a favourite in most northern regions. Ciabatta literally means "slipper", as it is a rather flat, stunted oval shape, although the name does not do justice to its feathery light texture or its delicious taste.

FILONE
A type of bread similar to a French baguette, but larger. There is also a smaller version, filoncino.

FRANCESINA
Similar to a French baguette, made in Lombardy. It has a hardish crust and a compact texture.

MANINA
A bread roll from Ferrara, a town that produces the best breads. It is made of a compact, yet light, dough.

MICHETTA
The classic Milanese bread roll. A michetta is a crusty round roll in the shape of a five-petal rose, which gives it its other name, rosetta. The bread inside is so highly leavened that the roll is almost hollow. A fresh and well-baked michetta is one of the most fragrant bread rolls available in Italy.

PAGNOTTA
A large round loaf, of which Pugliese pagnotta is the prime example. It is the oldest shape for a loaf. A pagnotta is traditionally sliced by the man of the household, who holds the loaf in the crook of his elbow, moving the knife towards his chest and slicing the bread thickly.

PAN CON L'UVA
Raisin bread from Lombardy. Pan con l'uva is made with dough containing butter and lots of raisins.

PANE DI ALTAMURA
Made in the eponymous town in Puglia, this splendid large bread is made with durum wheat flour, baked at length in a stone oven. It has a thick, smooth crust and a golden crumb with a most perfect wheaty flavour.

PAN DI MIGLIO
This traditional millet bread is more frequently made with maize flour (cornmeal) these days. It is traditionally eaten on St George's day (23 April). In Milan it is eaten with cream.

PAN DI RAMERINO

This sweet bread, from Tuscany, is made with rosemary (ramerino) and contains sultanas (golden raisins).

PANE INTEGRALE

Whole-wheat bread, usually shaped as a sandwich loaf or as small rolls. This bread is not very popular because its strong flavour detracts from the food it accompanies.

PANE PUGLIESE**

A large round loaf made in Puglia, with a crusty crust and a compact crumb.

PANE SICILIANO or PAN GAILLO

An oval shape, similar to ciabatta, but made with durum wheat flour.

PANE TOSCANO or PAN SCIOCCO

The only Italian bread that does not contain salt. It is particularly well suited to being eaten with the local salami* and the pecorino*.

PANETTONE

A traditional Christmas cake

This dome-shaped cake from Milan has conquered the world with its buttery flavour and light texture, studded with sultanas (golden raisins) and orange and citron peels. It has become *the* Christmas cake. In recent years the tall cylindrical shape, created by Motta in the 1920s, has been giving way to the original shape of a squat dome, much to the delight of all true Milanese. Panettone is never made at home because it would be too difficult a task, with the lengthy and numerous proving and rising steps needed.

There are now many kinds of panettone available on the market. It can be stuffed with, or coated with, chocolate, filled with zabaione* or mascarpone* cream and many other fancy treatments. I prefer to buy plain panettone and, with the last quarter, make my own pudding with it, as in the recipe on page 165.

PANFORTE**

Christmas cake from Siena

This is a hard, flat, highly spiced cake, today available from October to March, panforte is commercially produced and has become increasingly popular all over the western world. You can now buy panforte nero (black), which contains chocolate.

PANGRATTATO *Breadcrumbs*

These breadcrumbs are made with crustless white bread dried in the oven. Pangrattato is essential in most stuffings and is also used to thicken sauces, to coat food before frying, to sprinkle on gratin dishes and on buttered baking tine (pans) to prevent mixture (batter) from sticking. It is used in many pasta sauces from southern Italy, where it is sometimes added instead of the more expensive grated cheese.

PANINO *A filled roll*

Panino is generally taken to mean panino imbottito. Although all sorts of panini can be filled, the panino that is most commonly filled in bars is soft, and of a compact texture, similar to a bridge roll. Panini are not only eaten as snacks, they are now more and more taking the place of a proper lunch in towns and cities, where people do not have the time to go home.

PANISSA *Ligurian polenta*

This is a Ligurian polenta* made

with chick-pea (garbanzo bean) flour and water.

PANNA *Cream*

Although seldom used in traditional dishes, cream is now added to a number of pasta sauces to make them more liquid, yet denser. The best-known sauce based entirely on cream is used for dressing fettuccine*.

Cream is used in sweet preparations, although egg custard is often preferred, as it also is in the making of ice cream. There are two traditional desserts made entirely of cream and sugar: lattemiele* from southern Lombardy and panna cotta*.

PANNA COTTA

Literally, "cooked cream"

A mixture of cream, sugar and gelatine (gelatin), brought to simmering point and then poured into moulds to set. The traditional panna cotta from Piedmont and Val d'Aosta is flavoured with peach eau-de-vie. Panna cotta is served chilled and unmoulded and, traditionally, by itself, although there is now a trend to serve fruit purée with it or to surround it with fresh fruit.

PANZANELLA** *A bread salad*

A rustic, simple salad made all over central Italy, although it has gained popularity in other regions as well. Panzanella is essentially bread to which other things have been added. The bread should be the Tuscan unsalted white bread, preferably slightly stale. It is soaked in cold water, then squeezed and placed in a bowl. To this some fresh vegetables are added: ripe tomatoes, sweet red onions and a few leaves of basil or marjoram and/or sage. These are essential, but dandelion, cucumber, celery, parsley and anchovy fillets etc can be thrown in, too. The whole salad is dressed with the best local olive oil, wine vinegar, salt and black pepper.

PANZAROTTI, *or* PANZEROTTI

Savoury and sweet pastries

These are small, square or half-moon shaped pastries, made with bread dough and stuffed with various ingredients – usually a combination of tomatoes, mozzarella*, ricotta*, eggs and anchovy fillets, and flavoured with basil or oregano. The ingredients are characteristic of the central and southern regions where panzarotti are to be found. They are deep-fried in strutto* or olive oil. In Basilicata sweet panzarotti have a stuffing of sugared chick-pea (garbanzo bean) purée flavoured with chocolate and cinnamon.

PAPPA COL POMODORO

Bread and tomato soup

This is a classic Tuscan soup, of which there are as many versions as there are cooks. It combines two of the favourite Tuscan ingredients, bread and tomatoes. Pappa col pomodoro is good hot, warm or cold. The bread is Tuscan unsalted bread, one day old and lightly toasted.

PARMIGIANA DI MELANZANE**

Aubergine (eggplant) dish

This is a classic Italian dish, probably originally from Naples. It consists of slices of fried aubergine (eggplant), layered with mozzarella*, tomato sauce, Parmesan and basil. The dish is then baked. Now that fried food is less popular, the aubergine slices are often brushed with olive oil and grilled (broiled), usually to the detriment of the end result (see recipe page 149).

PARMIGIANO-REGGIANO *Parmesan cheese*

Parmigiano-Reggiano had its origins in the provinces of Parma and Reggio-Emilia, but nowadays it is also made in the provinces of Modena, Bologna and Mantova. It is still produced as it always has been, since it has been found impossible to achieve a hard, well-ripened cheese by industrial processes.

The milk used comes from local cows, the best Parmesan being made between April and November. The milk is from the morning and evening milking, and is partially skimmed but not pasteurized. Some whey from the previous batch is added to help the fermentation. The milk is curdled with calf's rennet, put into shapes and salted for 20 to 25 days.

The cheeses are large, weighing from 30–35 kg/66–77 lb and it takes 16 litres/28 pints/17½ quarts of milk to make 1 kg/2 lb 2 oz of cheese. The cheeses are matured in vast store rooms for different periods of time, and are named according to their age. Thus parmigiano nuovo is less than one year old, parmigiano vecchio is from one to two years old, and parmigiano stravecchio is two years old or more. No other cheese in the world is aged for so long. The stamp applied to its crust by the Consorzio guarantees that the quality of the cheese and the way it was produced meet stringent requirements.

Parmigiano-Reggiano has a lovely straw colour, with a crumbly texture and a mellow, rich and slightly salty flavour. It is widely used in Italian cooking and is a common flavouring for pasta; it is seldom used with fish and seafood sauces, but is used with most vegetable sauces. Parmesan is used in all stuffings, where it also acts as a binding agent; in risotti*, too, it has the added effect of making the risotto thicker and creamier.

Parmigiano-Reggiano, both young and old, is also an excellent table cheese. It can be broken into small pieces and goes particularly well with a glass of spumante or Prosecco•.

PASSATA

A purée of tomatoes – made with only tomatoes – bottled or packed in cartons.

PASSATELLI

A name for two different soups

The first version from Romagna is a mixture of dry breadcrumbs, bone marrow, Parmesan, nutmeg and eggs. The other from Marche also contains finely minced (ground) beef fillet (tenderloin). Both mixtures are pushed through the large holes of a food mill or a potato ricer directly into simmering stock, and the soup is cooked for a few minutes.

PASTA

Pasta is the generic word for any kind of dough, from pastry to bread dough. In these cases there is usually a qualifying adjective, as in pasta frolla* (shortcrust pastry/piecrust dough), or pasta da pane (bread dough). When the word is used on its own, however, it usually refers to pasta.

It used to be only in southern Italy that pasta was served daily, usually as a first course at lunch. But in the second half of the twentieth century pasta became the most popular start to a meal also in northern Italy, where it has ousted the local risotto*. A dish of pasta is now often served as a piatto unico (one-course meal), but never with salad. This is the typical meal of southern Italians, and it provides a healthy and well-balanced diet based on pasta plus a sauce consisting either of a small amount of meat, or some vegetables, pulses (legumes), cheese or eggs.

In Italy, pasta usually means dried pasta. Fresh pasta is eaten far less frequently and is by no means considered of higher quality, rather a different kind of food that can be better or worse, depending on how well it is made.

Fresh pasta: In Emilia-Romagna fresh pasta is made using only eggs and Italian 00 flour. The classic recipe for it is on page 70. In other regions one or two eggs may be replaced by water, which produces a rather bodiless and less tasty pasta. In the south the mixture is of durum wheat semolina, flour and water, which is hard to knead and shape. All these mixtures, at the dough stage, are called sfoglia*. Rolling pasta by hand is a difficult and time-consuming job, but there are many machines for making fresh pasta at home. The machine will not only roll but also cut the pasta. Pasta made with eggs is sold fresh or dried. More often than not a good brand of Italian dried egg pasta is far better than shop-bought fresh pasta.

Dried pasta: This is commercially made pasta, the composition of which is tightly controlled by law. It must be made only with durum wheat semolina and water. Equally important is the drying process, which must be gradual and lengthy. The best pasta is dried up to 80 hours, as opposed to 32 for the more mass-produced type. The dies through which the mixture is extruded also play an important part; for the best pasta bronze dies are used, giving a rough surface that is ideal for retaining the dressing.

Dried pasta comes in many shapes and sizes, most of which are best suited to a particular type of sauce. Generally speaking, long pasta, such as spaghetti, is suited to a sauce based on olive oil, as this allows the strands to stay slippery and separate. Thicker long shapes are best dressed with sauces based on butter, cream and cheese, which also go well with medium-sized tubular pasta. These shapes are also perfect dressed with vegetables or pulses (legumes), while the large rigatoni* and penne* are better for baked dishes.

Cooking pasta: Pasta may be everyday food, but it should be cooked with great care. It must be cooked in a large saucepan with plenty of salted water: there should be 1 litre/1¾ pints/1 quart of water to every 100 g/3½ oz of pasta, to which 10 g/¼ oz/1½ tbsp of salt is added when the water begins to boil, but before the pasta. When the water comes to a rolling boil, the pasta should be added to the pan and immediately stirred. The cooking time differs according to the shape and quality of pasta, and whether it is fresh or dried.

When the pasta is al dente† it is drained through a colander, or, for long pasta, by lifting it out with a long wooden fork or a spaghetti server. A little of the cooking water is sometimes reserved to add at the end, should the finished dish seem too dry. This is always done when cooking fresh pasta, since it absorbs more liquid.

Once drained, the pasta must be dressed immediately and should never be allowed to sit in the colander. It should not be dressed with too much sauce, nor should the sauce be watery.

Pasta Colorata or Aromatizzata Coloured or flavoured pasta. Pasta that is yellow (saffron), brown (fungi), red (tomato) or black (cuttlefish ink) has now become as widely available as the traditional green (spinach) pasta from Emilia.

Pasta Ripiena Stuffed pasta. Included under this heading is the range of different types of ravioli. The wrapping is made of egg pasta and the stuffing is different for each type of raviolo.

Pastina Only used in stock to make a minestrina*. There are all sorts of pastina: stelline ("little stars"), ave-Marie ("hail Marys"), risi (like grains of "rice"), farfalline ("little butterflies"), alfabeto ("letters of the alphabet"), anellini ("little rings") and many other tiny shapes.

Pastasciutta A term meaning pasta which, once cooked, has been drained and served with a sauce.

Pasta in Brodo is the opposite to pastasciutta, ie a dish of pasta served with the liquid in which it has cooked.

Pasta alla Norma In this dish from Catania, the pasta, usually spaghetti, is dressed with a fruity tomato sauce, slices of fried aubergine (eggplant) and grated salted ricotta*. The dish is so called because it is good enough to compare with Bellini's masterpiece of the same name, which in Catania (the composer's birthplace) is synonymous with perfection.

PASTA *Types and shapes of pasta*

AGNOLOTTI

These round or square stuffed shapes are traditional products of three regions: Piedmont – stuffed with braised meat and dressed with meat juice or butter and Parmesan; Tuscany – stuffed with veal, breadcrumbs and plenty of Parmesan; and Sardinia – where the stuffing is aubergine (eggplant), walnuts, ricotta and plenty of herbs. the dough of the Sardinian Agnolotti contains saffron.

ANOLINI**

Small stuffed pasta, half-moon shaped with ruffled edges, anolini originate from Emilia-Romagna, where they are cooked in meat stock and served as a soup. The stuffing can vary, but it always contains some type of meat or its juices. In timballo di anolini the cooked anolini are dressed with the juice of the meat, some butter and grated Parmesan cheese, and put in a pie dish lined with sweet pastry.

BIGOLI

The Venetian name for thick spaghetti* made (sometimes by hand) by pressing pasta dough through a small tool called a bigolaro. The original dough is made with flour, butter and eggs – which can be duck eggs. Originally made with soft wheat flour, bigoli underwent many local variations such as being made with whole-wheat flour. Most of the bigoli on the market are now made commercially, either with whole-wheat flour or with durum wheat flour. Bigoli are dressed with anchovy sauce or a sauce made with onion and mashed duck giblets.

BUCATINI

Thick, hollow spaghetti, a versatile shape that can be used instead of spaghetti with many sauces. It is a favourite pasta in central Italy, where it is used for amatriciana* ** and carbonara* or with other sauces of intense flavour.

CAPPELLACCI

One of the most delicious kinds of stuffed pasta, cappellacci, from Ferrara, are shaped like a large edition of cappelletti* or like a round raviolo*. They are filled with a mixture of puréed pumpkin, Parmesan, bread-crumbs, nutmeg and eggs. The best way to serve them is to pour melted butter over, and top plenty of Parmesan.

CAPPELLETTI

Stuffed pasta in the shape of little medieval hats (the meaning of their name). By tradition, cappelletti are served in brodo* (stock) made from capon stock, the most delicate of all meat stocks. When served asciutti† (literally dry, ie not in a soup) cappelletti are dressed with butter and Parmesan.

Cappelletti vary in shape and stuffing according to the region. The cappelletti from Gubbio, the richest of them all, are stuffed with a mixture of capon, pigeon, pork, brains and sausage, plus the usual eggs and Parmesan. Served in hot capon broth, they are traditional Christmas fare, but enough are made for them to be enjoyed at New Year and Epiphany, too.

The cappelletti from Reggio in Emilia, which are very small, have a succulent stuffing of different kinds of meat, prosciutto* and grated Parmesan. From Romagna come cappelletti di grasso, stuffed with capon breast, ricotta* and Parmesan, and also cappelletti di magro. These, as the name implies, contain no meat, being stuffed with ricotta and eggs.

CAPELLI D'ANGELO

Literally, "angels' hair"

Extremely fine strands of pasta, usually cooked and served in a light stock.

CASONSEI

This stuffed pasta is an ancient speciality of Bergamo and Brescia. They are an unusual shape, like a short fat sleeve, and are stuffed with sultanas (golden raisins), luganega*, Swiss chard, egg, Parmesan, and sometimes amaretti*. They are always served drained, dressed with melted sage-flavoured butter and grated Parmesan cheese.

CJALZÒNS

The ravioli* of Carnia, a province in the eastern corner of Friuli. Every town has its cjalzòn. The fillings and sizes are varied, but cjalzòns usually contain some savoury and sweet ingredients, showing the influence of Slav cooking. Ricotta*, often smoked, is sometimes present, as are potatoes, sultanas (golden raisins) and spices, especially cinnamon.

CONCHIGLIE

Literally, "shells"

A medium-sized, shell-like pasta shape, good for a meat ragù, vegetable sauces such as those containing broccoli or courgettes (zucchini), or with cheeses and ricotta*.

CORZETTI

Figure of eight-shaped pasta, popular only in Liguria. The traditional recipe, alla Polcevera (the name of their place of origin) suggests dressing them with rich meat juices or a fungi sauce.

CULURZONES *or* CULURGIONES

Culurzones are large Sardinian ravioli* stuffed with very fresh pecorino*, spinach, egg and saffron. The usual dressing is tomato sauce and grated mature (sharp) pecorino.

DITALI *and* DITALINI

Dried pasta in the shape of tubes. They can be rigati (ridged) or lisci (smooth). They are usually used in soups, the large size being suitable for pasta and bean soups and minestroni*, the smaller ones for pea or lentil soups.

FARFALLE
Butterfly
Dried pasta shapes that go particularly well with delicate creamy sauces. Farfalline, a small version of farfalle, are excellent in clear soup. Farfalle can be made from homemade pasta by cutting 5 cm/2 in squares and pinching them in the middle.

FETTUCCINE
These are the Roman tagliatelle*, traditionally a little narrower and very slightly thicker.

GARGANELLI
Homemade pasta from Romagna that is made into ridged, quill-like macaroni. Garganelli are excellent dressed with a meat ragù* which coats the ridges well. They are now also made commercially.

LAGANE *or* LAGANELLE
Wide tagliatelle* of southern Italy made with hard wheat semolina flour and water. The most common dish is lagane e ciceri – with chick peas (garbanzo beans). The chick peas and the lagane are cooked separately, and the two ingredients are then mixed and dressed with olive oil flavoured with plenty of garlic and chilli.

LASAGNE
Originally from Emilia-Romagna, these small sheets of pasta are made only with flour and eggs, no water and no salt. A few grams of cooked and chopped spinach are often added to the egg and flour mixture to produce lasagne verdi (green lasagne). Lasagne can also be bought fresh or dried.

Good-quality dried lasagne, made by Italian firms, is better than some of the fresh lasagne sold in shops.

Lasagne are traditional in many regions of Italy, but in each of these they are made with a slightly different dough, cut in varying lengths and widths, sometimes served straightaway and sometimes baked, and dressed with different sauces.

In Genoa, lasagne become narrow piccagge* and are served with pesto*. In Trieste the lasagne are dressed with butter, sugar and poppy seeds that have been previously sautéed in butter. In spite of the sugar, the dish is served as a first course. Lasagne al forno, the ubiquitous baked lasagne, comes from Emilia-Romagna. It is usually prepared with green lasagne, a rich and succulent meat ragù* ** and a velvety and delicate béchamel**. The traditional lasagne dish from Marche is particularly rich: it is vincisgrassi* **, in which the pasta dough is enriched with vin santo•. In Naples the traditional lasagne dish is lasagne di Carnevale, eaten at carnival time. These square lasagne are lavishly layered with local sausage, tiny fried meatballs, mozzarella*, ricotta* and hard-boiled (hard-cooked) eggs, all generously sauced with a classic Neapolitan ragù* **.

In modern cooking we have lasagne with fish, lasagne layered with red radicchio, béchamel and Parmesan, and lasagne alla boscaiola (with eggs, mushrooms, fontina* and Parmesan). Another fashionable dish is vegetable lasagne; when it is well made, it can be excellent.

LINGUINE *literally, "small tongues"* *or* BAVETTE
They are long flat pasta pieces. The traditional way to dress linguine is

aglio, olio e peperoncino – garlic, oil and chilli**. Another excellent way to serve linguine is with a sauce of fresh clams.

MACCHERONI

In everyday Italian, maccheroni is the word for a group of commercially made tubular pasta, which includes penne*, sedani, mezzani, ziti* and others. But in southern Italy, maccheroni is any kind of pasta made at home with a dough of durum wheat semolina, flour and water; a dough that is rather difficult to work.

The best-known pasta of this kind is maccheroni alla chitarra* **, with a shape like square spaghetti. The Sicilian maccheroni are long and thick, like ziti*, or spiral like fusilli*.

MACCHERONCINI *also called maccheroncelli, mezzi ziti or sedani*

A dried, commercially-made tubular pasta. In southern Marche, however, the maccheroncini are like tagliolini*. They are called maccheroncini di Campofilone, taking their name from a town near the coast, south of Ancona, where they are made. They are also made commercially, with an excellent egg dough, and are well known all over Italy.

MALTAGLIATI

Literally, "badly cut"; a homemade pasta shape. In Mantua the rolled-out dough is cut into long narrow triangles, while in Veneto and Emilia it is cut into small diamond shapes. Maltagliati are mainly used in soups.

MARUBINI

A pretty ravioli made only in the province of Cremona. By tradition they are served in meat stock, but nowadays they are also served asciutti†. They may be filled with minced (ground) braised beef, pork or veal and Parmesan, or with breadcrumbs, beef marrow, Parmesan and spices.

ORECCHIETTE
Literally, "little ears"

These are the traditional pasta of Puglia and Basilicata. Although they are also made commercially, they are still often made at home. The traditional way to prepare orecchiette is to cook them with turnip tops (greens), then drain and serve them together, dressed with salted anchovies pounded with garlic and chilli in olive oil. Another recipe is orecchiette with potatoes and rocket (arugula), in which rocket and orecchiette are added to the half-cooked potatoes. This dish is usually served as a thick soup, dressed with garlic and chilli sautéed in the local olive oil.

PAGLIA E FIENO

Meaning "straw and hay", this is an attractive egg pasta. It consists of yellow and green tagliolini*, hence its name, the green being made with spinach pasta.

PANSOTTI

Ligurian ravioli* in the shape of large triangles. The stuffing consists of chopped preboggion* – mixed wild herbs and greens – local curd cheese (farmer's cheese), Parmesan cheese, egg and a touch of garlic. Pansotti are dressed with salsa di noci** (walnut sauce).

PAPPARDELLE

Large tagliatelle* originally made at home but now made commercially. They are one of the few traditional pasta shapes from Tuscany, where they often accompany a rich hare stew, pappardelle con la lepre**.

PENNE

Literally, "quills", but in this context a shape of dried tubular pasta. Penne are particularly suited for rich meat sauces and for baked dishes. They are either rigate (ridged) or lisce (smooth).

PERCIATELLI

A type of spaghetti

The name used in southern Italy for bucatini (spaghetti with a hole).

PICCAGGE

A kind of large tagliatelle* made in Liguria with the local dough containing water as well as eggs. As a result the pasta is softer, less elastic and also less tasty. Piccage are usually dressed with pesto*, with roast juices or with a mushroom sauce.

PICI *also called* PINCI

A thick spaghetti made in Siena.

RAVIOLI

This is the name given to all stuffed pasta, from the small raviolini to the large raviolone, the favourite of most modern restaurants. There are some traditional ravioli made in Liguria, their recipe first appeared in the nineteenth-century book *La Vera Cuciniera Genovese.* These ravioli are stuffed with monkfish, batavia, borage, ricotta and Parmesan, dressed with the juices from fish heads and bones and fresh tomatoes.

RIGATONI

A name covering a few shapes of tubular, medium-sized pasta, always with ridges. They are particularly suited to being dressed with ragù*, sausages and other meat sauces. Rigatoni are the best pasta for baked dishes.

SPAGHETTI

This means little strings, which indeed, once cooked, it resembles. Experts maintain that spaghetti should not be drained in a colander, but rather lifted out of the water with an oversized slotted spoon made of wicker, or a long wooden fork or a spaghetti lifter, which looks like a long-handled hairbrush with wooden pegs in place of bristles. The reason for lifting the spaghetti out instead of draining it is to allow it to retain some moisture, since it should be quite moist *before* the sauce is added.

Of all pasta shapes, spaghetti is the most versatile. The best sauces are oil-based, as this allows it to remain slippery and separate.

Spaghetti alla Boscaiola A dish of spaghetti dressed with wild mushrooms sautéed in oil with garlic. Pasta and mushrooms should be present in equal proportions.

Spaghetti Cacio e Pepe A traditional recipe from Rome in which the spaghetti is dressed with an ample quantity of grated pecorino* and an equally generous grinding of freshly ground black pepper.

Spaghetti alla Carrettiera This Roman speciality is an oil-based sauce containing salted jowl or pancetta*, garlic and porcini*, to which roast juices are added and, right at the end, a little shredded tuna.

Spaghetti alla Siracusana In Siracusa the cooked spaghetti, which should be very thin, is stir-fried in a cast-iron pan in a soffritto* of oil, salted anchovies, black olives, chilli, garlic and parsley.

SPAGHETTINI

Thin spaghetti that is particularly

good with seafood or tomato sauces. In southern Italy, spaghettini is often called vermicelli*.

STELLINE

Tiny pasta star shapes used in clear soups.

STRASCINATI

A pasta from Basilicata made with semolina, water and melted rendered pork fat. The dough is rolled into thin sausages which are dressed with tomato sauce highly spiced with chilli. In Umbria strascinati are dressed with local sausage, egg and pecorino*.

TAGLIATELLE

Tagliatelle are made with the traditional Emilian dough of flour and egg, which should be rolled out so thinly that a newspaper could be read through it. It is then cut ("tagliare" is to cut) into strips 5 mm/¼ in wide.

Nowadays most cooks make tagliatelle by machine, and even more people buy them in specialist pasta shops. Tagliatelle made with egg is also available dried, and when produced by a good Italian manufacturer they are better than shop-bought fresh tagliatelle.

The classic Emilian dressing for tagliatelle is a Bolognese sauce* **. But tagliatelle goes equally well with other meat or creamy sauces.

TAGLIOLINI or TAGLIARINI

Long homemade pasta, thinner than tagliatelle*. They are ideal for soups or for a soufflé of pasta. See the recipe for Tajarin all'Albese on page 68.

TONNARELLI

Homemade pasta of central Italy, similar to square spaghetti*. When made in Abruzzo, this shape is called maccheroni alla chitarra* **. Tonnarelli are made with durum wheat semolina and water and dressed with most sauces suitable for spaghetti.

TORTELLI

Ravioli* stuffed with vegetables, these are made for eating on festive occasions. They are square-shaped and, like most stuffed pasta, they come from the Po valley.

Many different stuffings are used, but tortelli stuffed with spinach and ricotta* are the most popular of them all. The tortelli of Mantua are stuffed with the local pumpkin, plus amaretti* and mostarda* di frutta, while those of Reggio-Emilia and Ferrara (where they are called cappellacci) omit these ingredients but are more lavish with the Parmesan. All these tortelli are dressed only with butter and Parmesan.

The traditional tortelli of Bologna contain a mixture of ricotta, Parmesan, parsley and eggs, and they are dressed with a buttery tomato sauce made with a touch of onion.

There is also a different kind of tortelli made in Lombardy and Emilia-Romagna. These are fried sweet tortelli, similar to profiteroles without the filling but generously dusted with icing (confectioners') sugar. They are eaten hot at carnivals, on St Joseph's day (19 March) and often halfway through Lent, when traditionally the fast is temporarily suspended and the pleasures of the flesh can be enjoyed for 24 hours.

TORTELLINI

Small shapes stuffed with minced (ground) chicken, pork, prosciutto*, mortadella*, Parmesan and all the other usual flavourings. They are cooked, and served in stock, as a soup. Homemade tortellini are for festive occasions only, since making them entails hours of dedicated labour.

TORTELLONI

A large version of tortelli. As with tortelli, the most popular fillings are ricotta* and spinach, or ricotta, parsley and grated Parmesan, although these days it can be just about anything the cook fancies.

TORTIGLIONI

Large tubular pasta with spiral ridges, tortiglioni are ideally suited for a thick vegetable or meat ragù* and for making baked pasta dishes.

TROFIE

A kind of homemade pasta, a speciality of the eastern Riviera. Pieces of dough are dragged over the work surface with the fingers, so that they take the shape of a spiral. Trofie are now also available dried. They are traditionally boiled with a potato and some French (green) beans, and then dressed with pesto* **.

TRENETTE

A Ligurian pasta, similar to linguine*. Pesto* ** is the classic sauce for trenette, although a mushroom sauce could be contemplated by even the most stringent purist.

VERMICELLI

Literally "small worms", vermicelli is the name given to spaghettini* in southern Italy.

ZITI or ZITE

A thick, long, hollow pasta shape, traditional in Sicily and southern Italy, where they are served with a ragù*, with a sultana (golden raisins)

and breadcrumb sauce or with a tuna sauce**. They are usually broken into 10 cm/4 in pieces before they are cooked.

PASTA DI MANDORLE
Almond paste

Through the centuries nobody has surpassed the craftsmen and women of Palermo in modelling and colouring almond paste to make lifelike models of fruits, salami*, cheeses and all sorts of foodstuffs. (See Frutta di Martorana*.)

PASTA FROLLA *Sweet pastry*

Pasta frolla is mostly prepared for fruit or jam tarts, when it is usually flavoured with lemon zest. It is also used for timballi* and pasticci* (savoury pies traditionally made with sweet pastry). See recipe on page 155.

PASTA IN BRODO *Pasta in stock*

This is pasta served in the stock in which it has cooked. The pasta shapes used for this soup are pastina*, vermicelli* or capelli d'angelo* (angels' hair).

PASTA MARGHERITA
A type of cake

This cake is similar to pan di Spagna* (Madeira cake), but contains equal amounts of flour and potato flour.

PASTA SFOGLIA or SFOGLIATA *Puff pastry*

Pasta sfoglia is the natural successor to the filo (phyllo) pastry of the Middle East; a similar type of pastry was also used by the Etruscans and Romans.

PASTE *Little cakes*

This term refers to those attractive little cakes that you see in every pasticceria†. The most common paste are bigné (eclairs), cannoncini*, cannoli siciliani*, africani (rounds of sponge cake with a layer of cream and covered with chocolate icing/frosting), and tartlets filled with a selection of fresh fruit, almond cream etc.

PASTELLA *Batter*

The mixture for pastella varies according not only to the region and the cook, but also to the type of food with which it is to be used. It can be a mixture of egg, water and flour, water and flour only, or of milk, egg and flour. Whisked egg white is a common addition, as is yeast, Marsala• or vin santo•.

PASTICCIO *A baked pie*

This pie consists of pasta with vegetables and/or meat, even fish, bound together by béchamel* and/or eggs. It is sometimes contained in a pastry shell.

Traditional pasticci still made today include the pasticcio di tortellini* from Bologna, in which a sweet pastry case contains tortellini in a meat sauce. The pasticcio, or timballo, alla Napoletana is made with small maccheroni*, dressed with a ragù* of mushrooms, sweetbreads, chicken livers, cocks' (roosters") combs etc, all contained in a sweet pastry case (pie shell).

PASTIERA *A sweet tart*

An elaborate tart which, although first made in Amalfi, has since become particularly associated with Naples. It consists of a base of sweet pastry which is spread with a mixture of ricotta*, chopped candied fruits, sugar, eggs and grains of wheat boiled in milk, all flavoured with lemon rind, orange water and spices. Strips of pasta frolla* are laid in patterns over the filling and the tart is baked.

PATATA *Potato*

Potatoes never conquered Italy as they did other European countries. Perhaps for this reason they are treated as a dish in their own right and not just as an accompaniment to meat and fish. Tortini (pies) of potatoes are made with other vegetables – with onions in Lombardy, with green beans in Liguria (see recipe for Polpettone di Fagiolini on page 154) – or with other ingredients as in the Neapolitan gattò**. With fish they form the tielle* from Puglia, the recipe for which is on page 93. Potatoes are also used to make gnocchi* **. They are roasted, stewed (often with tomato**) and puréed, but seldom served boiled without any dressing. The best Italian potatoes are from Campania.

PECORA *Ewe*

Sheep and mutton is eaten in Abruzzo, Basilicata and Sardinia, but rarely elsewhere in Italy.

PECORINO *A ewe's milk cheese*

This cheese, produced in every region of central and southern Italy, is made from ewe's milk. The rennet used is the dried stomach of a milk-fed lamb. The best known kinds of pecorino are: romano, sardo, siciliano and toscano, all of which, although similar, have particular characteristics.

Pecorino Romano is the best for grating because of its strong piquant flavour. It is too strong for the table. Originally from Lazio, it is now produced mainly in Sardinia.

Pecorino Sardo can be eaten two weeks after being made and, when used as table cheese, should not mature for any longer than three months. It is a very tasty cheese, slightly salty and piquant, the piquancy increasing with age.

Some of the pecorini from Sardinia are smoked.

Pecorino Siciliano is the only one that can be eaten the day after it is made, when the flavour is at its milkiest; in this state it is called tuma. After a month it acquires a stronger, yet still milky flavour, that remains much the same for three months. After about the fourth month it becomes a grating cheese.

Pecorino Toscano is ripe after two weeks, when the inside of the cheese is creamy; it is then the most delicate of all pecorini. If it is aged, it becomes hard and piquant, but even then it is a table rather than a grating cheese. The pecorino delle crete senesi, a district south of Siena, is the favourite with real connoisseurs of pecorino. Another superb Tuscan pecorino is marzolino*.

Nowadays there is a considerable amount of factory-made pecorino toscano in which cow's milk is added to the ewe's milk.

PEOCI *Mussels*
The Venetian name for cozze* (mussels), with which they make the most delicious of all fish soups.

PEPE *Pepper*
This distinctive spice is not used as much in Italy as it is in the countries of northern Europe.

PEPERONATA
Italian ratatouille
Although made only with (bell) peppers and tomatoes, peperonata is prepared in the same way as its French cousin. Its origins are claimed by Emilia as well as by Naples, but it is now a popular way to cook peppers all over Italy.

Nearly all cooks have their own recipe for peperonata; the one on page 151 is a family recipe from my home. Leftover peperonata makes a perfect sauce for pasta.

PEPERONCINO *Chilli*
Chillies are mainly used dried as a flavouring for stews, sauces, fish, seafood etc and in salami* and sausages. Basilicata and Calabria are the homelands of peperoncino, or diavolicchio as it is called there, and it is the most common spice of those regions. This is also the case in Abruzzo, where many dishes are flavoured with it, including amatriciana** and arrabbiata* sauces for pasta. There are a few dishes containing it in Siena, but there, as elsewhere in Tuscany, it is called zenzero* (Italian for ginger), thus causing great confusion among foreigners!

Sweet (bell) pepper preserved in vinegar, usually the cigarette-shaped green pepper, is also called peperoncino.

PEPERONE *(bell) peppers*
The peppers usually associated with Italy are the sweet ones, known in the United States as bell peppers. Peppers grow everywhere in Italy, but the most highly prized ones come from around Cuneo and Asti in Piedmont, where they are an ingredient in the bagna caôda* **, and around Nocera in Umbria. The best of the small pointed kind are the sweet green peppers from Lombardy. While in other regions peppers are often eaten raw in salad, the Calabresi and Siciliani have always prepared them in many different ways. The simplest recipe of all is for peperoni arrostiti**. Then there are recipes for sautéed peppers**, for peppers cooked with eggs or mixed with sautéed potatoes, for stuffed peppers** and for the well-loved peperonata**.

Peppers are popular all over Italy, and most of today's leading chefs have created recipes for them, many matching peppers with pasta. This perfect combination has been popular in southern of Italy for centuries.

PEPOLINO *Wild thyme*

Also called serpillo, pepolino is the Tuscan name for a variety of thyme which grows wild in that region.

PERA *Pear*

The popular Italian varieties are Abate, Coscia, Decana and Passacrassana, some ripening in July and August in central Italy, while others (grown in northern Italy) are autumn (fall) or winter fruit.

The best recipe for a pear dessert is Pere al Barolo. The pears are stewed, unpeeled, in Barolo• wine with sugar and a flavouring of cinnamon and cloves. A highly regarded pear grappa* is bottled with a pear in the bottle.

PERNICE *Partridge*

There are three kinds of partridge in Italy: the real partridge, that is the red partridge; the grey partridge, also called starna; and the Sardinian partridge, which is a variety of the red partridge only found on the island and which has tasty, herby meat. The grey partridge is the least interesting, being mainly a farmed bird, but the most easily available. These partridges are good cooked in a casserole, stuffed with a few Muscat grapes and a little mascarpone*. The juices are then deglazed with red wine and brandy and a little more mascarpone is added for volume and sweetness.

PESCA *Peach*

Italy produces about half of the peaches of the European Union, the best being those grown in Romagna,

Marche and Campania. Peaches are white or yellow, the latter being the favourite of the producers because, being firmer, they are easier to handle, and they keep longer.

Pesche al vino is a good way to serve peaches. They are peeled and sliced, and then, just before eating, red or dry white wine is poured over. Some people sprinkle a little sugar on top. Another traditional way to eat peaches is pesche ripiene, for which the original Piedmontese recipe is on page 156. Peaches are delicious mixed with strawberries and dressed with lemon and orange juice. They are also used in ice creams, jams and jellies. Peaches are preserved in syrup, in alcohol or dried. White peaches are used to make a solid preserve called persicata.

A variety of peach used in the same ways as the common peach is the pesca noce or nettarina (nectarine). It is popular because it travels well.

PESCE *Fish*

Sixteen of Italy's 20 regions have a coastline, and the five others have lakes and rivers, so they can make up for the lack of sea fish with freshwater fish. Just to make sure that they always have their fish, Italians are also great importers of salt cod and stockfish.

In Italy a fish, unless it is a large specimen, is usually cooked and brought to the table with the head on. This is not only because the head imparts flavour during the cooking, but also because a decapitated creature is considered unattractive. In the best restaurants the fish is filleted at the table by the waiter.

PESCE PERSICO *Perch*

Perch is one of the best freshwater fish. It is caught principally in Lake Como, but it is also found in Lake Maggiore and Lake Garda. It has a white flesh and a non-fishy flavour suited to being cooked like veal. In Milan, in fact, the usual way to cook perch is "a cotoletta"† (filleted), coated in egg and breadcrumbs and fried in butter. The most traditional recipe is to serve shallow-fried fillets on a risotto* made with fish stock.

PESCE SAN PIETRO
John Dory
This fish has a tough skin, but excellent white flesh. The best way to cook John Dory is simply – either grilled (broiled) or lightly fried – and then serve it dressed with olive oil and flavoured with lemon juice.

PESCE SPADA
Swordfish
A very large fish, up to 4 m/4½ yd long, with a delicate flesh that can even be eaten raw (carpaccio of swordfish). Swordfish steaks are excellent marinated for an hour or so in olive oil, lemon juice, salt and pepper and then grilled (broiled). In Calabria swordfish steaks are steamed with olive oil, lemon, capers and salt, to which oregano and parsley are added at the end. A good Sicilian recipe is that of swordfish bundles, in which the fish, thinly sliced, is spread with a mixture of prosciutto*, mozzarella*, Parmesan and herbs and then rolled up and grilled. Another delicious way to cook swordfish is to thread it on a skewer with bay leaves and grill it. It can also be cooked "alla trapanese"** as in the recipe on page 97.

PESTO** *A basil sauce*
A sauce made with basil, olive oil, pecorino* and Parmesan. These are the basic ingredients to which walnuts or pine nuts may be added, depending on local tradition. Pesto is associated particularly with Liguria; the basil of Liguria being sweeter, yet more aromatic than that from elsewhere.

Pesto is used to dress trenette* and piccagge*. The pasta is traditionally cooked with sliced potatoes and, sometimes, green beans, and all three ingredients are dressed with pesto and eaten together. Pesto is also used to dress potato gnocchi* ** or to give a local touch – one spoonful is enough – to a minestrone*.

PETTO *Breast*
This, as in English, can be of beef, pork, lamb, turkey, chicken or duck. The popular breast of veal, a succulent cut, is either boned and stuffed and made into a roll, or it is roasted with the bones in place. Chicken or turkey breasts are boned and used for involtini*, or served with delicate sauces in place of the more expensive veal. An example of this is the popular dish petto di pollo alla valdostana, where the breadcrumbed fried breasts are covered with sliced ham and fontina* and then baked for a few minutes. A recipe for chicken breasts with porcini* is on page 106.

PEVERADA *or* PEARÀ
A pepper-based sauce
Peverada is a sauce from Treviso, now made all over northern Italy. Recipes vary, but the one essential ingredient that is always included is pepper in ample quantities. Peverada is a classic accompaniment to roast or boiled meats. My favourite recipe is on page 177.

PIADINA *or* PIADA
A filled bread snack
Piadina is made with flour, strutto*

(melted pork fat) and bicarbonate of soda (baking soda) or yeast. The kneaded dough is divided into small balls. Each ball is rolled out thinly and baked very briefly until slightly charred around the edges. While it is still hot, prosciutto*, salame*, sausages or a local cheese are laid on top and the piadina is folded in half. Piadina can also be fried. The end result is the most satisfyingly, tasty savoury snack imaginable.

PICCATA
A veal dish

This is a Milanese dish consisting of veal escalopes (scallops), floured and fried in butter and then finished with different flavourings. Different versions include piccata with lemon juice, piccata with Marsala•, and piccata with a selection of wild mushrooms, which are sautéed separately and then added to the meat.

PICCIONE *Pigeon*

Piccione refers to a domestic bird, the wild bird being called palombaccio*. There are two traditional recipes for pigeon: piccione coi piselli (stewed with peas), and piccione alla leccarda† (see Palombaccio).

PIEDINO
Pig's trotter (foot) or a calf's foot

Boiled, boned, sliced and dressed with a little lemon and oil sauce, pig's trotter (foot) or calves' feet are popular as an antipasto*, which is sold in Lombard delis by the name of nervetti*. They are also the necessary ingredients for making gelatine (gelatin). Pig's trotters are also included in the classic dish, cassoela ** (Milanese pork and cabbage stew).

PIGNOLATA *A Sicilian sweet*

This is a traditional Sicilian sweet. Its name stems from the fact that it is shaped like a pigna (pine cone). Pignolata is made up of many litttle balls of sweetened yeast pastry. Baked or fried, they are coated with plain icing (frosting) and/or chocolate icing.

PINOCCATA *An Umbrian sweet*

These are ancient sweets from Umbria made with pine nuts and sugar, which used to be sold at Christmas. They are now made commercially and are available in the shops for most of the year.

PINOLI
Pine nuts

These are the seeds of the stone pine, or *Pinus pinea*, which is the beautiful umbrella pine so characteristic of many stretches of the Italian coast. Pine nuts are an important ingredient in many dishes, the best known of these being pesto*, and sweet-and-sour dishes of Arab origin. They are also used in biscuits (cookies), cakes and other sweet preparations. To release their flavour, dry roast or dry fry them first in a low oven or in a dry, cast-iron frying pan (skillet) for a few minutes.

PINZA *A type of pizza*

In Veneto, Venezia Giulia and Trentino pinza is sweet, while in Emilia it is savoury, containing salame* and/or prosciutto* and pancetta*. The pinza of Veneto is made with wheat and maize flour (cornmeal), sugar, fennel seeds, a selection of dried fruits, grappa*, and butter. The pinza of Trentino consists of stale bread that has been soaked in milk and which is then mixed with sugar, dried figs and enough flour to make a dry dough.

PINZIMONIO *An olive oil dip*

This simple dip for raw vegetables consists of olive oil, salt and pepper, mixed together and served in a small cup – one for each diner. It is often served as an antipasto* in the summer.

PISAREI E FASÒ

Dumplings and peas

This is a peasant dish from Piacenza. The pisarei are tiny dumplings made with breadcrumbs and flour, kneaded with warm water. They are boiled and then mixed with a dish of fasò (cooked borlotti* beans) that have been previously stewed with tomatoes in a soffritto† of lard and the usual flavouring vegetables. Pisarei e faso is the traditional dish of this area which is now served in restaurants as an ideal one-dish meal.

PISELLI *Peas*

Peas are never boiled in water in Italy, instead they are poached in stock, often with onion and prosciutto (see Piselli a Prosciutto**). They are also used to make sformati† (moulds) and pasta sauces. The Veronese dish of tagliatelle* e bisi is the traditional Easter dish, the peas being cooked with spring onion (scallion), prosciutto or pancetta* and parsley. In Venice rice accompanies the peas in the classic recipe risi e bisi**.

PISSALADEIRA**, *also called* SARDINAIRA *A soft, thick pizza*

This is a pizza* from the western Riviera which is softer and thicker than the usual Neapolitan pizza**. It is in fact more akin to its French neighbour and near namesake, pissaladière, than to its compatriot from Naples. Pissaladeira is a popular antipasto* or a snack in Genoa and on the western Riviera.

PISTACCHIO *A nut*

Pistachio nuts link the Italian cuisine with that of the Middle East. Fresh, they are used in many Sicilian desserts and also in terrines, pâtés and galantines. But possibly the greatest use of pistachio nuts is in the making of the well-known ice cream. Salted pistachios, still in their shells, are a popular snack.

PITTA *A type of pizza*

Pitta is the Calabrese version of the Neapolitan pizza*. It is made with bread dough, to which a tablespoon of melted pork fat is sometimes added. The many toppings are usually different from those of a Neapolitan pizza. Two unusual pitte deserve a mention: one is with turnip tops (greens), a favourite vegetable of the region, and spicy sausage, and the other is with elderflowers scattered in the dough. A rolled pitta is made with potato dough and filled with caciocavallo* cheese and pancetta*.

PIZZA *Pizza*

There are innumerable pizzas, mostly savoury (see pizza rustica* **), but the most famous pizza is the Napoletana**. This was allegedly the brainchild of the ingenious Neapolitans, who gave new life to the plain, old-style pizza when they added the latest discovery, the tomato. It happened in the late eighteenth century, when a good strain of tomato, red, large and sweet, was developed around Naples. Tomatoes soon became the favourite topping for pizza.

A good pizza is not simple food, and it is not easy to make. It needs the hands of the Neapolitan pizzaiolo, who has learnt the secret of stretching the dough from countless cooks before him, and it needs the heat of a wood-fired oven. For this reason pizza is seldom made at home, nor is it usually eaten there; it is eaten in a pizzeria.

There is also pizza dolce, the traditional sweet bread prepared for village festivals. In Rome at Easter the tradition is to enrich pizza dolce with some ricotta* kneaded into the dough, which is flavoured with cinnamon and lemon rind. It is also made with polenta flour mixed with the ricotta and it contains pine nuts, ground cinnamon, and sugar.

PIZZAIOLA *A dressing for meat*

This sauce is used as a dressing for a slice of meat. It owes its name to the fact that it contains similar ingredients to a pizza topping – tomatoes, garlic and oregano. It is a speciality of Naples, but is quite common everywhere. Traditionally the meat is cooked in the sauce, but I prefer to fry the meat separately, as in the recipe on page 133.

PIZZELLA *A type of pizza*

This classic Neapolitan preparation is made with the dough of a Pizza Napoletana. The dough is rolled out in small rounds which are fried in olive oil and then covered with the usual tomato toppings. Then the pizzelle are finished off in the oven for 4 to 5 minutes. Pizzelle can also incorporate pieces of salami*, cheese or vegetables in the uncooked dough.

PIZZOCCHERI**

A buckwheat pasta and a type of dish
This is a kind of thick, large tagliatelle* made with buckwheat flour. It is the traditional pasta of Valtellina, an Alpine valley in Lombardy. Pizzoccheri is also a dish as in the recipe on page 75, the recipe itself being simply called pizzoccheri.

POLENTA
Ground maize (coarse cornmeal)
To be exact, polenta (coarse cornmeal) is not only the well-known yellow mixture of milled maize (corn) and water, but any other mixture of ground cereal or pulses (legumes) mixed with water.

Today, polenta is commonly understood to be a mixture of milled maize and water. The maize can be coarsely ground, as in the bramata of the Alpine valleys, or finely ground as in the polenta of central Italy. The proportion of water to flour can also be different, giving a thinner or thicker mixture. In Veneto and in Friuli there is also a delicate polenta bianca made with white maize flour, while in the Alpine valleys of Lombardy a polenta is made with a mixture of maize and buckwheat, a favourite of the real polenta connoisseur.

Polenta should be made in a paiolo†, the unlined copper pan that is just right for the purpose. With one hand a thin stream of ground maize is poured into salted boiling water (the proportion of salt is 1½ teaspoons per litre/1¾ pints/ 1 quart of water), while with the other hand the maize is stirred rapidly into the water with a long wooden stick or spoon to prevent lumps from forming. When all the maize flour has been

added, the mixture must continue to be stirred constantly for at least 45 minutes. The coarser the flour, the longer the cooking. But there is a quicker method, for which my recipe is on page 84.

There is on the market now a product known as polenta istantanea. It is part-cooked polenta, and only needs five minutes cooking time. The result, surprisingly enough, is good, even if not quite as good as traditionally prepared polenta.

Polenta is extremely versatile, as it becomes complementary to the flavour of the dish it accompanies. The afficionados like polenta dressed only with butter and gorgonzola*, crescenza* or other stracchino* cheeses. Those less keen on the basic flavour of polenta prefer it as an accompaniment to rich stews of meat or fish. Polenta is excellent with stewed cuttlefish, for instance, or with jugged hare or stewed venison. Polenta can be made in advance and, when cold, baked in layered slices with meat sauce, cheeses, béchamel** etc, when it is known as polenta pasticciata**. Sliced polenta is also grilled (broiled) or fried and served as an accompaniment to meat and game, or used as a base for bruschetta*.

POLLO or POLLASTRO
Chicken
Italian free-range chickens are maize-fed (corn-fed); they are yellow, fairly small and lean. The best chickens are bred in Tuscany, and because their chickens are so tasty, the traditional Tuscan recipes are very simple, for instance pollo alla Fiorentina (chicken portions coated in a light batter and fried), and pollo alla Toscana (portions cooked in wine with wild mushrooms and tomatoes).

Other Tuscan ways of cooking chicken, such as in fricassea* and alla cacciatora† ** are similar to recipes prepared all over Italy. In northern Italy chicken is often boiled as part of a bollito misto* (see Gallina). The pollo in potacchio from Marche is a local version of the cacciatora, which in Calabria and Sicily becomes pollo con le melanzane by the addition of some fried or grilled aubergines (broiled eggplant). In Lazio fried (bell) peppers replace the aubergines.

Most of the recipes mentioned above are made with the bird cut into portions, which is certainly the most popular way to cook chicken. It is cooked whole when roasted on the spit, pollo allo spiedo with some herbs and garlic and, often, a pricked lemon pushed into the cavity.

POLLO ALLA CACCIATORA
Chicken cooked the "hunter's way"
This recipe from central Italy is made slightly differently wherever one goes. Chicken portions are sautéed in oil and/or strutto*, then flavoured with mushroom and/or tomatoes and herbs. The recipe from Marche on page 105 is different from the usual one.

POLLO ALLA MARENGO
Chicken Marengo
This dish is one of the very few to which a precise date of origin can be ascribed. It was created by Napoleon's chef on 14 June, 1800, and eaten by Napoleon after he had won a bloody battle against the Austrian army on the fields of Marengo, a village in southern Piedmont. The traditional pollo alla Marengo consists of chicken portions, sautéed in butter, then splashed with white wine and cooked with

flavourings. Sprinkled with parsley, it is served surrounded by fried bread and shrimp poached in wine.

POLLO RIPIENO ALLA LUNIGIANESE *Lunigiana chicken*

Here, the stuffed chicken is cooked in the way of the Lunigiana, the valley of the river Magra in Tuscany. The chicken is filled with Swiss chard and wild greens, ricotta* and grana*, bound with egg. It is then boiled and served with the Tuscan salsa d'agresto, made with unripe grapes, walnuts, soft breadcrumbs, a little onion, parsley, sugar and garlic, all pounded together in the mortar.

POLLO ALLA DIAVOLA
"Devil's chicken"

This recipe is a classic of the Tuscan cuisine. The young chicken is cut in half down the breast, opened up like a book and gently flattened with a meat mallet (bat). Brushed with best olive oil, salt, pepper and chilli it is cooked on a grill over a wooden fire.

POLPETTE *Meatballs*

These are usually meatballs, although the word can refer to fish cakes or vegetable patties. In the case of polpette di carne, the particular meat used would be specified. The meat can be raw or cooked, when it is usually a leftover piece of boiled, roast or braised meat. Other ingredients go into polpette, some for binding – egg and/or béchamel**, or bread soaked in milk – and some for flavouring – grated cheese, spices, pine nuts, sultanas (golden raisins), garlic, onion and herbs. The polpette are coated in flour and/or egg and breadcrumbs, and then fried in butter and oil in northern Italy, or in strutto* and/or oil in central and southern Italy. When nicely brown all over, polpette are often finished with a splash of lemon juice, or a light mushroom or tomato sauce is added to the pan. The lemon juice dressing is very good with polpette made of raw beef flavoured with parsley and garlic (recipe on page 120). Polpette are particularly popular in Milan, where they are called mondeghili*.

POLPETTONE *A meatloaf*

This can be a meatloaf made with minced (ground) meat (which can be raw or cooked), salame* or mortadella*, bound with egg and flavoured with Parmesan and herbs. The most modest and humble polpettone is made with leftover boiled meat, to which egg, Parmesan and soaked bread are added. The polpettone is shaped like an oval, coated with flour and fried in butter. When cooked, the cooking juices are often thickened with eggs and lemon juice, and the sauce is spooned over the sliced polpettone. A recipe for a cold polpettone is on page 121.

In Liguria the word polpettone refers mainly to vegetable torte. The best known is the polpettone of green beans**, where a purée of beans mixed with mashed potatoes, egg and ricotta and flavoured with herbs and garlic is baked in the oven. Lastly there is also a polpettone of tuna; the fish is either mixed with potatoes or with eggs and Parmesan** and then poached in white wine, vinegar and water.

POLPO *Octopus*

Hardly the most attractive of creatures, but an octopus when well cooked can be delicious. The best-known recipe is polpo alla Luciana**. Octopus can also be boiled (preferably in sea water), then cut into small pieces and dressed with a light sauce of olive oil, lemon juice, parsley and a touch of garlic and chilli.

POMODORO *Tomato*

More tomatoes are eaten in Italy than any other vegetable. They are eaten in innumerable ways – raw in salad, baked with various stuffings, in sauces, with meat, fish, eggs, with other vegetables ... there is no end to the list.

Tomatoes are also processed to preserve them. The cultivation, processing and canning of tomatoes, mostly based in Campania, has become one of Italy's largest agriculture-based industries. The best tomatoes for canning are the San Marzano plum tomatoes, a great point in their favour being that they all ripen at more or less the same time; also they peel easily. The Italians always use these in winter for their sauces; they only use fresh plum tomatoes when they are in season and, if possible, locally grown.

In southern Italy and in Liguria tomatoes are also dried, both domestically by cutting them in half and spreading them out in the sun, and commercially. Dried tomatoes now constitute a large industry; they are exported everywhere, having become a favourite of chefs. My opinion is that they should be used with discretion.

To have real tomato sauce in the winter a preparation known as la salsa (the sauce), is made according to a ritual that takes place on a hot August day in every village in central and southern Italy. A large blue machine is brought out from its place of rest. Into the top goes bowlful after bowlful of the villagers' tomatoes, and out of the bottom flows a thick, seedless and skinless red liquid. This smooth liquid is then boiled with a little salt in large cauldrons. The next day the salsa is bottled, the bottles are sealed and boiled, the blue machine is washed and trundled back to its resting place, and for another year the villagers have the salsa that will make so many of their dishes taste so much better.

You can make a good plain tomato sauce at home. There are two recipes on page 176.

PORCETTO *A piglet*

This is a milk-fed piglet roasted on the spit or in the oven. Of all the porcetti, the Sardinian porceddu is the best. It is roasted on the spit over a fire of olive, myrtle or juniper wood. Porceddu is also eaten cold, after having been bundled up in myrtle branches for 24 hours.

PORCHETTA *A small roast pig*

Porchetta usually weigh about 50 kg/ 110 lb and are roasted in a wood-fired bread oven. Boned and stuffed with its own offal (variety meats), it is highly flavoured with garlic, pepper, wild fennel or rosemary and sometimes sweet spices. It is the great dish of central Italy, prepared for important occasions. Usually eaten cold, it is also the characteristic street food of those regions, sold from stalls in between two slices of thick country bread.

PORRATA *A leek tart*

The pastry for this traditional Florentine tart is made with egg and fresh yeast; it is then topped with pancetta* and leeks sautéed in olive oil and mixed with eggs.

PORRO *Leek*

Leeks are mainly eaten in northern Italy, although they are not a particularly popular vegetable. They are usually served gratiné with béchamel**. They are used in vegetable soups and also as a flavouring in some stews, braised meats, and meat and fish stocks.

PREBOGGION

A mixture of wild herbs and plants

May consist of beet, borage, dandelion, mint and is used for stuffing. Like many Ligurian preparations, preboggion is not found elsewhere in Italy. It is the main ingredient of the stuffing for local ravioli*, called pansôti*, for frittate* and soups.

PRESCINSENA *A curd cheese*

A curd (farmer's) cheese made in Liguria. It is often made at home from milk that has gone sour. Prescinsena goes into focaccia*, the stuffing of ravioli* and torta pasqualina*, into pesto* ** and walnut sauce.

PRESNITZ *A snail-shaped cake*

This traditional cake is made in Venezia Giulia for Easter and Christmas. A very thin puff pastry is stuffed with dried fruit, nuts, honey, crumbled biscuits (cookies), grated chocolate, moistened with rum.

PREZZEMOLO *Parsley*

The parsley used in every household, almost every day, is the flat-leaf variety. The curly variety is occasionally used for decoration, being prettier, but it lacks aroma and flavour. Chopped fine, usually with a mezzaluna†, parsley goes into many preparations, although it is seldom sprinkled over a finished dish. Oil, garlic and parsley is one of the most perfect flavour combinations of all.

PROSCIUTTO CRUDO

Cured ham

This is what, outside Italy, is known simply as prosciutto. It is taken from the hind thigh of a pig aged about eleven months. All types of prosciutto are cured in a similar way, but the curing time varies from 9 to 18 months, the average being 14 months. Prosciutti are still produced by traditional methods, and many are made domestically.

After the slaughtering of the pig, the prosciutto is kept in cold store rooms to harden the meat. It is then pressed and cleaned, and stripped of excess fat, before being given the characteristic shape. The salting, which comes next, is the trickiest process to get right, since one of the essentials of a first-class prosciutto is sweetness, but the more it is salted the better it will keep. After regular brushing, cleaning and resting, the prosciutti are ready for ageing. Finally each prosciutto is stamped with the Consorzio mark which guarantees quality and denotes origin.

Prosciutto di Parma accounts for half the total consumption of prosciutto in Italy. Prosciutto di San Daniele is considered by many connoisseurs to be equal to, if not better than, prosciutto di Parma. It has a characteristic sweetish side to its flavour, an orangey tinge to its colour and a guitar-like shape. Other prosciutti that can be compared, but are only found locally, are prosciutto di Norcia in Umbria and di Carpegna in Marche. Among many others are the prosciutto Toscano, tasty and on the salty side, prosciutto dei colli di Mantova and the prosciutto di Sauris in Friuli. In central Italy, locals keep pigs and make their own prosciutto, which is usually boned before it is cured, for easier keeping.

Prosciutto is still served at the beginning of a meal with melon or figs, or with other salumi*. It also goes into delicate fillings for stuffed pasta, it cover slices of veal to impart flavour, it is chopped in various sauces or it is used in elegant preparations such as mousselines and mousses.

PROSCIUTTO COTTO
Ham

The boned thigh of a pig is pickled with salt, saltpetre, sugar, juniper berries, pepper and other spices, and then cooked by steam and pressed into an oblong mould. It is ready to be eaten a few days after being cooked. Prosciutto cotto is no longer as popular as it used to be, having lost ground to the more fashionable prosciutto crudo*. It is only produced commercially, in Lombardy and Emilia-Romagna, although it is sold all over northern and central Italy. In southern Italy it is almost unknown.

PROVOLONE *A type of cheese*

This is a "plastic" curd cheese made with full-fat (whole) cow's milk. The cheese, once kneaded, is made into shapes, which can vary greatly both in size and in shape: they may be large or small, round, oval, pear-shaped or tubular. The small ones are called provolette, the middle-sized ones provole and the large ones provoloni. Provolone has a smooth, shiny crust that comes away easily. The cheese itself is buff-coloured and is hard, yet malleable.

There are two kinds of provolone: provolone dolce, made with calf's rennet and aged for about a month, although sweet is still tasty, and is softer than the more mature cheese; provolone piccante, made with kid's and lamb's rennet, is aged up to one year, and the longer it is aged the more piccante (pungent) it becomes. There is also smoked provolone.

PRUGNA, *also called* SUSINA
Plum

Plums are eaten as fresh fruit or they are poached in a cinnamon-flavoured wine syrup or used for making jam, which is a popular topping for tarts. Poached plums are called prugne giubellate or sciroppate and are kept for a year in sealed jars. When dried (prugne secche) they are usually eaten poached in red wine.

PUNTA DI PETTO
Boned breast of calf or ox

This is often served stuffed with minced (ground) pork and veal, prosciutto*, Parmesan, breadcrumbs, seasonings, herbs and spices. In the punta di vitello alla Parmigiana the meat is first sautéed in butter flavoured with parsley, rosemary, sage, cinnamon and onion and then cooked in the oven, basted with white wine, for about two hours. But the best known recipe for this cut is cima alla Genovese**.

PUNTARELLE
A variety of chicory (endive)

This chicory (endive), originally from Lazio is eaten as a salad. The spears are cut lengthwise almost to the root and then placed in cold water, until they become curly.

QUAGLIA
Quail

Farmed quail are more readily available than wild ones which are slightly larger and much tastier. (The quail farmed in Europe is not usually the native species.) Whether farmed or wild, quail are best eaten fresh, without being hung.

In a recipe from Veneto, quail, sautéed in oil, are roasted in the oven. At the end the cooking juices are sharpened by grappa. In Marche the birds are sautéed in butter and prosciutto* and then gently braised in wine. They are sometimes served on a mound of boiled rice, dressed with plenty of butter and Parmesan. The same method is used in Lombardy, where the quail are served with a creamy risotto alla Parmigiana*. A recipe for quail with balsamic vinegar is on page 111.

QUARTIROLO
A type of cheese
A cheese from Lombardy. Quartirolo is a fresh cheese with a milky flavour and a soft yet solid texture that almost literally melts in the mouth. Quartirolo belongs to the stracchino* family and it is similar to, but has less fat than, the better-known taleggio*. It is made in September and October when the cows feed on fodder of the quarto (fourth) mowing, hence its name.

RADICCHIO
A variety of chicory (endive)
This is the generic name for the red varieties of chicory (endive) which have been cultivated with a special method of forcing and blanching. Among these the most popular are the radicchio

rosso di Treviso, di Verona, di Castelfranco and the newly arrived di Chioggia. This last variety is extensively cultivated these days in greenhouses and is available all year around. It is pretty in appearance and crunchy in texture, but lacks the flavour of its older cousins.

The radicchio of Treviso, with its elongated leaves and broad white ribs, and that of Castelfranco with its exquisite round shape and variegated pink colour, are mainly used in cooking, while the radicchio of Verona and Chioggia are best for using in salads. On page 147 is the classic recipe for radicchio ai ferri – grilled (broiled) radicchio – a perfect accompaniment to grilled meats.

RAFANO *also* CREN *or KREN*
Horseradish
A native of eastern rather than southern Europe, horseradish is not widely used in Italy, although it appears in a few recipes from Venezia Giulia where it is always part of the traditional accompaniment to a platter of boiled pork meats.

RAGÙ *A pasta sauce*
Ragù is a rich sauce for pasta, traditionally made with meat. There are two basic ragù di carne, one alla Bolognese – the northern Italian ragù, and the other alla Napoletana – the favourite of the south.

Ragù Bolognese must be cooked very slowly for at least one-and-a-half hours, and should be cooked in an earthenware pot. It is the traditional dressing for tagliatelle* and tortellini*; the recipe on page 174 is my version of this classic sauce.

Ragù alla Napoletana is a quite different sauce, although still used to dress pasta. It shares the use of an earthenware pot with its northern cousin, and requires an even longer cooking time. Rrau (its dialect name) has long been one of the focal points of Neapolitan family life. This rich sauce is used to dress pasta eaten as the first course, while the meat from the sauce is eaten by itself, or with a vegetable, as the second course. The recipe on page 174 is from *Cucina Regionale Italiana* by Ada Boni.

Nowadays the name ragù is also applied to fish sauces that contain more than one kind of fish stewed with tomato and wine.

RANA *Frog*
Frogs are a speciality of Pavia and are excellent coated in a light batter, fried and served with fried freshwater shrimp. Other traditional dishes are rane in guazzetto† (frogs sautéed in oil and butter and then stewed in a tomato sauce containing wine and herbs), and frittata* di rane. The other great dish using frogs is risotto* con le rane, the rice being cooked with the frogs' legs in a stock made with the remaining parts of the frog.

RANA PESCATRICE *see* CODA DI ROSPO

RAPA *Turnip*
This root used to be very popular in Northern Italy, where many recipes are similar to recipes of the fifteenth and sixteenth centuries. Rape are not so fashionable now, but they are still used a lot in soups as in the Lombard Riso e Rape. But in Friuli-Venezia Giulia a dish made with fermented turnips is still very popular and is always served with boiled pork or added to Jota** (see page 59).

RASCHERA *A type of cheese*
Piedmont excels in the production of cheeses and raschera is among the top five. It is a DOC cheese made in the province of Cuneo in south-west Piedmont. Made with cows' milk, it is aged for at least one month. It is a splendid table cheese with a delicate and yet pronounced flavour.

RAZZA *also* ARZILLA *Skate*
An excellent fish that the Italians tend to ignore. It is most commonly cooked in a tomato sauce, or it is boiled and served with a hot butter and anchovy sauce.

RETE *Caul fat*
Caul fat is a fatty membrane lining the stomach of an animal, usually a pig. It is used to protect and to impart fattiness to the food it is wrapping. It is sold dried and folded in butchers' shops and it has to be moistened in warm water before it can be used. Its best-known use is for wrapping pig's liver (fegatelli di maiale*), one of the great Tuscan specialities.

RIBOLLITA
A type of soup
This thick soup is made in Tuscany. It was traditionally made in large quantities on a Friday, the fast day, so that it could be reheated on the Saturday, hence its name which literally means "reboiled". Ribollita is made with seasonal vegetables plus beans and cavolo nero*, the Tuscan cabbage. My recipe on page 57 also contains Savoy cabbage, which is included in the version made in Siena.

RICCIARELLI
Almond biscuits (cookies)
Soft almond biscuits (cookies) from Siena. Ground almonds and sugar are

moistened with egg whites and shaped into lozenges. The ricciarelli are baked on pieces of rice paper, the same size as the biscuits, in a cool oven until dry.

RICCIO DI MARE
Sea urchin

Common around the Italian coasts, sea urchins should not be cooked, only slit open and eaten raw with lemon juice. The best time to eat them is in the spring just before they breed, when the coral is full and ripe.

RICOTTA
A type of cheese

Ricotta is made from the whey after it has separated from the curd as a result of being heated. The strained whey is then heated again, which accounts for its name ("recooked"). The two traditional ricotte are the Piemontese and the Romana. The Piemontese, called Seiras, is creamy, looking a little like mascarpone*, although it is less rich. It can only be found in Italy and is not exported. Ricotta Romana is the kind sold abroad, although real Roman ricotta is made with ewe's milk (not with cow's milk as that available abroad) and has a much deeper flavour and lighter texture.

Ricotta, when good, can be eaten as it is with honey, ground coffee etc (see my recipe on page 157). It is also used in many cakes and desserts such as cassata Siciliana*, pastiera Napoletana and cannoli. Outside Italy the most easily available ricotta is a UHT product, which is only suitable for cooking, added to other ingredients.

Ricotta is also used in many savoury dishes such as vegetable pies and tarts. Mixed with spinach or Swiss chard it is essential in malfatti* **, the green gnocchi* from Emilia-Romagna and in tortelli di magro*. In central Italy, ewe's milk ricotta is added, crumbled, to vegetable soups such as fennel or spinach soup before serving.

In Sicily and Sardinia a whole ricotta is placed in the oven and lightly smoked with a little salt. It develops a dark crust but remains soft and creamy inside. Another type of ricotta is ricotta salata. This is hung to drain until dry, to be used, grated, over pasta al pomodoro (with tomato sauce) and it is an essential ingredient in a variety of Sicilian pasta dishes.

RISO *Rice*

Italy is the biggest producer of rice in Europe. Italian rice is a Japonica strain, of which four different types are grown, mainly in the Po Valley (see page 36). These are: ordinario, the short round rice used for puddings; semifino, a round grain of medium length suitable for soups, salads and some kinds of risotto*; fino, a less round grain that is good for risotti; as is the superfino, a long grain that is the best for any risotto. The best varieties of superfino are arborio, roma and carnaroli.

The better the rice, the longer it takes to cook, thus superfino takes about 18 minutes, while ordinario only takes about 12 minutes. The fino and superfino grades are used for making risotto because they absorb a lot of liquid during the cooking, and swell up without breaking. No other variety of rice has the same property, which is why risotto must be made with Italian rice.

Rice has certainly not conquered the south to anything like the extent that pasta*, from its base in southern Italy, conquered the north. In northern Italy rice is the main ingredient in an endless number of dishes, mostly risotti, but also soups, of which there are as many

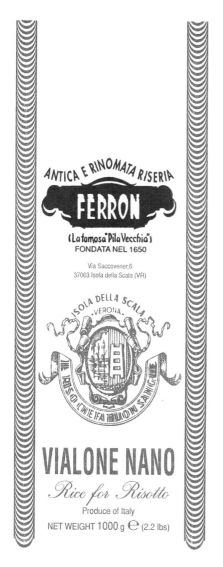

can be served simply boiled and dressed with butter and Parmesan; this is known as riso all'inglese ("made the English way"). It can also be prepared all'insalata (in salad).

Two new strains of rice are now cultivated in Italy: black rice (a hybrid of the Japonica and Indica varieties) and red rice (actually a grass, first grown in the the French Camargue and similar to that grown in California). Both varieties are best boiled and then sautéed with something light, such as shrimp or chicken, or served in a salad.

RISO IN CAGNONE
A traditional rice dish

A traditional dish made in Milan, Piedmont and Liguria. In the Milanese version the boiled rice is dressed with melted butter, sage leaves, a clove of garlic and Parmesan. The Piedmontese version also uses melted butter, but with fontina* cheese, while in the Ligurian recipe the parboiled rice is finished in a rich tomato sauce in which one or two sausages have been cooked.

RISOTTO
A savoury rice dish

This must be made with Italian rice (see Riso), which can absorb the liquid in which it is cooked without breaking or becoming mushy. To make a good risotto, the right saucepan is very important. Ideally, it must be heavy, and wide yet deep (about 25 cm/10 in) with a round bottom so that no grains can stick in the corners. Risotto cannot be left to cook by itself; it must be watched and stirred frequently. The basic recipe for risotto (risotto in bianco) is on page 80. Good risotti can be made with many ingredients. The Veneti excel in fish and vegetable risotti,

kinds as there are cooks. In soups the rice is usually matched with a seasonal vegetable, although several may be used together, as in minestrone*. Thus rice with chestnuts, turnips, potatoes, Savoy cabbage or parsley are classics of the cooking of the northern regions. One of the best soups is made by boiling rice in some homemade beef stock and serving it sprinkled with parsley and showered with best Parmigiano-Reggiano*. Rice for which they like to use Vialone Nano rice or other semifino varieties, while in Lombardy and Piedmont the traditional risotti are more geared towards meat, and the rice used is a superfino such as Arborio.

RISOTTO ALLA MILANESE *Traditional risotto*

Also known as risotto giallo (yellow) in its native city, this is one of the pillars of Milanese cooking. The saffron used is usually powdered saffron from crocuses cultivated in Abruzzo, which is of the highest quality. My recipe is on page 79. Risotto alla Milanese is the only risotto that is sometimes served as an accompaniment. By tradition it is served with ossobuchi* messicani* or with costolette alla Milanese*, although this is seldom done nowadays.

RISOTTO AL SALTO

A rice dish

This dish uses leftover risotto alla Milanese*. The risotto, spread and pressed into a buttered frying pan (skillet), is fried until a crust is formed underneath, then it is either turned over or grilled (broiled) to cook the top.

RISOTTO NERO

Black risotto

Venice has given us the best risotto recipes, especially those in which risotto is combined with fish. Risotto nero, also called risotto di seppie, is cooked with cuttlefish and includes their ink.

ROBIOLA

A type of cheese

This cheese is produced mainly in Piedmont and Lombardy, in cylindrical or square shapes of 300–500 g/ 10–16 oz. Commercially it is made with cow's milk, but some farm-made robiole are made with goat's or ewe's milk or a mixture of two different milks. After eight to ten days of ageing, the fresh robiola is soft but firm and has a delicate buttery taste. It becomes drier with age and develops a delightful piquant flavour after about six weeks. In both stages robiola is an excellent table cheese.

ROGNONE *Kidney*

Young calf's kidneys, which are sweet and tender, are usually eaten, though those of lamb, kid and pig are also used.

Lazio has more recipes for offal (variety meats), including kidneys, than any other region. Calf's kidneys, peeled, cored and sliced, are cooked rapidly in oil and butter and then splashed with Marsala• (rognoni al Marsala). Lamb's kidneys can be combined with sliced fungi sautéed in butter and lemon juice (rognoncini coi funghi). In Emilia, calf's kidneys are splashed with balsamic vinegar or lamb's kidneys are flavoured with lemon and anchovy fillets.

ROMBO *A type of fish*

The best Mediterranean rombi are the rombo liscio (brill), and the rombo chiodato (turbot). Rombo is usually marinated and flavoured with sage then cooked in butter. It is also gently grilled (broiled) and dressed with lemon juice.

ROSMARINO *Rosemary*

Rosemary is a perennial bush that grows wild, especially near the sea as its name implies, ros being the Latin for dew. It is one of the most used herbs in Italian cooking.

Rosemary is mainly used in the roasting of meats, but it is also used when roasting large fish and in bean soups, to which I add it at the end of the cooking, having sautéed it with garlic in plenty of extra virgin olive oil. Rosemary and garlic are one of the most successful combinations.

RUCHETTA
Wild rocket (arugula)
Wild rocket (arugula) is quite common in central Italy where it is used as part of the misticanza* salad. It has a pungent flavour similar to the cultivated rocket, but much stronger.

RUCOLA *Rocket (arugula)*
Rocket (arugula) has a delightfully pungent flavour which makes any salad far more pleasurable. Only one traditional recipe uses cooked rocket (arugula), a pasta sauce from Puglia – parboiled rocket is sautéed in olive oil with garlic and anchovy fillets. The pasta, cooked in the rocket water, is then layered with the salad with a generous splash of olive oil.

S

SALAMA DA SUGO
Cured pork meat
Salama, a speciality of Ferrara, is made from fat and lean minced (ground) pork, pig's livers and tongue, cut into small pieces and flavoured with spices and red wine. The mixture is pushed into a casing made from the bladder of a pig, and shaped like a small melon. It is dried and then cured for six or seven months. Salama is hand-made on a small scale rather than commercially. It

is sold uncooked, and has to be gently boiled for at least four hours.

SALAME *Salami*
This consists of minced (ground) or chopped pork, or pork and beef, flavoured with spices and herbs, well seasoned, pushed into natural or artificial casing and aged. Salami is made all over Italy in various sizes. Garlic, wine, peppercorns, fennel and chilli are used, each producing a different-tasting product. There are also excellent salami made from wild boar or from a boar/pig hybrid, a speciality of Tuscany and Umbria. Types include:

Salame Felino The most delicate of all the different types of salami. It is made near Parma, using the same large pigs from which prosciutto* is made. It contains only 20% fat, and is flavoured with just a soupçon of garlic and white wine.

Salame Milano A delicate-tasting salami, made with finely minced (ground) lean pork meat with tiny specks of fat and flavoured with a little

garlic and white wine. The other well-known Lombard salami is that of Varzi, which has the same flavouring as Milano, but the wine is red instead of white. It is a delicate and excellent product, still made on a relatively small scale.

Salame Toscano A robust salami, also called Finocchiona, flavoured with fennel and plenty of garlic.

Salame di Fabriano From Marche, this is the best salami of central Italy. The lean meat is coarsely minced (ground) surrounding white cubes of pure pork back fat, richly flavoured with pepper-corns and garlic.

Salame di Napoli The only well-known salami of southern Italy. The coarsely minced (ground) meat is flavoured with chilli to give it a spicy flavour, as indeed are all the locally made salami in the south.

Salame d'Oca Goose salami is pro-duced in some parts of the regions of Piedmont and Friuli. It is made with minced (ground) goose meat, plus the usual seasonings and, often, Marsala•, and is stuffed into the goose's neck. Salame d'oca and prosciutto* d'oca are traditional foods of Italian Jews.

This is only a short list of the most popular salami, but in every town, or even village, you will find salame nostrano (local salami) which is usually excellent and representative of the regional cuisine.

SALATINI
A savoury biscuit (cracker)
Salatini is the generic word for the small savoury biscuits that are served with aperitifs. Salatini can be flavoured with a variety of ingredients, which includes cheese, cumin seeds, fennel or herbs. They are usually bought loose in patisseries or bakers' shops.

SALE *Salt*
Ninety-five per cent of the salt consumed in Italy is sea salt. There are two grades, sale grosso (coarse) and sale fino (fine). Sale grosso is added to food that is boiled or cooked for a long time, and it is occasionally used at the table, where the crystals are served in a special dish. It is also applied directly to food to achieve the same effect as cooking in a clay pot, as when a fish or chicken is thickly covered in rock salt before being baked at a high temperature. The salt forms a crust around the bird or fish. Sale fino dissolves more quickly, and is used at the table, or in the kitchen in sauces and other preparations.

Salt is used as a preservative now, just as it was in the past, for preserving anchovies placed in layers in wooden barrels, for preparing bottarga* and mosciame* and for preserving many vegetables. Capers are much better preserved in salt than in vinegar, and basil and other herbs can be successfully preserved in layers of coarse salt.

SALMORIGLIO *A type of sauce*
This is a Calabrese and Sicilian sauce for grilled (broiled or barbecued) swordfish or tuna, or more rarely, for lamb or kid. It is a mixture of olive oil, lemon juice, oregano, parsley, salt and garlic.

SALSA *Sauce*
A salsa is either a juice derived in part from the cooking of the main ingre-dient, or it is a separate preparation served with the cooked dish to enhance its flavour. A pizzaiola*, for instance, is an example of the first type of sauce, since the meat is partly cooked in the sauce, thus imparting its flavour to it, whereas la peverada* **, a piquant relish

eaten with roast meats, comes in to the second category.

Italians dislike food that is swamped by a sauce. A roast will be served with only the de-fatted and deglazed meat juices, no gravy being made. It may not fill a sauceboat, but its taste will be of real meat. The greatest use of sauces in traditional cooking is for dressing pasta, and these are typically Italian, while most of the sauces which are served separately are of French origin.

The main sauces used in Italian cuisine are listed under their individual entries.

SALSA VERDE** *Green sauce*
Salsa verde originated in Lombardy, which has the sweeter and more aromatic parsley. It was, and still is, the indispensable sauce for a bollito misto*, or for any kind of boiled meat or boiled fish. Salsa verde is easy to make, you can adjust it to your own taste and be sure of a successful result as long as you use mild extra virgin olive oil, equally good wine vinegar and flat-leaf parsley.

SALSICCIA *Sausage*
This is one of the oldest staples. It is made in many different ways all over Italy, from the mild corda de Monscia (literally, "rope of Monza") in Lombardy to the highly prized salsiccia Calabrese, generously spiced with chilli. The classic salsiccia, of which luganega* is the most popular, is made with coarsely minced (ground) pork meat, two-thirds being lean meat and one-third fat. The meat is usually from the poorest cuts of the animal, such as throat and belly. The process of making sausages is very simple: the meat, coarsely chopped, or minced for a finer texture, is seasoned with salt and pepper and then pushed into the casing made from the gut of the pig. Different flavourings are added to the meat mixture, for instance white wine or grana* in south Lombardy, Parmesan in Emilia and garlic, chilli or fennel seeds in the south. Salsiccia is usually eaten soon after being made and is therefore not normally cured, although some kinds of salsiccia are cured and aged.

Although the classic salsiccia is made with pork, there are those made with wild boar, a speciality of Tuscany and Umbria, and the salsiccie di fegato (highly spiced sausages made with pig's liver).

Salsiccie usually need cooking, except for those which are cured and aged and can be eaten as they are. There are too many ways of cooking salsiccie to list. The salsiccia coi broccoli of Lazio is a classic, the sausage being fried in a little oil flavoured with garlic, and the blanched broccoli being added five to ten minutes later. The dish is finished on a gentle heat with the addition of a couple of tablespoons of dry white wine and a little water. In Calabria a similar dish is made with turnip tops (greens) and chilli. In Veneto salsiccie are sautéed with garlic and then splashed with red wine vinegar (salsiccie all'aceto). They are traditionally served with polenta*.

SALTIMBOCCA** *A veal dish*
This recipe consists of rolls of veal that are so tasty that, as their name declares, they "leap into the mouth". Thin slices of veal are covered by a slightly smaller slice of prosciutto* and a sage leaf. The meat is then usually rolled up and secured with a toothpick along the length of the roll. Saltimbocca is a traditional Roman dish, well-known all over Italy and abroad.

SALUMI *Cured meat*

Salumi is the collective noun for salame*, prosciutto* coppa*, cotechino* and all other products made by curing different kinds of meat in salt. There are two types of salumi, those made from one cut of the animal, such as prosciutto, and others made with minced (ground) meat stuffed into casing, of which salame is the prime example. Salumi of the first type are usually made with cuts of pork, or with pork meat, although a few are made with cuts of beef (eg bresaola*), roe deer, wild boar or goat. The other type of salumi are made with a mixture of minced pork, beef and/or wild boar.

SALVIA *Sage*

Sage is a herb that grows easily in Italy, and is used a lot in cooking, especially in the north and in Tuscany. It is used to flavour white meat, or in sauces in conjunction with butter, as in dressings for ravioli* and other homemade pasta. Sage is essential to fagioli all'uccelletto** of Tuscany and to saltimbocca**, but the dish totally based on sage is salviata**, a Tuscan speciality.

SANATO *Milk-fed veal*

Sanato is the highly prized Piedmontese calf, which is milk-fed until it is about ten months old. The meat is almost white, totally lean and delicate. Sanato can be used in all the recipes for veal, but there is a traditional recipe from Alba, roston all'albese, made with the fillet (tenderloin) which is braised with the usual flavourings in white wine, with porcini added half way through the cooking and truffle sliced over the top at the end.

SANGUINACCIO

Black pudding (blood sausage), or a sweet pudding

Sanguinaccio is a black pudding (blood sausage) in northern Italy, but a sweet preparation in the south. Both dishes use the first gift of the slaughtered pig, its sangue (blood). This should be used when it is still fresh and, if possible still warm. Milk is added to the pig's blood plus many spices and onions, the mixture being cooked and pushed into a casing.

The sweet sanguinaccio is rich, creamy and dark, with nuts and chocolate, as in the sanguinaccio from Naples, which contains crema pasticcera* in equal proportions with pig's blood.

SARAGO

A type of fish

Sarago is the name given to a few species of sea bream, of which the best are the Sarago Maggiore and the Sarago Fasciato – two-banded bream. They are both excellent fish with firm and delicate white flesh, and are excellent for grilling (broiling) or roasting. Saraghi are also added to fish soups, including the Tuscan cacciucco*. But the most interesting dish for saraghi is a roast on the spit, a speciality of the Tuscan coast.

Small saraghi, boned and stuffed with a piece of prosciutto* are threaded onto a skewer with slices of bread and sage leaves. Moistened with oil, the fish are roasted and basted with the cooking juices mixed with a little white wine.

SARDA or SARDINA *Sardine*
In correct culinary terms the first word refers to the fresh fish and the second to the preserved one. In Venice sardines are prepared "in saor" (see Scapece, page 314, and Sfogi in Saor, page 317). They are also fried with tiny artichokes or fennel wedges, while in Calabria fried sardines are served with a vinaigrette containing mint and lemon rind.

In Puglia one of the best local baked dishes is made with boned sardines layered with a mixture of breadcrumbs fried in olive oil, grated pecorino*, garlic and parsley, with beaten eggs poured over the top before baking. In Liguria, too, sardines are baked in a tortino* di sarde. Sicily offers some excellent recipes, among them sarde a beccaficu** and the pasta con le sarde* **.

Larger sardines can be stuffed in many different ways. In a recipe from Liguria they are stuffed with lettuce leaves and cheese. In the south sardines are traditionally stuffed with fresh breadcrumbs, egg, pecorino, capers and parsley.

The majority of sardines, though, are preserved in salt or oil, to which lemon juice or tomato is occasionally added. This is still an industry in Sicily, but now Spain is the main producer of canned sardines.

SARDE A BECCAFICU**
Baked sardines
In this well-known Sicilian dish the boned sardines are opened up flat, then rolled up and set in the dish with their tails in the air, making them look like little beccafichi (warblers) pecking at the dish.

SARTÙ *A savoury timbale*
This is the most sumptuous of all Neapolitan dishes. It consists of a timbale of boiled rice which is dressed with butter, Parmesan cheese and meat juices, spooned into a charlotte mould and filled with sautéed tiny meatballs, chicken livers, peas and dried porcini and diced mozzarella*. The timbale is then cooked in the oven for 30 minutes.

There are two versions of sartù, one without tomato (in bianco†), and the other, more modern, with a tomato sauce. This lavish dish is served at Christmas.

SAVOIARDI
Sponge fingers (ladyfingers)
These biscuits (cookies) are similar to sponge fingers (ladyfingers), but lighter and less sweet. They are served as an accompaniment to ice cream, sorbet (sherbet), fruit salad and creamy puddings. Savoiardi are also used for making layers in sweet prepartions, such as tiramisù* **.

SAVORE or SAPORE
A savoury sauce
This is a traditional preparation made in Emilia from grape must. It is used as an accompaniment to bollito misto* or as a filling for some kinds of ravioli* or tortelli*, such as pumpkin tortelli from Mantua. In Tuscany there

is an excellent savore of walnut made with verjuice, parsley and oil and served with boiled or roast meats.

SCALOGNO *Shallot*

Shallots are sometimes used in the preparation of a soffritto* because they soften faster than onion, and because of their delicate garlicky taste.

SCALOPPINA *or*
SCALOPPA *Escalopes (scallops)*

Scaloppine are thin slices of meat (usually veal, pork or turkey), cut against the grain from the boned top round of a young animal. It is then thinned with a meat mallet (bat) to a thickness of about 5 mm/¼ in. Scaloppine are used for many preparations, all quick and easy, such as scaloppine al limone or al Marsala•.

SCAMORZA *A curd cheese*

This is a plastic curd cheese, similar to mozzarella*, made with cow's milk. It is moulded to an attractive pear shape and a cord is tied around the narrow top. Each cheese weighs about 200 g/ 7 oz. Scamorza is white and creamy, quite dry, yet soft with a delicate milky flavour. It is eaten fresh. There are some smoked scamorze, and these can be distinguished from the fresh cheese by their brown rind.

SCAMPO *Scampi (jumbo shrimp)*

Mediterranean scampi have a thinner carapace than the Dublin Bay variety available in Britain. The usual method of cooking is to fry them, scampi fritti, the shelled scampi coated in egg and flour and fried in oil. New recipes such as spaghetti* agli scampi are trying to oust the traditional and inimitable risotto* di scampi. This dish is made to perfection along the coast from Venice to Trieste.

Scampi also make a good soup. They should be cooked whole, the carapace only split on the underside, so that the delicious juices of the heads and claws go straight into the broth (see recipe on page 102).

SCAPECE *A type of dressing*

A scapece refers to a method of preparing fish and vegetables in southern Italy and Sicily – the food is fried and dressed with a vinegary kind of sauce in which it sits for some time. It used to be a method of preservation. The same basic preparation is called saor (see recipe on page 95) in Venice and carpione* in Lombardy. The dressing varies from region to region, and the fish too. The vegetables are usually courgettes (zucchini) and pumpkin.

SCAROLA *Batavia endive (chicory)*

Eaten raw in salads and cooked in many ways, batavia endive comes mostly from southern Italy. Because of the slightly bitter taste it develops in cooking, batavia is used in many vegetable pies. In southern Italy batavias are also stuffed. A mixture of breadcrumbs, anchovy fillets, sultanas (golden raisins), pine nuts and capers is pushed between the leaves of small bunches of the blanched batavias, which are then braised in stock and olive oil.

SCARPAZZONE *A vegetable pie*

This is a vegetable pie from Emilia, and also from southern Lombardy where it is called scarpazza. It consists of a pastry crust made with rendered pork fat and a topping of Swiss chard, sautéed in oil and flavoured with garlic, nutmeg and Parmesan*. Sometimes pancetta* and parsley are added, while other versions use spinach instead of the sweeter Swiss chard.

SCHIACCIATA *A flat bread*

This is dressed flat bread, similar to focaccia**. Traditional schiacciata is made with bread dough and rendered pork fat, now often replaced by olive oil. There are numerous versions of schiacciata, all made in central Italy, many of them sweet such as that of Florence.

SCHIENALE *Spinal cord*

Also known as filone, this is the spinal cord of an animal. It looks like a long tube made of a substance similar to sweetbreads, to which it has a similar flavour. Schienali are from calves, oxen or lambs, the last being a favourite ingredient in Roman cooking.

SCORFANO *Rascasse*

There are two species of this fish around Italy, the black rascasse found in shallow waters and the red in deep waters. Rascasse nowadays is only used in fish soups. It thickens the soup and gives it a delicious flavour.

SCORZONE
A variety of black truffle

This is a black truffle, *Tuber aestivum*, which can be found all the year round except in spring. It has a pleasing flavour, but this is certainly not comparable to that of the real black truffle *Tuber melanosporum*.

SCORZONERA *Black salsify*

Black salsify, which is only black on the outside (the root, once cleaned, is of a beautiful butter colour), is popular in Piedmont, Liguria and Lombardy, but only to a limited extent elsewhere. It is cooked in similar ways to carrots.

SCOTTIGLIA *A large stew*

Also called cacciucco di carne, scottiglia is a large stew made with different types of meat and game in southern Tuscany. Medieval scottiglie are now reproduced for modern gourmets. Wild boar, lamb, venison, hare, rabbit pheasant, squab, thrush and skylark, separately sealed, are put in a large cauldron with tomatoes, wine and flavourings. When all the meats are cooked, toasted bread is placed in the bowls to absorb the rich stew, a typical Tuscan habit.

SCRIPPELLE *or* CRISPELLE 'NBUSSE
Pancakes (crepes)

These pancakes (crepes) served in stock are an old speciality of Abruzzo. The batter for the scrippelle contains chopped parsley. Once made they are rolled up and put in individual soup bowls. They are then sprinkled with plenty of grated pecorino* and Parmesan and covered with boiling capon or chicken stock.

SEDANO *Celery*

This flavoursome vegetable is usually braised in stock and dressed with Parmesan or covered with béchamel** and Parmesan. Blanched celery is also fried, coated in batter, or served raw in salad, dressed only with olive oil and, possibly, lemon juice. It is also often included in a bagna caôda* **. The greatest use of celery today, however, is in a soffritto* with onion and carrot. The green celery, leaves and all, is used, being more aromatic and smaller. Celery soups with pasta* or rice are a standby in every family.

SEDANO RAPA *or* SEDANO DI VERONA
Celeriac (Celery root)

Traditional celeriac (celery root) dishes are found in Piedmont and Veneto. An excellent recipe is for a soup in which the celeriac is sautéed with chunks of sausage and borlotti beans in a soffritto*. Meat stock is poured over and the soup is cooked for two hours, when tagliatelle* are added.

SEMIFREDDO

Soft ice cream

Semifreddo is the Italian ice cream *par excellence*. Made with egg custard, flavouring, Italian meringue and whipped cream, it is softer than ice cream because of the high content of sugar in the meringue. The most popular semifreddi are zabaione* and coffee.

SEMOLINA *Semolina soup*

Not to be confused with semolino*. Semolina is a soup made with semola, cooked in milk or stock. It is often given to young children, old people or invalids.

SEMOLINO/SEMOLA

Semolina

Semola refers to the ground durum wheat from which commercial dried pasta* is made, while semolino is the refined ground product used for making pasta at home, or in soups and other recipes.

A good dessert is made from semolina combined with eggs, sugar, butter, sultanas (golden raisins), candied peel and, sometimes, pieces of chocolate. The traditional dish made with semolina is gnocchi alla romana**.

SEPPIA

Cuttlefish

The use of cuttlefish in the kitchen is vast and varied. In Liguria they are cooked in zimino**. In Abruzzo they are marinated in oil, chilli and garlic and then stewed in wine until tender,

with a final addition of chopped parsley and lemon juice. In Venice cuttlefish are stewed in white wine to which a little tomato sauce and the ink of the fish is added. They are also fried, in which case the small young seppioline, fried whole, are the best.

Cuttlefish are ideal for stuffing. One of the best methods is to stuff them with their own cut up tentacles, some mussels, a squid, grated pecorino* and breadcrumbs, all bound with egg. They are cooked in olive oil in an earthenware pot. In Venezia Giulia there is a traditional recipe in which they are stuffed with the meat from a granceola*, mixed with the cut up tentacles, egg, butter and a little Parmesan cheese.

The best known cuttlefish recipe is risotto nero*, where the ink is used to flavour the risotto.

Seppie make an excellent sauce for spaghetti. The cuttlefish is cut up and stewed in white wine and then the ink is mixed in.

SFINCIONI
The focaccia of Palermo

There are two types of sfincioni, one similar to pizza and the other like a pie. The open sfincioni has a thick base of pizza dough and is covered with caciocavallo*, tomatoes, onions, anchovies, breadcrumbs and oil. The other type, called sfincioni di San Vito, is stuffed with minced (ground) pork, minced local sausage, ricotta* and breadcrumbs. The stuffing is first sautéed in oil and then placed between two thin sheets of pizza dough.

SFOGI IN SAOR**
Sole in sauce

This is one of the best-known Venetian dishes. Sfogi are sole, and saor is dialect for sapore, an old word for sauce. A dish of eastern origin, it is traditionally eaten during the day of the Festa del Redentore.

SFOGLIA *Pasta dough*

These rolled-out sheets of homemade pasta dough are made with flour and eggs, to which water and/or oil may be added, the mixture varying from region to region. The sfoglia of Emilia-Romagna, made with soft wheat flour and eggs, is the most popular (see recipe on page 72).

SFOGLIATELLE *Pastry cakes*

Puff pastry or short pastry cakes (cakes made with pie crust dough) from Naples with a filling of cooked semolina, ricotta*, candied fruit and spices.

SFORMATO *A savoury pudding*

Sformato is a pudding made with a coarse purée of vegetables, or occasionally of chicken, fish or sweet ingredients. It is bound with eggs and béchamel** and cooked in the oven, usually in a bain-marie. Sformato is traditionally made in a ring mould, so that the hole in the centre can be filled with a sauce before the dish is taken to the table. This might be a finanziera*, or a tomato sauce – or others, according to the main ingredient used for the sformato. Individual sformato can be made. (See recipes for Fennel and Spinach Sformato on page 141 and 147).

SGOMBRO *Mackerel*

A lovely looking fish with dark blue wavy stripes on its smooth, shining body. The best mackerel are caught in the Tyrrhenian sea.

One of the most traditional recipes for mackerel is from Liguria, mackerel with peas. The fish are sautéed in olive oil with garlic, onion and parsley and cooked with the peas in a tomato sauce. They are also excellent grilled (broiled) or pan-fried and finished off with a few drops of balsamic vinegar (see recipe on page 99).

SMACAFAM *A polenta dish*

One of the most basic dishes of the simple country cooking of Trentino, the name itself reveals the function of the dish; "smaca la fame" means that it "knocks out hunger". It consists of thick buckwheat polenta* mixed with sausage and onion. There is also a sweet smacafam prepared for carnival days – sultanas (golden raisins) replace the sausage.

SOGLIOLA *Sole*

Sole has many different regional names in Italy, the best known of these being sfogi* in Venice and sfoglie along the Adriatic coast.In Emilia-Romagna sole are cooked alla parmigiana (sprinkled with Parmesan after being sautéed in butter). In another recipe from the same region, sole, coated in flour, are put in an ovenproof dish with sage, onion, white wine, a couple of tablespoons of strong meat juices, lemon juice and parsley. They are baked, and served with small glazed onions. Further south, in Abruzzo, sole are roasted with olive oil, garlic, lemon juice and parsley. A few minutes before serving, lots of black olives and lemon slices are added. The most interesting recipe for sole, sogliole al basilico e pinoli**, is from Caorle, a town on a lagoon to the east of Venice.

SOPA COADA *Pigeon soup*

This is Veneto dialect for zuppa covada, literally broody soup. In spite of being quite elaborate, this soup has humble origins and comes from the countryside around Treviso, north of Venice. Sopa coada was devised to use up leftover roasted pigeons. The pigeons are put, with lots of Parmesan, in between slices of toasted bread. Stock is poured over them and the dish is placed in a very low oven to "brood" for at least four hours, during which time a little stock is added every now and then.

SOPPRESSA *A type of salami*

This is a popular salame*, now made in Veneto on a commercial scale. It is large, and made of coarsely ground pork; both lean meat and fat are used, the fat accounting for a third of the volume. Soppresse are cured for about a year in dark, dry rooms. They are eaten as an antipasto*, or as an accompaniment to grilled (broiled) polenta*.

SOPPRESSATA

A type of salami

Soppressata is made in central Italy. The most famous is the soppressata di Fabriano in Marche, still produced following an ancient recipe. It is a salame made with lean pork meat from the shoulder, mixed with fatty minced (ground) pancetta*, cut into sticks and packed into natural casing, which is washed in wine vinegar. It has a soft consistency and a delicate smoky flavour. There is also a soppressata of Siena, a wonderful large sausage made with the pig's head and spiced with the same spices as those used in panforte* **.

SORBETTO *Sorbet (sherbet)*

By the second half of the nineteenth century the word sorbetto had all but disappeared from cook books, the term gelati* being used to refer both to ice creams and to sorbets (sherbets). Recently, however, the word – and the sorbets – have experienced a revival, and today they are flavoured not only with the usual fruits but also with a variety of herbs and flowers. This revival is owing both to the modern desire for healthier foods that are light, clean and fresh, and to the increased availability of domestic ice cream machines that make it so much easier to make sorbets on a small scale.

SOTTACETI

A vegetable garnish

Made with all sorts of vegetables preserved in vinegar, sottaceti are used as part of an antipasto* and to garnish many cold meat dishes.

SOTTOBOSCO

Fruits of the forest

This could be translated as "from the woods" and refers to wild strawberries, wild raspberries, blackberries, blueberries and possibly some redcurrants. As a dessert, sottobosco is dressed with lemon juice and/or sugar or even, for

the purists, served as it is. Those who are less dedicated to purity ask for sugar and cream.

SPECK
A type of cured prosciutto

An Austrian type of smoked prosciutto* and a traditional product of Alto Adige. Recently it has become popular throughout the whole country. Speck now features strongly in antipasti*. It is also used successfully in pasta sauces**, it is kneaded into canederli* bread and is served with sauerkraut together with different cuts of pork.

SPEZIE *Spices*

The spices mainly associated with traditional Italian cooking are nutmeg, cloves, pepper and cinnamon. They are generally used sparingly. Chilli, however, has recently become popular in a selection of dishes, while the original spices have been largely superseded by a variety of fresh herbs.

SPEZZATINO *Stew*

The word comes from spezzare (to break), since the meat, usually a cheap cut, is cooked in chunks. Spezzatino is an everyday dish made at home, sometimes with potatoes, peas or (bell) peppers and usually containing tomatoes. Spezzatino is traditionally cooked in an earthenware pot. The meat is sometimes coated with flour before being sautéed in a soffritto*, and it is then cooked on the hob (stovetop) with wine. In southern Italy spezzatino is also made with lamb's or kid's offal (variety meats). The vegetables and flavouring vary, but there are some classic regional recipes, such as that featured on page 118.

SPIEDINI *Kebabs*

These are small skewers, but the word also refers to the food that is skewered. Meat, offal (variety meats), fish or vegetables are cut into small pieces and threaded on a skewer, with pancetta* and herbs placed between them. They are usually marinated in olive oil, salt and pepper and then they are grilled, preferably on wood or charcoal. The most popular spiedini are made with seafood.

SPIGOLA *Sea bass*

This is another word for branzino* (sea bass), the name by which the fish is most commonly known in southern Italy, where it is usually grilled (broiled) or baked.

SPINACIO *Spinach*

When cooked, spinach is dressed with olive oil and lemon juice, and perhaps a touch of garlic. All other recipes require further cooking. The best-known regional recipe is spinaci alla Fiorentina, where the chopped spinach is sautéed in butter and garlic and mixed into a béchamel** containing lots of Parmesan cheese, then the dish is baked in the oven.

Spinach is one of the ingredients most frequently used in fillings, as for ravioli*, agnolotti* Piemontesi, rotolo* di vitello* and pollo* ripieno. There are a number of spinach pies, of which scarpazzone* is the best known. Then there are gnocchi* with spinach and potatoes, gnocchi with spinach and ricotta* (see recipe on page 90) and endless other preparations using this popular vegetable.

Among the more modern ways of using spinach are as a very delicate pasta* dressing, and a risotto* verde. Chopped spinach is kneaded into pasta dough to make the only traditional coloured pasta (see Pasta).

Spinach is now available all year around, thanks to a number of new varieties. However the best spinach is still the winter one, and the first prize must go to the large, fleshy Gigante d'Inverno.

COMPAGNIA
DEI BUONI SAPORI

Frittatina di Spinaci
Spinach Omelette
PRODUCT OF ITALY

SPONGATA *also called*
SPONGARDA *A sweet pie*

Spongata consists of two thin layers of sweet pastry stuffed with a rich mixture of toasted bread, raisins, candied peel, walnuts, sultanas (golden raisins), mostarda* di frutta, cinnamon, nutmeg, coriander and mace, all bound in clear honey. The pie is lavishly sprinkled with icing (confectioners') sugar before it is served.

SPUMONE *A soft ice cream*

This very soft ice cream is originally from Naples and Sicily. The outside consists of a layer of vanilla ice cream, while the inside is a differently flavoured parfait. The more modern version of spumone is simply a kind of parfait (recipe on page 172). An old Piedmontese dessert made with mascarpone* and eggs is also known as spumone.

STECCHI *Traditional snacks*

These are snacks made in Genoa and Bologna. Stecchi means sticks, and on these short sticks, traditionally made of olive wood, a selection of sautéed morsels are threaded. They could include: veal, sweetbreads, brains, pickled tongues, artichoke segments, porcini and even slivers of truffle. The Ligurian stecchi are then coated in a mixture of breadcrumbs and egg and fried in olive oil, while the Bolognesi stecchi are dipped in a thin béchamel** and then coated with egg and breadcrumbs and fried.

STINCO *A cut of meat*

Although it is the same cut of meat as ossobuco*, shin (shank) is cooked in one piece and carved just before serving. It can be the shin of a young calf, a lamb or a pig. Calf shin is a speciality of Trieste, where it is generously brushed with olive oil or butter and flavoured with rosemary and lemon juice and roasted in a very low oven. Pig's shin (ham hock) can also be cooked in the same way or it can be pot-roasted with the usual flavourings, in white wine. Alternatively, it is cooked following a recipe from Alto Adige, where it is smoked and then eaten with sauerkraut.

STOCCAFISSO *Dried cod*

Stockfish is dried (not salted) cod. The cod (hake or ling is also occasionally dried) used is usually from Norway. The head is removed and the fish is air-dried — the result is a fish that is as hard as wood. The best stockfish is known as Ragno — it is white in colour and is very lean. Before cooking stockfish it must be beaten, to break the fibres, and soaked in several changes of water for at least 48 hours. In Italy stockfish is also sold already prepared for cooking. It is eaten in all regions of Italy, but especially in Liguria and Veneto, from where most of the traditional recipes come. In the south, baccalà (cod that is salted before being dried) is more popular. However confusion arises from the fact that in some places, and everywhere in Veneto, stoccafisso is called baccalà, and thus many of the recipes are wrongly named.

The two most popular recipes from Veneto are baccalà mantecato, similar to the French brandade, and baccalà alla Vicentina**. In Liguria a dish is made in which mashed stockfish is mixed with mashed potatoes. In another Ligurian recipe the stockfish is cooked, with cubed potatoes, in oil flavoured with mashed anchovy fillets. But in most regions stockfish is cooked "in umido"† (in a tomato sauce), flavoured with local herbs and/or spices.

STRACCHINO
A group of cheeses
This is the name of a group of cheeses, all made in northern Italy. Quartirolo*, robiola*, taleggio*, and gorgonzola* are all matured (sharp) stracchini, with particular charac-teristics of their own. Fresh stracchino is the same as crescenza*. These cheeses are nearly all made with full-fat (whole) cow's milk that is fresh and still warm, mixed with the milk from the previous evening.

STRACCIATELLA
A type of soup
A delicate soup made with the best homemade meat stock, top-quality Parmigiano-Reggiano* and good fresh eggs. These last two ingredients are beaten together, often flavoured with a touch of nutmeg. Stracciatella is a traditional soup from Lazio and Marche, where the nutmeg is often replaced by a touch of lemon rind.

STRANGOLAPRETI *or* STROZZAPRETI *A type of gnocchi*
Literally, "priest chokers". The name alludes to the reputation of priests to have a fondness for good food: they used to eat so many of these little gnocchi* that they choked on them. It is the name given to any type of gnocchi in southern Italy.

In Naples, strangolapreti are potato gnocchi and the dressing is a classic Neapolitan tomato sauce** or a Neapolitan ragù**, while in Basilicata they are made with pasta dough and dressed with a piquant ragù*. In northern Italy the name strangolapreti appears in Trentino, where it is applied once again to little gnocchi, this time made with a mixture of beet and bread soaked in milk or stock. They are served with melted butter and cheese.

STRUCOLO *A strudel*
Friuli-Venezia Giulia is the home of this strudel. There are two kinds; one sweet, with pastry similar to Austrian strudel but stuffed with ricotta*, breadcrumbs and sultanas (golden raisins); and one savoury (see the recipe for Potato and Spinach Roll on page 86).

STRUFFOLI *Neapolitan sweets*
These consist of little balls made with flour, egg and butter, flavoured with

orange and lemon. They are fried in oil and then coated in a hot syrup of honey, spices, candied peel and sugar. Once made, they are piled up to form a cone or made into a ring, and decorated. Struffoli are prepared in Campania at Christmas time and during the last week of carnival.

STRUTTO
Rendered pork fat

To make strutto, the fresh pork fat (sugna*) is cut into small pieces and cooked for a long time in an earthenware pot. It is then strained through a fine sieve (strainer) into a heated jar. Strutto has been the main cooking fat of central and southern Italy for centuries. Now, for health reasons, strutto is not so popular, yet it has not lost its property of making the food that is cooked with it very tasty.

SUGNA *Pork fat*

This refers to fresh pork fat, taken mainly from the back of the pig. Sugna is either used fresh, shortly after the killing of the pig, or it is rendered in an earthenware pot to make strutto*.

SUGO *Juice*

The liquid extracted from fruit, vegetables or meat during cooking is called sugo. There is some confusion, though, between the words sugo and salsa. What some call a sugo di pomodoro*, others call a salsa di pomodoro, and what is a sugo di carne* to some is a salsa di carne to others.

Sugo di carne is the cooking juice of a roast, a steak or an escalope (scallop). A Neapolitan ragù*, for instance, is also called sugo because the sauce, although it contains flavouring vegetables and spices, is made with the concentrated juices of the meat and cooked at length. Sugo di carne is used to dress pasta* or rice, as well as to serve with the meat itself.

SUINO or MAIALE* *Pig or pork*
Suino is mainly used as an adjective, for instance carni suine (pork meats).

SULTANINA
Sultanas (Golden raisins)

These are also known as uva passita, uva passa or uvetta. Sultanas (golden raisins) are used in cakes, biscuits (cookies) and desserts. They are also used in savoury dishes; saor (see recipe for sogliole in saor, page 95) is an example of this, as is caponata* ** and pasta con le sarde** and other southern Italian pasta sauces.

SUPPLI *A rice croquette*
These rice croquettes fried in olive oil are a speciality of Rome and central Italy. There are two versions. Suppli al telefono consist of little croquettes of risotto containing prosciutto* into which mozzarella* cubes are pushed. When you bite into them the melted mozzarella stretches into long threads, like telephone wires (hence the name). The other version is made with risotto dressed with a rich ragù*. Suppli are a popular snack found in most bars.

SUSPIRUS *Almond biscuits (cookies)*
Suspirus is Sardinian dialect for sospiri ("sighs"). They are little balls made

with ground almonds, sugar and egg white. What distinguishes suspirus from other almond biscuits (cookies) is that once baked they are coated with lemon icing (frosting).

T

TACCHINO *Turkey*

This bird is popular in northern Italy, where it is the traditional Christmas fare. In Lombardy a young hen-turkey is boiled with lots of vegetables and served with mostarda di frutta*. In Piedmont the young bird, stuffed with boiled rice, grilled (broiled bell) peppers, calf's liver and the bird's giblets, is roasted, basted with wine, and at the end the sauce is enriched by the addition of a cupful of cream. A recipe for stuffed roast turkey is on page 108.

The best recipes come from Venice: paeta (Venetian dialect for turkey) al malgaragno (with pomegranate), paeta alla schiavona and paeta col pien. In the recipe with pomegranate the bird is basted with the juice and served with a sauce of sautéed giblets sharpened by pomegranate seeds. In the second recipe, stuffed with celery, chestnuts and prunes, it is spit roasted. The third recipe is again for a stuffed, roasted bird, but the stuffing is typically Italian – prosciutto*, Venetian salame*, garlic, parsley and Parmesan, plus the Venetian sweet touch of candied peel and crumbled favarini (local soft biscuits/cookies). Turkey breasts and legs are very popular and are cooked in the same way as veal escalopes (scallops) or veal joints.

TACCOLA
Mangetout (snow peas)

A good recipe from Piedmont dresses blanched mangetout with a little butter and finishes them in the oven with a spoonful of creamy grated fontina and a few slices of white truffle.

TAGLIATA
Sliced beefsteak

A modern dish launched in restaurants and now quite popular. It consists of a T-bone steak, about 5cm/2in thick, grilled (broiled) or cooked on the griddle until still red inside. It is then sliced across diagonally to a thickness of 2 cm/¾in and served with best olive oil or aromatic butter and plenty of pepper.

TALEGGIO *A type of cheese*

This is one of the two best-known cheeses from Lombardy, the other being gorgonzola*. Taleggio is made from cow's milk and has a high fat content. It is ripe after two to three months. It is soft and buttery, with a very aromatic flavour and a reddish crust. A good taleggio is a highly prized table cheese. It is also used in cooking, for pizza* toppings, ravioli* fillings and frittate* etc.

TARALLO *and* TARALLUCCIO
Savoury biscuits (crackers)

Every town in Puglia offers the traveller the delight of its taralli – biscuits (crackers) shaped like rings, figures-of-eight or knots. The common denominator of most taralli is that they are not sweet, and they are cooked twice, either baked twice or first boiled and then baked. Taralli are made with a yeast dough enriched with egg or sweet white wine, and they can be flavoured with fennel seeds, cumin or chilli. They are eaten as snacks. Taralli are also part of the traditional cooking of Campania, where they usually contain chopped almonds.

TARANTELLO
A fish "sausage"

This is a tuna fish salami* made in Taranto, hence the name. The cured belly of tuna is minced (ground) and combined with spices, and then pushed into natural casing.

TARTUFO *Truffle*

Both white and black truffles are found in Italy, but it is the white that is the Italian truffle *par excellence*. The white truffle is known either as tartufo bianco or tartufo d'Alba, because the best of these truffles are found near Alba, in south-east Piedmont. They are also found in smaller quantities in Umbria, Tuscany, Emilia and Veneto.

The white truffle has an intense aroma that has been described as a perfect marriage between a clove of garlic and a piece of the best Parmesan. It varies in size from 2–15 cm/¾–6 in. It is found in woods, where it grows in symbiosis with poplars, willows, oaks and lime trees, between October and December. The white truffle is eaten uncooked.

The black truffle is known as tartufo nero or tartufo di Norcia. Outside Italy it is known as the truffe de Périgord. It is associated with hazel and oak trees, and is in season between October and March. The taste of the black truffle is milder than that of its white cousin, and it is usually brought out by cooking. Norcia is in Umbria, but this truffle is also found in Marche, Veneto and Lombardy. The black truffle is similar to another , the Scorzone* which is very common and is used a lot in sauces, oils etc. Its aroma and flavour are uninteresting. Small dogs are trained to find these buried jewels, but pigs are also occasionally used in Umbria.

The truffle is one of the most adaptable of all foods; it seems to keep its strong identity whatever food it is combined with. The white truffle is perfection on a delicate risotto* or on a dish of tagliatelle*, yet it can also improve the aggressive pungency of a bagna caôda* ** or the velvety richness of a fonduta*. A few shavings sprinkled over a Carpaccio* transform it into a gourmet dish. The milder-tasting black truffle makes a most delectable pasta sauce** (see page 65). A shaving of either kind of truffle gives any filling a lift. It changes the flavour of the simplest meatball, makes a gourmet dish out of a cheese frittata*, a polenta pasticciata** or even fried eggs.

TARTUFO DI MARE

A type of clam

Provided you know where it has been caught, the tartufo di mare is best eaten raw with a squeeze of lemon juice. It is used instead of vongola verace* to make pasta sauces.

TELLINE *A type of shellfish*

These attractive molluscs are like small vongole*, and are found mainly on the sandy beaches of the Tyrrhenian sea. They need a lot of cleaning to wash away the sand.

TESTINA *Head*

The head of a calf, a kid or a lamb has for centuries been regarded as a choice dish from court tables to peasant kitchens. In a favourite dish of central Italy, baby lamb's heads are simply grilled (broiled), flavoured with garlic and herbs. The head of an ox or a pig is called testa and it is mainly used for canned preparations and for making mortadella*. In central Italy a sausage (coppa di testa) is made with a pig's head (recipe on page 137). In Tuscany the same type of sausage is cut into cubes and mixed with chick-peas (garbanzo beans).

TIELLA *A boiled, layered dish*

A southern Italian word for a shallow ovenproof dish and, by extension, for a baked dish layered with many ingredients. A tiella will always contain potatoes, onions, garlic and olive oil, to which any of the following may be added: mussels, fish, pork, tomatoes, courgettes (zucchini), rice, wild mushrooms or celery. A tiella is baked in the oven, and it is done to perfection when the liquid released by the vegetables and/or the fish has been completely reabsorbed.

The best known of all of these dishes is one which comes from Bari, layered with rice, potatoes, mussels, tomatoes, onions and garlic, and a generous sprinkling of the local olive oil.

TIMBALLO *A savoury, moulded dish*

This is the name of a round mould, but the word is mainly applied to the dish that is made in such a mould. It is a rich, baked dish, sometimes contained in a pastry case. A timballo can be made with tagliolini*, tagliatelle*, maccheroni*, ravioli*, gnocchi* or rice. It may be served with rich sauce such as béchamel. A princely timballo is described by Giuseppe Tommasi di Lampedusa in his book *The Leopard*; the recipe on page 72 is my interpretation.

TIMO *Thyme*

Thyme is not commonly used, although it is one of the traditional flavourings for rabbit.

TIMPANO *A moulded dish*

A word used in Naples for a timballo*. The dish was given this name because timpani in past centuries were cylindrical pies in a pastry case, and were therefore drum-shaped like the percussion instrument.

TINCA *Tench*

Tench is a freshwater fish of the same family as the carp. It can have a muddy flavour, and so farmed tench might be preferable. A popular cooking method is in the oven, stuffed with Parmesan, breadcrumbs, garlic, herbs and spices.

TIRAMISÙ
A coffee-flavoured dessert

This needs no introduction. Oddly enough, in a country where the dishes are often centuries old, tiramisù is a relative newcomer. It was created about 30 years ago, allegedly by the owner of the El Toulà restaurant in Treviso. Tiramisù means "pick me up", which the pudding does as it is generously laced with coffee and some kind of alcohol. There are several versions of tiramisù and on page 158 you will find mine.

TOCCO *A savoury sauce*

Tocco is the name given in Liguria to sauces used to dress pasta or gnocchi. Tocco di carne (meat) is made with a piece of beef or veal that is slowly braised in butter and bone marrow with onion, carrot and celery. Splashed with white wine, it continues to cook with a little tomato purée, a selection of herbs, a few dried porcini and a grating of nutmeg. Water is added and the meat is given a further long, slow cook to add density and flavour to the tocco. The sauce is served with the pasta, while the meat is eaten as a second course. The other popular sauce is the tocco di funghi, which is made with sliced porcini, cooked in oil with onion, garlic and tomatoes.

TOMA *A type of cheese*

This cheese from Piedmont and Val d'Aosta is made from cow's milk and cream, and comes in a cylindrical shape. The methods of production are artisanal and the quality is controlled by legislation. Toma can be fresh with a milky yet slightly salty flavour, or aged for a few months, when it becomes quite strong. Fresh toma is sometimes used as a dressing for polenta*.

TOMINO *A type of cheese*

This is a round cheese, similar to toma*, but always eaten fresh. Some tomini are flavoured with pepper and served with a light dressing of olive oil and chopped herbs, as part of the unending list of Piedmontese antipasti*.

TONNETTO *A type of fish*

This is a kind of tuna found around the Italian coasts, but mostly in the Adriatic. It is the same beauriful shape as its larger cousin but usually about 60-70 cm/24–28 in long. A recipe from southern Italy combines the marinated fish with sliced potatoes which are then baked.

TONNO *Tuna*

A large fish which can be as long as 3 m/10 ft. It swims at amazing speed, its beautiful dark blue body looking like a torpedo flashing though the water. Tuna live in deep water but move near the shore in early summer to spawn. It is then that the Sicilian mattanza del tonno (slaughter of the tuna with harpoons) takes place.

Tuna has been compared to pork, both for its fatty meat and because it has no waste. It is popular in central and southern Italy, where it is mostly grilled (broiled or barbecued), but it is in Sicilian cooking that it comes truly into its own, with an array of recipes, some dating from Roman times. The Sicilian A. Denti di Pirajno boils the fish in a vinegary court-bouillon to which a thick paste of anchovy fillets is added, a flavouring similar to garum. Another southern recipe is tonno alla marinara. The tuna steaks are cooked in the oven in olive oil with black olives, tomatoes, capers, dried breadcrumbs and basil. The Calabrese add fresh chilli, their favourite spice.

Two recipes from Livorno are worth a special mention. The first, tonno ubriaco (drunken tuna) is made by frying the steak in oil with garlic and parsley and then cooking it in Chianti. In the other, tuna with peas, the fish is sautéed in olive oil with plenty of garlic and then braised with peas in a tomato sauce. In Veneto a similar recipe is prepared, with the fish and the peas being cooked in red wine instead of a tomato sauce.

In the old days, tuna was preserved in barrels, tonno sott' olio, the best part being the ventresca* (belly). In the best delis tuna is still sold by weight, and it is a much better product than tuna preserved in cans. Tonno sott' olio is used with beans and red onions in the Tuscan dish, tonno e fagioli**, known the world over. It also makes an ideal filling for hard-boiled (hard-cooked) eggs, mixed with the yolks and mayonnaise, or for ripe tomatoes.

Traditional pasta sauces made with tonno sott' olio are numerous in the south (see recipe on page 78), while in the north tuna is also used in a rice salad. Another excellent dish is polpettone di tonno (tuna roll) made with tuna, potatoes and eggs. The roll is boiled and then, when cold, served with a light mayonnaise or with an even lighter dressing of olive oil and lemon juice. You will find a recipe for tuna roll on page 100. A good bottarga* is made with the salted and pressed roe of tuna fish.

TOPINAMBUR
Jerusalem artichoke

In a nineteenth-century recipe, topinambur trifolati†, Jerusalem artichokes are first blanched and then sautéed in olive oil and butter, with parsley, shallot, garlic and anchovy fillets, still a popular recipe today. A simple way to prepare topinambur alla parmigiana† is to blanch them, sauté them in butter and then cover with a shower of Parmesan. They are excellent cold, previously boiled and dressed with salsa verde* **, or raw with bagna caôda* **.

TORDO *Thrush*

These attractive birds are considered a great delicacy in Italy. They have dark meat with a strong aromatic flavour, given by the berries they like to eat.

Thrushes are usually roasted on the spit, with slices of lardo and sage leaves. In Veneto, braised thrushes flavoured with juniper are boned and added to a risotto* in strips with the strained cooking juices. In Chianti they are cooked in oil with garlic, sage and black olives. Halfway through the cooking they added a handful of black grapes.

TORRONE
Italian nougat

This is the Italian version of nougat, a bar made with egg white, honey and toasted almonds, and flavoured with different essences (extracts), spices or liqueurs. The best-known torrone originated in Cremona, where the best producers are found. In Abruzzo, a softer torrone contains chocolate, in Sicily there are two torroni, one containing candied fruits and the other sesame seeds, while the torrone of Calabria is made with the excellent

local hazelnuts, honey and, often, figs. There is a recipe for a homemade chocolate torrone on page 170.

TORTA *A cake or pie*

There are few traditional cakes – the Italians do not eat many cakes, although they might occasionally have a slice at breakfast or tea-time.

Traditional regional cooking, however, is rich in vegetable pies which are called torta or tortino*, the latter usually referring to a dish without a pastry (pie) shell.

TORTA DI PANE

Bread pudding

A torta di pane is a traditional sweet preparation made with leftover bread – a popular dish in a country where so much bread is eaten! There are as many different torte di pane as there are households. Some are made with apples or pears, others are highly flavoured with spices, in medieval style. Others are studded with pieces of bitter chocolate and/or enriched with candied peel and nuts. The only ingredients that are always included are egg, milk, sugar and, of course, bread, which is

traditionally white. One special torta di pane from Veneto is made by soaking the stale bread in wine and sugar instead of milk and sugar; it is called torta di pane ubriaca* ("drunken bread pudding"). A recipe is on page 163.

TORTA DI RISO *Rice cake*

This rice cake is eaten unmoulded and cold. It may be made with or without a pastry (pie) shell. On page 159 there is my recipe for a torta di riso without a pastry shell.

TORTA DI TAGLIOLINI

A type of dessert

There are two kinds of this torta, one from Verona and the other from Modena. In both, very thin, homemade tagliolini* is placed uncooked, in layers, with chopped almonds, sugar, plenty of butter, lemon and orange juice and some liqueur. In the Veronese version the tagliolini are placed directly in a pan, while in the Modena recipe the tagliolini are placed inside a sweet pastry case (pie shell). Both torte are baked, covered with buttered foil.

TORTA PARADISO

A type of cake

This is a light Madeira-like cake, created by the Pasticceria† Vigoni in Pavia in the second half of the nineteenth century. The recipe is a well-guarded secret, and although torta paradiso has been copied by other pasticceri, the original is still the best.

TORTA PASQUALINA

A vegetable pie

The best known of vegetable pies, Torta Pasqualina is traditionally made at Easter, hence its name (Pasqua means "Easter"). It is a speciality of Liguria and, like many dishes from that region, skill, devotion and time are needed to make it. The dough is made with flour and water to which a little olive oil is added, to produce a pastry similar to filo (phyllo); like filo it is stretched until translucent.

The traditional filling is thinly sliced artichokes or Swiss chard sautéed in butter and onion and flavoured with marjoram. This is placed, with the local soft cheese, prescinsena*, butter, whole eggs and Parmesan, between many layers of the pastry and baked for an hour.

TORTA SBRISOLONA

A type of cake

This is a traditional cake from Mantua. Its name comes from sbriciolare (to crumble), because it crumbles when it is cut. In Mantua it is eaten with sweet wine. The recipe is on page 162.

TORTINO

A vegetable pie

A rustic vegetable pie, usually without pastry. Liguria is the homeland of tortini, where they are often called polpettoni*, a word which elsewhere in Italy means meatloaf. The tortini of Liguria are made with various vegetables: artichokes, green beans**, spinach, aubergines (eggplant), cardoons or courgettes (zucchini). In the tortino di carciofi*, which is also a speciality of northern Tuscany, the finely sliced artichokes are stewed in oil and water instead of being blanched.

A number of different tortini are made in other regions. You might, for instance, come across a tortino di patate* (potato pie) in central Italy made with mashed potatoes, eggs and pecorino*. Another variation on this theme is a tortino di zucchine* (courgette pie), in which tomatoes, not traditionally used in tortini, are included. In Lombardy there is a plain and simple tortino di patate e cipolle* (potatoes and onions) in which sliced boiled potatoes are sautéed in oil and butter with onion until a crust is formed. The tortino is then turned over, or put under the grill (broiler), to form a crust on the other side. A tortino di patate e carote* is made in the same way.

TOTANO *A cephalopod*

A totano is similar to a squid, but with a longer and tapered body which allows it to leap out of the water and glide through the air for short distances. It is found off the coasts of Sardinia, Liguria and Tuscany, where it is sometimes wrongly called calamaro*. Its flesh is tougher and less tasty than that of a squid, although it can be cooked in similar ways. Small totani (totanetti) are often part of a fritto misto*.

TRAMEZZINO

An Italian sandwich

A quick snack, usually eaten in bars, that can be filled with most things – from simple prosciutto* to quite elaborate mixtures.

TRANCIA *Fish steak*

A fish steak which comes from a large fish, be it tuna, swordfish or hake. The steaks are often grilled (broiled) and dressed with a lemony sauce such as salmoriglio*. They are also baked, or cooked on the hob (stovetop) in a large sauté pan in olive oil and white wine plus flavourings, or stewed, as in western Sicily, with tomato sauce, black olives, capers and cornichons (sweet dill pickles). Trance di tonno* are excellent fried and then finished in a sweet-and-sour sauce. Steaks of white fish are used in Puglia in their tielle*, sandwiched between two layer of potatoes.

TRIGLIA *Red mullet*

There are two varieties of this fish, triglia di fango (mud mullet) and triglia di scoglio (rock mullet). The latter, found in rocky seas, is more highly prized; it is redder and has golden stripes on its sides.

Red mullet is used in soups because of its strong flavour and its lovely colour, which it keeps during the cooking. It is excellent grilled (broiled), or wrapped in foil with herbs and wild fennel and baked, which is how it is cooked in Sicily. In Abruzzo red mullet is cooked in an earthenware pot, in white wine and olive oil, layered with slices of prosciutto* and bay leaves. In Puglia tiny triglie are floured and deep-fried. The best known of all the recipes, however, is triglia alla livornese**.

TRIPPA *Tripe*

In Italy, tripe is always sold already cooked. Just as in France, tripe is appreciated by Italian gourmets for its delicate flavour and its property of thickening and enriching the juices in which it cooks.

There are many excellent recipes for tripe, the best being from northern Italy, plus one or two from the central regions. All recipes are basically similar, since the sliced tripe is cooked with the usual flavouring vegetables and with wine and stock and, sometimes, tomatoes. In the Milanese recipe cooked beans are added 20 minutes before the end. Trippa alla Romana is flavoured with local wild mint and a lot of grated pecorino*, while in Siena and Arezzo they add a good amount of chilli. The trippa alla Bolognese is finished with beaten eggs and Parmesan. One of my favourites is the tripe recipe from Savona, a town on the western Riviera. The tripe is cut into strips and cooked in rich beef stock with cardoons, tomatoes and herbs. Some pasta, usually maccheroni*, is added at the end, and the soup is dressed with a generous amount of the superb olive oil from the local valleys.

TROTA *Trout*

When the trout is wild, small and fresh, there is no method of cooking better than the Milanese trotella al burro. The small trout, lightly coated in seasoned flour, and with a sprig of fresh sage in its cavity, is fried on both sides in plenty of hazelnut-coloured butter until a lovely golden crust forms. As it cooks, the fish retains its moisture inside this crust. In another simple recipe, from Piedmont, the fish is baked and finished with a sieved (strained) red wine sauce flavoured with anchovy fillets. In Abruzzo, where the local trout from the Sangro river are said to be among the best, the fish is cooked in an earthenware pot, lying in a tomato sauce made with fresh tomatoes, olive oil and garlic. This is one of the few recipes in which oil and tomatoes are used with trout.

TUORLO D'UOVO *Egg yolk*

Yolks are used a lot in Italian cooking; and are essential for binding stuffings. Yolks, rather than the whole egg, are also used to make the best pasta. Some cooks add one or two hard-boiled (hard-cooked) egg yolks to a salsa verde* ** to thicken it. Egg yolks are an essential part of that excellent dessert, bavarese lombarda, which consists of an outside of savoiardi* – sponge fingers (ladyfingers) moistened with liqueur, and a centre of pounded hard-boiled egg yolks, butter and cream.

U

UCCELLINI SCAPPATI
A meat dish
This name of this dish from Lombardy means "the little birds that have flown away". In fact the birds were never there, but the dish looks as if it was made with little birds, and this makes it popular with Italians.

The dish is actually made with an assortment of pork or veal, little pieces of pig's or calf's liver rolled into pancetta* slices and then skewered between sage leaves. The uccellini are sautéed in hot butter, and then cooked in white wine. They are always served with polenta*.

UOVA
Egg (of a hen if not otherwise specified)
Although eggs are used in interesting ways in a number of Italian dishes, the only really Italian egg dish is frittata*. Hard-boiled (hard-cooked) eggs, together with salame*, form the traditional antipasto* for Easter Sunday lunch.

In the south, an attractive dish is made with hard-boiled eggs, grilled (broiled bell) peppers and anchovy fillets; a mixture of scrambled eggs and peppers is also made by mixing eggs into a peperonata*. In a dish from Calabria, aubergines (eggplant), potatoes and peppers are stewed in oil and garlic, and the eggs are cooked whole at the end on the bed of vegetables. The same principle is used in a recipe called uova in Purgatorio: the eggs are poached in a tomato sauce flavoured with basil.

Uova al tegamino or al burro (fried eggs) becomes a gourmet dish with the addition of a few slivers of white truffle, which is how they are often eaten in Piedmont during the truffle season. In Umbria, black truffles and scamorza* cheese are sliced over the fried eggs. Other eggs, such as duck's, quail's or gull's, are served occasionally.

UVA *Grapes*
Grapes are not used as an ingredient in any traditional Italian dishes, although in Chianti black grapes are added to a dish made with thrushes. Generally, the Italians put them to their two best uses: they make wine with them or they eat them just as they are.

UVETTA *Dried grapes*
This term includes sultanas (golden raisins), raisins or currants that are used mostly in sweet preparations, but also in sweet-and-sour dishes.

VALERIANELLA or SONCINO

Lamb's lettuce (corn salad)

An early salad eaten for lunch on Easter Sunday, after the agnello* pasquale (Easter lamb).

VANIGLIA *Vanilla*

This is the fruit of a climbing orchid. Although vanilla is added to many sweet preparations, it is less common than other spices, such as cinnamon and nutmeg.

VENEZIANA

A sweet bun

Originally made in Venice on New Year's Eve, Veneziane are now found all year around, mainly in northern Italy. The dough is similar to that of a panettone*, but it does not contains sultanas (golden raisins) or candied fruit; it is flavoured with lemon and orange rind. Veneziane are covered with white sugar crystals, and sometimes with a few almonds.

VENTRESCA *Tuna belly*

This is the belly of a tuna, mainly used preserved. In Puglia, ventresca is used to make one of their delicious tielle*, in layers with sliced potatoes, chopped parsley, shreds of garlic and grated pecorino*. In central Italy the word ventresca is also used for belly (side) of pork.

VENTRIGLIO *Gizzard*

Cleaned and blanched gizzard is often added to a ragù* or to a sauce made with chicken livers.

VERDURE *Vegetables*

Vegetables are regarded not only as an accompaniment to meat, or occasionally fish, but as a dish in their own right. When one, or occasionally two, vegetables are served as an accompaniment they are lightly sautéed in butter or olive oil, so as not to interfere with the flavour of the main dish. But they come into their own when they are served as a separate course. They are prepared in sformati*, torte* or tortini*, fried in a light batter, stewed in tomato sauce or meat juices, stuffed, wrapped or roasted. They may be puréed, combined in earthy vegetable stews, or with pasta, rice or pulses (legumes).

VEZZENA *A type of cheese*

A cheese made in the area around Mount Vezzena in Trentino, where the herds are free to roam and the pasture is very mixed. Vezzena is similar to the better-known asiago*, and like asiago it is a table cheese when fresh (6–8 months) and a grating cheese when aged for 18–24 months.

VIGNAROLA *A vegetable dish*

This is a vegetable dish made in Rome – it is made with the new vegetables: broad (fava) beans, peas and wedges of globe artichoke added to gently fried onion. The dish is finished with lettuce leaves and sometimes is flavoured with a cupful of dry white wine.

VINCOTTO *Cooked wine*

This is a thick liquid made in all the

regions of southern Italy and in Emilia-Romagna. It is made by cooking the must from the grapes for a long time, until the liquid has the consistency of clear honey. Vincotto is used as an ingredient in, or an accompaniment to, sweet preparations.

VIRTÙ *A type of soup*

This soup, "le virtù" to give it its full name, is made in Abruzzo in May. It mixes seven of the previous year's dried pulses (legumes) – the fact that there are seven virtues gives the soup its name – with young new vegetables, which is why it is always made in May.

Other ingredients include a pig's trotter (foot), a piece of snout and some rind. When the dried pulses and the pork are cooked, and the pork bones removed, a soffritto* of onion, garlic, tomato paste and parsley is added to the mixture and the soup is livened by the fresh flavour of vegetables such as wild chicory, spinach, Swiss chard etc. Before serving the soup is thickened by a good handful of pasta, traditionally of seven different shapes.

VISCIOLA *A variety of cherry*

This is similar to morello cherry. It has quite a tart flavour and is used for making jam.

VITELLO *Veal*

The best meat comes from a calf slaughtered when still milk-fed yet large enough. The meat is pale pink, with only a little white, hard fat. Veal is popular in northern Italy, especially in Lombardy and Piedmont. Lombardy offers the best-known recipes, such as ossobuchi*, vitello tonnato*, fricandò and many others. The sophisticated cuisine of this region, based on butter, seems to highlight the delicacy of a piece of veal. But Piedmont rears the best calves – the Sanato*. A Piedmontese dish that takes pride of place is a pan-roasted breast of veal, a particularly moist cut full of flavour, which is stuffed with prosciutto*, fungi, white truffles and pickled tongue.

In Liguria the two traditional veal dishes are cooked in oil – the local cooking fat. They are tomaxelle** and vitello all'uccelletto, consisting of a piece of rump (round) flavoured with sage and pan-roasted in white wine. Emilia-Romagna shares many of the Lombard recipes, giving them the robust character of the local cuisine. Two examples are ossobuchi and cotolette, which, unlike the classic Lombard ones, are flavoured with tomatoes. Vitello al latte – cooked in milk in the same way as maiale al latte** is another speciality of Emilia-Romagna. Traditionally veal is found no further south than Emilia-Romagna, with the exception of the popular Roman dish saltimbocca* **.

VITELLO TONNATO
Veal with tuna sauce

There are two basic recipes for this dish, the old Milanese one and a newer Piedmontese version.

In the Milanese recipe the cooked veal is coated with a sauce made with mashed preserved tuna, anchovy fillets and capers diluted to the right consistency with the puréed cooking juices, lemon juice and cream. It is served hot.

The Piedmontese version calls for mayonnaise instead of cream, and it is served cold.

VITELLONE
A type of veal

This is the meat of a young calf, no older than three years, which has been allowed to graze. It is a favourite meat of northern Italy, where it is used in place of beef in many dishes such as arrosto morto, spezzatini* and even vitello tonnato*.

VONGOLA *Clam*

The more commonly found clam is the vongola gialla, also called simply vongola, while the more prized is the vongola verace (the "carpet shell"). The two differ in colour and size, the first being small with a yellow shell, and the other much larger with a grey shell with dark concentric lines.

All clams are cooked in the same way. In and around Naples you will eat the best zuppa* di vongole, ladled over toasted bread, and the best spaghetti alle vongole. Both these dishes come in two versions, with and without tomatoes. When vongole are used to dress pasta they are sometimes removed from the shell. An excellent spaghetti sauce is made by mixing vongole with mussels. Vongole make a delicious salad when dressed with extra virgin olive oil, a touch of vinegar, salt and black pepper and mixed with the diced heart of a celery.

In Venice vongole are used to make a perfect risotto*, risotto di caparozzoli (the Venetian name for vongole) in which the risotto is made with a fish stock and the filtered cooking liquid of the clam. The dish is finished with butter and some chopped parsley.

W

WÙRSTEL
A type of sausage

A small *wurst* or a small frankfurter, produced in Trentino-Alto Adige and also in Lombardy and Emilia. The meat used is beef, minced (ground) very fine and mixed with salted pork back fat flavoured with spices. Würstel are subjected to a special stewing process, after which they are ready to be eaten. They are traditionally served with sauerkraut and often with other pork products. A classic salad consists of boiled cubed potatoes and cut-up würstel, dressed with olive oil, vinegar and a teaspoon of French mustard.

Z

ZABAIONE *or* ZABAGLIONE
An egg-based dessert

Marsala• is the wine most commonly used in zabaione, as in the recipe** (on page 160) by the twentieth-century writer Ada Boni, but in Asti moscato is used, and Artusi suggests wine from Cyprus or Madeira. In Tuscany and Marche vin santo• is the popular wine.

Zabaione is one of the most popular of Italian dishes.

ZAFFERANO *Saffron*

During the Middle Ages and the Renaissance saffron was added to food as frequently as salt and pepper. Today it is no longer used so liberally. Its marriage with rice in risotto alla Milanese** is ancient and enduring, as is that with brodetti*, the fish soups of the Adriatic, and with fish stews. It is also used in some versions of the Sicilian pasta with sardines**. One of the newest and most fashionable recipes is pasta allo zafferano. The saffron is added to the dough or, if used with dried pasta, is put in the boiling water and a buttery sauce is made with a little extra saffron to add colour to the dish.

Saffron is grown extensively in Abruzzo, but to meet demand it is also imported from Spain. The spice actually consists of the dried, orange to red stigmas of the saffron crocus. It is still harvested by hand and it takes up to 250,000 flowers to produce 500 g/ 1 lb 2 oz of the spice – hence its high cost. It is sold in the form of dried stigmas – saffron threads – or, more commonly, as a powder.

ZALETI
Small yellow biscuits (cookies)

Venetian biscuits (cookies), with a name which, in the local dialect, means "little yellow ones". They are made with cornmeal, which gives them their colour. Zaleti are sold in every bread or cake shop in Venice, Treviso and other cities in Veneto. Zaleti are mostly eaten with a glass of wine, into which they are dunked. There is a recipe for zaleti on page 169.

ZAMPETTI *A trotter (foot)*

A zampa is a paw, thus a zampone* is a large paw, or trotter (foot), while a zampetto is a small one, ie a pig's, lamb's or calf's foot. There is a recipe from Piedmont for pig's trotters called batsoa – boiled and boned trotters, dressed with wine vinegar, are put in a bowl and pressed down. When cold, and looking like brawn (head cheese), it is cut into long slices, dipped in egg, breaded and fried in butter. See also Piedini.

ZAMPONE
A type of sausage

These are made with rind, lean pork meat and pork fat, all finely minced (ground) together and flavoured with nutmeg, cinnamon, cloves, salt and pepper. The mixture is pushed into the skin of a pig's trotter (foot) and then slowly stewed.

After that zamponi are sold raw for a lengthy cooking, after a previous overnight soaking; or precooked, needing only to simmer for about an hour. The final result is a deliciously tender, delicately flavoured sausage. Zampone is traditionally accompanied by lentils, spinach or potato purée.

ZENZERO *Ginger*

Ginger was one of the first spices to reach Europe from India. It was far more popular in the past than it is now. It appears rarely in the cooking of Venezia Giulia and Veneto. The word zenzero is the cause of great misunderstanding in Tuscany, where it is used instead of peperoncino* (chilli).

ZEPPOLE *Fritters*

These small Neapolitan sweet fritters are made with choux pastry. They are shaped into rings or buns. The bun-shaped zeppole can be filled with crema pasticcera*.

ZUCCA *Pumpkin*

The two most popular varieties are the large round pumpkin of northern Italy, with its bright yellow pulp and thick green knobbly (knobby) skin, and the long, pale green pumpkin of southern Italy, used to make a peculiar sort of jam and also, with a few tomatoes, to make a deliciously sweet pasta sauce.

In Mantova pumpkin tortelli* are made with the addition of amaretti* and mostarda* di frutta. In Reggio-Emilia those last two ingredients are replaced by a large quantity of Parmigiano-Reggiano*, a stuffing similar to the large cappellacci* of Ferrara. In Lombardy pumpkin risotto* is quite popular, the cubed pumpkin being added before the rice to the basic onion soffritto*. My favourite dish with pumpkin is gnocchi**, which appeared weekly on our table in Milan during the autumn (fall).

ZUCCHINA
Courgette (zucchini)

Courgettes (zucchini) are an extremely popular vegetable grown everywhere. In northern Italy, blanched courgettes are covered with a creamy béchamel** and a generous amount of Parmesan and then browned in the oven. They are also simply sautéed in butter and oil, usually cut into batons, cooked until quite tender and flavoured with oregano, a herb that combines particularly well with this vegetable. In Liguria courgettes, sliced on the diagonal, are sautéed in oil and garlic and then cooked with tomatoes and basil.

Courgettes are particularly well-suited to being stuffed. In Mantova the flesh of blanched courgettes is sautéed with onion in butter and then mixed with ricotta*, Parmesan, eggs and a few crumbled amaretti*. The mixture is piled into the halved courgettes and the dish is then baked. Other popular stuffings are béchamel, mushroom and ham, or a light ragù* of beef.

Courgette batons coated in light batter are fried and served as part of a fritto misto*. They make excellent sformati* with lots of Parmesan and a little nutmeg, perfect with fonduta**. A frittata* of courgettes is rightly popular, and nowadays sauces for pasta are successfully created with this delicate vegetable. Really fresh young courgettes are excellent steamed, cut in half and dressed with olive oil and lemon juice, a touch of garlic and oregano.

In a Sicilian dish, zucchine all' agrodolce†, fried courgettes are marinated in a sweet-and-sour sauce. In Naples zucchine a scapece† are similar to the Sicilian agrodolce, but while the Sicilian dish contains sultanas (golden raisins) and pine nuts, the Neapolitan vinegary sauce is flavoured only with mint and garlic.

ZUCCOTTO
A Florentine dessert

Zuccotto is a sponge cake filled with custard and whipped cream and studded with chocolate pieces, hazelnuts and almonds, or with candied peel. It is always served chilled. The top is decorated in alternate brown and white segments using sifted unsweetened cocoa powder and icing (confectioners') sugar that converge in the middle, a pattern that reminds the Florentines of the dome of their cathedral.

ZUPPA *Thick soup*

The word zuppa does not cover all kinds of soup – a zuppa is a thick soup, usually ladled over toasted bread. It is never a creamed soup nor does it contain pasta or rice, like minestrone. Zuppe tend to be quite simple dishes made with pulses (legumes) and one or two vegetables, or often just with lots of vegetables. The following are typical examples:

Zuppa di Verdura The vegetables used vary according to season and locality. The one thing they all have in common is that they must be cut into cubes or strips (in the case of cabbage, beets or lettuce leaves), cooked at length in light stock and ladled over toasted or fried bread to serve.

Zuppe di verdura are usually made a crudo (the raw vegetables are put straight in the stock or water without being previously sautéed). Local vegetables that are in full season and very fresh should ideally be used. When they are really fresh the zuppa is often made with water instead of stock, usually seasoned with Parmesan.

Zuppa di legumi are endless, sometimes with pasta, rice or farro*, sometimes containing a prosciutto bone or pork rind etc.

Zuppa alla Pavese In this soup boiling stock is poured over eggs and fried bread. The egg whites curdle but the yolks remain soft. Zuppa alla Pavese is a classic of Lombard cooking.

Zuppa di Pesce Fish soup. Zuppe di pesce are mostly local soups, sometimes with different names, and often varying in style from one place to another.

On the Adriatic, from Trieste to Puglia, the zuppa di pesce is called brodetto*, and it is supposedly the oldest of all fish soups, derived from the Greek soups. Although the name remains the same, the versions of brodetto are varied. The traditional version from Bari sees different molluscs and seafood placed on a soffritto* of onion, garlic, celery, carrot and parsley into which a good quantity of salted anchovies have been pounded.

In Taranto, on the Ionian Sea, the large variety of a rich sea catch is

Az. Agr. **Le Piagge**
Le zuppe Toscane
BIO
Zuppa di Farro

337

combined in the zuppa tarantina. The fish is sautéed in a soffritto of olive oil, garlic and parsley, then tomatoes are added and the soup is poured over toasted pane Pugliese*.

The infinite number of zuppe di pesce of Sicily are similar to those of the Tyrrhenian sea to the north, with the exception of a soup from Messina called zuppa di neonata – baby sardines and anchovies, known collectively as bianchetti* are cooked in water with olive oil and garlic.

The specialities of Naples and the nearby coastline are clam and mussel soups. In northern Tuscany, where the coast is rocky we find one of the best known of all Italian fish soups, the cacciucco* of Livorno, which contains chilli, as does the brodetto of Abruzzo**.

In Liguria there are many glorious fish soups including bagnun, from the eastern riviera from Genoa to Sestri Levante. It is a humble soup, made only with boned fresh anchovies cooked in white wine and olive oil, tomatoes, garlic and parsley, and more than the usual amount of black pepper. The bread here is brown, which distinguishes the bagnun from most other zuppe di pesce. Another soup from this coast is buridda*, of which there is one version made with many fish and another, older, version made only with stockfish, both containing porcini and pine nuts, two local ingredients. The last Ligurian soup to be mentioned is the ciuppin*, which is often puréed, but appears also, further to the west near the French border, with the fish cut into pieces – it is becoming increasingly similar to bouillabaisse.

In Sardinia there are zuppe di pesce similar to those found down the Tyrrhenian coast, plus the élite of all zuppe, the zuppa di aragosta (spiny lobster). The lobster, cut into chunks, is cooked in an oil-based tomato sauce flavoured with garlic and parsley.

ZUPPA INGLESE
Literally, "English soup"
This dessert is made, with variations, in many parts of central and southern Italy. In the south it often has a meringue topping, while in Emilia-Romagna it has layers of sponge cake and two differently coloured custards: egg custard and chocolate custard. In Tuscany, zuppa inglese is more liquid, thus lending credence to an explanation of its name, which is that English trifle came to Florence in the nineteenth century with the many English who settled there. The Florentines liked the dish, changed it a little, and named the result zuppa inglese.

A NOTE ON BUYING ITALIAN INGREDIENTS

Of course, many authentic Italian ingredients are widely available and extensively used elsewhere, notably fresh fruit and vegetables, such as watermelons and figs, or (bell) peppers and courgettes (zucchini). Cuts of meat do vary from country to country, but providing you select the right sort of meat – braising steak for slow cooking, for example – the results are likely to be satisfactory. Some kinds of game may be more difficult to obtain but if you want to try a recipe, it is worth seeking out a good supplier and asking his advice about a locally available substitute with similar qualities (take this book with you to help). Fish can also present difficulties although modern transporation means that more varieties are increasingly available. Even so, some Mediterranean fish simply don't travel well – it is hard, for example, to obtain fresh anchovies in northern Europe or the United States. Again, keen cooks seeking authentic flavours need to search for a good supplier who will be happy to advise and even willing to try to find more unusual ingredients. Specialist suppliers are the key to successful shopping for difficult-to-find ingredients – supermarkets are not the answer. This may be relatively straightforward advice for a city dweller but not so easy for people in more rural communities. An alternative would be to try the internet for mail order companies. Whatever your source, it is essential that you buy the best possible quality ingredients for an authentic Italian flavour.

For many store-cupboard (pantry) items it is worth spending time tracking down a reliable Italian delicatessen. Some large supermarkets do stock some Italian specialities but are unlikely to carry the same extensive range as a dedicated store. Moreover, in addition to standard items, such as dried porcini, Italian flour and stock (bouillon) cubes, their displays will probably include fresh cheese, prosciutto, salami, sausages, cakes and biscuits (cookies) and lots of other genuine Italian ingredients. An extra bonus is that you will probably have a further lesson in Italian ingredients and cooking thrown in for free. Italians are enthusiastic about food and if you are showing an interest, the proprietor and, very likely, the entire staff will be happy to offer advice and suggestions.

Terms & Techniques

ABBRUSTOLIRE
To grill or to bake

To grill, either on charcoal or over flames, or to bake in the oven. Used in connection with bread, which is first rubbed with garlic and doused with olive oil, as in the Roman bruschetta* and the Tuscan pannunta or fett'unta. Polenta slices are often abbrustolite, as are aubergines (eggplant) and (bell) peppers, a process which makes peeling easier: the vegetable is placed directly over the flame until its skin is black and charred. This gives a most delicious, slightly burnt taste.

ABRUZZESE, ALL'
In the style of Abruzzo

This implies a considerable use of chilli (the favourite local spice) combined with tomatoes. In spite of this, the cooking of Abruzzo is, in fact, extremely varied.

AFFETTATARTUFI
A truffle slicer

A small instrument for slicing truffles. Its main feature is that it can be adjusted to slice very thin slivers – necessary because of the high cost of truffles. It can also be used to slice raw mushrooms and Parmesan.

AFFETTATRICE *A meat slicer*

A rotary meat slicer, usually electric. As well as the familiar machine, seen in every Italian deli, there is a small version for family use. It is gaining popularity owing to the number of people choosing to buy whole prosciutti*, culatelli* or salami*. It is also useful for slicing roast meat.

AFFOGATO *Poached*

Food cooked in water, but usually applied only to eggs. The list of recipes for poached eggs is long, the principle being that they top delicious ingredients or can be served with many different sauces. Included among the best-known recipes are uova affogate con pomodori e mozzarella* (poached eggs with tomatoes and mozzarella); uova affogate alla Parmigiana* (poached eggs covered with melted butter and grated Parmesan) and uova affogate all'acciuga (served with a knob/pat of butter, anchovy paste and very finely chopped fresh parsley).

The other food that is affogato is ice cream. A scoop or two of vanilla ice cream is served covered with hot chocolate sauce. Or the ice cream is covered with hot coffee; called l'affogato al caffè – this modern concoction is one of Italy's most delectable treats.

AFFUMICATO *Smoked*

Smoked food does not play an important part in traditional Italian dishes. However, a few pork products are cured by smoking, the most common being pancetta affumicata* and speck*. Most smoked fish is of foreign origin, although around the lakes of northern Italy there is a tradition of smoking trout. Smoked swordfish is a fairly new product; it is excellent when properly smoked.

AGRO, ALL' *A sharp flavouring*

This is achieved by pouring lemon juice over boiled vegetables and sometimes lightly sautéeing them in olive oil. Asparagus, spinach, Swiss chard or broccoli are frequently served all'agro.

ARRABBIATA ALL'

"Angry", ie hot

In Italian gastronomy this refers to a hot tomato sauce for pasta flavoured with chilli, garlic and basil. The sauce originates from central Italy, probably Abruzzo, but recently it has become quite popular elsewhere in the country and, indeed, abroad.

ARROSTIRE *To roast*

Three basic methods of cooking come within the scope of this term. They are arrosto alla griglia (on the spit), arrosto al forno (in the oven) and arrosto in tegame or in casseruola (pot roast). Meat can be roasted by any of these three methods, but most fish can only be roasted by the last two; large and oily fish, however, can be roasted on the spit. Vegetables are roasted in the oven or in the pot.

Arrosto alla griglia is the oldest method of cooking, and still the best for a large piece of meat (porchetta* or abbacchio*) and most game, both furred and feathered. The meat is regularly moistened with its own fat which is collected in a container (leccarda†) placed underneath. A sprig of fresh rosemary is often used to flavour the meat and other flavourings are placed in the leccarda.

The meat roasted in the oven is usually a cut of beef, pork or lamb, but seldom veal, poultry or game, which are considered too lean for cooking that way. The meat may be flavoured with herbs, onion, celery etc and moistened with wine during the cooking. This method was the favourite of the great Artusi (see page 19), who, in his book *La Scienza in Cucina e l'Arte di Mangiar Bene*, wrote, "If I knew who invented the oven I would build a monument to him". He also cooks veal in the oven, but a milk-fed breast of veal or a leg, which are fattier cuts.

The most common method of roasting is on the hob (stovetop), the arrosto morto* being the most popular. The meat is cooked in a pan or in a casserole. It is first browned over a high heat and then, cooked on a lower heat, with the addition of wine, stock, balsamic vinegar and water, or a combination of these. These additions must be small — just enough to prevent the meat from burning. The meat must never braise, let alone stew. In another recipe the meat begins its cooking in liquid and is roasted at the end by removing all the juices and adding them to the pan very gradually, to brown the meat.

A large, delicate fish, such as sea bass or daurade, is best roasted in the oven (pesce al forno), while a smaller one is more suited to being cooked in the pan. The fish is usually marinated in oil, lemon, herbs and other flavourings.

Vegetables are cut into chunks and roasted in the oven. Three or four different vegetables are placed together, as in a dish from Umbria called la bandiera, the flag.

ASCIUTTO *Drained*

In a culinary context this word is only used in connection with pasta*, ravioli*, gnocchi* and rice that is drained of the water or stock in which it was cooked. Thus what is generally known as "pasta" is more properly called pastasciutta, to distinguish it from pasta in brodo (pasta in stock).

AVANZI *Leftovers*

Italians are masters at making the best of leftovers. They would, for instance, never serve the remains of a roast just as it comes from the larder (pantry). They would add other flavours and make polpette*, a juicy ragù* for pasta* or stuffing for ravioli*. A whole polpettone* is often made with leftovers from different meats, prosciutto* and other added ingredients. Cooked in a tomato sauce, it becomes an excellent dish in its own right. Another such is the bollito* rifatto alla Genovese. The leftover meat is cut into pieces and placed on a bed of crumbled crackers moistened with white wine. It is served with a vinaigrette and with chopped capers and garlic.

Many vegetables are stuffed with leftover meat that is minced (ground) and mixed with béchamel** sauce and other ingredients. Courgettes (zucchini) and onions are particularly good stuffed in this way.

Frittate* and tortini* are made with leftover pasta, rice or vegetables simply by adding eggs and, usually, Parmesan. Even leftover fish is used up. If fried it is prepared "in carpione"* (a sweet-and-sour sauce). If it has been cooked in tomato sauce it can be used to dress a dish of pasta, and if it was poached or grilled (broiled) it can be covered with a thin salsa verde*.

B

BAGNO MARIA *Bain marie*

The word refers to the cooking method and to the type of saucepan used. The gentle heat is suitable for making custard creams, some desserts, sformati* of vegetables or fish, or to keep food hot. It is also one of the best ways to melt chocolate.

BATTERIA DI CUCINA

Kitchen equipment

An old country kitchen is the best place to see the variety of utensils that come under this heading. What you would see, however, is nothing compared to what was considered necessary in a grand Renaissance house. Bartolomeo Scappi's (see page 13) list of implements needed in a well-equipped kitchen included 120 items, from the largest cauldron to various copper saucepans, strainers, knives, filters etc. Seven different sizes of skewer are listed, as are seven ladles and slotted spoons for different uses. Not to mention the moulds needed by chefs and confectioners.

Today's batteria di cucina, modest by comparison, might consist of the following items: two or three flame-proof earthenware pots in different sizes for soups, stews and ragù*, a set of three non-stick frying pans (skillets) and sauté pans with lids, one or two oval casseroles with lids for slow roasting, a few small saucepans of different sizes for sauces, and baking pans for lasagne. A large tall pan for cooking pasta* is essential, as is a large, deep, round-bottomed saucepan for risotti*. It is important to use the right type and size of pan as this can affect the final result of the dish.

An Italian kitchen is very often embellished with an array of brightly polished copper receptacles: pans, moulds, rings and a large paiolo† for making polenta*. The usual selection of knives includes a heavy, flat-bladed one for cutting tagliatelle* and a mezzaluna† for chopping vegetables and meats. A long matterello† for rolling out the pasta dough will be hanging in the corner, and there will be a large wooden board on which to make pasta. Also considered necessary are a food mill, a deep slotted spoon for retrieving gnocchi* and ravioli*, a large grater for Parmesan and a small one for lemon rind and nutmeg, plus a large colander with two handles, and feet, to stand in the sink when draining pasta. A batticarne†, to pound veal for scaloppine*, will also be present, while few Italian cooks would be without a mortaio† with its pestle. A food processor would never be regarded as an adequate alternative for some preparations.

Ovenproof dishes are not numerous, since Italian cooking is not particularly strong on oven cooking. The batteria di cucina also includes all the crockery (dishes), glasses, bowls etc which are used for the presentation of food.

BATTICARNE *Meat mallet (bat)*

This is found in most Italian kitchens and is essential for pounding veal slices in the preparation of scaloppine* (escalopes/scallops). A batticarne consists of a thick, heavy, metal disc of about 8 cm/3 in in diameter, with a handle fixed to the middle.

BATTUTO *"Beaten"*

Making a battuto is the first step towards cooking a great number of Italian dishes. It is the basis for soups, stews etc. Battuto, which means beaten, is a mixture of pancetta* or pork back fat with onion and/or garlic. Celery, parsley or other herbs are optional extras, depending on the final dish. These ingredients are finely chopped, so that they appear nearly pounded, and then they are gently sautéed. This transforms a battuto into a soffritto*. Battuto is sometimes used "a crudo", which means that it is added to the dish without being previously sautéed.

BIANCO *"In the white state"*

"In bianco" is a phrase used to describe food that has been prepared simply by boiling and then dressing with butter or oil. The expression is also applied to dishes that are more usually served "coloured", usually with a tomato sauce. Thus, spaghetti alle vongole*, when served without a tomato sauce, is called spaghetti alle vongole in bianco. Riso in bianco is another familiar dish in which the rice, simply boiled, and therefore white, is dressed with butter and Parmesan. Food prepared in bianco is particularly light and digestible and is therefore usually associated with people who are convalescing or on a diet.

BOLLIRE *To boil*

The definition of boiling is to render a food edible, or more pleasant to the palate, by the use of a liquid, usually water, maintained at simmering or boiling point. However, when referring to cooking meat, fish or vegetables in simmering water, the Italian word is

lessare†. So while pasta* and rice are cooked by the "bollire" method, bollito misto* (boiled meats) is cooked by the "lessare" method, when the water should never reach 38°C/100°F. The same cooking method also applies to fish.

BOLOGNESE, ALLA
In the style of Bologna

There are many dishes originating from the rich and varied cooking of this city. The best known are the ragù* (and therefore tagliatelle*, lasagne*, tortellini* etc alla Bolognese), the fritto misto* and the cotoletta*. The characteristic of the Bolognese style is food cooked at length in butter and/or lardo*, often with tomato purée, prosciutto*, onion and other flavourings. Chilli and even pepper hardly appear in the traditional cooking of this city, which rightly boasts one of the best cuisines in Italy.

BOMBA *A bomb-shaped mould*

A mould in the shape of a bomb, from which some preparations take their name. Bomba di riso, a speciality of Piacenza in Emilia, is made with half-cooked risotto* dressed with the juices of braised pigeons. The risotto is pressed around the side of the mould, the middle is filled with the pigeon meat, then covered with more risotto and the dish is baked. Other ingredients may be added – white truffles, sweetbreads, porcini*, peas, prosciutto* etc. A similar dish is made in Naples, called sartù*.

The sweet bombe are the bomba gelata and the bomba di mascarpone. The first consists of three different ice-creams lining the mould in concentric layers. The bomba di mascarpone is a mouthwatering concoction with the appearance of a dome-shaped cake. The cake – a shell of sweet yeast dough, contains mascarpone*, enriched by toasted hazelnuts, chocolate and candied fruit.

BOSCAIOLA, ALLA
A type of dish

The expression describes a dish that includes mushrooms (wild, dried or cultivated) and tomato sauce. It is a modern word with rather a loose meaning, used a lot on restaurant menus. It is not a specific preparation.

BRASATO *A method of cooking*

A dish and the method of cooking a cut of meat, often beef. The meat is usually marinated with all sorts of flavourings and red wine, and then cooked at length until tender (see brasato alla lombarda**).

BRODETTARE
A method of cooking

A method of cooking, mainly used for baby lamb, kid or rabbit, where the meat is cooked in broth and white wine. After cooking, egg yolks and lemon juice, and sometimes grated pecorino*, are added. It is a method common only in central Italy.

CACCIATORA, ALLA
Literally, "in the hunter's way"

A method of cooking applied to lamb, poultry and rabbit. When cooked alla cacciatora in northern Italy the meat or poultry is cooked in a little wine with tomato, onion, carrot, celery and mushrooms. In central and southern Italy, however, the flavouring is garlic, vinegar and rosemary, to which olives, anchovies and chilli are sometimes added. See recipes for agnello alla cacciatora and pollo alla cacciatora on pages 128 and 105.

The nineteenth-century writer Artusi gives a recipe called riso alla cacciatora in which a jointed chicken is sautéed in pancetta and parsley. When the chicken is lovely and golden, double the volume of water to rice and add the rice as soon as the water boils. So, alla cacciatora is a general term.

CAMICIA IN
Literally "in a shirt"

The term is only applied to poached eggs which, when cooked, are wrapped in egg white.

CARPIONE
A method of preserving fish

A northern Italian term for a method of preserving fish, which is similar to scapece* in southern Italy and Sicily, or saor* in Venice. Traditional carpione of Lombardy is made with freshwater fish.

(See recipe for Sogliole in Saor page 95).

CARTOCCIO *Literally, "paper bag"*

An ancient method of cooking food in the oven, tightly wrapped in greaseproof (waxed) paper or foil. Whole large fish are best suited to being cooked in this way. The most exuberant of all food al cartoccio is a sea bass or a daurade wrapped in paper together with all sorts of delicacies such as oysters, shrimp, clams and scallops. Another presentation, now fashionable, is spaghetti al cartoccio, the cooked spaghetti being dressed with seafood.

CASALINGA *or* CASARECCIA *Home cooking*

These two terms derive from casa (house or home), here with an overtone of "family". They are the attributes of the everyday cooking of a normal household. The best Italian cooking is casalinga, the cooking one rarely finds in restaurants. It is the type of cooking that is passed down from mother to daughter. Cucina casalinga or casareccia is now, often wrongly, used to describe only peasant cooking. It is not necessarily "peasant", but the word always conveys a feeling of simple food prepared with the utmost care and great love.

CENA *Dinner*

In northern Italy this meal takes place between 7.30 and 8.30pm, while in the south it is later, particularly in Rome, where it may be as late as 10pm. While in the country and in the provinces cena is the lighter of the two main meals of the day, in big cities nowadays it is the most important meal since most people tend to have a light lunch near their workplace. Cena also refers to an after-theatre supper, and cenone to a large buffet dinner.

CHITARRA *Literally "a guitar"*

In culinary terms it is the name of a device from Abruzzo for making a kind of pasta* called maccheroni alla chitarra**. It consists of a wooden frame with steel wires stretched taut across its length, the rolled-out sheet of pasta being pressed through the steel wires with a rolling pin. The resulting pasta looks like square spaghetti.

COLAPASTA *Colander*

Without this utensil no Italian kitchen could function, since (as its name explains) it is used for draining pasta*. A colapasta always has feet, or a round base – this is essential when you stand it in the sink to drain pasta. The colapasta is also useful for draining boiled vegetables, for dégorging slices of salted aubergines (eggplant) or courgettes (zucchini), for washing fresh fruits quickly and for other basic operations. A metal colapasta is much better than a plastic one.

COLAZIONE *Breakfast*

This is not a proper meal, rather a cup of coffee – usually with milk – or a cup of tea, with a biscuit (cookie) or two or a piece of cake. This quick breakfast is often taken at a bar on the way to work. However in hotels colazione usually means lunch, as it used to in northern Italy. Until some years ago, breakfast was known as prima colazione.

COTOLETTA
A food fried in breadcrumbs

Fried food that has been previously coated in egg and dried breadcrumbs. The ingredient can be a slice of meat, though never beef, an escalope (scallop) of poultry, a fish steak or a slice of vegetable such as aubergine (eggplant) or porcini caps. The best known cotolette are the Bolognese, covered with a slice of prosciutto*, flakes of Parmesan cheese and a spoonful of tomato sauce, and the Milanese, similar to the costoletta* but using an escalope rather than a chop. The latter is similar to the more famous Wienerschnitzel, the difference being that the Viennese escalope is first coated in flour and thus the crust formed by the egg and breadcrumbs does not adhere to the meat as it does in the Milanese version.

CRETA, ALLA

A method of cooking

This is an ancient method used for whole birds. The clay is moulded around the seasoned bird and baked. The clay is broken with a hammer. Several restaurants in northern Italy cook birds, especially guinea fowls, in this way. But nowadays the name also refers to the cooking of a bird in a bird-shaped clay container.

CROSTA *Crust*

"In crosta" is a way of cooking like the French en croûte, where the food is wrapped in a crust of pastry. The pastry can be a simple one of water and flour. This method, which is particularly suitable for cooking fish, keeps all the flavours sealed in, to produce a delicate and yet rich dish.

It was one of the favourite methods of the past when something in crosta, which was also called pastello, was served at every meal, from oysters to pears. The sixteenth-century writer Messisbugo(always put saffron in the pastry, both for colour and for a show of wealth.

CRUDO *Raw*

When cooking "a crudo" the main ingredient of the dish is placed in a pan together with the fat and flavouring ingredients (onion, garlic, herbs etc) that have not been previously sautéed. It is a healthy method of cooking.

CUCCHIAIO, AL

A type of dessert

"Al cucchiaio" refers to a dessert that can be eaten without being cut. Typical dolci al cucchiaio are sorbetti tiramisù*, bavarois and gelati.

CUCINA *The kitchen or cooking*

The word refers both to the kitchen and to the result of the activity which takes place there.

Cucina, the room, has undergone drastic changes through the centuries. The kitchen of the past was an important room, both in peasant families and in well-to-do households. A description of what a sixteenth-century kitchen in a grand household should be appears in *Opera* by Bartolomeo Scappi(. This kitchen had two water tanks, a grinder, a dough-chest, six trestle tables plus other occasional tables, built-in cupboards around the walls, an open fireplace, a large oven and a small brick construction alongside for cooking directly over the flame. It was dominated by a table "fifteen hand-spans long and three and a half hand-spans wide" on which the pasta was made. The kitchen, he wrote, should open out on to a small yard where birds can be plucked and animals can be killed, skinned and cleaned, after having hung in the winds coming from the north-facing yard. In the middle of this yard there should be a well and a large basin and many large buckets for washing fish and meat. Next to the kitchen there should be another room, much bigger than the yard, for storage.

A contemporary kitchen is a totally different affair; it may be small and inadequate in a town house, while in the country it is still the main room of the house and the centre of family life – as indeed it should be. The furnishing of the cucina differs, but the batteria* in it will include many similar utensils, pots and pans and gadgets. The cooker (stove) is usually large, with plenty of space between the rings to allow large pans to sit one next to the other. Traditional Italian cooking is mostly done on the hob (stovetop) and the oven is only used for baking.

Cucina is also the general term for cooking as a whole.

D

DENTE, AL *Literally "to the tooth"*

This expression is used only in connection with pasta* and rice. It means that the pasta or rice, though cooked through, still offers a little resistance to the tooth, this being an essential sign of being perfectly and properly cooked.

It is impossible to determine the perfect "al dente" point of cooking, as it depends on the different qualities and kinds of pasta or rice being cooked. To some extent it is a question of personal taste. A dish of spaghetti*, for instance, considered al dente outside Italy might be considered to be stracotto (overcooked) in Lombardy, and completely inedible in Naples.

Outside Italy, but not within Italy, the expression al dente is also used for vegetables.

DORARE *To gild*

In a culinary context the word means to turn food to a golden colour by deep or shallow frying, or baking with an egg yolk glaze. A costoletta alla milanese** or a good fritto* must be properly dorato: cooked until golden outside but with the inside still moist and not in any way overcooked.

Food that was dorato was very fashionable in the fifteenth and sixteenth centuries, a trend that began because doctors believed that gold (oro) was good for the heart. Chefs of the rich were instructed to cover the food with gold leaf, while the not-so-rich sought a similar result by frying the food or using saffron.

DOSE *Quantity*

When specifying quantities in recipes, Italian cookery writers used to be, and often still are, rather vague. They presume that their readers know the right proportions of the basic ingredients: butter, oil, onion, flour etc. So the quantities of some ingredients are often not given. When you ask an Italian cook how much stock he or she has added to that delicious sauce, the answer is "two fingers" or "half a glass" or "a bicchierino" (small glass). The size of the glass, or the fingers, is not specified! "A little chopped onion"; can be half a tablespoon, or as much as two tablespoons. It is all a question of experience, of "just knowing", which they presume everyone does.

DROGHERIA *Grocer's shop*

The word comes from droghe (drugs and spices). For me it conjures up an atmosphere of exotic smells mixed with the cheap toiletries, as well as visions of large glass jars full of sweets, nuts, spices, liquorice (licorice) sticks and candied fruits. These were the drogherie of my childhood; nowadays drogherie have largely been replaced by supermarkets. There are still a few, mainly located in provincial towns, but so many of their products are sold prepacked that half the pleasure in shopping in them has gone.

FERRI AI *Grilled or griddled*

This means grilled over embers or cooked in an iron pan. The fuel used to be wood or charcoal, and this is obviously the oldest method of cooking. Our ancestors threaded the raw food on wooden poles, later replaced by iron bars (ferri) which they held over the red embers.

FONDO *Cooking basics or juices*

The word has two meanings in culinary terms. First, it means the cooking basics, usually commercially prepared, which are added to a dish, at the beginning or end of the cooking to reinforce its flavour. Fondo also refers to the cooking juices, ie what is in the pan at the end of the cooking, the mixture of flavourings that gives the dish its particular flavour.

FORCHETTA *Fork*

While knives and spoons are as old as antiquity, the fork is a relatively modern tool which made its first appearance in Venice early in the eleventh century. Although in Italy the fork was in common use with the the aristocracy and upper classes by the sixteenth century, this was not the case elsewhere. As late as 1611 an English traveller wrote, "I observed a custome that is not used in any other country that I saw in my travels… the Italians doe alwaies at their meales use a little forke. The reason of this curiosity is because the Italian cannot by any means indure to have his dish touched with fingers, seeing all men's fingers are not alike clean".

FORNO *Oven*

By extension the word also means the shop attached to the oven (the baker's shop). The word is used for a baker's shop in a small country town or village; in a large town or city it is a panetteria*. Unlike the city panetteria selling bread of all shapes and sizes, the choice of bread in a country forno is limited. In addition to the local bread, which varies from region to region, there will be another two or three popular types and, on certain days, there will be some pizza* and/or focaccia*. In the past the forno was, in effect, the village oven, since the local women, few of whom had an oven of their own, took their cakes, pies stew, jams etc to the forno to be cooked (and to have a gossip). Although many more women now have an oven at home, the practice continues, partly for reason of economy (the baker's oven is always hot, and it's large) and partly because a wood oven cooks so much better than a domestic one.

As a method of cooking, baking is far less common in Italy than in northern Europe, and not many traditional recipes (cakes, biscuits/cookies and bread apart) use this method. Meat, for instance, is usually pot-roasted on the hob (stovetop).

FORMATO *Pasta shapes*

In a culinary context "formati" refers to the various shapes of pasta*.

FRANTOIO *An olive press*

This is where the olives are pressed, and olive oil is made. In more remote places a frantoio may be a small, one-room affair, while in larger olive-growing centres the frantoio is a sizeable commercial plant with a large output, some of which is exported. They are interesting places, and visitors are usually welcome. There are frantoi all over Italy, especially in Tuscany, Umbria and Puglia.

FRIGGERE *To fry*

A common method of cooking in Italy. Friggere always implies fast cooking in hot oil, butter or other type of solid fat, or a combination of these. The amount of frying fat used can vary, from about 0.5-1 cm/¼-½ in deep for shallow frying to 5 cm/2 in for deep-frying. The latter is used for preparing fritto*.

The frying pan (skillet) is usually an iron one with a long handle, called la padella* dei fritti. The fat used varies according to the region and the type of food. In Lombardy and Piedmont oil or butter and oil are used, while in Rome and Emilia-Romagna strutto* is the favourite fat. Oil is also used in Liguria, as it is in Naples, where they also use sugna*, this being melted pig's back fat traditionally preserved in pig's bladders. For health reasons, strutto and sugna are being replaced by vegetable oil, of which olive oil (not necessarily extra virgin) and groundnut (peanut) oil are the most popular.

FRIGGITORIA *A fried food shop*

This is the equivalent of a fish and chip shop, with the difference that a friggitoria sells other fried foods, such as tortelli, vegetables, meatballs etc in addition to fish and chips. In Piedmont, squares of semolina previously cooked in milk, fried and covered with sugar are also on sale, while Rome's speciality is fried salt cod. In Genoa, vegetables such as courgettes (zucchini), cauliflower, artichokes or tomatoes are the best choice in a friggitoria. Naples and Sicily have more friggitorie than any other region, partly owing to the local tradition of eating in the street.

In the past, the food used to be fried in cauldrons at busy street corners in the markets. The American traveller William Wetmore Story, in his book *Roba di Roma*, describes huge cauldrons in the Piazza Navona in the nineteenth century. "…these cauldrons bubble with hissing oil into which chopped vegetables and fritters are dropped and ladled out all golden and garnished with fried pumpkin flowers, upon shining platters."

FRULLATO *Whisked*

The word, which actually means "whisked", is used as a noun in the appellations frullato di frutta or frullato di caffè. These are the drinks made with iced milk, sugar and fruit juices or coffee and whisked until very frothy, in other words, milkshakes. The frullato di fragola (strawberry) is one of the most popular.

FRULLINO *Wooden beater*

A special wooden beater for zabaione and hot chocolate, consisting of a handle with a single or double wheel at the end. The frullino is held between the palms of the hands and twirled backwards and forwards to introduce air into the mixture. Although zabaione is now usually made with an electric beater, the traditional one made with this wooden frullino is less frothy but just as light.

FRUTTIVENDOLO

The greengrocer
One of the most important shop-keepers or stallholders. (Also known as erbivendolo or ortolano.) A good greengrocer will have a large selection of vegetables, which are by and large seasonal. Depending on the season he will have two or three kinds of onions, cabbages, broccoli, artichokes with or without thorns, yellow, red and green (bell) peppers, round tomatoes, oval tomatoes, knobbly (knobby) tomatoes, courgettes (zucchini) two or three varieties of aubergines (eggplant) … and so on.

Fruit is equally plentiful, and mostly seasonal. In recent years a glut of exotic fruits and vegetables has appeared to add prestige to the display, but the Italians are parochial where food is concerned, and they have not really taken to them. They also prefer to buy the fruit and vegetables that are in season, which means that they are almost certainly Italian produce picked at just the right point of ripeness.

Fruit and vegetables are also sold in supermarkets, but a reliable greengrocer is still preferred. He will provide bags for your purchases, he will advise you on the perfection of this or that melon, on the tastiness of the spring straw-berries that have just arrived, or on the best bargains of the day. But that said, the most enjoyable way to buy fruit and vegetables is at a street market.

FUNGHETTO, AL

Literally, "in the mushroom style"
Al funghetto is a method of cooking mushrooms, courgettes (zucchini) and aubergines (eggplant) identical to trifolato†. The expression is used particularly in Liguria.

G

GENOVESE, ALLA
In the style of Genoa
This implies a dish cooked in olive oil and containing pine nuts, herbs and garlic. Salsa alla Genovese, used for boiled fish, is similar to salsa verde* but also contains pine nuts and green olives. Finally there is the well-known pasta Genovese (a kind of sponge cake), which, however, has nothing to do with Genoa since it was created in the nineteenth century by a French chef.

GIRARROSTO
A rotating device for roasting
A device attached to a spit rotating over a fire, for roasting an animal or bird. In the old days, the girarrosto was worked by clockwork or was turned by a mechanism driven by a blindfolded animal walking around and around. Some girarrosti in old country kitchens were set over a large fireplace and operated by the rising heat. Modern girarrosti are set in the oven and worked by electricity.

GOCCIA *A drop*
This is used a lot as a measure. Italians love to give you recipes in which quantities are measured in terms of glasses, handfuls, fingers and drops. Una o due goccie (one or two drops) means a very little, just enough to give the dish a suggestion of another flavour, certainly not identifiable. It does not mean you

must measure the liquid with a drop counter. However, in the case of essences and extracts, una goccia does mean, literally, one drop.

GRATICOLA
A grill (broiler) or a cast-iron pan
Graticola means two things: it is another word for griglia† (grill/broiler), but a graticola is also a ridged cast-iron pan. This latter, however, can also be called a griglia.

GRATTUGIA *A grater*
One of the indispensable tools in any Italian kitchen, the grater is used almost daily. Parmesan cheese is sprinkled on most soups, pasta* and risotti*, and since it is never bought grated, the grattugia must always be to hand. Graters come in a variety of shapes and sizes, although the most common is that made purely for grating cheese, with only one size of hole. Nowadays you can buy electric cheese graters or beautifully designed graters which are put on the table next to a big wedge of Parmesan cheese. Most cooks also have a small grattugia for grating nutmeg and lemon and orange rind.

The grattugia is an ancient utensil. In the Etruscan museum at Chiusi there is a section from a tomb which shows a strainer, a ladle and a grater.

GRIGLIA *A method of cooking*
If food is cooked alla griglia, it is directly exposed to the embers, flames or other source of heat. It is one of the oldest ways of cooking, but was always considered to be a primitive method that did nothing to enhance the flavour of the food. Grilling (broiling) remained unfashionable all through the great cookery periods of the Renaissance up to the twentieth

century. Throughout that period it was deemed suitable only for peasants. Now the pendulum has swung the other way, and all the best restaurants will offer almost everything alla griglia. The point that these restaurants are making is that to be cooked alla griglia the food must be of prime quality, and therefore in keeping with the high standards of their establishment. Grilling is now popular not only in restaurants but also at home, where even in Italy fast food has become a necessity.

Although the food cooked alla griglia is generally meat or fish, vegetables are often grilled, too. Tomatoes, radicchio, aubergines (eggplant) and (bell) peppers are all excellent grilled. Peppers, in particular, lend themselves to grilling as they acquire a burnt taste which enhances their flavour.

The best-known grilled dishes originate from Tuscany, where the prime ingredients of the food are superb, while the cooking traditions are not so elaborate. Famous grilled dishes from this region include bistecca alla fiorentina**, made with a steak from a special breed of cattle, or pollo alla diavola* from the Valdarno, where the best Italian chickens are raised.

GUAZZETTO *A method of cooking*

"In guazzetto" means cooked in a light sauce based on two main ingredients — white wine and tomato. Frogs, seafood, fish or baccalà* are all cooked in guazzetto. The original recipe is for frogs, and it comes from south Lombardy, the area around Pavia where frogs abound. They are sautéed in a soffritto* of olive oil, chopped onion, celery and garlic. Splashed with white wine, the sauce is bound with a little flour and flavoured at the end with plenty of fresh parsley.

I

IMBOTTIRE *To stuff*

This term is used mainly in connection with (bell) peppers, bread rolls and focacce*. The recipes for peppers are nearly all from Rome and Naples, where they are meaty, with lots of flesh. The peppers are first burnt over a direct flame and peeled. Being a peasant dish, there is no definitive recipe for the stuffing. The usual ingredients are breadcrumbs (soft or dried), olives, capers, sultanas (golden raisins), anchovy fillets and parsley. An alternative stuffing is fried aubergine (eggplant) cubes and tomatoes. The peppers, sometimes topped with a tomato sauce if this is not already in the stuffing, are then baked.

A panino imbottito is a large snack eaten in a bar. The bread is white and soft and is either round or oval. The filling, often an assortment of ingredients, depends on the creativity of the chef. Focaccia is usually filled with a dry stuffing, such as prosciutto*.

IMPANARE

To coat with dried breadcrumbs

The word comes from pane (bread). It is the method for making a cotoletta*, which can be meat, vegetable or fish. The slice of food is first coated in egg and then impanato (breaded). The food is then fried or, less frequently, grilled (broiled) or cooked in the oven. The breadcrumbs protect the food, keeping it moist, and form a crust. The "impanatura" often contains a little grated Parmesan cheese in the proportion of one part of Parmesan to four of breadcrumbs.

IMPASTARE *To knead*
A verb incorporating the word "pasta", which is the key to the action. As well as the meaning of the word pasta that has become part of the English language, pasta in Italian means any kind of dough, from bread dough to puff pastry.

INGLESE, ALL' *In the English style*
Food dressed simply with butter. It applies mainly to boiled rice, pasta* and some vegetables. However, being an Italian adaptation of a foreign recipe, a generous amount of grated Parmesan is added for good measure.

INSACCATO *To stuff*
A generic name for all kinds of salami* and sausages. The word comes from sacco (bag) and means, literally, bagged. The bag in this instance is the casing for the meat and spices, which can be natural or synthetic.

INSAPORIRE *To make more tasty*
The word means to enhance the flavour of a dish during its preparation. This process plays an essential role in achieving the real Italian flavour. The word is used when the main ingredient of a dish is sautéed in an aromatic soffritto*. It is a stage in the preparation of a dish that should never be skimped, since it is the only way to give the right flavour to the finished dish.

L

LARDELLARE *To lard*
Large cuts of meat are often larded in Italian cooking (strips of fatty meat or fat are threaded through the meat to keep it moist as it cooks). This is because the cut of meat is lean, with very little, if any, fat, and also because it is cooked on the hob (stovetop), as with a pot-roast, which tends to dry the inside of the meat. Some meats are larded with a mixture of chopped pancetta*, herbs, salt and pepper, others with long pieces of carrot and celery, as well as strips of prosciutto*. A larding needle is used to insert the strips of fat into the meat. Larding not only gives moisture and flavour to the meat, it also makes it look attractive when sliced.

LECCARDA *A type of pan*
Also called ghiotta, a leccarda is a pan, rectangular or oval in shape, with a long handle. It is placed under the spit to collect the juices of the roasting meat, the juices being used to baste the meat.

LESSARE
A method of cokking meat, fish or vegetables in gently simmering water. See bollire†.

LESSO *Boiled*
As an adjective, lesso describes how the food is cooked. Pesce lesso is boiled fish, verdure lesse are boiled vegetables, patate lesse are boiled potatoes etc. As a

noun, it has a similar meaning to bollito, but it usually refers to a dish made with only one piece of meat. The Lombard lesso is possibly the best known; it is a piece of beef, usually boned, cooked in simmering water containing an onion stuck with one or two cloves, a celery stalk, a carrot and some parsley stalks. The carved meat is served moistened with its own stock and accompanied by boiled potatoes and carrots. Salsa verde* and mostarda* di frutta are the most common accompanying sauces.

LISTA *Menu*

Its full name is lista delle vivande, to distinguish it from the lista dei vini – the wine list. The lista does not have the same importance in Italian restaurants as in those of many other countries. In small restaurants or trattorias you are often not given one. Instead the waiter will tell you, often in a bored monotone, what there is to eat. You should not be put off by the absence of a written menu, as this is certainly no indication of inadequacy in the meal to follow. Menus are only written in Italian, even in the smartest restaurants, the Italians never having recognized the superiority of French gastronomy.

M

MACELLERIA *Butcher's shop*

This is usually the cleanest shop you will come across. In a city the window will have the meat beautifully displayed and arranged from palest pink to deepest crimson. The country shop usually has no window display. You walk in and there, on a higher level and behind a high counter stands the butcher in all his glory, deftly slicing the meat and at the same time preaching, chatting, advising the throng of local women waiting to be served.

Buying meat in an Italian village is a fascinating and educational experience, as long as you're not in a hurry. The piece is cut, cleaned, chopped or minced (ground) according to the most detailed specification. Italian housewives, always demanding, are particularly fussy when buying meat, a purchase that is expensive and over which much time and care must be spent.

MACINARE *To mince, grind or crush*

The most common use of the word, in a domestic context, relates to meat. Carne macinata is the mince (ground meat) obtained by putting the meat through the mincer (grinder), rather than by chopping it on a board; the meat is therefore minced small and uniformly. Meats, chicken, ham, salami* etc are all macinati to make polpette* and polpettoni* ripieni* and ragù*. Given the creativity and the thriftiness of

Italian housewives, leftovers and meats are often macinate to produce a completely new dish, rather than just being served up cold the next day.

A hand-cranked machine for mincing grinds the meat without reducing it to a pulp as electric machines do, which is why such a machine is still found in most Italian kitchens. Another popular gadget is the macinino del caffè (coffee grinder). It used to be a lovely wooden device with a drawer and an iron handle. Now it is a noisy electric affair which, however, takes a quarter of the time, and no effort.

MAGRO *Lean*
In culinary terms the word is applied to any lean meat, or food made from it. Magro also means meatless when applied to a dish for fast days, or indeed to the day itself, as with Ash Wednesday or Good Friday. Ravioli* di magro, for instance, are ravioli stuffed with spinach and ricotta* rather than meat, and brodo di magro* is stock made only with vegetables. Although there are a great many recipes for dishes "di magro" in old cookery books, the expression is little used nowadays because religious traditions are less frequently observed.

MANTECARE
To pound into a paste
The word comes from the Spanish "manteca" (fat). It means to pound into a paste, usually with butter, in the making of buttercreams (frosting) or ice creams. The word is also used in connection with many risotti* when butter and Parmesan are added at the end to make them creamy. The other dish that is mantecato is baccalà* (salt cod) a speciality of Venice (see Stoccafisso).

MARINARA, ALLA
In the sailor's style
This does not, in fact, refer to any particular combination of ingredients or method of cooking. Thus there is spaghetti* or vermicelli* alla marinara, with oil, garlic and, sometimes, chilli, or with a tomato sauce. The only proper recipe "alla marinara" is for pizza*, which is topped with tomatoes, garlic and oregano.

MARINATA *Marinade*
A mixture of ingredients, mostly liquid, in which meat or fish is steeped for a length of time. This can achieve several results, such as tenderizing or adding flavour, according to the marinade and the food in question.

A piece of beef is marinated to tenderize it, but also to add flavour. The marinade is usually red wine, to which onion, celery, herbs and other flavourings are added, the beef afterwards being braised or stewed. Boar, venison and hare are always marinated in wine to which some olive oil has been added. The same is done with kid and mutton. Pork is placed in a marinade of white wine or wine vinegar, plus the usual herbs and flavourings, to make it less rubbery, prior to cooking it in some special way, such as for maiale al latte**. Some Milanese cooks marinate veal cutlets in milk for costolette alla Milanese**, so as to make the veal whiter and more delicate.

An interesting Tuscan recipe for guinea fowl calls for the bird to be cut into pieces, fried in oil and then marinated in white wine, herbs and lemon juice for a few hours. Finally the guinea fowl cooks slowly in the marinade. Prepared in this way, a guinea fowl or chicken, which can otherwise be dry, remains moist and juicy. Fresh fillets of anchovies are marinated in lemon juice or wine vinegar for at least one day before being eaten raw.

MATTARELLO or MATTERELLO

Rolling pin

There are two kinds of this wooden tool in Italy; one is the short thick one which can also be found in kitchens in Britain and the United States and is used for pastry and biscuits (cookies). The other is a typical Italian tool. It is a stick made of smooth, well-sanded wood, about 80 cm/32 in long and 3.5 cm/1¼ in thick. It does not have handles, like the short one, but it sometimes has a knob at one end which is used for carrying it, with dough rolled round it, to a place where the dough is unrolled to dry out.

The longer rolling pin must have been in use in pre-Roman kitchens, as it is depicted in a bas-relief in a tomb of an Etruscan necropolis north of Rome, together with other tools for making pasta*. Centuries later it appears in an illustration in the sixteenth-century book by Bartolomeo Scappi, in which two men are working on thinning the pasta dough. One man is rolling out the round of dough, while the other is pressing it down so as to stretch it out as thinly as possible.

MENÙ *Menu*

Also referred to as the lista† delle vivande. If you happen to come across an old menù you will be amazed by the voracity of our ancestors. In *Il Cuoco Piemontese Perfezionato a Parigi*, written by an anonymous chef in the eighteenth century, a menu lists five "services" that were displayed on the table (the Russian service, with one course at a time, was not yet in use), each with at least five different dishes. And there were only 15 guests! In the nineteenth century, a dinner served à la Russe, given by the Italian Royal House, spanned at least eight courses, most of them made up of many parts. It consisted of two soups, two relevés, three entrées, two vegetables, a rest in the middle with some hors-d'oeuvres of prosciutto* and salami*, then on to the roasts of pheasant and snipe with truffles, and finishing with bavarois of peaches and pistachio, jelly of Alchermes liqueur, vanilla ice cream and apricot nougat! Even up to the First World War, dinners were gargantuan. Denti di Pirajno gives a menu for a dinner that took place in Venice in 1912 which consisted of twelve substantial courses. There are still those who can consume massive meals. I have it on good authority that in Puglia in 1977 members of the Accademia Italiana della Cucina managed to taste their way through 54 courses!

Nowadays, restaurants denote meals offered at different prices by describing them as the Menù this, that or the other. The cheapest is the Menù Turistico (especially for tourists), while the most expensive, and hopefully the best, is the Menù Gastronomico. In the most fashionable restaurants, where the chef is ready to express and promote his art, there is a new type of menu known as the Menù Degustazione.

MERENDA *Snack*

"The tray was piled high — tartine* with anchovy butter, smoked salmon, caviare, pâté de fois gras, prosciutto*, small vol-au-vents filled with minced (ground) chicken and béchamel**. On the trolley, jugs (pitchers), pots, glasses and mugs. And inside the china and pewter pots there was tea, milk, coffee;

in the jugs, lemonade and fruit juice." This sumptuous spread was the pre-War tea-time merenda that the privileged Finzi Contini children enjoyed on a summer afternoon, as described in *The Garden of the Finzi Contini* by G Bassano.

Merenda is eaten by all children, and by grown-ups too, but nowadays a spread such as that described above would appear only at a very grand party. Today's merenda for children might include crisps (potato chips), as well as focaccia* and a selection of miscellaneous snacks.

Country labourers refer to any sort of snack, taken at any time of day, as merenda. It usually consists of bread with some sort of salume* or cheese, and this merenda is frequently taken mid-morning, washed down by red wine. No one drink, however, is particularly connected with merenda.

MEZZALUNA
Literally, "half moon"
A knife with a crescent-shaped blade and a handle at each end, used for chopping. The curved shape of the mezzaluna makes it possible to chop by rolling the blade from left to right and back, without lifting it off the work surface. This makes it easy to control the fineness and uniformity of the chopped mixture.

MILANESE, ALLA
In the Milanese style
The expression does not apply to a particular method of cooking or to the use of special ingredients, but rather to food that is cooked according to an original Milanese recipe. That said, there is one common element in all cooking alla Milanese, and that is the use of butter as the cooking fat. There is risotto alla Milanese**, which is made with saffron, minestrone* alla Milanese, made with rice and pork rind or pancetta*, and costoletta alla Milanese**, when the cutlet is coated with egg and bread-crumbs and fried in butter. Asparagus** or leeks alla Milanese are served with butter and fried eggs.

MORTAIO E PESTELLO
Mortar and pestle
The pestle and mortar should be found in any respectable Italian kitchen. They are used for pounding herbs, anchovies, walnuts, pine nuts, peppercorns, juniper berries etc, in fact small quantities of any food that would be spoilt by using a food processor. In a mortar the food is bruised rather than chopped, thus squeezing out the juices and releasing more of the flavour.

norcini are employed on large farms to make the salami*, prosciutti*, coppe* and capocolli* that are then sent for sale to the norcinerie.

NAPOLETANA, ALLA
In the style of Naples
An expression which brings to mind gutsy tomato sauces, mozzarella*, garlic and oil. But in fact alla Napoletana is not a method that can be applied to different dishes, rather it describes the way a particular dish is made in Naples. Thus lasagne alla Napoletana is a rich lasagne dish made in Naples at carnival time. The lasagne are layered with mozzarella, ricotta*, tiny fried meat-balls and local sausages. Another example is minestrone alla Napoletana. This is similar to other minestroni, but it contains local pumpkin. The most famous dish alla Napoletana is the pizza – the topping is always made of tomatoes plus other ingredients.

NORCINERIA
A pork butcher's shop
A norcino (the name used in central Italy) is a pork butcher who slaughters the pig and produces various pork products. The norcineria is the pork butcher's shop. The origin of these words lies in the fact that the best pork butchers used to come from Norcia, a town in Umbria. The norcini carried on their migratory life until the Second World War. Nowadays some norcini practise their profession locally by going to various farms and villages to help with the killing of the pig. But pig raising is big business now, and most

O

P

ONDA, ALL' *Literally "wavy"*

All'onda, is an expression used in northern Italy to describe the ideal consistency of risotto*. It means creamily bound together; neither too liquid nor too dry.

OSTERIA *Inn*

An osteria is a place where men gather, and where women are not welcome. I do not recall ever having seen a local woman in a real old-fashioned osteria. Nowadays osterie are only found in small towns and villages. During the day their customers consist mainly of old men who sit there on their own in silence, staring into space, or who play scopa (a card game). In the evening younger men drop in and the atmosphere becomes more lively and noisier. Traditionally, wine is drunk. Simple local dishes are served, or bread rolls filled with salami*, or whatever else happens to be to hand. Sadly, the real osteria is dying out everywhere and is being replaced by the bar, with its pizzas* and panini*.

OVINI

Collective name for all sheep, kids and goats
A comprehensive word referring to baby lamb, lamb, mutton, castrated young mutton and kid.

PADELLA *Frying pan (skillet)*

The frying pan is an important part of the equipment of any Italian kitchen. In padella or spadellato is a way of cooking where the food is first sautéed and then finished off at a lower temperature, with the optional addition of some liquid. In many recipes for pasta*, the pasta, when drained, is finished off in the padella in which the sauce has been cooked. It is a traditional method for cooking many southern pasta dishes which have now become popular all over Italy.

PAESANA, ALLA

Cooked the peasant's way
The expression has no precise meaning, but it conveys rusticity and tradition. The ingredients used in a dish "alla paesana" are – or should be – locally grown or reared. One well-known dish that uses this epithet is risotto alla paesana** (a risotto with vegetables).

PAIOLO

A pot in which to cook polenta
This is the unlined copper pan in which polenta* is made. It is shaped like a large, round-bottomed bucket (pail) with a bucket handle. A paiolo is still a common fixture in most kitchens in Italy. It certainly can be found in all country kitchens in northern Italy, where it hangs over the fire in winter and is used almost every day for polenta.

A paiolo is a beautiful object, so beautiful in fact that a group of artists took it as their emblem and founded La Compagnia del Paiolo in the late fifteenth century. The members of the compagnia, of whom the painter Andrea del Sarto was one, gathered regularly to celebrate their mutual interests, chief among which, it seems, were the pleasures of the table.

An electric paiolo is now available – and very popular it is too, because its constantly revolving paddle relieves the cook of the work of mixing.

PANETTERIA *Baker's shop*
Panetterie have changed radically in recent times. While previously a panetteria was just an ordinary shop selling bread, focaccia* and some pasta, the new image of a panetteria in most towns is that of a "designer" shop, with shelf upon shelf filled with the most appetizing and appealing bread, as well as focaccia, pizze*, brioches, tarts, ravioli*, tagliatelle* etc. The windows of the smartest panetterie have elaborate and delightful displays of castles, farms and palaces – all made of bread.

When you enter the shop the all-pervading smell is so exquisite that it is impossible to buy only the bread you went in to buy. In the bread section alone the choice is bewildering: there is specialized bread from most regions, bread in every shape, colour and size, bread sprinkled with cumin or caraway seeds or studded with sultanas (golden raisins) or olives, all freshly baked at the back of the shop and quite irresistible.

PARMIGIANA, ALLA
"The way it is made in Parma"
This suggests a dish that contains Parmesan and possibly prosciutto*. Costolette* alla Parmigiana, for instance,

are breaded veal chops which are fried in butter and then simmered, with plenty of Parmesan flakes, in a little stock. Some recipes include slices of prosciutto between the veal.

PASSATO *Creamed or strained*
The word usually refers to vegetables, with a consistency halfway between a purée and a cream. The best-known passato is that of tomatoes, which now is simply called "passata*". A passato is usually made by pushing the food through a food mill or a sieve (strainer) or, less perfectly homogenous, in a food processor.

PASTASCIUTTA
Drained pasta
A slightly old-fashioned word for what is now usually called, simply, pasta*. The word pastasciutta is used to distinguish pasta served on its own, with a sauce, from pasta in brodo* (in stock). This distinction was more necessary when pasta in brodo was a common everyday dish, which it no longer is.

PASTICCERIA
Pastries, cakes and cake shop
The collective word for pastries and cakes and also the word for the shop where they are sold. Pasticcerie are always open on Sundays, and it is after church on Sunday that, traditionally, an Italian family buys pastries or cakes.

PASTICCIATA *A polenta dish*
A word used to describe polenta*. Polenta pasticciata** is a baked dish, usually made with leftover polenta cut into slices and layered either with a meat ragù* and/or with béchamel** and cheeses or mushroom and ham. It is a very common dish in northern Italy.

PASTO *Meal*

There are only two meals in Italy these days, lunch and dinner, and at these meals the family usually sits around the table together. Breakfast is hardly a meal as such, most of the time consisting of a cup of coffee and a biscuit (cookie) or two taken in solitary silence, or perhaps at a bar on the way to work. Children have caffè e latte* (coffee and milk) with bread, focaccia* or other bread-based snacks. Working people (except in large cities) and school-children go home for their lunch to enjoy together a plate of pasta, still the most common dish at midday.

The evening meal, often the lighter of the two, again finds the family around the table. The young are usually there too, often rushing out straight afterwards to meet friends for the cinema and then a burghi (hamburger) or a pizza*. Meals are not often taken in a restaurant even by the young, who soon realize that it is far cheaper, and often far better, to eat mamma's food.

The time of these two meals varies. In the north lunch is between midday and 1pm, while in the south, and especially in Rome, nobody sits down to lunch before 2pm, or to dinner before 9–9.30pm.

PENTOLA *Cylindrical saucepan*

A cylindrical pan used mainly for boiling, for some kinds of stewing and for making soups, in other words for cooking food in liquid. Italians are, rightly, fussy about their pots and pans and know how important it is to use the right sized pan made from the right material for the success of a dish. For instance, the pot for a risotto* must be large and deep with a round bottom, so that the mixing spoon can easily reach everywhere. The best metal for it is stainless steel with a copper bottom or heavy aluminium (aluminum).

A pentola's diameter is the same as its height. But a pentola for pasta is taller, and does not need to be heavy. A respectable family would have at least two, one for cooking pasta to serve up to four people and a large one into which 1kg/2¼ lb of pasta can be properly cooked.

All pentole have two handles or, more rarely, a bucket-type (pail-type) handle as in a paiolo†. This is a legacy of the past when the pot was hung on a hook over the fire.

PESCATORE, ALLA
Fish and tomato sauce

A name given to a sauce for pasta or rice containing some fresh fish in a tomato sauce.

PIATTO *Plate, dish or course*

You can have a primo piatto and a secondo piatto (first and second courses), more often than not referred to simply as the primo* and secondo. When vegetables are served separately from the meat this is regarded as another piatto, since it comes on a different dish.

The usual number of courses is two, with dessert or cheese and fruit to follow. But today a meal can consist of a piatto unico (one-course meal), followed by cheese and fruit. Each course is served on a large dish which is placed on the table, so that people help themselves. The practice of serving food on individual plates is considered suitable only for restaurants, not for homes.

PIZZICHERIA *A delicatessen*

A shop which sells every kind of salume*, cheeses, canned goods etc as well as a variety of mouth-watering prepared dishes. Another name for it is salumeria†.

PIETANZA *A second course*
This usually means a second course, ie the course that follows a soup, pasta* or risotto*.

POLPA *A piece of meat*
A general term for a piece of boned beef or veal, not necessarily a particular cut, but one that can be used for slicing thinly, for braising, stewing etc. The word polpa would never refer to a top quality cut such as fillet.

Polpa also means pulp, whether of tomatoes, aubergines (eggplant) or peaches, as well as the flesh of fish, seafood or crustaceans.

POTACCHIO *A sauce from Marche*
"In potacchio" is a sauce from Marche. Chicken or rabbit portions or cut-up lamb is sautéed in olive oil with onion and garlic, then cooked in thick tomato sauce and wine. A handful of chopped fresh rosemary is added about 30 minutes before serving.

PRANZO *The midday meal*
Pranzo means lunch, although some northerners might refer to the evening meal as pranzo, which was indeed the common practice until the 1960s. Rather confusing! Pranzo is eaten at home by families with young children (who come home from school to do so), and by everyone in the country or in smaller towns. In cities people have the midday meal at a restaurant near their work or in the company canteen.

While in the old days lunch was the main meal of the day, lately more and more Italians tend to have a quick, light lunch and to eat a proper meal in the evening. On Sundays, however, especially in the country and in the provinces, the midday meal is eaten at restaurants with all the family — from grandparents to babies.

PRIMIZIA *Early crops*
A word used to describe the early crop of fruit and vegetables when, at the beginning of their respective seasons, they first appear on the market. Primizie were more in evidence, and much more of a real treat, in the past when the produce in the shops was all locally grown, and thus only to be found in its real season.

PRIMO *The first course of a meal*
Short for primo piatto. The primi are the strength of Italian cooking, to the extent that many have been adopted by foreign cuisines and made into secondi† (second courses). Traditionally speaking, primi consist of all the different soups, pasta*, risotti*, gnocchi* and such like. Nowadays, when a meal is seldom more than three courses, some dishes that were once part of the antipasto* are occasionally served as primi.

PUREA *Pureé*
This is an italianization of the French word purée, meaning a pulp usually of vegetables reduced to a smooth cream. It is used mainly for potatoes, but many writers, myself included, prefer to use the French word which, in Italian usage, is sometimes spelt puré.

R

RIGAGLIE *Giblets*

A bird's liver, heart, stomach, unlaid eggs and cocks comb are all rigaglie. A light ragù* can be made with rigaglie, or tasty sauces such as the Piedmontese finanziera* for sformati* or risotti*.

RIPASSARE

Sautéeing cooked vegetables

A term for sautéeing previously boiled vegetables, a common procedure, especially for Swiss chard, spinach and other greens.

RIPIENO *Stuffing or filling*

This also applies to the food that is stuffed. Italians are masters of this art; suffice it to mention the endless varieties of stuffed pasta*, all traditional. Any cucina povera (poor cuisine) excels in creating this type of dish because of the need to make use of leftovers.

Aubergines (eggplant), courgettes (zucchini), (bell) peppers, tomatoes and onions are often stuffed, as are courgette flowers, mushroom caps, leeks and cabbage. Each vegetable is filled with suitable ingredients and then baked, stewed or occasionally, as in the case of courgette flowers, fried.

Fish comes stuffed, too. The grandest recipe is for branzino* stuffed with seafood, while the simplest recipe is for sardines stuffed with breadcrumbs, parsley and garlic.

There are some stuffed desserts too, like pesche ripiene alla Piemontese** and the large dried figs of Calabria stuffed with hazelnuts, candied orange peel and honey, then baked. A tremendous delicacy.

Stuffed food makes a most satisfying dish for the creative cook, who is able to successfully combine different tastes and textures.

ROSOLARE *To sauté*

A common method of cooking in Italy. When the battuto† (chopped mixture) is put on the heat with some butter and/or oil, it is rosolato to make a soffrito†, the starting point for most Italian dishes.

ROTOLO *A roll*

This usually refers to a pasta dish. A sheet of pasta is rolled out thinly and stuffed with Swiss chard, ricotta* and Parmesan, to which prosciutto*, mushrooms etc may be added. The pasta sheet is rolled up, wrapped in a cloth and then cooked for 30 minutes in boiling water.

The dough can also be a potato dough, like that for potato gnocchi* **.

Rotolo can refer to a meat roll: a thin slice of meat (preferably veal) is covered with other ingredients such as prosciutto*, thin frittata*, cheese etc and, when rolled and tied, is cooked in butter and wine.

S

SALMÌ *A cooking method*

A method of preparing game, both furred and feathered, similar to civet in France and jugged in Britain. Numerous spices are an integral part of a salmì, and grated chocolate is sometimes added to enhance the flavour and darken the sauce. Whatever the game, polenta is *the* accompaniment.

SALUMERIA *Delicatessen*

Known as pizzicheria† in southern Italy, this shop sells every kind of salumi*, cheeses, canned goods etc. In addition, it also offers an extensive variety of prepared dishes.

SCOTTARE *or* SBOLLENTARE *To blanch*

To blanch in salted and/or acidulated water (water with lemon juice). Less frequently scottare means to fry in very hot fat just long enough to form a thin crust on the food.

SECONDO *The second course*

The second course of a meal usually consists of a dish of meat or fish. In a lighter meal, a secondo can be vegetables or a frittata*.

SOFFRITTO *A cookery base*

This word crops up in Italian recipes more often than any other, for the simple reason that a soffritto is the starting point for innumerable dishes.

A soffritto normally consists of onion, celery plus sometimes carrot and garlic, a handful of herbs (such as parsley, sage, rosemary or others) and maybe a small piece of pancetta*, all finely chopped and gently sautéed in oil and/or butter until just beginning to colour. When the soffritto is ready, the meat, fish or vegetables are mixed in.

The word soffritto comes from sotto friggere (to under-fry), that is to fry very gently.

SOTT' OLIO
A method of preserving food in oil

This method is mainly used for vegetables, but pecorini* and some other fresh cheeses are also preserved in this way.

SOBBOLLIRE *To simmer gently*

To simmer so gently that bubbles only occasionally break the surface. This kind of very slow cooking is essential for many traditional dishes, including stock, bean and other soups, all stews and ragù*.

SORBETTIERA
An ice cream maker

This electric machine is also called a gelatiera*. More households used to have a sorbettiera in the past than now, when most people buy their sorbets and ice creams from the shops which advertise "produzione propria" which means that the products are made on the premises.

SPREMUTA *Pure fruit juice*

The two classic fruit juices, or spremute, are orange and lemon. While a sugo di frutta may be diluted, a spremuta is always pure juice. Spremuta is a drink, whereas the juice of a lemon or orange used in cooking is referred to as sugo*.

SPUNTINO
A light snack

A relatively modern word referring to a bite to eat that can be enjoyed at any time of the day. It can be anything from a piece of focaccia*, a mini-pizza, a sandwich or a piece of cake or even some fruit.

STRACOTTO
Literally, "extra-cooked"

This term refers to the dish as well as to the method of cooking. Stracotto is a popular braised beef dish of northern and central Italy, which differs from the other similar dishes, stufato* and brasato* in that the meat is not marinated in wine, the wine being added to the meat during the cooking.

Unfortunately, as is so often the case with Italian gastronomy, all is not quite as organized as it should be, and cookery writers use each of the three names in a loose way.

In a traditional stracotto from Emilia, the larded piece of beef is spiced with cloves and nutmeg. In Tuscany these spices are replaced by rosemary and other fresh herbs, and the stracotto is cooked in oil, thus being more in tune with the lighter local cuisine. The Tuscan wine used is lighter than the full-bodied Piedmontese one, fresh tomatoes are preferred to the tomato purée of the north and garlic is used much more generously.

STRASCINARE
To sauté blanched vegetables

A method of cooking favoured in central and southern Italy and used for green vegetables such as spinach, beet, chicory, turnip tops and broccoli. The blanched vegetables are quickly sautéed in oil, flavoured with garlic and sometimes chilli, by being strascinati (dragged) across the bottom of the pan.

STUFATO *A method of slow cooking*

A dish as well as a method of cooking meat. The meat, which can be one large cut or small pieces, is first marinated with all different flavourings in red wine and then is cooked in a covered container in the marinade for several hours. It is usually cooked on the hob (stovetop), not in the oven, so that more wine can be added gradually when needed. The end result must be meat that is pervaded by the taste of its rich sauce, and tender and juicy enough to explain the Milanese saying "El stua besogna mangiall con el cugiaa" (stew should be eaten with a spoon).

In northern Italy a stufato of beef in a single piece is often the Sunday dish in the winter, and in a locality north of Milan it assumes a festive role when it is cooked for the wedding dinner. A good stufato bodes well for a marriage.

Stufato can also be a dish made with vegetables which are braised in stock, milk or tomato sauce. In Tuscany there is a stufato di fave (broad/fava beans), in which the beans are cooked slowly in an earthenware pot on a bed of chopped pancetta*, oil, garlic and onion, moistened with meat stock. But the archetype of a stufato of vegetables is that from Basilicata, which is halfway between a thick soup and a vegetable dish. Onion, wedges of artichoke, potato, broad beans and diced pancetta are stewed in stock in an earthenware pot for several hours. At the end the pot is placed uncovered on a high heat to evaporate the extra liquid.

T

TAVOLA CALDA and TAVOLA FREDDA

Literally "hot table" and "cold table"

Tavola calda is a type of self-service establishment of recent origin, where hot dishes are served. There is now a tavola fredda where you can eat simple cold dishes and salads. These eateries are quite popular everywhere for a quick and reasonably priced meal with few gastronomic pretensions.

TEGAME *Shallow saucepan*

A shallow saucepan with straight sides and two "ear" handles. A tegame is one of the fixtures of any Italian kitchen because of its versatility. It is used for frying, sautéeing, for braising vegetables and for making frittata*.

A small tegame is called a tegamino and is used for the cooking and presentation of food directly to the table. A classic use of a tegamino is for frying eggs.

TEGLIA

A square or rectangular oven pan

In Puglia the local word for this type of oven pan is tiella*, and this is the name given both to the baking dish and to the special layered preparations that are baked in it.

TERRAGLIA *An earthenware dish*

Pots made of this material are widely used for soups, stews and all dishes which used a lengthy and very slow cooking. Usually these dishes are made with heatproof earthenware which means that they can first be set on direct heat and then, if necessary, be placed in the oven.

TIMBALLO *A type of mould*

A mould, as high as it is wide. The word also applies to the dish made in such a mould, consisting of a baked dish sometimes in a pastry case (shell). A timballo can be made with pasta or rice, dressed with meaty sauces or layered with vegetables. The most elegant timballo di riso consists of a thick outer casing of rice containing a rich ragù* of chicken livers, mushrooms etc.

TRIFOLARE *A method of cooking*

A method of cooking certain vegetables, such as mushrooms, courgettes (zucchini), aubergines (eggplant) and Jerusalem artichokes. The sliced vegetables are sautéed in olive oil, garlic and parsley; these are the basic elements to which anchovies, capers and wine may be added. In Liguria this method of cooking is called al funghetto. Oddly enough, only one meat dish shares the name and method: rognoni (kidneys) trifolati**.

TRITO *A mixture of chopped vegetables*

A chopped-up mixture, usually consisting of herbs, garlic, onion, celery and carrot, or any combination of these. A battuto* is similar, except that it should contain pancetta* or pork back fat, which a trito should not. A trito, or a battuto, is the basis of a soffritto* †, or it can be added "a crudo"† (just as it is) to dishes, soups or sauces.

U   V

UMIDO *To stew slowly*

To cook in umido is to stew very slowly in a small amount of liquid. This liquid is usually a tomato sauce, often with the addition of wine, a demi-glace or any concentrated meat juice. The food cooked in umido is generally meat which should "stew in its own juice", with a little extra liquid being added if necessary. By the end of the long cooking the juice should be dark and thick. Artusi(wrote: "Umidi are the dishes which generally are more appetizing, therefore it is appropriate to give them special care, so that they will be more delicate, will taste good and be easy to digest".

Spezzatini*, brasati* and stufati* are all part of the family of umidi. Each is made slightly differently, but the principle of slow cooking in a small amount of liquid is the same.

The fish that are most usually cooked in umido are stockfish and salt cod, in other words fish that must be cooked at length. Steaks from a large fish such as grouper or swordfish are also prepared in this way, as are the cephalopods. This method is also used for vegetables that are cooked at length in a tomato sauce (see recipe for Patate in Umido on page 146).

VAPORE A *Steam cooking*

A method of cooking that has recently become very popular for health reasons. The steamed food is usually dressed with best olive oil, but sometimes it can be flavoured with a light sauce or melted butter and cheese.

VENEZIANA, ALLA
Cooked the Venetian way

Although it might sound evocative, no specific method is implied with this term. The best-known dishes are fegato* (liver) alla Veneziana** and baccalà* alla Veneziana (see Stocafisso). The latter is similar to the Provençal brandade de morue.

Italy
Land of
Vines

The Origins

ALTHOUGH THERE IS EVIDENCE that some form of viticulture and winemaking was practised in Italy long before their arrival, it seems likely that the Greeks taught the local inhabitants this art.

In ancient times wine was almost universally considered a gift of the gods: the Greeks attributed it to Dionysus, the Indians to Soma, the Egyptians to Osiris and the Jews thought it contributed to stability and civilization.

Although we know that all this started as early as some 4000 years before the birth of Christ, it is difficult to establish the origin of the vine. The Bible tells us that, having ended up on Mount Ararat with the ark, Noah started to cultivate it. Vines and wine were considered to be symbols of prosperity and freedom in the Old Testament, while in the New Testament wine became mystically symbolic as Jesus offered it to his disciples as his blood, claiming himself to be the true vine.

The most active wine merchants in antiquity were the Phoenicians who shipped wine to Black Sea and Mediterranean ports, but it was the Greeks who, having occupied the southern part of Italy, known as Magna Graecia, made the most of the fertile terrain and favourable micro-climates to grow the vine. They were soon shipping wine back to Greece and it is said that one such wine, Cirò, was traditionally presented to the winners of the Olympic Games.

As for the rest of the country north of Naples, it seems that proper viticultural practices were introduced by the Etruscans, who settled there from the east around 700 BC Consequently the whole of the peninsula was soon covered with vineyards and became known as Enotria Tellus (land of vines).

When the Romans appeared on the scene some four centuries later, oenological practices were intensified and wherever the Roman legions went, so did the vine: the Romans introduced viticulture to Gaul and to Britain. In those days, wine was aged for long periods before drinking; indeed Cicero claims that he, and others, most enjoyed wines a century old. Originally, Roman women were not allowed to drink wine, as the commodity was often limited. In fact, by 92BC the Emperor Domitian was forced to restrict the cultivation of vines because their popularity was affecting the amount of wheat grown, which was much more important for the subsistence of his people.

THE POST-ROMAN ERA AND THE RENAISSANCE

AFTER THE ROMANS, viticulture suffered in Italy, particularly during the Middle Ages, when the local population was heavily engaged in fighting the invading barbarians, or running away from them. But there were some exceptions to that rule, perhaps the most outstanding example being that of Theodoric, king of the Goths, who, according to Cassiodorus, his historian, punished those who damaged the few remaining vineyards. Needless to say he greatly appreciated wine, especially that known as Acinatico, believed to be the predecessor of our present day Recioto•, a wine produced near Verona.

Apparently Charles the Great had a similar attitude towards hooligans damaging vines, whom he punished with heavy fines. But it wasn't until the fifteenth century or thereabouts that the cultivation of the vine came back into fashion as part of the revival of agriculture as a whole.

By the end of the sixteenth century wine had become extremely popular, and thus important commercially and, some 150 years later, the first agricultural academies were set up in the north of the country in Brescia, Conegliano, Veneto and Treviso, where studies included viticulture and oenology.

Soon, aristocrats and businessmen realized the business potential of wine and started to acquire land to plant vines. Under the supervision of skilled oenologists, they were soon producing enough wine even for export to remote places. But, by the late nineteenth century, phylloxera, a disease that wipes out vines, hit Europe, and Italian vineyards did not escape – they suffered the consequences until it was discovered that grafting vines onto American rootstocks would solve the problem. Production soon recovered and by the 1890s annual Italian wine production was some 30 million hectolitres (hl). Ten years later it had increased to nearly 45 million hl, and a decade on had exceeded 60 million hl, which is more or less Italy's average production at the beginning of the third millennium.

WINE LAWS AND LABELS

EFFORTS TO REGULATE the production of wines in Italy can be traced back to the first wine guilds of the Middle Ages and even to Roman times. But it is only much more recently, since the 1930s, that the legislation has been tightened up significantly, especially with the first royal decrees authorizing the formation of *consortia* among producers of particular wines, and the then Ministry of Agriculture and Forestry beginning to identify and officially recognize production areas.

The real breakthrough came in 1963 with Presidential Decree 930, which set out the regulations for the control of wine production in Italy and introduced Denominazioni d'Origine for wine produced in a specific area, from specific grape varieties, to specified yields, and aged and bottled in accordance with the regulations.

Since then, the classification of Italian wines has been further developed and now has a pyramidal configuration as follows:

Denominazione di Origine Controllata e Garantita or **DOCG** awarded to wines of outstanding quality with a DOC of at least five years.

Denominazione di Origine Controllata or **DOC** as explained above.

Indicazione Geografica Tipica or **IGT** introduced in 1992 to bridge the gap between DOC and Vino da Tavola. IGT is often used for wines sold under their varietal names and produced in larger production areas. IGT wines, unlike vini da tavola, are subject to yield limitations. **Vini da Tavola** or **VdT** is basic table wine category. However, some of Italy's best wines, made by dynamic producers who don't conform to Denominazioni d'Origine regulations (by using Bordeaux blends for example), cannot claim the quality designation.

THE COUNTRY

O NE QUARTER OF ITALY is made up of plains, three-quarters of mountains and uplands. The uplands, which account for two-fifths of the total area, are particularly suitable for vine growing – so vines thrive virtually everywhere in the country, owing to the nature of the soil and the ideal climatic conditions.

In the north, the Alps form a semi-circle from the Ligurian sea to the Adriatic sea, and are a natural border with neighbouring countries. In the west, they shelter the vineyards of Val d'Aosta and Piedmont (the latter one of the most important wine producing regions in the country) from the cold northwesterly winds. To the north, they guard the vineyards of Lombardy and Alto Adige. But viticulture is not only found on high ground: vines also grow on the fertile Po Valley (see page 374).

In the old days, rural communities used to be virtually self-sufficient. This meant they made their own wine, a habit which is regrettably dying out. It may not have been of high quality, but it was authentic and satisfying, accompanying every meal and appreciated by the whole family. Unfortunately this way of life has steadily disappeared. As young people leave the countryside for

the big cities, traditions are dying out, and the vineyards at the back of the village are being neglected.

Winemaking in Italy today is a sophisticated, almost clinical business, in response to a new generation of wine drinkers wanting to drink less, but better wine. Thus the overall quality of the wines has improved tremendously over recent years. Production has decreased dramatically as old vineyards have been uprooted, to be replaced by new but fewer vineyards, farmed more rationally to encourage the production of better grapes.

In spite of the improved quality, the average Italian is still not too bothered when it comes to matching wine with food. In fact, it is not uncommon to drink red wine with fish or to cool a light red wine in the summer. Wine drinking has always been regarded as a way of life, a simple beverage for all the family rather than a sophisticated luxury, particularly by the older generation. Even young children are offered light, or diluted, wine as part of their meal.

In any case, there cannot be strict rules as to what to drink with what and, at the end of the day, it is personal judgement that matters. In Italy eating habits still vary from region to region and yet there is a tendency towards uniformity. Visiting the country, if one has a chance, it is still worth searching out the odd *osteria*, or *locanda*, the classic Italian inn. Also, look out for basic roadside restaurants in out-of-the-way places, away from cities and motorways. As a rule, come lunch or dinner time, if you care more for the food than the décor, look for parked lorries: there will be a restaurant nearby, maybe modest but almost certainly both good and cheap!

THE REGIONS

Italy is made up of 20 regions, 18 on the peninsula and two major islands. Each of these regions produces wine — so there's something to suit every taste and palate.

THE NORTH

THE NORTH OF ITALY is characterized by high mountains and the dominating Po Valley. To the west is Piedmont, one of the best wine-producing regions in the country. As the etymology of the Italian name indicates, Piemonte is "ai piedi del monte" (at the foot of the mountain), and the Maritime, Cottian, Graian and Pennine Alps surround it to the south, west and north respectively. This is the second largest region after Sicily and it borders France to the west and Switzerland to the north. It is ideal wine country; indeed some of the top Italian red wines are

produced here, particularly on the hills of Monferrato and Langhe. Wines such as Barolo• and Barbaresco• are among the best known, as well as Asti Spumante•, the famous bubbly that has gained popularity outside the regional and national boundaries. All the region's wines can been seen and tasted at the Enoteca Permanente wine library in the castle of Grinzane, near Alba. In Pessione, the Martini & Rossi wine museum is worth a visit.

Good reds are also produced further east in the valley of

Valtellina in Lombardy. The wines here are made mostly from Chiavennasca, a close relative of Nebbiolo, which is responsible for the excellent reds of Piedmont. Lombardy is virtually in the middle of the Alpine chain and extends southwards to the river Po and beyond. The third largest region in Italy after Sicily and Piedmont, it was named after the Lombard people who had come to settle here from over the Alps and by the sixth century were in control of the Po Valley. Traditionally agriculture has concentrated on fodder and cereal crops, while winegrowing can be found at the periphery; to the north in Valtellina, to the south in the Oltrepò Pavese and to the east, near the western shore of Lake Garda.

At the other side of the lake is Veneto, one of Italy's largest wine-producing regions. Evidence of the vine in the area around Lake Garda has been traced back to the Bronze Age, as archaeological digs south of the lake have uncovered grape pips and fragments of wine vessels in pre-historic dwellings. Today it is an important centre for Italian wines, with Verona hosting Vinitaly, an annual international wine fair that attracts some 3,000 wine producers and over 100,000 visitors from all over the

world. Valpolicella•, Amarone• and Soave• are the best-known wines produced in Veneto, but there are many more coming to the fore; as indeed there are in Trentino-Alto Adige and Friuli-Venezia Giulia, the two small regions either side of Veneto, where wines such as Caldaro and Santa Maddalena, or Collio, are becoming increasingly popular.

Emilia-Romagna is a vast region producing an equally vast quantity of popular wine. Lambrusco•, in its various shapes and forms, is perhaps the most well known, and it goes hand in hand with the excellent, though rather heavy, local cuisine.

There is an Enoteca Regionale (a wine library) in the fourteenth-century cellars of Dozza's castle, near Bologna, where 600 wines from Emilia-Romagna can be sampled and bought.

THE CENTRE

To THE SOUTH, OVER THE APENNINES, IS TUSCANY, one of the most beautiful regions of Italy thanks to its varied landscape and the abundance of artistic treasures. This is where the Etruscans eventually settled, giving this region their name: Etruria. The climate is relatively mild, the summers tend to be long and dry and this, together with the suitable nature of the soil, make it the ideal habitat for vines, usually grown on hilly terrain at an average altitude of 450 m/1446 ft, and producing wines, particularly reds, of exceptional quality, such as Brunello di Montalcino•, Chianti• and Sassicaia (see Bolgheri•).

One of the most interesting and well-established wine routes of Italy must be the Chiantigiana that runs from Florence to Siena across the Chianti Classico district. Siena, a beautiful city of Etruscan origin, is home to the

Enoteca Italiana, located in the bastions that overlook the approach to the Medici fortress. Siena's Enoteca is actually the national wine library, a showcase of the country's finest wines, which are available for tasting.

Nearby is Umbria, a small, landlocked region, often referred to as the green heart of Italy because of its luxuriant vegetation. The best-known wine is named after the regional capital, Orvieto•. Agriculture prospers in the valleys and on the hills, where the vine and olive trees abound. The house of Lungarotti, well known for its fine wines, has set up a magnificent wine museum worth visiting in Torgiano, not far from Perugia.

Further east, between the Apennines and the Adriatic sea, is Marche. The best wines are produced along the upper reaches of the rivers Conca, Metauro, Tronto and in the area of Mount Conero, as well as that of the Castelli di Jesi and Cupramontana in the province of Ancona, the regional capital.

Further south in Abruzzo there are more excellent wines such as Montepulciano• and Trebbiano•. The economy of the region, which is fairly mountainous, is based principally on agricultural with vines cultivated mainly on the hillsides along the Adriatic coast and further inland where the soil is mostly of Pliocene origin and very rich in nitrogen.

Back on the other side of the Apennines, in Lazio, there are some good whites produced on the hills surrounding Rome including the Vini dei Castelli Romani (the wines of the Roman hills), such as Frascati• and Marino. Another well-known white, made near Montefiascone, is Est ! Est!! Est!!! The tale behind this unusual name is quite amusing. It is said that in the twelfth century, a German bishop who intended to travel to Rome for the coronation of Henry V sent his quartermaster to seek accommodation on the road to rest during the journey. Should the quartermaster find an inn dispensing good wine he was to chalk on the wall outside the Latin phrase "Vinum bonum est" ("the wine is good"). Apparently when he got to Montefiascone the diligent servant sampled the local wine and to make absolutely sure of its quality he drank rather a lot. Leaving the inn his mind was hazy and the only thing he could remember to write on the wall was "est". So, to make sure that his master would find the inn, he wrote on the wall Est! Est!! Est!!!, which has since become the name of the local white wine. Apparently, the bishop agreed with him to such a degree that he decided to end his days in Montefiascone – and never reached the holy city!

THE SOUTH AND THE ISLANDS

FURTHER SOUTH WE FIND OURSELVES IN CAMPANIA, where there are some excellent wines such as Greco di Tufo• and Taurasi•. This region extends from Latium to Basilicata along the Tyrrhenian sea and as far inland as Molise and Puglia. The Campania Felix (the happy land), as the ancient Romans called it because of its fertility, was in fact given its name by the Osci, the Oscan people who lived here in the fourth and fifth centuries BC. As for the Romans, this was the land of Falernum, celebrated by Horace and Martial, and that of Cecubo produced around Terracina. The black volcanic soil of the Campi Laborini, called Phlegraei by the

Greeks, was considerably more productive than the Roman soil and gave several crops a year. The climate here is mild, particularly along the coast and this favours agriculture in general. It is a beautiful land with picturesque bays such as the one at Naples, its capital, and charming islands like Capri and Ischia, the latter producing some delicious whites.

Over on the other side of the Apennines is Puglia, one of the largest wine-producing regions of Italy. The constant summer heat fully ripens the grapes giving wines with a high natural alcohol content. This is the easternmost region of Italy, which reaches southwards, in a slim peninsula extending into the Adriatic and Ionian seas. Compared with most other Italian regions there are virtually no mountains here but mainly uplands and lowlands. Viticulture and winemaking are the most important agricultural activities, first practiced by the Phoenicians who colonized the region some 2000 years BC.

The wines are rich, full-bodied and high in alcohol and for these reasons used to be exported in bulk to other Italian regions and beyond, mostly for blending with weaker, paler wines in need of strength and colour. But now the picture has changed and the local wines are sold on their own merits. The best, Copertino•, Primitivo di Manduria• and Salice Salentino•, have made an impression both in Italy and abroad. We shall certainly see more of them, and of other wines from Puglia, in the future.

Squeezed between Puglia and Calabria is Basilicata, almost entirely mountainous and virtually landlocked although it reaches both the Ionian and Tyrrhenian seas at the bays of Taranto and Policastro respectively. This is a land of fascinating natural beauty, with an ever-changing, mostly rugged, landscape. Mount Vulture, an extinct volcano, stands to the north, and on its slopes the grape variety Aglianico is grown with success thanks to the favourable microclimate and fertile soil. A robust yet velvety, delicately scented red, Aglianico del Vulture•, is also becoming better known.

Sicily, the largest island of the Mediterranean sea whose triangular shape earned it the ancient name of Trinacria, is one of the largest wine-producing regions in Italy. For the last couple of centuries its success in this field was closely linked to that of Marsala•, a fortified wine made famous at the end of the eighteenth century by the Woodhouse brothers from Liverpool, who even sold it to Nelson for his fleet. It is named after the port from which it was first exported. Today this aperitif or dessert wine is more popular with older generations, and is often used in cooking. In Marsala and elsewhere in Sicily, wine production is as sophisticated as anywhere else in the country and often results in wine, both red and white, of exceptional quality. Production is concentrated in the three corners of the island, as well as the tiny Lipari islands off the north coast, and the island of Pantelleria between Sicily and the northern coast of Africa (the island is actually closer to Tunisia than to mainland Italy) where an excellent dessert wine, Moscato Passito, is made. Contessa Entellina, produced in the Belice Valley, Alcamo and Etna (named after the volcano), are all DOC wines.

CANNONAU
di Sardegna
Denominazione di Origine Controllata

Dal 1899 Sella & Mosca, fedele interprete di un ambiente dove il vino è arte e vocazione, continua la grande

tradizione viticola sulle terre antiche e forti della Sardegna con Cannonau, vitigno nobile e di grande carattere.

Riserva
1997

IMBOTTIGLIATO NELLA ZONA DI PRODUZIONE DA
SELLA & MOSCA S.p.A.
ALGHERO - SARDEGNA - ITALIA

750 ml ℮   SELLA•MOSCA   13,5% vol
                 ITALIA

The vine is indigenous to Sardinia, the second largest island in the Mediterranean, with its rugged coastline, beaches of soft untrodden sand and dense woodlands where boars runs free. Various people migrated there over the centuries, and made their influence felt by grafting and cultivating the vine, gathering and pressing the grapes, fermenting the must and preserving the wine according to their habits. The red Cannonau• with its robust flavours, as well as the aromatic white Vermentino•, are typical expressions of Sardinia.

GLOSSARY

Abboccato *lightly sweet*

Amabile *semi-sweet*

Annata *vintage year*

Bianco *white*

Bottiglia *bottle*

Brut *dry, in sparkling wine*

Cerasuolo *cherry-coloured rosé*

Classico *the historic centre of a DOC zone*

Consorzio *consortium of producers*

Dolce *sweet*

Frizzante or **frizzantino** *fizzy or slightly fizzy*

Invecchiato *aged*

Liquoroso *strong wine, usually fortified, but sometimes naturally strong*

Passito *strong wine made from partially dried grapes*

Recioto *wine made from partially dried grapes, often sweet and strong*

Riserva *reserve for DOC or DOCG wines aged for a specified time*

Rosato *rosé*

Rosso *red*

Secco *dry*

Semisecco *medium sweet, usually in sparkling wine*

Spumante *sparkling wine, dry or sweet*

Superiore *in DOC wines denotes higher level of alcohol or ageing, or specific geographical origin*

Vecchio *old*

Vendemmia *harvest or vintage*

Vino novello *new wine, usually red, that is bottled soon after the harvest*

Wine Index

IT WOULD BE IMPOSSIBLE to list all Italian wines, but here are the major ones with suggested food matches. All recipes can be found on pages 52–189.

AGLIANICO DEL VULTURE DOC *Basilicata*

This unusual, full-bodied red wine is made from Aglianico grapes in the Vulture (in the province of Potenza). At times reminiscent of Barbera•, it can be aged for several years before drinking. Ruby-red in youth, Aglianico del Vulture turns garnet with age, and the initially delicate bouquet deepens. To taste, it is rich and dry, although there is also a slightly sweet type, suitably

FATTORIA PARADISO

PEZZI DI PARADISO°
Vigna dell'Olivo
1999

tannic yet velvety. It must be aged for a minimum of one year. When aged for three years or more it is called Vecchio and then, after five years, is known as Riserva.

Serve the dry type with: Roasts such as Arista alla Fiorentina and Braciole di Maiale alla Pizzaiola.

ALBANA DI ROMAGNA DOCG *Emilia-Romagna*

Somewhat controversially, this was the first white to be awarded the top DOCG status; controversial because it can be a rather neutral, dull wine. Standards have improved, however, in recent years. It is made from Albana grapes in an area of the Apennines east of Bologna, and can be secco, amabile, dolce or passito.

The secco (dry) is straw-yellow, turning golden with age, delicately scented, and dry, aromatic and warm to taste, with a hint of tannin. The amabile (semi-sweet) has similar characteristics to the secco, but tends to be more fruity and is slightly sweet, making it a light dessert wine. The dolce (sweet) has a higher degree of sweetness and enticing aromas. The passito must be aged for at least six months. It is golden-yellow to amber, wonderfully aromatic and is smooth and pleasantly sweet.

Serve the secco with: fish and vegetable dishes.

Serve the dolce with: Torta di Riso and Zaleti.

AMARONE DELLA VALPOLICELLA DOC VENETO (see Valpolicella)

ASTI OR ASTI SPUMANTE AND MOSCATO D'ASTI DOCG

Piedmont

Sweet, fizzy and low in alcohol, this Piedmontese white wine is produced exclusively from Moscato Bianco grapes grown in the provinces of Alessandria, Asti and Cuneo – all share this variety's distinctly "grapey" flavour. Moscato d'Asti, the gently fizzy dessert wine, is clear straw-yellow in colour, rich and fruity on the nose and has a sweet, aromatic flavour. It can be used to make the sparkling Asti (Asti Spumante) by allowing a second natural fermentation in the bottle, or in sealed stainless steel tanks. Asti Spumante has a fine, persistent mousse, a brilliant straw- to golden-yellow colour, extremely fruity aromas and a delicately sweet and balanced taste, making it an excellent light dessert wine.

Serve with: Budino di Panettone or Colomba.

BARBARESCO DOCG

Piedmont

This outstanding fruity red wine is made from the spicy Nebbiolo grape (more specifically from the subvarieties Michet, Lampia and Rosé) grown in Barbaresco, in the province of Cuneo. Often it is more approachable earlier than neighbouring Barolo, but the wine still needs age to soften its robust tannins – Barbaresco must be matured for at least two years before being released. Garnet-red in colour when young, it acquires orange tints with age, while the bouquet remains deeply fruity. It is a dry wine, full, robust, austere and yet also velvety and smooth. When aged for four years it can be called Riserva.

Serve with: roasted or braised red meat.

BARBERA D'ALBA DOC

Piedmont

The Barbera grape is found virtually all over Italy, yet it excels in the wines of Piedmont, and more specifically in the provinces of Alessandria, Asti and Cuneo. Barbera d'Alba is one of the best examples, with a deep ruby colour when young, turning to garnet with age. It is fruity, with a delicate aroma and a dry, soft, slightly tannic taste.

Serve with: Bollito Misto and Cassoeula. Excellent with mature (sharp) cheeses.

BARDOLINO DOC *Veneto*

Named after the lakeside town of the same name this light, bright, ruby-red wine is delicately scented, with a slightly bitter, almondy taste. It is made from Corvina Veronese, Molinara, Negrara and Rondinella grapes, with up to 15% of Barbera and Sangiovese. When vinified partly off the skins it is paler in colour and can be labelled Chiaretto which means "lightish" in colour. If bottled before the end of the year of production it can be labelled Novello.

Serve with: most dishes, apart from rich meat and oily fish. Ideal for pasta, risotti and gnocchi.

BAROLO DOCG *Piedmont*

Barolo is one of the great red wines of Italy, and of the world, and was always present on the dinner table of the Savoia, the Italian royal family from Piedmont. Like Barbaresco, this wine is made from subvarieties of the Nebbiolo grape, and it is named after the town of Barolo, in the Langhe area near Cuneo. The best examples of this rich, powerful (the minimum alcohol level is 13% abv) and tannic wine combine dry, almost austere character with deep, smooth velvety softness and a wonderfully fragrant nose. Barolo must age for at least three years. After five, it can be called Riserva.

Serve with: Fagiano alla Milanese, Stinco al Forno con Patate, Brasato alla Lombarda

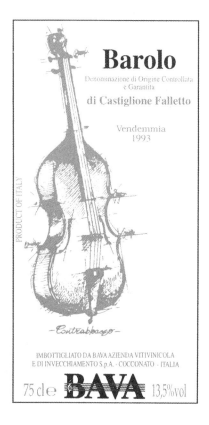

BIANCO di CUSTOZA DOC *Veneto*

This crisp, light white is made from several varieties: Cortese, Garganega, Tocai Friulano, Trebbiano Toscano and others, grown on sunny hillsides southeast of Lake Garda. Bianco di Custoza is a lightly scented and flavoured, bitterish wine. A sparkling version also exists.

Serve with: fish dishes, Polpettone di Tonno, Risi e Bisi, Gnocchi di Patate.

BOLGHERI DOC *Tuscany*

This is a fascinating DOC, and home to some of the country's top wines, including the world-famous Sassicaia. Because Sassicaia uses the non-indigenous grape varieties Cabernet Sauvignon and Cabernet Franc, it originally could not be awarded a DOC, and was simply labelled humble *vino da tavola*. In 1994, however, the area of Bolgheri was granted a DOC, which is now applicable to several locally produced wines. One such is Sassicaia, that now has its own subdenomination.

Many other excellent wines, often using international grape varieties, such as Ornellaia, are now included in this up-and-coming coastal DOC. The DOC itself applies to several wines as follows:

Bianco, a dry white wine made with Trebbiano Toscano, Vermentino and Sauvignon grapes.

Serve with: Sformato di Finocchi or fish.

Vermentino, a delicate white made from at least 85% of the eponymous grape. Serve with: Peperoni, Cipolline in Agradolce.

Sauvignon Blanc, a white, dry, slightly aromatic wine made from at least 85% Sauvignon Blanc.

Serve with: Risotto al Branzino, Gnocci di Zucca.

Rosso, a ruby coloured wine made from Cabernet Sauvignon, Merlot and Sangiovese.

Serve with: Fagioli all Uccelletto.

Rosato, a rosé made from the same grape as the red.

Serve with: Sgombri con le Cipolle.

Vin Santo Occhio di Pernice, a sweet, soft and velvety rosé dessert wine made from Malvasia and Sangiovese, with a minimum 16% abv.

Serve with: Torta di Riso, Torta di Mandorle.

Sassicaia, a superb deep ruby-red wine made with not less than 85% Cabernet Sauvignon. Elegant, dry, balanced and well-structured, this is a wine for special occasions and is suitable for ageing.

Serve with: Arista alla Fiorentina, Bistecca alla Fiorentina or lamb.

BRUNELLO DI MONTALCINO DOCG
Tuscany

The most aristocratic of Italian wines, Brunello di Montalcino has been produced for well over a century in the region of Montalcino, some 24 kilometres/33 miles south of Siena, from the Brunello di Montalcino grape, a clone of Sangiovese. Brunello needs a long maturation to soften its austere tannins, but when they do, the wine reveals a unique combination of flavours – bitter chocolate, cherry, earthy, dried fruit – that make the wait worthwhile. The minimum ageing is four years; with five it can be called Riserva.

Serve with: Spezzatino di Cinghiale, Stufato alla Napoletana, Coda alla Vaccinara and lamb dishes.

CALDARO DOC
Trentino-Alto Adige

Named after Lake Caldaro, a charming little mountain lake situated southwest of Bolzano, this ruby-red to garnet wine offers fruity aromas and a balanced palate, with a hint of almonds. It is made from Schiava Grossa and/or Schiava Gentile and Schiava Grigia, with the possible addition of Pinot Nero and Lagrein. The minimum alcohol content is 10.5% abv, and if it reaches 11.5% it can be called Scelto (selected). The Classico label is reserved for wine produced in a limited area within the production zone.

Serve with: Spezzatino di Manzo alla Bolzanese, Salsa allo Speck per Tagliatelle.

CANNONAU DI SARDEGNA DOC *Sardinia*

The grape variety Cannonau was imported years ago from Spain, where it was known as Alicante. Today it grows throughout the island of Sardinia (barring a few pockets here and there where the terrain is unsuitable), and produces a range of wine styles from dry to sweet. Generally deep ruby-red in colour, Cannonau has a pleasantly fruity aroma, and is dry to taste. With two years of ageing, it can be called Riserva. There is also a liquoroso, or fortified type, that can be secco (dry), or dolce naturale (naturally sweet), with an alcohol content respectively of 18% and 16% abv.

Serve the dry with: Coniglio ai Peperoni, Linguine all'Aglio Olio e Peperoncino and pasta dishes.

Serve the sweet with: Colomba and other cakes.

CARMIGNANO DOC
Tuscany

A red wine produced in a restricted area around Carmignano and Poggio a Caiano, near Florence, and made from Sangiovese, Canaiolo Nero, Cabernets Franc and Sauvignon, Trebbiano Toscano, Canaiolo Bianco and Malvasia del Chianti. These combine to give a dry, rich, soft wine with a lively ruby-red colour and an intense aroma of violets, developing greater finesse with age. It must be aged for at least 18 months; with three years it becomes Riserva.

Serve with: red meat (Bistecca alla Fiorentine) and boiled meat (Bollito Misto).

CASTEL DEL MONTE
DOC *Puglia*

Dry, well-balanced wines are produced under this DOC in the region of Minervino Murge (and parts of nine other regions) in Bari. The red is produced from Uva di Troia and Aglianico, has a ruby-red colour, an enticing vinous bouquet and is a lightish, rounded, if slightly tannic mouthful – perfect for drinking with a meal. With at least two years of age, it can be called Riserva, and this is especially

good with roast meat dishes. The pale-coloured white is produced from Pampanuto, Chardonnay and other white varieties which combine to give a fresh, rounded taste, ideal with fish.

Serve with: Orecchiette con i Broccoli, Funghi Trifolati.

CERASUOLO DI VITTORIA DOC *Sardinia*

Named after its deep red colour, Cerasuolo ("cherry colour") is a particularly strong wine with a minimum of 13% abv. This makes it suitable for long ageing. It is produced in the regions of Caltanissetta, Catania, and Ragusa, using Frappato and Calabrese grapes (with the optional addition of Nerello Mascalese). It has a delicate bouquet and tastes dry, full and well-balanced. A perfect wine with red meat dishes.

Serve with: Pasta con le Sarde, Caponata, Rognoncini Trifolata all' Acciuja e Limone and any sausage.

CHIANTI DOCG *Tuscany*

One of the best-known Italian wines, Chianti is produced in the Tuscan provinces of Arezzo, Florence, Pisa, Pistoia and Siena, from Sangiovese, Canaiolo, Trebbiano and Malvasia. (Although the increasingly fruity flavours now popular may include up to

10% of Cabernet Sauvignon, Merlot or Syrah instead of the traditional proportion of white varieties.) Chianti can vary in style from light, young and fresh to serious, intense wine for ageing. Better-quality Chianti Classico comes from the heart of the Chianti zone and is a lively, bitter-cherryish wine, often wonderfully scented with voilets. With age the dry, balanced, full, slightly tannic yet velvety palate becomes finer. Chianti Rufina, another sub-region, is also often better quality. With three years of age, Chianti can be called Riserva: a superb wine to drink with roasted or grilled(broiled) meats or poultry.

Serve with: Arista alla Fiorentina, Bistecca alla Fiorentina.

CINQUETERRE DOC
Liguria

For centuries a white wine has been produced in the part of Liguria known as Cinqueterre (five lands), a strip of land along the coast where viticulture is a real challenge as some vineyards are accessible only by boat. Cinqueterre is made from Albarola, Bosco and Vermentino grapes and is straw-yellow in colour, lightly scented and pleasingly dry to taste. It is an excellent accompaniment for fish dishes. Using the same grapes and letting them dry for a few weeks gives Sciacchetra, a wonderfully aromatic, golden-amber wine ranging from dry to sweet in style.

Serve dry Cinqueterre with: Pasta al Pesto.

Serve Sciacchetra with: Baci di Dama.

CIRÒ DOC *Calabria*

This DOC covers a red, a rosé and a white wine, made with grapes grown around Catanzaro (where the ancient Cremista, a temple dedicated to Bacchus once stood).

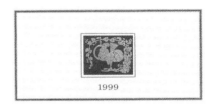

Dry Cirò rosso and rosato are made from Gaglioppo, fruity Cirò bianco is made from Greco Bianco.

Serve Cirò rosso with: meat dishes, Vincisgrassi.

Serve Cirò rosato with: Maiale al latte, Cinia all Genovese (although it is suitable throughout the meal).

Serve Cirò bianco with: fish dishes or polpetonne.

COLLI ORIENTALI DEL FRIULI DOC *Friuli-Venezia Giulia*

This is what I term a typical "umbrella" DOC (to the east of Udine) as it covers over 90 styles of red, white and rosè wine, depending on the grape variety used. Refosco dal Peduncolo Rosso is among the best reds, with a deep garnet colour and a dry, slightly bitter, warm palate. Of the whites Verduzzo Friulano and Ribolla Gialla are worth mentioning – the former is golden-yellow in colour, particularly fruity and is available both in a dry and a sweet version; the latter is aromatic, dry, fresh and balanced.

Serve Refosco dal Peduncolo with: game and meat.

Serve Verduzzo Friulano with: grilled (broiled) fish.

Serve Ribolla Gialla with: vegetable dishes or fruit.

COLLIO GORIZIANO OR COLLIO DOC
Friuli-Venezia Giulia

Collio is a small area to the west of Gorizia, a border town in the northeast, next to Slovenia. This DOC covers just under 40 types of wine including the famed and rather pricey Picolit, a white often compared to France's Château d'Yquem. It has an intense straw-yellow colour, wonderful aromas of acacia flowers, and a warm, sweet or semi-sweet taste. Pinot Grigio made here is also recommended, with lots of fruit and a full, well-balanced palate. Among the reds, Cabernets Franc and Sauvignon, and Merlot are also outstanding.

Serve white Collio with: Cavolfiore in Umido, Funghi Trifolati, Risotto alla Paesana.

CONTESSA ENTELLINA DOC *Sicily*

An excellent white wine made within the commune of Contessa Entellina, near Palermo, from Ansonica grapes blended with Catarratto Bianco Lucido, Chardonnay, Grecanico and Sauvignon Blanc and, occasionally, Müller Thurgau. Light in colour, this dry, crisp wine is an ideal companion to the local fish dishes.

Serve with: Trance di Tonno in Salsa Rinascimentale, Pasta con le Sarde, frittate* of any sort.

COPERTINO DOC *Puglia*

This DOC applies to wines made mainly from Negroamaro in Copertino and other areas around Lecce in southern Puglia. The rosso can offer interesting berryish flavours, and with two years of age becomes Riserva. The rosato is usually salmon-red to cherry in colour and dry to taste, with herbaceous tones, often accompanied by a pleasantly bitter aftertaste. Its easy-drinking quality makes it a wine to be enjoyed throughout a meal, especially with something like a robust pasta dish.

Serve with: Peperoni Ripieni di Pasta and pasta 'Ncasciata.

DOLCETTO D'ALBA DOC *Piedmont*

Sweet (dolcetto means "little sweet one"), soft wines are made from this early ripening red variety, with Dolcetto D'Alba one of the most highly regarded. Generally, they are easy, everyday wines, for drinking young.

Serve with: grilled (broiled) meat, agnolotti, paniscia.

FRANCIACORTA DOC
Lombardy

Franciacorta wines are produced in a hilly area south of Lake Iseo, in the province of Brescia. The best-known Franciacorta is the spumante. Like the bianco, it is made from Pinot Bianco and/or Chardonnay, with the optional addition of Pinot Grigio or Pinot Nero. It has delicate, fruity aromas and a fresh, fine, balanced taste with a touch of sweetness, making it suitable as an aperitif, or with dessert. Franciacorta Rosso is made from Barbera, Cabernet Franc, Merlot and Nebbiolo. It is almost purpley when young and has a dry, balanced taste – again a wine that's easy to enjoy throughout a meal. There is also a rosé sparkling wine, Franciacorta Rosato Spumante, made with the same grape varieties as the red, with the addition of Pinot Nero – this is a very fruity wine with a long-lasting froth to be drunk at the end of the meal.

Serve white sparkling with: Olives, focaccia or pizza.

FRASCATI DOC *Lazio*

The best known of the "Vini dei Castelli Romani" for several centuries, Frascati, once defined by Goethe as a heavenly wine, has long been the favourite wine of the Popes and the nobility of central Italy. This soft white wine is produced southeast of Rome in Frascati, Colonna, Grottaferrata, Montecomparti, and Monteporzio Catone, using Malvasia Bianca di Candia and Trebbiano Toscano grapes. There are three versions of Frascati: secco (dry), amabile (semi-sweet), or canellino (sweet). The dry is particularly suited to fish and white meat while the sweet or semi-sweet should be drunk at the end of a meal. "Superiore" means the wine has an abv of at least 11.5%, as opposed to 11%.

Serve with: fish, antipasti, Carciofi con Piselli, Rognoncini Trifolati all' Acciuga e Limone.

GATTINARA DOCG

Piedmont

This full-flavoured red wine has been made for centuries and is produced in small quantities from Nebbiolo grapes grown in Gattinara, near Vercelli. Garnet-red in colour, with an enticing aroma of violets, particularly when aged, Gattinara tends to be dry, with a slightly bitter finish – an excellent accompaniment for red meat dishes.
The minimum ageing is three years, and minimum alcohol level 12.5% abv, but with 13% abv and four years of age it can be called Riserva.

Serve with: Truffle dishes, Polenta Pasticciata, Fagiano alle Milanese.

GAVI OR CORTESE DI GAVI DOC *Piedmont*

A dry, balanced, fresh wine, Gavi is made from Cortese grapes grown in the hills around Alessandria. It has a brilliant straw-yellow colour, a delicate bouquet and a subtle creaminess when well made, and goes extremely well with white meat or fish dishes. There is also a sparkling version.

Serve with: antipasti and fish dishes, Polpettone di Fagiolini, and Trance di Pesce alla Casalinga.

GRECO DI TUFO DOC

Campania

Greco di Tufo is made from the grape of the same name and Coda di Volpe ("fox's tail"), in an area north of Avellino. This excellent white wine is regarded as one of the best from the south, and has a fruity, often herb-like taste.

Serve with: Mozzarella in Carrozza and Spaghetti alla Puttanesca and fish and seafood.

LAMBRUSCO DI SORBARA DOC *Emilia-Romagna*

There are several versions of this extraordinary frothy red wine (both dry and semi-sweet), named after the area in which they are produced; the better known are Sorbara, Castelvetro and

Santa Croce, all around Modena. Lambrusco is made from the Lambrusco grape, which gives a wine ranging from purple to pink in colour, and in style from dry to sweet. Most of the Lambrusco shipped abroad is amabile or semi-sweet, while the dry versions are drunk at home and, with their relatively high acidity, are perfect with the rich and fatty dishes of the area. There is also a Lambrusco Reggiano DOC and a Lambrusco Mantovano DOC.

Serve with: Anolini alla Piacentina, Lasagne al Forno and all salami, prosciutti and cheeses.

LOCOROTONDO DOC
Puglia

This pleasantly fresh southern white is named after the region of Locorotondo, some ten kilometres/six miles from Alberobello, famous for its "trulli" (traditional whitewashed buildings with conical roofs). The wine is made from Verdeca and Bianco D'Alessano grown in the communes of Locorotondo, Cisternino and part of the commune of Fasano. Greenish or straw-yellow in colour, with delicate aromas, it is lively and dry to taste.

Serve with: Caponata, Orata alla Pugliese and other fish dishes.

LUGANA DOC *Lombardy*

Grapes have been grown for centuries in this area south of Lake Garda, and the area gives its name to full, aromatic whites made from Trebbiano di Lugana. Straw-yellow or greenish in colour, turning light-golden with age, Lugana wines are pleasingly fragrant, and offer fresh, soft, almost creamy, buttery flavours, ideal to serve with the fish from nearby Lake Garda. A sparkling version is also available.

Serve with: most antipasti, risotti, such as Risotto alla Milanese, Minestrone alla Milanese.

MALVASIA

Malvasia is frequently found in various parts of the country (often combined with other grape varieties), but it excels on its own principally in Piedmont, as well as in Sicily and other nearby islands. Malvasia di Casorzo d'Asti DOC (Piedmont) is made from Malvasia Nera grown near Asti and Alessandria, and takes its name from the commune of Casorzo. It ranges from pink to ruby- red in colour, with the distinctive aroma of Malvasia grapes, while it is sweet and pleasantly aromatic in flavour. It is usually slightly spritzy, although there is also a fully sparkling version. From the Aeolian Islands off Sicily, also known as Lipari, comes Malvasia delle Lipari DOC (Sicily). When made from fresh grapes it has an attractive golden-yellow colour and is wonderfully aromatic, while if made with grapes left to dry for a time, it is sweeter and amber in colour.

Serve all with: cheese or desserts, depending on their sweetness.

MARSALA DOC *Sicily*

Marsala wine was first discovered by the Woodhouse brothers from Liverpool back in 1773 and is named after the port in which they established their cellars and warehouse. By the year 1800 they were supplying Nelson's fleet with what was to become a great naval drink, and later on a fashionable one in England, too. Marsala is a sweet fortified wine, produced and aged around Trapani, from Grillo and Catarratto grapes. Depending on their age Marsala wines are known as Fine (one year old), Superiore (two years old), Superiore

amount of other white varieties. It is a straw-yellow wine, and has light, fruity aromas, matched by a dry, fruity taste.

Serve the red with: Coppa di Testa, Lenticchie in Umido and rich pasta dishes.

Serve the white with: fish, prosciutto and light pasta.

Riserva (four years old), Vergine and/or Solera (five years old), Solera Stravecchio or Solera Riserva (at least ten years old). Marsala wines are also distinguished by colour: Oro (gold), Ambra (amber), Rubino (ruby), and by their sugar content: secco (dry), semi-secco (semi-dry) and dolce (sweet). Their alcohol content varies: Marsala Fine is not less than 17% abv, Marsala Superiore and Marsala Vergine or Solera are not less than 18% abv. Marsala wines are excellent served either as aperitifs or as dessert wine according to their degree of sweetness. They are also popular in cooking.

Serve with: desserts such as Gelato di Crema, Budino di Panettone.

MONTEFALCO DOC
Umbria

Two wines, a red and a white, are named after the town of Montefalco, in the province of Perugia. The red is made from Sangiovese, Sagrantino and other red varieties that give it a ruby-red to garnet colour and an intense, cherryish taste. The wine must be aged for 18 months before it can be sold and goes well with roast meat. The white Montefalco is made from Grechetto, Trebbiano Toscano and a small

MONTEPULCIANO D'ABRUZZO DOC
Abruzzi

Warm and full of flavour when well made, this amenable red wine is produced from the Montepulciano grape grown along the Adriatic coast, near Pescara. The variety was introduced in the area at the beginning of the nineteenth century. Today's wines are deep ruby-red, almost violety in colour, and are dry, soft and slightly tannic to taste. If aged for at least two years they can be called Riserva; excellent for roasts. There is also Cerasuolo, a cherry-coloured version which has a delicate aftertaste of almonds and should be drunk fairly young, ideally with soups or hors d'oeuvres.

Serve with: thick soups (such as La Ribollita), antipasti (Cipolline in Agrodolce) and rich pasta dishes (such as Bucatini all' Amatriciana).

MOSCATO DI PANTELLERIA DOC *Sicily*

An island of volcanic origin, often referred to as the pearl of the Sicilian channel, Pantelleria is part of the province of Trapani, although is closer to the Tunisian coast. This rich, golden dessert wine is made with Zibibbo grapes (the local name for the Muscat grown here) and offers the distinctive grapey aromas of Muscat, combined with an intensely sweet flavour. The passito version is made with Zibibbo grapes that have been partially dried, and is a perfect wine at the end of a meal with any type of dessert, such as Cassata di Sulmona and Tiramisù.

NEBBIOLO D'ALBA DOC
Piedmont

A red wine made from Nebbiolo grapes grown in the commune of Alba, near Cuneo. Nebbiolo is the great grape of Piedmont's famed reds, Barolo, Barbaresco and Gattinara. Here it gives a wine with a delicate scent of violets and a soft, velvety taste ranging from dry to slightly sweet. The dry version must be aged for at least one year, by which time the colour begins to acquire garnet tones. There is also a sparkling version.

Serve the red with: game and dishes with truffles.

Serve the sparkling with with canapés (as an aperitif), pizza, focaccia etc.

OLTREPÒ PAVESE DOC
Lombardy

This DOC applies to several wines made with grapes grown in an area known as Oltrepò Pavese, in the province of Pavia. Oltrepò Pavese Rosso is made from Barbera, Croatina, Pinot Nero, Uva Rara and Vespolina, and has a deep ruby-red colour, good body and is slightly tannic. Bonarda, another red, is made from Croatina and a small amount of Barbera. Intensely fruity, soft, lively, at times slightly spritzy, this wine can be dry or amabile. Among the whites are Riesling Italico, Riesling Renano and Cortese, the last made mainly with the grape of the same name and up to 15% of other white varieties. This soft yet lively wine has lots of fruit, and is also made in the full spumante style.

Serve the red with: roast meats, poultry, pasta and risotti.

Serve the white with: fish and seafood.

ORVIETO DOC *Umbria*

Smooth and easy-drinking when well-made (Orvieto Classico is usually best), this straw-yellow wine has been highly regarded for centuries, as the town of Orvieto was once a holy see and sent its wines to Rome to grace the table of popes, cardinals and princes. It is pro-duced from Trebbiano Toscano, Verdello and Grechetto and small quantities of other varieties grown in and around Orvieto. In style it ranges from dry (secco), with a slightly bitter after-taste, to semi-sweet (abboccato).

Serve the secco with: fish dishes such as Sogliole al Basilico e ai Pinoli.

Serve the abboccato with: most puddings such as Cassata di Sulmona.

PRIMITIVO DI MANDURIA DOC *Puglia*

This heady, spicy red wine is made from Primitivo grapes (now identified as California's Zinfandel). Deep red in

youth, the wine turns orangey with age, while the palate is generally full, balanced becoming velvety. The alcohol content is high: 14% abv.

Serve with: stewed and braised meats such as Filetto di Maiale alla Cavalcanti, Stufato alla Napoletana and with cheese.

PROSECCO DI CONEGLIANO VALDOBBIADENE DOC
Veneto
Softly sparkling Prosecco is made from grapes of the same name, grown on the hilly part of the Marca Trevigiana, between Conegliano and Valdobbiadene, near Treviso in northern Italy. (Up to 15% of Chardonnay, Pinot Bianco or Pinot Grigio, and Verdiso can also be included.) Characteristically light and fruity on the nose, the secco (dry) has a pleasantly bitter taste, while the amabile (semi-sweet) and dolce (sweet) are fruitier. When produced in the restricted area of Cartizze it can be called Superiore di Catizze. The most popular style is the frizzante (semi-sparkling), but there is also a full sparkling version. Both can be dry, semi-sweet or sweet.

Serve as an excellent aperitif.

ROERO DOC
Piedmont
Both red and white wines are made under this DOC on the hills surrounding Alba. The red wine is made from Nebbiolo and small quantities of Arneis and has a ruby-red colour with garnet hints when aged. Fragrant and fruity on the nose it is dry and velvety to taste.

White Roero is produced from Arneis grapes only and is straw-yellow in colour, with tints of amber. It has a delicate, almost grassy scents and a dry, slightly bitter taste; an excellent accompaniment to fish dishes.

Serve with: Calamari Ripieni, boiled meats (Bollito Misto), Casto lette alla Milanese.

ROSSO CONERO DOC
Marche
Rich, spicy Montepulciano grapes, and a small amount of Sangiovese, are at the heart of this big red wine, named after Mount Conero, situated just southeast of Ancona. (Conero was the name given by the Greeks to the cherry trees that still grow on the slopes of the mountain.) Rosso Conero is bright ruby-red in colour, and tastes dry, rich and full-bodied.

Serve with: Vincisgrassi and roast meats.

SALICE SALENTINO
DOC *Puglia*
This increasingly popular DOC applies to a red and a rosé wine made from Negramaro grapes grown in various regions around Bari and Lecce. The heat of the southern sun is reflected in the rosso, with its full, velvety, warm flavours. Salice Salentino Rosato is pink to cherry-red in appearance, has a fruity bouquet and a dry, velvety taste. A sparkling version is also available, an ideal aperitif.

Serve with: roasts or pasta, such as Orecchiette con i Broccoli.

SANGIOVESE DI ROMAGNA DOC
Emilia-Romagna

A popular, easy-drinking red, produced in the provinces of Bologna, Forlì and Ravenna from Sangiovese (with up to 15% of other red grape varieties allowed). The name Sangiovese appears to derive from the Latin *sanguis Jovis*, ("Jupiter's blood"). Sangiovese di Romagna, often delicately violet-scented, is dry, balanced, at times a little tannic to taste, with a pleasant bitter aftertaste. With 12% abv or more it can be called Superiore, and with two years of ageing, Riserva.

Serve with: pork dishes and rich pasta dishes (Lasagne al Forno).

SANT'AGATA DEI GOTI DOC *Campania*

This DOC covers several wines, named after the grapes from which they are made, produced in the commune of Sant'Agata dei Goti near Benevento. They are: Falanghina, a fresh, fruity and dry white wine (there is also a sweet version, Falanghina Passito); Greco, again a fresh white, pale and delicately scented; Forastera, a dry, well-balanced wine with fruity aromas; and Piedirosso or Per'e Palummo, a ruby-red wine with a pleasantly dry, tannic finish. There is also a sweet Piedirosso or Per'e Palummo Passito.

Serve with: fish and pasta dishes.

SANTA MADDALENA DOC *Trentino-Alto Adige*

Made from Schiava Grossa, Schiava Media, Schiava Grigia and Tschaggele grapes, Santa Maddalena is a lightish, tangy wine made in the Alto Adige, above Bolzano. It has a lovely ruby colour turning brick-red with age, heady scents of violets and almonds and a lightly aromatic taste, with the velvety flavour of almonds.

Serve with: red meats, fine game, Faraona con Mascarpone.

SOAVE DOC *Veneto*

The small town of Soave, some 32 kilometres/19 miles east of Verona, was named, apparently, after the Suavi, the people who occupied the area in the seventh century. Today it gives its name to a delicate white wine made from Trebbiano Toscano and Trebbiano di Soave grapes. Straw-yellow to greenish at times, the best examples of Soave are dry, well-balanced, clean, smooth, sometimes with a slightly bitter taste. With not less that 11.5% abv and five months of age, it can be called Superiore.

Soave Classico is made from grapes grown in a restricted area, and is often better.

Serve with: fish dishes, Fegato alla Veneziana and Pollo Arrosto.

TAURASI DOCG *Campania*

One of the best red wines of southern Italy, big, robust Taurasi is slowly gaining the reputation it deserves worldwide. This long-lived red is made mainly with Aglianico and needs to be kept for several years before it softens and releases its intense aromas and delicious burnt cherry flavours (a minimum of three years is required by law). The minimum alcoholic content is 12% abv but with 12.5% abv and four years of age it can be labelled Riserva.

Serve with: lamb, rich pasta dishes such as Bucatini all' Amatriciana.

TEROLDEGO ROTALIANO DOC
Trentino-Alto Adige

Bitter edges to this dry red wine make it a good wine for food, especially red meat dishes. It is produced in the north of the province of Trento, on an alluvial plain known as Campo Rotaliano, and using Teroldego grapes. Ruby-red, almost purpley in colour it has a deep, fruity aroma and a dry, slightly bitter and tannic taste, reminiscent of almonds. It is often referred to as the Prince of Trentino wines. With an abv level not less than 12% it can be called Superiore and, if aged for at least two years, Riserva, a perfect wine to serve with roasts. There is also a rosato version with much the same characteristics as the red but paler in colour and a little fruitier.

Serve with: Capriolo alla Alto Atesina, Cassoela.

TORGIANO ROSSO RISERVA DOCG *Umbria*

This commendable wine has gained a well-deserved reputation for some time now. It is made from Sangiovese and Canaiolo, and a small quantity of other varieties including Ciliegiolo, Montepulciano and Trebbiano Toscano, grown in the region of Torgiano, near

Perugia. It is limpid, has a vinous and delicate aroma and a dry, full-bodied flavour. It must be aged for at least three years, and makes a superb wine for red meat dishes.

While Torgiano Rosso Riserva is a DOCG, Torgiano as a DOC applies to a white wine, Bianco di Torgiano, a red, Rosso di Torgiano, a rosé, Rosato di Torgiano and others named after the grape variety from which they are made, such as Chardonnay, Pinot Grigio, Riesling Italico, Cabernet Sauvignon and Pinot Nero.

Serve with: fish, Pasta e Ceci, Fagioli all'Uccelletto.

There is also a Torgiano Spumante made from Chardonnay and Pinot Nero.

TREBBIANO D'ABRUZZO DOC *Abruzzo*

This somewhat neutral white wine is made from Trebbiano d'Abruzzo and/ or Trebbiano Toscano with the optional addition of up to 15% of other varieties grown on the hills throughout the region of Abruzzo. It is straw-yellow in colour, lightly aromatic, with a velvety, well-balanced taste.

Serve with: fish, seafood dishes, Pizza Rustica.

VALPOLICELLA & RECIOTO DELLA VALPOLICELLA DOC *Veneto*

Valpolicella and Recioto della Valpolicella are thought to be descended from ancient *retico*, well-known to the Roman emperors and mentioned by Virgil, Pliny and Martial in their works. Today it is made mainly from Corvina Veronese, Rondinella and Molinara, grown to the north of Verona.

Straight, well-made Valpolicella (ie not the cheap, over-commercial examples sold in large bottles) is generally a light red wine, with a characteristic aroma of bitter almonds, best drunk young to enjoy its dry, fruity, bitter-cherry flavours. Valpolicella Superiore must have 12% abv and be aged for one year.

Recioto della Valpolicella, a dessert wine, is made from the upper part of the bunch of grapes, the *recie* ("ears"in the local dialect), that tend to ripen best. The grapes are left to dry on the vine, to concentrate the sugars before vinification, resulting in a dark garnet wine with an intense bouquet and a semi-sweet taste. It has a minimum 14% abv.

A drier, more concentrated version of Recioto is Amarone ('bitter') della Valpolicella (formerly called Recioto della Valpolicella Amarone). This strong, long-lived wine is becoming more and more popular worldwide. It must be aged for two years and is a magnificent wine for special occasions.

Serve Valpolicella with: Baccalà alla Vicentina.

Serve Amarone with: game such as Lepre in Salmì.

VALTELLINA DOC *Lombardy*

The Valtellina Valley is where the river Adda flows towards Lake Como and the grapes grown on the slopes of its right bank make some of the best red wines of the region. The predominant grape variety is Chiavennasca (the local name for Nebbiolo) with a small percentage of other red grapes that produce a lively red wine with a dry, slightly tannic taste. The minimum alcohol level is 11% abv. From slightly dried grapes Sfurzat is made, a semi-sweet wine with not less than 14.5% abv. Valtellina can be called Superiore if the wine is made from not less than 95% Chiavennasca grapes, reaches 12 % abv and is aged for at least two years. With four years it can be called Riserva. The geographic subdenominations Grumello, Inferno, Sassella and Valgella are reserved for Valtellina made from grapes grown in the corresponding areas.

Serve with: rich meat dishes.

VERDICCHIO DEI CASTELLI DI JESI DOC
Marche

An excellent clean, crisp white wine made from Verdicchio grown predominantly in the province of Ancona. With a light straw colour, a delicate bouquet and a dry, balanced taste with a pleasantly bitter finish, this is the perfect wine to accompany fish dishes.

If produced with grapes grown in the old production area it can be called Classico. There is also a sparkling version.

Serve with: fish and seafood dishes, such as Scampi all'Abruzzese, Gattò di patate.

VERMENTINO DI GALLURA DOCG

Sardinia

Vermentino di Gallura is made in the Gallura area of northern Sardinia. The wine is strong, soft and straw-coloured, with powerful aromas and a dry, bitterish taste. The minimum alcohol content is 12% abv, but with 14% it can be called Superiore.

Serve with: fish soups and seafood, such as Aragosta al Forno, Sformato di Finocchi.

VERNACCIA DI ORISTANO DOC

Sardinia

Probably the best-known wine of Sardinia, this sherry-type speciality is made from Vernaccia di Oristano, a grape introduced to the island at the end of the fourteenth century. It is amber in colour, has delicate scents of almond tree flowers, and is a fine, warm wine to drink, with a bitter almond finish. The minimum alcohol level is 15% abv and with 15.5% and three years of age it can be called Superiore – and Riserva after four years. There is also a liquoroso dolce aged for two years with 16.5% abv, as well as a secco (dry), with 18% alcohol.

Serve the secco with: fish, such as Nasello alla Palermitana, Trance di Tonno in Salsa Rinascimentale.

Serve the sweet as an aperitif – with or without canapés.

VERNACCIA DI SAN GIMIGNANO DOC

Tuscany

This clone of Vernaccia was imported from Greece in the twelfth century and today is grown around the beautiful Tuscan town of San Gimignano. The wine itself is pale, with a fresh, dry, sometimes spicy taste. With one year of age it can be called Riserva.

Serve with: fish, such as Spigola al Forno, Dentice al Sale.

VINO NOBILE DI MONTEPULCIANO DOCG

Tuscany

This wine has been produced for centuries by Tuscany nobility, hence its name; apparently it was first produced by Jesuits as a wine for the Holy Mass. Today Vino Nobile di Montepulciano can be a truly impressive, full-bodied red, made mainly from Sangiovese grown on the hills of Montepulciano, not far from Siena, and Canaiolo Nero. Garnet in colour, turning brick-red with age, it offers aromas of violets and a strong, dry, slightly tannic taste. It must have an abv of 12.5% and at least two years ageing. With a third year it can be called Riserva. This is a superb wine to accompany roast meat and game.

Serve with: game and meat dishes, such as Spezzatino di Cinghiale, Arista alla Fiorentina, Fagiano alla Milanese

VIN SANTO DI GAMBELLARA DOC

Veneto

Vin santo ("holy wine"), an intense, aromatic dessert wine, is made from bunches of grapes hung up to dry in barns, (thus concentrating the sugars) before vinification. That of

Gambellara is perhaps the most worthy of mention, even if excellent vin santo is produced elsewhere in the country (in particular in Tuscany, where it is aged in small barrels known as caratelli: a must with the local cantucci, a type of hard biscuit traditionally dipped in the wine). The commune of Gambellara is near Vicenza, and its vin santo is made principally with Garganega grapes left to dry for several weeks after the harvest. The wine has a deep nutty aroma, at times reminiscent of berries, a straw-golden colour and is rich, smooth and sweet or semi-sweet, with a pleasantly bitter aftertaste.

Serve with: desserts and cakes such as Tiramisù, Cantucci and Torta Sbrisolone.

Bibliography

Accame, Franco; Torre, Silvio; Pronzati, Virgilio. *Il Grande Libro della Cucina Ligure* (De Ferrari Editore)

Adami, Pietro. *La Cucina Carnica* (Padova. Franco Muzzio Editore 1985)

Agnesi, Vincenzo. *Alcune Notizie sugli Spaghetti* (Imperia 1975)

Agnoletti, Vincenzo. *Manuale del Cuoco e del Pasticcere* 1852 (Reprint A. Forni 1983)

Alberini, Massimo. con ricette di Romana Bosco *Antica Cucina Veneziana* (Casale Monferrato. Piemme 1990)

Alberini, Massimo. *Storia del Pranzo all'Italiana* (Milano. Longanesi 1965)

Alberini, Massimo. *Liguria a Tavola* (Milano. Longanesi 1965)

Alberini, Massimo. *Piemontesi a Tavola* (Milano. Longanesi 1967)

Alberini, Massimo. *Emiliani e Romagnoli a Tavola* (Milano. Longanesi 1969)

Alberini, Massimo. *Mangiare con gli Occhi* (Modena. Edizione Panini)

Alberini, Massimo. *4000 Anni a Tavola* (Milano. Fabbri 1972)

Alberini, Massimo. *Cento Ricette Storiche* (Firenze. Sansoni 1974)

Alberini, Massimo e Giorgio Mistretta. *Guida all'Italia Gastronomica* (Touring Club Italiano 1984)

Alliata di Salaparuta, Enrico. *Cucina Vegetariana e Naturismo Crudo* (Palermo. Sellerio 1988)

Anderson, Burton. *Treasures of the Italian Table* (New York. William Morrow 1994)

Apicius. *Cookery and Dining in Imperial Rome* Edited and translated Joseph Vehling (New York. Dover Publications 1977)

Archestratus. *The Life of Luxury* translated G.Wilkins & S.Hill (Totnes. Prospect Books 1994)

Artusi, Pellegrino. *La Scienza in Cucina e Arte di Mangiar Bene* with Introductory Note by Piero Camporesi (Torino. Giulio Einaudi Ed 1985)

Baldassari Montevecchi, B. *La Cucina di Emilia Romagna* (Milano. Franco Angeli 1980)

Baldini, Filippo. *De' Sorbetti* 1784 (reprinted Firenze. Forni)

Bareham, Lindsay. *In Praise of the Potato* (London. Grafton Books 1991)

Benedetti, Benedetto. *L'Aceto Balsamico* (Consorteria dell'Aceto Balsamico 1986)

Benini, Zenone. *La Cucina di Casa Mia* (Firenze. Olimpia 1983)

Benporat, Claudio. *Storia della Gastronomia Italiana* (Milano. Mursia 1990)

Benporat, Claudio. *La Cucina Italiana del 400* (Firenze. Leo Olschki 1996)

Bergese, Nino. *Mangiare da Re* (Milano. Feltrinelli 1969)

Bevilacqua, Osvaldo & Mantovani, Giuseppe. *Laboratori del Gusto* (Milano. Sugar 1982)

Black, Maggie. *A Taste of History* (London. English Heritage 1993)

Boni, Ada. *Il Talismano della Felicità* (Roma. Carlo Colombo reprint 1984)

Boni, Ada. *Cucina Regionale Italiana* (Milano. Mondadori 1975)

Bonomo, Giuliana. *Il Grande Libro del Pesce* (Milano. Mondadori 1989)

Braudel, Fernand. *The Mediterranean & the Mediterranean World in the Age of Philip II Vol 1* (New York. Harper & Row 1976)

Brera, Giovanni & Veronelli, Luigi. *La Pacciada* (Milano. Mondadori 1973)

Brillat-Savarin, Jean Anthelme. *The Philosopher in the Kitchen* translated Anne Dayton (London. Penguin Books 1970)

Brydone, Patrick. *A Tour through Sicily and Malta* (Edinburgh 1840)

Bugialli, Giuliano. *Classic Techniques of Italian Cooking* (New York. Simon & Schuster 1982)

Campbell, Susan. *The Cook's Companion* (London. Macmillan 1980)

Camporesi, Piero. *Alimentazione, Folclore, Società* (Parma. Pratiche Editrice 1980)

Camporesi, Piero. *Il Paese della Fame* (Bologna. Il Mulino 1978)

Camporesi, Piero. *La Carne Impassibile* (Milano. Il Saggiatore 1983)

Capnist, Giovanni. *I Dolci del Veneto* (Padova. Franco Muzzio Ed. 1983)

Capnist, Giovanni. *La Cucina Veronese* (Padova. Franco Muzzio Ed. 1987)

Cardillo Violati, Leda & Majnardi, Carlo. *I Picchiarelli della Malanotte* (Foligno. Dell' Arquato 1990)

Carnacina, Luigi e Veronelli, Luigi. *La Buona Vera Cucina Italiana* (Milano. Rizzoli 1966)

Carnacina, Luigi e Veronelli, Luigi. *La Cucina Rustica Regionale Italiana* (Milano. Rizzoli 1966)

Carnacina, Luigi e Bonassisi, Vincenzo. *Il Libro della Polenta* (Firenze. Giunti Martello 1974)

Carnacina, Luigi e Bonassisi, Vincenzo. *Roma in Cucina* (Firenze. Giunti Martello 1975)

Castelvetro, Giacomo. *The Fruit, Herbs & Vegetables of Italy* Translated by Gillian Riley (London. Viking 1989)

Castiglione, Baldassare. *Il Libro del Cortegiano* (repr. Milano. V. Mursia 1972)

Cavalcanti, Ippolito. *Cucina Teorico-Pratica* (Napoli. De'Gemelli 1847)

Cavalcanti, Ottavio. *Il Libro d'Oro della Cucina e dei Vini di Calabria e Basilicata* (Milano. Mursia 1970)

Cato, Marcus Porcius. *On Agriculture* translated W.D. Hopper (London. Heinemann 1934)

Cerini di Castagnate, Livio. *Il Cuoco Gentiluomo* (Milano. Mondadori 1980)

Cervio, Vincenzo. *Il Trinciante* (1581) (reprinted Firenze. Il Portolano 1979)

Columella. *De Re Rustica* translated H.B.Ash (London. Heinemann 1934)

Conoscere i Salumi (Milano. Librex 1984)

Le Conserve della Nonna (Milano. Librex 1982)

Corrado, Vincenzo. *Il Cuoco Galante* (Napoli. Stamperia Raimondiana 1778)

Corsi, Guglielma. *Un Secolo di Cucina Umbra* (Assisi. Ed. Tipografica Porziuncola)

Couffignal, Huguette. *La Cucina Povera*

(Milano. Rizzoli 1982)

Cunsolo, Felice. *Guida Gastronomica d'Italia* (Novara. Istituto Geografico de Agostini 1975)

Il Cuoco Milanese e la Cuciniera Piemontese (Milano. Francesco Pagnoni 1863)

David, Elizabeth. *A Book of Mediterranean Food* (London. John Lehmann 1950)

David, Elizabeth. *Italian Food* (London. Macdonald 1954)

David, Elizabeth. *An Omelette and a Glass of Wine* (London. Dorling Kindersley 1984)

Davidson, Alan. *Mediterranean Seafood* (London. Penguin Books 1972)

Davidson, Alan. *North Atlantic Seafood* (London. Macmillan 1979)

Davidson, Alan. *The Oxford Companion to Food* (Oxford University Press 1999)

Davidson, Alan and Knox, Charlotte. *Seafood* (London. Mitchell Beazley 1988)

Davidson, Alan and Knox, Charlotte. *Fruit* (London. Mitchell Beazley 1991)

Del Conte, Anna. *Portrait of Pasta* (London. Paddington Press 1976)

Del Conte, Anna. *Secrets from an Italian Kitchen* (London. Bantam Press 1989)

Del Conte, Anna. *Entertaining all'Italiana* (London. Bantam Press 1991)

Del Conte, Anna. *The Classic Food of Northern Italy* (London. Pavilion Books 1995)

Denti Di Parajno, Alberto. *Il Gastronomo Educato* (Neri Pozza Editore 1950)

Dettore, Mariapaola. *Il Pane dall'Antipasto al Dolce* (Milano. A Garzanti 1979)

Di Corato, Riccardo. *451 Formaggi d'Italia* (Milano. Sonzogno 1978)

Di Corato, Riccardo. *838 Frutti e Verdure d'Italia* (Milano. Sonzogno 1979)

Dowell, Philip & Bailey, Adrian. *The Book of Ingredients* (London. Dorling Kindersley 1980)

Dumas, Alexandre. *Dictionary of Cuisine* translated L.Colman (USA Simon & Schuster 1958)

Eramo, Cia. *La Cucina Mantovana* (Padova. Franco Muzzio 1980)

The Faber Book of Food edited by Colin Spencer & Claire Clifton (London. Faber & Faber 1993)

Faccioli, Emilio. *L'Eccellenza e il Trionfo del Porco* (Milano. G. Mazzotta 1982)

Faccioli, Emilio. *Arte della Cucina* Vols I & II (Milano. Il Polifilo 1966)

Falavigna, Ugo. *Arte della Pasticceria a Parma* (Parma. Luigi Battei 1987)

Fast, Mady. *Mangiare Triestino* (Padova. Franco Muzzio 1993)

Field, Carol. *The Italian Baker* (New York. Harper & Row 1985)

Field, Carol. *Celebrating Italy* (New York. William Morrow 1990)

Francesconi, Jeanne Carola. *La Cucina Napoletana* (Napoli. Delfino 1965)

Goethe, J.W. *Italian Journey 1786-1788* translated by W.H.Auden and E. Mayer (San Francisco. North Point Press 1982)

Goria, Giovanni. *La Cucina del Piemonte* (Padova. Franco Muzzio 1990)

Gosetti della Salda, Anna. *Le Ricette Regionali Italiane* (Milano. Solaresi 1967)

Gozzini Giacosa, Ilaria. *Mense e Cibi della Roma Antica* (Casale Monferrato. Piemme 1995)

Grande Dizionario della Gastronomia (Milano. Readers' Digest Spa 1990)

Il Grande Manuale della Cucina Regionale edited by Stella Donati (Bergamo. Euroclub Italia 1979)

Gray, Patience. *Honey from the Weed* (London. Prospect Books 1986)

Grigson, Jane. *Fish Cookery* (London. David & Charles 1978)

Grigson, Jane. *The Mushroom Feast* (London. Michael Joseph 1975)

Grigson, Jane. *The Vegetable Book* (London. Michael Joseph 1978)

Grigson, Jane. *The Fruit Book* (London. Michael Joseph 1982)

Guarnaschelli Gotti, Marco. *La Cucina Milanese* (Padova. Franco Muzzio 1991)

Hazan, Marcella. *The Classic Italian Cookbook* (London. Macmillan 1980)

Hazan, Marcella. *The Second Classic Italian Cookbook* (London. Jill Norman & Hobhouse 1982)

La Cucina Piemontese 1798 (reprint Forni 1980)

Larousse Gastronomique

Lasøe, Thomas & Del Conte, Anna. *The Mushroom Book* (London. Dorling Kindersley 1996)

Liddel, Caroline & Weir, Robin. *Ices* (London. Hodder & Stoughton 1993)

Lombardi, Liliana. *Il Grande Libro della Pasta e dei Cereali* (Milano. Mondadori 1992)

Luard, Elisabeth. *European Peasant Cookery* (London. Bantam Press 1986)

Luraschi, Giovanni Felice. *Nuovo Cuoco Milanese* 1853 (reprint Forni 1980)

Maffioli, Giuseppe. *La Cucina Trevigiana* (Padova. Mursia 1981)

Maffioli, Giuseppe. *La Cucina Veneziana* (Padova. Mursia 1982)

Mantovani, Giuseppe. *La Cucina Italiana: origini, storie e segreti* (Roma. Newton Compton 1985)

Marinetti, Filippo. *La Cucina Futurista* (Milano. Stabilimento Grafico Matarelli 1932)

Mayer, Barbara. *Cakes* (London. Jill Norman & Hobhouse 1982)

McGee, Harold. *On Food & Cooking* (New York. Charles Scribner's 1984)

McGee, Harold. *The Curious Cook* (San Francisco. North Point Press 1990)

Medagliani, Eugenio & Gossetti della Salda, Ferdinanda. *Pastaio* (Cunsinallo. Alessi 1985)

de' Medici, Lorenza. *Florentines* (London. Pavilion Books 1992)

di Messisbugo, Christoforo. *Libro Novo* 1557 (reprint Forni 1982)

Metz, Vittorio. *La Cucina del Belli* (Milano. Sugar Co. 1984)

Il Mio Formaggio (Milano. Librex 1982)

Monelli, Paolo. *Il Ghiottone Errante* (Milano. Garzantti 1935)

Moretti, Maria Cecilia. *Sapori e Voci di Lago* (Foligno. Dell'Arquata 1985)

Naso, Irma. *Formaggi del Medievo* (Torino. Il Segnalibro 1990)

Norman, Jill. *The Classic Herb Book* (London. Dorling Kindersley 1990)

Novelli, Renato. *Le Marche a Tavola* (Ancona. Il Lavoro Editoriale 1987)

Olivero, Nello. *Storie e Curiosità del Mangiare Napoletano* (Napoli Ed. Scientifiche Italiane 1983)

Origo, Iris. *The Merchant of Prato* (Boston. David Godine 1986)

Owen, Sri. *The Rice Book* (London. Transworld 1993)

Pane Rita & Mariano. *I Sapori del Sud* (Milano. Rizzoli 1991)

Perna Bozzi, Ottorina. *La Lombardia in Cucina* (Firenze. G. Martello 1982)

Perna Bozzi, Ottorina. *Vecchia Brianza in Cucina* (Firenze. G. Martello 1975)

Petroni, Paolo. *Il Libro della Vera Cucina Fiorentina* (Firenze. Bonecchi 1974)

Petroni, Paolo. *Il Libro della Vera Cucina Bolognese* (Firenze. Bonecchi 1978)

Piccinardi, Antonio. *Dizionario di Gastonomia* (Milano. Rizzoli 1993)

Pisanelli, Baldassare. *Trattato della Natura de' Cibi et del Bere* 1611 (reprint Forni)

Platina, Bartolomeo. *Il Piacere Onesto e la Buona Salute* 1475 Edited by Emilio Faccioli (Milano. Einaudi 1985)

Plotkin, Fred. *Italy for the Gourmet Traveller* (London. Kyle Cathie 1996)

Plotkin, Fred. *Recipes from Paradise* (New York. Little Brown 1997)

Porcaro, Giuseppe. *Sapore di Napoli* (Napoli. Gallina 1985)

Rattazzi, Ilaria. *Tutti gli Usi della Frutta* (Milano. Sperling & Kupfer Ed. 1985)

Ratto, G.B. & Giovanni. *La Cuciniera Genovese* (Genova. Fratelli Pagano)

Righi Parenti, Giovanni. *La Grande Cucina Toscana Vols I & II* (Milano. Sugar Co. 1982)

Righi Parenti, Giovanni. *La Cucina degli Etruschi* (Milano. Sugar 1972)

Il Riso nella Ristorazione (Ente Nazionale Risi)

Roden, Claudia. *A Book of Middle Eastern Food* (London. Nelson 1980)

Roden, Claudia. *The Book of Jewish Food* (New York. Kopf 1996)

Root, Waverley. *The Food of Italy* (USA Random House 1971)

Roratro, Giampiero. *La Cucina di Carlo Goldoni* (Venezia. Stamperia di Venezia 1983)

Rossetto Kasper, Lynne. *The Splendid Table of Emilia-Romagna* (New York. William Morrow 1992)

Rumhor Von, Karl Friedrich. (1822) *The Essence of Cookery* translated B. Yeomans (Totnes. Prospect Books 1993)

Sala, Orietta. *La Frutta della Campagna* (Milano. Idealibri 1987)

Santich, Barbara. *The Original Mediterranean Cuisine* (Totnes. Proscpect Books 1995)

Santini, Aldo. *La Cucina Maremmana* (Padova. Franco Muzzio 1991)

Sassu, Antonio. *La Vera Cucina di Sardegna* (Roma. Anthropos 1983)

Scappi, Barolomeo. *Opera dell'Arte del Cucinare* 1570 (reprint Forni 1981)

Schneider, Elizabeth. *Uncommon Fruits and Vegetables* (New York. Harper & Row 1986)

Servi Machlin, Edda. *The Classic Cuisine of the Italian Jews* (New York. Dodd, Mead 1981)

Simeti, Mary Taylor. *Sicilian Food* (London. Random Century Group 1988)

Stefani, Bartolomeo. *L'Arte di Ben Cucinare et Instruire* 1662 (Reprinted Firenze. Forni 1983)

Steingarten, Jeffrey. *The Man Who Ate Everything* (USA. Knopf 1997)

Stobart, Tom. *Herbs, Spices and Flavourings* (The International Wine & Food Publishing Co. 1970)

Stobart, Tom. *The Cook's Encyclopedia* (London. Batsford 1980)

Tannahill, Reay. *Food in History* (USA. Stein & Day 1973)

Taruschio, Ann & Franco. *Leaves from the Walnut Tree* (London. Pavilion Books 1993)

Tasca Lanza, Anna. *The Heart of Sicily* (London. Cassell 1993)

Touring Club Italiano. *Guida Gastronomica d'Italia* (Milano. Touring Club 1931)

Vialardi, Giovanni. *Trattato di Cucina Pasticceria Moderna* 1854 (reprint Forni)

Westbury, Lord. *Handlist of Italian Cookery Books* (Firenze, Leo S. Olschki Editore 1963)

Wheaton, Barbara Ketcham. *Savouring the Past* (London. Chatto & Windus 1983)

Willan, Anne. *Great Cooks and their Recipes* (London. Elm Tree Books 1977)

Zaniloni Riveccio, Maria. *Polenta, Piatto da Re* (Milano. Idealibri 1986)

Index

PICTURE ACKNOWLEDGEMENTS

The publisher wishes to thank The Fotomas Index for their kind permission to reproduce the images on pages 2, 10, 22, 50, 190, 340, 370. Otherwise, all images copyright © Chrysalis Image Library.

Chrysalis Books Group Plc is committed to respecting the intellectual property rights of others. We have therefore taken all reasonable efforts to ensure that the reproduction of all content on these pages is done with the full consent of copyright owners. If you are aware of any unintentional omissions please contact the company directly so that any necessary corrections may be made for future editions.